S CHAND'S SUCCESS GUIDES
(Question and Answers)

MODERN INDIAN HISTORY

(For B.A. Pass & Honours Students of History. Based on U.G.C. Model Curriculum and also Modified Curriculum of Several Universities)

(Including Solved Long Answer Type, Short Answer Type, and Very Short Answer Type Questions)

J.C. AGGARWAL
Former Lecturer, Dayanand College
Hissar (Haryana)

S Chand And Company Limited
(ISO 9001 Certified Company)

S Chand And Company Limited

(ISO 9001 Certified Company)

Head Office: D-92, Sector–2, Noida – 201301, U.P. (India), Ph. 91-120-4682700

Registered Office: A-27, 2nd Floor, Mohan Co-operative Industrial Estate, New Delhi – 110 044, Phone: 011-49731800

www.**schandpublishing.com**; e-mail: **info@schandpublishing.com**

Marketing Offices:

Chennai : Ph: 23632120; chennai@schandpublishing.com

Guwahati : Ph: 2738811, 2735640; guwahati@schandpublishing.com

Hyderabad : Ph: 40186018; hyderabad@schandpublishing.com

Jalandhar : Ph: 4645630; jalandhar@schandpublishing.com

Kolkata : Ph: 23357458, 23353914; kolkata@schandpublishing.com

Lucknow : Ph: 4003633; lucknow@schandpublishing.com

Mumbai : Ph: 25000297; mumbai@schandpublishing.com

Patna : Ph: 2260011; patna@schandpublishing.com

First Edition 1999
Second Revised Edition 2002, Reprints 2004
Revised Edition 2007, Reprints 2018, 2019, 2020, 2021, 2022

Reprint 2024

ISBN: 978-81-219-1958-6 **Product Code:** H5MIQ41HIST40ENAC07O

PRINTED IN INDIA

By Vikas Publishing House Private Limited, Plot 20/4, Site-IV, Industrial Area Sahibabad, Ghaziabad – 201 010 and Published by S Chand And Company Limited, A-27, 2nd Floor, Mohan Co-operative Industrial Estate, New Delhi – 110 044.

Preface to the Revised Edition

The book has been revised in the light of the UGC Curriculum and also Modified Curriculum by various Indian Universities. The book, although does not claim any special superiority over similar books in use, certainly has some important merits. Chiefly, it is examination-oriented; it has constantly kept in view the requirements as well as the limitations of the students in preparing for the examinations and subsequently answering the questions. It attempts to ensure that only relevant and to-the-point material is included in the given answers.

The subject-matter of the course is so vast that on almost every topic several books have been written. It therefore becomes extremely important to sift the matter so that only the salient features are included, to be of immediate practical utility to the students. This book takes care of this point.

All redundant dates and details of conquests are excluded.

The questions included in this book have been selected from the previous question papers set in various examinations.

The book also highlights, along with the achievements of the rulers, the condition of the people in each period, along with their cultural, economic, political and social life.

Every possible effort is made to deal with each question critically and to the desired directions of the examiners.

Length of each answer is moderately exhaustive so that students are able to complete the paper within the prescribed time.

It is hoped that a thorough study of this book will enable students to obtain good marks in the examination.

Constructive suggestions for further enhancing the value of the book will be gratefully acknowledged and incorporated in the subsequent edition of the book.

J.C. Aggarwal

Contents

1

India in the Mid 18th Century, Political, Economic, Social and Cultural Trends

---

Q1. Bring out the main features of Indian economic and social life in the early 18th century. To what extent were they related to contemporary political developments?

or

Discuss the economic and social conditions in India in the first half of the 18th century. *(Delhi University 1992 and 1995)*

Ans. *Economic Life and Political Developments.*

The history of India during the eighteenth century was the history of decline - decline in almost all walks of national life. This decline may be attributed to the declining power of the Mughal rulers and resultant contemporary political developments.

The other two political developments were the emergence of a number of independent and semi-independent kingdoms and the greed of the European powers to have their foothold on India. All this resulted in firece struggles, conspiracies, battles and wars. Obiously, economic life was affected.

Some historians have termed the 18th century in India as the dark period of Indian history. India became a slave country of the British. The people had to fight a long battle for the liberation of the country from foreign domination. Likewise India had to struggle for getting back its territories from other European nations who had established their control.

Political and other Factors Affecting Economy

(1) Very little law and order and near political anarchy.
(2) Increasing revenue demands of the state on the people.
(3) Oppression of the state officials.
(4) Greed of the nobles and their demands on the people.
(5) The marches and countermarhes of the rival armies leading to destruction of crops in several areas.
(6) Loot and plunder of the foreign invaders.
(7) Trade routes infested with robbers.
(8) Growing interference of the European powers in the affairs of India.
(9) Extortion of money by the officials of the East India Company.

Chief Features of Indian Economy

J. N. Sarkar has depicted the economic conditions in these words, Thus ensued a great impoverishment of India - not only a decrease of national stock, but also a rapid lowering of mechanical skill and standard of civilisation, a disappearance of art and culture over wide tracts of the country."

The Indian economy was in a bad shape. Agriculture was very backward. The *zamindars* and *jagirdars* exploited the peasants. The English had captured the trade. Indian indigenous industries began to decline. The villagers were self-sufficient.

Bad shape of Indian economy. The Central Government was often on the verge of bankruptcy. Neither the emperor nor the officials were taking due interest in the economic development of the country. Corruption, indiscipline and inefficiency prevailed on large scale among officials at all levels.

Backward and stagnant Indian agriculture. Government had put heavy demands of revenue on the peasants. The officials oppressed the peasants and asked them to pay different kinds of tributes to them. The landlords did not take interest in providing better seeds, equipments and irrigation facilities.

Trade and commerce. Foreign trade was extensive and the balance of trade was favourable. Peter the great of Russia was led to exclaim, "Bear in mind that the commerce of India is the commerce of the world and he who can exclusively command it, he is the dictator of Europe." The foreign trade was gradually coming into the hands of the foreigners, who had secured somewhat favourable trading rights.

Decline in internal trade. Absence of a strong political control at the centre and in the provinces had led to the disruption of law and order in many areas. Roads were not safe and trade routes were infested with organised band of robbers.

Self-sufficient villages. The Mughal rulers in general did not interfere in the economic life of the villagers. Moreover the villagers remained isolated on account of the lack of means of communication. They were largely self-sufficient and imported little from outside.

State of industries. Although the state of industrial development had received great set-back, yet on account of the fame of Indian handicraftsmen, some industrial centres still enjoyed world-wide fame and attracted foreign markets.

India remained a large scale manufacturer of cotton and silk falerics, dyestuffs, jute, minarals, sugar and metal products like arms, metal-wares, saltpetre and oils.

Important centres of textile industry were :

Dacca and Murshidabad (Bengal),

Patna (Bihar),

Surat, Ahmedabad and Broach (Gujarat),

Aurangabad (Maharashtra),

Burhanpur (Madhya Predesh),
Lucknow and Agra (U. P.),
Masulipatnam, Chicacole and Vishakhapatnam (Andhra),
Bangalore (Karnataka),
Coimbatore (Tanjore) and Madurai (Tamil Nadu),
Multan and Lahore (Panjab).
Woollen industry flourished in Kashmir.

Indian ship building industry was very popular in European countries. In this regard, an English observer remarked, "In ship-building they taught the English for more than they learnt from them."

Economic contrast : Economic contrasts existed as those who had political powers in their hands mercilessely exploited the common man. The emperor, the royal families, the nobles, the mansabdars and the jagirdars enjoyed privileges. They were steeped in comfort and luxury.

The common man was highly exploited. He was required to face the heavy burden on account of the increasing expenditure, military needed for protection from foreign dangers and internal revolts. There were intrigues among the nobles for power and in this struggle, common man was the worst victim. Foreign invaders like Nadir Shah and Ahmed Shah Abdali plundred the Mughal treasury mercilessly and carried away enormous amount of wealth of India to foreign countries. Obviously the common man had to suffer when the government attempted to raise finances. Revenue officials and *Zamindars* extracted money on one or the other pretext.

Social Conditions

Main features of social life of the period in India are given below.

1. *Stagnating Indian society*. The period was marked by loss of creativity. While the 18th century brought about great scientific enlightenment to the nations in Europe, India witnessed conditions of inactivity, regimentation and indolence. Social evils and conservatism were clearly visible of a large magnitude. The altitude to life was fatalistic. There was gross inequality. The strong exploited the weak.

2. *Moral degeneration*. Moral degeneration was evident on accountof enormous wealth among the nobles. Most of them had scant regard for virtues like faithfulness, gratitute, honesty and loyalty. The dominant feature of life was single-minded pursuit for power and wealth. The common man, however was comparatively free from the declining morals.

3. *Great disparity*. There was great disparity in life style of the people. The rich lived in plenty and luxury and the poor who constituted about four-fifth of the population led a very miserable life.

4. *Four-fold social divisions*. The king and the princes constituted the upper most class. This class enjoyed an unparalleled status. The class of nobles, jagirdars and mansabdars enjoyed the patronage of the king. Most of

them lived a life of extravagance. Drinking was very common among them. They were generally corrupt. They readily accepted bribes and felt no hesitation in giving bribes. The middle class comprising the wealthy merchants, professionals and the petty mansabdars constituted the third strata of society. The lowest class comprised the artisans, cultivators, house-hold servants, shop keepers, small traders and slaves etc. The slaves were of diffenent categories. This class was condemned to live a hard life. Their clothings were scanty.

5. *Position of women*. The position of women was vulnerable. Following were the chief features of the status and condition of women:-

(1) Women in general possessed little individuality of their own.
(2) Polygamy was a common feature.
(3) Purdah was a general practice among the upper class women in the North.
(4) Women of upper classes were not supposed to work outside their homes. However, there were exceptions.
(5) Widow remarriage was uncommon. The life of a widow was very miserable.
(6) The practice of '*sati*' was prevalent in Bengal and some other parts of North India. It was mostly practised by upper classes.
(7) The practice of early marriage was common in several parts of India.
(8) Boys and girls were not permitted to mix with each other.
(9) Education of girls and women was neglected.
(10) Dowry system was prevalent.
(11) The evil of the sale of the daughter or the groom existed.
(12) Child marriages were common.
(13) At some places, killing of daughters at birth still existed.

6. *Hindu-Muslim relations*. Following were the chief features.

(*a*) Generally speaking, relations between the Hindus and the Muslims were very cordial.
(*b*) Important features were:
  (*i*) Urdu language served to unite the people. It was an important vehicle for interaction and also for the growth of composite culture.
  (*ii*) Several Hindu writers wrote in Persian and likewise many Muslim writers in Hindi, Bengali and other vernacular languages.
  (*iii*) Religious themes of each other's religion influenced both Hindu and Muslim writers.

(*iv*) The Bhakti and the Sufi movements helped in creating an environment of mutual respect and tolerance for each other's religion.

(*v*) The Muslim rulers and nobles participated in the Hindu festivasls like Durga Puja, Holi and Diwali etc. while the Hindu rulers in the Moharrum procession.

(*vi*) The lifestyles of the upper middle class Hindus and Muslims were very similar in several ways.

(*vii*) People of different religions had a lot in common irrespective of their caste and community.

(*viii*) Apart from civil posts, even in military, higher posts were given to the most competent persons irrespective of religion. Ibrahim Gardi, a Muslim was the commander of the artillery of the Marathas.

(*ix*) Alliances and wars in general were not made in the name of religion.

7. *Literacy and education*. Following were the important characteristics:

(*i*) *Elementary education.* Elementary education was wide spread. Elementary education for the Hindus was generally given in temples. The Muslims received elementary education in '*Maktabs*' attached with mosques.

(*ii*) *Higher education*. Education was primarily confined to higher castes. There were several centres of higher learning.

(*iii*) *Curriculum*. Emphasis was on law, literature, philosophy and religion rather than on geography, natural sciences, physical sciences and technology.

(*iv*) Maharaja Jai Singh had built five astronomical observatories. Nevertheless science remained neglected. Education was traditional and was not in tune with the rapid developments taking place in West at that time.

(*v*) *Women education*. Education of women was neglected.

(*vi*) *Financing of education*. Higher education was financed by richer sections, primarily Nawabs and *Zamindars*.

(*vii*) *Languages*. The Hindus generally received higher education in Sanskrit. For administrative work, both the Hindus and the Muslims learnt Persian.

8. *Social differences between the lower and the higher class and castes*:

(*i*) The higher class and castes had monopolised jobs, power and prestige.

(*ii*) While women of upper classes were not supposed to work outside their houses, peasant women usually worked in fields and women of the poor classes often worked outside their homes to supplement the family income.

(*iii*) Sati system was prevalent among the higher classes in north India but the people of lower class did not follow this in general.

(*iv*) Whereas the '*purdah*' system was common mostly among the women of higher classes, it had little relevance for middle classes.

(*v*) Widow remarriage was quite common among the people of the hill regions of the North and the Jats but in other parts and especially among higher class it was very rare.

2

Later Mughals and the Decline of the Mughal Empire

Q.1. Briefly describe the main events of the reign of Mughal rulers after Aurangzeb.

Ans. *Mughal Rulers after Aurangzeb*

After Aurangzeb's death in 1707, eleven Mughal rulers ruled for about 150 years *i.e.* upto 1857. As a matter of fact the Mughals had lost their power by 1739 when their rule wass confined to Delhi and its surrounding areas. Of the eleven Mughal rulers, five were murdered/deposed, three became pensioners of the East India company and three can be said to have ruled although they also remained almost powerless.

The English captured Delhi in 1803 and the last Mughal emperor Bahadur Shah (Zafar) was left only with the Red Fort of Delhi under him.

The following chart provides a brief account of the main events of the eleven rulers.

Chart Indicating the Period and main events of Rule of Mughal Emperors after Aurangzeb (1707 — 1857)

S. No.	*Emperor*	*Period of Rule*	*Remarks*
1.	Bahadur Shah	1707-12	Earned the nick-name of *'Shah-i-bekhabar'* (Headless king)
2.	Jahandar Shah	1712-13	(1) Wasted time in the company of his favourite concubine lady Lal Kanwar. (2) Strangled to death in the fort of Delhi.
3.	Farrukh Zafar	1713-19	(1) Owed his throne to two Sayyid brothers and was a puppet in their hands. (2) Deposed and put to death in a horrible way.

(contd.)

4. Rafi-ud Darajat	Feb. 28, 1719 to June 4, 1719	(1) Became emperor with the help of Sayyid brothers and puppet in their hands. (2) Suffered from consumption. (3) Deposed and died shortly.
5. Rafi-ud-Daula alias Shah Jahan II	June 5, 1719 to September 17, 1719	(1) Puppet in the hands of Sayyid brothers. (2) Suffered from consumption. (3) Deposed and died shortly.
6. Muhammad Shah	1719-48	(1) Got the throne with the help of Sayyid brothers but liquidated them in 1722. (2) Nicknamed '*Rangeela*' on account of his pleasures and loose habits. (3) Invasion of Nadir Shah in 1739 and general massacre in Delhi. (3) Loot and plunder by Nadir Shah.
7. Ahmad Shah	1748-54	(1) Deposed, blinded and imprisoned.
8. Alamgir	1754-59	(1) Had spent all his life in prison before becoming emperor. (2) Capture of Lahore by the Sikhs. (3) Under the influence of Marathas. (4) Saking of delhi by Ahmed Shah Abdali. (5) Was murdered.
9. Shah Alam II	1759-1806	4. Became a pensioner of the East India Company in 1808.
10. Akbar II	1806-1857	(1) A wanderer from place to place and reached Delhi in 1772. (2) Defeated in the battle of Buxer (3) Grant of Diwani to the Company. A Pensioner of the East India Company.
11. Bahadur Shah II	(1837-1857)	3. State prisoner of the British after 1857 (1) Emperor in name only. (2) Participated in 1857 revolt. (4) Died in Rangoon as an exile in 1862. (5) Last Mughal emperor.

Q.2. Write notes on

(1) The Sayyid Brothers
(2) Nadir Shah
(3) Ahmad Shah Abdali

Ans. *The Sayyid Brothers as 'King-Makers'*

The two brothers namely Sayyid Abdullah Ali Khan and Sayyid Hussain

Ali Khan are known as the '*King-Makers*' in history on account of their role in placing four Mughal emperor on the throne. These four were.

(*i*) Farrukh Siyar (1713-19), (*ii*) Rafi-ud-Darajat (Feb. 28, 1719 to June 4, 1719), (*iii*) Rafi-ud-Daula alias Shah Jahan *II* (June 5, 1719 to September 17, 1719) and (*iv*) Muhammad Shah (1719).

According to Prof. S. R. Sharma, "The history of nearly ten years from the accession of Farrukh Siyar (1712) to the discomfiture of Prince Sultan Muhammad Shah (1720) is very largely the biography of Sayyid Brothers as King-Makers. Abdullah Ali Khan and Hussain Ali Khan are familiarly known in history."

Sayyid Brothers' rise to power. After the death of Aurangzeb, the Sayyid Brothers gradually assumed power. They belonged to the group of Hindustani nobles and were opposed to the Turani or Irani group of nobles. They were Shias and were disliked by the Sunnis.

The Sayyid Brothers helped Farrakh Siyar in getting throne of Delhi. In 1713, they dethroned Jahandar Shah, (1712-13), the Mughal emperor and made Farrukh Siyar the emperor. As a reward of their services, the emperor appointed Abdullah Khan as his Prime Minister and Hussain Ali as the Commander-in-Chief of the Mughal army. The two brothers began to usurp all power. According to Dr. V. S. Smith, "During the scandalous reign of Farrukh Siyar, who was good for nothing and shameless debauch, the power of the government was mostly in the hands of two brothers.

The two brothers abolished the *'jazia'* and the pilgrim tax.

The two brothers attempted to conciliate and use the Rajputs, the Marathas and the Jats in their struggle against the rival nobles. On the other hand emperor Farrukh Siyar, being tired of the growing demands and influence of the two brothers tried to finish them. In this struggle, the two brothers won. They hatched a plot. The palace was surrounded by Sayyid troops. Farrukh Siyar was deposed, dragged out of *harem* and brutally strangled.

After Farrukh Siyar, the two brothers raised two puppet rulers, namely Rafi-ud-Darajat and Rafi-ud-Daula. Both these rulers ruled for about eight months only. They were very weak. They were suffering from T. B. They were deposed and after their deposition, they died very shortly.

End of the Sayyid Brothers. After three puppet emperors, the Sayyid Brothers made the 18-year Muhammad Shah, the emperor of India.

The deposition and murder of Farrukh Siyar had frightened several nobles including some ofthe Hindustani nobles. Their treatment with the other two emperors also invited hatred. The liberal religious policies followed by the Sayyid Brothers were not liked by the Sunni Musalmans. Thus an anti-Sayyid Brothers group began to emerge. The emperor Muhammad Shah also wanted to free himself from the control of two brothers. Conspiracies were planned against them. In 1720, his brother Sayyid Abdullah was made prisoner and he died in jail.

NADIR SHAH

Originally said to be a shepherd, Nadir Shah rose to become one of the greatest warriors of Persia and a merciless plunderer and killer in India. He is often called 'the Napoleon' of Persia. It is an irony of fate that the person who created fear and terror in India was in the end killed in his own state of Persia.

Nadir Shah is associated with the words like atrocities, cruelties and disorder.

Nadir Shah invaded India in 1739.

Causes of Nadir Shah's invasion

According to Dr. V. S. Smith, "When established on his throne (Persia), he easily found pretexts for the invasion and plunder of the rich and defenceless Indian plains.

Following were the important causes of his invasion on India.

1. Getting name and fame by conquering lands.
2. Weak Mughal ruler of India.
3. Lust for the fabulous wealth of India.
4. Mughal emperor's providing shelter to some Afghans who had opposed Nadir Shah.
5. Being angry with the Mughal emperor for not facilitating him (Nadir Shah) on the occasion of his accession.
6. Invitation from some nobles of the Mughal court to invade India.

Main events of the invasion

The defence of the North West Frontier was very weak. The roads and passes were neglected. No intelligence report was sent to the Mughal emperor by his governors. All the same, the Mughal emperor also did not call for any report.

In such a state of affairs, it became very easy for Nadir Shah to capture Kabul, Jalalabad, Peshawar and Lahore. The Governor of Punjab showed some resistance but was defeated. The pleasure-loving emperor failed to realize the danger in time.

Battle of Karnal (February 1739): At long last when Nadir Shah was marching towards Delhi, the Mughal emperor Mohammad Shah suddenly woke up and the imperial troops marched and camped at Karnal (about 40 km from the famous battle-field of Panipat).

The fight between the Mughal emperor and Nadir Shah lasted two hours. The imperial forces were routed. About 20,000 soldiers were slain. Mughal emperor Mohammad Shah made no further resistance and attended Nadir Shah in his camp.

Loot, Plunder and Massacre in Delhi

Nadir Shah agreed to return after getting handsome tribute from the Mughal emperor. Unfortunately rumour was spread that Nadir Shah was dead and a few Persian soldiers were killed by the inhabitants of Delhi. Nadir Shah became furious and on March, 11, 1739, issued a general order of slaughtering the inhabitants of Delhi.

According to contemporary accounts, the general massacre in Delhi lasted for about seven hours from eight in the morning till three in the afternoon. The Chandni Chowk, the Dariba Bazar and the buildings around the Jamma-Masjid were set on fire and reduced to ashes. People were butchered mescilessly.

Befor leaving Delhi, Nadir Shah crowed Mohammad Shah again as the emperor of Delhi.

Results of Nadir Shah's invasion

1. *Territorial losses* : Nadir Shah got the Mughal possessions lying into the west of river Indus. Afghanistan was virtually separated from India, West Punjab and Sindh were completely lost to the Mughal empire.

2. *Mughal power weakened* : The invasion of Nadir Shah gave a severe blow to the Mughal power and prestige.

3. *Independence of provincial governers.* Several provincial governments like those of Nizam-ul-Mulk in the Deccan, Saasdat Ali Khan in Oudh and Alivardi Khan in Bengl, Bihar and Orissa virtually became independent of the Mughal rule.

4. *Ground for invasions* : The weakness of the defence of the north-west was exposed and as a result it paved the way for the invasions of Ahmed Shah Abdali.

5. *Drain of wealth.* Nadir Shah went back with an enormous wealth valued at Rs. fifty to seventy crores—gold and diamond, 300 elephants, 10,000 horses, 10,000 camels etc. He also took away the famous '*Kohinoor*' and the '*Peacock Throne*'.

6. *Financial bankrupty of the treasury.* The Mughal emperor and his nobles had to part with a lot of money. The treasury almost became empty.

7. *New vocabulary.* The word '*Nadir Shah*' synonymous with 'cruelty, 'high-handedness' and disorder' became popular.

AHMAD SHAH ABDALI OR DURRANI (1748 TO 1767)

Early life and rise to power

Ahmad Shah Abdali, an Afghan Chief belonging to Abdali tribe was the most important and powerful general of Nadir Shah. Nadir Shah who was greatly impressed by the qualities of Ahmad Shah complimented him saying, "I have not found in Iran, Turan and Hind any man equal to Ahmad Shah in capacity and character." Ahmed Shah played a very significant role in Nadir Shah's invasion over India in 1739.

After the assassination of Nadir Shah in 1749, Ahmad Shah took advantage of the confusion and proclaimed himself the ruler of Afghanistan. He also captured Kandhar and Kabul.

Invasions Over India causes:

After establishing his position and power at home, he led seven expeditions to India between 1748 and 1767.

According to Elphinstone, Ahmad Shah's motives in invading India were, "Ahmad Shah must have entertained the desire of establishing political authority over at least a part of India, though there were other motives which led him to undertake these expeditions. These other motives must be financial gain, political ambitions and others."

Important causes of his invasions may be listed as under:

1. To increase prestige at home.
2. To gain control over some territories of India - Punjab and Sindh.
3. To obtain wealth from India.
4. To make use of the unstable political condition in India.
5. To derive the maximum benefit out of the declining power of the Mughals.
6. To avail of the invitation extended to him by Shah Nawaz, Governor of Punjab to invade India.

Ahmad Shah Abdali made three invasions in 1748, 49, 51, during the reign of Mughal emperor Ahmad Shah, two in 1756 and 59-61, during the rule of Alamgir II and again two in 1764 and 67 during the period of Shah Alam.

The fifth invasion was very decisive. The third Battle of Panipat was fought in 1761 between Ahmad Shah Abdali and the Marathas who had emerged as the strongest power in India. The power of the Marathas was almost crushed. (Details of this battle are given in a subsequent chapter.)

Effects of Ahmad Shah Abdali's invasions

1. *Rise of Sikhs in Punjab*: The invassions of Ahmad Shah Abdali contributed a good deal to the rise of Sikh power. As soon Ahmad Shah left India to go back to Afghanistan, the Sikhs captured Lahore and its surrounding areas.

2. *Great setback to the Marathas* : The invasions of Ahmad Shah Abdali in general and the third Battle of Panipat gave a stunting below to the quickly expanding power of the Marathas.

3. *Severe blow to the Mughal power* : The invasions of Ahmad Shah Abdali proved to be the last below to the totterng Mughal empire. It was confined to Delhi and a few surrounding areas.

4. *Gain and loss of wealth* : On the one hand, Ahmad Shah Abdali got a lot of wealth from India and on the other, India became a great loser of wealth.

5. *Opportunity to the East India Company* : It became easier for the East India Company to consolidate its position in India as the power of the Mughals and the Marathas received a great set back.

6. *Loss of life*. Thousands of innocent people were mercilessly murdered. Several Maratha generals and soldiers lost their lives.

Q. 3. Discuss the main causes for the decline and fall of the Mughal empire.

(Punjab University Oct. 1996 and Oct, 1998, Rajasthan 1995)

Ans. *Decline and Fall of the Mughal Empire*

There were seventeen Mughal rulers who ruled for about 332 years *i.e.* from 1526 A.D.to 1857 AD As a matter of fact effective Mughal rule lasted for about 150 years. *i.e.* from the reign of Akbar from 1556 to 1707 to the reign of Aurangzeb. By 1739 the Mughal authority was confined to Delhi and its surrounding areas. The last three Mughal emperors namely Shah Alam, Akbar *II* and Bahadur Shah Zafar were the British pensioners. The English captured Delhi in 1803. Thus, we can say that after 1739, the Mughal rule was on 'paper' and in name only.

Babar (1526-30) founded the Mughal empire in 1526 AD. Humayun (1530-40) and (1555-56) almost lost it in 1540 but again got in 1555 but could not strengthen it. Akbar (1556 to 1605) consolidated the Mughal empire and followed a policy of reconciliation towards the Hindus. On account of his benevolent rule and great qualities he came to be called 'Akbar the great.' Jahangir (1605- 1627) was mostly under the influence of his queen Nur Jahan. Shah Jahan (1627-1658) built several beautiful buildings including the famous Taj and his period is known as the 'Golden Period of Indian Architecture'. Aurangzeb (1658-1707) was the last strong Mughal ruler. He ruled over the vast empire ever ruled by an Indian ruler. All the same by his religious bigotry, he incurred the displeasure of the majority of his subjects. His rule was marked by several bloody conflicts. He, however, was able to overcome all the revolts but his actions led to the weakening of the foundation of the Mughal empire.

After Aurangazeb, eleven Mughal rulers ruled. Five were murdered/ deposed, and the last three became the pensioners of the British. The other were, by and large, nominal and figure-head rulers.

Causes of the Fall of the Mughal Empire

While discussing the causes of the downfall it must be borne in mind that there was nothing unusual about it. The rise and falls is the law of nature and this happened with the Mughal dynasty also.

Dr. V. A. Smith's observations on this issue make interesting reading "The Mughal Empire, like Asiatic depotisms, had shallow roots... the student who has acquired even a moderately sound knowledge of the history will be surprised that the empire lasted so long."

In the words of Edward and Garret, "A family in which fathers, sons and brothers regarded one another as enemies was inevitably doomed to lose its political supremacy."

Following were the important causes of the downfall of the Mughal empire.

1. *Aurangzeb's responsibility*. As observed by Khafi Khan, "Every plan and project that he formed came to little good; and every enterprise which he

took was long in execution and failed in its object." In the words of Dr. V. A. Smith, "From about 1698, if not earlier, Aurangzeb's prolonged campaigns may be described as complete failure." Aurangzeb's religious policy, Rajput policy, Jat policy Maratha policy, Sikh policy, North West Frontier policy and Foreign policy - all failed. Above all his suspicious nature and puritanic measures led to conflicts and rebellions which caused irreparable damage to the Mughal power and prestige.

2. *Very weak successors of Aurangzeb*. From the death of Aurangzeb in 1707 and upto 1759 *i.e.* about half a century, there were eight Mughal rulers.

(*i*) Bahadur Shah was known as '*Shah-i-bekhabar* (Headless king).

(*ii*) Jahandar Shah who was strangled to death spent most of his time in the company of lady Lal kunwar, his favourite concubine.

(*iii*) Farrukh Siyyar has been described by V. A. Smith as "good for nothing and shamelss debauch" He was a puppet at the hands of Sayyid Brothers, was deposed by them and put to death in a horrible way.

(*iv*) and (*v*) Rafi-ud-Darajat and Rafi-ud-Daula ruled for about six moths only. They also remained puppets in the hands of Sayyid Brothers. They were also deposed.

(*vi*) Mohammad Shah, nicknamed '*Rangilla*' on account of his loose habits saw the disintegration of his empire. In the opinion of Dr. K. K. Datta, 'Province after province slipped out of the imperial control'.

(*vii*) Ahmad Shah was deposed, imprisoned and blinded.

(*viii*) Alamgir was murdered.

(*ix*) and (*x*) Shah Alam II (1759 to 1806), Akbar II (1806 to 1837) and Bahadur Shah II (1837 - 1857) were the pensioners of the East India Company.

3. *Intrigues of nobles*. In the words of Edward and Garret, "The Chronicles of the Court of Delhi after the death of Aurangzeb offer an unbroken tale of plots and counterplots on the part of powerful nobles, culminating at intervals in open disorder and fighting with the titular emperor serving as the sport and plaything of the contending parties."

4. *Wars of succession*. In the words of Erakine, "The sword was the grand arbitar of right. and every son was prepared to try his fortune against his brothers."

5. *Inefficiency of the army*. Hunter has written about it as "The heroic soldiers of the early empire and their not less heroic wives had given place to a vicious and delicate breed of grandees."

6. *Degenerated Mughal nobility*. It is stated by J. N. Sarkar, "All the surplus produce of a fertile land was swept into the coffers of the Mughal nobility and pampered them in a degree of luxury not dreamt of even by kings of Persia or Central Asia."

7. *Financial bankruptcy*. Financial bankruptcy had began during the reign of Aurangzeb on account of his Deccan wars. It went on increasing year by

year. The emperors began to depend heavily on their *Vazirs*. "It is stated that Alamgir II (1759 to 1806) had no conveyance to take him to the Idgah and he had to walk on foot." This may be an exaggerated version but it certainly gives a fair account of the financial dependence and powers of the later Mughal emperors.

8. *Unwieldy size of the empire*. The Mughal empire had become too vast and only a strong, tactful and a diplomatic ruler could govern such an extensive empire. The later Mughal rulers lacked all these qualities.

9. *Wide-spread administrative corruption*. Officials and their subordinates -from the highest to the lowest made fortunes for taking brobes. It is stated that a personal attendant of Mughal emperor amassed Rs 12 lakhs in cash, besides several valuable articles and a house. Even the emperors were not above bribery.

10. *Mansabdari system and its drawbacks*. The Mansabdari system degenerated in the time of later Maghals. Mansabdars lived a life of luxury and the "mass of the people were human sheep."

11. *Alien Mughal rule*. The Mughal rule in India was foreign in origin. It did not take its roots from the soils of this land. The orthodox Muslims had their hearts in Arabia and Persia. An empire formed on such basis could depend only on its military strength.

12. *Invasions of Nadir Shah and Ahmad Shah Abdali*. These two invaders invaded India several times, defeated the Mughals, weakened the army, humiliated the rulers, looted the country and sounded the death knell of the Mughal empire.

13. *Lack of effective education and training*. There was no provision for good education and training for the sons of the Mughal nobles. According to J. N. Sarkar, "They were too much petted by eunuchs and maid servants and passed through a sheltered life from birth to manhood."

14. *Emergence of new powers*. With the weakening of the Mughal power, several new forces appeared on the scene for their supremacy. The Sikhs in the Punjab, the Marathas in the South, the Rajputs in Rajasthan, the Rohillas in Rohilkhand and the Jats in Agra and nearby areas established their own independent kingdoms. Nizam-ul-Mulk in Hyderabad, Ali Vardi Khan in Bengal and Saadat Khan in Oudh declared their independence.

15. *Coming of the European Nations in India*. Several European powers began to interfere in the affairs of India. Originally, their motive was to increase their trade but gradually they desired to enslave India. The English became a leading power after securing victories at Plassey in 1757 and Buxer in 1764 AD.

16. *Neglect of the sea power*. The Mughals did not realise the importance of a strong naval power. They, therefore, were defeated at the hands of the European powers.

17. *Impact of reformers*. In Maharashtra, the spirit of independence was

encouraged by religious and social reformers like Guru Ram Das. In Punjab, the Sikh Gurus emphasised the preservation of their faith against all odds. Likewise Satnamis and others kindled a spirit of freedom of worship etc.

18. *Stagnation and deterioration in agriculture*. There are several instances of peasant dicontent and oppression by the nobles which reslulted in the stagnation of agriculture.

19. *Absence of the spirit of political Nationalism*. According to Dr. Bipin Chandra, the absence of political nationalism among the people was an important cause of the downfall of the Mughal empire.

Summing up. In the end one can only say that rise and fall of the empires is a natural phenomenon and the Mughal empire was no exception.

3

Rise of Autonomous States in the Eighteenth Century

(The Marathas and Third Battle of Panipat)

Q.1. Briefly describe the political scenario that emerged as a result of the declining power of the later Mughals.

Ans. *Disintegration of the Mughal Empire and Rise of Independent States*

The Mughal empire founded by the bravery of Babur, extended and consolidated by the administrative ability, statesmanship and liberalism Akbar, maintained intact by Jahangir and Shahjahan, weakened by the faulty policies of Aurangzeb, disintegrated speedily after his death in 1707. Revolts and dissensions which were not unusual even during the heydays of the Mughal empire assumed alarming proportions during the period of later Mughals. The principle of 'survival of the fittest' became operative at the centre and in the provinces. The vast empire of the Mughals, within about three decades of Aurangzeb's death, ceased to exist as an all-India political unit and was split up into numerous independent states.

As observed by Dr. K.K. Datta, "Province after province — the Deccan, Oudh and Bengal — slipped out of imperial control. The Marathas established their power far and wide; the Jats became independent near Agra, the Ruhela Afghans founded the state of Rohilkhand in the north Gangetic Plain; and the Sikhs became active in the Punjab."

Important Provincial/Regional Independent Powers

Punjab: The narrow religious policy of Aurangzeb had given rise to Sikh power. After Guru Gobind Singh's death in 1708, the military and political leadership of the Sikhs for sometimes passed into the hands of Banda Bahadur. Banda Bahadur fought bitterly with the Mughal forces and won initial victories but lost to the Mughals and was executed in 1716. However, the Sikhs continued their struggle and established their hold in some parts of the Punjab.

In 1739, the Sikhs fell upon the rear of the army of Nadir Shah when he was returning from Delhi along with his booty and were successful in snatching away a part of the loot from the Afghans.

Ahmad Shah Abdali and the Sikhs came into conflicts several times. At one time he had to run away to save his life. In the end he was able to have an upper hand over them but failed to crush their power. After the return of Ahmad Shah Abdali to Afghanistan, the Sikhs emerged as a strong power in the Punjab. The Mughal Government lost its hold over Punjab.

Rise of Jats. During the reign of Aurangzeb, the Jats had rebelled but their revolts were crushed. After Aurangzeb's death the Jats were able to set up the Jat state of Bharatpur. The Jat power reached its highest glory under Suraj Mal (1756-63). The Jat kingdom included area covering Agra, Mathura, Hathras, Aligarh, Merrut, Rohtak, Rewari, Gurgaon and Mewat. After his death in 1763, the Jat kingdom was split up among petty Zamindars.

Rajput States. After Aurangzeb's death, the Rajput Chiefs of Marwar, Mewar and Amber became independent. They also played an important role in Mughal politics.

Rise of Marathas. After Shivaji's death, his kingdom could not survive for long as his successors proved to be very weak. The Marathas got divided. In due course, the real power came in the hands of the Peshwa (Prime Minister). The Marathas took full advantage of the weakness of the Mughal empire after the death of Aurangzeb and became a formidable power during the period 1713 to 1760. Their slogan under Peshwa Baji Rao was 'from Krishna to the Indus'. The Marathas extended their authority in the North upto the Punjab. However in 1761, in the third Battle of Panipat, they received a crushing defeat at the hands of Ahmad Shah Abdali.

Bengal. Bengal became independent during the period of later Mughals. The English first of all gained a foothold in Bengal.

Oudh. Saadat Khan, Safdar Jang and Shuja-ud-daula were the important rulers.

Deccan. Deccan became practically independent of Mughal control during the period of Farrukh Siyar.

Rise of Europeans. In the beginning of the 18th century, the Dutch, the Danes and the Portuguese had lot their influence. The English and the French contested against one another and the English routed the French.

Triangular Struggles in North and South India

In north India, a triangular struggle for supremacy ensued among three contenders *i.e.* the Marathas, the Mughals and the Afghans of Afghanistan. Marathas under the Peshwas (Prime Minister of the Maratha rulers) who wielded power, humbled the Mughals. In 1737 the Marathas raided Delhi. Likewise Nadir Shah and Ahmad Shah Abdali humiliated the Mughals. Thus there were left two contenders. Ahmad Shah Abdali, the Afghan ruler defeated the Marathas in the third Battle of Panipat in 1761.

In the South India also there was a triangular struggle among the Marathas, the Nizam of Hyderabad and the Sultan of Mysore.

There was another triangular contest in the South among the European companies — the Dutch, the English and the French. The six powers in the South entered into conspiracies and intrigues.

Thus there was a good deal of political chaos in the eighteenth century in India.

Q. 2. Write notes on:

(1) Banda Bahadur
(2) Suraj Mal
(3) Raja Sawai Jai Singh
(4) Safdar Jang.
(5) Shuja-ud-Daula.

BANDA BAHADUR (1670-1716)

Banda Bahadur whose original name was Lachhman Dass was a '*Bairagi*' (ascetic) who chose to bind himself (Banda) to Guru Gobind Singh, the tenth Guru of the Sikhs. Guru Gobind Singh baptised him in the '*Khalsa*' and asked him to wreck vengeance on the enemies of the '*Khalsa*'. A large number of Sikhs in the Punjab joined Banda. Banda captured Sirhand in 1710 after a bloody battle. It was a war of vengeance as the governor of Sirhand was regarded as the murderer of the sons of Guru Gobind Singh. The city was plundered and the Governor was killed mercilessly. After his victory, Banda Bahadur struck coins in the name of the Guru. He made Lohgarh as the centre of his administration.

Banda Bahadur appeared as a great champion of the Hindus and the Sikhs. He was a great organiser. According to a Sikh historian Dr. Ganda Singh? "It was through him that the path of conquest and freedom was discovered by the people of Punjab. He was the first man to deal a severe blow at the intolerant rule of the Mughals in the Punjab and to break the first sod in the conquest of that province by the Sikhs."

Banda Bahadur tried to ameliorate the condition of peasants by abolishing the *jagirdari* system. The Sikhs captured Amritsar, Kasur, Batala, Kalanaur and Pathankot — all important towns in the Punjab. Soon the Sikhs controlled practically the entire territory between the river Sutlej and Jammuna, reaching the neighbourhood of Delhi. The Mughal emperor Bahadur Shah took strong exception to it and in 1710 more than 60,000 soldiers were sent to subdue Banda Bahadur. Banda had to face defeat and he retired to the hills. Banda continued the struggle. Farrukh Siyar, the Mughal emperor who succeeded Bahadur Shah, made eleborate military arrangements to fight against Banda. Banda Bahadur and his army put up a strong resistance in the Battle of Gurdas Nangal but had to face defeat. Banda and some of his followers were captured and brought to Delhi. They refused to renounce their faith. They were tortured and executed in Delhi in July 1716.

SURAJ MAL (1707-1763)

On account of his political sagacity, steady intellect and clear vision, Suraj Mal is remembered as the 'Plato of the Jat tribe'.

Suraj Mal was the adopted son of Bandan Singh, the founder of the Jat state of Bharatpur after Aurangzeb's death. The Jat power reached its highest glory under Suraj Mal. He extended his authority over a large area which extended from the Ganga in the East to Chambal in the South, the province of Agra in the West to the province of Delhi in the North. The Bharatpur state included among others the districts of Agra, Mathura, Merrut and Aligarh.

After the Third Battle of Panipat, Suraj Mal was perhaps the strongest ruler in North India.

Suraj Mal was an able administrator, a great fighter and a wise statesman.

Bharatpur was the capital of the Kingdom.

After his death in 1763, the Jat kingdom was split up among petty zamindars

RAJA SAWAI JAI SINGH (1699 — 1743)

Several Rajput states emerged as independent states after the death o. Aurangzeb. Among the outstanding rulers of the 18th century, Raja Sawai Jai Singh of Amber occupies an important place. The remarkable ruler ruled for about 44 years-a very rare feat. He was a great astronomer, builder, engineer, jurist, social reformer and above all a wise statesman.

He distinguished himself as a man of science in an age when Indians were oblivious to scientific progress and thought.

Jai Singh erected five astronomical observatories on scientific principles at Delhi, Jaipur, Mathura, Ujjain and Varanasi. He designed a set of tables called '*Zij Muhammad Shahi*' to enable people to make astronomical observations. These observatories are known as *'Jantar Mantar'*

Jai Singh founded the city of modern Jaipur commonly known as the *'Pink city'*. The city was well-planned and built on scientific lines. Its wide roads crossing each other at right angles are a testimony to his engineering skill.

Jai Singh made Jaipur a great centre of art and science.

Jai Singh was a great literary figure. He got several important works of science and mathematics translated into Sanskrit. Among the important ones are Euclid's '*Elements of Geometry*' and Napier's work on the construction and use of logarithms.

Jai Singh was also an enlightened social reformer. He tried to enforce a law to reduce the extravagent expenditure which the Rajputs used to incur on their daughter's marriage. He also put a check on the killing of girls at birth by Rajputs.

SAFDAR JUNG

He was the Nawab of Oudh and also the '*Wazir*' of the Mughal emperor Ahmad Shah. He worked on this position for about six years from 1748 to 1754. Allahabad district was also under his charge.

A Good Administrator and a Tolerant Ruler. Safdarjung performed two functions. He was a Wazir of the Mughal king and the ruler of Oudh also. He gave a long spell of peace and economic prosperity to Oudh. He suppressed the rebellious Rohilla chiefs with the help of the Jats and Marathas. He organised an equitable system of justice and tolerance. He gave the highest rank of his administration to a Hindu name Maharaja Nawab Rai.

Patron of art and literature. He made Lucknow a great centre of art and literature. It almost rivalled Delhi in the development of music and art and language and poetry. The culture developed by him came to be known as 'Luckhnavi' culture. Lucknow also became famous for handicrafts.

SHUJA-UD-DAULA

Shuja-ud-Daula, son of Safdarjung succeeded him as the '*Wazir*' of the Mughal emperor and ruler of Oudh. He remained on this position for about twenty one years *i.e.* from 1754 to 1775 till his death.

Shuja-ud-Daula was so powerful at one time that the Mughal emperor Shah Alam *II* was living under his protection in Oudh.

In the Battle of Buxar in 1764, Mir Qasim, the Nawab of Bengal, Shuja-ud-Daula and Shah Alam *II* who had joined together against the East India Company were defeated. Under the Treaty of Allahabad. Shuja-ud-Daula received back the province of Avadh minus the districts of Kara and Allahabad but had to pay rupees fifty lakhs as war indemnity. Shuja-ud-Daula had to keep English troops for the protection of its frontiers. Thus Oudh came under the influence and semi-control of the English.

Q. 3. Examine the contribution of Balaji Vishwanath and Balaji Rao I in the rise and expansion of Maratha Power.

(Punjab University April 1996, Delhi University 1993)

or

Estimate the qualities and achievements of Peshwa Baji Rao *I*.

(Punjab University April 1997 and Oct 1997, Rajasthan 1990)

or

Give brief account of the rise of the Maratha power in India from 1717-1742 AD. *(Punjab University April 1998)*

Ans. *Setback to Maratha empire*. After the death of Shivaji, the Maratha empire received a setback. Shivaji's successors did not prove competent enough to maintain the empire intact. Shambuji, Shivaji son was killed by Aurangzeb and Shahu, Shambuji's son was put into prison.

Civil war among the Marathas. Raja Ram, the younger son of Shivaji carried on the struggle against the Mughals till his death in 1700 and Traradevi his widowed queen who acted as regent for his minor son Shivaji II offered resistance to Aurangzeb. After Aurangzeb's death, the Mughal empire also received some setback. In the confusion that followed, Shahu with the help of Balaji Vishwanath was able to free himself from the prison of the Mughals. War for supremacy among the claimants of Maratha empire ensued.

Balaji Vishwanath and his son Baji Rao I played an important role in reviving the Maratha glory

BALAJI VISHWANATH (1713-1720)

Balaji Vishwanath was chiefly responsible in making Shahu, the *'Chhatrapti'* Shahu. Balaji was a skilful diplomat and he won over Tara Devi's Commander-in-chief Dhanaji to Shahu's side and this had an upper hand over Tara Devi. Shahu gradually gave all his authority to Balaji on account of his great ability and devotion. Maratha energy received a new fillip.

Chatrapati Shahu appointed Balaji as Peswa (Prime Minister), an office that became virtually the supreme office and the Maratha king became a nominal ruler. All powers came to be vested in the Peshwa. This office or institution became hereditary.

Balaji was successful in uniting most of the Maratha chiefs under the leadership of Shahu.

Balaji also secured Shahu the financial support of rich Maratha bankers and this helped the state to ward off financial difficulties.

Balaji's deal with Sayyid brothers (king makers of later Mughals) brought riches to the Maratha king.

Balaji channelised the energies of the Marathas into the task of building a Hindu empire over the ruins of the Mughal empire.

Balaji restored peace and prosperity in the Maratha land which had been devastated by the evils of civil war.

BAJI RAO I (1720-40)

I. Policies

(1) *Incarnation of Hindu energy*. Baji Rao preached and popularised the ideal of *'Hindu-pad-padshahi'* or Hindu empire to secure the support of the Hindu chiefs against the common enemy *i.e.* the Mugal empire. He fully appreciated that the Rajputs, the Bundelas, the Jats and other Hindu chiefs were the natural allies of the Marathas in the struggle against the Mughals. The friendship of Sawai Jai Singh and Chhatarsal stood him in good stead.

(2) *Forward looking policy*. In his own words, "Now is our time to drive the strangers from the country of the Hindus and acquire immortal renown. Let us strike at the trunk of the withering tree, and the branches will fall of

themselves. By directing our efforts to Hindustan the Maratha flag shall fly from the Krishna (river) to Attock."

II. Main events of the rule of Baji Rao I

1. *Victory over the Nizam of the Deccan*. There were four important reasons that led to conflict with the Nizam of Deccan. (1) The Nizam of the Deccan who served as Viceroy of Deccan of the Mughal emperor wanted to establish his own independent kingdom. (2) He tried to sow dissensions among Maratha chiefs. (3) Although he accepted the claim of the Marathas to collect '*Chauth*' and '*Sardeshmukhi*' from the six provinces in the Deccan, he adopted dilatory tactics. (4) When Baji Rao was away from his headquarters and busy in Carnatic, the Nizam attached the territory of the Marathas. Baji Rao rushed from his campaign and inflicted a humiliating defeat on the Nizam in the battle of Palkhed in 1728. The Nizam entered into the Treaty of Mungi Shivagoan and agreed to recognise the undisputed claim of the Marathas regarding '*Chauth*' and '*Sardeshmukhi*' and to return all the territories captured by him in the absence of Baji Rao. Nizam also agreed to ramain neutral during Baji Rao's expedition to North India.

2. *Conquest of Malwa and Gujarat and Bundelkhand*. During the period 1724 and 1728, Baji Rao conquered and exercised influence over Malwa Gujarat and Bundelkhand by offering help to Bundela chief Chattar Sal.

3. *Raid on Delhi* (March 1737). During the Maratha campaign in northern Bundelkhand, a small troop of Marathas had to fall back under pressure. The Nawab sent exaggerated report to the Mughal emperor of his achievements.

Therefore, Baji Rao dashed to Delhi and terrorised the Mughal emperor.

4. *Battle of Bhopal* (December 1737). The Maratha power was increasing with great speed. This alarmed the Nizam. The Nizam with the help of the Mughal emperor attempted to drive out the Marathas from Malwa. Once again Baji Rao inflicted a crushing defeat on the Nizam in the Battle of Bhopal in 1737. On January 7, 1738, the Treaty of Duraha Sarai was entered into by the Nizam with Baji Rao. The Nizam agreed to pay a war indemnity of 50 lakhs of rupees. Besides, he accepted the full sovereignty of the Peshwa over the land between the rivers Narbada and Chambal.

About the significance of the Battle of Bhopal, Dr. Dighe writes, "Bhopal victory is the pinnacle of the victorious career of Peshwa. By defeating the confederate armies at Bhopal, the Peshwa established the supremacy of Maratha arms in India and announced the birth of a New Imperial war."

5. *Capture of Salsette and Bassein and concessions from the Portuguese*. The Marathas obtained from the Portuguese their northern possessions including four forts of strategic importance and also three hundred and forty villages.

6. *Poona and not Delhi as the political centre*. There is no doubt that with the phenomenal achievements of Baji Rao, the political centre in India shifted

from Delhi to Poona. It was not the Mughal emperor who was a supreme power but the Marathas.

AN ESTIMATE OF BAJI RAO

In guerilla warfare Baji Rao had no equal. He was next only to Shivaji. He possessed plenty of common sense, intelligence and very good physique. He was well-versed in diplomacy and administration. He correctly came to the conclusion that the Mughal power was declining and it was possible to snatch away the territories from it. He overran several kingdoms in the south as well as in the north. The Nizam of Hyderabad agreed to pay a war idemnity of Rs. 50 lakhs to him. He took the island of Bassein and other areas from the Portuguese. He tried to unite the Maratha chiefs. He put the Maratha power on strong footing.

Baji Rao's death at a young age of forty deprived not only the Marathas but also India as a whole of a great fighter and winner and also a wise strategist and statesman. He prepared the Marathas to fill up the vaccum created by the tottering power of the Mughals but his successors failed to reap the fruit of his labours.

Q.4. Discuss the causes and the results of the third Battle of Panipat.

(Rajasthan 1995 and 1996)

or

"The third Battle of Panipat was an important event of Indian history." Describe the causes of the defeat of the Marathas in this battle.

(Delhi 1985, 1983; Merrut 1980 and Punjab 1978)

Ans.

THE THIRD BATTLE OF PANIPAT (1761)

Causes of Battle

The Battle of Panipat fought between the Marathas and Ahmad Shah Abdali resulted in the victory of the latter. It was waged on account of the following reasons:

1. *Expansionist designs of the Marathas and Ahmad Shah Abdali.* The Marathas wanted to make the best use of the vacuum created in the political field by the tottering power of the Mughals. Ahmad Shah Abdali had already invaded India several times and was interested to strengthen his control over some parts of India in the north and particularly the Punjab.

2. *Growing influence of the Marathas over the Mughal emperor.* Alarmed at the growing power of the Marathas Nawab Safdarjung Wazir of the Mughal emperor entered into contract with the Maratha leaders Scindhia and Holkar on the following conditions.

(*i*) The Marathas would defend the Mughal emperor from internal and external dangers.

(*ii*) The Mughal emperor would pay fifty lakhs of rupees to the Marathas for their help.

(*iii*) The Marathas (Peshwa) would be given the right to collect *'Chauth'* from the Punjab, Sindh, and the Doab.

Though the agreement was not ratified by the Mughal emperor, yet it clearly showed the superiority of the Marathas. Obviously this was not in the interest of Ahmed Shah.

3. *Expulsion of the nominee of Ahmad Shah Abdali from the Mughal court.* In 1757, Ahmad Shah Abdali had left Najib-ud-Daula as his nominee to protect the Mughal emperor from the excesses of his *'Wazir'*. However, Najib proved to be worse than the *'Wazir'*. With the help of the Marathas, Najib was compelled to retire.

4. *Ill-feelings between the Marathas and the Rohillas.* The Mughal emperor had sought the help of the Marathas to put down the revolts of the Rohillas in the Doab. The Rohillas being Afghans had constantly poisoned Ahmad Shah Abdali (who was also an Afghan) against the Marathas.

5. *Over ambitious Marathas and jealousy of some powers.* It is alleged that the Marathas used to indulge in inflicting atrocities over their opponents who in turn invited Ahamad Shah to invade.

6. *Maratha's occupation of Punjab.* The Marathas occupied Lahore and Attock and drove away Timur, son of Ahmad Shah Abdali who, therefore was very eager to take revenge of the insult of his son.

Events

The conquest of Punjab by the Marathas brought them into conflict with Ahmad Shah Abdali who started from Afghanistan to recover the same from the Marathas. Ahmad Shah had under his command 40,000, cavalry and 35,000 infantry,. The Marathas under the leadership of Sadashiv Rao Bhau had 55,000 cavalry, 15,000 infantry and 15,000 Pandaris. The two armies faced each other on the battle field of Panipat in November 1760. Both sides negotiated for peace but no meeting ground was found. The battle was fought on January 14, 1761. It lasted for about 6 hours from 9. A.M. to 3 P.M. To begin with, the Maraths had an upper hand but later on, the Afghans carried the day. Sadashiv Bhao along with Viswas Rao, son of the Peshwa was killed. There was a terrible loss of life among the Marathas. This news reached Peshwa Balaji Baji Rao when he was coming to Panipat with reinforcement. However, it was too late. He retired broken hearted to Poona and died after a few days.

Important Causes of the Defeat of the Marathas

Important causes of the defeat of the Marathas were as under:

1. Mutual distrust and jealousy among the powerful Maratha leaders.

2. Outdated methods of warfare which could not match the modern warfare methods of Europeans.

3. Policy of aggression and plunder which created hatred for them among the neighbouring areas.

4. Lack of discipline and a unified command in the Maratha army.

5. Unfriendly relation and hostility of several Rajput states on account of the lack of diplomacy of the Marathas.

6. Lack of an efficient spy system to locate the weak and strong points of the enemy.

7. Neglect of sea power by the Marathas.

8. Lack of training in the open field but overconfidence of the Marathas.

9. Unsound financial position and dependence on plundering the neighbours.

Results of the third Battle of Panipat

1. The Marathas received a severe blow to their growing power.

2. The Mughal empire almost lost its significance.

3. Ahmad Shah plundered at will.

4. The East India Company, gained immensaly as the Mughals and the Marathas became very weak and the political situation turned very favourable to the Company.

5. It cleared the way for the rise of the Sikh power in the Punjab.

6. Internal dissensions among the Marathas increased.

Q.5. Discuss the significance of the Third Battle of Panipat.

(Rajasthan 1997)

or

Examine the causes that led to the failure of the Marathas to establish their stronghold in North India. Evaluate the consequences of the third Battle of Panipat. *(Delhi University, 1992 and 1996)*

Ans. *Causes of the failure of the Marathas*

It is common knowledge that all sorts of reasons are attributed to the failure of a ruler or his army. The Marathas are no exception. Likewise is the situation in the case of success.

Following were the important causes which contributed to the defeat of the Marathas:-

1. *Mistake of Bhau in the battlefield.* Viswas Rao, son of the Peshwa died in the battle field when he received a bullet. When Sada Shiv Bhau Maratha commander came to know of this, he dismounted the elephant to mourn over the death. This made him invisible which resulted in chaos in his army. Not only this in a fray, without any planning he plunged into the rank of Abdali's camp and lost his life.

2. *Overconfidence and complancency of Bhau.* While leading his army from Poona to Panipat, Bhau, the commander of the Maratha army met Suraj Mal, the Jat Raja on the way. The latter advised Bhau to leave at Jhansi or Gwalior all the multitude of women and children, the families of the officers

and the soldiers who accompanied the army — and the extensive beggage train of luxury — "Your troops" observed Suraj Mal," are more light and expeditious than those of Hindustan, but the Durrani's are still more expeditious than you." Bhau was also requested to drag out the campaign till the rains set in and then Abdali would be compelled to retreat. However Bhau disregarded all this. Instead he snubbed the Rajput ruler. Bhau showed a self-conceived conduct.

3. *Single-handed Campaign*. Kasi Raja Pandit, an eye-witness of the Battle of Panipat and also who took part in the peace negotiations with the Afghans has obeserved that Bhau "showed a capriciousness and self-conceited conduct and carried on everything by his own opinion alone."

4. *Mutual jealousies among Maratha commanders*. The team work among the Maratha commanders was lacking. Damaji Gackward, Jankoej Scidhia and Malhar Rao Holkar were extremely jealous of each other. Besides, Bhau was not held in high esteem by the commmanders.

5. *Failure to get cooperation of the Jats and the Rajputs*. The policy of indiscriminate plunder and overbearing attitude of the Marathas had alienated the Hindu powers.

6. *Lack of adequate discipline in the Maratha army*. The camping, campaigning, marching and discipline of the Afghan army were of a very high order.

7. *Lack of adequate equipment*. The Marathas fought mostly with lances and swords while the Afghan army used muskets.

8. *Lack of diplomacy*. The Marathas failed to realise the importance of the Sikhs who could prove very helpful in the Punjab. They were deadly against the Afghans. They would have gladly helped the Marathas in their struggle with the Afghans.

9. *Discarding guerilla warfare*. In spite of the advice of some Maratha leaders to Bhau not to fight a pitched battle as they were not well trained in this method of warfare, Bhau because of his unbending nature chose the other method.

10. *Help from Rohillas to the Afghans*. The Rohillas and Nawab of Audh joined the army of Ahmad Shah Abdali and this increased his strength.

11. *Afghan army greater in number*. J. N. Sarkar, on the basis of contemporary records has put the strength of Abdali's army at 60,000 as against 45,000 of the Marathas.

12. *Scarity of provisions for the army of the Marathas*. The Afghans very skilfully cut off the supply line of the Marathas in such a way that they could not get any provisions from Delhi. So desperate was the food situation in the Maratha camp on January 13, 1761 that some of the officers and soldiers approached Bhau and said, "It is now two days that no man among us got a grain to eat. Do not let us perish in this misery. Let us make a valiant struggle against the enemy and them what Fate has ordained will happen." As ob-

served by Dr. A. L. Srivastva, "Such a famished army was not likely to succeed against a well-provided and satisfied army."

13. *Ineffective Maratha artillery*. The Marathas had greatly depended on the artillery commander Ibrahim Gardi. But it proved ineffective against the Afghan's long swivel guns mounted on the moving camel backs.

14. *Stirring speech by the commander of Ahmad Shah*. Shah Wali Khan commanded the Afghan force at the centre, the right flank was guarded by the Rohillas. Ahmad Shah took his position at the back of the centre with reserve force. Bhau did not keep any reserve force. In the beginning, Bhau made a fierce attack at the centre and broke a few lines commanded by Shah Wali Khan. At this critical juncture, Shah Wali addressed his soldiers as, "Our country is far off, my friends whither do you fly." This infused a new life in the Afghan force. Simultaneously Ahmad Shah Abdali threw in his reserves. This turned the balance in favour of the Afghans.

15. *Mercenary soldiers of the Maratha army*. A substantial section of the Maratha army was a hired one. These soldiers fought for their salary and not for their motherland. They left the battle-field as soon as they found that Abdali's army had an upper hand.

16. *Abdali Vs Bhau as generals*. Undoubtedly Abdali was a far better military general than Bhau.

Significance/Consequences of the Third Battle of Panipat

1. *Great set-back to Maratha power*. In this regard two statements are generally made.

(*i*) "Two pearls are dissolved, twenty-seven gold *mohars* have been lost and about the silver and copper the total cannot be cast-up."

The statement signifies terrible loss of life among the Marathas. Two pearls refer to the Maratha Chief and Chief Commander Sadasiva Bhao and Visvas Rao, the son of the Peshwa; twenty-seven gold *mohars* imply Maratha Commanders, and silver and copper signify young Maratha soldiers who lost lives in the battle.

(*ii*) "The Third Battle of Panipat did not decide that who will rule after the battle over India but it decided who will not rule." This statement means that the third Battle of Panipat was not decisive as to who would rule India. It, on the other hand, decided that neither the Marathas nor the Mughals and nor the clan of Abdali would rule. The English who ruled India later on were not in the picture in the Battle of Panipat.

Historians have expressed divergent opinions regarding the loss to the Marathas. According to J. N. Sarakar. "The disaster was felt as personal by almost every home in Maharashtra". Sidney Own writes, "The Maratha power was, for the time being, shattered to atoms." Likewise Elphinstone has observed, "Never was a defeat more complete" Dr. A. L. Srivastva holds the opinion, "The Marathas legions which were hither to looked upon as invincible lost their reputation, militarily as well as politically."

On the other hand L. S. Sardesai states, "Notwithstanding the terrible loss in manpower suffered on that field by the Marathas, the disater decided nothing."

2. *Fatal blow to the Mughal empire*. The Mughal emperor was reduced to a mere figure head.

3. *Rise of the Sikhs in the Punjab*. The third Battle of Panipat paved the way for the rise of the Sikh power in the Punjab.

4. *Rise of the English power in India*. Sardesai has explained the position as, "It is significant that while the two combatants, the Marathas and the Muslims, were locked in deadly combat, in the field of Panipat (Clive the founder of the British Empire in India, was on his way to England to explain the feasibility of his dreams of an Indian Empire to the Great Commoner, Lord Chatham, the then Prime Minister. Panipat indirectly ushered in a new participant in the struggle for Indian supremacy."

5. *Rise of Hyder Ali*. With the declining power of the Marathas in the south, Hyder Ali consloidated his hold on Mysore and founded a kingdom there.

6. *Rise of Jats and Rajputs*. The defeat of the Marathas and the downfall of the Mughals provided opportunities to the Rajputs and the Jats to rise to power in Rajputana and territories around Delhi and Bharatpur.

7. *Loss of human power*. It is said, "There was not a single home in Maharashtra that was not mourning the death of a youngman." About 75,000 soldiers are said to have lost their lives.

8. *Blow to the unity of Marathas* The Maratha chiefs started quarrelling among themselves.

9. *Turning point in the history*. There is no doubt that the third Battle of Panipat changed the very history of India.

4

Beginning of the British Rule in India : Conquest of Bengal

(Tools of Expansion : War and Diplomacy)

Q. 1. What were the circumstances leading to the Battle of Plassey? State the events and results of this battle.

or

What were the causes of conflict between Nawab Siraj-ud-Daula and the East India Company? How did it come to an end? State its political significance.

Ans. *Causes of Battle of Plassey.*

The Battle of Plassey was fought between the Nawab of Bengal Siraj-ud-Daula and the East India Company on account of the following reasons:

1. *Imperialist design of the Company.* The East India Company was no longer a mere trading Company. It had already entered into war in Carnatic. Like wise it wanted to extend its influence to Bengal province which at that time was considered a very rich and fertile province. It may be noted that the Bengal province at that time comprised Bengal, Bihar and Orissa.

2. *Misuse of the Royal 'Firman' and Dastak'*. A 'Farman' was a royal decree issued by the Mughal Emperor. A 'Farman' of the Mughal Emperor Farrukh Siyar (1717) gave freedom to East India Company to trade without paying taxes.

'Dastak' a sort of pass issued by the Company to its employees, on the basis of 'Farman', allowing them free movement of Company's goods.

The servants of the East India Company began to misuse the royal orders. They indulged in private trade which was not allowed. Nawab Siraj-ud-Daula objected to the unfair practices of the servants of the Company.

3. *Fortification of Calcutta.* Without taking permission from the Nawab of Bengal, the Company began to fortify Calcutta in anticipation of their conflict with the French who had set up their factory at Chandernagar.

4. *English sympathy for the rival claimant.* The Nawab felt that the English were inclined to support the claim of his rival over the Nawabship of Bengal.

5. *Military weakness of the Indian rulers.* The Anglo-French struggle in Carnatic wars had shown the military and political weakness of the Indian rulers.

6. *Refusal to accept the authority of the Nawab.* The Company did not give due recognition to the authority of the Nawab. They did not give presents to the Nawab as was the custom at the tme of his coronation.

7. *Protection given to the accused.* A rich Bengali merchant Krishan Das had incurred the displeasuse of the Nawab. He fled to Calcutta with his family and wealth. The Company did not hand over him to the Nawab as requested by him.

8. *Capture of English factory.* The Nawab enraged at the above action of the English, captured their factory at Kasim Bazar and then attaked Calcutta.

9. *Black-Hole tragedy.* Historians have given conflicting views regarding this. It is said that the Nawab confined about 145 Britishers including women and children in a very small cell at Calcutta and made them to spend one summer night there. More than 120 people had died by morning and others were in very terrible conditions. This is known as the Black-hole incident. It is pointed out by the opponents that so many persons could not be bundled together in such a small cell.

10. *Treaty of Alinagar.* When the English in Madras learnt about the capture of Calcutta by the Nawab, they sent army under Clive and navy under Watson for recapturing Calcutta. Nawab Sirj-ud-Daula was forced to sign the Treaty of Alinagar. By its treaty, the English got back all their forts and also got the rights to fortify Calcutta.

11. *Conspiracy against the Nawab.* Taking advantage of the dissatisfaction in the court of the Nawab, Clive decided to dethrone Nawab Siraj-ud-Daula and raise to the throne Mir Jafar, the commander in-chief of the Nawab's army. In all four persons which included Mir Jafar, Rai Durlab, a Treasurer of the Nawab, Jagat Singh, the richest banker of Bangal and Amin Chand, an influential person, joined the conspiracy. This action of Clive has been universally condemned.

12. *Immediate excuse.* Clive blamed the Nawab that he had not carried out the terms of the Treaty of Alinagar and that he was conspiring against the English by writing letters to the French Company.

Events. Both the sides met for battle at the field of Plassey, about 20 miles from Murshidabad on June 23, 1757. The historic battle was fought in name only. The Nawab had about 50,000 troops as against about 3000 of Clive. Nawab's army led by traitors did not show any worthwhile resistance. Nawab was defeated and killed.

Causes of the defeat of Siraj-ud-Daula

1. Disputed claim of Sira-ud-Daula to become the Nawab resulting in mutual conflicts among the nobles of the court.
2. Diplomacy of the Company to win over some of the nobles to their side.
3. Conspiracy hatched out by Clive and the help of Seths and other influential persons.

4. Corrupt officers like Manak Chand who were looking after the affairs of the Nawab at Calcutta.
5. Treachery of the Commander of the Nawab's forces.
6. No help to the Nawab from the French.
7. Lack of confidence and courage in Nawab Siraj-ud-Daula.
8. Failure of the Nawab to understand the implications of the Treaty of Alinagar.
9. Superior naval power of the British.
10. Immaturity of the Nawab who was just 23 when he became the Nawab.
11. Clive a great military strategist.
12. Lack of intelligence system of Nawab's administration so as to get any clue of conspiracy against him.

RESULTS/CONSEQUENCES OF THE BATTLE OF PLASSEY

The Battle of Plassey had far reaching consequences. Some of the important ones are given here.

I. *Political Consequences.*

1. *A new chapter in the history of India.* In the words of Sir J. N. Sarkar, "On 23rd June 1757, the medieval period of India ended and the modern period started."
2. *A new chapter in the history of England.* According to Admiral Waston, "The battle of Plessey was of extra-ordinary importance not only to the Company but to the British Nation in General."
3. *Paved the way for the conquest of India.* The conquest of Bengal gave ample confidence to the Company that Indian rulers could be defeated without much force. This victory became the starting point of the British rule over India.
4. *Rise in Company's status.* It added to the political prestige of the Company.
5. *Political victory through conspiracy.* The English observed that there could be several Mir Jafars and Seths who could be helpful in overthrowing Indian rulers.
6. *New Nawab as a puppet.* Siraj-ud-Daula was put to death and the new Nawab became a puppet for sometime in the hands of the Company.

II. *Economic Significance*

7. *Drain of wealth.* The first instalment of wealth paid to the Company immediately after Plessey was a sum of Rs. 800,00 - all paid in silver coin. In the graphic language of Macaulay, "The fleet which conveyed this treasure to Calcutta consisted of more than a hundred boats."
8. *Commercial benefits.* The Company got control over the entire trade of Bengal.
9. *Control over the immense resources of Bengal.* The vast reasources of

Bengal greatly helped the English to conquer wars in the Deccan and extend their control over Northern India.

10. *Decline of Indian industries*. After this battle, the decline of Indian industries started rapidly.
11. *Private economic gains*. The Company's officials including Clive himself received huge bribes.

III. *Military Importance*

12. *Weakness of the army*. The victory of the Company in Bengal brought to light the weakness of the Indian armies.
13. *Confidence in military exploits*. The victory of the English filled them with great enthusiasm to fight against the French, the Marathas and the Sikhs and in fact all Indian rulers.

IV. *Moral side of the Battle*

14. It became evident that the English were determined to establish their hold by all means, fair of foul. They could resort to conspiracy, deceit, greed and bribery etc.

Summing up Col. Malleson has described the consequences as. "There never was a buttle in which the consequences were so vast, so immediate and so permanent," There may the some element of exaggeration in this statement but there is no doubt that the consequences for India were very grave.

Q.2. Write note on the significance of Battle of Buxar.

(Punjab University October 1996 and April 1997)

or

Discuss the causes, events and results of the Battle of Buxar.

or

Discuss the conflict between Mir. Qasim and the East India Company and indicate its results.

(Delhi University 1995)

or

Discuss the causes and consequences of Battle of Buxar.

(Rajasthan University 1996)

Ans. *Conflict between Mir Qasim and East India Company: Battle of Buxar*

The Battle of Buxar fought between the East India Company on the one hand and the combination of Mir Qasim, the ex Nawab of Oudh and Shah Alam, Mughal Emperor on the other hand, was won by the Company and it decided only the fate of Mir Qasim and others but also the whole of India.

Reasons of the Battle

1. *Imperialist designs of the East India Comany*. The East India Company, though formed as a trading Company had began to dream of controlling India politically also.

2. *The conflict for supermacy*. The Company wanted to exercise adminis-

trative control over Bengal but Mir Qasim was prepared to accept only the rights of the Company as a trading corporation.

3. *Trading equality*. Mir Qasim gave the same trading facilities to the Indian merchants as were available to the English. The English merchants would not tolerate equality. They wanted better facilities and demanded the reimposition of trading duties on Indian merchants which the Nawab had removed to bring them at par with the English merchants.

4. *Company's hopes belied*. The Company had dethroned Mir Jafar and enthroned Mir Qasim with the hope that he would be a puppet in their hands but Mir Qasim proved otherwise. In the beginning he did try to please the Company but there was no limit to Company's demands upon him. He had to look after the revenue of the state and the well being of his subjects. Thus the interests of the Nawab and the English were not compatible.

5. *Exploitation by the 'gomastahs'*. The methods of Engligh traders and their '*gomastahs*' (agents) were a growing menace to the political authority of the Nawab. Every servant of a British factory was armed with all the powers of his master and his master was armed with all the powers of the Company. It was used by Company's agents to hold a court under a tree and award punishment to the natives that suited their fancy.

6. *Murder of Ram Narain*. Clive had appointed Ram Narain as the Deputy Governor of Bihar. Ram Narain was a favourite of the English. His activities created suspicion in the mind of Mir Qasim. Finding an opportunity, Mir Qasim snatched all his wealth and got him murdered.

7. *Death of some Europeans*. In June 1763, Major Adams was sent to fight against Mir Qasim. Several battles took place. A number of English people were killed.

8. *Dethronement of Mir Qasim*. The Company reinstated Mir Jafar and dethroned. Mir Qasim as he proved inconvenient to them.

Events of the Battle of Buxar

Mir Qasim fought several battles against the Company but was defeated and he fled away to Oudh. There he organised a confederacy with the Nawab of Oudh and Mughal Emperor of Delhi with a view to drive away the English from Bengal.

The combined armies of the three powers numbering about 50,000 met the English army of about 7000 at the battlefield of Buxar on October 22, 1764. The English won the battle.

Results: The Treaty of Allahabad. The Treaty of Allahabad ended the struggle for power. Main provinsions of the treaty were as under:-

1. The *Diwani* (Revenue) of Bengal, Bihar and Orissa was entrusted to the Company by the Mughal emperor.

2. The Nawab of Bengal was to disband most of his army.

3. The Nawab of Bengal was to pay Rs. 15 lakhs to the Company.

4. The Nawab of Oudh was to pay Rs. 50 lakhs to the Company.

5. Shah Alam was to remain under British protection for six years at Allahabad.

6. The Company was to give a pension of Rs. 26 lakh to the Mughal Emperor Shah Alam.

7. The Nawab of Bengal was to administer Bengal through a Deputy *Subedar* to be appointed by the Company.

8. The English were permitted to carry on trade duty free in Oudh.

Political Significance of the Battle of Buxer.

1. The new Nawab of Bengal became a stooge of the English.
2. The Nawab of Oudh was at the mercy of the Company.
3. The Mughal emperor became a pensioner.
4. The whole territory from Bengal to Allahabad lay at the feet of the Company and the road to Delhi open.

Q. 3. Buxar completed the work of Plassey and made the British the masters of the situation." Comment.

(Rajasthan University 1997)

or

"Buxar deserves far more than Plassey to be considered as the origin of the British power in India." Explain this statement.

(Delhi University 1993)

The Battle of Plassey was decisive but not a great battle. Discuss

(Rajasthan University, Supp. 1997)

Ans. *Divergent views regarding the importance of the Battle of Plassey and Buxar*

Undoubtedly the work of Plessey was completed by Buxar and it made the British master of the situation. But it is not totally right to say that Buxar deserves far more than Plessey to be considered as the origin of the British power in India. Before we discuss the issue in detail, we may refer to the views of some historians in this regard.

According to Adimiral Watson, "The Battle of Plassey was of extraordinary importance not only to the Company but to the British nation in general."

In the words of J. N. Sarkar, "On 23rd June 1757, the medieval period of India ended and the modern period started."

Col. Malleson has described the consequences of the Battle of Plassey as, "There never was a battle in which the consequences were so vast, so immediate and so permanent."

On the other hand the following writers have laid more stress on the impact exercised by Buxar on the history of India.

1. According to Broome, "the fate of India depended on the battle of Buxar."

2. Sir James Stephan is of the view, "Buxar deserves far more than Plassey to be considered as the origin of the British power in India."

3. In the words of Ramsay Muir, "Buxar finally rivetted the shakles of Company's rule over Bengal.'

4. Battle of Buxar was important from military point of views. In this regard, Dr. R.C. Majumdar has rightly said, "The Battle of Plassey was decided more by treachery than by any inherent superiority of the British arms, and had the rights of the English in Bengal rested on that battle alone, their conquests of Bengal might partly has been attributed to a political conspiracy rather to any fair fight. But the defeat of Mir Qasim (and his associates) cannot be explained away by any sudden and unexpected treachery such as had over-whelmed Shuja-ud-Daulah. It was a straight fight between two rival claimants for supremacy, each of whom was fully alive to its possibilities and fore-warned of the consquences."

It has been rightly observed that the Battle of Plassey gave to the English "A place to stand and Buxar a province to rule." Plassey was a starting point of British's entry into India and Buxar a solid foundation for the British empire to be set up in India. The Battle of Plassey proved helpful to defeat the French in South India and Buxar to defeat all Indian rulers of the North and the South. The Battle of Plassey was not a battle in the true sense but it exposed the treacherous nature of the English imperialists. The Battle of Buxar reflected the better quality and strategy of the army of the English and exposed fully the poor quality of Indian armies. The Battle of Plassey had weakened the Nawab of Bengal only but the Battle of Buxar put the Mughal ruler who still claimed himself the Emperor of India at the mercy of the Company. The Battle of Buxar advanced the political frontiers of the English upto Oudh. The victory of the English in the Battle of Buxar sent a clear silent message throughout the country that the English were determined and destined to be the rulers of India in course of time. The march of the English to Delhi became very easy. The Diwani of Bengal and heavy war indemnities led to the beginning of `Wealth drain' from India to England.

According to Sarkar and Dutta, the battle of Buxar was "another step in advance from Plassey in the growth of British power in India." It is therefore not right to say that Buxar deserves far more than Plassey to be considered as the origin of the British power in India." Had there been no Plassey, there would have been no Buxar.

The Battle of Plassey laid the foundation and the Battle of Buxar raised on it the structure of the British empire. No doubt it was the real battle won by the British against the combined armies of two of the major Indian powers. It firmly established the British as masters of Bengal, Bihar and Orissa and placed Oudh and the Mughal ruler at their mercy.

From above, it can safely be concluded that the work of conquering. India by the British had its origin in the Battle of Plassey. Of course the Battle of Buxar placed them on a strong footing. Results of both the battles had their own importance and were of great significance for the British.

Q.4. How did the British manage to occupy Bengal by 1765?

(Delhi University 1997)

or

Give a brief account of the events during 1757 to 1765 that resulted in the establishment of British power in Bengal.

(Rajasthan University, 1995 and 1997)

Ans. *Bengal as the first province under the English rule.* From the very beginning of their trade and other operations in India, the British were interested in Bengal. Bengal was then the most properous province, industrially advanced and commercially vulnerable to foreign lust. It was considered as the central point to which all the riches of India were attracted. Its manufactures found their way attracted. Its manufactures found their way to the remotest part of India.

The vast resources of Bengal helped the English very much to conquer the wars in the Deccan and extend their control over Northern India.

The province of Bengal at that time included Bengal, Bihar and Orissa.

The first English factory in Bengal was set up at Hugli in 1651 during the rule of Shah Jahan.

Main events leading to the British control over Bengal

Following are the three main events during the period 1761 to 1765.

I. Battle of Plassey.
II. Battle of Buxer.
III. Dual Government of Bengal.

I. BATTLE OF PLASSEY (1757)

Parties and causes. The Battle of Plassey fought between the East India Company and Siraj-ud-Daula, Nawab of Bengal was won by the former.

There were three most important reasons of the Battle of Plassey. First, the servants of the East India Company had began to misuse the *'Firman'* and the *'Dastak'*.

The *'Firman'* or the royal decree issued by the Mughal emperor Farrukh Siyar which gave freedom to the East India Company to trade without paying taxes was misused. The servants of the Company indulged in private trade. Likewise the *'Dastak'* or the pasas issued by the Company to its employes on the basis of the *'Firman'* allowing them free movements of Company's goods was not properly used.

Secondly, the East India Company began to instigate the Hindu subjects of the Nawab and interfered in the internal affairs of the state.

Thirdly the English were determined to exercise control over Bengal.

Events. Lord Clive of the East India Company entered into conspiracy against the Nawab of Bengal by winning over his Commander-in-Chief Mir

Jafar, banker Jagat Seth, treasurer Rai Durlab. The details of conspiracy were settled through an influential person Amir Chand.

With only 3,000 soldiers, Clive defeated the army of the Nawab having 50,000 soldiers.

Mir Jafar, the Commander-in-Chief of Nawab's forces had already been won over by Clive. There was practically no fight.

Result. The vicory of East India Company under Clive paved the way for the conquest of India by the British.

Writing about the impact of the Battle of Plassey, Admiral watson wrote, "The Battle of Plasasy was of extra-ordinary importance not only to the Company but to the British nation in general."

II. BATTLE OF BUXAR (1764)

Parties. The Battle of Buxar was fought between the East India Company and the combined forces of Mir Qasim, deposed Nawab of Bengal, Nawab Shuja-ud-Daula of Oudh and Shah Alam, the Mughal emperor.

Causes of the Battle. Mir Jafar, the Commander-in-Chief of the Nawab's forces, who had entered into conspiracy against the Nawab of Bengal, Siraj-ud-Daual, succeeded him. However, he was dethroned by the British as he failed to meet the heavy financial demands of the Company. The Company, therfore, appointed Mir Qasim, the son-in-law of Mir Jafar. Mir Jafar though, appointed Nawab with the help for the Company did not like to work as a puppet. He tried to check the illegal trade carried on by the servants of the East India Company. He abolished all duties on internal trade, thus giving his own subjects a concession that the East India Company enjoyed. But the alien merchants (*i.e.* the English) were no longer willing to tolerate equality between themselves and the Indians.

Events. Mir Qasim was defeated in a series of battles and finally he fled to Patna and sought military assistance fron Shuja-ud-Daula. Nawab of Oudh. Emperor Shah Alam was also living there in those days. He also decided to help Mir Qasim. The British army with only 7,000 troops won against about 50,000 troops of the three Indian rulers.

Effects. The Treaty of Allahabad by which the Battle of Buxar came to an end, proved very helpful to the Company in exercising enormous amount of control and power in Bengal, Bihar, Orissa, Oudh and Delhi.

The victory of the English in the Battle of Buxar sent a clear message throughout the country that the English were determined and destined to be the rulers of India in course of time.

In the words of Ramsay Mair, "Buxar finally rivetted the shackles of Company's rule over Bengal."

III. DUAL GOVERNMENT IN BENGAL PROVINCE

After the Battle of Buxar, a new form of Govenment known as Dual Government was introduced. It remained in operation during 1765 and 1772. Under this type of government, the management of the state of affairs was divided between the Company and the Nawab of Bengal. The Company had the control of revenue collection and defence which other matters like law and order etc were under the Nawab. This arrangement all the more strengthened the control of the Company in Bengal.

Q.5. Why did India fail to provide a political power capable of providing a substitute to the Mughal empire in the 18th century?

(Delhi University 1986, 1988 and 1998)

Ans. *Dark Period in the History of India*

The history of India during the 18th century is usually regarded as the history of decline - decline in almost all walks of life and especially political. This decline has prompted some historians to view this century as the '*dark period*' in the history of India. This darkness in the political scenario prevented any Indian ruler to exercise its authority and face effectively the serious challanges posed by European powers and especially the British. India had to pay a heavy price for this. India became a slave country of the British for about two hundred years. The people of India had to fight a long and arduous batle for the liberation of the country from foreign domination.

Three major political developments in the 18th century. Eighteenth century was marked by three major political developments in India.

First, there was the decline and disintegration of the Mughal empire.

Second, a large number of independent and somi-independent kingdoms and powers had emerged.

Third, there was the greed of the European powers to have their foot-hold on India.

All this resulted in fierce struggles, conspiracies, battles and wars.

Emergence of Several Independent/Semi-independent Units

The perstige and power of the Mughal empire had received a great setback. In fact it existed on paper and in name only. Most of the rulers after Aurangzeb occupied the Mughal throne for very short period. Out of the eleven rulers, seven ruled for just 33 years *i.e.* each on an average less than five years. Many of them were very weak puppets in the hands of their nobles. They were mostly devoted to the pleasures of wine and women and neglected the affairs of the state. Several of them were victims of intrigues and faced unnatural deaths. The two Sayid brothers Muslim nobles emerged for some time as 'king makers'.

As observed by Dr. K. K. Datta, "Province after province — The Deccan, Oudh and Bengal slipped out of imperial control; the Marathas established their power far and wide; the Jats became independent near Agra; the Ruhela Afghans founded the state of Rohilkhand in the North Gangetic Plain; the Sikhs became active in the Punjab, and the invasion of Nadir Shah dealt a staggering blow to the Delhi Empire. Thus within three decades of Aurangzeb's death, the vast empire of the Mughals ceased to exist as an all-India political unit and was split up into numerous independent ststes."

Triangular Struggles for Supremacy in India

The Sikhs in Punjab had set up twelve strong but independent groups known as '*Misls*'. Maharaja Ranjit Singh (1780-1839) emerged as a strong ruler in the last decade of the 18th century and by that time, the English had already established their supremacy over all other Indian rulers. He was not in a position to pose a great threat to the English. At the same time, the English were not in a position to antagonise him. In a nutshell, there was no excuse for Ranjit Singh to challange the East India Company. Ranjit Singh, on his part, was fully conscious of his limitations.

The Marathas had emerged as a strong power during the downfall of the Mughals. They had received a big jolt when they faced a very humiliating defeat at the hands of Ahamad Shah Abdali in 1761 in the third Battle of Panipat. The Marathas were no longer a united power. Five distinct Maratha groups came into prominence. These were the Peshwas at Poona, Gackward at Baroda, Bhonsle at Nagpur, Holkar at Indore and Scindhia at Gwalior. The Maratha king lived at Satara. Thus the Maratha power was a divided one. The different Maratha groups did not present a united front.

1. *Triangular struggle among the Marathas, Afghans and Mughals.* In north India, a triangular struggle for an empire had began among three contenders-the Marathas, the Afghans and the Mughals. The size of the Mughal empire was decimated by the Afghans under Ahmad Shah Abdali and the Marathas. Later after defeating the Marathas, Ahmad Shah Abdali left India on account of internal conflicts in Afghanistan.

In such a situation, other powers, though did not play a major role but added to the political confusion.

The Indian powers weakened one another which facilitated the political ambitions of the East India Company.

On account of lack of diplomacy, the Marathas failed to get the cooperation of the Rajput states and the Jat state to face the challenges of the Afghans.

2. *Triangular struggle:Marathas, the Sultans of Mysore and Nizams of Hyderabad.* These three powers were usually at war path and occasionally changing sides.

3. *Triangular Struggle among : the British the rulers of Carnatic and the French.* The English made the best use of the war of succession to the thrones of Carnatic and Hyderabad.

4. *Triangular Struggle among : European powers of the Dutch, the English and the French.* The English ultimately won.

(5) *Triangular struggle among The Nawab of Bengal, Nawab of Oudh and the English.* In this case, the English were able to sow seeds of discord in the court of the Nawab of Bengal and by entering into conspiracy, defeated Siraj-ud-Daula in the Battle of Plassey in 1757 and thereafter in 1763, the confederacy of Mir Qasim, deposed Nawab of Bengal, Shuja-ud-Daula of Oudh and Shah Alam, Mughal Emperor.

Lord Clive with his realistic grasp of political and military state of affairs of Indian rulers, reduced the power of the French in South and of the rulers of Bengal, Oudh and Mughals in North and established the British supremacy. He showed the way and the successive Governor — Generals made the best advantage.

In short, the Marathas who could emerge as a supreme power in India failed to avail of the situation created by the tottering power of the Mughals.

Maratha kingdom was a confederacy. Power was shared by several Maratha chiefs who were independent rulers in their territories. King was the nominal head. The Peshwa of Poona was the head of the Maratha confederacy. Other members of the confederacy were, Gaekwrd of Baroda, Bhonsle of Nagpur, Holkar of Indore and Scindhia of Gwalior. The king lived at Satara. The English were successful in creating a wedge among these chiefs.

The Marathas could not rise equal to the occasion.

Following were the important reasons of the failure of the Marathas to fill the political vacuum caused by the decline of the Mughal power:

(1) No strong central power.
(2) Loose nature of Maratha confederacy.
(3) Mutual jealousies among the Maratha chiefs.
(4) Giving up '*guerilla*' warfare techniques.
(5) Neglect of proper military training by the Marathas.
(6) Lack of unity of command among the Maratha chiefs.
(7) Arrogance of the Maratha chiefs and their inability to develop friendly relations with other Indian rulers.

LACK OF NATIONAL CONSCIOUSNESS

At that time neither the common people nor the rulers and nor the soldiers had developed the consciousness of nationalism *i.e.* an integrated nation. Casteism, regionalism and provincialism dominated. Previous history repeated itself.

POLICY OF 'DIVIDE AND RULE'

The British were pastmaster in diplomacy. They were successful in creating all the more dissensions among the Indian rulers. The result was obvious. One by one, Indian rulers lost their states and surrendered, sometimes after fighting and sometimes without it.

SUPERIOR ARMY AND WAR TECHNIQUES

By and large, Indian rulers had not given proper attention to the discipline, training and equipment of the army.

Sometimes it is stated that Maharaja Ranjit Singh could make an attempt to drive away the British. But such a view has no force in it. By the time he gained strength, the East India Company had become very powerful. It was not, therefore, possible to fill up the vacuum caused by the disintegration of the Mughal empire. One cannot go by 'ifs' and 'buts'.

The Maharaja was a great statesman. He clearly and clevely came to the conclusion that it was practically impossible to make any headway against the English.

In short, it may be concluded that the Indian rulers, on account of their selfishness and individualistic approach and interests failed to offer a united front. At the same time no power was strong enough to bring other powers under one umbrella. Fortune favoured the English.

Q. 6. Explain the tools of expansion of the British empire with reference to war and diplomacy.

Ans. *War and Diplomacy as tools of expansion.*

The British established their empire by waging 4 Carnatic wars, 4 Anglo-Mysore wars, 3 Maratha wars, 3 Anglo-Burmese wars, 2 Afghan wars and two Sikh wars. Besides they fought several battles with other European powers.

Policy of Divide and Rule : Different Policies Towards Different States.

The British were past master in diplomacy. They were successful in creating dissensions among the Indian rulers among different castes, classes and religions. They incited one against the other. They favoured one group and discriminated the other. The result was obvious. The rulers of India as well as the people of India did not unite against the British.

Examples

1. *Second Carnatic war (1749-54).* In this war though the English were not responsible for the war of succession to the throne of Hyderabad and Carnatic, they made the best use of this event and sided with the parties that were opposed to the French.

2. *Battles of Plassey (1757) and Buxar (1764).* The British created divisions among the nobles of the Nawabs of Bengal.

3. *The First Anglo-Maratha War (1776-82).* The dissension at Poona among the Marathas gave the British much needed opportunity for profitable intrigues.

4. *Wellesley's Subsidiary Alliance System.* This system also created divisions among Indian rulers. Those rulers who joined the Alliance received British support and the others were on the other side of the fence.

5. *Mysore War.* The Nizam of Hyderabad, and the various Maratha groups failed to unite on account of the shrewdness of the British.

6. *Disunity in the Maratha Confederacy.* To a great extent, the Maratha unity failed by the policy of divide and rule of the British.

7. *Old and New Zamindars.* The revenue system introduced by the British created different classes of Zamindars.

8. Lord Dalhousi's Policies.

5

Anglo-French Struggle : Dupleix and Clive

(Carnatic Wars)

Q. 1. Describe briefly the different phases of the struggle between the English and the French for supremacy in India. What were the causes of the failure of the French in this struggle?

or

What were the Reasons for the Anglo-French struggle in the Carnatic? Briefly state the main events. What was the outcome of this struggle? Explain the main causes of the success of the English.

Ans. *Three Carnatic Wars or Three Phases of the Struggle between the English and the French*. The English and the French fought three wars during the period 1746 A. D. to 1763 A. D. and these wars ultimately resulted in the absolute supremacy of the English in India. The French power was wiped out in India.

Causes of the conflict. Following were the main causes of conflict between the English and French in India.

1. *Trade rivalry*. The English and the British Companies were formed to trade with India for the purpose of earning profits. Both were interested in the same type of trade goods.

2. *Close proximity of their settlements in India.* Both had established their settlements very close to each other and they were not good neighbours.

3. *Traditional rivalry*. England and France as neighbours in Europe had a long standing rivalry in Europe which reflected in their colonies also.

4. *Wars in Europe and their impact on India.* Wars fought in Europe like the Seven Years War and the Austrian War of Succession had their impact on their relations in India also.

5. *Political instability in India.* After the death of Aurangzeb, the Central authority disappeared from India. Several small independent and semi-independent states were set up.

There was no spirit of national unity.

The four strong kingdoms of South—Hyderabad, Maysore, Carnatic and the Maratha were occasionally at war on account of their desire to become the most important power.

There were fierce struggles for succession to the throne in Hyderabad and Carnatic.

The English and the French made use of these unstable political conditions and began to interfere in the political afairs of India.

FIRST CARNATIC WAR (1746-48)

Causes. The first Carnatic war was the projection of the Austrian War of Succession in Europe. The English and the French were on opposite sides in Europe. On account of this, war between them took place in India also.

Main Events. The French had an upper hand from the very beginning. The English attempted to capture Pondicherry, a settlement of the French but failed. On the other hand, the French captured Madras — a settlement of the English. The English appealed for help to the Nawab of Carnatic in whose territory Madras was located. The Nawab agreed to intervene.

Battle of St. Thome. The most important events of this war was the battle of Thome on the bank of the river Adyar. The French under the leadership of Dupleix who was the French Governor of Pondicherry defeated the Nawab's army of about 10,000 soldiers with a small force of just 230 French soldiers and 700 Indian soldiers.

The First Carnatic War came to an end with the termination of hostilities in Europe. Under the treaty, Madras was restored to the English.

Results of the war. It indicated the importance of sea power and the superiority of the well-disciplined and well-equipped European forces. It also revealed the political decay that had eaten into the heart of Indian state.

SECOND CARNATIC WAR (1749-54)

Immediate cause of the war. After the death of the rulers of Carnatic and Hyderabad, there was conflict among the claimants of the throne. With a view to strengthen their hold, the English and the French took opposite sides and accordingly supported the claimants.

Most important event: Clive's strategy. When the French under Dupleix were at the height of their success surprise strategy planned by Clive of the British won laurels. Chanda Sahib, the claimant of Carnatic, supported by the French was away from Arcot, his capital and had surrounded his opponent supported by the English. Clive with the help of just 30 soldiers captured Arcot. This demoralised the French.

In Hyderabad, the French had been successful in making Muzaffar Jang, the Nawab of Hyderabad. However, while the war was on, Dupleix, the Governor of the French Company in India was recalled by the French Government in France. The successor of Dupleix signed the treaty with the English on humiliating terms.

Results 1. The English established their supremacy in diplomacy and military.

2. The English got an opportunity to consolidate their power and influence in Bengal.

THIRD CARNATIC WAR (1757-1763)

Immediate cause. In 1757, the Seven-year War broke out in Europe. Conseqeuently in India also, the English and the French took opposite sides.

Main events. The French were finally defeated in the Battle of Wandiwash in 1760. In 1761, the French lost Chandernagar and Pondicherry. The Seven-year War in Europe came to an end with the signing of the Treaty of Paris. In India also, the war between the English and the French came to an end.

Results 1. Chandarnagar and Pondicherry were returned to the French with the condition that they would not fortify these places.

2. The French power was completely broken in India.

3. The British gained complete control over South India.

4. The experiences of war gained in South India proved very helpful to the English in conquering other parts of India.

VIEWS OF SOME HISTORIANS ON THE SUCCESS OF THE ENGLISH AND THE FAILURE OF THE FRENCH

Commercial Superiority. Regarding the commercial superioritiy and better financial position of the English Company, Movellet has observed, "The value of the sale of Indian goods in England between 1736 and 1756 was 41,200,000" while that of the French goods was 11,450,000".

Sea power. According to H. H. Dodwell, "The principal cause which had contributed to this complete victory (of the English) was certainly the relentless pressure of sea power."

Role of Clive. P.E. Roberts attributes the English viratory to the "masterful genius displayed alike in peace and war by Robert Clive."

Start from a sound base. V. A. Smith very emphatically observed, "Neither Alexander, the Great nor Napolean could have won the empire of India by starting from Pondicherry as a base and contending with the power which held Bengal and command of sea."

"Dupleix", writes Marriott, "made a cardinal blunder in looking for the key of India in Madras, Clive sought and found it in Bengal."

Resources of Bengal. According to Dutta and Sarkar, "In fact Plassey decided the fate of the Carnatic struggles and it was with the resources of Bengal that the English Company fought most of its wars and founded its dominion."

Rotten French Government. Alfred Lyall observed, "India was not lost by the French because Dupleix was recalled...It was through the short sighted, ill managed European policy of Louis *XV* that France lost her Indian settlements."

Causes of the success of the English and the failure of the French

S.No.	*Factor*	*The English Company*	*The French Company*
1.	Cooperation	Team sprit among the officials of the Company.	Lack of the Cooperation and team spirit.
2.	Diplomacy	Very superior.	Very weak.
3.	Financial position of the Company	Very Sound.	Very poor.
4.	European affairs	England comparatively free from wars and conflicts in Europe.	Active involvement of France in European affairs.
5.	Financial position	Very sound.	Not viable.
6.	Government's in-terest in the Company	British Government keenly interested.	Lakewarm attitude of the French Govenment.
7.	Independence of the Company	By and large independent.	Very dependent on the French Government.
8.	Military leadership	Clive's military strategy of a very high order.	Dupleix's weak command and arrogance. Likewise Lally made many mistakes.
9.	Naval power	Very superior.	Very weak.
10.	Organisation of the Company	Better organisation.	Poor organisation
11.	Shareholders of the Company	Shareholders taking keen interest.	Very little interest of the shareholders.
12.	Stability of the Government	More stable British Government in England.	Comparatively less stable.
13.	Political leadership	Very strong.	Very weak.
14.	Rich resource of Bengal	Conquest of Bengal provided very rich resources.	Lack of such a fertile are as with the French Company.
15.	British Government vs French Govenment	William Pitt, the war Minister in England kept the French busy fighting in Europe.	The French Government was not able to provide necessary help to the French Company in India. Moreover the ruler was a despot.

Q. 2. Briefly estimate the achievements and failures of Dupleix.

Ans. *Dupleix, Joseph Francois* (1697-1764)

A tragic figure. Dupleix began his career in commercial service with the French East India Company and rose to the Governor of Pondicherry and Director General of all the French factories in India. He was at the helm of affairs of the Company for about 12 years. (1742 to 1754).

Inspite of being a great administrator, a skilful diplomat and a born leader of men, Dupleix, will always remain a tragic factor in histroy. He was let down both by his fortune and his countrymen.

Foresight of Dupleix. According to Henri Martin, "Dupleix judged India to be destined to be conquered, not by other Asians, like those who had ravaged her before, but by Europeans. Dupleix was determined to give India to France." For the failure of Dupleix to achieve this ambitious project, Martin put the entire blame on the French Government and the Company. Lord Macaulay was also of the view, "The man who first saw that it was possible to found an European empire on the ruins of the Mughal monarchy was Dupleix."

Eliphinstone observed, "Dupleix was the first who made an extensive use of disciplined sepoys and marched an army into the heart of the continent."

Achievements of Dupleix

1. The Mughal emperor conferred on Dupleix the title of Nawab, an honour which greatly enhanced the prestige of Dupleix among the Indian princes.
2. Muzzafar Jang, the Subedar of Deccan invested Dupleix with the title of the Nawab of all the territories between the river Krishna and Cape Comrin including Carnatic.
3. He opened trade negotiations with countries in the Persian Gulf, with China and Tibet.
4. He strengthened the defences of Pondicherry.
5. He balanced income and expenditure of the French Company.
6. He captured Madras from the English during the First Carnatic war but had to return it when peace was made.
7. During the Second Carnatic war, he took up the cause of Muzaffar Jang and Chanda Shahib in Hyderabad and Carnatic respectively. His policy was successful at both the places in the beginning. The arrival of Clive upset his plan. Ultimately his policy was successful in Hyderabad but failed in Carnatic. Dupleix was called by the French Government at a time when he was needed most in India. The French government was of the view that Dupleix's policy was not in the interests of France. Dupleix's successor was a complete failure.

WAS DUPLEIXA FAI LURE?

Divergent views have been given by historians about the achievements of Dupleix.

Appreciation of Dupleix. According to Malleson, "If Dupleix had been able to continue in India for another two years, the rich heritage of Bengal would have fallen to France instead to his rivals." He further wrote, "We cannot but marvel at the blindness, the infatuation, the madness that recalled Dupleix."

According to James Mill, "The two great discoveries for conquering India, *i.e.*, the weakness of Indian armies against well-disciplined European forces and the ease with which Indians could be trained in the methods of European warfare, were made by the French under him."

Similarly Lord Macaulay and M. Xavier Raymond have praised Dupleix for his diplomacy and administrative qualities.

Critics of Dupleix. According to *Alfred Martinean*, "The blindness or the obstinancy was the principal cause of his failure."

Major Lawrance criticises Dupleix in these words, "It is my opnion that there never can be peace in the province while Dupleix stays in India. He neither values men nor money, nor any thing but what can gratify his own ambition."

Dodwell is of the view. "The policy of Dupleix indeed lacked the elements of permanent success and could never have survived a European war."

Dr. V. S. Smith takes the view. "The character and achievements of Dupleix hardly merit the admiration they have received." According to him, Dupleix was not a good general, because throughout his life he had been a business-man".

Causes of Dupleix's Failure

Causes of Dupleix's failure may be categorised under two under two heads.

(*a*) *Causes for which Dupleix was not responsible*

1. French Govenment did not give due support to the French Company in India.
2. French Government frequently interfered in the working of the Company in India.
3. The financial position of the Company was not sound from the very begining.
4. The sea-power of the French was very weak as compared with that of the English.
5. Dupleix could not get the cooperation from the French Government.

Causes for which Dupleix was responsible

1. Dupleix was not a good general. Clive proved far superior to him.
2. Dupleix was not a good executor of his plans.
3. Dupleix flung his net far beyond his resources.
4. Dupleix did not concentrate his attention to establish French influence in Bengal which was very fertile. He involved himself in the politics of Deccan which was not so rich.
5. Dupleix was very haughty and quarrelsome. He lacked the skill to get cooperation from his superiors as well as his subordinates.
6. Sending of Bussy to Hyderabad was not a correct decision.

Q. 3. What do you know about the Dual System of Government set up by Lord Clive in Bengal. Discuss its merits and demerits.

(Punjab University April 1995, Oct 1997)

Ans. *Meaning of the Dual Government.* In simple language dual government implied government of two powers. After the Battle of Buxar, this type of government was introduced in Bengal by Lord Clive in 1765 and it remained in operation till 1772 when it was abolished by Warren Hastings. Under this, the administrative affairs of the province were divided between the Nawab of Bengal and the East India Company. The East India Company had the control of revenue collection and defence and all other departments like law and order etc., were under the charge of the Nawab who was to get Rs. 53 lakh from the Company.

Structure of the Dual Government may be illustrated as under.

It may be remembered that Bengal province at that time included Bengal, Bihar and Orissa.

For the exercise of Diwani (collection of revenue), the Company appointed two Deputy Diwans namely Mohammad Reza Khan for Bengal and Raja Shitale Roy for the rest. Mohammad Reza Khan acted also as Deputy Nizam.

MERITS OF THE SYSTEM FOR THE EAST INDIA COMPANY

1. *Power of money of the Company.* The Company could exercise all power since it had the revenue with it.

2. *Indirectly all power with Company.* Lord Clive did not assume direct political control of the province as it could invite suspicion of territorial conquests. By this arrangement it became possible for him to exercise control indirectly.

3. *Throwing dust in the eyes of the natives.* It was a suitable means to throw dust in the eyes of the natives as Clive himself said, "Nawab had only the name and shadow of authority."

4. *Authority without responsibility.* The Company got complete authority without any responsibility.

5. *Saving of administrative expenditure.* The system relieved the Company from the task of administration to a considerable extent. The Company did not have the requisite number of officials to carry out this work.

6. *Economy.* The Company was relieved of the economic burden as the entire administration was in the hands of the Nawab who was to get a fixed

amount from the Company from the revenue of the province.

7. *No danger of conflict with the Marathas*. Direct assumption of authority of administration by the Company might have involved it into conflict with the rising power of the Marathas.

8. *Temporary arrangement*. It was a temporary settlement and suited to the Company as a matter of exigency.

Why was it introduced? Clive introduced this double government on account of two reasons:

(*i*) Clive hesitated to take the administration in his own hands as he feared that this step might be opposed by Indian rulers.

(*ii*) East India Company was basically a trading Company and it did not have the necessary administrative manpower and skill. Clive wrote to the Court of Directors of the Company even "three times the Present numbers of Clive servants would be insufficent for that purpose."

DEMERITS OF THE DUAL GOVERNMENT

1. *Breakdown of administration*. Since the Nawab depended for finance on the Company, he became powerless to run the administration efficiently and smoothly.

2. *Rampant corruption*. George Cornwall declared in the British House of Commons, "I do most confidently maintain that no civilised government even existed on the face of this earth which was more corrupt, more perfidious and more rapacious than the government of the East India Company from 1765 to 1784."

3. *Decline of agriculture*. In 1769, Richard Becher, a servant of the comapny wrote to its Directors, "This fine country which flourished....is verging towards its rain."

4. *Ruin of skill of the worksmen*. William Bolts, a contemporary has mentioned several methods of oppression inflicted by the '*gomastahs*' (agents) of the Company on the silk. Weavers of Bengal. "Should the weaver refuse to accept the control and receive advance money, he was usually tied in his girdles and flogged.. The rougery practised is beyond imagination." He further wrote, "Sometimes, the weavers were transferred from one merchant to another like slaves."

5. *Disruption of trade and commerce of Indian traders*. The Company's servants virtually monopolised the internal trade of Bengal. Clive himself referred to these abuses in the course of his speech in the House of Commons and said that Company is merchants traded not as merchants but as 'soverigns' and thousands of Indian merchants were 'reduced to beggary'.

6. *Diwani a little more than a deceptive camouflage.* Dr. Nandlal Chatterji stated that the system was "avowedly a device for hoodwinking the country's powers and the foreign nations whom Clive did not want to give umbrage.

The Nawab was now a pensioner of the state and had nothing but the name and shadow of authority." He further wrote, "At no period in the chequered annals of Bengal did the province suffer such flagrant spoilation as it did in the era of Clive."

7. *Illogical Scheme*. According to Nandlal Chatterjee, "The double government which Clive established was both illogical and unworkable. He forgot that division of power was impossible without creating anarchy and confusion. P.E. Roberts criticises the system in these words, "The unfortunate divorce of power from responsibility soon caused a recrudescence of the old abuses."

8. *Drain of wealth from Bengal*. It is eastimated that during the years 1766, 1767 and 1768, nearly 5.7 million £ were drained from Bengal.

9. *Famine in Benal*. The Bengal famine of 1770 took a heavy toll of life and produced untold miseries. It was observed by a servant of the Company." In several parts, the famine claimed one-third of population of Bengal.

10. *Frequent conflicts*. There were frequent conflicts between the officials of the Company and the Nawab.

11. *Fall in the income of the Company*. In spite of the oppression of the peasantry and hardships suffered by the people, the income of the Company fell as a result of the malpractices of the servants of the Company.

The critics of the Dual system tend to forget that Clive was determined to strengthen his control as well as Company's control over Bengal and accordingly he was least concerned with the niceties of the actions he took.

Q.4. Estimate the contribution of Clive to the East India Company.

or

How far do you agree with the statement that Clive was the real founder of the British empire in India? Discuss.

Ans. *Robert Clive* (1725-1774)

Founder of an empire. From Indian point of view as observed by K. M. Panikar in his book '*Survey of Indian History*,' "Clive was a gangster - a forgerer, a liar and a cheat" but there is no doubt that he founded in India a foreign empire that lasted for about two centuries. Clive with his realistic grasps of political and military state of affairs of Indian rulers, reduced the power of the French in South India, almost crushed the powers of Nawabs of Bengal and Oudh and also of the Mughal ruler in the North and established the British superemacy. It was by all means a spectacular success.

Brief life sketch. Clive served the East India Company first as a clerk, then as a trader, as a soldier, a commanding officer and twice Governor of Bengal (1757 to 1760 and 1765 to 1767). Bored with his routine in the office as a clerk, he twice tried to commit suicide but failed. Fate had destined him to be the founder of one of the mightest empires in the world.

Achievements of Clive. Clive's achievements may be categorised under the following four heads:

1. Military achievements.
2. Revenue achievements.
3. Administrative achievements.
4. Diplomatic achievements.

Military achievements of Clive. On account of his military skills and achievements, Pitt, the Prime Minister of England described Clive as a 'Heaven born general'. His important military achievements were as under:

(*i*) *Capture of Arcot*. Clive's successful conduct of the seize of Arcot (1751) with a few hundred soldiers turned the scales against the French in the first Carnatic war and gave a severe blow to their power. Subsequently Chanda Sahib was defeated at Trichinopoly. Thus he was responsible for establishing Muhammad Ali on the Throne of Carnatic.

(*ii*) *Winning the battle of Plassey*. In general he made an alliance with the dissatisfied nobles of the Nawab Siraj-ud-Daula and reduced the new Nawab Mir Jafar to the position of a puppet ruler. The battle of Plassey in 1757 paved the way for the conquest of India by the British. Clive made the Company the '*de-facto*' masters of Bengal.

(*iii*) *Blow to the power of the Dutch*. When Clive suspected that the Nawab of Bengal was in league with the Dutch, he attacked the Dutch, by land and sea. The Dutch made peace at Chinsura and agreed not to fortify their settlements in India.

(*iv*) *Capture of Northern Cicars*. Clive captured this territory from the French.

Clive's two victories at Arcot and at Plassey with just a handful of troops demonstrates his extra-ordinary skills in military affairs.

Revenue achievements. With the Treaty of Allahabad in 1765, the Company obtained the '*Diwani*' *i.e.* revenue rights from the Mughal ruler. The resources of Bengal, enabled the English to conquer South India and they routed the French—their political rivals in India.

The Treaty of Allahabad proved very useful for the Company. The grant of '*Diwani*' in Bengal (Bengal, Bihar and Orissa) made the position of the Company legal. The titular Mughal ruler became a pensioner of the Company.

Administrative achievements. 1. By introducing the system of Dual Government in Bengal, Clive strengthened his hold over Bengal. Seen from the point of view of the British, this system served the purpose for which it was introduced in the then existing situation in India. Clive was a realist and he knew well that the time was not ripe to take over the administration of Bengal directly under the control of the Company. Moreover this was a temporary arrangement.

2. Clive asked all the servants of the Company to sign a declaration that they would not accept any gift from anyone.
3. Clive took several stepts to check the private trade of the servants of the Company.

4. He made proposals to the Directors of the Company to raise their salaries so that they were not tempted to accept gifts and indluge in private trade. It is important to note that the servants of the Company were very low paid.
5. With a view to helping the servants of the Company, Clive formed a Society of Trade in 1765. The profits from this trade were given to the servants of the Company.
6. Clive laid the foundations of a postal or '*dak*' system on which the modern postal system was subsequently built up by his successors.

Achievements as a statesman. Clive depended upon more on diplomacy than on wars. He was aware of the fact that owing to the heavy requirments of the Company's own investments, it was very difficult to find enough money for war. He also realised that the hazards of war could not be conducive to the growth of the Company's trade. The wars which he waged were won by him with the minimum loss of men and money. It is true that for the achievements of his objectives, he could go to any extent. His military diplomacy paid him dividends at Arcot. His diplomacy (conspiracy) made him victorious at Plassey, with little cost. The Treaty of Allahabad strengthened his hold on the Nawab of Oudh, Bengal and Mughal emperor. He showed the wisdom in not annexing Oudh. By forming a Dual Government in Bengal, he made the Company a supreme political as well as an administrative power.

VIEWS OF SOME HISTORIANS AND OTHERS ABOUT THE CHARACTER AND ACHIEVEMENTS OF CLIVE.

Admirers of Clive

1. Clive as a "heaven born general."—William Pitt Prime Minister of England.
2. "Our Island (England) scarcely ever produced a man more truly great, either in arms or in Council."— Lord Macaulay.
3. Lord Clive settled great foundations."— Burke.
4. "Clive was as great as Frederick the Great of Prussia."—Lord Chatham.
5. "Clive was high-spirited, courageous, indefatigable man to whom above all others, the English are indebted for the foundation of their empire in India."— Alfred Lall.
6. "His military genius and his gift of leadership were abundantly manifested both in the Penisula and in Bengal." Dr. V. S. Smith.
7. "He had the resolution of a taskmaster, the sternness of a dictator and the efficiency of a supervisor."—Dr. Nandlal Chatterjee.
8. "A military genius."—Lord Curgon

Critics of Clive

(*i*) "There is little trace of skilful combination in his plans."— Sir Charles Wilson.

(*ii*) "Clive was a gangster who achieved glory as a forgerer, a liar and a cheat."—K. M. Panikar.

(*iii*) Clive was "unscrupulous and devoid of a fine moral feeling, narrow and illiberal in his outlook." Nand lal Chatterjee.

(*iv*) "Dual system of government was a complete failure." Ramsay Muir.

(*v*) Daul system made confusion worse confounded and corruption more corrupt."—Key.

Balanced assessment

(*a*) "Clive was a man of insight rather than of foresight."—Dodwell.

(*b*) "Clive was not a founder but a harbinger of the future. He was the forerunner of the British Indian empire."— Percival Spear.

Summing up. There is no doubt that Clive transformed a mere trading body that the East India Company was into a territorial power with the role of 'King-maker' in Bengal. He outdid the French adversary Dupleix and achieved permanent results.

Clive believed in the dictum 'end justifies the means' and for this he resorted to forgery and treachery. But whatever he did was in the interest of his mother country. Of course while doing so he amassed enormous wealth through unfair means.

Sad end. On his return to England after his second governership of Bengal, Clive was charged of abusing his powers. After a lengthy debeate in the House of Commons, the folowing resolution was unanimously carried, "That Robert Clive at the same time rendered great meritorious services to his country." Clive was honourably acquitted. But the proceedings and charges so much injured him that in 1774, he committed suicide. That Clive was greatly emotional is evident from his earlier two attempts to end his life by suicide when he felt frustrated with his non-achievements before the sieze of Arcot. After retirement when his achievements were not fully appreciated by a section of his countrymen in England, he felt frustrated and ended his life.

6

Anglo-Mysore Relations : Hyder Ali and Tipu Sultan

Q.1. Examine the Anglo-Mysore relations during the times of Lord Cornwalls and Lord Wellesley.

or

Describe Anglo-Mysore relations from about 1767 to 1799 A.D.

or

Discuss the British relations with Hyder Ali and Tipu Sultan.

(Delhi University 1992)

Ans. *Four Mysore Wars*

Four Mysore were fought between the rulers of Mysore and the English during the period 1767 to 1799. The first two Anglo-Mysore Wars were fought in 1767-69 and 1780-84 between. Hyder Ali the ruler of Mysore and after his death by Tipu, his son and the English. The Third Anglo-Mysore War (1790-92) and the Fourth Anglo-Mysore War (1799) were fought between Tipu, the ruler of Mysore and the English. At the time of the third war, Lord Cornwallis was the Company's Governor General and at the time of the fourth war, Loıd Wellesely held this post.

After the and of the fourth war, which gave a decisive victory to the English, the Company annexed large territories of Mysore Kingdom. The remaining territory was given to a child of the Hindu family dethroned by Hyder Ali.

One of the most important causes of the defeat of Mysore rulers was that the English were able to isolate Hyder Ali as well as Tipu from the Marathas and the Nizam of Hyderabad. Their policy of 'Divide and Rule' paid rich dividends to them.

FIRST MYSORE WAR (1767-69)

Causes. 1. Hyder Ali had fully realized the designs of the English and he was strengthening his position. His sudden rise had given much anxiety to his neighbours and the English.

2. The Nizam of Hyderabad hated Hyder Ali as a man of low birth.
3. The Marathas regarded Hyder Ali as their enemy as he had refused to pay the Chauth to them.

Events. The English won over the Nizam and there after the Marathas and attacked Mysore. Hyder Ali was a shrewd statesman and he bought off the Marathas for about Rs. 35 lakhs and broke the alliance. He won over the Nizam also. But after sometime the Nizam deserted Hyder Ali. However Hyder Ali proved too strong and forced the English to sign peace treaty on his own terms.

Results. The Treaty of Madras (1769) which ended the war had the following provisions:

1. Both returned the territories conquered from each other.
2. The English were to help Hyder Ali if he was attacked by any power.

SECOND MYSORE WAR (1780-84)

Causes. 1. The English did not help Hyder Ali when he was attacked by the Marathas. This was in gross violation of the Treaty of Madras.

2. War broke out between the English and the French. The English captured the port of Mahe, through which Hyder Ali was getting his supplies.

Events. In the beginning, Hyder Ali inflicted one defeat after another on the British armies. But thereafter Warren Hastings' (1772-85) diplomacy saved the English. He bribed the Nizam and made peace with the Marathas. Hyder Ali had to face defeat. After Hyder Ali's death, his son Tipu carried on the war.

Results. Peace was restored by the Treaty of Mangalore between Tipu and the English as no party was in a winning position. The clauses of the treaty were as under:

1. Both sides returned the territories conqured from each other.
2. Both sides released the prisoners of war.

THIRD MYSORE WAR (1790-92)

Causes. 1. The real cause was the distrust between Tipu and the Company.

2. Lord Cornwallis (1786-93), the Governor General of Bengal worked on the anti-Tipu suspicion of the Nizam and the Marathas and arranged a Triple-Alliance (1790) with them against Tipu.
3. Tipu sought the help of the French King.
4. Tipu attacked the Raja of Travancore as according to Tipu, the Raja had violated an earlier arrangement. The Raja was an alloy of the English.

Events. Cornwallis himself marched and captured Bangalore and approached Srirangapatam but for want of military help, the English had to vacate Bangalore. The English, with the support of the troops of the Marathas and the Nizam again moved towards Srirangapatam.

Results. Sultan Tipu was forced to sign the treaty of Srirangapatam which contained the following terms:

(*i*) Tipu had to part with half of his territory which was divided between the English and the Marathas.

(*ii*) Tipu had to pay the war indemnity of three crores of rupees which was equally divided among the allies.

Cornwallis summed up the Company's gains, "We have effectively crippled our enemy without making our friends too formidable."

FOURTH MYSORE WAR (1799)

Causes. 1. Lord Wellesley (1798-1805), the Governor General of Bengal who succeeded Cornwallis was determined to extend the influence of the Company in India. He wanted complete submission of Tipu.

2. With a view to strengthen the position of the English, he devised a new system known as *'Subsidiary System'*. He made Subsidiary Alliance with a number of Indian States including the Nizam. Tipu Sultan was also asked to join it but he refused.

3. Tipu had lost half of his territory as a result of the Third Mysore War and was burning with revenge. He wanted to take back his territory and for achieving this objective, he entered into negotiations with the French and the ruler of Kabul.

Events. Mysore was attacked from two sides, *i.e.,* Bombay and Madras. Tipu fought with great courage but of no avail. He was besieged at Srirangapatam. He was offered peace on payment of £ 2,00,000 and surrender half of his kingdom. He did not accept these terms and fell fighting. Srirangapatam, the capital of Mysore was captured.

Effects

1. Welleseley retired the sons of Tipu to Vellore on pensions.
2. He did not annex the Mysore kingdom but divided it.
3. The Mysore districts in the north-west bordering the Kingdom of Nizam were awarded to the Nizam but he had to surrender them to the Company the following year.
4. Wellesley offered the areas lying in the middle of the English East India Company's Empire and the Nizam occupied terrtories, to the Peshwa who declined to accept them. These areas were, therefore, equally shared by the English and the Nizam betwen themselves.
5. The Company annexed Coimbatore, Kokinada and Srirangapatam districts into the empire.
6. The remaining part of the Kingdom was granted to the member of the former Adiyar Hindu royal family of Mysore, the family dethroned by

Hyder Ali.

7. Wellesley admitted Hindu Raj of Mysore into the Subsidiary Alliance system. The Raja accepted the Kingdom of Mysore as a Jagir from the Company which could be taken away from in him case of maladministration.

The political position of the Company became very strong in India. In this way the Mysore Kingdom lost its identity.

Q. 2. Assess Hyder Ali as an administrator, ruler and Statesman.

(Rajasthan University 1996)

or

Write a short note on Hyder Ali. *(Delhi University 1997)*

Ans. **HYDER ALI (1722-82)**

Hyder Ali as a ruler and an empire builder. By dint of his military skill he rose from a petty official in the army of the Mysore to the Nawab of Mysore. The King Chikka Krishna Raj had been reduced to the position of a mere puppet by his two ministers.

Hyder Ali on account of his qualities of leadership became the commander-in chief of Mysore army and overshadowed the two ministers. Earlier while he was a *Faujdar* of Oindigal he misappropriated the revenue and' managed to raise on independent army for himself. Finding a suitable opportunity he made the Hindu Raja a prisoner and himself became the ruler of Mysore. He captured a number of places and enlarged his Kingdom.

Taking advantage of the political confusion among the Marathas, he acquired Cuddaph, Bellary, Gooty, Kurnool and important territories in the Krishna-Tungabhadra Doab.

Ruler with a foresight. It is usually believed that Hyder Ail was among the first to realize the danger posed by the English to India. He realised fully that to meet several challenges, he must improve the finances of the state and strengthen his military force. He therefore introduced several revenue and administrative reforms. He organised his administrative set up into 18 departments of which the police and the finance departments were the most important. In general, he preferred the Hindus for carrying out civil administration and the Muslims to discharge military functions.

Hyder Ali kept a large disciplined army. With the help of the French Officers, he built a modern arsenal (an establishment for the manufacture and storage of arms).

He also trained over one lakh cultivators in military venture during the idle months of the agriçultural season.

He established his firm control over the rebellious sections of the population.

Hyder Ali as a statesman. It is accepted by historians of all shades that Hyder Ali was a ruler of great merit. He was endowed with immense strategic insight and diplomacy of a high order. Though unlettered, yet he possessed a large measure of commonsense. He seldom lost his balance of mind whether in victory or in defeat.

Hyder Ali had learnt the art of permutation—combination of the diplomatic chessboard and tried to outmanoeuver his adversaries in the game.

DIPLOMATIC VICTORY OF HYDER ALI IN THE FIRST MYSORE WAR (1767-1769)

The English forged an alliance with the Nizam of Hyderabad and advanced into Mysore territory. The Marathas also created trouble for Hyder Ali. Hayder Ali was faced with a very serious situation but he rose equal to the occasion. He won over the Marathas by promising them a sum of Rupees 23 lakhs. He also managed to reconcile with the Nizam. The result was that the English were left alone. Hyder Ali proved very formidable. Hyder Ali's forces reached near Madras (the main city of the English in the South) and plundered its subburbs. The English authorities at Madras became panicky and begged for peace. Hyder Ali virtually dictated the terms of peace. The treaty demonstrated that Hyder Ali was a military strategist and a diplomat. His resounding success was also due to the efficiency and superiority of his cavalry which made it possible for him to campaign on an extensive scale. The Court of Directors of the East India Company had to admit that the war had been "very improperly conducted and most disadvantageously concluded."

Amicable relations with the French and the Dutch. Hyder Ali took many French military personnel in his service to train his army and also secured arms and stores from the French. He also made friendship with the Dutch.

Grand Quadruple Alliance. Hyder Ali formed an alliance consisting of Nizam, the Poona Government of the Marathas and Bhonsle of Nagpur but it was short-lived.

SECOND MYSORE WAR (1780-84)

The English were able to break the quadruple alliance. They also did not adhere to the earlier settlement arrived at after the First Mysore War. So conflict became inevitable. During the early phase of the war, Hyder Ali's army won victory after victory. Hyder Ali's war-machine wrought havoc on the English. Hyder Ali was so near Madras that several of its residents ran away in panic. Hyder Ali occupied Arcot, the Capital of Carnatic. But in the end, Hyder Ali had to face defeat. In spite of reverses, he continued to fight. But fate was not with him. He was suffering from cancer and died on December 7, 1782. After his death, his son Tipu continued the struggle.

It is very unfortunate that the Indian rulers in the South *i.e.* different factions of the Marathas, the Nizam of Hyderabad and Hyder Ali failed to present a united front. Hyder Ali did not prove himself as diplomatic as the English. He had to face wars with the English single handed. Same was the case with other Indian rulers. Nevertheless, it must be admitted that Hyder Ali was a terror to the English and excited dread in their hearts.

Q.3. Discuss the resistance of Mysore under Tipu Sultan against the British and explain why Tipu failed where Hyder Ali had succeeded.

Rajasthan University 1996, 1994)

or

Give an estimate of Tipu Sultan's achievements and failures.

Ans. *Tipu Sultan and the English*

After the passing away of his father Hyder Ali, Tipu Sultan succeeded him to the throne of Mysore and continued the struggle against the English.

During his father's time, he had also fought against the English.

Tipu Sultan fought three wars and in the end he lost his life while fighting.

While the Second Mysore (1780-84) was on with the English, Hyder Ali died in 1782 on account of cancer. Tipu Sultan did not lose heart. He fought the war. The war was not decisive. Therefore, both the parties ended the war and signed the Treaty of Manglore (1784). Both agreed to restore their mutual conquests and accepted the position that existed before the start of the war. They also agreed to exchange prisoners of war.

The Second Mysore had ended without any decision. The Treaty of Mangalore was short-lived. The English as well as Tipu Sultan was in the look out of an opportunity to start to struggle again. Tipu Sultan sent his emissaries to Paris and Constantinople for developing friendly relations and this aroused suspicion in the minds of the English.

Lord Cornwallis who had succeeded Hastings as Governor-General of India was determined to increase the influence of the Company in India. He organised in 1790 an anti-Tipu alliance with the Marathas and the Nizam. Cornwallis himself led the army and captured several places. Supported by the Nizam and Nizam's troops, the English advanced towards Sringapatam, the capital of Mysore. The third war lasted for about two years (1790-1792). Tipu offered tough resistance but ultimately had to enter into a very humiliating Treaty of Sringapatam.

Tipu had to surrender half of his territory to the English. He was also required to pay over three crores of rupees as war indemnity. The English gave some portion of Tipu's territory to the Nizam and the Marathas.

The last phase of the struggle ended with the Fourth Mysore War (1799). Lord Cornwallis had been succeeded by Lord Wellesley. He was an expansionist. He was determined to wipe out the independence of Tipu altogether. He devised a new scheme known as Subsidiary Alliance System. The new system was accepted by the Nizam and the Marathas.

Though defeated badly in the Third Mysore War, Tipu was determined to take revenge of his defeat. He made efforts to increase his friendship with France, Kabul, Arabia and Constatinople (Turkey etc.).

Lord Wellesley asked Tipu to join the Subsidiary Alliance and on his refusal to do so, he attacked Mysore from two sides *i.e.* Madras and Bombay. The armies of the Marathas and the Nizam also joined the English. Thus Tipu was surrounded from all sides and his capital was seized. The English asked him to sign a treaty under which Tipu was required to surrender half of his territory as well as to pay 20,000,000 but Tipu refused to accept these terms. At last he died fighting.

Results of the wars. The Kingdom of Mysore lost its independence. A major chunk of the territory of Tipu was divided among the British, the Marathas and the Nizam. A small portion was given to a child of the old Hindu dynasty which ruled over Mysore before Hyder Ali.

ACHIEVEMENTS AND FAILURES OF TIPU SULTAN

Divergent views have been expressed by the historians regarding Tipu's achievements and failures. Before arriving at some conclusion, we may very briefly review his achievements also. We have already referred to his failures in wars against the British.

Tipu Sultan tried to provide strong administrative, economic and military base. He encouraged trade and commerce issuing a new currency and weights and measures. He developed trade links with France, Turkey, Iran and other countries. He established trading Company on the model of European companies. He encouraged the growth of indigenous industries. He made various efforts to build modern army and navy on European lines. He strengthened the arsenal set up by his father Hyder Ali. He established two dock yards for modernising navy.

Inspite of the fact that on account of his daring courage and strength, Tipu Sultan is usually called the `Tiger of Mysore', he was responsible for the liquidation of the kingdom of Mysore. True, he was an able administrator, great innovator, far-sighted statesman and yet he failed to protect the kingdom established by his father. Fortune was against him.

There is no disagreement on the statement of Wilks, "Hyder Ali was born to create an empire, Tipu to lose one." There is no doubt that Tipu had to face heavy odds. It is also equally true that his father Hyder Ali started from a scratch and was able to build up a strong empire. During his life time, he was able to keep his territory intact.

Tipu placed too much reliance on the French at a time when their power had almost disappeared from India.

Tipu failed to cultivate friendship with the Nizam and the Marathas.

There is a great controversy regarding his views about religion. While on the one hand, the Muslim historians regard him as the champion of Islam, the European writers describe him as a cruel tyrant and a die-hard Muslim fanatic. No such controversy is seen in the case of Hyder Ali who was tolerant towards all communities and religions. His first Diwan and many senior officers were Hindus. It is said that Tipu gave money for the construction of the image of goddess Sharda in the Shringeri Temple.

Views of some historians on Tipu

Critics. V. A. Smith regarded Tipu as a man "full of whims and caprices."

According to Major Dirom Tipu's "cruellies were inflicted upon those whom he considered his enemies."

According to Alfred Lyall, "He had no political ability of higher sort".

Wilks went to the extent of saying, "Hyder was born to create an empire, Tipu to lose one."

Supporters of Tipu

Sir John Shore commented, "The peasantry of Tipu's dominions were well protected and their labours encouraged and rewarded."

Mill writes, "As a domestic ruler he (Tipu) sustains an advantageous comparison with the greatest princes of the East."

Moors praises Tipu for his "congenial form of government."

Dr. Ishwari Prasad has explained the hostile attitude of the British historians in these words, "The fear with which the English regarded Tipu is the measure of his greatness. They dreaded him and hated him. That state has found expression in the character which the English historians have pointed to Tipu."

According to Sayed Abdul Qadir, "The character of Tipu Sultan stands out in marked contrast to that of his more celebrated father. Personal courage he certainly possessed and he is said to have been a good rider and a skilful marksman. His pen was the most prolific. He is said to have written to his officers both civil and military detailed instructions on every conceivable matter. He pronounced decided opinions on science, medicine, commerce, religious observance, engineering, military establishments and a host of matters with equal facility."

Tipu was definitely deficient in the skills of war strategies which eminently distinguished his father. Tipu lacked diplomatic skill in comparison to his father.

There is no doubt that ultimate end is the index of the greatness of a person. Tipu's end was tragic. He lost his life as well as the kingdom established by his father. On account of this he may be pronounced as a failure.

7

Anglo-Marathas Wars: Success of the English

Q.1. Critically assess Nana Phadnavis' character and policies. How did he affect the future of the Maratha state? *(Rajasthan University 1996)*

or

Trace the phases of struggle between Nana Phadnavis and British power. *(Rajasthan University 1991)*

Ans.

NANA PHADNAVIS (1742-1800)

Head of the Council of Regency. Nana Phadnavis played a very crucial role in the Maratha affairs for about 38 years from 1762 to 1800 *i.e.* till his death. During the period of Peshwa Madhav Rao Narain (1774-95), Nana Phadnavis was the `*de-facto*' Peshwa. In fact it was he who after the death of Peshwa Narayan Nao, favoured his posthumous son Madhav Rao to succeed and gave a call to Maratha chiefs to accept him as the Peshwa. The new Peshwa was just a new borrr baby and therefore a council of regency was required. Nana Phadnavis was made the head of the council.

Raghoba or Raghunath Rao, uncle of Peshwa Narayan Rao was the other claimant of the post of the Peshwa. Sir Jadunath Sarkar, the noted historian has described Raghoba as the 'most infamous character of Maratha history.' Nana made all efforts to protect the Maratha power from the evil designs of Raghoba who sought help from the English East India Company.

First Maratha War (1775-82) and Nana Phadnavis.

There were two important reasons for the First Maratha war with the English. From the very beginning, the English had evil designs over India. They had already become the supreme power in the North. In the South, the Marathas were a great force to reckon with. An opportunity came to them when Raghoba, a disgruntled and an ambitious chief approached them for help to become the Peshwa. The Bombay Governor-General of the Council and in violation of the Regulation Act of 1773, made the Treaty of Surat with Raghoba in 1775. The Treaty included the following provisions:

(*i*) Raghoba to be made the Peshwa.

(*ii*) Raghoba to be supported by the English troops and their expenses to be borne by Raghoba.

(*iii*) Bassein and Salsettle territories to be given to the English.

Nana Phadnavis guided the affairs of the Maratha power. For a while he was very successful in uniting almost all the Maratha chiefs against the English. But the English were successful in dividing the Maratha chiefs. However in the war fortunes wavered on both sides and the two parties realised the futility of war. A peace treaty at Salbai (1782) ended the war.

The Treaty of Salbai secured peace between the Marathas and the English. The English had to bribe Bhonsle, the Maratha chief of Nagpur to make peace. The Company was to keep Salsette with it. Raghoba claim on the throne of Peshwa was not accepted and he was given a pension. Warren Hastings, the Governor-General of Bengal discribed the peace treaty as, "successful negotiation of peace in the most desperate period of his distress." Such was the success of the diplomacy of Nana Phadnavis.

Maratha and Mysore. Nana Phadnevis wanted to increase the Maratha influence in the South. Hyder Ali fought three wars with the Marathas in 1764, 1767, and 1770-71 lost all the wars and had to pay huge war indemnity to the Marathas. After his death, he ultimately signed a treaty in 1792 and as a result, the Marathas got huge territories from him.

Battle with Nizam of Hyderabad. Although the Nizam had joined the Marathas against Tipu, he was still their enemy. When Nana pressed the Nizam for the tax arrears, he refused and declared war on the Marathas in 1794. The battle was fought at Kharda in 1795. Nana was able to unite Maratha chiefs against the Nizam. Nizam was defeated and agreed to clear the arreas of Chauth and Sardeshmukhi and to give some territory also to the Marathas. Nana played an important role in the struggle against the Nizam.

CHARACTER AND PERSONALITY OF NANA PHADNAVIS

Nana was very studious and regular in his work habits. He attended to all the details of the administration. He was always serious and he was hardly seen laughing. He was usually reasonable and fair in his dealings. He was afraid to commit treachery.

Nana always worked in secret. He was a stern taskmaster and therefore was not liked by several Maratha chiefs. He did not want to share power with others. He loved money too much. He did not subordinate his love of power and money to the service of the nation. He was often in danger of assassination. On about 20 occasions, attempts on his life were made. However, each time he had a miraculous escape.

(*a*) *Admirers of Nana*

(*i*) *Captain Browing*. "Nana is gone and with him the Brahman Raj. Poona has fallen."

(*ii*) *Palmer*. "With Nana had departed all the wisdom and moderation of the Maratha Government."

(*iii*) *Richard Temple*. "Maratha administration lost all vestige of honesty and efficiency by the death of its great minister."

(*iv*) *Grant Duff*. "Nana doubtless shines out as the last genius produced by the Maratha nation."

(*b*) *Critics of Nana*. According to Sardesi, "Nana would have acquired a much higher place in history if he had subordinated his love of power and monetary interest to the service of the nation."

Grant Duff, while praising Nana as a great statesman, has criticised him "for want of personal courage and having an ambition not always restrained by principles."

Q.2. Discuss the role of Mahadaji Scindhia in Maratha affairs.

(Rajasthan University 1996)

Ans. **MAHADAJI SCINDHIA (1727-1794)**

Brief life sketch. Mahadaji Scindhia played an important role in strengthening the Maratha power in the last quarter of the 18th century. He served the Maratha state faithfully. The life of Mahadaji was one long period of strenuous activity. It can be divided into four parts. During the first part upto 1761, he was an obscure figure. He was one of the few Marathas of note who escaped his life during the third Battle of Panipat in 1761, although permanently lamed by a severe wound.

During the second phase he emerged as one of the four territorial chiefs who shared power with Peshwa-Scindhia of Gwalior, Holkar of Indore, Gaekwad of Baroda and Raja of Nagpur. During this period he acquired the supreme fitness which later on helped him to cooperate with Nana Phadnavis to defeat the English during the First Maratha was and arrive at settlement.

During the third phase he made his mark in two dimensions. He helped Shah Alam, the titular Mughal emperor, when he quitted British protection in 1771 and escorted him to re-enter Delhi. During this phase, he proved himself to be a great negotiator with the British in the First Maratha war.

He won the confidence of the British who were very keen to arrive at some amicable.

Settlement with the Marathas. Realising the no-win position and futility of the war, he prevailed upon the Peshwa to enter into a peace treaty. So the Peace Treaty was signed in 1782 at Salbai, a village in Scindhia's territory. This treaty enhanced his influence greatly.

The fourth phase of Scindhia's career began after the First Maratha War. During this period, he created a kingdom which he left for his children. It may be noted that the kingdom created by him lasted till the marger of Indian states immediately after independence.

HISTORIANS ON THE ACHIEVEMENTS OF SCINDHIA

Achievement of his two objectives. According to Malleson, "In his life he had two main objects, the one to found a kingdom, the other to prepare for the contest for empire with the English. In both, it may be said he succeeded."

Establishment of Maratha control. In the words of J. N. Sarkar, the noted historian and an authority on the subject, "He towers over Maratha history in solitary grandeur." He further states that inspite of several challenging situations, "...in the end he triumphed over all." According to the same author, "In establishing Maratha control over the Imperial Government of Delhi (Mughal Government) and wipping off the disgrace of Panipat, Mahadaji Scindhia had to labour alone, nay in the teeth of pinpricks and convert opposition by the court of Poona (Peshwa's court)".

Survival of Maratha power. It is pointed out by Sardesai that if Mahadaji and Nana Phadnavis had not acted in concert and brought all their resources to bear on the First Maratha war there would have been an end of the Maratha power.

Successful ruler. According to Keene, "He was an Indian ruler of successful capacity in times of exceptional difficulty."

A tolerant ruler. It is accepted that Mahadaji was free from caste and religious bias. He was equally respected by the Hindus and Muslims. He employed Brahmans, the Prabhus, Marathas and Maharas.

Mahadaji suffered from one drawback. He did not manage his financial affairs properly.

Mahadaji's greatness may be summed up in the words of Malleson, "By the death of Mahadaji Scindhia, the Marathas lost their ablest warrior and their most foreseeing statesman."

Comparison between Mahadaji Scindhia and Nana Phadnavis

Mahadaji and Nana, though differed greatly in their mental cast and physical features, but had one common bond-loyalty to the Peshwa and consolidation of Maratha power. Both played an important role in meeting the challenge of the British in the First Maratha War. The Marathas maintained their power and territory through a partnership between the brilliant military commander Mahadaji Scindhia, who operated in the north and Nana Phadnavis who shrewdly maneuvered through the conflicts between Hyderabad. Mysore and East India Company in the South.

An eminent historian has described the difference between these great Maratha leaders in these words, "While Nana was by nature strict and serious, regular and hardworking, abstemious in words and actions, difficult for approach, and never given to sport, mirth or company, hardly ever seen to laugh and of an extremely delicate and then constitution. Mahadaji was, on the other hand, of jovial and merry temperament, ever surrounded by crowd of people, talking, joking, laughing and enjoying company, taking counsel with all, but always so cautions as to set people entirely on a wrong scent, never to let other fathom his real intentions or plans, in fact an exact antithesis of Nana."

Q.3. "The year 1818 marked the end of Maratha empire." Explain

or

How many Anglo-Maratha wars were fought? What were their consequences? Why did the English succeed against the Marathas?

or

Explain the nature of Maratha confederacy. How did the English bring about the destruction of Maratha confederacy?

or

Give a brief account of the Anglo-Maratha relations from 1802 to 1818 and also the causes of the defeat of the Marathas.

Ans. *Rise and Fall of the Marathas*

The rise of Maratha power is associated with Shivaji (1627-1680). He welded the scattered Marathas into a mighty nation. He broke the power of the mighty Mughal Emperor Aurangzeb in the Deccan. After his death, the Maratha power received set back for a few years. Baji Rao I (1698-1740) who succeeded his father Balaji Vishvanath in 1720 formulated a bold plan of expansion of the Maratha power. He said, "Let us strike at the trunk of the withering tree (tottering Mughal empire). The branches will fall of themselves. Thus would Maratha flag fly from the Krishna (river) to the Indus." He achieved great success during his life time. His successor also tried to enhance the Maratha power. For a while it appeared that Marathas would dominate the entire North India. The Marathas even became the protectors of the Mughal emperor. However they were defeated by Ahmad Shah Abdali in the third Battle of Panipat in 1761. Their defeat put an end to their ambition of becoming a supreme power in India.

Emergence of Maratha Confederacy and the conflict with the English

Maratha confederacy comprised a group of powerful Maratha chiefs, namely Bhonsle with his headquarters at Nagpur, Peshwa at Poona, Gackward at Baroda, Scindhial Gwaliar, Holkar at Indore, the Peshwa being the nominal head of the confederacy. The foundation of the Maratha Confederacy was laid by Balaji Rao, the second Peshwa (1720-1740). He discarded the practice of paying cash to his chief officers and instead granted jagirs. The offices became hereditary. After the defeat of the Marathas in the Third Battle of Panipat in 1761, the Maratha power declined greatly and so was the case with the power of the Peshwa. Gradually, the Marathas again enhanced their power and the members of the confederacy became more independent of the influence of the Peshwa. The members of this group, some time collectively, sometimes individually and sometimes at variance with each other, fought with the

English but ultimately the Marathas lost to them. The primary reason of the conflict with the English was their desire to establish empire in India.

Four phases of Anglo-Maratha conflict

Following were the four phases of the Anglo-Maratha struggle.

1. First Maratha War (1775-1782 A. D.).
2. Second Maratha War (1802-1804).
3. Third Maratha War (1803-1805).
4. Fourth Maratha War (1817-1818).

FIRST MARATHA WAR (1775-1782)

The East India Company determined as it was to enhance its power in India, interfered in the internal affairs of the Marathas. They sided with one disgrunted Raghoba, a Maratha Chief and a claimant of the office of the Peshwa. Nana Phadanavis and Mahadaji Scindhia proved too strong to the English.

Treaty of Salbai (1782). Of the 17 terms of the treaty which ended the war, following were the most important:-

(*i*) Claim of Raghoba to the office of the Peshwa was not accepted. He was given a pension.

(*ii*) The English occupation of Salsette was accepted.

SECOND MARATHA WAR (1802-1804)

Causes. With the death of Nana Phadnavis, `departed all the wisdom and moderation in Maratha politics. Holkar became so powerful that the Peshwa entered into subsidiary Alliance with the English under the Treaty of Bassian (December 1802) on terms which were humiliating to the Maratha pride. The Maratha Chiefs were greatly annoyed by this treaty.

Events. Scindhia and Bhonsle combined. Holkar and Scindhia patched up their differences. However, he and Gaikward did not join Scindhia and Bhonsle in their struggle with the English. Of course, they did not side the English. Bhonsle was defeated and made the Treaty of Deogaon under which he entered into the Subsidiary Alliance and ceded Cuttack to the English.

Scindhia also faced defeat and made the Treaty of Arjungaon by which he entered into Subsidiary Alliance. He also ceded Broach, Ahmednagar and the territories between the Ganges and the Jamuna including Agra and Delhi.

Results. (*i*) The English gained complete control over the coast of Orissa and the territories between the Ganges and the Jamuna.

(*ii*) The Peshwa became a disgruntled puppet in their hands.

THIRD MARATHA WAR (1803-1805)

Now Holkar alone was left in the field. Lord Wellesley turned his attention on him but he proved more than a match for the British. He made friendship with the Raja of Bharatpur. Besides he employed traditional Maratha tactics of mobile warfare. The finances of the Company had dwindled on account of constant wars. In Europe, Napoleon posed a major threat to the British power. Wellesey was therefore, recalled and the Company made peace with Holkar by the Treaty of Rajghat giving back to Holkar the greater past of his territories.

FOURTH MARATHA WAR (1817-18)

The Maratha Chiefs combined together and made the last attempt to regain their old prestige. However, they failed to evolve a well-thought out war strategy.

Results

1. Like rulers of other Indian states, the Maratha Chiefs now existed at the mercy of the British power. The Maratha confederacy was altogether destroyed.
2. Peshwa was dethroned, given pension and sent to Bithur near Kanpur. His territories were annexed.
3. The Company became a paramount power in India.
4. Bhonsle and Holkar lost several territories.
5. A small kingdom of Satara, formed out of Peshwa's territories, was given to The Maratha King as a complete dependent of the British. Presumably, this war done to satisfy Maratha pride.

Causes of the Failure of the Marathas Against the British

These may be divided under five broad heads; namely administrative, economic, military, political and miscellaneous.

I. *Administrative Cause.*

1. No cohesive and unified administrative system.
2. Neglect of public welfare programmes.
3. Very weak central administration.

II. *Economic causes.*

4. Poor resources of Maharashtra.
5. Very little industrial development.
6. Dependence on loot and plunder.
7. Heavy reliance on *`Chauth*' and *`Sardeshmukh*'.
8. Lack of a viable economy.
9. Constant wars resulting in a great economic burden.

III. *Military causes.*

10. Old weapons.
11. Loose army discipline.
12. Neglect of military science.
13. No unified command of action.
14. Mercenary soldiers.
15. Abandonment of guerilla warfare.
16. Neglect of artillery and navy.

IV. *Political causes.*

17. Loose federation of powerful Maratha groups.
18. Mutual dissentions.
19. Absence of a charismatic or towering personality.
20. Lack of foresight and diplomacy.
21. Want of national sentiment and priority to regional pride.
22. Revival of feudalism.

V. *Miscellaneous causes*

23. Lack of education.
24. Neglect of science.
25. Inadequate espionage system.
26. Narrow mindedness - lack of due consideration to non-Marathas.
27. Treachery of some Marathas chiefs.
28. Superior resources of the English.
29. Untimely deaths of effective leaders.

(For details see next question)

Q.4. What were the causes of the failure of the Marathas against the British? *(Rajasthan University 1997)*

or

Explain the term Maratha Confederacy. Discuss the causes of its break-up.

or

State how the English were able to defeat the Marathas and establish their supermacy.

or

Discuss the causes of the downfall of the Maratha power.

(Delhi University 1992 and 1996)

Ans. *Maratha Confederacy*

The Maratha confederacy comprised a group of powerful Maratha Chiefs namely Bhonsle with his headquarters at Poona, Gaekwad at Baroda, Scindhia at Gwaliar, Holkar at Indore, the Peshwa being the nominal head of the confederacy. After four wars the Marathas lost to the British.

Downfall of the Maratha Power/Maratha Confederacy

About the rise and fall of the Maratha power, Dr. K. K. Datta has observed, "The fabric of the Maratha empire which the genius and military ability of Shivaji had brought into existence and which after a short period of decline was revived by Baji Rao I and competed with the English for political supremacy for about forty years now collapsed most ignominiously. This was primarily due to certain inherent defects in the character of the Maratha state particularly during the eighteenth century though there were other factors as well."

Following were the important causes of the fall of the Marathas:

1. *Maratha state was not well-knit.* About the middle of the eighteenth century, the Maratha state had become a loose federation. The authority of the Peshwa was nominal. Powerful Maratha chiefs like the Bhonsle, Gaikeward, Holker and Scindhia carved out semi-independent kingdoms for themselves and paid `lip-service' to the authority of the Peshwa. Maratha power was shared by many Maratha chiefs. Malet wrote about the Maratha confederacy, "The seeds, however, of domestic dissensions are thickly and deeply shown in the Maratha system (if system it may be called)."

2. *Lack of effective leadership.* The total absence of first rate leadership after the demise of Nana Phadnavis and Mahadaji Scindhia towards the end of the eighteen century became an important cause of the fall of the Maratha power. They were succeeded by unworthy successors. About Daulat Rao Scindhia who succeeded Mahadaji Scindhia, Broughton wrote, "A tiger or a pretty face, an elephant fight or a new supply of paper kites have each sufficient attraction to direct his chagrin." Likewise Peshwa Baji Rao II (1795-1818) had a criminal stain in his character. Sardesai writes about these two leaders, "Their misdeeds brought the Poona court and society to such a moral degradation that no one's life, property or honour was safe. People even in distant parts of the land had to suffer terrible misery through misrule, oppression, plunder and devastation."

3. *Selfishness of Maratha Chiefs.* Often the Maratha Chiefs took sides against each other, much to the detriment of the interest of the state. There was a lot of hostility between Holkar and Scindhia while the Bhonsle of Nagpur claimed the kingship of the Maratha empire. Mutual jealousies prevented the Maratha Chiefs from offering a united front to the East India Company. In 1803 when the Scindhia and the Bhonsle went to war against the Company, Holkar kept aloof waiting for the outcome. In 1804 Holkar himself was drawn into a conflict with the Company and single-handed. Likewise in the Fourth Maratha War, all the chiefs did not combine against the common enemy.

4. *Lack of cohesion in Maratha state.* According to J. N. Sarkar, the religion- national movement which was very active in Maharashtra in the seventeenth century and which had worked in the destruction of the Mughal empire

almost disappeared in the eighteenth and nineteenth century.

5. *Lack of a viable economy*. The Maratha empire subsisted not on the resources of Maharashtra but on the tribute levied upon newly acquired territories. In the absence of any industry or foreign trade, fighting and looting were the major lucrative opening of the youth. Collection of *`Chauth'* and *Sardeshmukhi*' had limitations.

6. *Constant wars a great economic burden*. The Maratha leaders indulged in civil wars as well as wars of expansion or defence. This ruined their economy and had on adverse effect on their treasury. Wellesley wrote, "They have eaten the forage and the grain, have pulled down the houses and have used the material as firewood and the inhabitants are fed with their cattle."

7. *Defective military system of the Marathas*. Though not lacking in personal prowess and valour, the Marathas were inferior to the English in organisation, in war strategies, in disciplined action and effective leadership.

8. *Treachery in the Maratha ranks*. Treachery in the Maratha ranks played havoc on them.

9. *Abandonment of Guerilla system of war*. Arthur Wellesely, Alfred Lyall and Munro and several other writers and authorities on military affairs of the time have pointed out that the Marathas lost important battles by not following their guerilla warfare. However it is also pointed out that Marathas" fault lay not in abandoning their traditional system of warfare but in inadequate adoption of the modern techniques of warfare.

10. *Neglect of artillery*. the Marathas did not attach adequate importance to the development of a powerful artillery. The importance of a powerful British artillery is realised when we consider how British artillery easily reduced many Maratha forts which had baffled the Mughal armies under Aurangzeb.

11. *Unbalanced development of the army wings*. There is no doubt that the best results could have been achieved in a coordinated development of all the three wings of the army, viz., infantry, cavalry and artillery.

12. *Inferior Maratha diplomacy*. The Marathas were poor in diplomacy as compared with the British. Who at once accepted Raghoba as their ally. In the Second Maratha War, they won over Gaekward and the Southern Maratha jagirdars on their side. Peshwa was their ally by the Treaty of Bassein.

13. *Maratha espionage Vs English espionage*. The Marathas were indifferent to military intelligence. It is pointed out that every English officer who toured any part of India and especially Maharashtra used his eyes and afterwards his tongue and pen and while a number of Britishers could speak and understand Marathi, the Marathas knew very little about the British system of Government, their factories and settlements etc. in India. As against this, the Company's spy system was perfect. C. W. Malet while stationed at Surat collected detailed information about the families of Scindhia and Holkar.

14. *Lack of liberalism*. J. N. Sarkar points out that growth of orthodoxy and

Brahman-Maratha differences sapped the vitality of the Maratha state.

15. *Revival of feudalism.* S. N. Sen attributes the fall of the Maratha military power to the revival of feudalism after the death of Sambhaji.

16. *Neglect of scientific progress.* According to S. N. Sen, the failure of the Maratha leaders to keep pace with the scientific progress in other parts of the world also contributed to their fall.

17. *Lack of National sentiment.* V. V. S. Khare thinks that among other reasons of their failure, their lack of national sentiment was also responsible.

18. *Defeat in the Third Battle of Panipat.* The defeat of the Marathas in the Third Battle of Panipat had robbed them of the cream of their youth — their fighting force.

19. *Faulty administration.* The Marathas did not pay much attention to effective administration. They neglected public welfare works.

20. *Narrow ideal of the Maratha rule.* The Marathas began to illtreat non—Marathas, so much so that they even plundered the territories of non-Maratha Hindus *i.e.* the Rajputs and Jats. Hence the Marathas failed to get their cooperation in the Third Battle of Panipat and afterwards.

21. *Subsidiary System of Lord Wellesely.* The system lured several rulers to seek friendship with the Company. It greatly increased their military strength.

22. *Superior Geographical knowledge of the English.* The English were quite familiar with the physical features of the Maratha territory. They always selected battle fields keeping geographical factors in view. The Marathas neglected this aspect.

23. *Superior navy of the English.* The English possessed a strong navy and could bring reinforcement from England at anytime.

24. *Lack of definite law of succession.* There were several claimants to the office of the Peshwa and it led to civil war.

25. *Hereditary succession to high posts.* The hereditary successions to the higher posts in Maratha confederacy resulted in loss of efficiency.

26. *Superior resources of the English.* The English in course of time came to possess superior resources. They had become the masters of Bombay, Madras, Bengal and Bihar. Their resources were very vast and compact. T' ey could count upon help from England. The resources of the Marathas were comparatively less. No wonder the English triumphed against the Marathas.

27. *Unfortunate Northern venture.* The Marathas tried to spread their net beyond their capacity and resources. They had enemies nearer home like the Nizam. Instead taking on them effectively, they turned their attention to the North and which proved disastrous.

28. *Blind towards the foreign danger.* The Marathas failed to gauge the foreign danger and ignored the growing power of the English. They did not realise that the English had become a superior power in North India through their victories in the Battles of Plassey and Buxar and that they would do the same in South India. The Marathas failed to join together even during the

national emergency. They failed to help one another against their common enemy and the result was that all of them were defeated one by one by the English East India Company.

29. *Lack of system.* In the Maratha organisation or system, there was little unity of command, little distribution of work and power and no clear cut assignment of duties. Every important Maratha Chief pulled in his own direction.

Summing up. The internal dissensions of the Marathas, lack of a systematic organisation, poor espionage, weak finances, inferior diplomacy, neglect of latest military science, want of national sentiment were the important causes of their failure against the British.

Before entering into conflict with the Marathas, the English obtained detailed information about the Marathas, their confederacy, their leaders and differences among themselves, Maratha chiefs who could be won over, Maratha Forts and their positions, means of communication and strategic points etc. For seven years they collected this type of information and thereafter they were to make elaborate preparations to meet the Marathas whom they considered a formidable force. On the other hand, the Marathas almost ignored this aspect. Besides the English turned to the Marathas after their defeat in the Third Battle of Panipat.

The British overpowered the Maratha confederacy by the following methods.

(*i*) By sowing dissensions among the members of the Maratha confederacy.
(*ii*) By buying peace through Treaty of Salbai.
(*iii*) By Subsidiary Alliance.
(*iv*) By wars.

8

Maharaja Ranjit Singh: Anglo-Sikh Relations Annexation of Punjab

Q.1. Give an account of the achievements of Maharaja Ranjit Singh?

or

How did Maharaja Ranjit Singh come to power? How was he able to save Punjab from the English?

Ans. MAHARAJA RANJIT SINGH (1780-1839)

Brief Life Sketch. On the death of his father in 1793, Ranjit Singh became Chief of the Sukherchakia Misl at the age of twelve. It may be noted that Sakherchia was one of the twelve Misls of the Sikhs which had their power in Punjab and its authority extended over a few districts of the Rachna and the Chaj Doab. He was betrothed at the age of six and married at the age of sixteen. He had a severe attack of small pox which resulted in the loss of one eye. He started accompanying his father at the age of ten. At the age of seventeen he became independent of the Council of Regency consisting of his mother, mother-in-law and Diwan Lakhpat Rai who controlled the affairs of the state.

Achievements of Maharaja Ranjit Singh: Lion of Punjab

Maharaja Ranjit Singh like Akbar showed an early grasp of political affairs. Like Shivaji in Maharashtra, Ranjit Singh wedded together the petty Sikh Misls into a strong kingdom. Ranjit Singh was brave, courageous and fearless. He was a great diplomat, a stateman, a military leader and a benevolent ruler. He was the only Indian ruler who preserved his independence when almost all other rulers submitted to the British. On account of his daring exploits and fearlessness, he came to be known as the 'Lion of Punjab'. Probably he was the only one-eyed as well as illitrate Indian ruler who established a strong empire.

Achievements of Maharaja Ranjit Singh may be categorised under the following heads.

1. Military achievements
2. Administrative achievements
3. Religious achievements: Toleration
4. Diplomatic achievements: relations with the English

Military Achievements

It goes to the credit of Ranjit Singh that he was always successful in his military exploits. He was a very shrewd and skilful commander. First, he conqured Lahore and then Amritsar, thereafter he established his authority over the entire territory from the Sutlej to the Jhelum. He conquered various territories in cis Sutlej- Malva. He captured Doladhi, Ludhiana, Dakha, Rai Kot, Jagraon, Wadni, Naraingarh, zira, Kot Kapura etc.

Ranjit Singh got Kangra from the Dogras and Attock from the Afghans. He conquered Kashmir and Peshawar.

He gave shelter to Afghan ruler Shah Shuja and got the precious diamond 'Koh-i-Noor' from him.

Administrative Achievements

(1) *Nature of State: Ranjit Singh a benevolent despot.* The Maharaja was the embodiment of all civil and military authority in the state. He, however, worked for the welfare of his people. He considered himself as the servant of the Khalsa or the Sikh Commonwealth and acted in the name of the Khalsa. He struck coins in the name of Guru Nanak and Guru Gobind Singh.

Ranjit Singh was known for his accessibility, his just and fair administration.

(2) *Council of Ministers.* The Maharaja was assisted by a Council of five ministers. The Maharaja used to give due consideration to the advice of his ministers.

(3) *Provincial and local administration.* The kingdom was divided into four provinces namely Lahore, Multan, Peshawar and Kashmir. The provinces were divided into Parganas or districts. The districts were further divided into Taluquas. Each taluqua had between 50 to 100 villages.

There was a *panchayat* in each village. Each village was self-sufficient.

(4) *Financial administration.* Land revenue was the chief source of income. It varied between 33 per cent to 40 per cent depending upon the fertility and richness of soil. The Maharaja had given strict orders to the marching armies not to damage crops in any way.

(5) *Judicial administration.* There were no written laws. Law was based on customs of the people. Fines were imposed in most cases. The administration of justice was more of a local concern than national concern.

(6) *Military Administration and Reforms.* Ranjit Singh gave his maximum attention to maintain a strong and well-disciplined army. His army proved an effective fighting force against the Misls, the Afghans the Dogras and the Gorkhas.

He introduced the following reforms in the army:-

(*a*) He created a regular standing army.

(*b*) He introduced the system of monthly payment to his army-a unique feature at that time.

(*c*) He employed about fifty European Officers to train his army - French, Russion, Germans, English etc.

(*d*) He gave adequate care to provide adequate equipment.

(*e*) He ensured that the mobility of the army was swift.

Diplomatic Achievements: Relations with the English

Ranjit Singh's ambition to acquire the cis-Sutlej states (Sikh states to the east of the river Sutlej) brought him face to face with the East India Company—a power that was also expanding its territories in India. Both the parties realised the importance of mutual goodwill. Both realised their assets and limitations and entered into a Treaty at Amritsar (1809). According to the treaty, Maharaja Ranjit Singh was free to expand his territories to the west of Sutlej. Both adhered to this arrangement during the time of Ranjit Singh. Although there were small matters which led to some problems from time to time but they were solved mutually. Writers have expressed divergent views on this treaty.

An Assessment of Ranjit Singh

Maharaja possessed exceptional qualities of military leadership, diplomacy and administration. He was a just and fair ruler. He showed religious toleration.

He created a strong and peaceful state in an area that had known prolonged periods of disorder and strife.

Despite his small stature and one eye, he had a commanding presence and became something of a legend in the history of Punjab.

Some Opinions

Admirers (*a*) Lepel Griffin calls Ranjit Singh "The beau ideal of a soldier - strong spare, active, courageous and enduring."

(*b*) According to Baron Von Hugel, "Never perhaps was so large an empire founded by one man with so little criminality."

(*c*) Cunning has summed up his achievements as "He consolidated the numerous petty states into kingdom. He wrest from Kabul its fairest provinces."

(*d*) In the word of Jacquemont, "He knew the name, position and history of ten to twelve thousand villages of his kingdom."

(*e*) Sinha observes, "His conversation was a nightmare even to a man of intellectual capacity of Jacquemont."

(*f*) Dr. R. C. Majumdar describes the achievements of Ranjit Singh in these words, "A born ruler of men, Ranjit Singh is entitled to fame chiefly for his success in effecting the marvellous transformation of the warring Sikh states into a compact monarchy."

(*g*) Baron Hagel has remarked, "During the time when the Punjab was under Ranjit Singh and India was under British Government, the Punjab definitely enjoyed more prosperity and peace than India."

Critics

(*i*) N. K. Sinha states, "In his relations with British Government, Ranjit Singh is seen at is worst."

(*ii*) Dr. G. L. Chopra observes that Ranjit Singh's despotic rule "was certain to bring a rapid paralysis of the central authority after is death."

Q.2. Examine critically the relations of Maharaja Ranjit Singh with the English? What was their impact on the Sikh power and the English power in India. *(Rajasthan University 1995)*

or

Trace the relations of Maharaja Ranjit Sing with the English from 1800 to 1839 A. D.

or

Examine critically Ranjit Singh's policy towards the British. How did it affect the fate of Punjab after his death?

(Rajasthan University 1995)

Ans. *Maharaja Ranjit Singh's Relations with the English*

At the outset it must be admitted that it goes to Ranjit Singh's credit that he was the only Indian ruler who remained independent when others fell a prey to the expansionist and imperialist designs of the East India policy. He has been unduly criticised by a section of historians that he followed a weak policy towards the English.

Following were the important phases of the relationship between Maharaja Ranjit Singh and the British.

I The British Mission (1800)
II Treaty of Lahore (1806)
III Sir Charles Metcalf's Mission (1808)
IV Treaty of Amritsar (1809)
V Durbar of Rupar (1831)
VI Triple Alliance (1839)

I. *British Mission (1800)*

The first contact between Maharaja Ranjit Singh and the English took place in the year 1800. There were two important reasons. India was threatened by an invasion of Zaman Khan (Shah) of Kabul who had been invited by Tipu Sultan, a bitter enemy of the British. At the same time Maharaja Ranjit Singh was also expanding his Kingdom. The British, therefore, sent Munshi Yusaf Ali to the court of Ranjit Singh with rich presents to win over him to their side. However, the danger of Zaman's invasion receded and Yusaf Ali was recalled.

II. *Treaty of Lahore* (1806)

In 1805, Jaswant Rao Holker, a prominent Maratha chief who was hotly pursued by the British came to Amritsar to seek his help against the British. Ranjit Singh at that time was busy in his plans of expansion in the west. He, therefore, did not think it prudent to help him. Moreover the English also desired that Ranjit Singh should not help Holkar. Accordingly agreement between Ranjit Singh and the British was made in 1806. Its important terms were as under:

(*i*) The English to withdraw their troops from the Punjab.
(*ii*) Ranjit Singh to force Holkar to leave Amritsar.
(*iii*) The English not to attack Ranjit Singh's territory if he remained friendly with them.

Evaluation of the treaty. Opinions are sharply divided on the issue. On the one hand it is argued by some historians that it was prudence for Ranjit Singh to have friendly relations with the British as he had not yet become very strong. Ranjit Singh also realised that Holkar was spent up force and he was without any worthwhile resource. Moreover in case he had helped Holker, Punjab and not Maharashtra would have become a battle field between the Marathas and the British. In this way, the fertile province of Punjab would have been ruined.

On the other hand, it is argued that by helping Holkar, Ranjit Singh would have applied a brake to the growing power of the British.

III. *Sir Charles Metcalf's Meeting with Ranjit Singh* (1808)

The 1806 agreement did not contain any clause regarding the eastern limit of Ranjit Singh's territory. He, therefore, decided to bring the Cis-Sutlej Sikh States of Patiala, Nabha and Jind under him. Ranjit Singh led expeditions to Malwa and he occupied a few places. This alarmed the Sikh rulers of Malwa and they approached the British Resident at Delhi. In the meanwhile the British felt alarmed on account of the fear of Franco-Russian invasion of India. They therefore sent Sir Charles Metcalf to negotiate a treaty of friendship with Ranjit Singh. Maharaja agreed to enter into treaty on two conditions–one condition was that the English would remain neutral in case of Sikh-Afghan war. The other was that the British would recognise Ranjit Singh the sovereign of the entire Punjab including the Malwa (Cis-Sutlej) territories. The negotiations did not succeed.

IV. *The Treaty of Amritsar* (1809)

Ranjit Singh continued his policy of expansion in the Cis-Sutlej area and he captured Faridkot, Malerkotla, Ambala and other places. The rulers of these places approached Metcalfe who protested but Ranjit Singh paid no head. In the meanwhile, situation in Europe became favourable for the British. The fear of France-Russian invasion disappeared. The British now thought of adopting a tough attitude towards Ranjit Singh. Ranjit Singh agreed to start negotiations and the Treaty of Amritsar was signed.

Terms of the Treaty of Amritsar

(*i*) River Sutlej became the boundary line between the territories of Ranjit Singh and the British.

(*ii*) The British were not to interfere in the affairs of Ranjit Singh.

(*iii*) Ranjit Singh was not to acquire territories on the left bank of the river Sutlej.

(*iv*) The cis-Sutlej Sikh states (states in Malwa) were to enjoy British protection.

(*v*) There was to be a perpetual friendship and amity between the British and Ranjit Singh.

Why did Ranjit Singh Sign the Treaty of Amritsar?

1. *The defeat of the Akalis.* In a local clash between the Akalis who were in large numbers and a small body of English troops, the Akalis on whose strength Ranjit Singh depended to a great extent, lost heavily. This incident convinced Ranjit Singh that the English army was far superior to the Sikh army.

2. *Firm policy of the British.* There was a great change in the situation in Europe on war front which made the British adopt a stiff attitude towards Ranjit Singh.

3. *Fear of the Cis-Sutlej rulers joing the British.* The rulers of Patiala, Nabha and Jind had expressed their intention to seek the protection of the English. This discouraged Ranjit Singh to join issue with the English.

4. *No check on his expansionist policy.* Ranjit Singh knew that if he entered into treaty of friendship with the English, he would be in a position to expand his kingdom in the north and also consolidate it.

Impact and Significance of the Treaty

Historians have expressed divergent opinions regarding the impact and significance of the Treaty of Amritsar. Some of the historians have sharply criticised Ranjit Singh for entering into this treaty. A more rational view is that the treaty had merits as well as demerits.

Advantages to Ranjit Singh and Sikh Cis-states

Treaty gave the following advantages :-

1. *Expansion of his territories.* It became possible for Ranjit Singh to expand his territories to the west. Within a few years after this treaty, he conquered Multan, Derajat, Kashmir and Peshawar etc. and greatly enlarged his sphere of influence.

2. *Avoidance of war.* The British had vast resources at their disposal. Their forces were well-disciplined. Ranjit Singh, on the other hand had limited resources. In case of defeat, he would have lost some territories or like other rulers would have lost his identity.

3. *Independence of Sikh Cis-Sutlej States.* In the long run, the treaty proved useful to the Sikhs. It is said that if these states had become a part of Ranjit Singh's kingdom, these would have been annexed by the British with the rest of the Punjab in 1849. As observed by Syed Abdul Qadir, "If the Government of Lord Minto (the British) had not intervened, Ranjit Singh would have taken under his control the cis-Sutlej territory as he did the rest of the Punjab and in 1849, from the Jamuna to the Khyber, not even one yellow spot would have been left."

Advantages to the British

1. *Diplomatic gain.* The British gained in diplomacy. They had an upper hand. They became the protectors of Cis-Sutlej states of Sikhs.

2. *Territorial gains.* The frontier of the British in India was pushed from the Jamuna river to the Sutlej.

3. *Greater scope for further expansion.* Now the British became free from the hostility of the Sikhs and they waged successful wars in other parts of India. It helped them to defeat the Gurkhas of Nepal and the Marathas in the Fourth Maratha war.

Disadvantages to Maharaja Ranjit Singh

1. *Lowering the prestige of Ranjit Singh.* It became clear that the entire state of Punjab would not come under his domination.

2. *Brought the English very near to the territory of Punjab.* The design of the British became more definite. They were allowed to station some troops at Ludhiana - a place very suitable to the British from military point of view.

3. *Set back to the expansion of his kingdom.* Ranjit Singh could not become the ruler of all Sikh states of the Punjab. The Sikh states of Patiala, Malerkotla and Jind remained independent of his control.

In the words of N. K. Sinha, "In this Anglo-Sikh alliance, the British Government was the rider and Ranjit Singh was the horse...In his relations with the British Government, Ranjit Singh is seen at his worst. He never grandly dared. He was all hesitancy and indecision."

According to Sinha the Treaty of Amritsar was diplomatic defeat for Ranjit Singh. He had to put his pride in the pocket and eat a humble pie."

About the consequences of the treaty, Dr. N. K. Sinha has observed, "His failure to absorb the Cis-Sutlej states was a tragedy of Sikh militant nationalism and the success of the cis-Sutlej Sikhs with the aid of the British Government marked the disruption of the great creation of Guru Gobind Singh."

It appears Dr. Sinha has not been quite fair to Ranjit Singh in his criticism.

He did not fully appreciate the situation in which Ranjit Singh was placed. The dark side of the picture is that Ranjit Singh's defeat at the hands of the British would have enabled them to annex Punjab as early as the first quarter of the 19th century. It goes to the credit of Ranjit Singh that a major part of Punjab could be kept independent by 1849 Maharaja Ranjit Singh realised his limitations and took the right decision.

V. *Durbar at Rupar* (1831)

Apart from minor irritants on some matters, relations remained somewhat friendly. It is true that inspite of the Treaty of Amritsar (1809), mutual suspicion did not vanish. Each side was in the look out of an opportunity to have an upper hand but no party was prepared for a showdown. Maharaja Ranjit Singh and Lord William Bentinck met at Rupar and both parties professed friendship for each other. Abdul Qadir made the followship remarks about this meeting, "William Bentinck was then lulling Ranjit Singh to sleep at Rupar so that he may steal a march upon Sind and bring it under British sphere of influence."

Next year in 1832, the British entered into a commercial treaty with the Amirs of Sind. Ranjit Singh grew suspicious but he was assured that the treaty was purely commercial.

VI . *Tripartite Treaty of 1839*

In spite of friendship treaty, the British took three steps against the wishes of Maharaja Ranjit Singh. These were (*i*) Commercial treaty with the Amirs of Sind (*ii*) Capture of Shikarpur (*iii*) Occupation of Ferozpur and converting it into a military cantonment. Maharaja made several protests but with no response. The same thing happened in 1839 when Tripartite Treaty was signed between Ranjit Singh, Shah Shuja, a claimant of the throne of Kabul and the British. The Maharaja while agreeing to the Treaty, refused to give passage to the British army through his territories.

Summing up. After taking into consideration the superior military strength of the British, the decision of the Cis-Sutlej Sikh states to seek British protection, and the limited resources of Ranjit Singh, one is not inclined to accept these views of Dr. Sinha, "...In the last decade of his career, Ranjit Singh is a pathetic figure, helpless and inert....He feared to expose his kingdom he had created to the risk of war and chose instead the policy of yielding, yielding and yielding." On the other hand it may be stated that Maharaja was a great statesman. He clearly came to the conclusion that it was practically impossible to make any headway against the mighty power of the British. He tried to get as much as he could from the British Government. He kept his kingdom intact. One should not go by `ifs'. Ranjit Singh followed the path of wisdom.

If Punjab was annexed by the British after the death of Ranjit Singh it was not his fault. His successors turned out to be very weak. It is not necessary that a worthy father should be followed by a worthy son. Ranjit Singh was not alive when intrigues and plots took place in Punjab. Friendship with a very weak ruler like Holkar who was already on the run, would not have yielded the desired results. Of course Ranjit Singh did not demonstrate marked diplomacy in dealing with the 'rulers of Sikh Cis Sutlej states. Perhaps friendship with them would have strengthened his position.

Q.2. Write an essay on Anglo-Sikh relations. *(Delhi University 1997)*

or

Discuss the circumstances leading to the annexation of Punjab by the British. Was it morally justified?

(Rajasthan University 1996 and 1997)

Ans. *Anglo-Sikh Relations and Annexation of Punjab*

With the annexation of Punjab on March 29, 1849, the entire Indian subcontinent excepting Avadh came under British dominion. Avadh, as a matter of fact had been controlled and indirectly governed by the British at least since 1801.

The history of Punjab in the years following the death of Ranjit Singh is the history of plots and counter-plots, murders and assassinations, of desertions and treachery—all undermining the stability of the state and culminating in the annexation of the Punjab by the British.

Two Broad Phases of Anglo-Sikh Relations

Anglo-Sikh relations may be studied under two broad heads:

1. Relations of the British with Maharaja Ranjit Singh.
2. Anglo-Sikh relations after the death of Ranjit Singh.

First Phase: Relations of the British with Maharaja Ranjit Singh.

These can be categorised under six phases. (*i*) The British Mission (1800), (*ii*) Treaty of Lahore (1806), (*iii*) Sir Charles Metcalfe's Mission (1808), (*vi*) Treaty of Amritsar (1809); (*v*) Durbar at Rupar (1831); (*vi*) Triple Alliance (1839).

There is no doubt that the British were par excellent in diplomacy. They had their eyes set upon Punjab, and they waited patiently for a suitable opportunity. In Maharaja Ranjit Singh, they found a very formidable enemy. So long as he was alive, they made no attempt to annex Punjab. Maharaja Ranjit Singh also realised that the British were very powerful. Thus both the parties tried to avoid conflict and cultivated friendship with each other. Apart from minor irritants, the relations between the two remained nearly friendly.

(*i*) In 1800, the British sent a good will mission to the court of Maharaja Ranjit Singh.

(*ii*) In 1806, a treaty of friendship was made at Lahore and Maharaja agreed not to render any help to the Maratha Chief Holkar who was being chased by the British. The English on their part withdrew their forces from Punjab which were following Holkar.

The Treaty proved helpful to both *i.e.* Ranjit Singh and the British.

(*iii*) Realising the danger of Franco-Russian invasion on India, the British sent Chales Metcalf to meet Maharaja Ranjit Singh. The mission was not fruitful.

(*iv*) Ranjit Singh continued his policy of expansion which sent alarm bells to Sikh cis-Sutlej states of Patiala, Nabha and Malerkotla who approached the British for protection. In the meanwhile, the Franco-Russian danger had vanished. Negotiations between the British and Ranjit Singh resulted in the Treaty of Amritsar (1809). According to this treaty, the Maharaja was free to expand the territories to the west of Sutlej the British were not to interfere in the affairs of Ranjit Singh. The cis-Sutlej Sikh states were to enjoy protection.

The treaty was in the interest of both the parties. Ranjit Singh, thereafter expanded his kingdom, in the rest of Punjab. The British also pursued their policy of expansion in other directions.

(*v*) Relations between the two remained in general friendly, notwithstanding minor conflicts. In 1831. Lord William Bentinck and Ranjit Singh met at Rupar and exchanged pleasantries.

(*vi*) In 1832, much against wishes of Ranjit Singh, the British entered into commercial treaty with the Amirs of Sind. In 1839, the British, Shah Shuja, a deposed ruler and claimant of Kabul and the British entered into treaty of friendship. However, Maharaja did not agree to give passage to the British army through his territories in case of attack on Sind or Kabul.

Second Phase of Anglo-Sikh Relations between 1839 and 1849: Annexation of Punjab.

There are three stages in the second phase: (*i*) First Sikh war (1845-46), (*ii*) Treaty of Bhairowal (1846), (*iii*) Second Sikh War (1848-49) and annexation of Punjab.

FIRST SIKH WAR (1845-46)

Causes. For six years, after the death of Ranjit Singh, there was chaos and confusion in Punjab. Several warring groups in the royal family and the Khalsa army emerged. There were conspiracies and intrigues. The Khalsa army became more powerful and it made and unmade rulers of Punjab. There was an intense struggle for succession to the throne. There was a spate of murders of the claimants of the throne. Ultimately in September 1843, Dalip Singh a minor son of Ranjit Singh was proclaimed as the Maharaja and Rani Jindan as regent and Hira Singh Dogra as Wazir. Hiza Singh himself fell a victim of court intrigues and was murdered. The main problem was to check the growing power of the army.

The English were closely watching the happenings in Punjab. In 1842, their troops passed through Punjab in the First Afghan War disregarding the Tripartite Treaty of 1839. They began to make military preparations. They had lost prestige in the First Afghan war and wanted to re-establish their supremacy by capturing Punjab.

In 1843, the British had annexed Sind. The Sikhs began to fear the designs of the British all the more. The Lahore Durbar (ruling group) wanted to reduce the power of the Khalsa army. The ruling Sikh Sardars thought that the victory of the Khalsa army would mean expansion of the territory and its attention would be diverted from politics. In case of defeat, its strength would be reduced and it would become less dangerous.

Events. The Khalsa army, encouraged by Lahore Durbar crossed the river Sutlej. Thereupon, Lord Harding, Governor General declared War. At that time, the Khalsa army was without a general or any rate without one supreme controlling authority.

Four battles fought at Mudki, Ferozshah, Buddewal and Aliwal did not decide the issue. The final battle at Sabraon (Feb. 10, 1846) proved decisive. The English army captured Lahore.

Causes of the defeat of the Sikhs. At the time of the Anglo-Sikh conflict, selfish and shortsighted person were at the helms of affairs at Lahore Durbar and the army. Lal Singh and Teja Singh, the commanders of the Sikh army proved treacherous and they gave all vital information regarding their trenches to the English.

Results and Treaty of Lahore (March 1846). Following were the main provisions of the treaty:

1. The Maharaja renounced all claims to the Sikh territories on the left bank of the River Sutlej.
2. The English were given all the territory lying between the Sutlej and the Beas rivers.
3. Lahore Durbar was to pay an indemnity of one and a half crores of rupees. The Sikhs had only fifty lakhs of rupees. They gave the State of Jammu and Kashmir to Maharaja Gulab Singh for one crore of rupees.
4. A limit was placed on Khalsa army. It was not to exceed 22,000 infantry and 12,000 cavalry.
5. The Sikhs had to surrender all the guns used by them against the English.
6. The Lahore Government was not to employ any European witout the consent of the English.
7. The British troops were to be given passage through the Punjab whenever required.
8. A British force was to remain at Lahore till the end of the year. Henry Lawrence was appointed Resident at Lahore.

9. The minor Dalip Singh was recognised as the Maharaja with Rani Jindan as Regent of the state and Lal Singh as Wazir.

Result. The victory of the British greatly enhanced their power and the Sikh power was reduced substantially.

TREATY OF BHAIROWAL (DECEMBER 1846)

After the treaty of Lahore, things did not work smoothly. Lal Singh and some other Sikh leaders were opposed to the handing over of Jammu and Kashmir to Gulab Singh. They encouraged the Governor to rise against Gulab Singh. The revolt was put down by the British forces. Lal Singh was removed from his position and sent to Banaras. Jammu and Kashmir was handed over to Gulab Singh.

Thereafter the Treaty of Bhairowal was signed. Its terms were as under:

(*i*) A Council of eight pro-British Sikh Chiefs was to administer the affairs of Lahore kingdom during the minority of Dalip Singh.

(*ii*) The Council was to act under the advice of the British Resident.

(*iii*) A British force was to be kept at Lahore and the Sikh Government of Lahore was to pay Rs. 22 lakhs a year for its expenses.

(*iv*) The arrangement was to continue till 1854 when Maharaja Dalip Singh was to become major.

SECOND SIKH WAR (1848-49)

Causes. The second Sikh war was inevitable. The British were in the look out of an opportunity to capture Punjab. However, following were the main causes of the second Sikh war.

(*i*) Humiliating of the Sikhs and their desire to wipe off the disgrace.

(*ii*) Confidence of the Sikh soldiers in their bravery and their view that defeat of the Sikh army was on account of the treachery of their leaders in the army. The Sikh soldiers, therefore wanted to exchange arms with the British once more.

(*iii*) Harsh treatment of Rani Jindan by the British.

(*iv*) Resentment of the people against the set up established after the Treaty of Bhairowal.

(*v*) Harsh treatment with the Governor of Multan by the Lahore Darbar and the British Resident.

(*vi*) Refusal of Sher Singh, a Sikh chief to put down the revolt.

(*vii*) Friendship of the Sikhs with the Afghans by surrendering Peshawar Lord Dalhouse declared war and said, "The task before me is the utter destruction and prostration of the Sikh power, the subversion of its dynasty and the subjection of its people." He declared it the "war of vengeance."

Events. Four battles were fought at Ramnagar, Chillianwara, Multan and finally at Gujrat which is also known as 'the battle of guns. In this battle, the Sikhs also got the help of the Afghans. The Sikh army had to surrender at Rawal Pindi after the last battle.

Results. The Sikhs of Punjab lost their sovereignty and Punjab was annexed on March 29, 1849 by the British. This was the last war fought by the British in India for the extension of their empire.

Dalip Singh was given a pension of £ 50,000 per annum and sent to England.

Was the annexation of Punjab justified?

Critics

Several historian have criticised the British for their annexation of Punjab.
Major Even Bells terms the annexation as "sacred breach of trust."
According to Trotter, it was "unprincipled and unjustifiable."
Following arguments are put forward in this regard:-

(*i*) It is argued by the critics that after the Treaty of Bhairowal, it was the responsibility of the British to crush revolts in Punjab during the minorship of Maharaja Dalip Singh. Instead of accepting this responsibility in word and spirit, they allowed the matters to take a serious turn. Maharaja Dalip Singh had no responsibility in this regard. He should not have been deposed after the Second Sikh War.

(*ii*) It was unjust to ask Mulraj of Multan to render account for the last ten years when he had been governor for four years.

(*iii*) Murder of two British officers was no justification for declaring war.

Justification. Critics often forget that the British conquest of India was based on the basis of their imperialistic designs. There was no question of 'justification or non-justification' in their policy. One may ask this question: "In what way were the British justified in bringing India under their domination?" In this context one is reminded of proverbial story of the wolf and the lamb: the British wanted to have their domination over Punjab and so they annexed it.

9

Anglo-Sind and Anglo-Oudh Relations

Q.1. Why did the English annex Sind? Was it a moral Act?

or

Give an account of the British policy towards Sind leading to its annexation.

or

Do you agree that annexation of Sind was a sequel to the Afghan problem? Comment.

Ans. ANNEXATION OF SIND (AUGUST 1843)

Strategic Importance of Sind. Sind occupied a strategic position. It lay on the route from British India to Afghanistan through the Bolan pass. The French, and the Russian invasions and their influence from this side always haunted the British. They were also apprehensive that Maharaja Ranjit Singh might increase his influence over Sind.

During the beginning of the 19th century, Sind was ruled by a number of tribes who had come from Baluchistan. The most important states were Khairpur. Mirpur and Hyderabad. The Amir (Chief) of Khairpur claimed nominal sovereignty over the other two kingdoms.

Phases relating to the annexation of Sind.

Following were the important phases in this regard:-

1. Treaty of Friendship (1809)
2. Mission of Sir Alexander Burnes (1831)
3. Meeting of Lord William Bentinck and Maharaja Ranjit Singh (1831)
4. Anglo-Amirs Treaty (1832)
5. Tripartite Treaty (1838)
6. Treaty with Amirs (1838)
7. First Afghan War (1839-1842)
8. Annexation of Sind (1843)

1. *Treaty of Friendship* (1809). The treaty signed between Lord Minto and the Amirs of Sind included the following :

(*i*) There would be mutual intercourse through envoys.

(*ii*) The Amirs would not allow the French to settle in Sind.

The treaty was renewed in 1820.

2. *Mission of Sir Alexander Burnes* (1831). Alexander Burnes went to Maharaja Ranjit Singh with presents through Sind. The basic idea to pass through Sind was to know the commercial as well as military importance of Sind. The people of Sind could scent the game of the British. When Burnes entered the Indus, a Sind soldier observed, "The mischief is done, Alas! Sind is now gone as it has been seen by the British." Subsequently this proved true.

3. *Meeting of Lord William Bentinck with Maharaja Ranjit Singh* (1831). The same year Maharaja Ranjit Singh and Lord William Bentinck met at Rupar. The Sikh ruler proposed that Sind should be partitioned between the Sikhs and the British. However, the Governor General William Bentinck did not discuss this issue.

4. *Anglo-Amirs Treaty* (1832). The British had been carrying on talks with the Amirs for sometime and in 1832 concluded a treaty which contained the following terms:

(*i*) A free passage for English travellers and merchants would be given through Sind.
(*ii*) Indus would be used for commercial pursuits.
(*iii*) No war vessel would pass through the Indus river.
(*iv*) No military use would be made of this river.
(*v*) No English merchant would be settled in Sind.
(*vi*) Travellers and visitors would he required to have pass permits.
(*vii*) The old treaty of friendship was confirmed.

5. *Tripartite Treaty* (1838) *and Afghan Affairs*. To counter Russian influence, the British wanted to obtain a counteracting influence over the Afghans. Ranjit Singh was too powerful to be coerced. The weakness of the Amirs of Sind came very handy to the British. Thus, consolidation of British influence in Sind was considered a necessary preliminary to control Afghanistan.

Ranjit Singh had taken Rojhan, a town on the Sind frontier and also at one time had thought of invading Sind. The Company started negotiations with the Amirs and agreed to have a British Resident at Hyderabad. In the meanwhile the dispute over the claim of rival parties in Afghanistan assumed serious proportion, Shah Shuja, a claimant approached the British. With a view to solve the Afghan problem, the British were able to persuade Maharaja Singh to sign a Tripartite Treaty between the British, the Maharaja and Shah Shuja. By this treaty the Maharaja accepted British mediation in his dispute with the Amirs of Sind. Shah Shuja agreed to relinquish his sovereign rights on Sind on condition of receiving the arrears of tribute. The Amirs produced documentary evidence to show that Shah himself had exempted them from all claims. Maharaja Ranjit did not accept the condition of allowing, British forces to pass through his territory in case of war with Afghanistan.

6. *Treaty with the Amirs* (1839). Under the threat of superior power, the Amirs accepted a treaty according to which a British force was allowed to be

stationed at two places in Sind and its cost of maintenance also to be borne by them.

7. *First Afghan War* (1839-1842). During the First Afghan war, the British, in complete disregard to the Treaty of 1832, mobilised their troops through Sind. Sind was made the base of operations for waging war against Afghanistan. The Amirs faithfully honoured the treaty. They remained quiet even when the British suffered reverses in the Afghan war and at the same time had not honoured their treaty. The Amirs made no attempt to exploit the situation.

8. *Annexation of Sind Sequal to the Afghan issue*. During the First Afghan War, the Amirs of Sind found themselves saddled with the general liability to help the British. As already mentioned, the British were determined to annex Sind on account of its military importance. With their serious reverses in the Afghan War, they wanted to avenge their humiliation by annexing Sind on the one or the other pretext. The British, therefore, sent Sir Charles Napier to tackle the affairs of Sind. He was given complete civil and military authority. He blamed the Amirs for their disloyalty towards the British. He demanded from the Amirs:

(*i*) the right to mint coins.
(*ii*) to supply coal to the British ships passing through the river Indus.
(*iii*) To surrender Thatta, Sakkar, Bakhar, Karachi, Rohri etc.

The British also began to interfere in the internal affairs of Sind.

The Amirs accepted the above mentioned terms. However, Napier suspected that the Amirs were preparing for war. Even during negotiations, he inflicted several acts of aggression in Sind and captured Hyderabad. This enraged a section of the population and rebellion broke out. Napier continued his atrocities. The British declared war on the Amirs of Sind and inflicted heavy casualties on them and they occupied Hyderabad and Milani. The Amirs were made captives and banished from Sind. Napier himself accepted, £ 70,000 as a sort of booty from the plunder of Sind. Sind was annexed in 1843. Thus the annexation of Sind was sequel to the Afghan war. Treaty after treaty was forced on the Amirs to meet the changing Afghan situation. The failure of the British in the First Afghan war had increased their necessity of increasing vigilance on the frontier.

Criticism of the British policy in Annexing Sind

1. It openly violated the terms of the treaty of 1832.
2. The Amirs were forced to pay money even though Shah Shuja had agreed to give up all claims.
3. The Amirs were asked to sign a new treaty which virtually put an end to their sovereignty.
4. The Amirs were stopped from coining their currency.
5. Even during negotiations, Napier took possession of some territory of the Amirs.

6. The British levelled vague charges against the Amirs.
7. The Amirs were not responsible when the British Residency was attacked by some people who had felt aggrieved at the cruel actions of Napier.
8. The English wanted to make Sind as the base of their operations against the possible invasion of Russia.

Select Views of Historians and others on the Annexation of Sind

1. Napier himself (the villain of the drama of annexation) wrote in his diary, "We have no right to seize Sind, yet we shall do so, and a very advantageous, useful, humane piece of rascality it will be."
2. *"The Bombay Times'* wrote, "Alas! that this man bears the name of Englishman: Alas! that he is born in the glorious age of Wellington, which he disgraces."
3. *'The Times of London'* described this affair as "rotten throughout."
4. Henry Lawrence wrote, "I do not think that Government can do better than restore it to the Amirs."
5. Inne, a renowned historian observed that the case of annexation of Sind was "more or less deliberately manufactured."
6. According to Ramsay Muir, "Sind is the only British acquisition in India of which it may fairly be said that it was not necessitated by circumstances, and that it was therefore an act of aggression."
7. In the words of W. A. G. Archbold, "The real cause of the chastiment of the Amirs consisted in the chastisement which the British had received from the Afghans."
8. Dr. V. A. Smith has remarked, "Lord Auckland had broken treaties with the Amirs of Sind in a most cynical fashion. Lord Ellenborough went further and deliberately provoked a war in order that he might annex the province."

Summing up. The wolf (the British) wanted the lamb (the Amirs) and had it.

Q.2. Give a brief account of the process of the decline of Oudh's power during the first half of the nineteenth century and its ultimate annexation by the British. *(Rajasthan University 1994 and 1997)*

or

Sketch the history of the annexation of Oudh by the British.

(Rajasthan University 1996)

Ans. ANNEXATION OF OUDH (1856)

Annexation in the name of God. Before deliberating upon the history of annexation of Oudh, it would be of interest to mention the argument of Lord Dalhousi who ordered its annexation, "The British Government would be guilty in the sight of God and man if it were any longer to aid in sustaining by its countenance an administration fraught with suffering to millions." One may aptly counteract this statement by remarking that the British statesmen always put all sorts of strange arguments in the justification of their acts. One may ask, were they not guilty in the eyes of God when they inflicted unparalleled atrocities on the people of India by enslaving them? Was it God's will?

Brief history of Oudh. After the death of Aurangzeb in 1707, the Mughal power declined rapidly and a number of independent kingdoms sprang up in the country and Oudh was one of these.

Shuja-ud-Daula was the Nawab of Oudh when the first encounter with the British took place in 1764 in the Battle of Buxar. In this battle, the British defeated the combined forces of the Nawab of Oudh, Shah Alam Mughal Emperor and Mir Qasim , the Nawab of Bengal. Since then the British had been extracting money from the Nawab on one or another pretext. All sorts of demands and pressures had been put on the Nawab. Nevertheless, the Nawab of Oudh had remained the British allies since the Battle of Buxar.

Lord Wellesley (1798-1805) made heavy demands on the Nawab. Although the Nawab had paid his subsidies regularly, Wellesley demanded and got the surrender of Rohhilkhand and the southern districts between the Ganges and the Yamuna. All this amounted to about one-half of his territories.

Lord Hastings (1813-23) who fought against Nepal, got a good deal of money from the Nawab on the plea that the defeat of Nepal would contribute to the security of Nepal.

The British Governor Generals started interfering in the internal affairs of Oudh and even took part in throning and dethroning Nawabs with the result that administration of the Nawab became very weak.

LORD DALHOUSI (1848-56) AND ANNEXATION OF OUDH

Lord Dalhousi was an expansionist through and through. He applied the 'Doctrine of Lapse' to achieve his aggressive ends. The Doctrine of Lapse could not be applied to Oudh as the Nawab had several heirs to the throne. So Lord Dalhousi annexed Oudh on the pretext of 'good of the governed.' Annexations, whether by the Doctrine of Lapse or on the pretext of good of the people were in fact based on the old doctrine of 'might is Right.'

The main excuse for annexation of Oudh was the continuation of misrule by the Nawabs. The fundamental fact that British intervention had been greatly instrumental for misrule was ignored. But what was the guarantee that the British rule would be beneficial? This fact was totally ignored.

There is no denying the fact that the Nawab of Oudh Wajid Ali Shah (1822-

1857), the last Nawab was a very weak administrator although a scholar of eminence and author of over 100 books in Persian and Urdu. All efforts to train him as a ruler had failed. The supreme passion of his life was *'Ishq'* or (making love). He surrounded himself with beautiful women (*'Paris'*) and put them in a special palace called *'Parikhana'*. They were handsomely paid and were his special possessions. Corruption was rampant in his administration. It is stated that once when his chief Minister was going to see him, he was caught by four ruffians and he was not let off till they were paid a handsome amount as ransom. There may be an element of exaggeration but it indicates a sorry state of affairs.

As the administration of Oudh was very inefficient, Lord Dalhousi gave Wajid Ali a warning.

Dalhousi skilfully planned the annexation of Oudh. He sent special officers to investigate the charges of misrule in Oudh. The officers deputed by him sent report about the rottenness of government administrative machinery. Colonel Sleeman, the Resident of Lucknow wrote lengthy reports about the prevalence of misgovernment in Oudh. Nevertheless he was not in favour of annexation and he favoured strict control of the administration through their agency. He wrote, "Were we to annex or confiscate Oudh or any part of it, our good name in India would undoubtedly suffer," Sleeman was replaced by Outram.

Tutored by exaggerated reports of lord Dalhousi, the Court of Directors gave their verdict in favour of annexation of Oudh. On the refusal of Nawab Wajid Ali Shah to sign the abdication document, Lord Dalhousi annexed Oudh on February 13, 1856 and proclaimed that the annexation was desired by God to save Oudh from misrule.

Criticism of annexation of Oudh. The annexation of Oudh has been criticised on the following grounds:

First, in the earlier treaties with Oudh, there was no provision for annexation.

The Nawab had been very loyal to the British.

Third, the people of Oudh did not want annexation. They preferred the misrule of the Nawab to the rule of the British.

Fourth, it was a gross violation of international law.

Fifth, the responsibility of misrule in Oudh was in part that of the British who had since 1803 controlled and indirectly governed Oudh.

Even a section of the Directors of the court of the East India Company was against annexation and brought a censure motion against Lord Dalhousi on this issue, John Shepherd, a Director of the Company commented that the annexation would be "as liable to destroy the liberties of Indians so as to promote their rights and welfare." As a matter of fact it was the enormous potential of Oudh as a market for Manchester goods which excited Dalhousi's greed to annex Oudh.

Immediate consequences. The annexation of Oudh caused dissatisfaction and alarms among several sections and especially the rulers of the surviving Indian states. The people of Oudha were so much outraged that they took a prominent part in the events of 1857.

10

Growth of Colonial Administrative Apparatus

(Administrative Control of the British Government over East India Company)

Q.1. State briefly the nature of the rule of the East India Company in India. Explain the steps taken by the British Government to extend its administrative control in India upto 1800 A. D.

or

Why did it become necessary for the British Government to control the affairs of the East India Company and pass the Regulating Act of 1773 and Pitt's India Act of 1784.

or

Write short notes on (*i*) Regulating Act of 1773 (*ii*) Pitt's India Act of 1784.

Ans. *The nature of the British rule in India during the period 1757 to 1857*

Technically speaking it was not directly British rule. India was ruled by a private English Company which was registered in England for the purpose of trade in the eastern countries.

The objectives of the administration of the Company

(*i*) To increase Company's profits for its shareholders.

(*ii*) To enhance the profitability of its Indian possession for Britain.

(*iii*) To maintain and strengthen the British hold over India.

Reasons of the British Government's interference in the affairs of the Company

(*i*) The Company which was a trading one began to perform administrative functions.

(*ii*) The employees of the Company became very rich by adopting unfair means.

(*iii*) It was feared that the Company might interfere in British politics.

Two Parliamentary Acts passed before 1800 dealing with the control of the

British Government over the country.

1. Regulating Act of 1773
2. Pitt's India Act of 1784

Reasons for passing the Regulating Act (1773)

(*i*) Radical change in the nature of work of the Company. It had become a political power in India and ruled over millions of people. It also engaged itself in military pursuits.

(*ii*) Growing corruption among the employees of the Company.

(*iii*) Difficulties arising out of the Daul Government introduced by Lord Clive in Bengal.

(*iv*) The amassing of wealth by the Directors of the Company and employees led to political rivalries in England.

(*v*) Large scale private trade and huge profits of the officials of the Company brought home (England) excited the jealously of other sections of the British society.

(*vi*) Company's request for loan from the British Government.

Main Provisions of the 1773 Act.

1. Governor of Bengal became the Governor-General of India.
2. To help the Governor-General a Council of 4 members was set up. The decisions were to be made by the majority vote. The Governor-General was given the right of his casting vote.
3. The Supreme Court was set up at Calcutta to administer justice.
4. The right to elect the Court of Directors was give to shareholders.

This was the first major step taken by the British Government. The Act passed by the British Parliament reduced the power and influence of the Court of Directors of the Company by subjecting their functioning under the supervision and scrutiny of the government. It was made compulsory for the Company to put up a report about its working before the British Government. The right of the Parliament to interfere into the affairs of the Company and to legislate was recognised. The Act made provision for liberal salaries for the officials of the Company. It sternly prohibited them from accepting gifts or rewards directly or indirectly.

Pitt's India Act 1784

The Pitt's India Act (on the name of Prime Minister of England) was passed to remove some of the shortcomings of the Regulating Act of 1773 and to make the functioning of the East Company more efficient and also to increase the control of British Parliament on the East India Company.

Main Provisions

(*i*) The Board established a Board of Control including two Cabinet Ministers for regulating the functioning of the East India Company.

(*ii*) The number of Members of the Governor-General's Council was reduced to three.

(*iii*) The Governor of Madras and Bombay were made subordinate to the Governor-General.

(*iv*) The Company's political work was separated from its commercial work.

Significance

The administration of the Company in India came under the overall control of the British Parliament. The Company became answerable to British Parliament.

The Board was given the power to superintend control and direct all acts and operations relating to civil, military and revenue administration of the British territories in India. The Governor-General of India was to be appointed by the Board of the Company with the approval of the Crown. Later on the President of the Board of Control became the Minister for Indian affairs. The arrangement to control the affairs of the Company remained the basis of the British administration in India.

While Pitt's Act laid down the general framework in which the Government of India was to be carried on till 1857, later enactments brought about several important changes which gradually diminished the powers and privileges of the Company. In 1786, the Governor General was given the authority to overrule his Council in matters of importance affecting security, peace or the interests of the Empire in India.

In the words of Prof. Keith, "The Act altered the constitution of the Company at Home (in England), changed the structure of the Company in India, subjected in some degree the whole territory of India, and provided in a very efficient manner for the supervision of the Company by the Ministry."

Q. 2. Write short notes on:

1. Charter Act of 1793
2. Charter Act of 1813
3. Charter Act of 1833
4. Charter Act of 1853

or

Explain the various steps taken by the British Government to extend its control over the East India Company during 1800 and 1857.

Ans. *Extending Control by the British Government on the East India Company*

From time to time, the British public opinion was putting pressure upon the British Parliament to end the trade monopoly of the East India Company. There was also a strong feeling that in view of expanding territorial control of the Company in India, there was a great need to tighten the control of the British Government over the Company which by its nature of work was a trading agency.

There were two aspects of the control.

(*i*) Working of the Company in India: Governor General and its Council: Governor-General and other Governors.

(*ii*) Control of the British Government/Parliament over the Company.

The Regulating Act of 1773 and Pitt's Act of 1784 were passed for the realisation of the above mentioned objects. Still there was need for making further changes.

CHARTER ACT OF 1793

Circumstances leading to passing of the Act. The East India Company was granted the monopoly of Eastern trade in 1773 for 20 years. It was to expire in 1793 and hence it had become necessary to renew the Charter. The condition of the Company had improved after 1773 and the Ministers in England were favourably inclined to the renewal of the Charter. England had got involved in a life-and-death struggle with revolutionary France and the attention of the nation was pinned upon the struggle. Hence there was not much opposition to the renewal of the Charter.

MAIN PROVISIONS OF THE CHARTER

The most important provisions of this Charter were the following:

1. The Company to have the monopoly of carrying on trade with the East for twenty years.
2. The payment of the members of the Board of Control and their staff to be made out of Indian revenues.
3. The Governor-General of Bengal and the Governors of Bombay and Madras to have only three members in their Councils. Each of the members must have resided in India for at least twelve years before appointment.
4. The Commander-in-Chief not to be member of the Council, unless specially appointed its member by the Court of Directors.

5. The Governor-General and the Governors could over ride their Councils on their responsibility.
6. Emphasis on the control of the Governor-General over the Presidencies of Madras and Bombay.
7. The Governor-General authorised to appoint a Vice-President of the Executive Council from amongst its members to preside during his absence.
8. Stress on non-interference in the affairs of Indian States.

CHARTER ACT OF 1813

Circumstances leading to the Passing of The Act. The Charter Act of 1813 was passed after a great deal of controversy. This was due to several reasons. Firstly there was a great demand for abolishing the trade monopoly of this Company. The Company's territories in India had expanded so much that it was found difficult for it to continue both as commercial body and a political sovereign. Secondly, trading classes of England now clamoured that the Company's monopoly of trade with India should come to an end and they also should be allowed to trade with India.Thirdly, while the British people wanted free entry into India, the British missionaries also demanded permission to preach Christianity among the Indian people. But the Company opposed any such move fearing that such a step would offend the Indian people. Nevertheless, the British opinion was in favour of the Charter being revised to ensure their an easy entry on the India soil.

Main Provisions of the Act

1. The Charter was renewed for 20 years.
2. Trade with India, excepting in tea was thrown open to all Englishmen.
3. The monopoly of Company of trade with China was retained.
4. British merchants and missionaries could come to India and settle by getting a licence.
5. The Company was required to maintain its commercial accounts separate from territorial accounts.
6. The shareholders were granted a dividend of $10\frac{1}{2}$ per cent out of the revenue of India if the commercial accounts failed to provide that amount.
7. One lakh of rupees was to be spent on the education of the Indians.

Significance of the Act. The Charter Act of 1813 is important in several respects.

Firstly, the subjects of His Majesty could trade with India, except in tea. It gave a great impetus to British trade with India.

Secondly, it showed the deference of Parliament to public opinion because the monopoly of Company's trade with India was cancelled, except in tea, in spite of the defence put forward by the Board of Control.

Thirdly, the provision for spending one lakh of rupees a year on the education of Indians meant that the Company must work for the uplift of the Indians by making arrangements for their education.

Fourthly, a large number of missionaries began to come to India and they also started schools and colleges.

CHARTER ACT OF 1833

Circumstances leading to the passing of the Act. Under the Act of 1813 the Company retained its monopoly of trade with China and tea trade with India. The ideas of free trade were gaining ground in England very swiftly. Hence, the people there were vehemently opposed to the continuance of its monopoly.

Main Provisions of the Charter Act of 1833. 1. The Company was deprived of its commercial privileges.

2. Company's monopoly of trade with China came to an end.

3. The territories and the revenues of India were granted to the Company for twenty years.

4. President of the Board of Control now became Minister for Indian affairs.

5. The licensing system was abolished and now any Englishmen could come to India, settle and acquire property.

6. The powers of the Governor-General were greatly increased.

7. Services were thrown open to all irrespective of caste, colour and creed.

SIGNIFICANCE OF THE CHARTER ACT OF 1833

1. The Charter Act of 1833 was a measure of great importance. At Home one of the most important developments was that the Company was relieved of its monopoly of trade in India as well as with China, and this completed the work of the Charter Act of 1813, thereby changing the character of the Company from commercial to administrative and political.
2. The Charter Act of 1833 made certain important changes in the recruitment policy of the Government of India. This Act declared "No native of India shall by reason of his religion, place of birth, descent or colour be disabled from holding any office under the Company." This

colour be disabled from holding any office under the Company." This declaration found appreciation in various quarters. Ramsay Muir described it as an `unparalleled declaration which a ruling class can announce in regard to its recently conquered subjects'. Macaulay styled it as a wise, benevolent and noble clause of the Act. According to Prof. Sri Ram Sharma, "It was a grandiose gesture worthy of the first reformed Parliament." But the actual progress towards the declared policy was heart breakingly slow and insipid. According to Dr. Ishwari Prasad "The declaration was more honoured in the breach than in the observance by those who were entrusted with the governance of India."

3. It marked the beginning of the Indian legislature.
4. The Act also abolished Company's monopoly of tea trade and trade with China. It was deprived of all its commercial privileges which were left to it by the Charter Act of 1813.
5. The huge inflow of Europeans in India while on the one hand brought Indians into closer contacts with the Europeans, which contributed to their general improvement and prosperity, on the other hand the Europeans also exploited the Indian masses.
6. Due to this Act, Indian Penal Code and the Codes of Civil and Criminal Procedure came into existence.
7. This Act was also a definite step towards the unification of British possessions in India and the establishment of a strong Central Government in this country.

CHARTER ACT OF 1853

Circumstances leading to the passage of the Act.

1. The Act of 1833 had placed the Presidencies under the Governor-General-in-Council, thus depriving them of their independence which now they clamboured to obtain again.

2. The Charter Act of 1833 had thrown open jobs to the Indians but the new policy was honoured more in breach than in spirit. The Indians got no jobs other than the categories of jobs held by them before 1833. Punniah has rightly remarked that this clause "remained for long in the tantalising realm of unfulfilled aspiration." It gave legitimate cause of grievance to Indians.

3. There was also growing demand that the dual government at Home should be abolished; as the Court of Directors had out lived their purpose, and this institution coupled with the authority of the Board of Control made the handling of the Indian problems more difficult, involving unnecessary

dian Presidencies which demanded the appointment of a Secretary of State with an Indian Council to handle the business.

Main provisions of the Act

1. The Charter was not renewed for a definite period. The Company was allowed to hold the territories in India as a trust for Her Majesty. Earlier each Act was reviewed for twenty years.

2. The Civil Service was thrown upon to all.

3. The Act created for the first time a Legislative Council for India.

4. The Governor General was empowered to veto the bill passed by the Legislative Council.

Significance of the Act

1. The Act marked the beginning of a Parliamentary structure of Government of India.

2. The Act by not being renewed for a definite period gave indication of the fact that the Company's rule would not last long.

Demerits 1. The Legislative Council was created but it had no Indian members.

2. Examinations were held in England and the age limit was low. Hence it was not possible for a large number of Indians to competitive.

11

Administrative, Judicial and Land Revenue Reforms

(Reforms of Warren Hastings and Lord Cornwallis)

Q.1. "Warren Hastings was the real builder of the modern Indian administrative system." Discuss.

or

"Hastings' fame rests on his administrative work." Explain.

or

Give an account of the administrative reforms introduced by Warren Hastings. *(Delhi University 1996)*

Ans. *Warren Hastings (1772-1785) as the Builder of British Administrative System in India*

Undoubtedly the achievements of Warren Hastings in India rest on the foundation that he laid of the administrative system rather than on the criteria usually applied to an empire builders *i.e.* the number of battles won and enemies vanquished, the number of square miles of territory conquered and annexed, the plunder and the riches amassed.

According to J. S. Cotton, "Indians and Anglo-Indians alike venerate Hastings' name, the former as their first beneficent administrator, the latter the most able and the most enlightened of their own class." He further observed, "If Clive's sword acquired the Indian empire, it was the brain of Hastings that planned the system of civil administration."

Davies in his book '*Warren Hastings and Oudh*' has written, "He laid some of the foundations of our rule and traditions in India."

While pointing out some defects of Warren Hastings' personality and character, Lord Macaulay praises him for his "administrative skill."

Penderal Moon in '*Warren Hastings and British India*' writes that he "rescued the Company's Government from bankruptey and chaos." He further attributes to him "The establishment in India of an essentially British administration."

According to Alfred Lyall, "Warren Hastings showed a genius for pioneering administration that would have won him distinction at any epoh of our Indian history...his public acts brought him to the verge of private ruin."

Dark Side of his revenue reforms. In 1782 Sir John Shore stated, "The real state of the districts in now less known and the revenue less understood than now." He went on to say that Warren Hastings left behind him "a dark trail of misery, insurrection and famines."

How unsatisfactory the land revenue policy was, may be clear from the remarks of Cornwallis, made in 1789, "one-third of the Company's territory in Hindustan is nonojungle, inhabited only by wild beasts."

Administrative reforms introduced by Warren Hastings

Tasks and difficulties before Warren Hastings. With a view to have a clear perspective of the reforms introduced by Warren Hastings, we may, in brief, refer to the then prevailing situation in India.

1. On account of the numerous corrupt practices indulged in by the employees of the Company, its financial position had greatly deteriorated.

2. Though the Company was enjoying the right of Diwani of the rich provinces of Bengal, Bihar and Orissa, it had reached the state of financial bankrupty and it had requested the Government of England for a loan of £ 10 lakhs.

3. The Dual Government in Bengal had failed miserably.

4. The system of levying the land-rent and its collection was very defective.

5. Arrangement for proving justice to people suffered from several counts.

6. Apart from financial and administrative problems, there were many political issues which needed a close examination.

7. Lord Clive's time and energy were mostly spent in waging wars in India and had very little time for administrative work.

Six-fold division of Hastings' reforms

I. Administrative reforms.
II. Judicial reforms.
III. Financial reforms.
IV. Revenue reforms.
V. Commercial reforms.
VI. Miscellaneous reforms.

1. *Administrative reforms.* These included the following:

(*i*) Abolition of the dual system of administration which was the root cause of confusion and disorder that prevailed.

(*ii*) Taking up all responsibilities of administration by the East India Company on its own shoulders.

(*iii*) Removal of Indian Deputy Nawabs and appointment of English collectors in their places.

(*iv*) Shifting of treasury from Murshidabad to Calcutta as it was easier to exercise control from this place.

(*v*) Reorganisation of Nawab's affairs by appointing Munni Begum, widow of Mir Jafar as Regent and Superintendent of household affairs.

II. *Judicial Reforms*. These were as under:

(*i*) abolishing the judicial function of the zamindars.
(*ii*) Setting up civil and criminal courts in each district.
(*iii*) An English Officer to preside over the Civil court and also to collect the land rent in his district.
(*iv*) Indian collecter to look after criminal work.
(*v*) Bringing the judicial proceedings in writing.
(*vi*) Justice to be administered in accordance with the Hindu and Muslim laws.
(*vii*) Preparing a code of laws to administer justice.
(*viii*) Fixing a definite time limit for giving judgements.

III. *Financial reforms*. Important financial reforms were:

1. Reducing the pension of Nawab of Bengal from Rs. 32 lakhs to Rs. 16 lakhs per annum.
2. Stoppage of tribute of Rs. 25 lakhs payable to Shah Alam, the Mughal emperor of Delhi as he had gone over to the protection of the Marathas.
3. Taking over two districts of Kara and Allahabad from Shah Alam and selling to Shuja-ud-Daula Nawab of Oudh in return for the payment of Rs. 30 lakhs.
4. Substantial reduction in pension given to the servants of the Company.
5. Securing Rs 40 lakhs from the Nawab of Oudh by giving him help against the Rohillas.
6. Improving currency.
7. Sending trade mission to Bhutan and Tibet for improving trade relating with them and thus improving the finances of the Company.
8. Closing uneconomical and insecure offices of the Company.

IV. *Revenue reforms*

(*i*) Appointment of British Land Revenue Collectors for the collection of land revenue and carrying out land reforms.
(*ii*) Appointment of a Board of Revenue for exercising complete supervision over the whole system of land revenue.
(*iii*) Introduction of five-year land revenue settlement.
(*iv*) Abolition of the five-year settlement after sometime and introduction of one year settlement on the basis of highest bidding.
(*v*) Appointment of Naib Diwans in each district for the assistance of Collectors.
(*vi*) Appointment of an Indian Officer called Rai Rajan to maintain the revenue record.
(*vii*) Appointment of an Accountant-General.

V. *Commercial reforms*

(*i*) Abolition of a large number of Chowkies or custom houses which were hampering the growth of trade in the country. Only five custom houses at Calcutta, Hugli, Patna, Dacca and Murshidabad remained.
(*ii*) Sending commercial missions to Bhutan, Tibet and Egypt.
(*iii*) Forbiding the use of '*dastak*' by the servants of the Company.
(*iv*) Charging duties on their personal goods from the servants of the Company. This provided a good deal of revenue to the Company.
(*v*) Reduction in expenditure.
(*vi*) Reduction in duty by 2 1/2 per cent on all goods except salt, betelnuts and tobacco.
(*vii*) Checking exploitation of weavers by the Company's agent.

VI. *Miscellaneous reforms*

(*i*) Opening of a mint at Calcutta.
(*ii*) Issue of coins of definite shape and weight having the same value. Earlier the value of a rupee differed from place to place.
(*iii*) Introduction of the banking system.

Summing up. Lord Clive laid the foundations of territorial expansions of the British in India and Warren Hastings laid the foundations of the British system of administration in India. Warren Hasting, however, gave no place to the Indians in the positions of trust and responsibility. From the point of view of the British, it was necessary to do so. How could they assign such positions to Indians when their stakes were very high?

Q.2. Discuss the social and administrative reforms introduced by Lord Cornwallis. *(Punjab University April 1995, Oct 1998)*

or

Give an account of the administrative and judicial changes made by Lord Cornwallis. *(Rajasthan University 1992)*

or

Give your assessment of the administrative, revenue and judicial reforms of Lord Cornwallis. *(Delhi University 1997)*

or

Describe Lord Cornwallis role in strengthening English empire in India. *(Delhi University 1997)*

Ans. *Strengthening the Administrative Structure* by *Cornwallis* (1786-93)

While Lord Clive laid the foundations of the British territorial expansion in India, Warren Hasting laid the foundations of the administrative set up and Lord Cornwalis strengthened it and which remained substantially in force till 1858. Cornwallis has left his imprint on the administrative system and his methods of administration came to be remembered by the dignified name of the 'Cornwallis system' or the 'System of 1793'. He left behind him a tradition of service which was of lasting value in Indian administration.

It is said that with great difficulty he was persuaded to accept the office of the Governor-General of India. It is generally admitted that he was "the first honest and incorruptible Governor General India ever saw and after his example hardly any Governor General dared to contemplate corruption."

Tasks before Lord Corwallis. Cornwallis had the following tasks before him:

(*i*) To establish an efficient and honest administrative system.
(*ii*) To establish a judicial machinery which could provide justice to the people.
(*iii*) To find out a satisfactory solution of the land revenue system.
(*iv*) To reinstate British reputation of honesty.

Reforms of Lord Cornwallis

Regarding the reforms of Lord Cornwallis Dr. Ishwari Prasad has observed, "With him begins the formation of the essentials of the administrative system which with certain modifications ruled India till recently. His reign of seven years was one of peace with the exception of the third Mysore war. His fame rests not on his foreign policy but on his interval reforms."

As observed by R. C. Dutta, "He did not believe the expectations formed of him and his rule afforded a gleam of sunshine in India after much of darkness and storms."

Reforms of Cornwallis may be studied under the following broad heads:

I. Public Service reforms.
II. Judicial reforms.
III. Commercial reforms
IV. Police and army reforms.
V. Revenue reforms.

1. *Public service reforms.* There is no denying the fact at the time of assuming the office of the Governor-General of the India, by Cornwallis, the whole system of government and its administration was corrupt and full of abuses. Quickly get rich mentality was the order of the day at every level. The servants of the company were both corrupt and inefficient. Lord Cornwallis set his personal example of honesty and always remained above the greed for money that had tarnished not only the names of Clive and Warren Hastings but also of the character of the British in this regard.

Cornwallis took the following measures to provide a clean and efficient administrative machinery.

1. Increasing the salaries of the servants of the Company as it was very low and it tempted them to indulge in corrupt practices.
2. Forbidding the servants of the Company to undertake private trade.
3. Checking all unofficial perquisites enjoyed by them.

4. Stopping their all underhand dealings.
5. Requiring every servant to declare his property under oath before he left India.
6. Recruiting able servants on merit and disregarding recommendations. He is said to have set aside the recommendations of the President of the Board of control of the Company. Not only this, he resisted the recommendations of the Prince of Wales.
7. Setting personal example of honesty and integrity.
8. Reducing the number of servants.
9. Europeanisation of services in highs posts as he did not consider Indians worthy of trust.
10. Separating civil administration from judicial administration.

II. *Judicial reforms: Cornwallis Code.* Cornwallis' judicial reforms were embodied in the famous 'Cornwallis Code.' This Code prepared in 1793 was meant for the guidance of the people working in the judicial department. It set fixed laws for land revenue, police, civil and criminal justice and other allied subjects. It defined in clear terms the rights of the authorities and established an organised system of appeals. It made a clear distinction between the administrative and commercial services. It ushered in the system which formed the steel frame of British-Indian administration.

Following were the major judicial reforms introduced by Cornwallis.

1. He separated the judicial and executive powers.
2. He took away the judicial powers from the revenue collectors who used to enjoy judicial powers. Earlier, the powers of the Collector, Magistrate and Judge were concentrated in the hands of one person. Carnwallis removed this defect.
3. He set up the hierarchy of civil courts as illustrated below.

HIERARCHY OF CIVIL COURTS

Involving disputes over Rs 5000		King in Council
Involving disputes upto Rs 5000		
	6	Sadar Diwani Adalat at Calcutta
	5	(Presided over by the Governor-General and his Council
Involving dispute upto Rs 1000	4	Four Provincial Courts at Calcutta, Murshidabad, Dacca and Patna.
Involving disputes upto Rs 500	3	District Courts or City Courts (Presided over by District Judges)
Involving disputes upto Rs 200	2	Courts of Registrars (Presided over by Europeans)
Involving disputes upto Rs. 50	1	Munsif Courts (Presided over by Indians)

4. Salaries of the judicial officers were increased.
5. Court fèes paid by the litigants were abolished.
6. Legal fees charged by the lawyers were moderately prescribed.
7. Circuit Courts which moved from one place to another for dispensing justice were established in districts under English judges.

III. *Commercial reforms*. Cornwallis found corruption rampant in the commercial/trading department of the Company. He remarked, "The warehouses at Calcutta were a sink of corruption." He introduced the following reforms:

1. The method of procuring supplies through contracts was given up and the method of procuring supplies through commercial Residents and Agent, was started. The commercial Residents made advances to the artisans and settled prices with them. The Company started getting supplies at cheaper rates.

2. Cornwallis abolished the monopoly of trade earlier given to some agents and employees.

3. Cornwallis reduced the strength of the Board of Trade from eleven to five members.

4. He reduced the number of Collectors from 36 to 23.

5. He imposed a nominal tax on every big shop in big cities and towns.

IV. *Police and army reforms*

(*i*) *The organization of regular Police Force.* Formerly, the powers of the police were exercised by Zamindars. Lord Cornwallis organised a police force, established *Thaas* for every twenty square miles, and put *Darogas* in charge of them. The District Judges had the powers of Magistrates and control over the police.

(*ii*) *Incentive for the police.* To make the police arrangements more efficient, the District Magistrate were allowed a 10 percent commission on the recovered property. Similarly they would get a fixed amount when they arrested robbers and dacoits.

(iii) More English soldiers. The number of English soldiers in the army was increased.

IV. *Revenue reforms*: *Permanent Settlement of Bengal* (Bengal at that time comprised Bengal, Bihar and Orissa).

Cornwallis found several defects in the prevailing system of land revenue. The income of the Company from land revenue was uncertain. The Company had tried various systems like fixing land revenue on annual basis, on 10-year basis and also on the auction system but these arrangements did not prove successful so as to ensure a definite income on permanent basis. Yearly fixation of land revenue led to lot of inconvenience. It increased the administrative work enormously. Besides it was far easier to have transaction with the *Zamindars* whose number was small.

Main provisions. The new system known as Permanent Settlement of Bengal had the following provisions:

1. *Zamindars* were recognised as the owners or proprietors of the land.
2. *Zamindars* were given the right to transfer the land.
3. *Zamindars* acted as agents of the government for the collection of revenue from the cultivators who became their tenants.
4. *Zamindars* gave 10/11 of the revenue collected by them from the cultivators to the government.
5. The amount to be paid by them was fixed on a permanent basis.
6. *Zamindars* had to pay the land revenue in time even if the crops failed for some reasons.
7. If the revenue increased on account of improvement in agriculture or extension of cultivation etc., the Zamindar was allowed to keep the entire increased revenue for himself.

Merits of the permanent settlement of Bengal. Following were the main advantages.

(i) Political Advantages. The East India Company created a new class of *Zamindars* that became very loyal to the Company. The new class of *Zamindars* believed that owed their existence to the Company.

(*ii*) *Financial Security*. Earlier, the income of the Company from land revenue was uncertain. Now it became certain.

Overall estimate of Cornwallis' reforms. Here we quote the views of Lord Curzon and Ishwari Prasad, which are quite balanced.

According to Lord Curzon, "The administration of Lord Cornwallis,... was remarkable for his internal reforms, in which, with a courage that cannot be over-praised, he set his face against the jobbery and corruption. The civil and criminal courts were reformed." He was, of course critical of permanent settlement of Bengal and termed it as `a mistake.'

Dr. Ishwari Prasad has given his estimate of the achievements of Lord Carnwallis in the following words: For twenty years after the departure of Carnwallis the system in its entirety remained sacrosanct. These twenty years demonstrated both its merits and demerits. The Permanent Settlement was given up as ruinous to the state as well as the ryots. It was realised that the establishment of courts of justice does not necessarily mean justice. What was essential was a court of law in conformity with the notions of the people to be governed. The Europeanisation of the services had proved uneconomic and Indians had to be brought in. But the merits outweighed the demerits. Carnwallis will ever remain a great name among the builders of the British administrative system. The defects in that system only serve to remind us that he was human. But his distrust of Indians equalled by perhaps Lord Curzon was reflection of the English character continued for long after Carnwallis had left the shores of India. It was responsible for the racial bitterness of the later years."

Q. 3. The Permanent Settlement of Bengal was the most unfortunate scheme that ruined a country. Explain.

(Rajasthan University 1993 and 1997)

or

Why did Lord Cornwallis introduce the System of Permanent Settlement of Bengal? What were its chief features? Point out its merits and demerits.

Ans. *Permanent Settlement of Bengal*

Background of the Permanent Settlement of Bengal. After the Battle of Buxar, the Company secured the Diwani (land revenue) of Bengal, Bihar and Orissa. At that time according to the prevailing practice, the ryot or the cultivator paid a fixed share of the produce of his land either in cash or kind to the Zamindar. The zamindar received the revenue, to the state and kept some part of the revenue for himself. He was also responsible for maintaining peace within his jurisdiction. However, his office gradually became hereditary. The Directors of the Company felt that the Company was not getting the amount due to it and that a part of the revenue was being misappropriated by the zamindars. So Lord Clive appointed English supervisors to exercise control over them but things did not improve. Warren Hastings introduced the system of bids. The lands were given to the highest bidders. The highest bidders began to extract more and more revenue from the cultivators which resulted in great hardship to them. Then the revenue was fixed on annual basis and on 10-year basis but all these arrangements did not prove successful so as to ensure adequate revenue to the Company.

When Carnwallis came to India, he found agriculture decaying, coultivators sinking into poverty, Company losing revenue and money lenders flourishing. The Directors of the Company were also alarmed at the steady deterioration of the revenue collection. Under these circumstances, Permanent Settlement of Bengal was introduced.

Chief features of the system of Permanent Settlement of Bengal

1. The zamindars were recognised as the owners or proprietors of the land.
2. The zamindars could sell their lands and were given the right to transfer them.
3. The zamindars acted as the agents of the government for the collection of revenue from the cultivators.
4. The cultivators became the tenants of the zamindars.
5. The zamindars gave 10/11 of the revenue collected by them from the cultivators to the government.
6. The revenue to be paid by the zamindars was fixed on a permanent basis.
7. The zamindars had to pay the revenue even if the crops failed for some reasons.

8. If the revenue increased from the land on account of improvement in agriculture or extension of cultivation etc. The zamindar was allowed to keep the entired increased revenue for himself.
9. In case the zamindars did not pay the land revenue, a part of their land was to be disposed of to recover the land revenue.
10. The magisterial powers were taken away from the zamindars.
11. The zamindars were left with no police work.

MERITS OF THE PERMANENT SETTLEMENT OF BENGAL

I. *Administrative Merits*

1. *Simplification of work.* Permanent Settlement did away the enormous administrative work related to periodical settlement.

2. *Better use of Company's servants.* Permanant settlement set free a large number of able servants of the Company for judicial work. Formerly they had to waste a lot of time every year in allotting the work of collection of revenue to the highest bidder and realising the same amount.

3. *Simplified method of collection.* Before Permanent Settlement, method of collecting land revenue was rather very cumbersome. The Company was required to maintain a big establishment for carrying out its work in the field of revenue assessment and collection.

II. *Political Merits*

4. *Creation of a faithful class.* The Permanent Settlement created a loyal class of zamindars. The zamindars who were made the owners of the land by the Company could be counted upon to defend the rule of the Company against its rivals. It was found that the zamindars as a class proved loyal to the British Government during the Rebellion of 1857.

III. *Economic and Revenue Gains*

5. *Assured revenue.* The Government was assured of a certain amount of revenue from the land. It now did not depend upon the results of annual bidding.

6. *Saving in expenditure.* Yearly assessment led to economic dislocation and expenditure. Now with Permanent Settlement these factors and hurdles disappeared.

7. *Merits of a permanent tax.* It is usually accepted that a permanent tax is inexpensive, uniform and certain. It has all the advantages stated by the famous economist Adam Smith.

IV. *Miscellaneous gains*

8. *Land improvement.* The landlords knew that they had to pay a specific amount of revenue to the Government. They, therefore, tried to bring about

improvement in land to get more income. They brought more land under cultivation and for this they were not required to pay any additional revenue to the government. The zamindars adopted several methods to increase agricultural output.

9. *Increase in commerce, industry and trade*. The zamindars became wealthy and secure. They could now make more investment in commerce, trade and industry. Thus the economy prospered.

10. *Possibility of additional revenue*. Though the Government could not enhance the land revenue yet indirectly the scheme proved useful. With economic prosperity, Government could tax them in several ways.

11. *Increase in the value of land*. The value of land increased in view of increased production.

12. *Economic stability of the Government*. Since the prosperity of the people increased in the province of Bengal, it gave more stability to the Government.

Demerits of Permanent Settlement

1. *Neglect of the peasants*. The system overlooked the interests of the cultivators who cultivated the land. It deprived them of their hereditary rights in the land.

2. *Oppression of the zamindars*. The system placed the cultivators on the mercy of the zamindars. The zamindars used all sorts of oppressive methods to collect as much revenue as possible from the cultivators.

3. *Absentee landlords*. The zamindars in several cases left the tenants in the hands of middlemen who exploited them and extorted revenue according to their whims.

4. *Extravagant lives of the zamindars*. By leaving the work of collection of revenue to the middlemen, the landlords shifted to the towns and cities and spent money on luxuries and pleasures.

5. *Little improvement in lands*. Cornwallis had expected that after being assured of the proprietorship of the land, the zamindars would take interest in making improvements in the land. However these hopes were belied.

6. *Limitation on Government revenue*. The Government could not enhance the land revenue but its expenditure was increasing, several new ventures had to be undertaken by the Government for which more money was needed.

7. *High revenue demands*. The land revenue demanded from the zamindars was very high. Several of them could not realise that amount from the cultivators with the result that they had to sell their lands. The condition of the zamindars became miserable when the crops failed but they had to pay the revenue to the Government.

8. *Heavy taxes on non-agricultural classes*. The amount of land revenue to be collected by the Government from the zamindars was fixed but the expenses of the administration of the province increased with the passage of time. The gap or the deficit had to be made good by taxing non-agricultural classes.

Supporters of the Permanent Settlement of Bengal

1. Marshman. "It was a bold, brave and wise measure. Cultivation has been extended and a graduate improvement has been visible in the habits and comforts of the people."

2. R. C. Dutt. "If the prosperity and happiness of a nation be the criterion of wisdom and success, Lord Cornwallis' Permanent Settlement of 1793 is the wise and the most successful measure which the British nation had ever adopted in India."

Crtitics of the Permanent Settlement of Bengal

1. Holmes. "The Permanent Settlement was a blunder. The interior tenants derived from it no benefit whatsoever. The zamindars again and again failed to pay their rent charges and their estates were sold for the benefit of the Government."

2. Munro. "It seemed extraordinary that it should ever have been conceived that a country could be as much benefited by giving up a share of the public rent to a small class of zamindars."

3. Dr. Tara Chand. "The Permanent Settlement deprived the state of share in the increase of rent which resulted from the improvement of the economic conditions.

4. S. R. Sharma. "There can be no greater criticism on the Permanent Settlement of Bengal that being found defective and uneconomic, it was not introduced in other provinces of India."

5. Sir Edward Calebrook. "It was a great mistake to have sacrificed the interests of the peasant class in the country. It deprived the occupiers of land of their hereditary rights in the soil."

Mixed Comments

(*a*) Setton Carr. "The Permanent Settlement somewhat secured the interests of the zamindars, postponed those of the tenants and permanently sacrificed those of the state."

(*b*) Baden Powell. "The Permanent Settlement disappointed many expectations and several results that were not anticipated....The Permanent Settlement in contrast to the chaotic system which it supplanted had fairly obvious advantages."

Q.4. Explain the land revenue policy of the British Government in India.

Ans. *Different Land Revenue Policies in States*

There was no uniform land revenue policy in the whole of India. On the one hand there was the Permanent Settlement of Bengal which included the territories of Bengal, Bihar and Orissa, on the other hand, there was *Ryotwari* system in South-Western India and *Mahalwari* system in some North Indian states. In general, it can be stated that these policies were followed to realize maximum revenue and to send a part of it directly or indirectly to England. The interests of the peasants or the cultivators were also ignored to benefit the Zamindars. On account of this discriminatory treatment, the peasants suffered and the Government created a loyal class of zamindars who always supported the British Government. Several small landowners in systems other than Permantant Settlement were forced to mortgage their lands to the moneylanders or mahajans as they were required to pay revenue to the Government by a fixed date. In the process land got fragmented into small pieces also.

LAND REVENUE SYSTEMS AT A GLANCE

Permanent Settlement of Bengal	*Ryotwari System*	*Mahalwari System*
1. *Zamindars* owners of the land and cultivators as tenants.	Cultivators owners of the land.	Cultivators as the owners of the land.
2. Revenue collected from the tenants by the *Zamindars* and deposited in the treasury after keeping with them some share.	Revenue paid by the cultivators themselves.	Revenue collected on the basis of the village as a unit and deposited in the treasury by the representatives of the village.
3. System prevalent in Bengal, Bihar and Orissa.	Bombay, Madras, Berar, Sind, Assam.	North West Province, Punjab, parts of Central India, Gangetic Valley.
4. Covered 19 per cent of British India.	Covered 30 per cent of British India.	Covered 51 per cent of British India.

PERMANENT SETTLEMENT OF BENGAL
(ALREADY DISCUSSED)

THE RYOTWARI SYSTEM

Main features. The system derives its name from the word 'Ryot' which means a 'cultivator-peasant'. It had the following main features.

1. The cultivators were the land owners.
2. The land revenue was raised after every 20 to 30 years.
3. The cultivators themselves deposited the land revenue.

Merits 1. The Company gained financially as it could increase the land revenue.

2. The peasants had the satisfaction that they had become the owners of the land.

3. The peasants were freed from the tyranny of the Zamindars.

Demerits 1. The Company had to deal with a large number of cultivators instead of a few zamindars.

2. In most cases, very exhorbitant land revenue was fixed. In Madras, it was fixed as high as 45 to 55 per cent of the gross produce of the land. The situation was no better in Bombay and other places.

3. The peasant had to pay the fixed land revenue even when his produce was partially or wholly destroyed by flood or drought, etc.

4. The Government retained the right to enhance the land revenue.

THE MAHALWARI SYSTEM

Meaning. The system derives its name from the word *'mahal'* which means an estate or a village. Under this system, land revenue was charged on the estate or the village as one unit. It could be collected through the representatives of the village. The land revenue was periodically assured.

Q.5. Write a critical note on the changes brought about by Warren Hastings and Cornwallis in the administrative system.

(Rajasthan University 1996)

Ans. *Warren Hastings as Forerunner of Cornwallis*

As Sher Shah was a forerunner of Akbar in matters of land revenue administration, Warren Hestings was the forerunner of Cornwallisa in matters of administration. Warren Hastings laid the foundations of the British administrative system in India and Cornwallis improved upon it and strengthened it. It goes to their credit that with some modifications necessitated by changes in the political situation, the system continued till the British left India. Cornwallis could achieve substantial results on accounts of three factors. First, he enjoyed the confidence of both the Court of Directors and the President of the Board of Control. Second, foundations of the administrative structure had already been laid by his predecessor. Thirds Cornwallis himself was far ahead of Hastings in matters of honesty and integrity.

Following were the main areas of administrative reforms:

1. In 1772, Warren Hastings initiated the policy of assuming direct responsibility for the Government of Bengal, Bihar and Orissa by abolishing the Dual Government set up by Lord Clive in 1765. The constitutional process was further completed by Cornwallis through his judicial and police reforms.
2. Warren Hastings sought to check the growing 'get rich quick attitude' of the Company's servants. He compelled them not to indulge in private trade or accept presents. Cornwallis increased their salaries and allowances. At the same time, he required each officer of the Company to declare his property on oath before he left India. He strictly enforced his orders even though he had to dismiss some high officers.
3. In the matter of land revenue administration, Warren Hastings had tried some experiments to streamline it and Cornwallis greatly profited

from these. However, both could not achieve much success in their efforts to bring about substantial improvements.

4. The separation of revenue administration from civil jurisdiction, the most important feature of the Cornwallis Code of 1793 was also begun by Warren Hastings.
5. Warren Hastings laid the foundation of a new judicial system in 1772 when he established two district courts of justice—one civil or *Diwani Adalat* for settling disputes relating to property, marriage, inheritance etc., and the other criminal or *Faujadari Adalat* relating to cases of forgery, murder, robbery and violence etc. Likewise two courts of appeal were established at Calcutta.

   In 1790, Cornwallis abolished two district courts and established four courts—one in each division at Calcutta, Murshidabad, Dacca and Patna. Appeals from these courts could be heard by the Governor-General in Council.

   Cornwallis also established sub-ordinate courts. He also gave licences to educated Indians to act as Vakilas on behalf of the people.
6. Warren Hastings vested English judges of the civil courts with magisterial powers. Lord Cornwallis took the next step of appointing European officers to Faujdari Adalats also.
7. Cornwallis substituted English criminal law for Mahammedan law. (For details see Q. No. 1 and 2 of this Chapter)

12

Administrative, Judicial, Economic, Educational Reforms of William Bentinck

Q. 1. Give an account of administrative, judicial economic, educational and social reforms of William Bentinck.

(Punjab University April 1996)

or

Discuss the reforms of William Bentinck.

(Punjab University, April 1997)

or

Is it correct to describe William Bentinck as the true liberal of his age? *(Delhi University 1995)*

Ans. *Administrative Reforms of William Bentinck* (1828-1835)

In the history of India, Bentinck's name will be long remembered for the introduction of a number of reforms in several fields which have played a significant role in modernising India. No previous Governor-General of India had ever tackled social problems with greater courage than Bentinck did.

The system of education as introduced by him in accordance with the recommendations of Lord T.B. Macaulay has received both praise and blame of equal intensity.

Lord Macaulay, the Law Member and the President of the Committee of Public Instruction during Bentinck's time wrote that William Bentinck "never forgot that the end of the government is the happiness of the people"

From the following reforms carried out by Bentinck it is obvious that he was a true liberal. Bentinck's reforms may be classified under the following heads:

I. Administrative reforms.
II. Educational reforms.
III. Financial reforms.
IV. Judicial reforms.
V. Press reforms.
VI. Public works reforms.
VII. Social reforms.

I. *Administrative Reforms*

1. *Employment of Indians*: Bentinck reversed the policy of Lord Cornwallis

of not appointing Indians in the service of the East India Company. This was done in view of three considerations. First, salaries given to the Europeans was very high which put heavy drain on government treasury. On the other hand, Indians could be employed on low salaries. Second, with the passage of time, some Indians had acquired the knowledge of English and they could work in offices. Third, Indians would be pleased by the prospect of employment.

The Charter Act of 1833 laid down, "No native of India nor any natural born subject of His/Her Majesty should be disabled from holding any place, office of employment by reason of his religion, place of birth, descent or colour." Bentinck followed this policy.

2. *Setting up separate Board of Revenue* : The territories of the Company had become very vast and a single Board of Revenue located at Calcutta could not cope up with the work efficiently. So a separate Board of Revenue was set up at Allahabad.

II. *Educational Reforms*

The modern system of education in India is the legacy of the period of William Bentinck. The period saw a controversy regarding the implementation of the provisions of the Charter Act of 1813 which had provided for a sum of Rs. one lakh a year for the "revival and promotion of knowledge of the sciences among the inhabitants of the British territories." Two schools of thought had emerged regarding the implementation of this provision. There were the Orientalists who insisted on the spread of knowledge in the medium of oriental languages like Arabic, Persian and Sanskrit. On the other hand, the Anglicists were for the use of English. Some prominent Indians like Raja Rammohan Roy were in favour of English language. To settle the controversy, the Government appointed a Committee of Public Instruction. Lord T. B. Macaulay, the Law Member was the Chairman of the Committee in 1835. He wrote a famous Minute in 1835 which contained his recommendations which were accepted by Lord Bentinck. On March 7, 1835, Resolution was passed which contained that all funds meant for education would be best employed on English education alone and that European literature would be promoted in India. Thus originated the system of education in India on modern lines. With slight modifications, it still continues in India.

The system of education as outlined by Macaulay was intended to serve two important objects. One, to produce an educated class that was 'Indian in blood and colour but English in manners and tastes." Second, to prepare an educated class to take up administrative jobs in the Company.

III. *Financial Reforms*

William Bentinck inherited a deficit of Rs. one crore and for providing a viable financial structure, he constituted two Committees to go into the various aspects of income and expenditure of the Government and to suggest measures for improvement. On the basis of the recommendations of these Committees, Hastings took steps which converted the deficit of Rs. one crore into a surplus of Rs. two crore.

Following reforms were introduced by Bentinck.

1. *Reduction of employee's allowance* by half.
2. *Reduction of Sinecure jobs* - jobs with salary but without any work.
3. *Appointment of Indians* who worked at far lower salaries than the English. This resulted in a good deal of reduction in the cost of administration.
4. *Abolition of the Provincial Courts* of Appeal which had negligible work as compared to the expenditure incurred on them.
5. *Verification of the Claims of tax free land.* The native rulers had given lands to several people by way of reward or charity. These lands were free gifts and no revenue was charged. Bentinck investigated into all such claims. Those people who could not furnish any proof were deprived of their lands. On other lands, reasonable amount of taxes were levied.
6. *Regulating of opium trade of Malwa* by issuing licenses which added revenue to the Company.
7. *Revenue settlement of Northwest Province* which led to improvement of soil and consequently addition to revenue of the Company.
8. *Classification of land on the basis of its productivity* which yielded more revenues.

IV. *Judicial Reforms*

1. *Simplification of the cumbersome judicial process* by the abolition of Provincial Courts of appeal and Circuit and transferring their functions to the Commissioners who supervised the work of the Collectors of Revenue and the police within their jurisdiction.
2. *Increase in the power of Magistrates* to award punishments upto two years.
3. *Summary disposal of rent cases* by the collectors under Regulation of 1831.
4. *Appointment of Indian Judges on fixed salaries.* However, these could not try cases in which American and European critizens were parties.
5. *Introduction of Jury System* under which European Judges could take the assistance of respectable Indians in deciding cases.
6. *Adoption of veranacular as court languages* in place of Persian. This proved useful for common people.
7. *Codification of law* which enabled the lawyers to have a more clear perspective of law.

V. *Press Reforms*

Bentinck's policy towards the press was characterised by a liberal attitude.

He considered the press to be a 'safty-valve' for discontent. He, however, could not tolerate Government officials making use of official information to criticise the act of Government.

VI. *Public Works Reforms.*

1. Improvement in the canal system of North West Province.
2. Construction of Grand Trunk Road from Calcutta to Delhi.
3. Starting the construction of a road from Bombay to Agra.
4. Introduction of steamship navigation on the Ganges.

VII. *Social Reforms*

Lord William Bentinck adopted several measures in the social field which went a long way in eradicating social evils which in due course had plagued the Hindu society, in particular.

1. *End of 'Sati' practice*: The term '*Sati'* literally means 'a pure and virtuous woman.' It is used in the case of a devoted wife who contemplates perpetual and uninterrupted conjugal union with the husband, life after life, and as a proof thereof burns herself with the dead body of her husband.

Several enlightened Indian rulers had taken steps to abolish this cruel practice in their dominions. Emperor Akbar had attempted to restrict it. The Marathas had forbidden it in their dominions.

Early British Governor-Generals like Cornwallis, Minto and Hastings had taken some steps to restrict this practice. Several Indian reformers led by Raja Rammohan Roy urged William Bentinck to take necessary steps to declare the practice of 'Sati' as illegal.Many Indian newspapers also supported the proposal.William Bentinck provided the necessary legislative corrective. Regulation No. *XVIII* of December 1829 declared the practice of *'Sati'* or burning alive of widows illegal and punishable by the criminal courts as culpable suicide. A few orthodox Bengali families vainly made an appeal to the Privy Council against Government interference in their religious customs.

2. Stoppage of infanticide *i.e.* system of killing their own daughters - a practice prevalent in some tribes of India, especially among illiterate Rajput families.

3. Suppression of human sacrifices prevalent mostly among wild tribes of Orissa to win the favour of gods and goddesses.

4. Suppression of *'Thugi'* - Cruelties of bands of robbers and murderers which had made travelling most insecure in several parts of India. The *'Thugs'* moved in disguise and sometimes in numbers as large as three hundred. Strict measures were taken to liquidate them.

5. Reform in the Hindu law of inheritance which declared that any person who embraced anyother religion would have full rights in his share in the property. This law was greatly criticised as it encouraged conversion to Christinanity.

An Estimate of Reforms of William Bentinck.

Admirers of William Bentinck

1. *Lord T. B. Macaulay.* In praise of Lord Bentinck.

"Who infused into Oriental despotism the spirit of British freedom;

Who never forgot that the end of the government is the happiness of the governed;

Who abolished crude rites,

Who effaced humiliating distinctions;

2. *P. E. Roberts.* "Bentinck was a true liberal of his day...He was undoubtedly the first Governor General openly to act on the theory that the welfare of the subject people was perhaps the primary duty of the British in India."

3. *Thompson and Garratt.* "The arrival of Lord William Bentinck marked the beginning of a new era in numerous ways. His seven years' rule proved a peaceful interlude between two periods of severe and costly campaigning. He initiated new policies in the sphere of finance, justice and education."

4. *A. L. Srivastva.* "William Bentinck was the first Governor-General in India to have carried out important reforms for the benefit of the people."

5. *E. Thorsan.* "Lord William Bentinck had come to India as a reformer."

6. *Dr. Ishwari Prasad.* "Bentinck's glories were the glories of peace.'

7. *B. C. Dutt.* "He promoted English education in India and endeavoured to carry out the maxim that the administration of India was primarily for the interest of the people."

Critics of William Bentinck

1. *Thornton.* He described the period from 1828 to 1835 as "blank achievements" and the Governor-General "having done less for the interest of India and for his own reputation than any who had occupied his place since the commencement of the nineteenth century, with the single exception of Sir George Barlow."

2. *R. C. Muzamdar.* "The rule of Hindu law by which a convert to any other religion forfeited his claim to paternal property was abrogated by a new regulation of Bentinck's zeal was not shared by many."

3. *Sir T. Wellesley.* "This (law) was the most daring interference with religious and social customs undertaken by the Company's Government."

Balanced view of Grenville. "He (Bentinck) is a man whose success in life has been greater than his talents warrant for he is not right-headed and has committed some great blunder...but he is simple in his habits, popular in his manners and liberal in his opinions".

13

Economic Impact of the British Rule: Drain of Wealth

Q. 1. Give a critical assessment of the commercial and economic policies of the British Government in India.

or

"The rich and prosperous India was converted into a country of hewers of wood and drawers of water." Explain this in the context of commercial, economic and industrial policies followed by the British Government in India.

or

Discuss the economic impact of the Colonial British rule on India's agrarian economy and traditional handicraft industries.

(Rajasthan University 1996, Delhi University 1992 and 1993)

or

"The British converted India into a colonial appendage of the British economy." Explain

(Rajasthan University 1995)

Ans. *Indian Economy Subservient to British Economy*

The rule of the East India Company was the rule of British traders and every effort was made by them to earn maximum profits. Accordingly the agricultural, commercial and industrial policies of the Britishers in India during the Company's rule upto 1857 and after the Crown rule upto 1947 were exploitative of the Indian economy.

The British derived enormous economic benefits in several ways from their Indian empire. Starting by making profits from trade with India, the British made India a major market for goods manufactured in England and a source of raw materials for their British factories.

Four phases of the commercial and economic policies followed by the British in India

First pahse from 1600 to 1757. The East India Company was, by and large, a trading organisation. It marketed Indian goods abroad and earned profits.

Second phase from 1757 to 1813. Apart from trading with Indian merchants, the Company began to compel the Indian artisans and craftsmen to sell their products at very cheap rates to them. All sorts of pressures were exerted upon them in this regard. A radical change took place in their policies after 1757, on account of the following factors:

1. After the Battle of Plassey, the Company also became a great political force in India.
2. (*i*) The Company after its political control over Bengal, used its power to gain monopolistic control over India's trade and production.
   (*ii*) The Company's resources increased with the revenues of Bengal.
3. The artisans and peasants were forced to sell their goods at cheaper rates to the Company.
4. The Indian traders were prevented from competing with British exports from India.
5. India's trade was also opened to the private English traders which dealt a massive blow to the Indian traders.

*Third phase from 1813 to 1857.*The Charter Act of 1813 curtailed the monopoly of trade of the Company.

Fourth phase from 1858 and effects of Industrial Revolution on Indian economy. Now finished goods manufactured in England began to be sold in India. Raw materials were exported from India.

Two fold strategy to impoverish Indian economy

The British rulers adopted the following strategies to enrich their economy and impoverish Indian economy (*i*) Discriminating duties (*ii*) Monopoly of raw materials.

Discriminatory duties. The British Government was determined to protect its growing machine-made industries. Heavy import duties on the Indian made goods in Britain were imposed. As a result, Indian imports to England declined. India was forced to export only raw materials like cotton and silk.

During the second quarter of the 18th century, laws had been passed in Britain which forbade the wear and use of printed or dyed cotton cloth. In 1760, in Britain, a lady had to pay a fine of £ 200 for possessing an imported piece of a handicraft from India.

The British Government levied such high duties on several categories of Indian goods that their imports to Britain virtually ceased. For example in 1824, a duty of 67 1/2 per cent was levied on Indian calico and a duty of 37 1/2 per cent on Indian muslins. Indian sugar had to pay an import duty in England that came to be over three times its cost price. In several cases, duties in England went up as high as 400 per cent. No such duties were levied on machine made goods imported in India from England.

Monopoly of raw materials The Industrial Revolution in Britain completey changed the economy towards the end of the 18the century. The British industry expanded rapidly on the strength of their modern machinery and other technological advances. A powerful group of manufacturers in Britain emerged. They were in a position to influence the commercial and economic policies of the Company. They also found support from the British Government. They prevailed upon the Company to follow such a policy that encouraged the import of raw materials in Britain from India and export of manufactured goods from Britain to India. This continued till the end of the British rule in India.

H. H. Wilson, the co-author of James Mill, in '*The History of India*' has summed up the impact of discriminatory treatment met out to Indian trade and industry by imperial Britain, "Had this not been the case, had not such prohibitary duties and decrees existed, the mills of Manchester would heve been stopped in their onset, and could scarcely have been again set in motion, even by power of steam. They were created by the sacrifice of the Indian manufacture. Had India been independent, she would have retaliated, would have imposed prohibited duties upon English goods and thus would have preserved her own productive industry from annihilation. This act of self-defence was not permitted to her, she was at the mercy of the stranger. British goods were forced upon her without paying any duty, and the foreign manufacturer employed the arm of political injustice to keep down and ultimately strangle a competitor with whom he could not have contended on equal terms."

British policies and impoverishment of Indian people

1. Lack of incentive to the development of indigenous industries with the result that they began to decay. The craftsmen were unemployed and consequently became poor.
2. Collection of revenue through heavy taxation on the people of India.
3. Neglect of modern industries in India as the raw material of India was used for the industries in England.
4. Heavy drain of wealth from India on account of salaries of the British employees working in India, their pensions etc.
5. Neglect of Indian agriculture and breakdown of agraian structure.
6. Exploitation of the peasants by *Zaminadars*.
7. Frequent occurrence of man-made famines.

Factors that were responsible for the stagnation of agriculture in India.

1. Absentee landlords.
2. Growing pressure on land on account of the decay of Indian crafts and decline of trade.
3. Fragmentation of land resulting in small holdings or pieces of land.
4. Lack of irrigation facilities and dependence of agricultural on monsoon rains.

5. Poverty of the cultivators to use new agriculture implements, better seeds and manure etc.
6. Higher rates of revenue on land.
7. Indifference of the government towards agriculture.

British economic policy and the impoverishment of Indian peasantry?

1. The peasants were overburdened with land revenue. The land burden became so heavy that the peasants had to leave their lands in Bengal to find employment in other pursuits. One-third of Bengal in the early period of British rule was transformed into jungles inhabited by beasts.
2. Different systems of land revenue were tried but all had adverse effects on the peasants.
3. Powerful sections of the society like the landlords, the money-lenders and the government officials put heavy demands on the peasants.
4. Very little was done for the improvement of Indian agriculture and to increase production.

Irrigation facilities were not improved. New implements were not used.

British industrial policy and backwardness of Indian industries

It was not in the interest of the industrial development and economic progress of England that India should develop industrially. Their main focus was to get its raw material resources in abundance for their industries. Following were the important reasons for the industrial backwardness of India.

1. Ruin of Indian cottage industries on account of the decline of rulers who patronised Indian artisans and craftsmen.
2. Lop-sided industrial policy of the Company and thereafter also no encouragement to the development of industries.
3. Primitive techniques of Indian industries which were no match to British industries.
4. Lack of technical education.
5. Cheaper machine-made goods.
6. Discriminatory tariff policy.

Q. 2. Briefly discuss the British economic policies in India with special reference to the destruction of indigenous industries and drain of wealth to England. *(Punjab University Oct. 1997)*

or

"British rule led to the impoverishment of India." Discuss.

(Rajasthan University 1997)

or

Explain the concept of 'Drain of wealth'. What were its consequences?

(Rajasthan University 1994 and 1997)

or

What were the various channels through which Indian wealth was drained out during the British rule.? *(Rajasthan University 1996)*

or

What was drain of wealth? What were its effefcts?

(Rajasthan University, 1996)

Ans. *Drain or Wealth or Economic Drain*

Meaning of Drain of Wealth. Drain of wealth implied outflow or carrying away of India's enormous wealth to England by the English through various means. It led to the extreme form of exploitation of India's resources for the benefit of the people of England. Drain of wealth occurred on account of the policies of the British rulers. It may be observed that the East India Company came to India as 'a hawker and pedlar', not for the good of India but for the goods of India.

The 'golden sparrow' (India) was caged and starved by the British rulers.

Some of the Mughal rulers spent huge amounts of money on their wild pursuits but the Money remained in India. It did not go out. India became a plundered nation in the hands of 'ruthless plunderer's *i.e.* the British. It was a constant plunder that continued for about two centuries. The economic drain reduced Indians to the position of 'hewers of wood and drawers of water.

History of 'drain of wealth The drain started after the Battle of Plassey. The victory led payment of £ 234,000 to Lord Clive, huge amounts to army and naval officers, £ 8 lakh to the Company and substantial amount to the Members of the Calcutta Council. The drain increased tremendously when the Company obtained the Diwani of Bengal in 1765. There was limitless plunder by the servants of the Company. Nearly one-third of revenues of Bengal was sent away to Britain.

English merchants and their 'gomashatas' (agents) arbitrarily decided every thing; the goods to be delivered, the price to be paid, and even the weavers to be flogged. Normal trade had become almost a plunder.

The English used several dubious methods of exporting wealth from India. It is estimated that by 1840 two to three million sterling (£) was annually transmitted to Britain every year. It is observed that "the British administration was like a sponge which absorbed everything from the banks of the river Ganga and squeezed it on the banks of the river Thames (in Britain).

Estimate of Wealth drain. Clive estimated the total revenue of Bengal at £ 4 million which after defraying all administrative expenses left a net surplus of £ 1,650,000. The quantum of surplus increased due to increase in rate of land revenue demand and ruthless method of collection of land revenue from the farmers.

Lord Ellenborough, Chairman of the Select Committee of the House of Lords, and later Governor-General of India, admitted in 1840 that India was "required to transmit annually to this country (England) without any return except in the small value of military stores, a sum amounting to between two and three million sterling (£)."

R.C. Dutt (1848-1909) a noted Civil Servant who after retirement pursued literary and political activities presented a well documented exposition of India's economic drain in his two volume *'Economic History of India'* (1902). Dutt was the President of the Indian National Congress in 1899. He pointed out that the annual remittance of 17 million sterlings in 1901-02 for Home Charges represented nearly one-half of India's net revenue annually sent out to England without any return. He showed that these charges were neither just nor necessary.

Home Charges/various channels of economic drain. These included the following:-

1. Pensions and gratuity of thousands of Britishers who served at various posts.
2. Savings sent by the British officers, out of their fat salaries.
3. Dividends paid to the shareholders of the East India Company.
4. Marine Charges for British ships anchored in Indian's seas.
5. Establishment of the Secretary of State for India.
6. Money spent on foreign wars in Afghanistan, Tibet and Persia, etc. not concerned with the interests of India.
7. Interests on Public Debt of India incurred for internal wars in India and suppression of Rebellion of 1857.
8. The working expenses, interest on capital invested and profits guaranteed to private companies operating railways and public works.
9. Huge amounts received as presents and illegal gratifications.
10. Enormous gains made by the servants of the Company through private trade.

Evil Consequences of Economic Drain

Dadabhai Naoroji (1825-1917), a pioneer in political and economic awakening of the Indian masses, was the first to bring to the notice of the people that India was being made 'economically destitute' on account of constant draining of her revenues to alien coffers. His book *'Poverty and Un-British Rule in India,* published in 1901 became a classic. He explained India's poverty as a consequence of continuous exploitation of the Indian people for the exclusive advantage of a privileged minority *i.e.* the English people. On the basis of detailed comparisons of national and per capita income in fifteen countries, estimates of agricultural and non-agricultural produce, foreign trade figures, estimates of domestic prices and taxation, he concluded that British rule produced a 'drain of wealth' or unilateral transfer of capital from India to Britain without concomitant measures of economic development in India. The theory of 'wealth drain' became the credo of the Indian National Congress for many years.

M. G. Ranade (1842-1901), a venerated figure in public life, Judge of the Bombay High court and one of the prominent founders of the Indian National

Congress, deplored that commerce and industry were passing out of the hands of India.

In the words of Dr. Tara Chand, a noted historian, "Imperial Britain treated dependent India as a satellite, whose main function was to sweat and labour for the master, to subserve its economy and to enhance the glory and prestige of the empire."

Following were the major consequences of drain of wealth from India:-

1. Poverty of the people of India.
2. Disruption of Indian economy.
3. Ruin of artisans and craftsmen.
4. Stagnation and deterioration of Indian agriculture.
5. Impoverished peasantry.
6. Outflow of capital and its paucity to undertake public works.
7. Backwardness of Indians industries.
8. Chain of famines — 17 famines during 1859 to 1909 which hit almost all parts of the country and led to the death of about 55 lakhs of people.

Causes of the decay of indigenous handicrafts

1. High handedness of the British rulers. After the battles of Plassey and Buxar, the English turned trade into plunder. They committed all sorts of atrocities on the Indian craftsmen. They even went to the extent of cutting off their thumbs if they refused to work for the Company.
2. Lack of partronge of Indian rulers who began to imitate their masters.
3. Policy of free trade in India and its reverse in England.
4. Cheaper machine -made goods.
5. Neglect of industrial development in India.
6. Loss of raw materials.

Summing up. Indian economy became a handmaid of British economy. The British exploited Indian resources and carried away Indian's wealth. The self-sufficiency of Indian economy, which was like a milch cow now became barren, all devoid of its glarious past. The blossoming economy of India, which attracted the British, became its own enemy. A substantial part of the population of India was reduced to abject poverty.

(See also Chapter 21)

14

Cultural, Religious and Social Awakening in India

(First Half of the 19th Century)

Q. 1. Raja Rammohan Roy was the "Father of Indian Renaissance and Prophet of Indian nationalism." Discuss. *(Rajasthan University 1997)*

or

Discuss the statement that Raja Rammohan Roy was the "Father of Modern India." What was his attitude towards the British rule?

(Rajasthan University 1997)

or

Do you agree with the view that Raja Rammohan Roy was the "Father of Modern India'? *(Rajasthan University 1996)*

or

"Raja Rammohan Roy's contribution in the making of modern India was many sided." In view of the above statement describe the progressive steps taken by him.

Ans. *Many-Sided Contribution of Raja Rammohan Roy* (1772-1833)

Raja Rammohan Roy is called the "Father of Indian Renaissance' and "Prophet of Indian Renaissance' in view of his great contribution in national awakening. There was no important area of national life that he left untouched. He was convinced that many-sided attempts were needed to bring about a new vigour in the people of India. It was Raja Rammohan Roy writes Rabindranath Tagore, who "inaugurated the modern age in India." In the political, religious and social field — in fact in every field, the Raja was the first among the Indians who worked for the advancement of his country. He was very anxious that the essential conditions for the political awakening of the Indians should be created as early as possible.

Commenty on the Renaissance in India, initiated by Raja Rammohan, Prof. J.N. Sarkar described it as "The beginning...of a glorious dawn, the like of which the histroy of the world had not seen elsewhere - truly a Renaissance, wider, deeper and more revolutionary than that of Europe after the fall of Constantinople. Raja Rammohan Roy laid the foundations for the reform of

Indian society through his crusades against religious orthodoxy, social evils and illiteracy. He raised his voice against the economic and political exploitation of the Indians. He promoted national consciousness among the Indian people.

Rammohan Roy's family name was Bannerjee. His great grandfather was conferred with the title of 'Raja' by Mughal emperor Akbar. Hence Raja Rammohan Roy.

A rationalist. He was keen to dispel ignorance and orthodoxy without denationalising the people. He accepted the supermacy of man's reason and conscience over the dictates of priests or scriptures. He applied a rational approach to all aspects of reforms including religion. He wanted his countrymen to accept the rational and scientific approach and the principles of human dignity and social equality of all men and women.

Synthesis of the East and the West. He pleaded that India should acquire the treasure of knowledge and wisdom both of the East and the West, on the basis of reason. He wanted India to learn from the West but through the process of intellectual openness. Indian culture was to be renovated through the creative process. He stood for the reform of Hindusism and a the same time, he adopted an extremey friendly approach to other religions.

Religious reform. He wanted to bring about reforms in Hinduism by getting rid of idolatory, sacrifices and caste regidity. He studied the Vedas and the Upanishads and proclaimed that all the Hindu scriptures preached worship of one God. He aimed his guns at the priests for encouraging practices like endless rituals, belief in several gods and goddesses and untouchability. In the process, he read voraciously, wrote abundantly and propagated fearlessly. In 1815, he established the *'Atmiya Sabha'* to spearhead a movement for socio-reform and to launch a counter-attack against orthodoxy. In the same year, he published two books–the *Vedanta Grantha* in Bengali and the *Vedantasara* in Sanskrit to propagate his views. In 1828, he founded the Brahmo Samaj on the twin pillars of reason, the scriptures *i.e.* the Vedas and ther Upanishads.

Promoter of education Rammohan Roy was himself a great scholar. He knew more than a dozen languages such as Sanskrit, Persian, Arabic, English, French, Latin, Greek etc. He studied the culture, philosophy and sciences of the East and the West. It is therefore, no wonder that he took a keen interest in the promotion of education. He was convinced that without the spread of education, the task of national awakening and religious and social regeneration could not be accomplished. He took the following steps in this regard.

1. He advocated the rapid spread of Western education and English in India.
2. He maintained at his own cost an English school at Calcutta. In this school, he introduced among other subjects like the philosophy of Voltaire—a western scholar.

3. He opened a collge which offered both the Indian and the western literature and sciences.
4. He took several steps for the promotion of Bengali language and also wrote a book on Bengali grammar. He even wanted the English people to learn this language.
5. He gave his full support to all those who stood for the introduction of the English language and Western sciences.
6. He believed in imparting liberal education to the people and worked for the realisation of this objective.
7. He translated the Vedas and some of the Upanishads into Bengali and English.
8. He penned down several historical, literary, philosophical and religious books in Bengali for enlightening his countrymen.

Social reformer. He severly, criticised social evils like the practice of '*Sati*', advocated equal status for women and condemned child marriage.

Raja Rammohan took the following steps for raising the status of women and their education.

1. Rammohan worked ceaselessly for advancing the status of women in society. He quoted extensively from the Vedic literature in the support of his views for securing a place of honour for women.
2. He extended his full cooperation to Lord William Bentinck in passing the law declaring 'Sati' as unlawful.
3. He himself saved several widows from being burnt alive.
4. He preached in favour of widow remarriage.
5. He demanded for women the right of inheritance to property.
6. He condemned polygamy.
7. He laid great stress on women's education for enabling them to fight social evils.

Promoter of the freedom of press. He carried on a vigorous agitation against the Press Regulation of 1823. His Bengali journal '*The Samvad kaumudi*' was the earliest Indian edited newspapers. He submitted a memorial to the Supreme Court in which he dealt upon the benefits of a free press.

Raja Rammohan Roy's attitude towards English rule: His Political Thought

Raja Rammohan believed that the British in India were by a divine dispensation. They had a mission to perform in this country and, therefore, they must continue till that mission is fulfilled. He was in favour of the Indians getting political rights but according to him only such rights could be given to them as they were competent to enjoy or in other words, he stood for a steady political reform in India. At the same time, he was very anxious that the essential conditions for political awakening of the people of India must be created as early as possible. He therefore, supported the introduction and promotion of English education in India. He believed that English education would throw open the floodgates of the liberal and democratic thought of the English in India. He sponsored the opening of the Hindu College in 1819 for educating the Indians on modern lines. He also assisted Alexander Duff and John Wilson to start an English school.

The Raja stood and fought for the freedom of the press.

He was anxious to brinbg about reform in the administrative structure of the country and perhaps was the first Indian to be consulted by the British Parliament on Indian affairs. He gave evidence before a Select Committee of the British House of Commons.

Raja Rammohan Roy's contribution to political awakening of India

1. *First to enunciate the duties of the British rulers.* Miss Collect wrote about the political view of Raja Rammohan as, "Before the time of Raja Rammohan Roy's public activities in Calcutta, there was no glimmering of a political life in the country. People had no conception of their civil rights and privileges; no body ever thought of approaching government to make known their grievances and ask for redress. Raja Rammohan Roy was the first to enunicate rights and privileges of the people and in the name of the nation to speak to the government of their duties and responsibilities as the sovereign power."

2. *Freedom of Press: Memorandum to the Supreme Court.* He was the first to submit in his own name and his five friends a memorandum to the Supreme Court in Calcutta on March, 31, 1823 against the Ordinance of the then acting Governor General. He pleaded for the freedom of the press in the memorandum. On rejection of his appeal, he filed his case before the King-in-Council. and wrote, "Freedom of expression is an invaluable privilege firmly secured to us by the laws of the land which we had so long enjoyed and could not be changed."

3. *Raja Rammohan's love for liberty*. Speaking on the Reform Act of 1832, he wrote, "The struggles are not merely between the reformers and the antireformers but between liberty and oppression throughout the world, between justice and between right and wrong.

Select opinions on the work of Raja Rammohan Roy

1. *Bentham* The famous English philosopher and a contemporary of the Raja described him as his "internsely admired and dearly beloved corraborator in the service of mankind."

2. *Miss Sophia D. Collect.* The editior of '*Life and Letters of Raja Rammohan*' wrote, "Raja Rammohan Roy was the first to enunciate the rights and privileges of the people." "Rammohan stands in the history as the living bridge over which India marches from her unmeasured past to her incalculable future. He was the arch which spanned the gulf between ancient and modern humanity, between superstition and science, between despotism and

democracy. The Raja was a link between reaction and progress."

3. *B.C. Pal* "The Raja worked both for personal and social reform."

4. *S.N. Bennerjee*. "Raja Rammohan Roy was not only the founder of the Brahmo Samaj and the pioneer of all social reform in Bengal, but he was also the Father of Constitutional Agitation in India."

5. *Brajendranath Seal in 'Raja Mohanroy: the Universal Man'* descibes him, "Prophet of Humanity - the civiliser and enlightener of the Asiatic nationalities, a golden link between the far East and the Far West."

6. *Sir Monier Williams* describes the Raja as "The heralder of new age. He was a great investigator of science and comparative religion."

7. *Subash Chandra Bose*. "Raja Rammohan Roy stood out as the apostle of religious revival."

Q. 2. Discuss the origin of the Brahmo Samaj Movement with special reference to the contribution of Raja Rammohan Roy.

(Punjab University, 1997)

Ans. *The Brahmo Samaj: Notable Role in Indian Renaissance*

The Brahmo Samaj has played a remarkable role in the Indian Renaissance. In the words of H.C.E. Zacharias, "Rammohan Roy and his Brahmo Samaj form the starting point of all the various reform movements — whether in Hindu religion, society or politics — which have agitated modern India." (*'Renascent India'*).

For some time it seemed that Indian youth was completely cut off its moornings and bowled over by new Western ideas and values in life. At such a critical movement, the Brahmo Samaj emerged as a great religious and social reform movement in the field of religious reform. The main significance of Brahmo Samaj, according to the majority of the scholars, lay not in what it retained of traditional Hinduism but what it discarded of the old.

Raja Rammohan founded the Brahmo Samaj in August 1828. The Trust Deed executed in 1830 contained the object of the Brahmo Samaj as, "the worship and adoration of the Eternal, Unsearchable, Immutable Being, Who is the Author and Preserver of the Universe."

Before founding the Brahmo Samaj, Raja Rammohan made a deep study of the scriptures. He studied the Vedas and the Upanishads and proclaimed that the Hindu scriptures preached worship of one God. He aimed his guns on the priests for encouraging practices like endless rituals, belief in several gods and goddesses and untouchability. In the process he read voraciously, wrote abundantly and propagated his views fiercely.

His knowledge of several languages such as Sanskrit, Persian, Arabic, French, Latin, Greek and Bengali greaty helped him to understand and preach religious principles and values. He studied the culture, philosophy and sciences of the East and the West. It is, therefore, no wonder that his pursuits led to the founding of the Brahmo Samaj.

Before starting Brahmo Samaj, he established the 'Atmiya Sabha' in 1815 to spearhead a movement for socio-reform and to launch a counter attack against orthodoxy. In the same year, he published two book namely, *The Vedanta Grantha'* in Bengali and the *'Vedantsara'* in Sanskrit to propagate his views.

It should be clearly understood that Rammohan Roy never intended to establish a new religion. He only wanted to purge Hinduism of the evil practices that had crept into it. Roy remained a devout Hindu till the end of his life.

Important principles of Brahmo Samaj

Following were its important principles:

1. Belief in one God.
2. Repudiation of the doctrine of polytheism (worship of several gods and goddesses).
3. Equality of all men.
4. Opposition to useless rituals and sacrifices.
5. No caste system.
6. Improvement in the status of women.
7. No idol worship.
8. Society based on the true teaching based on the Vedas and the Upanishads.
9. Rational approach to the affairs of the society.
10. Abolition of child marriage.
11. Widow remarriage.
12. Saction for all sections of the society for sea-voyages.

Leaders of Brahmo Samaj. Most of the important leaders of the Brahmo Samaj had received education through the English medium and had absorbed Western liberal thought. They wanted to introduce liberal ideas into the philosophy of Hinduism that was stagnating.

Debendra Nath Thakur (1818-1905), Keshv Chsndra Sen (1838-1884), Justice Mahadev Govind Ranade (1842-1901), R.G. Bhandarkar (1837-1925) and N.G. Chandavarkar (1855-1923) were its prominent leaders.

Spread of Brahmo Samaj. The energy, vigour and persuasive eloquence of some of its leader like Debendra Nath Thakur and Keshav Chandra Sen popularised the movement and its branches were opened in U.P., Punjab, Bombay, Madras, and other towns. In 1865, in Bengal, there were 54 branches. Brahmo Samaj opened several educational institutions in different parts of India.

Q. 3. Write notes on :

1. Ishwar Chandra Vidya Sagar.

2. Henry William Derozio and his Young Bengal Movement.

3. Social and religious reformers in Western India.

Ans. I. *Ishwar Chandra Vidya Sagar* (1821-92)

Ishwar Chandra Vidya Sagar made a great contribution to the making of modern India.

Vidya Sagar was a great humanist, a renowned scholar and a powerful social reformer. He was born in very poor family and studied while standing under a street lamp. By din of his hard work, he won several scholarships and rose to become the Principal of a Sanskrit College. He was, therefore, naturally interested in the promotion of education.

Contribution to the field of education

1. Organised 35 girls schools.
2. Introduced a new method of teaching Sanskrit.
3. Introduced the study of Western thought in the Sanskrit College.
4. Opened the gates of the Sanskrit College for Non–Brahmans.
5. Granted scholarships to the poor.
6. Secretary of the first women's college—Bethune College in Bengal.
7. Evolved a modern prose style in Bengali.
8. Wrote articles on history, grammar and Epics.

Vidya Sagar's Contribution to Social Reforms

1. Advocated powerfully the cause of women uplift.
2. Attacked polygamy.
3. Carried a crusade for widow remarriage.
4. Provided financial help to the couple at the occasion of widow remarriage.
5. Prostested against child marriage.
6. Worked for the promotion of female education.

II. *Henry William Derozio and his Young Benal Movement*

The Young Bengal Movement was started by Henry William Derozio, who taught at the Hindu College, Calcutta from 1826 to 1831. A native of Scotland, he permanently settled in India. The movement started by him is called Young Bengal Movement as he himself was very young (He died at 22) and his followers were bright and fiery young students.

The Young Bengal Movement was devoted to the following ideas:

1. Truth must conform to human reason.
2. Truth drives away superstitions.
3. Promotion of female education and raising the status of women.
4. Protection of peasants from the tyranny of *Zamindars*.
5. Freedom of the press.

Henry expressed his love for India in his poetry. For example, in 1827, he wrote.

My country! in the days of glory past
A beauteous halo circled round thy brow,
And worshipped as a deity thou wast,
Where is that glory, where that reverence now?

And one of his pupils Kashi Pershad Ghosh, wrote in 1830 A. D.

Land of the gods and lofty name;
Land of the fair and beauty's spell;
Land of the bards of mighty fame;
My native land; for e'er farewel!

The orthodox Hindus of Calcutta were greatly alarmed by his radical views like showing no respect to religious idols, beef eating, etc. They, therefore, brought pressure on the authorities of the Hindu College Calcutta to dismiss him. Therefore, he was removed from service of the Hindu College. The same year, he died of Cholera at the young of 22.

III. *Social and Religious Reformers in Western India*

Gujarat

1. Bal Shastri Jambekar was one of the first reformers in Bomaby (Earlier Bombay was a part of Gujarat State). He attacked orthodoxy of Brahmans. In 1832, he founded a weekly of Brahmans called *Darpan* with the objective of removing superstitions from the minds of the people and shedding new light on social and religious issues.
2. Karsondas Mulji started the '*Satya Prakash*' in Gujarat in 1852, to advocate widow remarriage.
3. Dadabhai Naoroji (1825-1917), a Parsi devoted himself to several reforms. He championed the cause of female education. He was instrumental in establishing prominent societies like the students Literary and Scientific Society, the Bombay Association and the Widow Remarriage Association etc.

Maharashtra

In 1849, the Paramahansa Mandali was founded in Maharashtra. Branches of the Mandali were formed in several towns like Poona and Satara in

Maharashtra. The chief objectives of the Mandali were (*i*) Breaking caste system (*ii*) Widow remarriage.

In 1851, Jotiba Phule and his wife started a girls' school at Poona and soon many educational institutions came up. Jotiba Phule, born in a low caste Mali family, carried a campaign against the domination of upper classes and Brahmanical supermacy.

Gopal Hari Deshmukh (1823-1892), popularly called Lokhitwadi, advocated widow remarriage. He vehemently criticised social evils like child marriage, shaving of the heads of the widows, caste distinctions etc. He started a '*Punar-Vivaha Mandal*' (Widow Remariage Institute). He contributed funds for educational institutions, orphanages, public wells etc. He wrote several books and started newspapers to promote his views.

15

Lord Wellesely and Lord Dalhousie Subsidiary Alliance: Doctrine of Lapse

Q. 1. Write a note on Subsidiary Alliance.

Ans. *Lord Wellesely (1798-1805)*: Originator of *the subsidiary Alliance*

Lord Wellesely was an expansionist and he adopted three methods to increase British power in India. These were (*i*) Adoption of Subsidiary Alliance Policy (*ii*) Outright Wars (*iii*) Assumption of the territories of previously subordinated rulers.

Meaning of Subsidiary Alliance. The Subsidiary Alliance was a sort of agreement between the British and an Indian ruler on the basis of mutual understanding for performing administrative, military and political functions.

Provisions of the Subsidiary Alliance

(*i*) The Indian ruler accepting the Alliance would not enter into alliance with any other power.

(*ii*) The Indian ruler would not declare war against any power without the permission of the British.

(*iii*) The Indian ruler would allow the British Resident to stay in his state. The British Resident was a senior officer to safeguard the interests of the British in the state.

(*iv*) The Indian ruler, in case of any conflict with any other ruler, would accept the decision of the British.

(*v*) The Indian ruler would acknowledge the East India Comapny as the paramount power.

(*vi*) The Indian ruler would maintain some British force at his own expense.

(*vii*) In return for accepting all these conditions, the British would protect the Indian ruler from internal and external danger.

Advantages of the Subsidiary System to the British

(*i*) The British were able to bring under control several rulers.

(*ii*) They were able to raise army at the expense of the Indian rulers.

(*iii*) They were successful in checking the French influence on Indian rulers.

(*iv*) Their prestige increased.

(*v*) They increased their hold without waging wars.

States entering into Subsidiary Alliance

(i) The Nizam of Hyderabad.
(ii) The Nawab of Oudh.
(iii) Peshwa Baji Rao II.
(iv) Gaekwad of Baroda.
(v) Several Rajput States.

Demerits of the system

The independence of the Indian States was diluted. They leived several charges on their subjects for the maintenance of the British army. The British Residents interfered in the day-to-day administration of the rulers.

Q. 2. Write notes on :

1. Doctrine of Lapse. 2. Main events and reforms of Lord Dalhousie. 3. Development of means of Transport and Communications by Lord Dalhousie 4. Commercial Reforms of Lord Dalhousie.

or

Critically discuss the reforms of Lord Dalhousie.

or

"Lord Dalhousie was splendid in the organisation of reforms." Describe his important measures of reforms.

Ans. *Lord Dalhousie as a Reformer*

Lord Dalhousie is remembered not only for his wars, conquests and annexations but also for his reforms and development schemes. He is both greatly praised and condemned. While some thinkers regard him as the greatest administrator sent by the Company, others regard him as an expansionist and imperialist through and through. His critics state that whatever benefits India got from his reforms, they were incidental and bye product of his efforts to establish a strong and unirorm administrative set up in India, conducive to British rule. His sole objective was to promote British interests in India. As observed by Sir Richard Temple, "as an imperial administrator he had never equalled by any of the illustrious men whom England has sent forth to govern India."

1. *Doctrine of Lapse*

The Doctrine of Lapse meant that "if the ruler of a state should die without any heir (*i.e.,* son), his adopted son would not succeed him but that state would lapse and go back to the British Company." Of course, heir could be adopted with permission.

Lord Dalhousie was a great imperialist and would not miss any opportunity to extend British empire. The Doctrine of Lapse came as a handy instrument for this purpose. He annexed the states of Satara, Nagpur, Jhansi, Jaitpur Sambalpur, Baghat and Udaipur.

The annexation policy created a great unrest among the Indian rulers. It became one of the important reasons of 1857 Revolt.

(For details see next question)

2. *Main Events and reforms of the Reign of Lord Dalhousie*

Main events of the reign of Lord Dalhousie may be categorised under two heads.

(*a*) Expansion of British dominions in India.
(*b*) Reforms in various fields.

(*a*) *Expansion of British dominions in India*

Lord Dalhousie was an imperialist and an annexionist. He adopted the following measures to expand British territories and influence in India:

(i) Policy of Doctrine of Lapse.
(ii) Expansion by conquests.
(iii) Expansion on grounds of mal administration.
(iv) Expansion on account of default in payment.
(v) Expansion by abolishing titles and pensions.

Reforms of Lord Dalhousie

(*i*) He founded the first Indian railway.
(*ii*) He set up the post and Telegraph Department.
(*iii*) He established the Public Works Department.
(*iv*) He introduced the system of competitive examination for selection to Civil Services.
(*v*) He made Simla as the summer capital of India.
(*vi*) He set up the Education Department (Discussed in detail separately).
(*vii*) He established Universities at Bombay, Madras and Calcutta.

Regarding the contribution of Dalhousie in undertaking reforms in several fields. K.M. Pannikar has observed, "Dalhousie was a remarkable personality, remembered now only for numerous annexations especially of Oudh. But his achievements in the sphere of administration are more notable than those of any of the Governor-General or Viceroy. The Central Legislative Council of India owed its existence to him. The first railway line was laid by him. The first telegraph line was due to his direct initiation and a half anna postage was his reform. The great Ganges Canal, the first of the mighty irrigation schemes was his handiwork. The Grand Trunk Road in its modern shape was begun by him. In fact, politically and administratively, Dalhausie is the greatest of Indians pro-consuls. His humane interests were no less notable. At his own personal cost, he maintained the Women's College which his collegue Betheric had founded. The great Roorkee Engineering College owes its existence to him. India owes a heavy debt of gratitude to this great Scotsman."

3. *Development of Means of Transport and Communications by Lord Dalhousie*

Two extreme contradictory views are expressed by several Indian scholars on the reforms of Lord Dalhousie. On the one extreme is K.M. Pannikar who is all praise for him. (See his views as above). On the other hand there is Dr. Ishwari Prasad who is a vocal critic of his reforms.

Railways, Roads and Post and Telegraph. Lord Dalhousie paid his special attention to the means of transport and communication not because of his love for the welfare of the Indians but because of the interests of the British. Their improvement was considered essential for strengthening the hold of the British. They were necessary for the defence of the country and in the maintenance of peace and order. With their improvement, army and police could be made more mobile. At the same time, Dalhousie wanted to encourage British investment in India through these means. Lord Dalhousie provided all the facilities and guaranteed interest to the English business and trading corporations. The Government became responsible of the profits which the corporations might make themselves. Dr. Ishwari Prasad in this context has remarked, "As an instrument of imperialism the state guarantee to the contractors was ingenious. As a business proposition it was fradulent to the tax payer. A few strategic lines were laid at enormous cost to India and extreme profit to the English capitalists."

In may be remembered that the broad outlines of the railway lines were laid down by Lord Dalhousie in his famous Railway Minute of 1853 which formed the basis for the future railway extension in India. The first railway connecting Bombay with Thane was laid down in 1853. In 1854, a railway line was built from Calcutta to the Rani Ganj coal-fields.

Besides encouraging trade and facilitating commerce, the railways have gone a long way in uniting India.

Dalhousie may be regarded as the 'Father of Electric Telegraph in India', Nearly 4,000 miles of electric telegraph lines connected Calcutta with Peshwar, Bombay and Madras and other parts of the country.

Lord Dalhousie also laid down the basis of the modern postal system also.

4. *Commercial Reforms*.

Lord Dalhousie followed a free trade policy which could serve trade and industrial interests of the people of England. It suited most to the British manufacturers who could manufacture goods on a large scale and sell in India. In this regard, Dr. Ishwari Prasad has observed, "The aim of Dalhousie to introduce commercial reforms was to throw open the produce and market of India to the exploitation of the English capital. In this he was successful beyond his expectations. His reforms were inlets through which economic imperialism riveted its hold upon India, evalution of military imperialism into economic imperialism. The doctrine of Free Trade, was introduced and proclaimed as one of the maxims of trade applicable to every country and every clime. All parts of India were declared free. The necessary improvements in light houses and harbour accommodations were undertaken. All checks and hindrances that impeded the flow of goods and capital were removed. The result was that all the industries of India slipped into the hands of English capitalists. Indian capital and enterprise already shy due to the constant wars of British aggression were weighted by Dalhousie's commercial and trade innovations. Their results however were far reaching and they are writ large upon the face of India—industrial poverty, extreme dependence on agriculture and an unbalanced economy. The following figures quoted by Sir. W.W. Hunter, one of his apologists as indicating the success of Dalhousie's commercial reforms tell their own tale of economic exploitation from the Indian point of view. Export of raw cotton rose from 1-1/2 million sterlings to 3-1/2; export of grain rose from 89 million sterlings to 290 million; the total exports of merchandise rose from 13-1/2 million sterlings in 1848 to over 23 million in 1856. On the other hand the total imports of English manufactured goods rose from 10-1/2 to 25-1/2 million sterlings during the same years."

Q. 2. Write a critical note on the Doctrine of Lapse and its applications.

(Punjab University Oct. 1996)

or

Write a note on Doctrine of Lapse.

(Punjab University, 1996, and Oct. 1998)

Ans. *Doctrine of Lapse*

Meaning and origin of Doctrine of Lapse. Lord Dalhousie, the Governor-General of India (1848-56) was an annexationist and an imperialist through and through. His name is famous for the application of Doctrine of Lapse in the annexation of a number of states in India. The objectives of the policy of annexation adopted by Lord Dalhousie become very clear in his two statements. He declared that the "extinction of all native states of India is just a question of time." He also declared, "No man can deprecate more than I do any extension of the frontiers of our territory which can be avoided or which may not become indispensably necessary for consideration of our own safety, and of the maintenance of tranquillity of our provinces. But I cannot conceive it possible for anyone to dispute the policy of taking advantage of every '*just opportunity*' which presents itself for consolidating the territories which already belong to us by taking possession of States which may lapse in the midst of them." Dalhousie's *but and just opportunity* - the words used by him in the above statement demonstrated his intentions very clearly. Dalhousie's clear conviction was the old system of ruling through `sham royalties' and "artificial intermediate powers" was not suitable and it resulted in the misery of the people.

The Doctrine of Lapse states, "If the ruler of a dependent state should die without any heir (*i.e.* son), his state would lapse or go back to the British Company."

Dalhousie was the implentor and not the creator of Doctrine of Lapse

The Directors of the English Company had declared as early as in 1834 that permission to adopt on the failure of natural heirs "should never be granted but as a special mark of favour or approbation." In 1841, it was declared that every effort should be made to abandon "no just and honourable annexation of territory or revernue." Dalhousie employed this doctrine in as many cases as possible.

The basis of the Doctrine was that as the English Company was the *Paramount power*' in India, the '*dependent*' states could not pass on to the adopted son without the sanction of the paramount power and the latter had the right to withold the sanction.

Three fold categorisation of States and Doctrine of Lapse. According to Lord Dalhousie; three categories of Indian states were as under:

(*a*) Those states which were not tributary and which were not and never had been subordinate to a paramount power.

(*b*) Hindu Princes and Chieftains who were tributary and owned subordination to the British Government as their paramount power in place of the Emperor of Delhi or the Peshwa etc.

(*c*) Hindu sovereignities and states which had been created or revived by the '*Sanads*' (grants) of the British Government.

According to Dalhousie, the paramount power could refuse adoption in case of states covered by categories (*b*) and (*c*) and declare the states having passed back or 'lapsed' to the paramount authority. In such case the 'Right to Adoption' - a Hindu law was substituted by the paramount power's, Right of Lapse

Dalhousie recognised the right of the adopted son to succeed to the personal property of the prince or the chieftain but drew a distinction between succession to private property and the succession of the royal '*gaddi*' (throne).

States annexed by Lord Dalhousie through the application of the Doctrine of Lapse.

Following were the states annexed (*i*) Satara (1848), (*ii*) Jaitpur in Orissa (1849), (*iii*) Sambhalpur (1849), (*iv*) Baghat near Simla (1850), (*v*) Udaipur (1852), (*vi*) Jhansi (1853), (*vii*) Nagpur (1854).

Of these seven states, Satara, Jhansi and Nagpur were more important states while the other four were very small principalities.

In case of Bhagat (Punjab Hills) and Udaipur, the decision of Dalhousie was afterwards reversed by Lord Canning. The Home Government did not accept Dalhousie's proposal to annex the small Rajpat state of Kasauli on the ground that it was a protected ally and a dependent state.

Criticism of Dalhousie's annexation policy. The Doctrine of Lapse under which Dalhousie annexed several princely states is criticised on the following grounds.

1. The application of the Doctrine of Lapse was against the customs and traditions of the Hindus because the adoption of a son according to the Hindu law was always regarded as valid.
2. The distinction between independent allies, dependent and subordinate states was only an artificial one. Any state could be annexed by merely stating that it was a dependent state.
3. Lord Dalhousie applied the doctrine to server the imperial designs. His high handedness becomes quite evident from the fact that some of his decisions were set aside by the court of Directors. They did not allow the annexation of the state of Kasauli.
4. Lord Canning (1856 to 1862) did not find justification in the annexation of Bhagat and Udaipur and reversed the decision of Dalhousie.
5. Dalhousie's Doctrine of Lapse was based on the doctrine of 'Might is Right.'

View of Historians and statesmen on the Doctrine of Lapse

1. *Arnold*. "The annexation of Satara was "a rich but not a lawful prize".

2. *Kaye*. "But lapse is a dreadful and an appalling word, for it pursues the victim beyond the grave".

3. *Edward*. Burke in one of his speeches said, "From Himalaya to Cape Comorin, there is not a single prince, great or small, in India, with whom the English have come into contact, whom they have not sold."

4. *Basu*. "Every word of what Burke says was true, as its truth was painfully exhibited in Dalhousie's regime. The descendants of those princes with whose help the English succeeded in establishing their power in this country were very shamefully treated and on their death their principalities annexed in the teeth of existing treaties on the ground of alleged want of heirs. This sort of annexation was the euphemistic name of Lapse."

5. *Inne*. "His (Dalhousie's) predecessors had acted on the general principle of avoiding annexation, if it could be avoided: Dalhousie acted on the general principle of annexing if he could do so legitimately."

6. *Lee Warmner*. He feels constrained to admit that "in the cases of Satara and Nagpur, imperial considerations weighed with him."

7. *P. E. Roberts*. "Whatever might have been the facts" writes Roberts, "the natives did undoubtedly believe' that the existence of all native principalies was threatened."

Results of the Docrine of Lapse

(*a*) *Point of view of the British*. Undoubtely Lord Dalhousie succeeded in adding important territories to the British dominion without waging wars.

(*b*) *Point of view of Indians*

(*i*) All the princes who were deprived of their states became staunch enemies of the British.

(*ii*) Dalhousie's policy of annexation became one of the major causes of the Rebellion of 1857.

(*iii*) The armies of the annexed states were disbanded. The retrenched soldiers were ever ready to create trouble. They played a significant role in 1857.

(*iv*) Several officers and influential nobles who lost patronage of the princess whose states were disbanded turned against the British.

(v) The annexation of states created a feeling of insecurity and uneasiness in the minds of the rulers of the surviving states. They began to fear that the British Government would sooner or later find an excuse to annex their states also.

Q. 4. How far was Lord Dalhousie responsible for the out-break of Rebellion of 1857?

Ans. *Lord Dalhousie as an Annextionist and Imperialist.*

Lorie Dalhousie has received a great praise at the hands of some historians and scholars for his pro-British attitude. Such historians usually describe him as an imperial administrator who always worked from the point of view of British interests. Obviously, he sacrificed the interests of the people of India. His annexations of Indian states-right and left on one or the other pretext gave rise to discontent and resentment in the country against him.

Since people of India suspected his intentions, his reforms were also not appreciated. Therefore, his annexations, introduction of reforms and western innovations were, to a large extent responsibles for the uprising of 1857.

Let us for a moment analyse the attributes paid to Lord Dalhousie by Sir Richard Temple. According to Sir Richard Temple: "As an imperial administrator, he has never been surpassed and seldom equalled by any of the illustrious men whom England has sent forth to govern India. While Lord Clive made the English power in India and Wellesley made them a supreme power in this country, Dalhousie completed the work and made the English theonly power in India. Expansion of territory, unification of territory and the drawing forth of material resources–these were the three labours given to Lord Dalhousie to accomplish in India and in the three words — Conquest, consolidation and development – his work can be summed up."

Thus he was praised for extension of territory — extension for whom; extension for the benefit of the people of England and in other words deterimental to the interest of the people of India.

The unification of territory again implies the uniform application of English laws, manners and customs.

The word 'development' here means the development of British commerce, trade and economy.

'Conquest' means bringing more and more Indian territory under the control of the British.

'Consolidation' implies strengthening political as well as economic gains of the people of England in India.

Annexation of Lord Dalhousie creating unrest

Dalhousie's annexations added between a third and a half to the territorial size of British India of 1848. In the north-west the British became the warden of the Passes, in the north the boundaries of British India became contiguous to Tibet and the Chinese empire, in the south-east the British controlled the entire coastal line on both sides of the Bay of Bengal. Within Indian subcontinent, the British empire touched its 'natural frontiers' bounded by the oceans and the mountains.

Dalhousie was an expansionist, imperialist and annexationist. He would seize every opportunity to grab territories in India. He took recourse to every means, fair or foul, to expand the boundaries of the British empire. The following chart ilustrates his mehtods of annexation and the effected states/territories/individuals.

Method of Annexation	*Effected states/Territories/Individuals*
1. Policy of Doctrine of Lapse	(*i*) Stara (*ii*) Jaitpur (*iii*) Sambalpur (*iv*) Baghat (*v*) Udaipur (*vi*) Jhansi (*vii*) Nagpur.
2. Expansion by conquest	(*a*) Punjab (*b*) Burma (*c*) Sikkim
3. Expansion on ground of mal administration	Oudh
4. Expansion on account of Default in payment	From Nizam of Hyderabad Berar
5. Expansion on account of abolishing Pension and titles	(*i*) Nana Saheb's pension denied. (*ii*) Abolished the pension and title of Nawab of Carnatic. (*iii*) Abolished the pension and title of Raja of Tanjore.

View of historians on annexations. (See the views of historians and statesmen in question No. 2)

Reform of Lord Dalhousie and their effect in creating unrest. (See the views of Ishwari Prasad in Q. No. 2)

Smith's view regarding Dalhousie's reposibility for the Robellion of 1857. The storm gathering in India for a number of years burst out in 1857, a year after Lord Dalhousie's departure from India. The ruling princes in the words of V.A. Smith, "Knew nothin about substle distinitions of dependent and subordinate states..They simply saw that principality after principality was escheated and annexed for one reson or another, so that no ruler of a native state felt safe, the pace was too fast and the cumulative effect of the transactions profoundly was unsettling."

V.A. Smith blames Lord Dalhousie for lack of foresight, "The out going Governor-General certainly had not the slightest provision of the storm that was to break the next year in May, and had not made any arrangement to meet it... he must share with his predecessor the censure due for permitting the continuance of a most dangerous military situation in India. He had not taken any precautions to protect the enormous store of munitions at Delhi which was left in the hands of the native army or to secure the essential strategical position of Allahabad. Whatever thought was devoted to military preparation in India was directed to the Punjab. Everywhere else the old haphazard distribution of the troops continued, and nobody in authority military or civil seems to have realised the obvious perils incurred."

T.R. Holmes believes that the rebellion that broke out in Oudh was not due to annexation but to the harshness with which the Taluqdars were treated. *Sir John Kaye* says, "But in neither way did Dalhousie even come to understand the genous of the people with whom his lot was cast..His advisers insisted upon the duty of universal usurpation...The sight of the clerk section sealed their sympathies."

Speaking about Lord Dalhousie's responsibility for the Mutiny of 1857, *P. E. Robert* say, "Dalhousie had very well prepared the ground and now only a pretext was required for the great upheaval. The greased cartridges served as the immediate cause for the outbreak of the great rising and naturally precipitated the crisis, the discontent and resentment which were really responsible for the trouble were in stock as the result of wrong and misguided policy of Dalhousie. It was not for nothing that Lucknow, Jhansi and Kanpur became the chief centres of mutineers. each explosive material for discontent was ready. It needed but to ingnited. The terrible blunder of greased cartridges fanned into a fierce and devouring flame all this smouldering discontent and served as a match to a magzine."

Dr. Ishwari Prasad writes about the responsibility of Lord Dalhousie for the mutiny, "There has been a great controversy regarding the exact responsibility of Dalhousie' for the events of 1857. Dalhousie was neither responsible for the Mutiny, not could he have averted it. The Mutiny was the natural reaction of a people against foreign rule. Dalhousie's responsibility was in accelerating the outburst of that reaction. His breathless conquests galvanised the latent spirit of the people, gave unity to those who before had been divided by being placed under different systems of administration. His onslaughts on ancient royalties spread a wave of rebellion which culminated in the events of 1857. His responsibility, however, ends here: at the most it can be said that he precipitated the forces, a revolution that had been working beneath the surface. The Mutiny would have occurred, may be at a later date, even if Dalhousie had never ruled over the destinies of our people."

In short, following were the effects of the policies followed by Lord Dalhousie and for which he is held partly responsible for the Rebellion of 1857

1. All the princes who were deprived of their estates became staunch enemies of the British Government. Rani Laxmi Bai became the leader of the mutineers in Central India. Nana Sahib, the adopted son of Peshwa Baji Rao II became an arch enemy of the British because he was denied his pension of Rs. 8 lakhs a year. He was also deprived of the title of Peshwa. He became the leader of the mutineers at Kanpur.
2. The retrenched soldiers of the armies of annexed states became unemployed and were ready to create unrest and trouble.
3. Several influential as well as common people lost their jobs as a result of the annexation of States. They also turned hostile to the British.
4. Many Zamindars who lost their lands when the settlements of territories of annexed states were made, were also very angry with the British.
5. The '*taluqdars*' of Oudh lost considerable influence and power. They took an active part in the Rebellion.
6. The distinction between '*dependent*' and '*protected*' states was not clear to the Indian rulers. They began to fear that the British Government would sooner or later find an excuse to annex their states.
7. The too rapid introduction of reforms by Dalhousie did not appeal to the deep-rooted conservative attitude of the Indian masses.

To sum up, the minds of the people were full of so much discontent and uneasiness that even a slight pretext or provocation was enough to set ablaze the long smouldering fire.

16

Overviews of British Expansion in India (1757 to 1856)

Q. 1. Trace the growth of the British power in India from 1757 to 1856.

Ans. *Growth of the British Power in India*

1. *Beginning and end of the British rule in India.* With their victory in the Battle of Plassey on June 23, 1757, the British started their process of conquering India and completed it on February 7, with the annexation of Oudh by Lord Dalhousie. (1848-1856)

Lord Clive (1757-1760 and 1765-1767) who won the Battle of Plassey was the founder of the British rule in India and was the first Governor of Bengal which at that time comprised Bengal, Bihar and Orissa.

Lord Mountbatten (1900-1979) was the Past Viceroy of India (1947-48). He had taken over as viceroy from Lord Wavell in March 1947.

2. *Extent of East India Company's Territories* (1772-1790). In 1785, the British Dominion in India extended over Bengal, Bihar and Orissa, Banaras, and Ghazipur, Northern Sarkars, part of Salsette (acquired from the Marathas from the Treaty of Purandhar in 1776), apart from the harbours of Madras, Bombay and some minor ports.

By the Treaty of Faizabad (1775), the East India Company, had acquired Banaras and Ghazipur from the Nawab of Oudh.

3. *Extension of British Rule* (1790-1804). *Territorial agains from Anglo wars.* After the third Anglo-Mysore War (1790-92), the English acquired Malabar on the west, Dindigul and the surrounding districts in the south and Baramahal districts in the east.

After the Fourth Anglo-Mysore War (1799), the English annexed the south Kanara Coast, Wynand in the southwest, Coimbatore and Dayapuram in the south-east besides Serirangapanam.

Gains from Nizam. In 1800, the Nizam of Hyderabad ceded to the company the districts of Bellary and cuddaph by the subsidiary Treaty.

Gains from Oudh. In 1801, the Nawab of Oudh surrendered the territories of Rohilkhand, Farrakhabad, Mainpuri, Etawah, Fatehgarh, Allahabad, Azamgarh, Basti and Gorakhpur to the Company.

Territorial gains from the second Anglo-Maratha war (1802-03). The Company's gains included the Upper Doab (territory between the Ganges and the Jamuna), all territories north of the Rajput states of Jaipur, Jodhpur, the part of Broach, the forts of Ahmednagar, district of Cuttack in Orissa.

In 1805, the Company's dominion extended along the whole sealine of India from Sind frontier at the mouth of the Indus down to western coast upto the Cape Comorin and then east ward along the Bay of Bengal to the Frontier of Burma. In northern India, the Company's political jurisdiction extended from Bengal to the deserts bordering upper Sind and Punjab.

The princely states of Oudh, Nagpur, Gwalior, Indore, Baroda, Hyderabad, Mysore, Travancore and others accepted the protection of the East India Company.

4. *Extension of British Dominion* (1805-1817). *(i) Political influence of the Company in Punjab* (1809). The East India Company declared its protectorate over all cis-Satluj states by a treaty with Maharaja Ranjit Singh.

(iii) Gains from Anglo-Maratha war (1814-16) The Gurkha ruler surrendered the territories of Kumaon and Garhwal to the Company. The Comapny now acquired sites for the development of hill stations like Simla, Mussoori, Ranikhet, Iadour and Nainital.

(iii) Gains from the Third Anglo-Maratha war (1817-18). The Peshwaship was abolished. The entire dominion belonging to the Peshwa in western India was acquired by the Company and merged in the Bombay Presidency. The Company also acquired the Peshwa's political rights over Bundelkhand and Malwa.

The Maratha Chiefs like Scindhia, Bhonsale and Holkar ceded important territories north and south of the Narbada, besids Ajmer.

Within the natural boundaries of India bounded by the ocean and the mountains, the British soverign influence extended from Assam in the east to the river Sutlej and the uper Sind desert in the west and from the Himalayas in the north to Cape Comorin in the south.

5. *Growth of British Power in India* (1818 to 1856). (*i*) *Gains from the First Anglo-Burmese war* (1824-26). The English got Assam, Arakan and the coastal strip of Tenasserin.

(*ii*) *Victory over Jat ruler*. The English made the best use of the struggle over the succession issue of Bharatpur. In 1826, the fort of Bharatpur regarded as impregnable, was captured by the British.

(*iii*) *Annexation of Cachar and Coorg*. The British annexed Cachar in 1832 and Coorg in 1834.

(*iv*) *Annexation of Punjab* (1845 to 1849). After the First Anglo-Sikh War (1845-1846), the Company acquired the Jullundur Doab (territory between the river Beas and the Satluj) besides hill areas situated between the Satluj and the Indus.

After the Second Anglo-Sikh War (1848-49), the entire territory of Punjab was annexed.

(*v*) *Second Anglo-Burmese War* (1852). After their victory, English annexed Lower Burma (Pegu).

(*vi*) *Annexation of Sind* (1843). The English annexed Sind by defeating the Amirs of Sind. This was in violation of all treaties entered into between the Amirs and the Company.

(*vii*) *Annexation of territories by Lord Dalhousie.* Lord Dalhousie (1848-56) was an expansionist and an imperialist. He took recourse to every means, fair or foul to expand the boundaries of the British empire. Under him, the British dominion in India reached its pinnacle.

He followed the following policies in this regard.

(*a*) *Expansion through the policy of Doctrine of Lapse.* Lord Dalhousie annexed the following states. (*i*) Satara (1848). (*ii*) Jaitpur (1849). (*iii*) Sambalpur (1849). (*iv*) Baghat (1850). (*v*) Udaipur (1852). (*vi*) Jhansi (1853) and (*vii*) Nagpur (1854)

(*b*) *Expansion by Conquests.* (*i*) Punjab (1849). (*ii*) Lower Burma (1850). (*iii*) Sikkim (1850).

(*c*) *Expansion on account of default in payment.* Berar (1853) from the Nizam of Hyderabad.

(*d*) *Expansion on ground of maladministration.* Oudh (1856)

Summing up. The Company was able to exercise its control over India on account of its superior diplomacy and statesmanship (Divide and Rule Policy), lack of unity among Indian rulers and use of new war weapons and techniques. After the Revolution of 1857, the rule of the East India Company came under the direct domination of the British Government in Britain.

17

Popular Resistance to Company's Rule : Revolt of 1857

Q. 1. Illustrate in brief the causes, events, centres of events, leaders and the result of the events of 1857.

Ans. *Struggle for Freedom 1857*

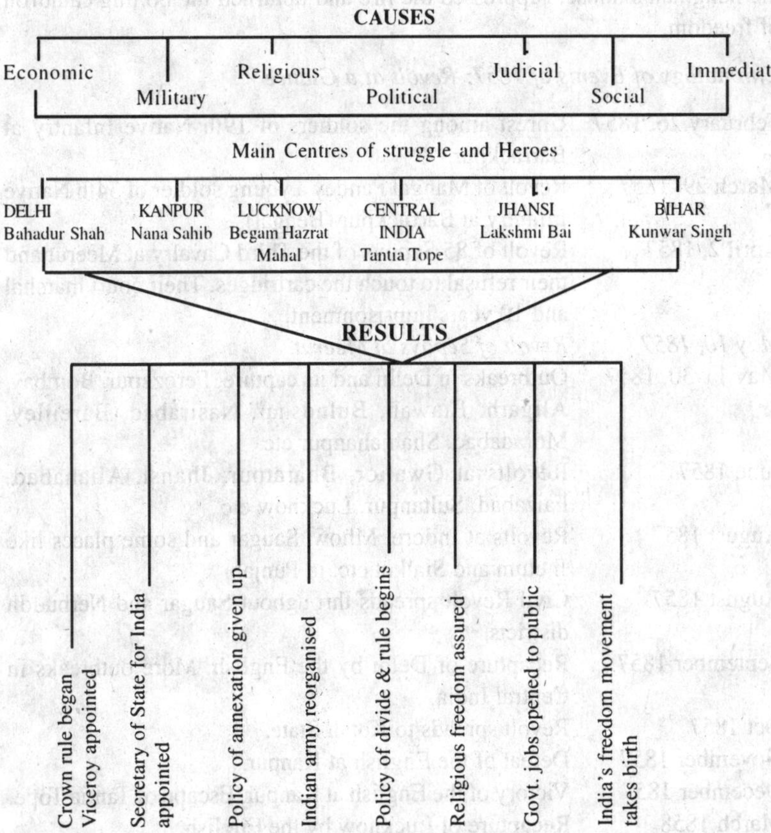

The revolt began at Meerut, 58 km from Delhi on 10th May 1857, and then gathering force it rapidly embraced a vast area from the Punjab in the north to the Narmada in the south, and from Bihar in the east to Rajputana in the west. But the ruthless repression of the British, with heap over heap of atrocities ended the chapter of the revolt with the hanging of Tantia Tope on 18th April 1859.

The causes were various that fermented. The first blast and its fury spread like fire under the patriotic blaze and heroic valour of great leaders at different places which were soaked by the blood and sanctified by the sacrifice of thousands of martyrs. Thus, thousands of mothers lost their beloved sons, thousands of children mourned their fathers loss, and thousands of young widows sobbed in choked silence and, with their shattered life and broken bangles, paid the price for India's first great fight to break the chains of slavery of their motherland. But the British might with bayonets, bullets, bombs and the hangman's noose, suppressed the fire and upturned the boiling cauldron of freedom.

Chronology of Events of 1857: Revolt at a Glance

February 26, 1857	Unrest among the soldiers of 19th Native Infantry at Barrackpur.
March 29, 1857	Revolt of Mangal Pandey a young soldier of 34th Native Infantry at Barrackpur (Bengal).
April 2, 1857	Revolt of 85 Sepoys of the Third Cavalry at Meerut and their refusal to touch the cartridges. Their court marshal and 10 years imprisonment.
May 10, 1857	*Revolt of Sepoys at Meerut.*
May 11-30, 1857	Outbreaks in Delhi and its capture, Ferozepur, Bombay, Aligarh, Etawah, Bulndshar, Nasirabad, Bareilley, Moradabad, Shahjahanpur etc.
June 1857	Revolts at Gwalior, Bharatpur, Jhansi, Allahabad, Faizabad, Sultanpur, Lucknow etc
August 1857	Revolts at Indore, Mhow, Saugar and some places like Jhelum and Sialkot etc. in Punjab.
August 1857	Civil Revolt spreads throughout Saugar and Nerbuddh districts.
September 1857	Recapture of Delhi by the English. More outbreaks in Central India.
Oct 1857	Revolt spreads to Kotah State.
November 1857	Defeat of the English at Kanpur.
December 1857	Victory of the English at Kanpur. Escape of Tantia Tope.
March 1858	Recapture of Lucknow by the English.
April 1858	Victory of the English at Jhansi. Revolt in Bihar by Kunwar Singh.
May 1858	Recapture of Bereilli and Jagdishpur by the English Guerilla warfare by the rebels in Rohilkhand.

June 17, 1858	Death of Rani Jhansi while fighting at Kalpi.
July-December	Re-establishment of English authority in India.
1858 April 1859	Capture and hanging of Tantia Tope on April 1859.

Q. 2. Analyse the political, socio-religious and immediate causes of the Mutiny of 1857. What were its results?

(Punjab University, April 1998, Oct. 1997)

or

Discuss the causes of the uprising of 1857. What led to its failure?

(Punjab University 1997)

or

Discuss the causes and results of the uprising of 1857.

(Punjab University 1991)

or

How would you explain the failure of the Revolt of 1857?

(Rajasthan University 1997)

Ans. *Manifold Causes of the Revolt of 1857*

The Revolt of 1857 was an eruption of the volcano of the various pent-up forces and feelings of the people of India. It came as a culmination of popular discontent with the British policies which had led to a great exploitation of the people. There were several cultural, economic, military, political, religious, social and immediate causes of the Revolt.

As a matter of fact even before 1857, several revolts on a minor scale but in different parts of the country by several sections had taken place and which were ruthlessly crushed. Discontent has been brewing since the conquest of Bengal. For about 100 years the people of India had witnessed the enormous loot and plunder of wealth from India to Britain. Every policy of the British *i.e.*, cultural, educational, military, political and social was aimed at the benefit of the British people. Several sections of population felt suffocated under the tyranny of the foreign rulers. They, therefore, revolted and attempted to free themselves but failed in 1857.

Views of some historians in this regard are given below.

1. *Dr. Ishwari Prasad* points out two most important reasons of the Revolt.

(*i*) Disregard of Indian philosophy and culture by the English and

(*ii*) Economic drain.

Regarding the cultural policy of the British rules, he writes. "The Engligh happy, in their ignorance of Indian philosophy attempted to introduce western notions of inheritance, marriage and succession and thereby consciously and unconsciously trampled upon the most sensitive portion of a Hindu's life. This was great degradation and was the result of a well settled policy. It has been a common belief of all imperialism that to degrade the conquered, to disrupt their social system, to make them forget their past, to impoverish them and then to lure them to the religion of the conquerer is better guarantee of stability than mere military strength. In its application to Indian society, however, the policy recoiled on its promoters. It stirred the people, brought back to them the reminiscences of their glorious past and cemented the causes of rebellion."

2. About the impact of the economic drain, *Ishwari Prasad has observed*, "The political changes prior to the advent of the British, the rise and fall of empires in Delhi had little or no effect upon the economic structure and life of the people. The reason for this was that the wealth remained in the country and whatever power ruled over Delhi it had no sympathies beyond the boundaries of India. With the English, however, it was quite different. Though paramount in India, they were subordinate to the Crown of England and their economic policy was subservient to their mother country. Indian wealth flew out of the country. Indian economy began to be fashioned to meet the needs of Industrial England. With the Industrial Revolution of the early 19the century, England ceased to be a mere commercial nation and was transformed into a manufactory of the world. Raw material for her factories and markets for her finished goods became England's prime needs. British policy in India was developed to meet those needs. The once famous Indian industry died of English competition and neglect; the burden on agriculture increased and India became a land exporting raw materials and importing finished goods. English capital flowed into the country and as it carried away both interest and profits, the results were ruinous. India became a milch cow to feed England while her own sons were gradually pushed to the verge of strarvation."

3. About the use of cartridges, *Lord Roberts* in his book "*Forty years in India*" has remarked: "The recent reserches of Mr. Forrest in the records of Government of India prove beyond doubt that the lubricating mixture used in preparing the cartridges was actually composed of the objectionable ingredients-cow's fat and lard and that incredible disregard of the soldiers religious prejudices was displayed in the manufacture of these cartridges."

4. Regarding cruel treatment towards the Indians, *Sir Thomas Munroe remarked,* "The foreign conquerors have definitely treated the Indians very cruelly, but never was such a humiliating treatment meted out to them as we have done unto them. Never have they been charged that their whole nation was dishonest and was not worthy of confidence and that they would never get any job in the administration unless there was no way out for the British East India Company."

5. *Dr. V.S. Smith observes that,* "The movement was a revolt of the old against the new, of Indians' conservatism against aggressive European innovation."

6. The assertion of Mangles, the Chairman of the Court of the Directors of the Company regarding conversion of Indians to Christianity is that it had created fears. According to him, "Providence has entrusted the extensive empire to England in order that the banner of Christ should wave triumphant from one end of India to the other. Every one must exert all his strength that there may be no dilatoriness on any account in continuing in the country the grand

work of making all Indians Christians."

7. *Major Edwards had openly declared, "The conversion of all Indians to Christianity was the ultimate aim of our occupation of India."*

8. To the same effect *wrote Rev. Kennedy.* "Whatever misfortune may come on us, so long as our Empire in India continues, so long let us not forget that our chief work is the propagation of Christianity in the land until Hindustan from Cape Commorin to the Himalayas, embraces the religion of Christ and until it condemns the Hindu and Muslim religions, our efforts must continue persistently. For this work we must make all the efforts we can and use all power and all the authority in our hands."

Following were the important causes of the Revolt.

1. *Cultural factors.* The foreign rulers wanted to impose their culture *i.e.,* their etiquettes and manners on the people of India. Lord Macaulay very emphatically stated that through the introduction of the new system of education, there in India would emerge as a class of people Indian in blood and colour but English in manners and tastes etc. Lord Macaulay also used very uncalled for remarks when he termed Indian arts, literature and sciences as 'false'.

2. *Economic factors.* These included: (*i*) Ruin of Indian economy (*ii*) Wealth drain from India (*iii*) Decay of indigenous crafts (*iv*) Stagnation of agriculture (*v*) Decline of Indian industries on account of discriminatory import and export duties on the manufactured Indian goods (*vi*) High revenue demands and impoverishment of Indian peasants (*vii*) Lack of irrigation and other facilities (*viii*) Poverty and famines.

(3) *Military Causes. (i)* Cruel treatment of Indian soldiers by foreign officers (*ii*) Lack of promotional prospects (*iii*) Anti-religious rules like denial of putting sectarian marks on their foreheads, shaving off their beard, crossing the sea, an act which was considered by soldiers as against their religion (*iv*) Non-provision of special allowance for serving in distant lands (*v*) Lord Canning's General Service Enlistment Act under which all the soldiers had to march wherever ordered (*vi*) Forcible annexation of Oudh and discontentment among Oudh soldiers.

4. *Political Causes.* (*i*) Annexation policy of Lord Dalhousie (*ii*) Denial of adoption to several Indian rulers like refusal to continue the pension to Nana Saheb, the adopted son of the Peshwa Baji Rao II, Rani Lakshmi Bai of Jhansi, (*iii*) Annexation of Oudh.

5. *Religious Causes*, (*i*) Anti-Indian religion activities of the Chrisian missionaries (*ii*) Interference in religious customs of the people (*iii*) Displacement of 'Mullahs' and 'Pandits' from employment and prestige with the introduction of the new system of education based on the supremacy of the English language and European arts, literature and sciences.

6. *Social Causes.* (*i*) Abolition of the Sati Practice (*ii*) Prohibition of child marriage (*iii*) Widow remarriage (*iv*) Breaking barriers of caste system through

the introduction of railways (*v*) Racial arrogance of the English people.

7. *Immediate Cause*. Introduction of cartridges smeared with cow's and pigs' fat and resultant unrest among Hindu and Muslim soldiers.

8. *Psychological Causes*. A general belief prevailed among the people that the British rule in India would last for a century. The foundation of this rule had been laid in 1757. Therefore, the year 1857 was considered to be the last year of the British rule in India.

Beginning and ending of the Revolt. Usually, the beginning of the Revolt is attributed to the Third Cavalry whose sepoys at Meerut on May 10, 1857 revolted and killed some British officers.

The first shot of revolt was fired in March 1857 by Mangal Pandey, a sepoy at Barrackpore in Bengal when he refused to use the greased cartridges. He was hanged and he became the first martyr. On May 9, 1857, 85 sepoys of 3rd Cavalry at Meerut were jailed for refusing to use the greased cartridges. On May 10, 1857, sepoys at Meerut rose to a man, attacked their officers and released their coleagues from jail and marched towards Delhi. The 85-year Mughal Emperor Bahadur Shah II was proclaimed the Emperor of India. Thus began the Revolt which gradually spread to other areas.

At Kanpur, the Revolt was led by Nana Saheb, the adopted son of Peshwa Baji Rao II. He was assisted by his trusted general Tantia Tope and and other officer Azimullah Khan.

At Lucknow, Hazrat Mahal, the Begum of Oudh, led the Revolt.

Rani Laxmi Bai of Jhansi was the leader at Jhansi. Her courage and military skill inspired her countrymen. She fought gallantly but Jhansi was captured by the English with the help of some traitors. She died fighting on June 17, 1858.

Bakhat Khan led the Revolt at Bareilly.

A Rajput Zamindar Kanwar Singh of Arrah (Bihar) led the movement in Bihar and at several places in Central India. Though he was nearly 80 year of age at that time, he was perhaps the most outstanding leader and strategist of the Revolt.

The Revolt began at Meerut, 58 km, from Delhi on 10th May 1857, and ended on April 18, 1859 with the hanging of Tantia Tope.

Delhi became the centre of the Revolt and Bahadur Shah its symbol. Bahadur Shah wrote letters to all the chiefs and rulers of India asking them to fight against the British regime.

The entire Bengal army rose in Revolt. Oudh, Rohilkhand, Bundelkhand, Central India, several parts of Bihar and East Punjab shook off British authority. In several states in India, the rulers remained loyal to the British Government but their soldiers revolted. Several chiefs in Rajasthan and Maharashtra revolted. In several territories common people rose up in arms and fought with their axes and spears, bows and arrows etc.

Causes of the Failure of the Revolt

Even though popular and widespread, the Revolt of 1857 failed. Historians' have attributed several causes of the failure of the revolt, Among the important ones were:

1. *Lack of Central leadership.* The rebel leaders, by and large, lacked national perspective. They were fighting for the restoration of their lost privileges. The sepoys of Meerut who came to Delhi declared Mughal Emperor Bahadur Shah II as their leader. Very few leaders who led the movement fought under his leadership. There was no central leadership to guide the rebel sepoys and civilians. There was no war strategy.

2. *Lack of Common Cause.* The Revolt was not inspired by a common cause. In the beginning, the sepoys of Meerut, on their arrival at Delhi declared the Mughal Emperor as the Emperor of India but after his capture by the British, this common cause was lost.

3. *Lack of National Consciousness.* At that time neither the common people nor the rulers and nor the sepoys (soldiers) had developed the consciousness of nationalism *i.e.*, of integrated nation. Regionalism, provincialism and casteism prevailed.

4. *Uncoordinated Efforts.* There was no central leadership to provide coordinated strategies to fight. The struggle depended upon the local people.

5. *Absence of Effective Leadership.* There was a lack of a chain of inspiring leaders. Emperor Bahadur Shah aged 82, was the weakest leader. He lacked leadership qualities. After his arrest, there was no central leader to guide the movement.

6. *Lack of Nationwide Dimensions.* The movement remained confined to a few areas. The South India virtually remained unaffected. Sind was quiet. Rajputana was loyal. Central and Eastern Bengal remained undisturbed. Punjab, by and large remained unaffected.

7. *Loyalty of Several Rulers to the British.* Most of the Sikh states of Punjab sided with the rulers. The Gorkhas of Nepal rendered meritorious services to the British. The Nawab of Bhopal and Nizam of Hyderabad showed loyalty to the British.

8. *Lack of Resources.* The rebels did not possess sufficient war material and equipment as compared with the British.

9. *Lack of Good Generals.* There is no doubt that Nana Saheb, Tantia Tope and Rani Lakshmi Bai were brave and full of courage but they were no match against the British generals who had fought several battles.

10. *Jealousy of leaders.* The leaders at different places were jealous and suspicious of one another and often were at daggers drawn. The only thing common was their own interest against the maltreatment of the British rulers to them.

11. *Regular Supply to the British Forces.* The means of communications developed by the British proved very useful to them. They were able to send

reinforecement within no time.

12. *The British Supremacy of the Sea*. The British with their control of the sea power were able to bring in more than one lakh soldiers in India.

13. *British Diplomacy*. The British used the Sikhs, the Pathans and the Gorkhas etc. to fight against each other at their will.

14. *Hostility of Several Sections*. The big *Zamindars*, the moneylenders and the educated Indians remained hostile to the rebels.

15. *Lack of a forward looking programme*. Once the rebels overthrew the British power from an area, they did not know what sort of political power or institution to establish there.

16. *Premature Revolt*. It is said that the Revolt broke out before the fixed date of May, 31, 1857. The date fixed for the Revolt was known only to a few leaders. But certain events like the trial of Mangal Pandey and his execution and the disbandment of the 19th and 34th Indian regiments made the Indian soldiers lose their patience. The Revolt began before the duc date.

17. *Old verses new weapons*. The rebeltion soldiers had to fight with traditional weapons which were no match to the modren weapons possessed by British forces.

An Analysis of the Causes of Failure of the Revolt

According to *Dr. Smith*, "The jealousy between the Hindus and the Muhammadans, the political rivalry between Peshwa and Badshah, and innumeral animosities of various kinds so divided the rebels everywhere that they never were able to combine effectually for the execution of a well considered plan."

Maulana Abul Kalam Azad, a prominent freedom fighter and author of '*India Wins Freedom*' also observes, "As I read about the events of 1857, I am forced to the conclusion that Indian national character had sunk very low. The leaders of the revolt could never agree. They were mutually zeolous and continually intrigued against one another. In fact these personal jealousies were largely responsible for the Indian defeat."

Dr. R.C. Majumdar attributes the failure to the lack of planning. The most important cause of the failure of the mutiny was the lack of a general plan and a central organisation guiding the whole movement. A number of isolated outbreaks without any link or a common plan between them could harly succeed against the British forces, directing with a strong will and derermintation by a central organisation which could command the resources of India, and later of Britain."

Lord Canning who was the Governor-General of India when the Revolt broke out was of the view that the fate of the English in India would have been different had the native rulers supported the rebels. He had expressed his feelings as, "It Scindia joins the rebels, I will have to pack off tomorrow."

Sir Russel also wrote "Yet it must be admitted that with all their courage, the English would have been quite exterminated if the natives had been all together and hostile to them. The desperate defence made by the garrisons was no doubt heroic but the natives shared their glory and they by their aid and presence rendered the defence possible. Our seize of Delhi would have been quite impossible if the Rajas of Oudh and Patiala had not been our friends and if the Sikhs had not been recruited in our battalions and remained quiet in the Punjab. The Sikhs at Lucknow did good service and in all cases our garrisons were helped, fed and served by the natives as our armies were attended and strengthened by them in the field."

Dr. Ishwari Prasad is of the view that the revolt began prematurely, "As events proved, the Meerut accident by precipitating the Revolt saved the British Raj from the ruin which Nana Saheb and his colleagues had planned.

Wilson, Whites and Malleson, three noted historians of the Revolt agree in regarding Meerut outbreak as fortunate for the Company and fatal to the revolt. It upset the whole plan of the rebels, deprived them of a concerted action and in many places the local leaders did not know what to do. This led many to spontaneous and unpremeditated action."

Treveleyan has gone to the extent of observing that Nana was too ambitious, "Nana's object, was to lay the foundations of his future sovereignity at Cawnpore (Kanpur). The mighty power exercised by the Peshwa was to be restored to himself, the architect of his own fortunes, would bring the glory of replacing the vanished scepter. There can be no doubt that some such thought influenced him."

Summing up the analysis of the causes of the failure of the revolt. Maulana Azad's analysis seems very weighty, "In the light of the available evidence we are forced to the conclusion that the uprising of 1857 was not the result of careful planning nor were there any masterminds behind it. Besides, the natives spying for the British were at work inside and outside the Fort, among whom the Maulvi Rajab Ali stands out as the most notorious. On the other hand, the English had the advantage of having very capable leaders and generals like the Lawrence brothers, Outram Haveloch, Nicholson, Neil, and Edwards. This was really fortunate for the British Government. It were these British leaders and generals who resisted the mutineers very stubbornly in the early stages of the Mutiny and who were thus in a position to control the situation. They had received a substantial aid from their homeland in the later stages of the mutiny. Otherwise also, they were far superior to the Indian leaders in military and political qualitits. All of them had only one object before them and that was the defence of the British Government in India. They, had unity of purpose. They were not divided in their political aims."

Results of the Revolt of 1857

The Revolts had far-reaching effects on the political, administrative, military, and social set-up of the country.

1. *Contitutional and political effects*.

(*i*) The Mughal rule came to an end.

(*ii*) The rule of the East India Company in India came to an end.

(*iii*) The entire administration of India came into the hands of the British Crown and the British Parliament.

(*iv*) The Indian princes were assured that the policy of annexation would not be followed.

(*v*) It was ensured to the Indian rulers that all the agreements and treaties that they had entered with the East India Company would be fully honoured.

(*vi*) The right of the Indian rulers to adopt sons was accepted.

2. *Religious effects*. Indian people were assured of full religious freedom.

3. *Administrative*. The people of India were assured that they would be given opportunity to hold higher posts of responsibility under the government.

4. *Military*.

(*i*) The strength of the European army stationed in India was increased and the artillery was put under their exclusive charge.

(*ii*) A number of Indian communities were debarred from joining the armed forces.

5. *Emergence of heroes*. The heroes of the revolt soon became household names in the country and they even now inspire bravery and patriotism.

6. *Indian nationalism*. The struggle of 1857 sowed the seeds of Indian natioinalism and freedom which led to a continuous struggle and culminated in the freedpm of the country from the British rule in 1947.

7. *Social effects*. The Revolt widened the gulf between the Europeans and the Indians.

Q. 3. While discussing the causes of the revolt of 1857, describe the part played by educated Indians, state rulers and Sepoys.

(Delhi University 1997)

Ans. *Causes of the Revolt of 1857*

The causes of the Revolt were various. It was the culmination of the people's mistrust of the British and of their discontent and dissatisfaction, hardships and the suffering caused under the oppressed British rule. However, for the sake of convenience, the causes may be grouped under seven heads, namely economic, military, political judicial, religious,social and immediate.

Economic. The peasants which constituted the vast majority of the people had to face several famines on account of poverty, unavailability of essential commodities and hunger. Besides there was an economic drain from the country.

Military. There was a general feeling among the Sepoys that they were discriminated in several matters and that their foreign counterparts enjoyed far more facilities. There were very few opportunities for their promotion. Their living conditions were very hard. They were given a very humiliating treatment.

Religious. A general impression among the masses belonging to the Hindus as well as the Muslims seemed to have developed that the British in India were motivated towards converting them to Christianity. The social reforms were also seen in this very perspective.

Political. The political credibility of the British suffered a great deal as they had broken their oral and broken pledged, maltreated the Indian rulers, annexed their territories, imposed their own nominees on the throne, disregarded the Hindu law of adoption as successor to the throne, stopped pensions and withdrew titles etc. Lord Dalhousie's Policy of Doctrine of Lapse had created great unrest among Indian rulers.

Judicial. Lawas discriminated between the Europeans and the Indians. The judicial process was very complicated and costly also.

Social. The Europeans considered themselves very superior and often treated the Indians with contempt and arrogance. The middle and upper classes found themselves excluded from high posts.

Immediate. By 1857, the ground for the rebellion was ready and only a spark was needed to set it on fire. Since the conquest of Bengal, there had been several rebellions of a local nature in different parts of the country. The spark came in the form of greased cartridges the tip of which was said to have been composed of fat derived from beef and pork. The Hindu and the Muslim soldiers found it offending to their religious belief.

(For details of the causes of the Revolt, refer to question No. 2 of this chapter).

ANALYSIS OF THE ROLE OF THE EDUCATED INDIANS, STATE RULERS AND SEPOYS

Role of the educated Indians in the Revolt

The educatied Indians in general did not support the Revolt primarily on account of two reasons. First, the rebels were opposed to progressive reforms in the social life of the people. Second, the educated Indians, in general thought the British rule to be beneficial. In the 1830's Raja Rammohan Roy had advocated the British system of education in India and he was also of the view that India would benefit from the British rule.

Role of the Indian rulers in the Revolt

Broadly speaking the role of Indian rulers can be divided into two categories. One group of rulers actively involved in driving away the British from India. Under this category are placed Rani Jhansi, Nana Saheb, Mughal Emperor Bahadur Shah, Begums of Oudh, the Mughal Empress Zeenat Mahal, Zamindar Kunwar Singh of Bihar and Tantia Tope, the right hand of Nana Saheb.

The other group was of those rulers who supported the British for they felt that once the English were thrown out, their existence would vanish. This group included the Scindhia of Gwalior, Nizam of Hyderabad, Nawab of Bhopal, Holkar of Indore, several rulers of the Punjab and Rajputana and the Gorkhas. The most important cause of the failure of the Revolt was the valuable help rendered by Indian rulers to the British.

Lord Canning, the Governor-General of India, when the Revolt broke out, was of the view that the fate of the English in India would have ben different had the native rulers supported the rebels. He had expressed his feelings in these words, "If Scindhia joins the rebels, I will pack of of to—morrow."

Role of the Sepoys in the Revolt

Perhaps this is the only instance of its kind, that a 'popular revolt' which took place in different parts of India was led by Sepoys — by and large illiterate section of the society. The struggle for Indian independents, was thereafter, led by educated Indians — in several cases educated Indians who had received their education in England and other countries.

Even before 1857, there had been a number of Sepoy revolts on account of low pay, distant postings, hurt of religious sentiments, bad food, insults and discrimination between the Europeans and Indian Sepoys. There was a revolt at Vellore in 1806 by the Hindu Sepoys, Native infantry, stationed at Barrackpur revolted in 1824 when asked to proceed to fight the first Burmese War. In 1838, there were sepoy revolts at Sholapur, Secundrabad, Milligaon and Hyderabad. Madras Cavalry revolted in 1843 at Jabalpur. All these revolts were crushed.

In the 1857 Revolt, the sepoys were in the vanguard and had taken the initiative. Following were the important causes:

(*i*) No promotional avenues. A soldier entered as a soldier and except in few stray cases, retired as a soldier.

(*ii*) Disparity in pay. The highest pay attainable by a Subedar of the infantry was less than the minimum of a newly European recruit.

(*iii*) Lack of trust on Indian soldiers and strict supervision on them.

(*iv*) Trampling self-repest of Indian soldiers. Use of epithets like '*Suar*' or '*Pig*'. Soldiers treated as an inferior animal.

(*v*) Annexation of Oudh and discontent among Oudh soldiers in the army of the British. Oudh was the nurscry of soldiers.

(*vi*) Crossing of sea or '*Kala Pani*' was pollution to orthodox Hindu soldiers. Refusal of soldiers to cross the sea.

(*vii*) No adequate allowance for distant postings.

(*viii*) Encouragement from the British casualties in several wars and confidence of the Indian soldiers in their capacity to win.

(*ix*) Fear of the Sepoys that they would be converted to Christianity.

(*x*) Use of new cartridges smeared with the flesh of the cow and the pig.

Sepoy mutiny. In view of the initiative taken by the soldiers and their active involvement in the 1857 events, most of the British historians and scholars are of the view that the outbreak of 1857 was a 'Mutiny by the Sepoys' of India. The trend was originally set by the Government of the day. Earl Stanley, the then Secretary of State for India, while reporting the events of 1857 to Parliament, used the term 'Mutiny' and thereafter this term began to be used by most of the English writers like Charles Bell, C.W. Forrest, T. R. Holones, M. Innes, J.W. Kaye, G. Macmunn, G. B. Malleson, C.T. Metcalfe, Earl Roberts and several others. Sir John Lawrence was of the opinion that the Mutiny had its origin in the army and its cause was the greased cartridges and nothing else.

The view of Sir John Seelay was that the Mutiny was "Wholly unpatriotic and selfish sepoy mutiny with no native leadership and no popular support."

It is of great interst to refer to the views of the Governor-General of the day. While the then Secretary of State for India, Early Stanley used the term 'mutiny,' Lord Canning, the then Governor-General of India stated that it was 'more like a national war.'

However, it is wrong to term it as a 'Sepoy Mutiny' as several sections of population participated in the struggle. At several places peasants played a significant role. Several zamindars also took part. It was organised in the rural areas also where there were no sepoys. Many rulers took part in the movement. (For details see next question)

Q. 4. Describe the nature of the uprising of 1857. What were the causes of its failure? *(Punjab University 1995)*

or

Discuss the nature and causes of Great Rebellion of 1857 *(Punjab University 1996)*

or

Discuss the nature and causes of the Uprising of 1857. *(Punjab University 1998)*

or

Analyse the causes and character of the Revolt of 1857. *(Delhi University 1997)*

or

Explain the nature and results of the outbreak of 1857. *(Rajasthan University 1997)*

or

What were the causes of the outbreak of 1857? Was it the first war of Indian Independentee? *(Rajasthan University 1996)*

or

Discuss the nature of the Revolt of 1857. Briefly explain its impact on British attitude towards India. *(Rajasthan University 1995)*

Ans. *Nature and Character of Uprising of 1857*

Diametrically views have been expressed by historians, scholars, statesmen and writers on the nature and character of the events of 1857. Popular terms used are the following:

1. Army Mutiny/Army Revolt/Army Uprising.
2. Hindu Conspiracy.
3. Muslim Conspiracy.
4. Mutiny.
5. National War.
6. Popular Uprising/Popular Revolt.
7. Rebellion.
8. Revolt.
9. Religious war.
10. Rural-based Revolt.
11. Sepoy Rebellion/Sepoy Revolt/Sepoy Uprising.
12. Soldier - peasant struggle.
13. Uprising.
14. War of Indian Independence.

Here we shall examine some views in detail.

First View

Army Mutiny/Army Revolt/Army Uprising/Sepoy Mutiny/Sepoy/Revolt/ Sepoy Rebellion/Sepoy Uprising.

(See previous answer also)

Supportes of the View

Sir John Lawrence was of the view that the events of 1857 had their origin in the army and their cause was the greased cartridges and nothing else.

According to Sir John Seelay it was "Wholly unpatriotic and selfish sepoy mutiny with no native leadership and no popular support."

Prof. P.E. Roberts accepts the views of John Lawrence and Seelay and observes that the Mutiny was mainly military in origin but it occurred at a time when for various reasons there was social and political discontent in the country and the mutineers took advantage of the same.

Marshman called it as "the savage muting of a hundred thousand sepoys."

The view of Dr. Alexander Duff is that the revolt was the spontaneous outcome of the fraternity of sepoys of all castes and creeds.

Why is it called a Military Revolt?

Several reasons are given for it. (*i*) There had been several such revolts even before 1857 and it was just one of such revolts (*ii*) The revolt was basically confined to the soldiers (*iii*) The revolt was restricted to a small area in North India and most of the other parts of the country remained unaffected (*iv*) Only a few rulers like Bahadur Shah, Rani of Jhansi and Nana Saheb took part in the revolt (*v*) Some rulers as those of Patiala, Kapurthala, Gwalior, Bhopal,

Hyderabad and Nepal sided with the British and helped them to suppress the revolt (*vi*) The revolt was mostly concentrated in and around cities of North India and several villages remained unaffected (*vii*) The rulers who led the revolt were initially motivated by the fear that they might lose their territories on some pretext, as was the fate of other dispossessed rulers. (*viii*) A sepoy was swored at. He was treated wrongly. He was addressed as '*Suar*' or Pig. He was treated an inferior animal.

Why is it not called a Sepoy/Military Revolt? (See other parts of the answer)

Second View: Conflict Between Civilizations

Some historians led by *T. R. Holmes* are of view that the Revolt of 1857 was "a conflict between civilization and babarism." This point of view smacks of narrow racialism. It may be noted that both the English and the Indian were guilty of murder of innocent people.

Third View: Hindu Conspiracy

A few historians call it a Hindu Conspiracy. It is contended by them that it was initiated by Mangal Pandey - a Hindu. It was engineered by the emissaries of the Peshwa under the guidance of Nana Saheb.

There is no basis for such a theory. The Hindus and the Muslims worked shoulder to shoulder.

Fourth View: Mohammedan Conspiracy

Outram holds the view that "it was a Mohammedan conspiracy making capital of Hindu grievances." This view is basically made on the English diplomacy of "Divide and Rule.' The explanation is extremely in adequate and unsatisfactory. If it were a Muslim conspiracy, the Nizam of Hyderabad would have been induced not to remain neutral. Mangal Pandey, Nana Saheb, Tantia Tope, Rani Laxmi Bai, were not Muslim leaders.

Fifth View: National Uprising/War

Lord Canning, the Governor-General of India, in whose rule, the events took place observed, "The struggle which we have had, has been more like a national war than a local insurrection. It its magnitude, duration, scale of expenditure and in some of its moral features, it partakes largely of the former character."

Benjamin Disraeli, a contemporary conservative leader in England, describes it as "a nationsl rising." He contended that the so-called Mutiny was no sudden impulse but was the result of careful combinations, vigilant and well-organised, on the watch for an opportunity the decline and fall of empires are not affairs of greased cartridges..such rebellions are occasioned by adequate causes and accumulation of adequate cause."

Ashok Mehta, a great national leader points out the national character of the movement in his book "*1857: The Great Rebellion*."

Sixth View: Popular Revolt

Arguments in Favour of Popular Revolt

1. *Participation by Civilians.* No doubt, the sepoys were the backbone of the revolt and they bore the brunt of the struggle to break the chains that imprisoned India. They became its shield and spear. However, besides the sepoys, millions of Indian took part in the revolt. The number of the civilians killed was as large as that of the sepoys.

The rapidity with which the struggle for freedom spread shows that in several areas, it enjoyed mass support. At some places the civilians were more active and aggressive than even the sepoys. At some places, those who sided with the British faced boycott from the community. At places boatsmen refused to ferry British army across the river. Several sections of population participated in the struggle.

2. *Common Symbol.* The circulation of '*Chapatis*'— the symbol of revolts in different parts of the country by the 'Sadhus' and others point to the popular upsurge for freedom.

3. *Involvement of Several Regions.* The movement was not confined to one region or city or province. It was widespread.

4. *Hindu-Muslim Unity.* The religious harmony among the Hindus and the Muslims was quite evident during the movement. The Mughal Emperor prohibited the cow slarghter throughtout the country to conciliate the Hindus. In a letter to Rajas of Rajputana, he pleaded that the different forces of the nation must unite and wage the Revolutionary War. He further wrote, "I have no desire left of ruling over India after the expulsion of the English for my own aggrandizement. If all of your native Rajas are ready to unsheath your sword to drive away the enemy, then I am wiling to resign imperial powers who are chosen to exercise it." Several Hindu rulers responded to the offer of the Muslim ruler.

Arguments Against Calling it Popular Revolt

The rebel leaders by and large lacked national perspective. They were fighting for the restoration of their lost privileges. Thc sepoys of Meerut who came to Delhi declared Mughal emperor Bahadur Shah II as their leader. Very few leaders who led the movement fought under his leaderhip. There was no central leadership to guide the rebel sepoys and civilians. There was no war strategy. The movement was unplanned and uncoordinated.

The leaders at different places were jealous and suspicious of one another and often quarrelled. The only thing common was their own interest against the maltreatment of the British rulers to them.

Patriotism merely meant regionalism. There was no all-India consciousness or modern type of nationalism.

The Revolt in the absence of any unity of purpose did not embrace the entire country. Major parts of South India, East India and West India remained unaffected. It was primarily restricted to North India.

Some of the Indian rulers supported British.

Quite a large number of big *Zamindars* sided with the British.

Propertied class in general kept itself aloof from the mutineers.

Modern educated Indians did not provide help to the rebels.

Seventh View: Religious Uprising

It is believed by some historians and thinkers that it was a religious uprising. Their contention is that the greased cartridges smeared with animal fat - cow and pig had led the sepoys to suspect the intentions of the British rulers to convert them to Christianity. They, therefore, rose in rebellion as their religions *i.e.,* Hinduism and Islam were against such things.

This theory is discounted with the argument that had this been a religious crusade, several, Hindu and Muslim rulers and other sections would not have rendered any help to the British. Moreover, there were no religious clashes between the Christians and others.

There is no doubt that religious cause was one of the reasons of the widespread Revolt but not the sole cause.

Eighth View: Revolutionary War

Justin McCarthy in his '*History of Our Time*' records, "The fact was that throught the greater part of the Northern and North Western provinces of the Indian Peninsula, there was a rebellion of the native races against the English power. It was not alone the sepoys who rose in revolt - it was a combination of grievances - national hatred and religious fanaticism against the English occupation of India. The native princes, and native soldiers were in it. The Meerut sepoys found in a moment a leader, a flag and a cause and the mutiny was transferred into a revolutionary war."

Usually revolutionary wars are the outcomes of some philosophical and sociological principles advocated by philosophers and sociologist. In this struggle, such principles were missing.

Ninth View: Rural Revolt

S.B. Chaudhuri points out that the rural areas arose as one man and the principal cause was the loss of land rights to the urban moneylender and traders under pressure of British land revenue system.

Erick Stokes, on the other hand, points out that rebellions were often the fierest and the most protracted where land transfers were low and the hold of the moneylender the weakest.

Kye has observed, "Not only in the districts beyond the Ganges but in those lying between the two rivers, the rural population had arisen - and soon there was scarely a man of either faith who had not arraigned against us."

Rural unrest was, no doubt,one of the important causesbut to name it Rural Revolt would be unfair. Several sections of the Population, other than the rural ones were actively involved in it.

Tenth View: War of Independence

Why is it Called as the War of Independence?

It was a people's movement on account of the following factores.

1. It was the result of a widespread public reaction against the British rule as secret emblems in the form of 'chapatis' and 'red lotuses' were used to carry the message of freedom by the wandering 'sanyasis' and 'faqirs' and also the 'madaris' from village to village throughout the country. These groups represented the common people of India.
2. May 31, 1857 was fixed as the day for the revolt throughout the country. However, it broke out earlier and full preparation could not be made throughout the breadth and length of the country.
3. The Indian Chiefs who took part in the revolt proclaimed their loyalty to the Mughal King, who was considered as the symbol of political and national unity of the country.
4. The revolt spread quickly in Oudh, Rohilkhand, the Doab, the Bundelkhand, the Central India, large parts of Bihar and the East Punjab. Many small Chiefs of Maharashtra and Rajasthan revolted with the support of the people who disliked the British rule. Local rebellions also occurred in Bengal and Hyderabad.
5. The entire Bengal army rose to revolt. Although many of the rulers of the princely states remained loyal to the British, their soldiers revolted or remained on the brink of revolt.
6. The common people in several areas rose up in arms, often fighting with axes, spears and arrows, lathis and sickles etc. The peasants, the artisans, the shopkeepers, the day labourers provided strength to the freedom movement, espeacially in the areas at present included in Bihar and Uttar Pradesh. It is of some importance to note that in many of the battles with the British armies, commoners even outnumbered the sepoys who participated in the revolt. It is estimated that in Oudh alone, over one lakh people died fighting. An Indian boatman refused to ferry General Havelock and his troops across the river.
7. The commoners at various places who did not actively participate in the revolt, showed great sympathy for the rebels. They rejoiced at the victory of the rebels. They even boycotted those sepoys who remained loyal to the British.
8. There was remarkable Hindu-Muslim Unity to face the Britishers during this struggle. Hindus and Muslims were well represented at all levels of leadership.

9. This revolt would not have spread so swiftly had there been no popular support behind it.
10. The movement was so popular that even women put on men's attire to take part in it.
11. "*Feringee Bhagao*" (Drive away the English) was the common slogan.

Why is it not Called the War of Independence?

1. There was no common objective before the rebels when the struggle started at Meerut.
2. The movement did not embrace all regions of the country.
3. All sections of the population were not represented in the struggle.
4. The leaders had selfish motives and were fighting to regain their own power, privileges and status.
5. It was a feudal fight, some rulers fought against the British while others sided with the British.
6. The movement was not centrally planned.

War of Independence: Select Views

V.D. Savarkaar, a great nationalist revolutinary Peader and an eminent writer, after a good of research, wrote his book '*The Indian War of Independence*' which was published in London in 1909. He described the uprising of 1857 as a "planned wár of Indian Independence"; and attempted to prove that the uprisings of 1826-27, 1831-32, 1848 and 1854 were reharsals of the great drama played in 1857. Later on several leaders of the freedom struggle further developed the theme of the popular character of the Revolt and it cited as a shining example of the perfect accord and harmony between the Hindus and the Muslims in the fight for freedom from British domination.

Dr. S.N. Sen, in his book "*Eighteen Fifty Seven*" is inclined to believe that the Uprising of 1857 was a War of Independence. He concludes that revolutions are mostly the work of a minority, with or without the active support or sympathy of the masses. Such was the case with the American Revolution as well as the French Revolution. Dr. Sen observes, "The Mutiny became a revolt and assumed a political character when the mutineers of Meerut placed themselves under the king of Delhi and a section of the landed aristocracy and civil population declared in his favour. What began as a fight for religion ended as a war of independence for there is not the slightest doubt that the rebels wanted to get rid of the alien government and restore the old order of which the king of Delhi was the rightful representative."

Dr. R.C. Majumdar gave his analysis of the events of 1857 in his book "*The Sepoy Mutiny and the Revolt of 1857*" and subsequently he elaborated his arguments in the chapter he contributed to the Bhartiya Vidya Bhawan's "*British Paramounty and the Indian Renaissance*. Vol, IX. He writes, "Whatever might have been the original character it soon became a symbol of challenge to the mighty British power in India. It remained a shinning example before nascent nationalism in India in its struggle for freedom from the British yoke and was invested with the full glory of the first War of independence against the British." However he has also stated, "It is difficult to avoid the conclusion that the so-called First War of Independence of 1857 is neither First nor National, nor War of Independence."

Prof. S.B. Chaudhari, in his book *"Theories of the Indian Mutinies"* has observed, "First War of Independence it certainly was, as in the whole canvas of the recorded history of India it would be difficult to find a parallel to this gigantic anti-foreign combine of all classes of people and many provinces of India. There was never a war in India lasting continuously for more than a year and simultaneously in all the regions which had for its objective the abasement and ejectment of the alien ruling power."

Pt. Jawaharlal Nehru in his *Discovery of India*' remarks, "It was much more than a military mutiny and it spread rapidly and assumed the character of a popular rebellion and a war of Indian Independence."

Dr. Rajendra Prasad in the President's message broadcast from All India Radio on August 14, 1957 stated, "It is a historical fact that the movement of 1857 was the most determined and widespread of the risings which had taken place till then against the East India Company. There is little wonder if writers and historians have described this movement as a national war of independence."

In the opinion of *K.M. Panikkar,* "It is true that all leaders of the rebellion came from among the dispossed, but all were united in the object they had in view, the expulsion of the British and the recovery of national independence."

Ashok Mehta, a freedom fighter has observed, "The rebellion of 1857 was more than a mere sepoy Mutiny, was an eruptaion of the social volcano wherin many pent-up forces found vent. After the eruption, the whole social topography had changed. The scars of rebellion remained deep and shinning."

Summing up. From the letter written by Mughal emperor Bahadur Shah to the Rajas of Rajputana, it becomes clear that the struggle was for the independence of the country. The letter reads, "It is my ardent wish to see that the '*Feringee*' (English) is driven out of Hindustan by all means and at any cost. It is my ardent wish that the whole of Hindustan should be free, but the Revolutionary war that is being waged for the purpose will not be crowned with success unless a man capable of sustaining the whole burden of the movement, who can organise and concetrate the different forces of the nation and unify the whole people in himself, comes forward to guide the rising. I have no desire left of ruling over India after the expulsion of the English for my own aggrandizement. If all of your native Rajas are ready to unsheath your sword to drive away the enemy, then I am willing to resign imperial powers and authority in the hands of any confederacy of native princes who are chosen to exercise it." Several sections of Hindus responded to this. All this shows that it was the war of independence or national rising, although on a limited scale.

Q. 5. Write notes on
(1) Bahadur Shah (2) Rani of Jhansi (3) Nana Saheb (4) Tantia Tope (5) Begam Hazrat Mahal (6) Kanwar Singh (7) Maulvi Ahmad Shah.

Ans. 1. *Bahadur Shah* (1775-1862)

The last Mughal emperor and the 19th in the line of Babur, occupied the throne of Delhi from 1837-58, but in name only. In fact, he was the pensioner of the British and his domain hardly extended beyond his palaces.

Bahadur Shah became the symbolic head of the Great Rebellion of 1857. Delhi was captured for a short while by the rebels.

Babadur Shah's two sons and a grandson were shoot dead by the British near Delhi Gate. The place is known as '*Khooni Darwaja*' (Bloody Gate). The British recaptured, imporisoned the emperor and exiled him to Rangoon, Burma.

Bahadur Shah's chief claim of his last words reflected his agony when he wrote the couplet, "Zafar was indeed so unfortunate for he was not granted even a six feet grave in the streets of his beloved Motherland." (English translation). Fame is not as a political figure but as a poet. He wrote in Persian and Urdu, using the pseudonym '*zafar*'.

He was a patron of the arts and literature.

Galib, the great poet of Urdu and Persian adorned the court of Bahadur Shah.

2. *Rani of Jhansi* (1835-1858)

Lakshmi Bai, popularly known as Rani of Jhansi came from a Brahman family of Satara (Maharashtra). She was brought up in the household of the Peshwa Baji Rao II. She was married to Maharaja Gangadhar Rai of Jhansi. She was widowed at the age of 18. After the death of her husband, she became the Regent of her adopted son aged five. However, the British refused to recognise the adoption and Jhansi was annexed by Lord Dalhousie under his 'Doctrine of Lapse.'

The Rani of Jhansi was the most colourful personality of the uprising of 1857. She like Nana Saheb and other Indian rulers similarly affected by Dalhousie's policies of territorial expansion joined the struggle against the British.

She was very brave, highly energetic, fearless and resolute. She fought stoutly, with swords in both hands and the reigns of the horse in her mouth. She was helped by Tantia Tope and brave Afghan soldiers.

The Rani was a great booster of her sepoys' morale. She herself went round to inspire her men with zeal and resoluteness.

On June 4, 1857 the Rani was forced by the strong British assault on the fort of Jhansi to go out of the fort and re-fight the British on the Kalpi-fields. The Rani rode forward at might with her adopted child Damodar Rao being on her back, tied in a silk '*dhoti*'.

The Rani and Tantia Tope marched towards Gwalior to seek the help from the Maharaja of Gwalior but without any success. Maharaja Scindhia of Gwalior fought with the Rani but was defeated, most of his troops deserted to her and he took refuge at Agra.

Rani Jhansi died at Kalpi near Jhansi fighting on the battle-field on June 17, 1858.

Tales of her bravery, patriotism military skull have inspired generations of Indians ever since then. Rani of Jhansi had said, "To fight against the English has become my *dharma*."

V.D. Savarkar in the *Indian War of Independence* pays the following tribute to her, "One such life vindicates the whole existence of a nation, the flame of patriotism was burning in her heart. It is very rarely that a nation is fortunate to be able to claim such an angelic person, as a daughter and a queen."

An eminent Hindi novelist Vrindavan Lal Varma in his novel sums up the work of Rani Jhansi in these words, "The Rani fought for Swarajya, died for Swarajya and turned herself into a stone for the foundation of Swarajya."

The famous heroic song of poetess Subhadari Kumari Chauhan sings her glory in those words, "*Khub Ladi Mardani, Woh to Jhansi Wali Rani Thi*". (The mainly queen of Jhansi fought so undauntedly").

3. *Nana Saheb* (1800-1859)

Govind Dhondu Pant, popularly known as Nana Saheb was the adopted son and heir of the last Maratha Peshwa Baji Rao II. Nana Saheb succeeded to the Peshwa's title and residence at Kanpur (Cawnpore) in 1851 but he was refused the annual pension of Rs. 800, 000 pledged by the East India Company. This action of Lord Dalhousie found expression in the Great Uprising of 1857.

Nana Saheb is reported to have toured the country in the early months of 1857 to spread the message of struggle against the British rule.

Nana Saheb accepted Bahadur Shah as the Emperor of India and declared himself to be a '*Subedar*' (Governor) of Bahadur Shah. He was assisted by his two very capable officers Tantia Tope and Azimulla.

Nana Saheb was defeated at Kanpur. Thereafter, he joined the forces of Oudh, led by Begam Hazrat Mahal, wife of the deposed ruler. After the failure of the uprising, he is said to have escaped to Nepal.

Nana refused to surrender and his last words to the British were, "Life must be given up some day. Why then should I die dishounoured?"

It is stated that Azimullah Khan, the agent, of Nana Saheb and Rangoji Bapu, the '*Vakil*' of the dispossessed Raja of Satara had planned the Revolt in England and attempts said to have been made to enlist the suppport of foreign powers like Russia, Italy and Egypt. It was commonly believed during the Revolt that Garibaldi, the Italian hero had promisded to aid and that a treaty of alliance had been concluded between the Kaiser (Ruler) of Russia and Nana Saheb. But conclusive proof in this regard is missing.

Treveleyan has stated, "Nana's object, then was to lay the foundations of his future sovereignty at Cawnpore. The mighty power exercised by the Peshwa was to be restored to himself; the architect of his own fortunes, would bring the glory of replacing that vanished scepter. There can be no doubt that some such thought influenced him."

Kayes has also accepted the major role of Nana Saheb in organising the Revolt of 1857.

"It was no sudden thought, born of the accident of the greased cartridges, that took the disappointed Brahmin and his Mohammedan friend to Lucknow in the spring of this year of trouble. For months, for years indeed, ever since the failure of the mission to England had been apparent, they had been quitely spreading their network of intrigue all over the country. From one native court to another, from one extremity to another of the great continent of India the agents of Nana Saheb had passed with overtures and invitations discreetly, perhaps mysteriously, worded to Princes and Chiefs of different races and religions but most hopefully of all to the Marathas. There is nothing in my mind more substantiated than the complicity of Nana Saheb in widespread intrigues in the outbreak of the mutiny. The concurrent testimony of witnesses examined in parts of country widely distinct from each other takes this story altogether out of the regions of the conjectural."

4. *Tatya Tope or Tantia Tope* (1814-59).

Tatya Tope was the popular name of Ramchandra Pandurang. He was the most loyal general of Nana Saheb and was the moving spirit behind his army.

Tatya tope, a great expert in guerilla warfare became famous for his explo its during the Great Uprising of 1857. He tried to capture Kanpur but failed. He took Gwalior fort, rendered great help to Rani Lakshmi Bai of Jhansi and called upon the Marathas from all over the Deccan to rally against the British. He and his small army used guerilla tactics against the superior British forces and avoided direct combat.

Tatya Tope carried on his fight with the British in the vast regions of Central India, Malwa, Bundelkhand, Rajputana and Khandesh. Nevertheless he was no match for the mighty power of the British. He was hotly pursued by the British. At last worn out with fatigue, he hid himself in the jungles. It so happened that Man Singh, a chief who had been deprived of his estate by the Maharaja of Gwalior was also wandering in the same jungle met Tatya Tope by chance and became friendly. However, Man Singh proved a traitor and informed the British about the hidding place of Tatya Tope. The sepoys captured him while he was asleep. He was tried and hanged.

5. *Begam Hazrat Mahal*

After Oudh's annexation by Lord Dalhousie, the deposed Nawab was in exile at Calcutta. The struggle was taken up in Oudh by his wife, Begam Hazrat Mahal. She declared her son Birjis Kadar as the Nawab of Oudh. She was a moving spirit behind the Uprising in Lucknow. The British Residency at Lucknow was besieged by the rebel sepoys on June 30, 1857. Sir Henry Lawrence, the Resident lost his life while defending the British interest. For several months, struggle went on. Begam Hazrat Mahal demonstrated great bravery but could not succeed. She was given an offer of amnesty by the Queen, but as she had no faith in the Britishers, she escaped to Nepal.

6. *Kanwar Singh* (1778-1858)

A Rajput zamindar, Kanwar Singh was the chief organiser of the Revolt in Bihar. Although, he was nearly 80 years of age at that time, he was perhaps the most outstanding military leader and the strategist of the Revolt. He waged a fierce struggle against the British in Bihar and also campaigned in Oudh and Central India. He was successful against the British forces near Araah in Bihar. However, there he sustained a fatal blow while fighting.

5. *Maulvi Ahmad Shah*

Maulvi Ahmad of Faizabad (Fyzabad) was one of the important leaders of the Uprinsing of 1857.

About Maulvi, *Malleson* writes: "Before the Mutiny broke out, the Maulvi travelled throughout India, on a roving mission to excite the minds of his compatriots to the steps then contemplated by the master spirit of the plot. Certain it is that, in 1857, he circulated seditious papers throughout Oudh: that the police did not arrest him, and, to obtain that end, armed force was required. He was then tried and condemned to death. But, before the sentence could be executed. Oudh broke out into revolt and like many a political criminal in Europe, he steeped at once from the floor of a dungeon to the foot step of a throne."

Q. 6. Write a note on the Peasants and Tribal movements in the rule of East India Company.

Ans. *Peasants and Tribal Movements in the Rule of East India Company.*

Several revolts of peasants and tribals took place during the Company's rule. These revolts were the forerunners of the revolt of 1857. Important revolts were as under :

1. *Chuar Risings.* In 1768, famines, enhanced land revenue demands and economic distress led to the revolt of Chaur aboriginal tribesmen of Midnapur district.

2. *The Hao and Munda Tribesmen Revolt.* Several revolts of the tribesmen of Chhota Nagpur and Singhbum took place in the first half of the 19th century.

3. *Santhal Revolts.* The Santhals of Rahmahal district in Bengal revolted under the leadership of Sidhu and Kanhu and declared themselves independent in 1855. The government pacified them by creating a separate district of Santhal parganas.

4. *Bhil Uprisings.* In Western India, the Bhils, an aboriginal tribe of Western ghats revolted in 1817-19.

5. *Surat Salt Agitation.* The raising of salt duty was vigorously opposed in 1844.

6. *Kolapur Revolt.* Faced with the spectre of unemployment, the Gotkaris revolted in 1844.

18

Impact of the Revolt of 1857

(Government of the India Act, 1858 and Queen's Proclamation, 1858)

Q. 1. What was the impact of the Revolt of 1857 on the Government of India? *(Delhi University 1995, 1998)*

or

Write Notes on:

1. Government of India Act, 1858

2. Queen's Proclamation 1858

Ans. *Government of India Act, 1858.*

Circumstances leading to the Act. The events of 1857 gave a fillip to the demand in Britain that a trading company i.e. the East India Company should not be allowed to exercise political control over India. After a good deal of debate in Parliament, it received the Royal assent on August 2, 1858.

Main provisions of the Act and their Implementation.

1. India came to be governed in the name of the Queen.
2. The administration of territories of India was transferred from the Company to the Crown.
3. The military and naval forces were transferred to Queen.
4. The Government of India began to be carried out by the Viceroy on behalf of the Queen.
5. The Board of Control and the Court of Directors of the Company were abolished and all the powers possessed by them were given to the Secretary of State for India and his Council.
6. The Secretary of State was to be a member of the Cabinet. His salary and allowances were made a charge on the revenues of India.
7. The Secretary of State was given the power to overrule his Council.
8. The Secretary of State for India was given the power of sending to and receiving secret messages from the Viceroy of India and was not expected to communicate these to the Indian Council.
9. The British Parliament got control over Indian affairs. The Members of Parliament could ask questions from the Secretary of State on matters of Indian administration.

10. The Secretary of State for India was to submit a report every year to the British Parliament (House of Commons) on the moral and material progress of India.
11. The Act laid down that except for the purpose of repelling invasion or any other sudden or urgent necessity, Indian revenues were not to be employed for military operations outside India without the consent of Parliament.
12. Appointments to the convenanted Civil Services were to be made by open competition.
13. The assumption of the powers by the Crown was to be announced to the princes and the people of India by Queen's Proclamation.

Significance of the Act. The 1858 Act opened a new chapter in the history of India.

1. The rule of India by the Company came to an end. Now India was placed under the Crown.
2. The control of the Secretary of State for India increased over the affairs of India.
3. A new policy towards Indian States was evolved. The policy of annexation was discarded.
4. Employment in Civil Services became open through competition.
5. An additional revenue burden on India was put on account of the establishment of the office of the Secretary of State for India.

Thereafter Indian Council Acts 1861, 1892, 1909 1919 and 1935 were passed to bring about changes in the structure and functioning of the Government of India.

Queen's Proclamation of 1858

Importance : Queen Victoria's Proclamation read at a Durbar held by Lord Canning (1856 to 1862) at Allahabad on November, 1858 is a great landmark in the history of Indiia. Ths poclamation remained the basis of Indian administration upto 1917. This proclamation was circulated very widely in India and translated into the varnacular languages.

The issuance of the proclamation became necessary in veiw of the radical changes that took place in India after the Revolt of 1857.

Significant features of the proclamation

Assurance to the Princes. "We hereby announce to the Native Princes of India that all treaties and engagements with them by or under the authority of the Honourable East India Company are by us accepted, and will be scrupulously maintained and we look for the like observance on their part".

No territorial extension. "We desire no extension of our present territorial possession, and while we will permit no aggression upon our dominions or our rights to be attempted with impunity we shall sanction no encroachment on those of others."

Respect for Rights and Dignity of Princes and others. "We shall respect the rights dignity and honour of our Native Princes as our own, and we desire that they as well as our subjects, shall enjoy that prosperity and that social advancement which can only be secured by internal peace and good government."

Religious freedom. " We declare it to be our royal will and pleasure that none be favoured, none moldested or disqualified by reason of the religious faith and observances, but that all shall alike enjoy the equal and impartial protection of the law, and we strictly charge and enjoy all those who may be in authority under us that they abstain from all interference with the religious belief or worship of any of our subjects on pain of our highest displeasure."

Equal opportunity in Administrative Services. "And it is our further will that so far as may be, our subjects of whatever race or creed be freely and impartially admitted to offices in our services, the duties of which they may be qualified by their education, ability and integrity, duly to discharge".

Due regard to ancient culture. "We know and respect the feelings of attachment with which the Natives of India regard the land inherited by them from their ancestors and we desire to protect them in all rights connected therewith subject to the equitable demands of the state and we will do that generally in framing and administering the law, the regard to be paid to the ancient rights, usages and customs of India".

Welfare of the people. "It is our earnest desire to stimulate the peaceful industry to promote works of public utility and improvement and to administer its government for the benefit of all our subjects. In their prosperity will be our strength, in their contentment our security, and in their gratitude our best reward.

Pardon to the guilty: "We desire to show our mercy by pardoning the offences of those who have been misled but who desire to return to the path of the duty". Our clemency will be extended to all offenders save and except those who have been or shall be convicted of having directly taken part in the murder of British subjects. With regards to such, the demand of justice forbids the exercise of mercy".

Q. 2. State the changes that took place in India after the Revolt of 1857.

or

State the significance of the Revolt of 1857.

or

What were the administrative, constitutional, political and religious effects of the Revolt of 1857?

or

"The Great Revolt of 1857 marks on epoch in the British Indian History". Elucidate this statement.

Ans. *Epoch Making Changes*

The administrative, constitutional, military, political, religious and social structure of India underwent radical changes after the Revolt of 1857. The British Government took two important steps to bring about changes. These were. (*i*) The Government of India Act, 1858 (*ii*) Proclamation of the Queen of England.

The psychological environment in India also changed considerably after the Revolt of 1858.

1. *Administrative changes.* (*i*) The Company's administration and control over India came to an end (*ii*) Now Indian affairs came under the Crown of England (*iii*) The designation of the Governor-General of India was changed into the Viceroy of India (*iv*) The control of the Secretary of State for India-a newly created post (a Cabinet Minister of England) over the Viceroy of Indian was greater than the control of the President of the Board of Control over the Governor - General of India.

2. *Constitutional changes.* (*i*) All territories in India under the control of the East India Company came under the Crown of England (*ii*) The Biritish Parliament could excercise more control over Indian affairs (*iii*) All the treaties and agreements made by the Company with the Indian rulers were to be honoured by the Company.

3. *Educational changes.* Universities were established at Calcutta, Madras and Bombay in 1857.

4. *Judicial changes.* (*i*) The Penal Code on which Lord Macaulay's Commission had begun work so many years before became the law of the land (*ii*) Crown's Supermen Court and Company's Sadar Courts were amalgamated in the High courts which were now established at each Presidency.

5. *Military changes.* (*i*) Increase in the number of European troops. It was laid down that at least one third of the army in India and must consist of Europeans (*ii*) Placing artillery exclusively under the Europeans. (*iii*) Increase in military expenditure on account of higher emoluments to Europeans (*iv*) Distinction between Kings, troops and Company's troops was abolished.

6. *Political changes.* (*i*) India remaining under the British domination on account of the failure of the Revolt (*ii*) No further expansion of territories in India under British Rule (*iii*) No application of Doctrine of Lapse (*iv*) Assurance to Indian rulers for fair treatment. Regarding this, the Queens' Proclamation of November 1858 said, "We hereby announce to the Native Princes of India that all treaties and engagements made with them by or under the authority of the East India Company are by us accepted and will be scrupulously maintained and we look for the like observance on their part. We desire no extension of our present territorial possessions and while we will permit no aggression upon our dominions or our rights to be attempted with impunity, we shall sanction no encroachment on those of others.

We shall respect the rights, dignity and honour of Native Princes as our own; and we desire that they as well as our own subjects should enjoy that prosperity and that social advancement which can only be secured by internal peace and good government.

We hold ourselves bound to the native of our Indian territories by the same obligations of duty which bind us to all our other subjects, and those obligations, by the blessing of almighty God, we shall faithfully and conscientiously fill".

7. *Religious Change.* The British rulers declared very emphatically their policy of non - interference in the religious affairs, customs and traditions of the native Indians. The Queens Proclamation read, "Firmly relying on ourselves on the truth of Christianity and acknowledging with gratitude the solace of religion, we disclaim alike the right and the desire to impose our convictions on any of our subjects. We declare it to be our royal will and pleasure that none be favoured, none molested or disqueted by reason of their religious faith or observances but that all shall alike enjoy the equal and impartial protection of the law and we do strictly charge and enjoin all those who may be in authority under us that they abstain from all interference with the religious belief or worship of any of our subjects.

And it is our further will that, so far as may be our subjects of whatever race or creed be freely and impartially admitted to office in our service, the duties which they be qualified by their education, and ability and integrity only to discharge.

We know and respect the feelings of attachment with which the natives of India regard the lands inherited by them from their ancestors, and we desire to protect them in all rights connected therewith, subject to the equitable demands of the state and we will do that generally in framing and administering the law due regard be paid to the ancient rights, usages and customs of India".

8. *Sociological Change.* The Revol of 1857 widened the gulf between the Europeans and the Indians. Social estrangement between the two started (*ii*) It is stated by the some writers that the relations between the Hindus and the Muslims became sore as each claimed more participation in the Revolt.

In the words of *K.M. Pannikar,* "On the Indian side also the Mutiny loomed large. The rebels had been put down with a heavy hand. The atrocities of the White terror rankled long in Indian minds and poisoned the relations of the two races for decades" (*iii*) The Muslim Renaissances received more set back as compared with Hind Renaissance. According to *C.F. Andrew* "It is not difficult to trace fatal havoc to budding spiritual life which one year of mutiny wrought . Decay immediately overtook the revival of learning in Delhi (center of Muslim learning) from which it never recovered. Calcutta the centre of Hindu Renaissance escaped the horrors of the Mutiny and was saved".

Miscellaneous Change. (*i*) Services were opened to all. The Proclamation of 1858 contained an assurance that services would be open to all irrespective of race or creed. To give effect to this policy, the Indian Service Act of 1861 was passed which provided for an annual competitive examination to be held in London.

(*ii*) The feudal and reactionary elements became the favourite and privileged sections of the Biritish rulers. In the words of *Pt. Nehru,* these taluqdars took pride in calling themselves the "Barons of Oudh" and became one of the pillars of British Rule.

(*iii*) The era of territorial aggrandisement gave place to the era of economic exploitation.

Summing up : It is a matter of great regret that "The Rebellion of 1857" the Sepoy Mutiny, or simply the Mutiny, the Popular Outburst, the Uprising, the First War of Indian Independence–assorted names given by different thinkers over the past hundred and fifty years failed in its objectives. For about another hundred years, India was destined to suffer under the foreign domination. The hold of the British over India was all the more strengthened. Before 1858, India was under the East India Company and after that there was only a change of '*master*'. The 'Drain of Wealth' became very acute and several famines took place which caused untold misery to the people of India.

19

Lord Ripon and Lord Curzon: Their Reforms

Q. 1. Lord Ripon was a liberal statesman. In the light of this statement, discuss the administration of Lord Ripon. *(Delhi University 1994)*

or

Explain the reforms of Lord Ripon. Was he a different person in that imperialist era? *(Rajasthan University 1992)*

Ans : *Lord Ripon (1880-1884)*

Won affection from Indians and hatred from his country men

The Governor-General Lord Ripon and Viceroy of India received so much admiration for his administrative reforms and his friendly attitude to the people of India that at the time of his departure from India to England, his journey from Simla to Bombay has been described as "a triumphant march such as India has never witnessed". In contrast to this his tenure in India was described in Britain, "as one of the most successful failures of history". From Indian point of view, he has been hailed as. Ripon the Good' In the words of *P.L. Roberts* "If Lord Ripon had forfeited popularity among his countrymen he had at any rate won by his championship of their causes, the enthusiastic devotion and support of men of Indian birth. On his resignation in 1884, the route of his journey to Bombay was lined with acclaiming and admiring crowds and his name has ever since been enshrined in the hearts of the nationalists in India as the great Champion of their cause on the Viceregal throne".

Many Fold Reforms of Lord Ripon

Lord Ripon within a period of just four years, carried out far-reaching reforms in the administrative structure, educational system, financial matters, social field and political system.

I. *Reforms in Administrative Structure*

1. *Local administration* : Lord Ripon has been called the 'Father of Local Self-Government'. The most notable work of Ripon was the Government Resolution (1882) on local self Government according to which local bodies were to be developed throughout the country. The Resolution stands out as a

landmark in the development of local self-government in India. According to Lord Ripon himself, "It is not primarily with a view to improvement in administration that the measure is put forward and supported. It is chiefly desirable as an instrument of political and popular education".

Following were the major provisions of the Resolution .

(*i*) The Provincial Governments were required to set up a network of Local Board in every district.

(*ii*) The majority of the members were to be non official.

(*iii*) Official members not to exceed one third of the total members.

(*iv*) The system of election was to be introduced wherever possible.

(*v*) The local boards were to be charged with specific duties and entrusted with suitable sources of revenue.

(*vi*) There was not to be undue interference of the Government in the functioning of the local bodies.

(*vii*) The number of Municipal Committees was to be increased.

2. *Reforms in Civil Service Recruitment*: Before Lord Ripon, competitive Civil Service examinations used to be held at London and the age limit for candidates was 18 years. Lord Ripon felt that these two factors put the Indians at a great disadvantage. It was very expensive for the Indians to go to London for appearing in the test. On account of general overall low standards in education and on account of several other factors, Indian young men at the age of 18 were not sufficiently mature. Lord Ripon, therefore, pleaded the cases of the Indians. He was successful in getting the age limit raised from 18 to 21 years.

3. First Population Census in India was conducted in 1881.

II. *Economic, Commercial and Financial Reforms*

1. Revenues of the state were divided into three categories, namely Imperial Heads, Provincial Heads and Divided Heads.

(*a*) *Imperial Heads of Revenue* : These included income from customs, posts and telegraphs, railways, mint, salt, land revenue etc. The revenue from these services went wholly to the Central Government and the Central expenditure was to be met out of this fund.

(*b*) *Provincial Heads of Revenue* : Under the head fell revenues received from roads, printing and general administration etc. These were to go to Provincial Governments to meet their expenses.

(*c*) *Dividcud Heads:* Revenue from excise, forests, stamp duties, registration etc. was equally dividcd between the Central Government and Provincial Governments.

Deficit of the Provincial Government was to be met by transferring some portion of land revenue.

2. Lord Ripon continued the free trade policy followed by his predecessors. Import duties were abolished on several articles. These were however retained on spirits and wines etc. On arms and ammunition duties were retained for political considerations.

III. *Educational Reforms*

With a view to spread education in the country, Lord Ripon appointed a commission under the chairmanship of W.W. Hunter. The Commission made the following important recommendations:

1. The Commission emphasised the Government's special responsibility towards the extension and improvement of primary education.
2. The Commission recommended the control of primary education to be transferred to the newly set up District and Municipal Boards.
3. For secondary education, the Commission recommended two divisions one literary education and the other commercial and vocational education.
4. The Commission made important recommendations for the spread of female education.
5. The Commission recommended that private enterprise should be encouraged in the field of education.

IV. *Industrial Reforms*

For improving the lot of factory workers, the Government passed the first Factory Act (1881). The Act prohibited the employment of children under the age of seven. It limited the number of working hours for children below the age of twelve. The Act required that dangerous machinery should be fenced. It provided for the appointment of inspectors to supervise the implementation of these measures.

V. *Judicial Reforms: Ilbert Bill Controversy (1883-84)*

A Bill for judicial reforms known as Ilbert Bill after the name of Sir C.P. Ilbert, the Law Member of the Viceroy's Council was introduced in the Legislative Council in 1883. The Bill aimed at placing the Indian and European judges on equal footing. According to the existing provisions except in presidency towns, no magistrate or sessions judge could try a European or British subject unless he himself was a European or British subject by birth. Indian judges could not try European or British subjects. This Bili raised a very strong protest from the European and the Anglo-Indian community. Meetings were held the against this Bill. Abuses were hurled upon Ripon. The protesters even raised the slogan "European women in danger", Other slogans raised by them were: "Shall we be judged by the Nigger. Shall he send us to jail? Shall he put in authority over us? Never! it is impossible! Better that British rule in India should end than that we should be obliged to such humiliating laws." Ripon submitted to the storm of agitation and a compromise was reached. The amended offenders could demand trial by jury of which at least half the members must be Europeans or Americans.

VI. *Military Reforms*

Lord Ripon brought to an end to the second Afghan was which had been waged by his predecessor.

VII. *Political Reforms*

(*i*) *Mysore* : Mysore had been annexed by Lord William Bentinck on account of maladministration. Subsequently it was found that the reports of maladministration were exaggerated. Lord Ripon, restored the throne to the adopted son of the Maharaja, of course with certain conditions.

(*ii*) *Kolapur* : Lord Ripon followed the similar policy in the case of Kolapur.

(*iii*) *Hyderabad*: When the prince became major, he was duly installed on the throne.

The policy of returning Indian States to their rightful owners made Lord Ripon very popular.

VIII. *Press Reforms (1882)*

The Press Act of 1878 had put several restrictions on the newspapers published in vernacular languages and the English press was free. There was a great resentment against this discriminatory treatment. Lord Ripon appreciated the sentiments of the Indians and repeated this Act.

Estimate of Lord Ripon

As already mentioned, Lord Ripon has been greatly admired by the Indians and equally detested by the British in general.

Ripon is being remembered by the Indians as 'Ripon the Good' and 'Ripon the Virtuous.'

Pandit Madan Mohan Malviya in his presidential address at the Indian National Congress Session at Lahore in 1909 referred to Ripon "as the greatest and the most beloved Viceroy whom India had known."

According to *S. Gopal,* the noted historian "1883 saw the beginning of Indian political organisation and nationalist endeavours". "*P.I. Roberts* has observed.

He was a truly liberal. He was determined to take some forward steps in the direction of liberalizing the Indian Government".

Florence Nightingale called Ripon "the Savior of India".

Arnold White, a great critic of Ripon said that he had "opened the door to the loss of India".

Q 2. Review the administration of Lord Curzon. ***(Delhi University 1984)***

or

"Curzon did not follow the policy of reforms as Ripon did. On the contrary he believed in supervision, official interference centralization and creating dissentions". Explain

(Rajasthan University 1996)

or

Give a critical estimate of the administration of Lord Curzon. What were the reactions of the Indian leaders to it?

Ans: *Two-fold Division of Curzon's Reforms (1899-1905)*

With a view to having a clear perspective of the reforms undertaken by Lord Curzon, we may divide the reforms under two heads namely (*i*) The administrative reforms and (*ii*) The political cum-administrative reforms.

As far as his reforms from administrative points of view are concerned, broadly speaking they deserve appreciation, On the other hand, his reforms made outwardly from administrative considerations but in reality political considerations implied therein invited so much criticism that his good work done on the invited administrative side receded to the background and he became a villain in the eyes of Indians in general. Lord Ripon though made limited reforms yet became popular with the Indians on account his being considerate and receptive to the needs of the people of India. His liberal approach won affection and regards of Indians. Before giving an analysis, it is considered appropriate to give his reforms in various fields.

Guiding Principles of Curzon's Administrative Reforms

Following were the guiding principles :

1. *Efficiency as the watchword* : Curzon was very clear about the work in hand. In his own words, "If I were allowed to narrate in a nutshell the entire work of my administration in India in one word, that will be efficiency."

2. *Overhauling of the administrative machinery*: In the course of a conversation in London in July 1904 he said that "epochs arise in the history of every country when the administrative machinery requires to be taken to pieces and overhauled and readjusted to the altered necessities or the growing demands of the hour".

3. *Reforms in Several Fields* : Lord Curzon was convinced that there was scarcely a department of the Government or branch of the service which should escape his attention.

4. *Methodical process of reforms* : Curzon's method was to appoint an expert commission to go into the working of a department in depth and then carry out necessary reforms by enacting legislation where needed.

5. *Centralisation of Work:* The trend of his reforms was towards 'officilization' and 'centralisation'.

Manifold reforms.

1. Agricultural reforms.
2. Archaeological reforms.
3. Army reforms.
4. Economic reforms.
5. Educational reforms.
6. Famine relief reforms.
7. Local self government reforms.
8. Police reforms.
9. Railway reforms.
10. Political-cum-administrative reforms.

1. *Agricultural Reforms*

The reforms included the following:

(*i*) *Punjab Land Alination Act (1900)* : According to this Act, a non agriculturist could not purchase land from an agriculturist without the permission of the Government. The land of an agriculturist could not be attached in payment of debt.

(*ii*) *Cooperative Societies Act (1904)* : The Act provided for the formation of cooperative credit societies in rural and urban areas. The main objective was to give relief to rural indebtedness.

(*iii*) *Agricultural research :* To quote Curzon, "Our real reform has been to endeavour for the first time to apply science on a large scale to the study and practice of Indian agriculture" He took the following measures in the regard:

(*a*) Appointment of an Inspector General of Agriculture.

(*b*) Establishment of an Agricultural Research Institute at Pusa in Bengal.

(*iv*) *Irrigation Facilities* : A Commission was appointed to look into the various issues involved in irrigation. As a result of its recommendations, the cana system in Punjab was improved. The construction of the Upper Chenab, Canal, the Upper Jhelum Canal and the Lower Bari Doab Canal was started.

(*v*) *Land Revenue*: Greater elasticity in revenue collection was made by the Land Resolution of 1902. The policy of reduction in land revenue was formulated in case of failure of crops.

2. *Archaeological Reforms*

For the protection of historical monuments, an Ancient Monuments Protection Act was passed. The Act made it an offence to do any harm to the monuments declared as preserved by the Government.

Old sites were to be excavated by the Department of Archaeological Survey.

3. *Army Reforms*

(*i*) Grouping of army into two commands—the Northern Command with its headquarters at Muree and the Southern Command with its headquarters at Poona.

(*ii*) Three brigades, two of native battalion and one of British Battalion.

(*iii*) Setting up of a training college for officers at Quetta.

(*iv*) Supply of superior arms to British battalion.

(*v*) Reorganisation of the army transport system.

4. *Economic Reforms*: *Financial Reforms*

(*a*) Establishment of a new Department of Commerce and Industry.

(*b*) Passing of the Indian Coinage and Paper Currency Act of 1899 and making British Sovereign legal tender in India. at the rate of Rs. 15 to a Sovereign.

(*c*) India put on a gold standard.

(*d*) Raising the limit of taxable income from Rs. 500 to Rs. 1000.

5. *Educational Reforms*

(*i*) Appointment of a Universities Commission to suggest reforms.

(*ii*) Passing of Indian Universities Act (1904).

(*iii*) Indian Universities Act 1904 increased Government control over Indian Universities. (Discussed Separately).

(*iv*) Appointment of Director General of Education to coordinate the educational activities of the provinces.

7. *Judicial Reforms*

(*i*) Increase in the number of judges of the Calcutta High Court.

(*ii*) Increase in the salary and pension benefits of the Judges.

(*iii*) Revision of the Indian Code of Civil Procedure.

6. *Famine Relief*

(*i*) Appointment of a Famine Commission to suggest measures to provide relief.

(*ii*) Assistance to be taken from non-official agencies.

(*iii*) Construction of more railways for speed transport of food stuffs to famine stricken areas (About one million people said to have lost their lives out of about 60 million people affected by famine in various parts of India)

8. *Local Self-Government*

(*i*) Reduction in the number of elected members of Calcutta Corporation.

(*ii*) Majority of nominated members in the Calcutta Corponation.

9. *Police Reforms*

(*i*) Direct recruitment to higher posts.

(*ii*) Raising the salary of policemen - not to be less than Rs. 8 per month.

(*iii*) Establishment of training schools.

(*iv*) Setting up a Criminal Investigation Department.

10. *Railway reforms*

(*i*) Appointment of a Railway Commission.

(*ii*) Establishment of a Railway Board.

(*iii*) Opening of new railway lines.

(*iv*) Railways to be run on commercial lines.

11. *Political-cum-administrative reforms*

(*i*) *Partition of Bengal* : Lord Curzon felt that Bengal which at that time included Bengal, Bihar and Orissa, was too big to be properly administered by a Lt. Governor. It was, therefore, divided into two provinces: (*i*) Bengal and (*ii*) Eastern Bengal and Assam in 1905. Curzon described The Partition of Bengal as a mere readjustment of administrative boundaries'.

The province of Bengal comprised the western districts of Bengal proper, Bihar and Orissa. The other called the Eastern Bengal and Assam comprised the eastern districts of Bengal proper and Assam. The Bengali Hindus became a minority and the Muslims a majority in the newly called East Bengal and Assam province. (Discussed separately in detail).

(*ii*) *Status of Presidency Governors*: Lord Curzon believed in the policy of centralisation in every field. He put forward a proposal to reduce the powers of Governors of Bombay and Madras but this was not accepted by the British Cabinet.

Comparison between Lord Curzon and Lord Ripon : Lord Ripon was liberal in his outlook and he was genuinely interested in the welfare of the Indians. On the other hand, Lord Curzon was very arrogant and he held the Indians in contempt. In his convocation address to the Calcutta University in 1905, he declared " I hope I am making no false arrogant claim when I say that the highest ideal of truth is to a large extent a Western conception ..... Undoubtedly truth took a high place in the moral code of the West, before it had been similarly honoured in the East where craftiness and diplomatic while have always been held in much repute".

Lord curzon believed that Providence had appointed the Englishmen to carry on the administration of India and he would be going against the will of God if he gave any concessions to the people of India.

In those days, it was said by several sections of the people of India that "Lord Curzon loved India as one loved his dog, a useful and faithful slave". According to Curzon, the Congress was "tottering to its fall, and one of my great ambitions while in India... is to assist it to peaceful demise."

About the Partition of Bengal, *S.N. Banerjee* wrote "The announcement fell like a bombshell". We felt that we had been insulted, humiliated and tricked. We felt that it was a deliberate blow aimed at the growing solidarity and self-consciousness of the Bengali-speaking population. The Partition of Bengal became a national movement which agitated the minds of all the Indians. No wonder, the partition had to be cancelled in 1911.

In the Calcutta Corporation, the reforms were so conducted that the actual control over the affairs of the Corporation was transferred to the executive committee largely British in Character and composition.

The report of the Universities Commission was also not appreciated by educated Indians. In the words of H.C.E. Zacharias. "The Act of 1904 certainly left the Indian University to be an institution meant not for the fostering of love for learning but for the providing of efficient hurdles in a race after jobs". *S.N. Banerjee* observed that the report of the Commission "convulsed educated Indians from one end of the country to another"

Curzon was a great imperialist. His every reform, however, good was looked upon with suspicion. He used to say, "India is the pivot of our empire. We have not the smallest intention of abandoning our Indian possessions".

Curzon's foreign and domestic policies were motivated by the urge to make the British position in India impregnable.

Earl of Ronald Ohay in his book *"Life of Curzon"* has observed, "Lord Ripon's ideal was to secure, by slow degrees, autonomy of the *Indian People.* Lord Curzon's was to secure it for the *Indian Government"*. Lord Ripon's reforms in the local self government, Repeal of Vernacular Press Act, Ilbert Bill employment of Indians to higher posts, ending of conflict with Afghanistan and restoration of states to Indian princes earned him the gratitude of the people of India.

20

British Policy Towards Indian States

Q. 1. Discuss the relations of the East India Company with the Indian States before 1857.

(Punjab University 1992; Delhi University 1995)

Ans : *No Uniform Policy Before 1857*

There was no uniform policy of the British which determined their relations with the Indian States. The relations depended upon the exigencies of the situation. In the words of *K.M. Pannikar,* "The authorities of the East India Company were wavering with every passing way as to whether the rulers were Zamindars, feudatories, tributaries or independent sovereigns, and each Governor-General and each President held and enforced his views". Sometimes a Governor-General followed earlier precedents and at other times created new precedents. Likewise *Prof-Dodwell* has very aptly observed, "Besides the rights vested by treaty in the Company there had arisen, under no sanction but of superior power on the one side and reluctant acquiescence on the other, a body of precedents relating to successions and to interference in the internal administration of the states. Together these constituted the Company's paramountcy undefined, undefinable, but always tending to expand under the strong pressure of political circumstances".

The motives of the British were purely imperialistic and as Marx wrote in 1853. "As to the native states, they virtually ceased to exist from the moment they became subsidiary to or protected by the Company."

The nature of relations depended upon the personality of the Governor/Governor-General, his Resident and the native ruler. While discussing the relations between the Company and the Indian princes, it must always be remembered that the Company though in the beginning had commercial interests only but in due course, in the first stage it tried to interfere in the succession issues of some states and thereafter it began to extend its military and political domination and control. It may be mentioned here that with the decline of the Mughal power, innumerable states had emerged. It is very difficult to give the number of these states. There was so much confusion that the phenomenon of the creation, merger, integration, enlargement, and dissolution had assuming an alarming proportion. Each of about 600 states had its own unique problem and set-up with which the Company had to deal.

Several approaches/stages/phases of the relations

1. Policy of each Governor/Governor-General.
2. Stagewise study.
3. Phasewise study.
4. Man theories or principles of approach.

In fact, there is no watertight compartment among the stages. All are correlated.

Policy of each Governor/Governor-General of Bengal and Governor-General of India

Of the five Governors of Bengal, policies of two Governors, namely Clive (1757-60 and 1765-67) and Warren Hastings (1772-74), deserve special mention. Of the nine Governors-General of Bengal, Warren Hastings (1774-85), Wellesely (1798-1805), Lord Minto (1807-13), Hastings (1813-23) and Willam Bentinck (1828-33) took special interest in this issue. Of the six Governor Generals of India, Lord William Bentinck (1833-35) and Lord Dalhousie (1848-56) need special mention.

Stagewise Study

Sir William Lee — Warner in his book '*The Native States of India*' published in 1910 mentioned the following three stages:

(*i*) The policy of Ring Fence down to 1813.
(*ii*) The policy of Subordinate Isolation, 1813-57.
(*iii*) The Policy of Subordinate Union from 1857 onwards.

Four Phase of Company's Relations with the Indian States (1768 to 1800)

Alfred Lyall has mentioned four stages in the Company's participation in Indian wars with the states.

In the first stage, the Company undertook to lend its troops to a friendly Indian prince to assist him in his own wars - for instance the Treaty with the Nizam (1768).

In the second stage, the Company's troops took the field on their own account with the assistance of an Indian ally who made common cause with them.

In the third stage, the Indian ally was not to supply troops but money. The Company undertook to raise, train and equip an army under English Officers and make available to the ally a fixed number of troops, as for instance in the treaty with Hyderabad (1798).

The final stage was the logical step. The Company undertook to defend the territory of an Indian ally and for that purpose statined a subdiary force in the territory of the state. The Indian ally was asked not to pay money but surrender territory from the revenue of which the expenses of the subsidiary force were to be met, for instance Treaty with Nizam (1800).

Usually following stages are mentioned by several writers :

(1) East India Company's struggle for equality with Indian States (1740-65).

(2) The policy of Ring Fence (1765-1813)

(3) The policy of Sub-ordinate Isolation (1813-57).

(4) The policy of Sub-ordinate Union (1857-1935).

(5) The policy of Equal Federation (1935-1947).

1. *East India Company's Struggle for Equality (1740-1765)*

This period includes the role of Lord Clive also. This period may be divided into two periods ie. 1740 to 1756 and 1757-1765.

The East India Company was a commercial body with some political ambition. The French Company and the English Company were trade rivals. Dupleix and Clive became the leaders of the opposite parties. With the capture of Arcot in 1751 and the victory in the Battle of Plassy in 1757, a new chapter began in the history of East India Company and the history of India. The English Company acquired political influence also and stood at equal footing with Indian princely states. Clive transformed a mere trading body into a territorial power with the role of king-maker in Bengal.

2. *Policy of Ring Fence* (1765-1813)

The Company became an important power after the Battle of Buxar in 1765 when the Mughal Emperor Shah Alam - II granted the Diwani (the right to collect the fund and revenue) of Bengal, Bihar and Orissa. With this settlement of land revenue, Clive became the founder and a harbinger of the future British rule in India.

Warren Hastings (1774-1785) also showed the British aggressive side to India. He created Oudh as a 'buffer state' for the territories of the Company. At the same time the Company adopted a policy of 'Raising Fences' around its frontiers to survive safely within the 'ring-fence. The Company was not in a very strong position to spread wide its net. The English felt that any attempt to go out of they fence' would may prove harmful and eventually may cost their own territory. The defence of Oudh from the attack of Rohillas and the Marathas constituted the defence of Bengal. Similarly the state of Carnatic was made to act as a 'fence' against the Sultan of Mysore.

Subsidiary Alliance of Lord Wellesley (1798-1805). Wellesley had a very clear mission before him. He wanted to make the East India Company a Supreme Power in India by adding to its territories and reducing all the Indian states to a position of dependence on the Company. He gave up the policy of non-intervention in the affairs of the states. In fact he followed the policy of war and more wars if the native rulers did not accept his policy of Subsidiary Alliance. His considered view was that the policy of non-intervention would only strengthen the enemies of the Company. In his 'forward policy' he was backed by the War Ministry in England. He adopted an offensive attitude towards Indian rulers. He described himself as a 'Bengal tiger' and was always looking for a prey. He made no secret of his views that he considered the annexation of Maratha territories as very conducive not only to the Company but also to the people of these territories. The Subsidiary Alliance System proved very helpful in bringing Indian states within the orbit of British political power. It served the objective of asserting British supremacy in India. Wellesely offered princes a choice of signing of a permanent treaty of subordinate alliance with the Company or facing distablization of the Kingdom and likely dethronement.

The boundaries of British control in India were significantly extended by Wellesely

3. *Policy of Sub-Ordinate Isolation (1813-1857)*

(*a*) *Lord Hasting's Policy towards the Princely States (1815-23).* Sir George Barlon (1805-07) strictly followed the policy of non-intervention. He was succeeded by Lord Minto (1807-13) who was also in favour of following the policy of non-intervention but had to modify his policy in certain cases. His most important achievement was the Treaty of Amritsar (1809) with Maharaja Ranjit Singh. The treaty of friendship was observed by the Company and the Maharaja for about 30 years.

Hastings' policy was guided by a two-fold objective (*i*) To destroy the independence of the Maratha Chiefs and make them accept the Company's supremacy (*ii*) To bring under the Company's protection all harmless states. There were three most important Maratha Chiefs namely the Scindhia, Bhonsle and the Holkar. Since the object of destroying their power could not be achieved through negotiations, Hastings resorted to war. The Maratha Wars resulted in the realisation in great measure the aim of Hastings. Not only was the Maratha power considerably reduced but also vast territories were added to the Company's possessions.

Hastings looked upon the Rajput States as their "natural allies and the natural enemies of the Marathas". Agreements of Friendship were signed with a large number of Rajput States. Nevertheless these agreements were taken as 'subordinatc cooperation' and were rather harsh to the Rajput States.

Lord Hastings brought into the subsidiary alliance 145C states in central India, 145 states in Kathiawar and 20 in Rajputana. He enunciated the policy of complete sub-ordination and Isolation but he avoided the annexation of the Indian States.

(*b*) *Lord Bentinck's Policy towards Indian States (1828-35)* : In difference to the wishes of the Court of Directors of the Company, William Bentinck followed the policy of non-interference into the affairs of Indian states as far as possible. Bentinck, however, departed from the policy of non-intervention and annexed Mysore (1831), Coorg (1834) and Cochin (1834) on the plea of maladministration.

(*c*) *Lord Dalhousie's Policy towards Indian States (1848-56)* : Eight years of Dalhousie's rule are full of important policy decisions and events in every field and especially in the field of expanding British Control and power in India. About his annexation policy, Inne has very aptly remarked, "His predecessors had acted on the general principle of avoiding annexation if it could be avoided, Dalhousie acted on the principle of annexing if he could do so legitimately." Dalhosie's annexations were both of 'war' and 'peace'. While embarking upon the path of annexations, he never bothered about 'violent breach of trust'. Dalhousie's annexations added between a third and a half to the territorial size of British India of 1848. His Policy of Doctrine of Lapse marked a new epoch.

His annexations included the following:

(*i*) Punjab after the victory of the English in the Second Anglo Sikh War (1848-49).

(*ii*) Portion of Sikkim in 1850.

(*iii*) Lower Burma in 1852 after the Second Anglo Burmese War (1852).

(*iv*) Berar in 1853 after a new treaty was forced upon Nizam.

(*v*) Satara (1848), Jaitpur (1849), Sambhalpur (1849), Baghat (1850), Udaipur (1852), Jhansi (1853) and Nagpur (1854) by the application of 'Doctrine of Lapsed.'

(*vi*) Oudh in 1856 on the pretext of misgovernment.

Dalhousie's policy of expansion became one of the important reasons of the 1857 Revolt. Thereafter, a radical change occurred in the policy of the British towards Indian States.

Q. 2. Analyse the Changing attitude of the British towards the Indian States between 1858 and 1935. *(Delhi University 1990, 1992, 1997)*

Ans : *Chief Features of the British Policy Towards Indian States (1858 to 1935)*

After the Revolt of 1857, major changes took place in the policy of the British rulers towards Indian States. Important features of the policy may be summarised as under:

1. The Doctrine of Lapse was given up.
2. No Indian state was to be annexed to the British territory in India.
3. The Indian princes were permitted to adopt.
4. The policy of non-intervention in the affairs of the states was given up.
5. Direct relation between the Crown and the Princes was established.
6. All the Indian States were placed at the same level *i.e.*, the old distinction between the allied and the feudatory states, between dependent and protected states was removed.
7. Government began to get more and more cooperation from the rulers of the states.
8. In due course, an organisation of Indian States was created to discuss

common problems.

Important policy decisions and documents governing relations

1. Queen's proclamation (1858)
2. Lord Canning's policy (1852-62)
3. Trial of Gaekward of Baroda during Northbrook (1874)
4. The Royal Titles Act (1876)
5. Renditions of Mysore (1881)
6. Manipur State Case (1891)
7. Lord Curzon and Indian States (1899-1905)
8. Chamber of Princes (1919)
9. The Butler Committee (1927)
10. Simon Commission (1928)
11. Round Table Conferences (1930-32)
12. Government of India Act (1935)
13. The British Policy vis-a-vis Congress policy on Princely States
14. Indian independence Act 1997

The policy of subordinate Union (1857-1935).

Queen's Proclamation (1858). The Queen's proclamation included, "We hereby announce to the Native Princes of India, that all treaties and engagements made with them by or under the authority of the East India Company are by us accepted, and will be scrupulously maintained, and we look for the like observance on their part".

The Proclamation further said, "We desire no extension of our territorial possession...... We shall respect the rights, dignity and honour of our Princes as our own".

The Proclamation aimed at removing the fear of the Indian Princes.

Lord Canning's Policy (After 1858). Lord Canning gave practical shape to Queen Victoria's Proclamation by granting 140 '*Sanda's* (Instrument or Grants of Adoption) to Hindu and Muslim Princes. He also showed favour to the Indian Princes who had rendered useful service to the British during the Revolt of 1857.

Trial of Gaekward of Baroda (1874). The new policy was to punish the ruler for misgovernment but not to annex the state. The Gaekward of Baroda was tried by a Commission on charge of misgovernment. He was found guilty and removed from his position. A child of the royal family was placed on the throne with a Maratha chief as Prime Minister.

The Royal Titles Act (1876). The Indian Princes standing on a status of equality with the Crown came to an end with the Royal Titles Act. The Title of Empress of India (Kaiser-i-Hind) was conferred on Queen Victoria. Lord Lytton held a magnificent Durbar at Delhi to proclaim the assumption of the new title by the Queen.

Rendition of Mysore (1881). William Bentinck had deposed the Prince of

Mysore on account of misadministration and the state was placed in the hands of English Officers. Lord Ripon reinstated the adopted son of the ruler and this made him very popular with the Indians.

Manipur State Case (1891). There was trouble in the state regarding succession. The British Government sent the Commissioner of Assam with some troops to settle the dispute. He was treacherously murdered by the Commander-in-Chief of Manipur at the time of interview. The British occupied Manipur and put the guilty to death. A minor member of the royal family was put on the throne and the state was not annexed.

In 1891, the Government of India, laid down the following principles.

(*a*) The Government of India have the undoubted right to settle the succession and intervene in the case of rebellion against the chief.

(*b*) Principles of International law could not apply to Indian states.

(*c*) Resistance to the Imperial Orders constitutes rebellion.

(*d*) The Paramount Power (The British Government) has the right to inflict punishment on those who put to death its Agents while discharging their lawful duties imposed on them.

Lord Curzon and Indian States. Lord Curzon followed the policy of patronage' and 'intrusive surveillance.' He issued a circular desiring Indian Princes to devote their energies not in pursuit of pleasures but in the welfare of their subjects and administration. He put restrictions on their trips to Europe. Long absence from India was regarded as dereliction of duty.

Chamber of Princes (1921)

Background the growth of political unrest in British India had put the Government of India on the defensive and the Government thought it expedient and prudent to obtain the support of Indian Princes to counteract progressive and revolutionary developments. The authors of the Montag. Chelmsford Reforms (1919) were of the view that time had come to end the isolation of the Indian rulers and something should be done to provide for joint consultations and discussion between them.

In augurtation of the Chamber : The Government of India consulted the Indian rulers and ultimately the Chamber of Princes was set up on February 8, 1921 by a Royal Proclamation. The ceremony of its inauguration was performed by the Duke of Connaught on behalf of the King of England in the Diwa-i-Aam of the Red Fort in Delhi.

Aims and Objects

A passage of the Proclamation was as "My Viceroy will take its counsel freely in matters relating to the territories of Indian States generally and in matters that affect these territories jointly with British India or with the rest of my empire. It will have no concern with the internal affairs of individual states or their rulers or with the relations of individual states with my Government, while the existing rights of these states and their freedom of action will in no way be prejudiced or impaired".

The Chamber of Princes was the advisory body. Yet it proved very useful to have a common forum to discuss their common problems.

Membership. The Chamber of Princes consisted of 120 members. Out of these 12 members represented 127 states. The remaining 108 members were in individual capacity, being the ruler of important states. As many as 327 states were not given any representation. Some important states did not become its members. Ordinarily the Chamber met once a year and was presided over by the Viceroy. The Chamber elected a Chancellor who presided over the meeting in the absence of the Viceroy:

Evaluation of the Work of the Chamber

The establishment of the Chamber of Princes marked an important step in the development of relations between the Crown and the states for it involved a departure in the earlier policy according to which it was rather the aim of the Crown to discourage joint action and joint consultation between the Indian states and to treat each state as an isolated unit apart from its neighbours. Nevertheless it remained an advisory body only. It did not treat each state on equal footing as the system of representation differed widely. Moreover more than half of the states were not given any representation. Some of the important states did not join it.

The Chamber of Princes accomplished one purpose which was to end the isolation of individual princely states. But it was unable to fulfil its large purposes, that of evolving a common set of principles for the princes to follow and of bridging the gaps between Princely States and British India.

The Butler Committee (1927)

As the nationalist movement in the country gathered momentum, the Government of India appointed the Indian States Committee (after the name of its Chairman Butler), to make recommendations as to how the British hold over the Indian Princes could be perpetuated.

The recommendations of the Committee were criticised by the Indians of all walks of life and especially the nationalist leaders. According to *C.Y. Chintamani,* "The Butler Committee was bad in the origin, bad in time chosen for its appointment, bad in its terms of reference, bad in its personnel and bad in its line of inquiry while its report is bad in reasoning and bad in its conclusions".

According to *Sir Visvesvaryya,* "In the Butler Committee Report, there is no hint of a future for the Indian States people. Their proposals are unsympathetic, unhistorical, hardly constitutional or legal... There is no modern conception in their outlook. Certainly nothing to inspire trust or hope".

Simon Commission (1928). The Simon Commission recommended the creation of a Federation of the Indian States and the Provinces of the British

India as a final choice of the problem.

The Policy of Equal Federation (1935-1947)

Round Table Conferences (1930-32). A series of meetings held in Britain between the British members of Parliament and the representatives of Indian political parties and the Princely States to discuss issues relating to the political set up of India were known as the Round Table Conferences.

Government of India Act 1935 : In the federal structure proposed for the whole of India under the Government of India Act 1935, the Indian States were to be allotted 125 out of 375 seats in the Federal Assembly and 104 out of 260 seats in the Council of States.

The Federation did not come into existence as the requisite number of states did not agree to joint it.

British Policy vis-a-vis Congress policy on Princely States : During the course of the Second World War (1939-45), the All India Congress refused to cooperate in the war efforts of the Government. In 1942, it passed the 'Quit India Resolution'. The British Government put forward several schemes to satisfy the Indian leaders. A section of the Indian Princes was for having independent states even after British India gained independence. The British Government proposed the Cripps Mission (1942), the Wavell Plan (1945) and the Cabinet Mission Plan (1946). In all these proposals, it was held that the British Paramountcy over the Princely States would lapse as soon as India, gain independence but the proposals did not specify the relation of the Princely States vis-a-vis British India.

On the other hand, the All India Congress Committee had declared in a resolution on June 15, 1947 that they cannot admit the right of any Princely State in India to declare its independence and live in isolation from the rest of India". Pt Jawaharlal Nehru declared categorically," We shall not recognise the independence of any state in India; further any recognition of any such independence by any foreign power will be considered an unfriendly act".

Indian Independence Act 1947 : The Act provided that the suzerainty of His Majesty over the Indian States lapses and with that all treaties and agreements in force on that date also lapse. As a result of this provision, the Indian Princely States became completely independent and the Governments of India and Pakistan did not inherit the rights or authority of the former Government of India i.e. British Government. In a nutshell, the Indian Princely States were free to join any dominion they liked, India or Pakistan.

21

Educational, Industrial (De-industrialisation) and Press Policy of the British

Q. 1. Write a critical essay on the System of Education as introduced by Lord Macaulay during the period of Lord William Bentinck.

Ans. *Macaulay's System of Education*

Background. The Charter Act of 1813 had stipulated that "a sum of not less than one lakh of rupees in each year shall be set apart and applied to the revival and improvement of literature and for the introduction and promotion of knowledge of the sciences among the inhabitants of the British territories in India." However, substantial progress could not be made.

Lord T.B. Macaulay's Minute. A sharp controversy had been going on in India on the interpretation and implementation of the policy as contained in the Charter of 1813. With a view to sort out matters during the period of Lord William Bentinck, Lord Macaulay, the Law Member was appointed the Chairman of Public Instruction Committee. Lord Macaulay gave his recommendations in a document which came to be known as Lord Macaulay's Minutes and these Minutes became the basis of the modern system of education in India.

Points of Controversy

1. Who were learned native Indians?
2. What should be the contents of education?
3. What is the meaning of art, literature and science?
4. What should be the medium of instruction?

The Orientalists considered learned Indians having the knowledge of Vedic or Muslim scriptures; art literature and science meant Indian perspective. The medium of instruction should be Indian classical languages like Sanskrit, Persian and Arabic. On the other hand, the Anglicists emphasised knowledge of Western art, literature and science through the medium of English.

Macaulay's Views on Indian and European literature

1. "A single shelf of a good European literature was worth the whole native literature of India and Arabia."
2. Condemning Indian art and literature and sciences he wrote, "We are to

teach false history, false astronomy, false medicine, because we find them in the company of a false religion."

Macaulay's Arguments in Favour of English

Macaulay rejected the claims of Arabic and Sanskrit as against English, because he considered that English was better than either of them. His arguments in favour of English were:

1. It stands pre-eminent even among the languages of the West....It is likely to become language of commerce throughout the seas of the East.
2. In India, English is the language sponsored by the ruling class.
3. It would bring about renaissance in India, just as Greek or Latin did in England or just as the languages of Western Europe in civilising Russia.
4. The natives are desirous of being taught English and are not eager to learn Sanskrit or Arabic, and that demand of the latter was maintained artificially through, "bounty money".
5. It is possible to make the natives of this country good English scholars, and to that end our efforts ought to be directed.

Implications of Macaulay's Policy

It was impossible to educate the body of people, but it was possible through English education to bring about "a class of persons Indian in blood and colour, but English in tastes, in opinions, in morals and in intellect" and that education was to filter down from them to the masses.

Shortly before Macaulay left for England, he expressed before the House of Commons on July 10, 1837, "It may be that the public mind of India may expand under our system until it has outgrown that system, that by good Government we may educate our subjects into a capacity for better government; that having become instructed in European language, they may in some future age demand European Institutions. Whether such a day will ever come I know not. But never, will I attempt to avert it or retard it. Whenever it comes, it will be the proudest day in English history."

Religious Prejudices of Lord Macaulay and Education. In a letter to his father in 1836, Macaulay wrote, "Our English schools are increasing with leaps and bounds and now the condition has reached to a position that it has become difficult to accommodate the students. Hindus are much influenced with education. There is no Hindu who may keep real faith in his religion after studying English. I have full confidence that if our education policy succeeds, then no idolator will be left in Bengal. All this will be done naturally, without any religious preaching and interference.

Acceptance of Macaulay's Minutes and Lord William Bentinck's Resolution of 7th March, 1835. Following points were incorporated in the Resolution.

1. "that the great object of the British Government ought to be the promotion of European literature and science amongst the natives of India and that all funds appropriated for the purposes of education would be best employed on English education alone;
2. "that while the colleges of oriental learning were not to be abolished, the practice of supporting their students during their period of education was to be discontinued;
3. "that Government funds were not to be spent on the printing of oriental works; and
4. "that all the funds at the disposal of the Government would hence forth be spent in imparting to the Indians a knowledge of English literature and science."

Thus William Bentinck's Resolution of 1835 became the basis of future educational policies and programmes of the British Government in India.

Positive effects of the English system of education

(*i*) Spead of modern ideas.
(*ii*) Spread of democratic values.
(*iii*) Generation of anti-imperialistic ideas among a section of the educated Indians.
(*iv*) Promotion of ideas of economic and social equality.
(*v*) Creating awakening leading to religious and social reforms.
(*vi*) Developing spirit at emotional and national integration.
(*vii*) Widening of mental horizon and contact with the western world.

Negative effects of the system of education

(*i*) Neglect of women's education.
(*ii*) Neglect of scientific and technical education.
(*iii*) Overemphasis on Western thought and culture.
(*iv*) Overstress on English language.
(*v*) Creation of unemployment among the educated Indians.
(*vi*) Neglect of Indian culture.
(*vii*) Neglect of Indian languages.
(*viii*) Neglect of mass education.
(*ix*) Indirect spread of Christianity in India.

Q. 2. Write an essay on the policy and growth of education during the British period.

or

Write note on the Education policy of the British from 1813-1904.

(Delhi University 1996)

or

Discuss the development of education between 1854 and 1928.

(Delhi University)

Ans. *Development of the Education Policy of the British in India*

Beginning of the policy (1813). The beginning of the State System of Education in India by the British rulers may be traced back to the year 1813. Its foundations were laid in 1835 by the Minute of Lord Macaulay. This system continud fill India became force.

Clause 43 of the Charter Act of 1813 stated, "It shall be lawful for the Governor-General in Council to direct that out of any surplus which may remain of the rents, revenues, and profits arising from the territorial acquisitions, after defraying the expenses of the military, civil, and commercial establishments and paying the interest of the debt, in manner, here in after provided, a sum of not less than on lakh of rupees in each year shall be set apart and applied to the revival and improvement of literature and encouragement of the learned natives of India and for the introduction and promotion of a knowledge of the sciences among the inhabitants of the British territories in India."

Lord Macaulay's Minute and Lord William Bentinck's Proclamation (1835)

Macaulay's Minutes. Lord Macaulay came to India as a Law Member of the Council of Governor-General on 10th June 1834. He was appointed the Chairman of the Society of the Public Instructions of Bengal by Lord William Bentinck. At that time a violent Oriental and Occidental controversy regarding medium of education in India was very evident. Lord Macaulay was asked to give his advice on the following two issues:

1. Could the granted money of Rs. 1,000,00 be spent in any other way also besides the oriental education?
2. What was the actual meaning of the Article of the charter of 1813.

Lord Macaulay submitted his Minutes on 2nd February 1835 which contained the scheme of education to be followed in India. In his Minutes, he supported the Western education through English medium in India. His Minutes was accepted and Lord William Bentinck issued his Proclamation in March 1935 which set all the controversies and led to the formulation of a policy which became the corner stone of all educational programmes during the British period in India.

Wood's Despatch (1854)

Wood's Despatch came to be known after Charles Wood who was the President of the Board of Control. It was written by John Stuart. It began to guide educational policy in India.

Objects of Educational Policy: Diffusion of European Knowledge. The Despatch observed, "The system of science and philosophy which forms the learning of the East abounds with grave errors, and Eastern literature is at best very deficient as regards all modern discovery and improvement"; and concluded the discussion with the following declaration:

"We must emphatically declare that the education which we desire to see extended in India is that which has for its object the diffusion of the improved arts, sciences, philosophy and literature of Europe; in short, of European knowledge."

The Despatch had the following objectives in view:

1. To confer upon the natives of India those vast and material blessings which flow from the general diffusion of Western knowledge:
2. Not only to produce a high degree of intellectual fitness but also to raise the moral character of those who partake of the above advantages;
3. To supply the East India Company with reliable and capable public servants; and
4. To secure for England a large and more certain supply of many articles, necessary for her manufactures and extensively consumed by her population, as well as an almost inexhaustible demand for the produce of British labour.

In 1857, Universities of Bombay, Calcutta and Madras were established.

Hunter Commission (1882)

Lord Ripon appointed the first Indian Education Commission, known as Hunter Commission, on February 3, 1882, with William Hunter as its Chairman and it came to be popularly known as 'Hunter Commission' after the name of its Chairman.

Terms of Reference of the Commission. "It will be the duty of the Commission to enquire particularly into the manner in which effect has been given to the principles of the Despatch of 1854, and to suggest such measures as it may think desirable in order to the further carrying out of the policy therein laid down."

"It is the desire of the Governor General-in-Council that the Commission should specially bear in mind the great importance which the Government attaches to the subject of primary education. The development of elementary education was of the main objects contemplated by the Despatch of 1854....; the principal object, therefore, of the enquiry of the Commission should be the present state of elementary education throughout the Empire and the means by which this can everywhere be extended and improved."

Policy. Regarding the policy of Government towards primary education, the Commission recommended.

(*i*) That primary education be regarded as the instruction of the masses through the vernacular in such subjects as will fit them for their position in life, and be not necessarily regarded as a portion of instruction leading up to the university.

(*ii*) That while every branch of education can justly claim the fostering care of the State, it is desirable, in the present circumstances of the country, to declare the elementary education of the masses, its provisions, extension, and improvement, to be that part of the education system to which the strenuous efforts of the State should now be directed in a still larger measure than heretofore.

The Hunter Commission anticipated a diversified course for Secondary education.

Indian University Commission (1902)

The Commission appointed by Lord Curzon defined the territorial jurisdiction of each University.

It stressed the need for a strict and systematic supervision of the affiliated colleges by the University....

The secondary schools were to be recognised by the Universities.

Gokhale's Resolution on Primary Education (1913-14)

The Imperical Council rejected G.K. Gokhale resolution on making primary education free and compulsory.

Sadler Commission or Calcutta University Commission (1917)

The Commission was appointed under Dr. M.E. Sadler, of the Leeds University.

The Commission held that for the improvement of University education, reform at the secondary stage was very essential.

A curriculum spreading over three years should be prescribed for the degree of B.A.

The stage of admission to the University should be Intermediate and not Matriculation.

'*Purdah* Schools' for girls upto the age of 15 or 16 should be provided.

It recommended that a Special Board of Women's Education should be set up at Calcutta University to meet educational needs of women.

The Hartog Committee Report (1929)

The Committee is particularly known for its emphasis on primary education. It drew attention to the enormous amount of wastage and stagnation at this stage.

Abbot and Wood Report (1936-37)

The report made recommendations on the development of technical and vocational education.

Basic Education (1937)

Gandhiji was the originator of the system of Basic Education. According to him seven years of free and compulsory primary education should be made craft-centred and self-sufficient to meet its expenditure. Some progress in this direction was made when Congress Ministries were formed during 1937-39 but after that it made no impact.

Post-War Education Scheme or Sargent Report on Education (1944)

The main feature of the report was its suggestion that free and compulsory primary education, would be made available over a period of forty years.

Table 1. Expansion of Primary Education (1881-82 to 1946-97)

Year	*No. of Primary Schools*	*No. of Pupils*
1885	2810	155,000
1881-82	83,000	2,000,000
1901-02	93,004	3,000,000
1921-22	156,007	6,000,000
1936-37	190,000	10,000,000
1945-46	167,000	13,000,000
1946-47	135,000	10,000,000

Note. *It is difficult to compare the statistics of 1946-47 with those of 1936-37 on account of the creation of Pakistan. But the figures of 1945-46 which are of undivided India show that there was a fall in the number of schools but some increase in the number of pupils.*

Table 2. Expansion of Secondary Education and Higher Education.

Type of Institution	*1855*	*1921-22*	*1936-37*	*1946-47**
1. Universities	Nil	10	15	19
2. Arts Colleges	21	165	271	297
3. Secondary Schools	280	2,200	4600	3600

*(*Statistics for Independent India).*

Q. 3. State briefly the positive and negative effects of the British System of Education in India.

Ans. Regarding the role of the British Government in India, Howell has observed, "Education in India under the British Government was first ignored, then violently and successfully opposed, then conducted on a system now universally admitted to be erraneous and finally placed in its present setting".

Main Drawbacks of English System of Education in India

1. It was not related to the needs of India.
2. It was an urban system of education in rural country.
3. English dominated the curriculum.
4. System of education was too bookish.
5. System was examination-oriented.
6. System was very wasteful.
7. System produced clerks by and large.
8. System followed a single track.
9. System was unplanned.
10. System neglected vocational, commercial and technical training.
11. System was very expensive.
12. System was not in accordance with the needs of a free, secular and democratic character.

Prof. Aparna Basu of Delhi University has summed up the positive and negative aspects of English education in India as under.

Positive Aspects of English Education. The introduction of English education was one of a series of acts which collectively opened the doors of the West to the East. In every sphere of modern Indian life, though the influence of tradition persists, the impact of the West can also be traced. Much of the organization of the democratic state, its secular character, the structure of its institutions and the political principles underlying them are all largely European in inspiration. Similarly, the social reforms in Hindu society, the movements for the emancipation of women and for the removal of untouchability reflect western influence to a considerable extent.

Negative Effects of English Education. Negative effects are fairly obvious. The educational system by building up an educated class strengthens the barrier between the upper classes and the masses. The use of English raised the class barrier even higher. The low rate of literacy, the method of teaching, neglect of training of teachers, contempt for manual works, emphasis on a literary education and neglect of technical education which was inevitable in a colonial context and the creation of a gulf between an elite educated in English and the masses—all these constituted formidable obstacles in the path of development.

Q. 4. State the industrial policy and development of industries in India during the British rule.

Ans. *Industrialisation/Deindustrialisation of India* Paradoxically, sometimes the term 'deindustrialisation' is used to denote the state of industrial development during the British rule in India. This is so because the traditional Indian small-scale and cottage industries which were an important source of the import of the wealth from outside, decayed and declined. On the other hand, their place was not filled up by the development of modern industries. This was on account of the discriminatory policy of the British rulers.

Secondly, Whatever Indian industries were developed, they, by and large, were developed with British capital, under British control and for British profit.

Thirdly, the member of workers which the modern industries employed was far less the number of artisans and craftsmen they displaced.

Thus, in the balance, India was getting deindustrialised.

Impact of the 'De-industrialisation' of India. Following were the consequences.

1. There was a heavy drain of India's wealth to England.
2. The working force in the industries went on decreasing. It is estionated that just 03.3 per cent of the people were employed in industries during the period 1911 to 1921. This percentage fell down to 1.00 per cent by 1947.

3. The working force in agriculture increased greatly. The population dependent on agriculture increased from nearly 61 per cent in 1891 to 73 per cent in 1921.

Industries which were almost non-existing during the British rule. Following industries were almost non-existing in India:

(1) Agricultural tractors (2) Automobile tyres. (3) Earth-moving equipment. (4) Cement industry. (5) Medicines. (6) Machine tools. (7) Cotton textile machinery. (8) Jute mill machinery. (9) Sugar mill machinery. (10) Petroleum production. (11) Railway wagons. (12) Motor Cycles. (13) Scooters.

Brief History of Development of Industries in India (Upto the First World War)

Year	*Development of Industries*
1853	Starting of the first cotton textile mill in Bombay by Cowasjee Nanabhoy.
1855	First Jute mill in Risra (Bengal).
1879	56 cotton textile mills in India, employing about 43,000 persons.
1882	20 Jute mills, most of them in Bengal, employing about 20,000 persons.
1901	36 jute mills employing nearly 6,00,000 persons.
1905	206 cotton mills, employing nearly 2,00,000 persons.
1906	Coal mining industry, employing about 1,00,000 persons.
1914	264 cotton mills.

Main Characteristics of Development of Industries in India

1. Lopsided development of modern industries in India. Large parts of the country remained totally undeveloped.
2. Modern industries usually owned or controlled by British capital.
3. Development of large-scale, machine-based industries and not machine-making industries.
4. In several cases even Indian-owned industries controlled by foreign-owned or controlled managing agencies.
5. Slow and stunted growth of modern industries.
6. High profits made by foreign capitalists who invested capital in industries.
7. Easy credit facilities to foreigners and very few for Indians.
8. Predominance of foreign banks. In 1914 foreign banks held over 70 per cent of all bank deposits in India. By 1937, their share had decreased to 57 per cent.
9. Low railway freight rates for British goods and higher for domestic products.
10. Almost complete absence of heavy or capital goods industries; no big plants to produce iron and steel or to manufacture machinery.
11. Lack of basic industries such as steel, metallurgy, machine, chemicals

and oil.

12. Little development of electric power.
13. Growth of plantation industries such as indigo, tea and coffee—almost under European ownership — almost all items of export on a large scale.
14. Development of modern industries without government help and often in opposition to British policy.
15. Paltry development of industries in India as compared with other countries.
16. Employment in modern industries to only about 23 lakh people out of India's total population of 3570 lakhs.
17. Very negligible opportunities of employment to those artisans and craftsmen who were displaced from their traditional industries. According to the estimates of the Indian Planning Commission, the number of persons engaged in processing and manufacturing industries, fell from 10.3 million in 1901 to 8.8 million in 1951, even though the population increased by nearly 40 per cent.
18. Indian trade and industry etc. determined by British interests.

Important Causes of Slow Growth or Backwardness of Industries

1. Discriminatory policy of the British rulers.
2. Export of raw materials from India for providing raw materials to British industries.
3. Lack of capital in India to invest in industries as a result of drain of capital from India and its export to England.
4. Lack of credit facilities.
5. Neglect of technical and vocational education in India.
6. Heavy import duties on Indian goods in England.
7. Restrictions on the sale of Indian goods in England.
8. Higher freight charges of Indian goods by the railways in India, as compared with lower freight charges on foreign goods transported to various parts of India.
9. Policy of free trade followed in India and lack of protection to Indian industry against unfair competition of foreign goods.
10. Competition from machine-made manufactured goods abroad.

Q. 5. Write a note on the growth of Press in India.

Ans. *Growth of Press in India*

Broadly speaking, press performs three functions. *One*, it conveys government policies to the public, *Second,* it keeps government informed of public needs and reactions to government policies. *Third,* it keeps the public and government informed of events and happenings at home and abroad. Press also serves cultural educational, political, religious interest etc also.

At present, their are more than 2000 daily newspapers published in India in different languages with a circulation of over twenty-two million, nearly 8000 weekly journals with a circulation of over seventeen million and over 8000 monthly journals with a circulation of over ten million. The Hindi-language press holds the first position in terms of number of publications well as circulation, followed by the English language press.

The year 1780 saw the publication of a weekly '*The Bengal Gazette*' by J.A. Hickey. For his outspoken criticism, his press was seized in 1782, then came the '*Calcutta Gazette*' in 1784.

In 1823, several restrictions were imposed upon the press. However these were relaxed in 1835.

During the Revolt of 1857, restrictious were reimposed.

The Vernacular Press became critical of the policies of the government after the Revolt of 1857. To check this, Lord Lytton passed the Vernacular Press Act of 1878. This Act discriminated between the English Press and the Vernacular Press. it was nicknamed as 'Gagging Act.' There was wide-spread agitation against it and Lord Ripon repealed it in 1881.

Unpopular acts of Lord Curzon resulted in the growth of anti-government press and the Extremist leaders vehemently criticised the government.

Several restrictions were put on the Press under the Newspaper Act of 1908 and 1910.

After the introduction of 1919 Reforms, the Press Act of 1910 was repealed in 1922.

The Congress started the Civil Disobedience Movement in 1930 and restrictions were again imposed under the Indian Press Act (1931). This Act gave sweeping powers to the government to control the Press.

During the Second World War, government assumed special powers to control the Press. These powers were withdrawn in 1945 when the war ended.

In independent India, Press enjoins a fair degree of freedom. It is free and vocal. It has shown healthy and vigorous growth as an institution.

Many prominent leaders of the freedom movement started newspapers to promote their ideas and awaken the people of India. For instance, Tilak started '*Kesari*' and '*Mahratha*'. Gopal Krishna Gokhale edited the '*Quarterly*', Lajpat Rai Started '*Bande Mataram*' and '*People*' and Gandhiji promoted his views through his numerous journals like '*Indian Opinion*'; '*Young India*', and *Harijan*.

Q. 6. Give a brief account of the development of modern means of transport and communication of India under British Rule.

(Punjab University 1997)

or

Write a short note on development of transport and communication under the British rule in India. *(Punjab University 1998)*

Ans. *Transport Policy*

Transport policy of the British rulers in India was guided by British interests. They realised that a cheap and speedy system of transport was a necessity if British manufactured goods were to flow on a large scale in India and at the sametime India's raw materials secured for British industries. The other consideration for the development of communication was to invest British capital in the railways and to earn huge profits. Still another factor in this regard was the necessity to deploy forces speedily whenever and wherever needed.

Pressure was mounting from British capitalists, industrialists and manufactures on the Government of India and it fell in line with these views as it thought that the development of transport and communication would enable it to administer the country more effectively and efficiently and to protect their rule from internal rebellion or external aggression by enabling more rapid mobilisation and movement of troops.

Railways were also helpful in other ways. They encouraged trade and were helpful in mitigating rigours of caste system because people of different castes travelled in the same compartment.

Development of railways. It was decided that the Indian railways would be constructed and operated by private companies and they would be guaranteed a minimum profit of five per cent on their capital by the Government of India. The first railway line running from Bombay to Thana was opened to traffic in 1853 during the period of Lord Dalhousie. Calcutta was connected with Raniganj coal fields by rail in 1854.

Lord Dalhousie (1848-56) paid special attention to the development of railways. In his famous Minute of 1853, he laid down an extensive programme of railway development. He proposed a network of four railway lines which would link the interior of the country with various parts of the country.

After 1880, railways were built through private enterprise as well as state agency.

Discriminatory policy : The railway policy of the British Government discriminated against Indian manufacture and enterprise. Railway freight rates encouraged foreign imports at the cost of domestic products. It was more costly to transport Indian goods than to transport import goods.

In planning, construction and management, the economic and political development of India and its people was not given due consideration. On the contrary, the primary consideration was to serve the economic, military and political interests of British imperialism in India.

Roads

The first step in the development of roads was taken in the construction of the Grand Trunk Road from Sonargaon near Calcutta to Delhi in 1839 and it was completed in the 1850s later it was extended to Peshawar.

Calcutta had the first metalled road in 1825.

The first motor bus was introduced in Bombay in 1826.

Posts and Telegraph

The first post office was established by the East India Company in Calcutta in 1727.

The first telegraph line from Calcutta to Agra was opened in 1853.

Lord Dalhousie reformed the postal system. A uniform rate of half anna per letter not exceeding half tola was fixed.

22

British India's Foreign Policy (Afghanistan, Burma, Nepal and Sikkim)

Q. 1. State the basic factors which governed India's relations with its neighbours before 1947. Explain its relations with Nepal, Sikkim and Tibet.

Ans. *Background.* India's neighbours with which it had relations of war and peace were: Afghanistan, Bhutan, Burma and Nepal.

India in the east is separated from Burma (Myanmar) by a series of mountain ranges. In the north it is adjoined by Sikkim, Bhutan, Nepal, Tibet and China. In the north west, Afghanistan is India's neighbour. The Gulf of Manner and the Palk Strait separate India from Ceylon (Sri Lanka). This is the picture of British India's neighbours before the formation of Bangladesh and Pakistan and the control of China over Tibet.

Focus on the Foreign Policy of the British Government

India was a prized possession of the British. The British domination in India gradually extended its natural geographical boundaries from the trading factories on the sea-coasts to the ice capped Himalayan hills. The British, therefore, were out to exert a preponderant position in all the adjoining countries, namely Nepal, Burma, Sikkim, Bhutan, Tibet and Afghanistan, They would not allow any other imperialist power to intrude not only into India, but also into her neighbouring countries. Thus, the guiding principles of the British rulers in India were:

(*i*) To maintain their political and economic stronghold in India.
(*ii*) To prevent any other power to make commercial profits at their cost.
(*iii*) To expand their sphere of influence in the neighbouring countries of India and to check the influence of other European or foreign powers.
(*iv*) To expand their empire by capturing India's neighbouring countries.

India's Relations with Nepal

Background. Nepal is in north of India with an area of 1,41,000 sq km

(55,000 sq miles) and a population of about 23 million. Its capital is Kathmandu. The highest mountain in the world, Everest stands just within its frontiers. The Gurkhas, known for their breavery and toughness as soldiers, came from Nepal to join the British army in India. Nepal has the unique distinction of being the only Hindu kingdom in the world.

War with Nepal (1814-16). The Gurkhas had grown in strength by slow degrees and embarked upon a programme of expansion. They established their control over the hilly region, from the frontier of Bhutan in the east to Sutlej in the west. The Gurkhas occupied the districts of Butwal (north of Basti District) and Sheoraj (East of Butwal). These districts were under the British influence. The British reoccupied these areas. This led to more border clashes and war in 1814.

Nepal was invaded by four armies from four different directions. The three British armies had to suffer heavy losses partly because of the bravery of the Gurkhas, and partly on account of lack of knowledge of the topography of the area. The fourth army, however, was successful and the famous Gurkha General, Amar Singh, was defeated. The Gurkhas had to surrender.

Treaty of Saguali (1816): This treaty between the Gurkhas and the British proved very useful to the latter. Following were the outcomes of this treaty:

(*i*) The provinces of Garhwal and Kumaon came under the British rule (*ii*) The British got several hill stations such as Simla. Mussoorie, Almora, Ranikhet, Nainital, Dehradun and Landour (*iii*) The Gurkhas withdrew from Sikkim (*iv*) The Gurkhas abandoned their claim to the Tarai areas (*v*) The Gurkhas accepted to keep a British Resident at Kathmandu.

Importance of the Treaty

(*i*) The treaty of 1816 established an abiding friendship between India and Nepal (*ii*) The recruitment of the Gurkhas in the British army added strength to the British empire (*iii*) The British gained facilities for trade in Central Asia (*iv*) The British got a large territory from Nepal (*v*) The British got several important hill stations (*vi*) Sikkim came under the complete control of the British (*vii*) Nepal served as a buffer state between India and China.

Relations with Sikkim

Background: Sikkim became an integral part of India in 1975. It has an area of 7,300 sq. km with a population of about 4 lakhs. Gangtok is its capital. Sikkim lies in the heart of the towering Himalayas. Kanchenjunga, situated on Sikkim's western border with Nepal, dominates the land.

In the earlier times, the kingdom of Sikkim served as a buffer between India and China. It controlled the trade routes between India and Tibet. In 1835, the Raja of Sikkim was persuaded to cede Darjeeling to the British for an annual payment of Rs. 3,000, which subsequently was raised to Rs. 30,000.

In 1849, a military action was taken against Sikkim as the Sikkim authorities had arrested two British travellers. Some hilly areas of Sikkim were annexed to the British empire. In 1860, Sikkim became a British protectorate when again military action was taken against it.

RELATIONS WITH TIBET

Background: The whole of Tibet covering an area of 1,222,000 sq. km. is a part of the Himalayas. It is the highest country in the world. For centuries, it remained virtually cut off from the outside world. Its population is about 18 lakhs Lhasa its capital. The people of Tibet are the followers of Buddhism with lamas as priests. In 1950, the Peoples Republic of China claimed the country as a province and a few years later, its spiritual leader , the Dalai Lama, came to India and settled down here.

Policy Considerations: The British policy of Tibet was guided by four factors (*i*) Safety of the north frontiers of the British Empire in India (*ii*) Weak hold of China over Tibet (*iii*) Lure of trade and (*iv*) Mineral resources of Tibet. All these factors necessitated some sort of political influence over Tibet.

Events: The conflict with Tibet started in 1887, when the Tibetans invaded Sikkim, which was a protected state under the British. The attack, however, was repulsed. The British tried to establish commercial relations with Tibet but it showed no interest. The British felt that Tibet had been gradually coming under Russian influence. In 1904, Lord Curzon sent an expedition to Tibet and a treaty was signed.

This *Treaty of Lhasa* (1904) contained the following.

(*i*) A war indemnity of Rs. 25 lakhs was imposed on Tibet (*ii*) The Chumbi Valley in Tibet was to be vacated by the British (*iii*) Russia was assured that there would be no interference in the affairs of Tibet by the British (*iv*) The Tibetans assured that they would not allow any foreign power to set their foot in Tibet.

Q. 2. Explain Anglo-Afghan relations. What were the causes of the failure of the British policy in Afghanistan.

or

What were the chief considerations governing Afghan policy of the British rulers in India? To what extent were they successful?

General Background: Afghanistan is an independent nation in Central Asia to the north and north-west of India (now north and north-west of Pakistan). It is land of barren mountains. Although the country is a little larger than France, it has only about 20 million inhabitants, almost all of whom are Muslims. The Pathans among the inhabitants are the most prominent. Dried fruits and lamb skins are the chief exports. Its capital, Kabul, stands on the river of the same name.

Factors Governing India's Relations with Afghanistan

Afghanistan had a crucial importance for the British on account of the following considerations:

1. It could serve as an advanced post outside India's frontiers for checking Russia's military threat.
2. On account of its geographical location, it could conveniently become' a buffer-between the two hostile powers — the British and the Russian.
3. It was placed in such strategic position that it could serve commercial interests of the British in Central Asia.
4. The British wanted to weaken and end Russian influence in Afghanistan.
5. The British wanted to keep Afghanistan a weak and divided country so that they could exercise their influence on it.

Three Afghan Wars: These were fought in 1839-42, 1878-80 and in 1919. The British failed to conquer Afghanistan and it remained an independent country.

The First Afghan War (1839-42)

Forward Policy' of the British and its Failure

Lord Auckland (1836-42), the Governor General of India proposed a resolution on the basis of Subsidiary Alliance to Dost Muhammad, the ruler of Afghanistan, which the latter rejected as it interfered with the freedom of Afganistan. Dost Muhammad's request for compelling Ranjit Singh to return Peshawar to him was not acceptable to Lord Auckland. This led to the first Afghan War.

With a view to exercise their influence in Afghanistan, the British signed an Alliance. The three parties in the Alliance were Shah Shuja, the deposed ruler of Afghanistan, Maharaja Ranjit Singh and the British. The terms were:

1. The British and Ranjit Singh Singh would help Shah Shuja to regain power in Afghanistan.
2. Shah Shuja would formulae his foreign policy according to the British and Ranjit Singh.

Events : The forces of the British, Ranjit Singh and Shah Shuja got victory in Afghanistan. However when the British forces were returning, only one out of 16000 soldiers could survive when attacked by the Afghans.

About the fate of the British in the First Afghan War, it is stated, "The retreat became a rout, the rout a massacre."

It was like a funeral procession.

'*Masterly Inactivity*' of *John Lawrence and others in relation to Afghan Policy after First Afghan War.*

Masterly in activity implied non-interference in the affairs of Afghanistan for about 22 years (1864 - 1874). John Lawrence, the Viceroy of India (1864-69) was the originator of this policy.

After the death of Dost Muhammad' in the war of succession among his sixteen sons, the British adopted the policy of neutrality.

The Second Afghan War (1878—79)

Reason: *Forward Policy in Afghanistan*. There was a change of Government in Britain and the new Government wanted a vigorous policy to be adopted towards Afghanistan. Lord Lytton (1876-80) the Viceroy of India followed the new policy. The new ruler Sher Ali (Son of Dost Mahammad) was asked to accept new terms and on his refusal to do so, an attack was launched upon Afghanistan. The British were successful. Sher Ali fled from Afghanistan.

Treaty of Gandamak This treaty was signed with Yakub Khan, son of Sher Ali. It had the following provisions.

(*i*) Yakub Khan was recognised as the ruler (Amir) of Afghanistan.
(*ii*) The Amir was to conduct the foreign policy under British advice.
(*iii*) A British Resident was to stay at Kabul.
(*iv*) Yakub was to get a subsidy of Rs. six lakhs annually.
(*v*) The districts of Kuram, Pishin and Sibi of Afghanistan were to be ceded to the British.

The treaty of Gandamak was hailed as a great achievement of Lord Lyttons Afghan policy. He very proudly remarked, "We have achieved all that we wanted," In England, Lord Disraeli made a similar statement when he said, "We have acquired the scientific and the most appropriate boundaries of our Indian Empire."

The British success, was, however, very short lived. The national pride of the Afghans had been hurt and once again they rose to defend themselves. In 1879, the British Resident and his escorts were killed. Afghanistan was invaded and the Afghans were defeated but the situation remained war-like. The British ruler's object keeping a British Resident at Kabul was not achieved, Likewise the object of separating Kandhar was not fulfilled. The war at the same time cost a good deal of money. Lytton's Afghan policy was greatly criticised.

Conciliary policy of Lord Ripon

There was a change of Government in Britain and Lord Lytton in India was replaced by Lord Ripon, The Secretary of state for India announced his policy as, "As soon as it is possible let us create those conditions in Afghanistan which existed before the War," Lord Ripon ended the hostile environment and created peaceful conditions.

Third Afghan War (1919)

During the period between 1879 and 1919, relations between Afghanistan and the British remained comparatively cordial. Russia's defeat at the hands of Japan in 1905 and the Anglo-Russian Alliance of 1907, eased the pressure on the Afghan frontiers. Russia accepted Afghanistan outside its sphere of influence and the British also agreed not to change the political status of Afghanistan.

Causes of the Third Afghan War : The First World War (1914-18) and the Russian Revolution (1917) again created bitterness in the Anglo-Russian relationships which in turn affected Anglo-Afghan relationship. The Russian Revolution inspired the Afghans to be completely free from British influence. The Afghan policy of the British to interfere in Afghan affairs annoyed the Afghans. The Afghans raised a revolt against the British. This is called the Third Afghan War.

Treaty of Rawalpindi (1919): The Afghan War ended with this treaty and Afghanistan became completely free in her foreign affairs also.

Failure of the British Policy in Afghanistan

Following were the chief reasons for the failure of the British to conquer and influence Afghanistan:

1. The people of Afghanistan, by nature, were freedom loving. They could be defeated or subdued, but not kept under control for a long period.
2. Afghanistan being a mountainous country, it was not possible to conquer it with ease and once it was conquered, it was not possible to hold it long.
3. The geographical location of Afghanistan is such a strategic one, that it could get assistance from countries like Persia and Russia.

Q. 3. Explain Lord Auckland's policy of Afghanistan. What were its consequences?

or

Discuss the causes and the results of the First Afghan War.

(Delhi University 1992 and 1997)

Strategic Position of Afghanistan and British Policy

Afghanistan situated between Persia, Central Asia and India, occupies a very strategic position on the north-west frontier of India. In the 18th century, Ahmad Shah Abdali had attacked India many times. In the beginning of the 19th century, the fear of Russian expansion loomed large. The Russians defeated Persia in 1826, and the British in spite of their agreement with Persia, did not support it. In view of the fear of Russian invasion on India, the British had to safeguard its nortwest frontier.

Three Anglo-Afghan Wars took place in 1838, 1877-1879 and 1919.

Causes of the First Afghan War. There were five important considerations.

1. There was the fear of Russian invasion on India and it could take place through Afghanistan.
2. There was internal struggle for the throne of Afganistan and the British wanted to exploit this situation.
3. Dost Muhammad Khan, the ruler of Afghanistan was harassed by Maharaja Ranjit Singh who had captured Peshawar. Therefore, he wanted British support.

4. The Persian army was being trained by Russian experts and the army also threatened Hera.

In vies of above, Lord Auckland wanted to have friendly relations with the Afghans but this did not materialise. Dost Muhammad Khan said that he was prepared to enter into friendly alliance with the British provided they would exert influence on Ranjit Singh to get back Peshawar for him. This was not acceptable to Lord Auckland, the Governor-General of India. Then Dost Muhammad Khan entertained the Russian agent. Auckland made a treaty with Shah Shuja, a claimant of the throne of Afghanistan. Ranjit Singh did not agree to allow British troops to pass through his territory. It was, therefore, decided to attack Afghanistan through Sind much against the wishes of the Amirs of Sind and in violation of the Treaty of 1832.

Main events of the War (*i*) *Initial success of the British*. The British forces accompanied by Shah Shuja marched through Sind and occupied Kandhar, Ghazni and Kabul. Dost Muhammad Khan surrendered and was sent to Calcutta as a State prisoner. The British had won the first round of the struggle.

(*ii*) *Unpopularity of Shah Shuja*: *British casualties*. Trouble soon started. Shah Shuja became unpopular as he had become the ruler with the help of the British. The British troops encamped in the open. The number of British troops was reduced in Afghanistan to effect economy. The attitude of some of the British officers was very hostile which irritated the Afghans. Alexander Burnes, one of the most influential English officers was attacked at his residence by the Afghans and cut to pieces. Akbar Khan, son of the deposed ruler Dost Muhammad called upon the British political agent for interview and murdered him. The Afghans attacked the British troops and out of a garrison of 16,000 troops, only one managed to escape and to tell the sad story.

(*iii*) *Recall of Auckland*. When the news of this disarter reached England, Lord Auckland was replaced by Lord Ellenborough.

(*iv*) *Dost Muhammad Khan becoming the Afghan ruler*. Another attack was planned and made. The British forces sacked Kabul. Shah Shuja had already been murdered before the renewed attack. Dost Muhammad was set free and he became the ruler of Afghanistan. He remained friendly with the British till his death.

Criticism of the British in Waging Afghan War

1. Dost Muhammad Khan was an independent ruler and he had every right to make friendship with any power including Russia.
2. The fear of Russian invasion was without any basis.
3. Even if there was any danger of Russian invasion, the powerful Sikh kingdom lay on the way.
4. Dost Muhammad Khan was very popular in Afghanistan. Shah Shuja, the other claimant was no match to him and he was without any worthwhile resources. He was never welcomed in Afghanistan.

5. The British, by sending their troops through Sind, violated the 1832 Treaty.
6. There was little coordination of command. English military officers were not always unanimous on their military strategies.
7. The British officers showed scant regard for Afghan sentiments.
8. Lord Auckland was led away by ill-chosen and unwise advisers.
9. About twenty thousand lives were lost but not even a single inch of territory was gained.
10. The expedition was economically ruinous. About fifteen million stering was spent without my gain.

Some Comments

1. *J. N. Kaye,* in '*History of the War in Afghanistan*' has observed, "No failure so total and so overwhelming as this is recorded in the pages of history."
2. *Trotter* describes this policy as "baneful, lawless and blundering."
3. According to *Dr. V.S. Smith, Lord Auckland* "had, not the sense to see the truth," He termed it as "fantastic policy."
4. *P.L. Roberts* has criticised the Afghan policy in these words, "The Afghan policy of Lord Auckland has met with practically universal condemnation at the hands of historians and every rereading of the evidence deepens and strengthens the conviction that the war was politically one of the most disastrous and morally one of the least justifiable ever waged by the British."
5. *Dr. Ishwari Prasad* has remarked, "Even the Home Authorities (authorities in England) advised caution but Auckland refused to give up his project."

Causes of the Failure of Afghan policy

(*i*) Incapable advisers of Auckland.
(*ii*) Lack of military strategy.
(*iii*) Long journey of the army as Maharaja Ranjit Singh did not permit the British troops to pass through his territory while moving into Afghanistan.
(*iv*) Unpoplarity of Shah Shuja among the people of Afghanistan.
(*v*) British repression on the people of Afghanistan after their initial success in war.
(*vi*) Capability of Akbar Khan, son of Dost Muhammad Khan, who assumed the role of a national leader in the absence of his father and arousal of Afghan sentiment by him.

Q. 4. How and why was Burma important for the British? Critically examine their policies towards the country in the later half of the 19th century? *(Delhi University 1998)*

Ans. *Anglo-Burmese Relations*

Introduction: Three Wars with Burma.

Burma has an area of 678,000 sq km (262,000 sq miles) which is more than five times as large as England. Before 1824, it was an independent state. The British fought three wars in 1824-26, 1852 and 1885 respectively after which the entire territory of Burma came under the British and it became a province of India with a special status. After the passing of India Act of 1935, it was separated from India in 1937. It became an independent nation on January 4, 1948.

Burma's tropical forests produce valuable wood such as teak. Rice is the principal crop. The country is rich in minerals, including precious stones and oil.

During the Second World War, Burma was occupied by the Japanese, but after the defeat of Japan, it again became a part of the British empire.

Burma's importance for the British and Anglo Burmese Wars

Both the powers *i.e.* Burma and the East India Company were imperialist by nature and were trying to extend their influence and control over neighbouring areas. The frontiers of Burma and India were in close proximity with each other. Hence a conflict between two expanding powers was inevitable.

Burma had occupied Manipur and Assam etc. Its boundary touched the territory of the East India Company in India.

The eastern boundary of Bengal remained undefined. So border clash between Burma and the East India company was natural among the competing powers.

The Burmese had the notion that no troops could stand against them.

Following were the important causes of conflict:

(1) Imperial design of the British to expand their empire (2) Checking the influence of the European powers in Burma (3) Procuring profitable commercial opportunities for the British traders by taking advantage of the forest wealth of Burma and also using Burma as a market for their goods (4) Checking the imperialistic desire of the Burmese rulers to expand their kingdom, as by conquering the neighboring territories had already reached the border of British India.

First Anglo-Burmese War (1824-26)

Immediate Causes of the War. There two major reasons.

(*i*) The Brmese made advances on the Chittagong frontier. The fugitives who ran away from the territories conquered by the Burmese took shelter on the British border and began to use it as their base to reconquer their lost territories. The East India Company declined to surrender them to the Burmese Government.

(*ii*) The Burmese occupied the island of Shahpuri, a small island near Chittagong and the Burmese threatened an invasion of interior Bengal.

Main events. In 1824, the First Burmese War broke out. After some initial reverses, the British forces drove the Burmese out of Assam, Cachar, Manipur and Arkan. Rangoon was occupied and the British forces reached very near Alva, the capital of Burma.

Treaty of Yandabo

According to this treaty, the Burmese Government agreed (*i*) to pay one crore of rupees as war compensation (*ii*) to part with its coastal provinces of Arakan and Tenasserim (*iii*) to abandon all claims on Assam, Cachar, and Jaintia (*iv*) to recognise Manipur as an independent state (*v*) to negotiate a commercial treaty with Britain (*vi*) and to accept a British Resident at Alva, the capital of Burma.

The Second Burmese War took place in 1852, primarily on account of the imperialist and expansionist policy of Lord Dalhousie. Of course, the excuse, was that the Burmese ruler did not honour his commercial commitment. This time, the War was shorter than in 1824-26. The British annexed Pegu, the only remaining coastal province of Burma. The Burmese fought guerilla war for about three years but without any success.

After the annexation of Pegu, relations between Burma and the British remained cordial for about two decades.

The Third Burmese War was fought in 1885 on account of two reasons. one, the Burmese king wanted to establish commercial relations with France — an action not liked by the British. Second, the Burmese ruler imposed a heavy fine on a trading company associated with the British. The British forces attacked Burma and with two weeks of fighting, Burma was captured and annexed to India.

Results of the Burmese Wars

1. Upper Burma was annexed by the British and this completed the conquest of the whole of Burma.
2. The British made Rangoon as the capital of Burma.
3. Now the British empire extended upto China.
4. Burma was made a province of the British India. (It was separated from India after the Indian Act of 1935).
5. India had to bear a very heavy economic burden on account of Burmese wars. The entire expenditure incurred on 40,000 soldiers who were deployed in the Burmese wars was borne by India without any benefit to its people. Hundreds of soldiers also lost their lives.

Critism of the Burmese policy of Lord Dufferin

The Burmese policy of the British rulers has been greatly criticised by historians. The critics, however, forget that the imperialist powers have there own yardsticks and they always justify their actions. *P. E. Roberts* has very aptly remarked, "The ethics of the relations between powerful western empires and weak Eastern nations are admittedly difficult to disentangle but it is to be feared that the abstract rights of semi-civilised countries receive scant recognition, when great colonising powers converge upon them." While agreeing with the remarks of Roberts, one fails to understand when he uses the term 'semi-civilised.' In other words, the British rulers were civilised although they were plundering the weak countries. "Might is right" is the dictum that determines their ethics. It was true in the past, is true in the present and perhaps will remain true for years to come.

Following are the points of criticism of British's Burmese Policy:

First, it is said that the Burmese ruler was a tyrant and the British wanted to teach him a lesson. It is argued against this that it was an internal affair of Burma and the British had no right to interfere in the internal affairs of an independent country. Second, it is said in the defence of the British, that the British merchants were not properly treated. This, however, did not justify war. The merchants could have stopped trading with Burma if circumstances were not favourable to them.

Third, the British had the suspicion that the ruler of Burma was in communication with the French - the sworn enemies of the British. In this context, it is stated that every country is free to make friendship with country of its own choice. The Burmese ruler was a sovereign and was free to have relations with any foreign power.

The fact is that the proverbial story of 'wolf and the lamb' presented the ideal before the British rulers in their dealings with the week and the helpless.

23

Socio-Religious Movements : Indian Renaissance : Status of Women

Q. 1. Discuss the features of some of the leading religious reform movements in the nineteenth century. *(Delhi University 1997)*

or

Discuss the various socio-religious reform movements in the 19th century India to reform religion and society. *(Delhi University 1995)*

or

What were the distinctive features shared by the major socio-religious reform movements of the nineteenth century.

(Rajasthan University 1993)

Ans. *Socio-religious Reform Movements*

Interlinked Social and religious reforms : The social and religious movements in India in the nineteenth century were interlinked. These movements were complementary as well as supplementary. By and large, all the reformers of the nineteenth century emphasised religious and social reforms.

Circumstances leading to the emergence of religious and social movements.

The nineteenth century was marked by strenuous attempts to rediscover, reassess and regenerate Indian society by eschewing orthodoxy and eradicating social evils which had been eating the very vitals of the Indian society and especially the Hindu society. The religious and social reformers emphasised that the truths revealed by the sages and theologians of ancient ages in India, should be seen in the right perspectives.

The main streams of the new movements may be summed up as purging of society of superstitutions reaping the fruit of science and restoration of the ancient glory of the society. There were movements in almost every part of India. The leaders of the movements made missionary tours over different regions of the country for promoting a rational outlook.

Leaders of the movement : Raja Rammohan Roy (1772-1833), Keshav Chandra Sen (1838-1878), Mahadev Govind Ranade (1842-1900); Swami Dayanand (1825-83), Ramkrishna Parmhansa (1836-1886) and Swami Vivekanand (1863-1902) were the most outstanding reformers among the Hindus.

Among the Muslims, Sir Syed Ahmed Khan (1817-1898) was the chief reformer

Narayan Guru (1854-1928) made a great contribution to the emancipation of the oppressed sections of the society in Kerala.

Jotiba Phule (1827-1890) was a great religious and social reformers of Maharashtra.

Important religious and Social Movements.

These were as under:

1. The Brahama/Brahmo Samaj.
2. The Arya Samaj.
3. The Ramkrishna Mission.
4. The Aligarh Movement.
5. The Theosophical Society.
6. The Rehnumai Mazdayan Sabhi among Parsees.
7. The Namdhari Movement among the Sikhs.
8. The Singh Sabha Movement (among the Sikhs).
9. Satya Shodak Samaj.
10. The Veda Samaj.
11. The Prarathna Sabha.

Common features of the social reform movements of the second half of the 19th century.

(*i*) The movements were concerned with the regeneration of society through educational and social reforms.

(*ii*) They were based on religious scriptures.

(*iii*) These were not confined to the people professing one particular religion. The covered almost all religions.

(*iv*) They laid stress on the emancipation of women, promotion of their education, raising the status of widows, abolition of the practice of *Sati* and removal of *Purdah* etc.

(*v*) Belief in one God and His worship.

(*vi*) Abolition of caste system and untouchability.

(*vii*) No image worship.

(*viii*) Rationalism and scientific attitude.

(*ix*) Universal brotherhood.

(*x*) Service to the needy.

Common important ideas that influenced the religious and social reform movements of the 19th century.

Rationalism and universalism were the two important ideas that influenced the movements in the religious and the social field.

Rationalism implied acceptance of ideas by reasoning and not by blind faith. It meant repudiation of supertition.

Universalism meant a belief in the unity of brotherhood as well as godhood.

It was inherent in showing love and respect for the beliefs and ideas of others.

Social Reformers As Well As Religious Reformers

(*i*) The social reformers were religious reformers also. They tried to promote social reforms on the basis of religious scriptures. For instance, Swami Dayanand, the founder of the Arya Samaj worked for the eradication of ritualistic dogmas and superstitious practices by quoting the Vedas. He made the Vedas as the foundation and the basis of social reforms. He proved from the study of Vedas that women should be given an equal status with men. He worked for the abolition of caste system as it had no sanction of Vedas. In the same way, other reformers encouraged interpretation of religious texts based on rational and scientific thinking. At no stage, the social reformers disregarded religious books and their teachings.

(*ii*) The social reformers struck a balance between religion and social reforms as under:

  (*i*) All religions advocate welfare of humanity. So welfare schemes such as opening of hospitals were encouraged.

  (*ii*) All religions call for the removal of ignorance. So social reformers advocated the opening of educational institutions.

  (*iii*) All social reformers encouraged scientific education to dispel superstition.

  (*iv*) All social reformers laid stress on equality. Thus they condemned caste system and untouchability.

  (*v*) They encouraged Indians to develop self-confidence to improve their lot rather than depend upon destiny.

No Desire to Start New Religions

A perusal of the life, works and teachings of reformers who worked for religious and social reforms in the Hindu society clearly establishes the fact that they desired to purify the Hindu religion. They based their teachings on the Vedas, the Upanishads and several other Hindu scriptures. They asked their followers to interpret the ideas contained in these books on the basis of reason. Swami Dayanand and Swami Vivekanand stressed that the Vedas preach the worship of one God, provide equality to all sections of society, accord respectable position to women, and emphasised the well being of all. They quoted the scriptures to show that there is no place for superstition, caste system and untouchability.

Effect of the religious and social reform movements on national awakening?

The religious and social reform movements especially the Arya Samaj and the Ramakrishna Omission under the dynamic and inspiring leadership of Swami

Dayanand and Swami Vivekanand respectively attempted to glorify the past cultural, philosophical and other achievements of India. They held out the promise that Indians by their own efforts and with self-confidence were capable enough to countercheck the influence of the foreigners and raise the countries to new heights of glory.

The reformers like Raja Rammohan Roy promoted the ideals of equality and fraternity which helped 'national awakening'. Some of the Western educated reformers began to visualize the evil consequences of the economic exploitation of India by imperialist rulers.

Important Regulations Relating to Social Reforms

(*i*) *Checking Female Infanticide.* The Bengal Regulations of 1795 and 1804 made female infanticide equivalent to committing murder and punishable accordingly.

(*ii*) *Banning 'Sati' Practice.* In 1829, Wiliam Bentinck banned the *'Sati'* practice.

(*iii*) *Restriction on Child Marriage.* In 1872, the Native Marriage Act was passed which disallowed the marriage of girls below 14 and boys below 18 years. But its enforcement was limited to a few sections of society. The most effective step was taken in 1930 when the Sarda Act was passed which raised the marriage age of girls to 14 and of boys to 18. In 1978, the marriage age of girls was raised to 18 and of boys to 21.

(*iv*) *Widow Remarriage.* The Hindu Widow's Remarriage Act of 1856 legalised marriage of widows. The Hindus were not covered by this Act.

Main Limitations of the Movement

1. They were mostly confined to urban areas.
2. They covered a fringe of population of the country.
3. The villagers remained on the mercy of priests.
4. The reforms had legal force behind them.
5. The reforms overemphasised the past glory which developed a false sense of pride.
6. Sometimes reforms created hatred among different sections of population.
7. The overzealous protagonists of reforms sometimes created walls of separation among the orthodox and the progressive people.
8. Occasionally reforms led to severe clashes resulting even in deaths sometimes.

On the whole, reforms gradually led to a new awakening.

Q. 2. "Dayanand's revivalist movement was accompanied by a radical social message". Comment. *(Rajasthan University 1995)*

or

Evaluate Swamy Dayanand's contribution to social and religious reform movement. *(Delhi University 1995)*

SWAMI DAYANAND (1825-1883)

The great path finder and path maker. Born in a Brahman family of Gujarat, Dayaram Mulshankar who later on became Swami Dayanand, from the very beginning was seized of the desire to fathom the mysteries of life and death. At the age of 19, he left home and wandered almost all over India in quest of knowledge and truth. At last he found his 'guru' in Swami Virjanand. To his master, he pledged to devote his life to disseminate truth, to wage unremitting war against falsehood and to work for the establishment of a right religious and social order in the society. He found the true way of life in the Vedas. In the Vedas, he sought the solution of the problems of human ignorance and misery. He spent his entire life in preaching, teaching and writing books to disseminate true knowledge. He emitted a lot of thunder and light. His goal was to dispel darkness and pessimism and to spread light and optimism, to destroy superstitious mentality and fraud and instead to develop a scientific temperament and rationalism, to annihilate bigotry and encourage liberalism. He was a nationalist to the core and was opposed to foreign rule. He declared as early as 1875 that a 'good government' was no substitute for 'self-government'.

On account of his valuable contribution to the religious and social field, Rabindranath Tagore has paid him a glorious tribute as, "The great path-maker in northern India, who through bewildering tangles of creed and practice, the dense undergrowth of the degenerate days of our country - cleared a straight path that was meant to lead the Hindus to a simple life of devotion to God and service for man".

Go back to the Vedas : Vedic Wisdim. Swami Dayanand's interpretation of Vedas has brought a new vista of knowledge in the sphere of religious and social reform and educational reconstruction. His belief in the Vedas has been hailed by savants of the East and the West. Sri Aurobindo has said, "There is then nothing fanatical in Dayanand's idea that the Veda contains truth of science as well as truth of religions. I will even add my own convictions that the Vedas contains other truths of a science which the modern world does not at all possess and in that case, Dayanand has rather understated than overstated, the depth and range of the Vedic wisdom." *Edward Carpenter* in his *'Art of creation'* has observed, "The same germinal thoughts of the Vedic authors came all the way down history even to Schopenhauer and Whitman, inspiring philosophy after philosophy and religion." It would, therefore, not be superstition to discover the echoes of the Vedic past reverberating in his religious, social and educational thinking and practice.

Swami Dayanand's emergence at a critical juncture : Swami Dayanand, according to Dr. S. Radhakrishnan emerged at a time when there was spiritual confusion in our country, when many of our social practices were in the melting pot, when we were overcome by superstition and obscurantism, this soul came forward with staunch devotion to truth and a passion for social equality and enthusiasm and worked for the emancipation of our country".

Swami Dayanand as a religious reformer

1. *Universality of True Religion.* Dayanand's conception of the religion in his own words was, "I believe in a religion based on universal and all embracing principles which have always been accepted as true by mankind and will continue to command the allegiance of mankind in the ages to come".

Describing the aim of his life, he wrote, "The sole aim of my life, which I have also tried to achieve, is to help to put an end to the mutual wranglings, preach universal truth, bring all men into the fold of one religion whereby they may cease to hate each other and instead, may firmly love one another, live in peace and work for their common weal. May this doctrine, through the grace and help of God and with the support of all truthful, honest and learned men, who are devoted to the cause of humanity may reach every nook and corner of this earth so that all may acquire righteousness".

2. *Conception of One God* : There is only one God and Who is the source of all true knowledge. He is Existent, Conscious, All Beautilude, Formless, Almighty, Just, Merciful, Unbeggotten, Infinite, Unchangeable, Beginning less, Omniscient and Controler of all form within, Evermature, Imperishable, Fearless, Eternal and Creator of Universe. To Him alone is worship due.

3. *The Vedas–source of all knowledge.* He observed, "My conception of God and all other objects in this universe is founded on the teachings of the Vedas and other *shastras* (scriptures)". From where should men derive courage and inspiration to attain the ideals of their lives? From the Vedas, is the answer.

4. *No belief in endless rituals.* He propagated the view that the long established Brahmanical practices of '*Karmakanda*' (ritualism), '*moortipooja*' (idol worship) and '*avtaravad*' (theory of incarnation) are not the essence of Hindusism.

5. *Faith on transmigration of Soul.* Dayanand believed in the doctrine of transmigration of soul or rebirth and of '*Karma* (fruit of one's deeds).

6. *Harmony between the knowledge of the Vedas as science.* Finding the faulty existing commentaries on the Vedas, he himself wrote commentaries on them and pointed out that the knowledge contained in the Vedas is in complete accord with science.

7. *Synthesis between the Spiritual and Material :* He maintained that the Vedas contain the basic principles of spiritual as well as practical wordly knowledge and that they should be suitably harmonised in our daily lives.

8. *Practical ways of life.* He pointed out that the Vedas were not meant for recitation on religious and social occasions but they were meant to guide us in

our daily activities as householders and as social beings. They were also to govern the relations of the rulers and the governed.

Swami Dayanand as a social reformer

By quoting the relevant portions of the Vedas, Swami Dayanand showed that there was no place for social evils like caste system, child marriages, polygamy, custom of '*Sati*', and inferior status of women and untouchability.

Dayanand emphasised that women, beings the emblem of creative power and representative of motherhood must be treated with respect. He advocated equal rights for men and women in all respects: in marriage, in the matter of property and in the study of the Vedas and Shastras. Discarding *'Purdah'* completely, he believed in the complete emancipation of women.

It was Dayanand's belief that the division of the Hindu society into innumerable caste and communities was one of the causes of India's downfall. A friend of the *'depressed'* or the so called untochables, he raised his strong voice against the social and religious inqualities from which they suffered. He advocated treating them on equal basis and taking special steps to improve their lot.

Dayanand appealed to the people to open orphanages and widow homes.

Dayanand as an Educational Reformer

Dayanand considered education as the most important instrument of religious and social reforms in the society. Only education could dispel darkness and bring light to the ignorant. While he wanted traditional subjects to be taught he was equally in favour of modern subjects to be taught. He maintained that all sections of the society had full right to education. He specially advocated the education of girls and women. He was convinced that unless education was given on right lines and the boys and girls led a life of complete *'brahmcharya'* (celebacy), the nation would not be able to become happy and prosperous.

Right conduct of life for rejuvenating religious, social and national life

For all the people belonging to four *Ashramas'–'Brahamacharis* (Students), *'Grihasthis'* (Householders), *'Vanaprasthis'* and '*Sanyasis*', Swami Dayanand laid down the following ten characteristics.

1. Cultivation of firmness of mind and contentment.
2. Cultivation of the spirit of forgiveness under all circumstances - whether one be censured or praised, honoured or dishonoured etc.
3. Devotion of mind to virtue and abstinence from sin and vice, that is refraining from the entertainment of sinful thoughts even for one moment.
4. Non-acquisition of a thing without the permission of its owners or fraud, hypocrisy, or breach of faith or by teaching falsely or in any other way that is condemned by the Vedas which is called dishonesty or theft. The reverse of it is called honesty.

5. Mental purity which consists in freedom from inordinate love or hatred, from prejudice or injustice, etc. Bodily cleanliness which consists in keeping the body clean.
6. Direction of the senses in the path of rectitude, and freedom from sin.
7. Development of one's intellect by abstaining from intoxicants and other things that are prejudicial to its growth, from the company of the wicked, from sloth, negligence, etc and by using things possessing healthful properties, associating with men of noble character and by the practice of yoga.
8. Acquision of correct knowledge of all things.
9. Truthfulness in the harmoney of thought, word and deed.
10. Freedom from wrath and other evil habits and the cultivation of calmness of mind and other good qualities.

Spread of his teachings by Swami Dayanand

Swami Dayanand adopted the following measures for the spread of his message

1. Lectures at various places
2. Debates and discussions
3. Publication of Journal
4. Personal example
5. Founding of the Arya Samaj
6. Publications, Swami Dayanand published more than twenty books and periodicals. His most important publication is *'Satyarth Prakash'* (Light of Truth).

The *Satyarth Prakash,* the monumental work of Swami Dayanand consists of the following chapters.

Chapter 1.	Deals with the Vedic concept of God.
Chapter 2.	Describes the care and education of the children.
Chapter 3.	Outlines recommendations for a system of education as well as for religious and social observances.
Chapter 4.	Discusses the '*varna*' or caste system.
Chapters 5, 6, 7.	Contain views on *'ashrams'*, government and theology.
Chapter 8.	Deals with the theory of creation.
Chapter 9.	Explains the concepts of true knowledge, ignorance and salvation.
Chapter 10.	Incorporates the rules of conduct.
Chapters 11,12,13 and 14.	Include a critical commentary on various religious systems in India.

Contribution of Swami Dayanand

The force of his logic, the power of his oration, the depth of his scholarship, the dazzle of his intellect, the compassion of his heart, the sincerity of his purpose, the overpowering spirituality of his multi-dimensional personality and his profound mastery over the language swayed the masses and evoked spontaneous reverence from them. It is, therefore, natural that a band of devoted workers gathered around him and promoted his teachings.

About the contribution of Swami Dayanand, *Sir Jadunath Sarker* has observed, "When the history of India's growth comes to be written, the high rank will be adjudged to the '*naked faquir*' Dayanand Saraswati. He rescued the heart of Hindustan from atrophy; he linked it with the spirit of eternal progression ruling the outerworld; he proved that whatever is best and truest in the legacy of ancient sages of Aryavarta, is possession open to the entire human race and not confined to any twice born or the sacred soil".

Swamy Dayanand was truly a shining star of Indian Renaissance. He had the rare qualities of religious path maker, an enlightened social reformer and a political philosopher - all combined into one.

Q.3 Describe the origin and growth of the Arya Samaj with special reference to its contribution in the field of socio-religious, educational and political reforms. *(Punjab University, Oct. 1998)*

Ans: *Arya Samaj : A Reformist Movement*

Background of the founding of Arya Samaj. By the middle of the nineteenth century, India found itself bewildered in a welter of cultural ideas. Politically powerless under the British rule, it yielded to the way of a foreign civilization which in many respects was not in accordance with its honour. A moral breakdown had shaken its faith in the potency of its old age culture and civilization. The First War of Independence was an attempt to find an anchorge, but its failure swept it off the old cultural moorings. What remained was a moral anguish shrouded with the heavy gloom of despondency. Indian culture, religion and philosophy were under severe attack at the hands of the Christian missionaries. Under the impact of Western thought, several sections of the educated Indians also began to lose their faith in this past glory. Under such a situation a great prophet emerged in Swami Dayanand who founded the Arya Samaj in 1873 to provide a new direction to the Hindu society by reinterpreting the Vedas and bringing into light the splendid thoughts contained therein.

Mission of the Arya Samaj: The Arya Samaj is envisaged to awaken India through its past, to arouse the pride of the Hindus in their cultural heritage and adhere strictly to the Vedas which it holds to be the sole source of all knowledge.

The message of Arya Samaj as will be seen from its '*Ten Principles*' is universal and meant for the welfare of mankind. It tends to make all people

Aryas (noble people), physically and spiritually developed, materially prosperous, mentally and morally uplifted and socially, nationally and internationally united.

Ten Principles of the Arya Samaj

1. God is the primary source of all true knowledge and of all that can be known through it.
2. God is Existent, Intelligent and Blissful. He is Formless, Almighty, Just, Merciful, Unborn, Infinite, Unchallengeable, Beginningless, Incomparable, the Support and Lord of all, Omniscient, Imperishable, Immortal, Fearless, Eternal, Holy and the Maker of universe. To him alone worship is due.
3. The Vedas are scriptures of true knowledge. It is the duty of all Aryas to read them, hear them being read and recite them to others.
4. We should always be ready to accept the truth and give up untruth.
5. All actions should be performed in conformity with Dharma, that is, after due consideration of right and wrong.
6. The primary aim of the Arya Samaj is to do good for all, that is, promote their physical, spiritual and social well-being.
7. We should treat all people with love, fairness and due regard for their merit.
8. We should aim at dispelling ignorance and promoting knowledge.
9. One should not only be content with one's own welfare, but should look for it in the welfare of others also.
10. One should regard oneself under restriction to follow altruistic rulings of the society, while all should be free in following the rules of individual welfare.

Contribution of Arya Samaj to the field of education

Realising that lack of education as an important cause of India's backwardness, Swami Dayanand laid great stress in the spread of all types of education including industrial and vocational.

D.A.V. Schools

On June 1, 1886, the followers of Swami Dayanand founded the D.A.V. School, Lahore under the leadership of Mahatma Hansraj (1864-1938) in memory of Swami Dayanand. This school later on was upgraded to a college. Since then this movement has assumed gigantic proportions and at present there is a long chain of D.A.V. (Dayanand Anglo Vedic) institutions spanning the country avowedly with the following objectives.

1. To encourage, improve and enforce the study of Indian literature.
2. To encourage and enforce the study of classical Sanskrit and of the Vedas.

3. To encourage and enforce the study of English literature and sciences, both theoretical and applied.
4. To provide means for giving technical education not inconsistent with the above three aims.

Arya Schools and Colleges

Several educational institutions are also run under the name of Arya Schools and Colleges and which are not managed by the D.A.V College management Trust but by other Arya Samajs established at local or provincial level.

Gurukuls

Swami Shraddhananda (1857-1926) another devoted follower of Swami Dayanand, chose to establish a Gurukula patterned on the ancient system of Ashrams in the Sylvan surroundings of the Kangri village on the eastern bank of the Ganges near Hardwar. In this institution, a great emphasis was laid on the teaching of Vedic scriptures while at the same time modern sciences were not ignored and were duly included in the curriculum. This movement also gathered momentum in course of time and now well nigh about hundred Gurukuls are dotted all over the country separately for boys and girls.

One section of Arya Samaj led by Lala Lajpat Rai and Mahatma Hansraj established D.A.V. Schools and colleges, while the other section led by Swami Shraddhanand established Gurukuls.

The number of D.A.V. institutions in united Punjab of British days (before 1947) was so large that it exceeded those established by all other denominations put together. The number of graduates in Punjab who had received education in D.A.V institutions was also so large that in the election to the Senate of Punjab University at Lahore, the majority used to consist of those who were associated with D.A.V. institutions.

On the organisational side, who worked to strengthen it, two names stand out. They were Lala Sain Das (1841-90) in Punjab and Pandit Bhagvandin Mishra in UP.

Work of Arya Samaj in the Social Field

Arya Samaj has produced a galaxy of social reformers. It has been doing a lot of humanitarian work. Arya Samaj's social work includes opening of orphanages, widow homes, oldage homes, service during national calamities like earthquakes, epidemics, floods and droughts etc. It has helped scores of poor families at the time of the marriages of their daughters.

It has been working towards the eradication of caste distinctions, untouchability, raising the status of women and increasing the age of marriage.

It has been making efforts towards equality of sexes, justice and fair play between man and man.

Arya Samaj has opposed polygamy, *'parda'* system and the practice of *'Sati'* by spreading education. It has attempted to develop social awakening. Arya Samaj supports social equality.

Work of Arya Samaj in the field of religion

The Arya Samaj emphasises the teaching of the Vedas. It promotes the concept of one God - God that is Omnipotent, Light behind all lights. Force behind all force. It provides an ethical and spiritual code. It attempts to present the noblest aspects of Hinduism. It works for the stoppage of idol worship.

It also strives to prevent the conversion of Hindus to other religions. It takes up the *'Shuddhi'* work i.e. reconversion of non-Hindus to Hindus.

It advocates *'Sandhya'* (Worship of God) every morning and every evening.

It emphasises the importance of *'Swadhya'* (self study) of portions of scriptures everyday.

It attempts to promote the ideal of service to humanity and considers it a very sacred religious duty.

Work of Arya Samaj in the Political Field

The Arya Samaj, though primarily a religious and social organisation indirectly greatly contributed to Indian nationalism. Swami Dayanand, its founder was the first to use the word *'Swaraj'* (self rule) and declared Hindi as the national language of India. He clearly stated that the foreign rule even when "imbued with parental justice and kindness, could not be substitute for self rule. Foreign government cannot be perfectly beneficial even when it is free from religious bias and race prejudice". He further observed, "Regeneration of India is difficult to achieve without having one language, one faith and one aim". Many leaders of the Arya Samaj were in the forefront of the freedom struggle of the country. Among the important leaders, mention may be made of Lala Lajpat Rai, the 'Lion of Punjab', Ajit Singh (Uncle of Bhagat Singh), Bhagat Singh and Lala Hardyal. Veer Savarkar, Shyamji Khosla, B.G. Tilak and Gopal Krishna Gokhale were also influenced by the philosophy and principles of Arya Sabha. About Arya Samaj's influence on him, Lajpat Rai said, "All that was good and creditable to me, I owe to the Arya Samaj.... It was the Arya Samaj that instilled into me, love for the nation.. I learned my lessons in public life from and in the Arya Samaj. It was there that I saw the models of purity in public life and there I made my dearest friends. I am under enormously heavy debt to the Samaj. I should not be able to pay back what I owe". Bhagat Singh, 'the martyr among martyrs' was the product of the D.A.V. College, Lahore.

Thousands of students who had received their education in the D.A.V institutions took part in the freedom struggle and in various other programmes of national development.

Spread of Arya Samaj

The Arya Samaj has established a network of its units in India and abroad. There are about 5,000 Arya Samajs in India and abroad, 200 provincial and district councils, 300 Arya Vir Dal units, 200 Arya Kumar Sabhas (for boys and girls); 1000 colleges and schools, 2000 primary and middle Schools, 100 Gurukuls, 300 Sanskrit *pathshala*, 10 technical institutions, 200 orphanages, several charitable dispensaries, women homes, old age homes, *goshalas*, newspapers, periodicals and reading rooms etc.

About the work done by the Arya Samaj, *Jawaharlal Nehru* wrote in the *'Discovery of India'* as, "it has done very good work in the spread of education both among boys and girls, in improving the condition of women and in raising the status and standards of the depressed classes"

Q. 4. Write an essay on the role of Swami Vivekanand in the awakening of India. *(Rajasthan University 1995)*

or

Explain the contribution of Swami Vivekanand to religious and Social reform. State the main functions of Ramakrishna Mission founded by him.

Ans: *Swami Vivekanand (1863-1902)–Prophet of New Awakening : Chief Contributions*

1. *Clarian Call to the nation*: Swami Vivekanand was keenly interested in the development of all aspects of national life. He was a 'Karma Yogi' who believed in ceaseless constructive action. He drew the attention of his country men to the various ills from which it was suffering and gave a clarion call "Arise! Awake and Stop not till the goal is reached".

Swami Vivekanand has been hailed as "Awakener of Modern India', Nation Builder', 'Man-Maker', 'Synthesiser of Science and Religions. Synthesiser of the Moral and Material and Synthesiser of Intellect and Physique'.

2. *Love for the Motherland* : To him love for the motherland was the first commandment and religion came next. In her book, "*The Master' I Saw him*" sister Nivedita wrote, "Throughout those years in which I saw him almost daily the thought of India was to him like the air he breathed. True, he was a worker at foundations. He never used the word 'nationality' nor proclaimed an era of 'nation making'. 'Man-making', he said was, a his task. But he was born lover and the queen of his adoration was his Motherland."

3. *What is national awakening and love for the motherland?* Swami Vivekanand was not content merely with preaching but his message was the service of the poor and the lowely and he called upon his countrymen to shake off the age-old lethargy, remove the abuses which had crept into their society and work for the reconstruction of their country.

He appealed to the educated, "So long as the millions live in hunger and ignorance, I hold every man a traitor who, having been educated at their expense, pays not the least heed to them. I consider that the greatest national sin is the neglect of the masses and that is one of the causes of our downfall."

Swami Vivekanand repeated his theme, "O India ! Forget not that the lower classes, the ignorant, the poor, the illiterate, the cobbler, the sweeper are thy flesh and blood". Indeed Swami Vivekanand was the greatest well wisher of the down-trodden. He further said very emphatically, "I call him a Mahatma who feels for the poor". His religion consisted not in dogmas and rituals but doing service to the poor and raising their standard. He said, "Service to mankind is the highest goal of religion".

4. *Our duty towards national awakening and development* : Swami Vivekanand reminded us that the nation lived in the cottages and, therefore, it was the duty of every educated youngman to go from village to village and make the people understand their real condition, awake them from their long slumber and advise them how to improve their own miserable lot. The sunken vitality of the helpless victims of social justice was to be restored physically, intellectually as well as spiritually.

5. *Faith in ourselves* : Vivekanand awakened faith in ourselves. "Anything that makes you weak physically, intellectually and spiritually, reject as poison". He quoted Swami Ramkrishna, his master, "He who thinks himself weak will become weak and this is true. If a man day and night thinks that he is miserable, low and nothing, nothing he becomes".

6. *Strength is life* : Swami Vivekanand gave the message of courage and strength. His advice was "be strong, my young friends. You will be nearer to heaven through football than through the '*Gita*'. You will understand '*Gita*' better with your biceps, your muscles a little stronger. You will understand the '*Upnishads*' better and the glory of '*Atman*' when your body stands firm upon your feet and you feel yourself as man". His main '*mantra*' was "Strength, Strength. Strength is Goodness, Weakness is Sin".

Weak minds can never understand or grasp mighty ideas. In their attempts to do, they dilute such ideas with their own littleness. Only the elephant knows the strength of the lion and not the mosquito. Only the mighty can understand the '*Gita*'. The '*Gita*' is meant to wake us from our slumber and to invigorate us and to make us think and enable us to come out from our old ruts.

7. *Fearlessness:* According to Jawaharlal Nehru, 'Vivekanand spoke of many things but one constant refrain of his speech and writing was '*Abhaya*' (Fearlessness)". Fearlessness comes from faith and strength. Swami Vivekanand asked his countrymen to stand upon their own legs and not look to others for help in the task of national reconstruction.

8. *True religion:* According to Swami Vivekanand, service to mankind is the highest goal of religion. He further said that the best image for worshipping God is man who resides in every heart. It is on account of this conception of religion and God that he called upon his countrymen to work cealessly for the poor and the down-trodden.

9. *Religion is not in the kitchen* : He saw the problem of India as too much religion of the wrong kind. He declared we should discard such concepts as "our religion is in the kitchen. Our God is in the cooking pot and our religion is 'don't touch me, I am holy". According to him religion consisted in equality of men, the supermen virtue of comparison, work without attachment, devotions with renunciation of the personal ego, and service of all men and especially of those who were poor or illiterate or disinherited. He strongly decried 'touch-me-not' attitude of the Hindus in religious matters. He frowned at religion's tacit approval to the oppression of the poor. He believed that it was an insult to God and humanity. He saw the 'divine' in the form of the poor whom he called '*Daridra Narayan*'.

10. *Religion as social service and a great cementing and unifying force* : According to Swami Vivekanand, religion does not consist in doctrines and theories, however beautiful they may be. Religion has to be practised if it was to have meaning, and the practice has to take account of the call of social reality. "I do not believe in God or religion which cannot wipe the widow's tears or bring a piece of bread to the orphan's mouth". He emphasised, "It is man-making religion that we want".

Swami Vivekanand, in his famous address at the Parliament of Religions in 1893 at Chicago summed up his message and philosophy by saying that upon the banner of every religion will soon be written 'Help and not Fight', 'Assimilation and not destruction, 'Harmony and Peace and not Dissension' Religions of the world are not contradictory but they are various phases of our eternal religion. I accept all religions".

Swami Vivikanand, therefore, stressed that for national reconstruction, all religions in India should work for social harmony and moral uplift of the people.

11. *Education for National awakening and national reconstruction* : Vivekanand was a firm believer in education as an instrument of betterment. He was greatly distressed to see the denial of literacy and education to the vast population of India. He at the same time wanted a thorough re-orientation of the system of education. He declared, "We must have man-making education. We want that education by which character is formed, strength of mind is increased, the intellect is expanded and by which one can stand on one's own foot". Education must make people self-reliant and cultivate in them spirit of service.

Vivekanand gave importance to the education of the masses. He asserted, "The great national sin is the neglect of the masses and that is one of the causes of our downfall. No amount of politics would be of any avail until the masses in India are more educated, well fed and well cared for. If we want to regenerate India, we must work for them".

12. *Learning from others but keeping our own:* While Vivekanand welcomed the use of Western thought and technology for our national reconstruction, he cautioned his countrymen against being dazzled by its materialist

success. When we take anything from others we must mould it after our own way.

13. *Social action* : Above all, Vivekanand stressed social action. Knowledge unaccompanied by action in the world in which we live was useless, he said.

For giving a concrete shape to his teachings and the teachings of his 'guru' Swami Ramakrishan Pramhansa, he founded the Ramakrishna Mission as a centre of service.

Ramakrishna Mission

Swami Vivekanand, the ardent disciple of Ramakrishna Parmhansa (1834-86), established in 1897, the Ramakrishna Mission to promote his teachings in an easy and understandable language and to give a practical shape to them. It was formerly registered as a Charitable Society in 1909. In 1899, the Belur *'Mutt'* was built near Calcutta to house its headquarters and a monastery founded in the Kumaon Hills of North to train the spiritually hungry young men who joined the new organisation.

Mission's programmes are:

1. Mission's objectives include, "The first and foremost task in India is the propagation of education and spirituality among the masses. It is impossible for hungry men to become spiritual unless food is provided to them".
2. It carries out Ramakrishna's injunction, "Service of man, for man is God".
3. Hence our paramount duty lies in showing new ways. It propagates the principles of Vedanta, including the equality of all religions in the search of Absolute.
4. It has adopted a progressive attitude of accepting science and reaping the fruits of modern science and technology from its beginning, without, however neglecting spirituality.
5. As an organised monastic order, the Ramakrishna Mission trains a body of active ascetics for whom prayer and meditation go hand in hand with the material alleviation of suffering.
6. It carries out multifarious activities in several kinds of relief work, rural development, dispensaries and hospitals etc.
7. It opens reading rooms and libraries.
8. It starts and maintains educational institutions at the school and college level.
9. It is active in several countries of the subcontinent as well as in America, Europe, South-east Asia and Oceanic.

Q. 5. Analyse the role played by the Aligarh Movement in the progress of the Muslim Society with special reference to Sir Syed Ahmed.

(Punjab University, Oct. 1996 April 1998)

Ans: *Sir Syed Ahmed Khan (1817-1897)*

A great reformer of the Muslim Community : Sir Syed Ahmed Khan, undoutedly, finds the most important place among the Muslim reformers of the nineteenth century. His influence on the coming generation has also been greatly marked. He was firmly convinced that the Muslims could progress only by reconciling the Islamic thoughts with modern scientific thought. Among the Muslims, he was the harbinger of the Renaissance. He urged the people to develop a critical and rational outlook. Promotion of science and modern education among Muslims remained his primary task throughout his life.

While serving in the judicial department of the East India Company for about 38 years (1832 to 1870), he took a keen interest in initiating several measures for the improvement of his community. As a member of the Viceroy's Legislative Council for four years from 1878 to 1882, he never for a moment forgot his duty to the Muslim community.

Sir Syed's keenness to uplift Muslims : He always aimed at raising the Muslim intelligentsia to a better status. With this objective in view, he always looked to the British for support. He was unhappy about Britisher's callousness towards Muslims after the Revolt of 1857 and he strove for reapproachment. He was successful in weaning the British Government from the policy of suppressing the Muslims by convincing them that the Muslims were not primarily responsible for the Revolt. In his book *'Causes* of *the Revolt'*, he attempted to establish that the events of 1857 were the result of accumulation of many grievances which had been haunting the minds of the Indians in general. He strove to show that the Indian Muslims were loyal to the British Government. He emphasised that if some Muslims were misled by the mutineers by coaxing and cajoling, they could be won back to the faith of loyalty. He did not hesitate in exhorting his co-religionists to extend full cooperation to the British and derive maximum benefit out of the blessings of the British Raj.

Cautious approach : He was keen to eradicate social evils which had crept into Muslim community, However, he did not believe in sweeping changes. He wanted the reforms to be effected cautiously and peacefully without affecting the fundamentals of Islam. He condemned the institution of slavery and described it un-Islamic. He opposed the system of *'piri'* and *'muridi'* (mystics and their followers). He urged the Muslims to give up medieval customs. He advocated the removal of *'purdah'* and pleaded for the spread of education among Muslim women and raising their status. He condemned the practice of polygamy and early divorce among the Muslims.

Spread of education among Muslims : Though he lacked formal education in English, he established while in the judicial service, English medium schools at Moradabad and Ghazipur in the 1860s.

He worked very hard for a number of years to open the Muhammadan-

Anglo-Oriental College (M.A.O. College) at Aligarh in 1875 with Theodore Beck of Cambridge as its principal. By the end of the century this institution became the heart of higher education and political awareness for Indian Muslims. It gained its present day status of Aligarh Muslim University in 1920.

Associations and Societies : In 1864, he set up an organisation called the 'Scientific Society' for the promotion of scientific thought among the Muslims. The society published Urdu translations of English books on science and other subjects. He established many associations.

Journals. He promoted his views on social reforms through his magazine '*Tahzib-ul-Akhlaq*' (Improvement of Manners and Morals).

Two phases/faces of Sir Syed Ahmad's personality and work: Muslim interests first

Sir Syed Ahmed displayed nationalist sentiments in some of his early speeches. In a speech in 1883, he observed, "My Hindu brethren and my Muslim co-religionists breathe the same air, drink the water of sacred Ganga and the Yamuna... live and die together." Further he declared, "Our land of India is like a newly wedded bribe whose two beautiful and luscious eyes are the Hindus and the Mussalmans."

On account of his utterances, Sir Syed Ahmed was regarded an undisputed leader of both the Hindus and the Muslims. During his trip to Punjab in 1884, for the collection of funds for the Aligarh College, several addresses were presented to him both by Hindus and Muslims praising his services to the nation.

Under the growing influence of Beck, Principal of the Aligarh College, a nationalit in Sir Syed Ahmed was substituted by a communalist. He defined the Congress movement as "a civil war without arms." His contention was that if India was to be given an elective system based on worth or education, "the whole Council will consist of Babus so and so and all Muslims hated these fish-eating Babus of Bengal."

Sir Syed Ahmed began to oppose the Congress very vehemently and he laid the foundations of the Indian Patriotic Association with the objective of publishing and circulating pamphlets, opposing the policies of the Indian National Congress and bringing it to the notice of Members of Parliament in England and English journals.

Sir Syed Ahmed also laid the foundations of the Annual Muslim Educational Conference in 1886, a year after the establishment of the Indian National Congress.

In 1893, he set up the Mohammedan Defence Association of Upper India for the purpose of safeguarding the Muslim interest.

Summing up: Leaving aside his opposition to the Congress, there is no doubt that he rendered a great service to the Muslim community. He told the Muslims that Prophet Mohammed had said, "For getting knowledge go as far as the Chinese Wall and even beyond that Wall". Throughout his life he tried to accomplish two objectives namely, better relations between the Muslims and the British Government and providing modern education to Muslims. A renowned historian S.C. Sir, Syed Ahmed as an 'apostle of reconciliation' who established on 'working harmony between East and West".

Aligarh Movement

The Aligarh movement or Aligarh School derives its name from the MAO College founded by Sir Syed Ahmed Khan in 1875 and reconstituted as Aligarh Muslim University in 1920. A legacy of the Revolt of 1857 was that the British rulers had got the impression that the Revolt of 1857 was spear-headed by the Muslims and they were its arch consperators. This suspicion of the British was confirmed by the Wahabi Movement (movement launched by a section of the Muslims in Punjab and which was crushed by British in the 1870s. Sir, Syed Ahmed was convinced that the Muslims could advance only under the patonage of the British rulers. W.W. Hunter, a Britisher in his book 'The Indian Musalman' made a strong plea for reconciling and rallying the Muslims round the British Government through concessions. This was greatly welcomed by a section of the Muslim Community led by Sir Syed Ahmed. This school of thought felt that the Muslim community would be deprived of its rightful share in the administrative services if they confined themselves in a shell and resisted modern thought. This came to be termed as Aligarh Movement.

Principal Beck of the MAO College, Aligarh played a leading role in wining over the Muslims to English side. He was able to create a band of workers of this school of thought under the leadership of Sir Syed Ahmed. As a result the Aligarh Movement was used to keep the Muslims away from the Congress. The influence of Beck was so great on Sir Syed Ahmed and his followers that the letter began to attack the Congress.

Among the important leaders of the Aligarh Movement were Maulvi Chiragh Ali, Alif Hussain Hali (an Urdu Poet, Nazir Ahmad, Maulana Shibli Nomani and Khuda Baksh. It is generally believed that the most of the members of the Aligarh school or Aligarh Movements were guided by the idea of separation and they helped the British rulers in weakening the national movement.

The Aligarh Movement had two objectives: One, advancement of the Muslim Community and two, opposing the Indian National Congress.

Maulvi Chiragh Ali (1844-1885), one of the front leaders of the Aligarh Movement who sought to reform the Muslim society and modernisi it was in the service of the East India Company and later the British Government of India after 1857). He was very keen that his co-religionists must reconcile themselves to British rule and get the right place in the administrative services. He stood for Monogamy and a better status for Muslim women in the society and tried to promote these through his literacy works.

After Beck, the next principal the Morrison also adopted the policy of instigating the Muslims against the Hindus and the Indian National Congress.

Q. 6. Explain how Brahmo Samaj and Arya Samaj represented two streams of Renaissance movement in India. *(Rajasthan University, 1994)*

Ans: *Renaissance Movement in India*

The nineteenth century in India was the century of unprecedented intellectual ferment in the field of religious and social reforms. It was the century of introspection, reassessment, reinterpretation and regeneration of ancient thought and culture in the light of western thought and culture. There emerged a number of reform movements in Hinduism . All these contributed in various ways to the furthering of Indian Renaissance. Of these, two the Brahmo Samaj and the Arya Samaj, Played major role in redepening the principles and practices of Hinduism.

Brahmo Samaj

Brahmo Samaj was founded in 1828 by Raja Rammohan Roy, who has been hailed as the father of 'Indian Renaissance' and 'Prophet of Indian nationalism'. He is regarded as the 'promulgator' of modern age in Indian history, an advocate of religious and social reconstruction and a supporter of Western education. He worked for the intellectual, political religious and social regeneration of India.

Brahmo Samaj became an important vehicle of reforming Hindu society by removing serval ills that had crept into it with the passage of time.

After Raja Rammohan Roy, the Brahmo Samaj was promoted by Devendranath Tagore and Keshub Chandra Sen. The Samaj influenced some of the greatman like Dr. J.C. Bose, Rabindra Nath Tagore and Bipan Chandra Pal.

The Brahmo Samaj consisted of worshippers of one God. The first temple of the Samaj was opened in 1830 at Calcutta. The eternal and Supereme being was not to be worshipped under any designation or little adopted by any particular sect and no name was given to it. Idolatory was not to be allowed in the temples nor any sacrifice was to be made therein. Anything against any religion could not be contemptuously spoken. The temples were for all without any discrimination. Brahmo Samaj was to be a tolerant body devoted to the promotion of piety, virtue and benevolence. It was meant for consolidating the bounds of union between men of all religious persuations and creeds. It stood for strengthening the solidarity of the current religious of the day.

Basic Principles of Brahmo Samaj

(*i*) Monotheism : God is one. He is all powerful. We should worship one God only. No worship of gods and goddesses.

(*ii*) No caste system.
(*iii*) Soul is immortal.
(*iv*) Stress on human dignity.
(*v*) No domination of priestly class.
(*vi*) No image worship
(*vii*) Widows remarriage
(*viii*) No *Sati* practice
(*ix*) Raising the status of women

Debendranath Tagore and Keshub Chandra Sen in the promotion of Brahmo Samaj

After Raja Rammohan Roy, the Brahmo Samaj movement was promoted by Debendranath Tagore and Keshub Chandra Sen.

Debendranath Tagore (1818-1905), born in affluence shunned all luxuries. He came into contact with Rammohan Roy and wrote a number of tracts on Brahmoism. Through *Tattwabodhni;* a society founded by him and through his journal *Tattwabodhni Patrika,* he preached liberal ideas and rejected *idolatory.*

Keshub Chandra Sen (1838-1884) travelled widely and made Brahmo Samaj an all India organization by establishing 65 centres in different parts of India. He arranged nineteen Brahmo marriages. During his life time, a split also occurred in the Brahmo Samaj when he married his minor daughter.

THE ARYA SAMAJ

The Arya Samaj was founded in 1873 by Swami Dayanand, a great Vedic scholar. It was intended to reform the Hindu Society on the philosophical thought contained in the Vedas. Swami Dayanand found the Hindu Society broken up into castes and sub-castes, each of which looked down upon the others in the spirit of hatred rivalry. Castes were determined on the basis of birth. Any violation of the rules of caste was punishable by ostraism. The life of the *shudras* was intolerable. The Hindu Samaj suffered from many religious ills like idolatory, worship of several gods and goddesses, performance of many costly rites and rituals and even human sacrifices. The Hindus were gradually losing their faith in their capacity to meet the challenge of Christian missionaries. They had forgotten the true spirit and truth contained in the Vedas. Under such a situation, Swami Dayanand reinterpreted the Vedas and in its light started the work of reforming Hindu Society by setting up the Arya Samaj.

Arya Samaj has been working for the regeneration of the Hindu society through its manifold activities in the field of cultural, educational, political, religious and social reconstruction.

Principles of Arya Samaj

Life is one integrated whole. All aspects of life are interlinked and interrelated. Therefore, a comprehensive view of man's relations with God, with his self and with others must be taken. Accordingly the Arya Samaj has formed ten principles to guide the life of its members in various areas for leading a happy, peaceful and balanced life.

Following are its principles.

1. Parmeshwar (God) is the fountain of all true knowledge.
2. Worship is alone due to Ishwar (God), Who is all Truth, All Knowledge, All Merciful, All Omnipotent, All Omniscient, All Immortal.
3. The Vedas are the books of true knowledge, and it is the paramount duty of every Arya to read or hear them read, to teach and preach them to others.
4. An Arya should always be ready to accept truth and renounce untruth when discovered.
5. Truth should be the guiding principle in all matters.
6. The primary object of the Samaj is to do good to the world by improving the physical, intellectual, spiritual, moral and social condition of mankind.
7. An Arya should manifest due love for all and appreciation of justice in his behaviour towards others.
8. An Arya should endeavour to diffuse knowledge and dispel darkness.
9. He should not be content with his own improvement, but look for it in that of others.
10. In matters which affect the general social well being of our race, he ought to discard all differences and not allow his individuality to interfere, but in strictly personal matters, every man may have his own way.

A perusal of the above principles of the Arya Samaj would reveal that they are cosmopolitan in character. They are equally applicable to all tends and peoples of all ages.

Impact of the Brahmo Samaj and the Arya Samaj

The Brahmo Samaj and the Arya Samaj have played a significant role in raising the status of women, in removing evils of caste system and in spreading education.

The work of these two organisations may be summarised as:

1. They have advocated spread of education among women.
2. They have encouraged widow remarriage.
3. They have condemned the practice of *'Sati'*.
4. They have prevented female infanticide.
5. They have pleaded for the abolition of *purdah.*
6. They have condemned child marriage.
7. They have worked for the enforcement of monogamy and condemned

polygamy.

8. They have set up several educational institutions for the girls and women.
9. They have pleaded for the right of inheritance for women.
10. They have decried dowry system.

It was the untiring efforts of Raja Rammohan Roy that in 1829, William Bentinck could declare *Sati* against law. Ishwar Chandra Vidyasagar, performed the marriages of 25 widows between 1855 and 1860. It was through his efforts that a large number of petitions from Bengal, Madras, Bombay, Nagpur and other cities were presented to the government asking it to legalise the widow remarriage. Swami Dayanand proclaimed that the Vedas provide for an equal status for women. The Arya Samaj founded by him has been playing an important role in this regard. Hundreds of Arya and D.A.V. educational institutions have been opened. Annie Besant and Jotiba Phule also rendered a great service to the various causes of women. Sir Syed Ahmad Khan demanded ban on Purdah system and polygamy among the Muslim women.

Factors that have led to the loosening of caste system in India: The religious and social reformers have exercised a tremendous influence in loosening the caste system in India. They have emphasised that all human beings are equal and none is socially high or low. The worst off shot of the caste system is untouchability practice. On account of this, the untouchables i.e. the people belonging to lower castes were denied entry to temples, to sacred places and public wells etc. The nineteenth century and the twentieth century are marked by the emergence of several forces which helped to mitigate the evil consequences of the caste system. Some of these are listed below:

1. Compaign against the caste system by religious and social reformers like Raja Rammohan Roy, Swami Dayanand, Swami Vivekanand, Mrs Annie Besant and Gandhiji.
2. Efforts of religious and social organisations like the Brahmo Samaj, the Prarathna Samaj, the Veda Samaj, and the Arya Samaj etc.
3. Scientific interpretations of the religious scriptures like the Vedas and their dissemination.
4. Development of means of transport and mixing of people of different people.
5. Spread of Western education and liberal ideas.
6. Industrialisation and urbanisation leading to more mobility.
7. National movement and mass participation in it.
8. Indian Constitution and its following provisions.

Art. 14. Equality before law.

Art. 15. Prohibition of discrimination on grounds of religion, race, caste, sex or place of birth.

Art. 16. Equality of opportunity in matters of public employment.

However, inspite of all this, caste system still exists to a considerable extent. Vigorous efforts are needed to mould public opinion. Perhaps spread of education among the vast number of illiterates in the country is the need of the hour.

Q. 7. Write notes on :

(*i*) **The Theosophical Society**

(*ii*) **Namdhari Movement**

(*iii*) **Singh Sabha**

(*iv*) **The Prarathna Sabha**

(*v*) **Rehnumai Mazdaysen Sabha**

Ans: *The Theosophical Society*

Founding of the Theosophical Society:

The Society was founded by Madame H.P. Bavastsky (1831-1891) of the Russo-German birth in 1875 in the United States. Later Colonel M.S. Olcott (1832-1907) of the U.S. Army joined her, In 1882, the headquarters of the Society were shifted to India at Adyar, an outskirt of Madras. Swami Dayanand had invited both the leaders to visit India. Though it gained some following but it could not take firm root in India.

It was a movement launched by Westerners who glorified Indian philosophy and religion. The society helped Indians to recover their self-confidence. The society wanted the Indians to get rid of social evils. It drew inspiration from the philosophy of the Upanishads and the Vedanta school of thought. The movement came to be allied with Hindu Renaissance.

Main teachings of the Theosophical Society

1. Belief in the doctrine of the transmigration of the soul.
2. Attainment of the knowledge of God through spiritual ecstasy.
3. Belief in incarnation.
4. Faith in the theory of '*Karma*' (theory of actions)
5. Brotherhood of humanity without distinction of race, creed, sex, caste or colour.

The Theosophical Society's Work in India

Mrs. Annie Besant (1847-1933), an Irish lady who came to India in 1883, became the moving figure behind the society. She remained the president of the Theosopical Society of India from 1907 till her death in 1933. She was one of the very few Westerners who came to India, settled here and adopted it as their home. She worked for about fifty years for the regeneration of India in cultural, political, religious and social fields. (A detailed description of her work is given separately.

Sikh Reform Movements

Among the Sikhs, two important movements emerged.

The Namdari Movement/Kuka Movement. The Namdari Movement was founded in 1857, at Bhaini, 16 miles from Ludhiana in the Punjab, by Bhai Ram Singh, an ex-soldier of the Khalsa Army. The movement was the outcome of the degeneration set in the path of morality among the followers of Sikkism after the death Maharaja Ranjit Singh. Several social evils like Sati, dowry and sales of girls etc. had crept into the society. Satguru as Ram Singh was called, asked his followers to observe the following (*i*) giving up drinking, (*ii*) Giving up drugs (*iii*) No dowry (*iv*) No polygamy (*v*) No sale of daughters (*vi*) No Worship of *'pirs'* (mystics) at their graves, (*vii*) Use of *'Swadeshi'* goods (*viii*) No female infanticide etc.

The Namdharis initiated the cheapest system of celebrating marriages.

The Namdharis are supposed to be vegetarians and cow protectors.

The Namdharis are expected to do a lot of meditation and charitable work. Common kitchen is another characteristics of the Namdharis.

The British rulers looked upon the Namdharis with suspicion. Heavy atrocities were inflicted on them. In 1872, more than sixty Namdharis were tied to the mouth of the gun and blown off. This cruel action shocked the entire nation, Even the conscience of some sections of the people in England was stirred up. Guru Ram Sing was exiled to Burma. The Namdharis were not deterred and they took an active part in the national movement.

The Singh Sabha Movement

The Singh Sahba movement was started in the Sikh Community in 1873 at Amritsar with the two-fold objective. It aimed at reaping the benefit of the Western enlightenment through modernising the system of education. It also countered the proselytizing activities of the Christian missionaries.

The Singh Sabha opened a network of Khalsa Schools and Colleges throughout the Punjab.

The Prararthana Samaj

In Maharashtra, Prarathna Samaj was founded in 1849 under the inspiration of Keshub Chandra Sen of the Brahmo Samaj. The followers of the Samaj believed that the true love of God lay in the service of God's children. They did not have confrontation with the Hindu orthodoxy and they relied upon education and persuation.

In the field of social reform, the focus of the Samaj was on four objectives (*i*) Disapproval of the caste system (*ii*) Raising the age of marriage both for males and females (*iii*) Widow remarriage (*iv*) Women education.

Justice Mahadev Govind Ranade (1842-1901) and R.G. Bhandarkar (1837-1925) were its great leaders.

Rehnumai Mazdaysan Sabha

Among the Parsis in 1851, a group of educated persons organised the

Rehnumai Mazdaysan Sabha (Religious Reform Association) for the renovation of their religion and society. Among the focal points of the movement were: improving the status of women. Abolishing the '*Purdah*', raising the age of marriage and promoting female education. For the promotion of these objectives, the Association started a newspaper '*Rast Goftar*' (Truth Teller). Among its important leaders were Naoroji Furdonzi, Dadabhai Naroji and K.R. Cama. In due course, the Parsis became of the most modern sections of the Indian Society and played an important role in national awakening. The famous revolutionary Madam Bhikaji Cama was the daughter-in-law of K.R. Cama.

Q. 8. Write Notes on:

(*i*) **Ramakrisna Pramhansa**
(*ii*) **Mahadev Govind Ranade**
(*iii*) **Jotiba Phule**
(*iv*) **Annie Besant**
(*v*) **Narayan Guru**

RAMAKRISHNA PARMHANSA (1836-1886)

Apostle of Spirituality **:** The unlettered Ramakrishna whose original name was Gadadhar and who was a priest in a temple at Dakshineshwar, near Calcutta, became the embodiment of spiritual enlightenment. His ardent disciple Narendra Dutta, afterwards Swami Vivekanand made a mark of his learning, oratory, scholarship and wisdom at the Parliament of Religions held at Chicago in 1893. Ramakrishna is regarded as the personification of the highest and the best in Indian culture and tradition. On account of holy life, simplicity of character, extraordinary skill in explaining complicated religious mattes in a very simple language and his catholic outlook, he became a great source of inspiration for the seekers of truth and for those who wanted to realise divinity.

Search for God: three experiences: In his search for religious truth, Swami Ramakrishna, lived with the learned persons and saints of different faiths. He was not content with experiencing only the Hindu modes of approach to God or the Divine. He searched for God through all faiths practised the teachings of Islam, Christianity and Buddhism and through each of them, he reached the goal which these faiths promised to their followers.

One goal and several paths : He again and again emphasised that there were many roads or paths to God and salvation. He said, "*Jato mat, tato path*" (There are as many ways as there are creeds) to reach God and there is no conflict in them.

No criticism of any religion : He did not criticise any religion. He accepted that if followed sincerely, every religion would lend to salvation.

Meditation and Service : He stood selfless devotion to God and sought religious salvation in the traditional Indian ways of renunciation, meditation and devotion.

He also believed that service to man was service of God and that it would also lead to salvation.

Faith in Indian culture: From his teachings, the comtemporary Indian intellectuals whose faith in their own culture had been shaken by the challenge of the West, found reassured from his teachings.

Ramakrishna was a pioneer in the Renaissance Movement in India.

The Ramakrishna Mission is founded in his memory to promote his teachings in India and abroad.

MAHADEV GOVIND RANADE (1842-1901)

Many sided Personality : M.G. Ranade was a champion of social amelioration, guide of men, distinguished judge, eminent economist, enlightened thinker, noted historian, progressive religious reformer and a patriot. Ranade dedicated his entire life for the regeneration of teeming millions in all respects. He was one of the prominent founders of the Indian National Congress. On account of his profound intellect, he was called the 'Socrates of Maharashtra'.

Interdependence of reforms : Ranade was convinced that all areas of national life i.e. educational, economic, political and social needed substantial changes. He said, "You cannot have a good social system when you find yourself low in the scale of political rights nor can you be fit to exercise political rights and privileges unless your social system is based on reason and justice. You cannot have a good economic system when your social arrangements are imperfect. If your religious ideas are low and grovelling, you cannot succeed in social economic or political spheres. This interdependence is not an accident but is the law of nature".

Social Reformer : Ranade ceaselessly worked for social reforms. He became an active member of the Prarathna Samaj in Maharashtra - a counterpart of the Brahmo Samaj of Bengal. According to Ranade, politics and social reforms were interwined. As a reformer, he tried to convince the people that the desired social reforms were in consonance with the Vedas and Smritis. He worked for inter-caste dining, inter-caste marriages and remarriage of widows. Under his leadership, the work of social reform was made more broad-based.

Methods of Social Reform : Of the four methods advocated by social reformers i.e the traditional method, the conscience method, the legislative method, and the rebellion method, he stood for the first three methods. About widow remarriage he remarked, "There is the express permission in the Vedas, express permission in the Shruties".

Contribution of Ranade to associations and organisations. He was the main source of the Deccan Education Society. He was the brain behind the Sarvajanik Sabha of Poona, engaged in the awakening of the social and political conscience of the people and representing to the Government the needs and the aspirations of the people. He was an active member of the Brahmo Samaj. He was associated with the Widow Marriage Association. He extended whole hearted cooperation to Swami Dayanand when the latter went to Poona for propagating social and religious reforms. He took the initiative in founding the Indian National Congress. Ranade was the soul of the Indian Social Conference, founded in 1887 and which worked for the abolition of caste, support to inter-caste marriages, raising of the marriageable age, discouragement of polygamy, widow remarriage, women's education, improvement in the condition of the so-called outcastes and settlement of disputes between the Hindus and the Muslims by the appointment of Panchayats.

Starting his career as a teacher, he rose to the position of a judge of the Bombay High Court, an office which he retained till his death in 1901.

JOTIBA PHULE (1827-1890)

Work for the Depressed Classes **:** A great social and religious reformer of Maharashtra, Jotiba Phule was greatly inspired by the ideals of Shivaji. He belonged to a low caste family of '*flower suppliers*' to the house of the Peshwas. Thus the family had come to be known as '*Phule*'. Jotiba and his wife devoted their lives for the uplift of the depressed classes and women. Jotiba rejected caste distinctions and the supermacy of the Brahmans over non-Brahmans.

Work for female education: In 1851, Jotiba opened a girl's school at Poona. Thereafter several schools came up.

Jotiba established a good library for the low caste and a night school for adults.

Social reforms: Jotiba opened orphanages and widows homes. He encouraged the adoption of children of the widows. He took a keen interest in improving the living conditions of the mill workers. He condemned the practice of child marriage, infanticide and shaving the heads of the widows.

Jotiba wanted to keep out the priests from performing marriage ceremonies.

In 1873, he founded the Satya Shoddak Samaj (Truth Seeking Society) for securing social justice for the weaker sections.

Jotiba put forth his views in his book '*Gulam-geri*' (1872). His other publications include '*Dharma Tritiya Ratna*' (Exposure of the Puranas '*Ishara*' (A Warning) and '*Life of Shivaji*'

On account of his sterling qualities of his character, Jotiba was called '*Mahatma*' (Great Soul) by his followers.

MRS. ANNIE BESANT (1847-1933)

A Foreigner who worked for India's regeneration. Born and brought up in Ireland, she came to India in 1893, settled here and adopted it as her home. She became a great lover of Hinduism and claimed that she was a Hindu in her former birth. She wore the Hindu costumes and adopted Hindu ways of life. She made a great contribution to the enrichment of India's life in cultural, educational, social and political, fields. She wrote a number of books on Hindu philosophy and translated the Gita into English.

Mrs. Annie's Contribution to Social Field : She became a member of the Theosophical Society in 893, and remained its President from 1907 till her death in 1933. She condemned early marriage and forced widowhood in society. She stood equality for women in India. She established Women's Indian Association which later on bloomed as an All India Women's Conference an organisation for the uplift of women. She founded the Indian Boys Scout Association.

Mrs. Annie's Contribution to education: Mrs. Annie Besant had a deep insight to understand the needs of the masses of India and she prepared a national scheme of education based on the fundamental principles of Indian culture. She also urged that the students should be made conscious and proud of the glory of the country. She established the Central Hindu High School of Benares. She established a National University at Adiyar, near Madras.

Mrs. Annie Contribution to National Struggle : She entered the freedom struggle on the eve of the First World War. She concluded a lengthy statement in London on behalf of India in June 1914, "India works only that she shall be recognised as a nation, shall be given self-government and shall form an integral part of the empire, composed of self-governing communities. She asks no more than this"

For building up a vigorous movement of Home Rule, she started a daily paper '*New India*' in Madras in 1914. In 1916, she started the Home Rule League and established its branches throughout the country.

She travelled all over India and called upon the people to wake up from their slumber.

She was elected the President of the Indian National Congress in 1917.

About her role in the struggle for freedom, Pt. Jawaharlal Nehru once said, there could be no doubt that in India's journey for freedom her part was a considerable one".

NARAYAN GURU (1854-1928)

Narayan Guru's greatest contribution was his work for the emancipation of the oppressed sections of the society in Kerala. Born in a family of untouchables, he became very sensitive to their degraded position in the society.

Narayana Guru set up the Sri Narayan Dharam Paripalna Yogam — an organisation which worked for the uplift of Ezhavas—depressed class.

He started establishing temples without images. The first temple built by him contained the following words, "Here is the place where all people live in fraternity without caste distinctions". He attacked the priestly class for their endler's rituals to maintain their supermacy. However, he believed in the method of persuation and not hatred.

Narayan Guru attained a state of very high spiritual awareness by practising austerities.

Q. 9. What do you mean by Indian Renaissance? In what way this was a major event of the nineteenth century? *(Rajasthan University, 1996)*

Ans: *Indian Renaissance*

Meaning: The 19th century was at once a watershed dividing the dark ages and the age of enlightenment. Its hundred years, heralding the Indian Renaissance, changed the face of India. This century represented an encounter of two differing cultures — One, the Indian, chiefly spiritual, rich with its hoary tradition, but disfigured with the accumulated dust and rust and the other, European or Western, comparatively new, pragmatic, enterprising but materialistic enriched by the discoveries in the realm of science. The synthesis of the old and the new was the story and romance of the 19th century. Raja Ram Mohan Roy (1772-1833), Ishwar Chandra Vidya Sagar (1820-1891), Debendranath Tagore (1818-1905), Swami Dayanand (1824-83), Swami Vivekanand (1863-1902), Annie Besant (1847-1933) and others represented this century at the fullest; sticking to the old traditions and yet moulding the traditions to renew in the light of Vedic thought and Western impact. Even though they lived in the 19th century and dealt with its problems, they were figures who looked beyond their age to the millenary to come. Among the Muslims, Sir Syed Ahmad (1817-1898) held the faith that the religious and social life of the Muslims could be improved by reconciling the Islamic thought with the modern Western thought. He interpreted the '*Quran*' in terms of rationalism and science.

Social Perspective of Renaissance

When the Britishers came to India, they saw a rigid caste system, many social evils and customs which had been hallowed by *"Dharma"* but which were considered inhuman in most other parts of the world. Such customs were: '*Sati*' practice, early child marriage, enforced widowhood, infanticide, temple prostitution '*devdasis*', an injunction against travel overseas involving loss of caste etc.

These Hindu practices became the targets of attack by Christian missionaries as well. This naturally led the social reformers of the 19th century to have a new look at their socio-religious customs. The first of the reform movements to take the field was the Brahmo Samaj, founded by Raja Rammohan Roy and its inspiration was Western but Raja Rammohan was widely travelled and a great scholar of several languages. It was largely due to his efforts that the burning of widows with their dead husbands was made illegal in 1829, just four years before his death. Keshub Chandra Sen (1838-84), another leader of the Brahmo Samaj, on his return from England, campaigned against child marriage and persuaded the Samaj to celebrate the remarriage of widows and marriages between different castes. it was largely due to the efforts of Kesub Chandra that the Government passed an Act in 1872 not only making Brahmo marriages legal but also abolishing child marriage and the remarriage of widows. The Prarathna Samaj of Bombay, an institution on the pattern of Bramo Samaj, under the leadership of Mahadev Govind Ranade (1842-19007) compaigned against the evils of child marriage and the prohibition of remarriage of widows.

Swami Dayanand, after a deep study of the Vedas came to the conclusion that such practices were against the teachings of Hindu Shastras and he, therefore rejected them. He proved from the study of the Vedas that women should be given equal status with men. He worked for the abolition of caste system as it had no sanction of the Vedas. The Arya Samaj founded by him has been playing an important role.

Swami Vivekanand's call to the nation was, "O India ! forget not that the lower classes, the ignorant, the poor, the illiterate, the cobbler, the sweeper are thy flesh and blood". He further declared, "I consider that the great national sin is the single neglect of the masses and this is one of the causes of our dawnfall". "I call him a Mahatma who feels for the power". He founded the Ramakrishna Mission in the memory of his guru Ramakrishna Paramhansa.

Jotiba Phule (1827-1890) was a great religious and social reformer of Maharashtra. He was a pioneer of the widow remarriage movement and uplift movement of the lower classes in Maharashtra. He established an organisation called Satyashadak Samaj (Truth Seeking Society).

Among the Parsis, social reform movement was started by Naoroji Furdonji, Dadabhai Naoroji and K.R. Cama with the formation of Rehnumai Mazdayasan Sabha or the Religious Reform Association. In the social field, the focus was on improving the position of women, abolishing '*Purdah*' and raising the age of marriage.

In South India, social reform movements were led by Chembati Sridharalu, the most prominent leader of the Veda Sabha.

Narayan Guru did a commendable work for the emanicipation of the depressed sections of the society in Kerala.

Kandukukari Veeresalingam was an important social reformer in Andhra.

Bhai Ram Singh, founder of the Namdhari movement among the Sikhs in Punjab emphasised these points (*i*) No dowry (*ii*) No worship of *Peers'* graves (*iii*) No female infanticide (*iv*) No polygamy.

Singh Sabha movement founded at Amritsar in 1874 aimed at the preaching of Sikh tenets and production of religious literature of the Sikhs.

Religious Perspective of Renaissance

It may be remembered that all social reformers were also religious reformers. They based their teachings on their religious scriptures and proved that they did not sanction several religious practices in vogue. Swami Dayanand, the founder of the Arya Samaj worked for the removal of ritualistic dogmas and superstitutious practices by quoting the Vedas. He made the Vedas as the foundation and the basis of religious reforms. The Ramakrishna Mission emphasised the teachings of Upanishads.

About the catholicity of Hindu religion, Swami Vivekanand, in his inaugural address at the World Parliament of Religions at Chicago (1893), quoted the *'Shivamahima Stotra'*, "You alone are the object of all human quest, the way all rivers merge into the ocean. They follow straight or winding path because their routes happen to vary." Vivekanand highlighted the *stotra* to emphasise the point he subsequently made in his speech: "We do not merely tolerate all religions, but accept them all to be true". He was merely re-stating the philosophy of his guru, Sri Ramakrishna Paramahansa, who, in one of his famous Bengali epigrams, had said: "*Jato mat, tato path* (there are as many was as there are creeds)".

In an inimitable folksy analogy, Ramakrishna had commented, pointing to rain water coming out of gargoyles at a disciple's house, that different people have different words for water, but water doesn't change its character from one place to another. As Vivekananda explained to one of his first American disciples, Ole Bull: "My master used to tell us that Hindu, Christian, etc, are but different names of the same truth". He summed up his message, "Upon the banner of every religion would soon be written, in spite of resistance, help not fight, Assimilation and not Destruction, Harmony and Peace and not Dissension". In 1894, in a speech, he explained his concept of a true religion, "I do not believe in a God or religion which cannot wipe the widow's tears or bring a piece of bread to the orphan's mouth. However sublime the theories, however well spun may be the philosophy, I do not call it religion as long it is confined to books and dogmas. Religion is in being and becoming."

Educational Renaissance

The religious and social reformers of the 19th century were not theorists only. They were pragmatists also in their approach. They were convinced that education was a very important instrument of bringing about the needed religious and social reforms: They therefore, stressed upon the necessity of opening educational institutions which would impart Eastern and western thought. The chain of DAV institutions (Dayanand Anglo Vedic Institutions) existing all over India is a great tribute to the memory of Swami Dayanand.

Causes which led to Renaissance in India

Following were the important causes:

1. Rediscovery of India's past by foreign scholars like Max Muller and others.
2. Spread of Western thought and education.
3. Propaganda of Christian missionaries and their provocation to the Indians.
4. Contacts with foreigners: rationalists and humanists.
5. Economic exploitation of the people of India by the British.
6. Inspiration from the rise of modern Japan.
7. Emergence of religious and social reformers in India; reinterpretation of Indian philosophy and religion.
8. Role of the press.
9. Role of the literature.
10. Work of several religious and social organisations.

24

National Awakening : Indian National Congress (1885-1904)

Q. 1. Give the causes of the rise of Nationalism in India. What was A.O. Hume's role in the birth of the Congress?

(Delhi University 1997)

or

Examine the factors which led to the growth of national conscious ness in India. *(Delhi University 1995)*

or

Enumerate the factors that led to the rise of Indian nationalism during the second half of the nineteenth century.

(Rajasthan University 1995)

Ans: *Rise of Nationalism in India*

National awakening or nationalism was the outcome of a large number of factors. The national awakening, witnessed in the great upheaval of 1857' was the beginning.

After the events of 1857, several associations came up for promoting national awakening among the people of India. Among the important ones were the following:

1. East Indian Association, London (1866).
2. Poona Sarvjanik Sabha (1870).
3. Indian Association, Calcutta (1876).
4. Madras Mahajan Sabha (1884).
5. Bombay Presidency Association (1885).
6. Indian National Congress.

Usually national awakening is associated with the Indian National Congress, although other associations also contributed to it in some degree but their role was very limited. The role of the Congress eclipsed all other associations.

Main features of national awakening : National awakening had the following characteristics: One, it was, in some significant way, motivated by the Sepoy Revolt of 1857, though it was of a different nature. It was not led by the Sepoys or the Indian rulers but was basically started by intellectuals. Second, it was a movement in which, all people and sections of society living in different parts of the country became united against the common enemy. Third, the national struggle for the freedom of India was not confined to Indians living in India but also abroad. Fourth, it was mostly non-violent. Fifth, after 1920 or so, it was dominated by Gandhiji. Sixth, it was the outcome of a large number of factors.

Factors that Led to National Awakening

Following were the important factors that gave rise to national awakening:

1. *Very nature of foreign rule :* The very intrinsic nature of the foreign rule with its expansionist, exploitative, imperialistic and oppressive designs created hatred for it. The British never treated India as their country. They came to India as foreigners, ruled India as foreigners, lived in India as foreigners and also left India as foreigners. They considered it their 'divine right' to plunder India and take away its enormous wealth to Britain.

There is no doubt that the foreign character of the British domination in itself produced a nationalist reaction, since foreign regime invariably generates patriotic feeling in the hearts of a subject nation.

2. *Evil consequences of foreign domination* : A foreign domination, always, directly or indirectly proves very harmful to the country under its control. There is invariably clash of interest between the foreign rulers and the natives. Experience shows that the welfare of the ruled class suffers. There is a hardly any area of life of the ruled people that is not adversely affected by the selfish policies of the foreign rulers. The British rule became a stumbling block to India's overall development i.e. cultural, economic educational, intellectual, political, social and spiritual. In fact, every action or policy of the British, even for the good of the Indian people was looked down upon with suspicion.

3. *Exploitative economic policies and Ruin of Indian Economy :* The exploitative economic policies of the British resulted in enormous economic drain from India to Britain, appalling poverty of the masses and recurrence of famines claiming crores of lives (human and animals), and destruction of crops. There was hardly a section of population which did not suffer from the economic oppression of the foreign rule.

A large number of cultivators became landless as they were required to pay very high land revenue . Their lands became less productive for want of facilities like improved seeds, irrigation facilities. etc. They had to mortgage their lands and homes etc.

The Indian artisans and craftsmen lost their means of livelihood and were left on the brink of starvation.

The Indian traders suffered on account of unfair competition from British traders.

The Indian industrialists were at a great disadvantage compared with foreign industrialists who received all types of financial and other help in setting up industries.

The old Zamindars were deprived of their lands and their place was taken up by new Zamindars who were also being plundered by unscrupulous government officials.

The workers, especially plantation workers were ill-paid and ill-treated. They led a very miserable life.

4. *Recurring famines :* There were widespread famines during the second half of the 19th century when crores of people lost their lives on account of famines. The famines were followed by epidemics. The hardships faced by the Indian people convinced them that the British rule in India was the major cause of their starvation, misery and death. It is estimated that during 1860 and 1900, about 15 million people died on account of famines.

5. *Indian Renaissance and recovery of India's past glory :* The strenuous efforts made to study the ancient culture, literature, philosophy and religion by the British and Indian scholars, including indologists and archaeologists like Max Muller, John Marshall, Dayaram Sawhney, Wheeler and R.G. Bhandarkar helped profoundly, to bring to light, the richness of the ancient heritage of India. Masses began to feel proud of India's advances in arts, astronomy and sciences of ancient India. They began to take pride in the Indus Valley Civilization. They were thrilled to know that when the great Vedic Civilization flourished, England was inhabited by semi-barbaric tribes. They started reacting sharply to the western criticism of India's culture and civilization. They began to discard their sense of inferiority.

6. *Role of religious and social leaders.* Leaders like Swami Dayanand, Ramakrishna Paramahans, Vivekanand and others infused a new spirit of faith and courage. Besides reminding the people of the glory and greatness of India's past, they declared that there was no substitute for self-government. Swami Vivekanand, in his own way, exhorted the people of India to be strong and brave. It is said about him, "The queen of his adoration was motherland". He asked the educated people of India to be sensitive to the weak and the illiterate. He called for ceaseless efforts to rise and bring glory to the motherland. The founders of the Theosophical Society of India and Mrs. Annie Besant made their own contribution to the cause of national awakening.

7. *Impact of western thought* : A large number of educated Indians who came into contact with western thought, were greatly influenced by the democratic, nationalist, rational and political outlook. Philosophers like John Stuart Mill (1806-1873) became their guides. Nationalist leaders like Mazzini (1805-1872) and Garibaldi (1807-1882) of Italy became their political heroes.

8. *Spread of Education* : Spread of education became an important factor in the promotion of national consciousness among the Indians in a number of ways. First, modern education gave the educated Indians access to the liberal ideas of the West. They became acquainted with the ideals of democracy and human freedom and received inspiration from the nationalist movements and freedom struggles taking place in countries outside India. Second, the edu-

cated people were in a better position to make others aware of the evils of the foreign rule. Third, the growing middle class of western educated young people got disillusioned with the recruitment and racial policies of the British. Fourth, Universities of Bombay, Calcutta, Madras, Punjab and Allahabad were to produce graduates, quite a large number of whom were aspirants to high posts in civil services. They, however, found that the policy of discrimination followed by the British was a great barrier in their career. They, therefore, felt the need for an organised united action for national resurgence. In course of time, the best among them became the leaders of national movements. Fifth, English, as the medium of higher education created a certain community and unity of outlook and interests among the educated Indians. It became the medium of communication and exchange of ideas among educated Indians belonging to different regions.

9. *Role of literature :* The literature that was produced during the period, accelerated the spread of national consciousness among the masses of India. Novels, plays, poems and stories written in various Indian languages greatly helped in national awakening. The novel *Anand Math* and the composition *Vande Matram* of Bankim Chandra, the famous Bengali writer, became a great source of inspiration to the people. For the first time, it was sung at the annual session of the Indian Congress in 1896. Vast literature produced by Bhartendu Harish Chandra in Hindi, Vishnu Shastri Cheplunkar in Marathi, Subramanya Bharati in Tamil, Rabindranath Tagore in Bengali and Altaf Hussain Hali in Urdu, helped in stirring the hearts of the Indian people and stamped their minds with the ideals of freedom.

The appalling condition of the masses, as depicted in the well documented and scholarly writings of Dadabhai and R.C. Dutt, touched the conscience of the intellectuals and made them aware of the exploitative nature of the British economic policies.

10. *Role of the Press*: The contemporary press, newspapers and magazines, served a powerful media for mass awakening, infusing political ideas and patriotic sentiments. The Government tried but failed to subdue or purchase the press. It was very vocal in its criticism of the policies pursued by the British in India. The editors wrote fearlessly and exposed freely the evils of foreign rule. Editors like Lala Lajpat Rai of the *Bande Matram* and *The People* and Bal Gangadhar Tilak of *Kesari* and *Maratha,* suffered deportation. Five editors of *Yugantar* were put behind the bars. By the year 1905, India had over 700 newspapers and an equal number of periodicals. The nationalist press had to pay a very heavy price for its nationalist views.

11. *Development of means of transport and communication:* All major parts of the country were inter-connected with railways, postal services and other communication. Hence it became easier to spread the nationalist sentiments easily, to every nook and corner of the country.

12. *Administrative and economic unification of the country :* The British introduced a uniform system of administration throughout the country. It was based on a hierarchy of administrators right from Governor-General/Viceroy to the village patwari. The entire territory was divided into convenient units of administration, called provinces which were subdivided into smaller administrative units. Laws were duly codified. Uniform legal procedures and precedents were followed. There developed a strong centralised administrative set-up which kept provinces under strict discipline.

Setting up industries and trade helped to bring about an economic unification. Economic self-sufficiency of the village was replaced by its dependence on market forces.

13. *Racial discrimination against the Indians and their maltreatment* : The British always assumed an air of racial superiority and openly insulted even the English educated Indians. An Indian could rarely expect justice in a case involving a British citizen. The Criminal Procedure Code of 1873 had put such restrictions that Indian judges in general were not permitted to decide cases in which Europeans were involved. Ilbert Bill (1882), which provided for bringing the Indian and European magistrates on the same footing, generated a lot of opposition from the British community and ultimately it had to be modified. Indians could not travel in certain railway compartments, and visit entertainment clubs and restaurants. All this created a feeling of hatred for the British rule.

14. *Heavy war costs :* The British continued to wage a number of wars with other countries like Nepal, Tibet and Afghanistan and the cost of these wars was met out of the taxes collected from the Indians.

15. *Apathy of the British:* The period from 1876 to 1884 has been called the seed time of Indian nationalism. It was the period of passing the notorious Vernacular Press Act, which put restrictions on the press to curb Indian sentiments. The Second Afghan War brought untold suffering to the army people. There was the Ilbert Bill controversy. Lakhs of Indians died in the famines that took place during the period. Lord Lytton held his famous Delhi Durbar and the people wondered at his collousness.

16. *Discrimination against the Indians with regard to their appointment in Government Services :* In the beginning no Indians were appointed on high posts. The British thought that Indians were not capable of any trust and faith. The Proclamation of Queen Victoria in 1858 declared that henceforth Indians would be appointed on high posts on the basis of their merit irrespective of their caste, religion or race. Inspite of this Proclamation, this policy was not properly implemented. In 1868 Surendra Nath Banerjee passed the ICS Ex-

amination yet he was not given any high position. When Queen's Bench Division gave its decision in his favour, he was appointed an Assistant Collector in November 1871. But two years after this he was removed from service. This discriminatory, arbitrary and unjust policy of the Government created a great discontent and unrest among the educated people of India. They started taking active part in the National Movement with the aim of driving away the British from India.

In 1897, Gopal Krishna Gokhale gave a very convincing evidence before the Royal Commission which proved that there was a great need for providing adequate opportunity of appointment to the Indians on higher posts. In the civil department, these were only 55 Indians out of 1276 officers. In military, only one officer out of 856 was in the same bracket income. In Police, out of 230 District Superintendents of Police, there were just 3 Indians.

Role of Hume in National Awakening

Allian Octavian Hume (1829-1912), a retired British Official of the Indian Civil Service (ICS), was one of the prominent founders of the Indian National Congress in 1885. He inherited his attitude of taking up noble causes from his father who himself was a prominent Scottish patriot and reformer. Hume himself was witness to the violence and the spirit of revenge on the part of the British as well as the rebels. His life had been saved by some Indians when the rebels in 1857 attacked him. Hume appreciated the sentiments of the Indians and therefore he formed an organisation to present the sentiments of the people through peaceful means and to avoid the recurrence of 1857 events accompanied by bloodshed.

After his retirement, he devoted the rest of his life to the cause of Indian welfare. On March 1 1883, he exhorted in a letter to the Calcutta University graduates, to work for the uplift of their motherland, "Even if fifty among you cannot be found with sufficient power and sacrifice and love and pride in your country... there is no hope for India". He addressed the following lines to the people of India.

"Sons of Iand, Why sit ye idle?
Wait ye for some Deva's aid?
Buckle to be up and doing!
Nations by themselves are model"

The early Congress leaders regarded Hume as a 'Lightening Conductor'.

Hume published a pamphet entited *An Old Man's Hope* in which he made an appeal to the people of England in these words, "Ah Men! Well fed and happy ! Do you at all realise the dull misery of these countless myriads? Toil, Toil, Toil; Hunger, Hunger Hunger; Sickmen, Suffering, Sorrow, these alas, alas, alas are the key notes of their short and sad existence.

Q. 2. Why was the Indian National Congress founded? What were the factors leading to its emergence? State its initial objectives. Briefly mention the various phases of its work for the national awakening and freedom struggle of India.

or

Write an essay on the work of the Indian National Congress in National awakening and struggle for independence of India in its earlier phases.

Ans: *Congress as the Architect of India's Freedom Struggle*

There is no doubt that the Indian National Congress, during the course of time, played the most prominent role in the freedom struggle of India. It gathered together under its banner lakhs of people who made invaluable sacrifices and underwent even inhuman suffering and sorrow to keep alive the flame of freedom. It is rather paradoxical that the organisation founded by a British national, A.O. Hume, a retired Civil Servant, blessed by Lord Dufferin, tenth British Viceroy of India and first presided over in 1885 by W.C. Bannerjee, a British loyal barrister of Calcutta, spear-headed the struggle against the British. Later on Dufferin turned into the bitterest critic of the Congress.

Factors leading to the founding of the Indian National Congress : The national awakening witnessed in the great upheaval of 1857 was the beginning. In due course several local organsations in different parts of the country took up reforms in piecemeal manner without having a larger national perspective and without co-ordination with the efforts of other associations. A need for a well-knit organisation that could embrace in its fold, several sections of population belonging to different religions and regions was acutely felt. This need led to the founding of the Indian National Congress. The Indian National Congress attracted in the beginning, only educated classes, but in due course, it became a mass organisation under whose umbrella all sections of the population fought for the freedom of the country.

Congress as a 'Safety Valve' : Hume and others of his way of thinking did not want the repetition of the events of 1857. They wanted to provide an 'outlet' for the expression of the feelings of discontentment and distrust among the Indians and to find suitable solutions to their problems. This 'outlet' was provided by founding an organisation of the Indian intelligentsia which included senior retired officials, leading lawyers, prominent political persons and others representing different walks of life. The founders of the Congress wanted a gradual regeneration of the Indian nation. They were keen to established cordial relations between the officials and non-officials. They stressed that the British rule must be based on enlightened principles and all this could be achieved by setting up a forum which found its birth in the formation of the Indian National Congress.

According to Dr. Pattabhai Sitaramaya, a former President of the Congress and the author of '*History of the Indian National Congress*', the origins of the Congress are "shrouded in mystery".

Initial aims of the Congress: These were as under:

1. Promotion of friendly relations among nationalist political workers of different parts of the country.
2. Development and consolidation of the feelings of national unity, irrespective of caste, region or province.
3. Formulation of popular demands of the people and their presentation before the government.
4. Organisation of public opinion in the country.

Official/Government attitude towards the Congress : During the first two years of its inception (1885-87), the British response was well disposed towards its activities. The viceroy, Lord Dufferin, had entertained the Congress leaders at a garden party, at Calcutta in 1886. The Governor of Madras had also organised a similar party in 1887. However, the growing demands of the leaders for a representative and responsible government alarmed the authorities. In 1888, the Congress started a paid agency in London, for political propaganda, for the welfare of the people of India. This all the more irritated the British rulers. Pro-government papers also began to criticise the Moderate leaders. On the demands of the moderate leaders for a representative government in India, Lord Dufferin criticised the activities of the Moderate leaders in 1886 with these words, "Congressmen are seeking to sit in the Chariot of Sun. How can any reasonable man imagine that the British Government would allow this microscopic minority to control the administration of that majestic and multi-form empire".

In 1897, the Secretary of State for India, George Hamilton, referring to the Congress demands, said in the House of Commons, "The liberties of the British Constitution did not apply to criminal lunatics".

The British officials branded the Congress leaders as "disloyal babus", "Seditious Brahmans" and "violent villains". The Congress was described as a "factory of sedition." Lord Curzon, the Viceroy of India, declared in 1900, "The Congress is tottering to its fall and one of my great ambitions, while in India, is to assist it in a peaceful demise".

The British rulers began to describe it as the organisation of the Hindus and followed the policy of "Divide and Rule". They tried to drive a wedge between the Hindus and Muslims.

The history of the Congress became almost the history of the struggle for independence. The programme and activities passed through phases.

PHASES OF THE WORK OF THE CONGRESS AT A GLANCE

Phase/period	*Main objective*	*Prominent Leaders*	*Nature of the Programme*
1. 1885-1904	Gradual introduction of reforms	A.O. Hume Dadabhai Naoroji, Surendranath Banerjee, Gopal Kirshna Gokhale, Badru-ud-din Tyabji (Moderate leaders)	1. Organisation of public opinion through meetings etc. 2. Passing resolutions. 3. Sending Petitions. 4. Constitutional means.
2. 1905-1918	Seeing Salvation of motherland	1. Bal Gangadhar Tilak 2. Lala Lajpat Rai. 3. Bepin Chandra Pal (extremists militant leaders).	1. Swadeshi Movement. 2. Boycott and hartal. 3. Non-cooperation. 4. Fiery speeches through public platform and press.
3. 1919-1927	Greater control in the working of the Government	Gandhiji's leadership	1. Technique of Satyagraha. 2. Use of Khadi 3. Slogan of Hindu-Muslim Unity 4. Mass agitation 5. Non-cooperation Movement
4. 1928-1947	Goal of Porna Swaraj (Complete Independence)	1. Gandhiji 2. Jawaharlal Nehru 3. Subhash Chandra Bose 4. Sardar Vallabhbhai Patel 5. Maulana Abul Kalam Azad	1. Demonstrations, hartals 2. Participation in Government. 3. Congress Ministries in several provinces. 4. Civil Disobedience Movement 5. Satyagra has, Fasts 6. Quit India Movement 7. Negotiations for Independence.

Congress as the Representative of the Cross-Section of India's Population

The composition of delegates of the first session of the Congress held at Bombay indicates that it included people from different walks of life, regions and communities. The first session in 1885 attended by 72 delegates was held at Bombay, the second at Calcutta attended by 434 delegates, the third at Madras which drew 607 delegates, the fourth at Allahabad with 1248 delegates.

The first session was attended by editors, lawyers, retired civil servants, scholars, writers etc.

Some of the important leaders who attended the first session included Dadabhai Naoroji, Badr-ud-din Tyabji, Subramania Iyer, Dinsha Wacha, Ranade, Pherozeshah Mehta etc.

Q.3. What did the national movement in its early phase (1885-1905) try to achieve? How far did it succeed? *(Delhi University 1993)*

or

Give an account of the policies of the Indian National Congress upto 1905. *(Delhi University 1996)*

or

What did the national movement in its early phase (1885-1905) try to achieve? What are the achievements of the moderate leaders.

(Rajasthan University 1997)

Ans: *Moderate Leaders, Moderate Aims, Moderate Methods and Moderate Achievements: Policies of the Indian National Congress*

Moderate Leaders and Moderate Aims and Objectives

The early nationalist movement during 1885-1905 in India was guided by leaders who were called moderates or moderate nationalists on account of their cautious, cooperative and conciliatory approach to national issues. These leaders included: A.O. Hume (1829-1912), Dadabhai Naoroji (1825-1917), Badru-ud-din Tyabji (1844-1906), Pherozeshah Mehta (1845-1915), Surendranath Banerjee (1848-1925) and Gopal Krishna Gokhale (1866-1915).

The Moderate leaders had faith in the British Government that it would gradually redress the grievances of the people of India. Their approach was constitutional. They did not ask for complete independence.

A.O. Hume's appeal to the British rulers was,

"Ah Men! Well fed and happy ! Do you all realise the dull misery of these countless myriads? Do you at all realise these countless myriads? Toil, Toil; hunger, hunger, sickness, sorrow, suffering: these, alas-alas, are the keynotes of their short and sad existence".

Dadabhai observed, "Europeans occupy almost all the higher places in every department of government directly or indirectly under its control. While in India they acquire India's money, experience and wisdom and when they go, they carry both with them".

Surendra Nath Banerjee's approach was, "There are occasions when we must not cooperate and follow it as protest. But I altogether repudiate persistent policy of non-cooperation, especially, when the government is prepared to move along progressive lines"

Gopal Krishna Gokhale wrote, "The Englishman who imagines that India can be governed much longer on the same lines as in the past, and the Indian who thinks that he must seek a destiny for his country outside this empire of which now for better or worse, we are a part-both sides alike show an inadequate appreciation of the realities of the situation.'

Safety Valve and Congress's birth: According to some thinkers "The Indian, National Congress was founded to provide an outlet for the feelings of discontentment and distrust that has been brewing in India against the exploitative and imperialistic nature of the British rule. This outlet was provided by providing a suitable organisation of the Indian intelligentsia which included senior retired officials, leading lawyers, prominent political persons, and other representing different walks of life. In fact in the beginning the movement was supported by Lord Dufferin, the then Viceroy of India (1884-1888)

But the attitude changed soon after the Congress session at Madras. The British realized that the Congress leaders might promote nationalism among the people and make them very hostile to the British rule. Lord Dufferin ridiculed it as representing a "microscopic minority of the people". Its leaders began to be described as "seditious, double sided character", branded as "disloyal babus", and "violent villains".

Main Objectives of the Moderates

The moderates had three main objectives before them (*i*) To build up a strong public opinion in India by arousing the consciousness of the people towards administrative, economic and political reforms (*ii*) To unite the people on one political platform irrespective of caste, religion and region (*iii*) To persuade the British Government and British public opinion to introduce reforms.

Main demands of the Indian National Congress during 1885 to 1905

1. Wider employment of Indians in higher offices in the public sector.
2. Establishment of representative institutions.
3. Rapid development of modern industries.
4. Tariff protection to Indian industries.
5. Stopping economic drain of India by England.
6. Improvement in the condition of work of the plantation labourers.
7. Reduction of heavy land revenue.
8. Provision of irrigation facilities.
9. Abolition of salt tax which hit the poor and middle class.
10. Freedom of speech and the press.
11. Expansion of educational facilities.

The Methods Used by the Moderates to Achieve their Objectives

The methods used by the Moderates may broadly be expressed in terms of 6Ps i.e. Pen, Press, Platform, Posters, Playcards and Prayers to arouse public opinion to national causes and to get redress from the British. In 1888, it is estimated that Hume organised about 1000 public meetings. A paid agency was established in England for this purpose. Several papers were founded. Numerous prayers on people's demand were sent to the Government for necessary action.

2. *Constitutional Methods* : The moderates believed in adopting constitutional agitation within the ambit of law and slow orderly political progress.

3. *Careful resolutions* : They framed their resolutions with utmost moderation and clarify.

4. *Delegates*: They sent delegations to England to educate British public opinion.

5. *Publication of Books* : The moderates brought out a good deal of literature for highlighting the need of removing the economic hardships of the people.

Contribution of the Moderates

In spite of the limitations of the Moderates, they were able to contribute a lot for national awakening. Their major achievements are given below:

1. *Laying the Foundations of Indian independence.* The Moderates planted the seeds of liberty with great care and thus they laid a simple but firm foundation of India's freedom.

2. *Political Education.* The Moderates educated the people politically about their rights. For this objective, they took the aid of 6 P's i.e. Pen, poster, platform, press; playcards and petitions.

3. *Beginning of National Unity and Emotional Integration.* The Moderates brought together people from different parts of India at one platform. The organisation included people belonging to different regions, religions, castes, creeds and occupations also.

4. *Pointing out Drawbacks of Administration* The Moderates openly opposed the unjust actions of the government.

5. *Link between the Government and the People.* The Moderates on the one hand advocated the people's causes and on the other also presented the government's view before the people. Thus they intended to serve a bridge between the government and the people.

6. *Nurturing Popular Democratic Ideas.* The Moderates attempted to popularise the ideas of civil liberties, equality and freedom, etc. among the masses.

7. *Poineering work in Presenting True Economic Picture.* The Moderates brought out convincing literature on the extreme form of economic exploitation of the people of Indian by the British rulers. Dadabhai wrote pamphlets and books like '*England's Debt to India*', '*Poverty of India*' and *Poverty and Un-British Rule in India.*

8. *Evolving Common Economic and Political Programme.* For the first time, a common economic and political programme for the uplift of the Indian people was prepared.

9. *Secular Outlook.* The Moderates prepared their programme not on the appeals to religious or shallow statements but on secular lines.

10. *Constitutional Reforms.* The passing of the Indian Councils Act of 1892 was regarded as the first fruit of the efforts of the petitions and resolutions passed by the Congress at its sessions. In its sessions the Congress had asked for the expansion of the Councils.

Q. 4. Who were Moderates? State their objectives and the work done by them in national awakening.

Ans: *Moderates as the Founders of the Indian National Congress*

The Moderates were the intellectuals who founded the Indian National Congress. They were greatly moved at the impoverishment of the Indian people caused by the economic policies of the British rulers. They felt that heavy taxation, exploitation and the stagnated and backward agriculture had made the conditions of the peasants miserable.

The free trade policy, the gradual evolution of colonial pattern of trade and disappearance of support of local chiefs and nobles, ruined the artisans and the handicraftsmen.

The workers at the plantations and the modern industries had to work under very uncongenial conditions. Their wages were also very low. They lived from hand to mouth.

The British rulers drained the country's wealth and material resources to increase the wealth of England.

Early Congress leaders had faith in the British Government that it would gradually redress the grievances of the people of India. They, therefore, used to send representations, hold meetings, publish articles and go to England to mould public opinion. Their objectives as well as methods were moderate in nature. They wanted the betterment of the economic conditions of the people and more employment to them. Their approach was constitutional. They did not ask for complete independence. Hartals, demonstrations etc., were usually not resorted to.

Chief objectives and demands of the Moderates : The Moderates worked for the gradual introduction of reforms in the working of the administration of India. They asked for more powers for the Indians to the Legislative Councils and election of members. They also demanded major changes in the economic policies of the government for facilitating the growth of industries in India. Other major demands included providing more opportunities for Indians to compete for higher posts in administration, freedom of speech and expression etc.

Moderates as path finders and torch bearers: Their contribution to national awakening : The Moderates, the founders of the Indian National Congress, played a significant role in National awakening. They were the path finders and the torch bearers. They were aware of their limitations and accordingly initiated a moderate action. Perhaps time was not ripe for a revolutionary approach. Without minimising the important significant role that the Moderates played in the freedom struggle, it must be admitted that it took four decades after 1907, the year when the Extremists came into prominence, to achieve independence. Even Extremists could not achieve substantial results. The last phase of struggle for freedom was led not by an extremist but by a leader who believed in the power of *satyagraha*. There is no doubt that the

Moderates, the Extremist, the militants and the revolutionaries and the Gandhivadis, all contributed to the nationalist movement.

2. *Contribution of Moderates to consitutional reforms.* The Moderates had complete faith in the solemn pledges given by the British Government to the people of India from time to time. Surendranath Banerjee regarded the Queen's Proclamation of 1858 as "The Magna Carta of rights and liberties". For constitutional reforms, the Moderates believed in constitutional and orderly agitation. Badru-ud-din, the Congress President in 1887 said, "Be moderate in your demands, just in your criticism, correct in your facts and logical in your conclusions".

As a result of the pressure brought by the Indian National Congress, under the influence of the Moderates, the government passed the *Indian Council's Act of 1892.* The Act enlarged the functions of the Legislative Councils. They were authorised to discuss the annual financial statement under certain conditions. The members of the Councils were given the right to ask questions from the government on matters of public interest. The number of members was increased.

The 1892 Act fell short of expectations. Dadabhai Naoroji, in his presidential address of the Indian National Congress in 1893 at Lahore, termed provisions of the Act as 'arbitrary'. About elections to the Councils, R.C. Dutt observed, "Half a dozen members elected under somewhat complicated rules can scarcely express the views of the people of a province with a population of 30 to 40 million or more".

Budget could now be discussed but there was to be no voting. The Congress leaders termed the Act as a 'hoax'. They raised the slogan associated with the War of American Independence, "No taxation without representation". By the beginning of the 20th century, the demand for self government within the British empire was made from the Congress platform by Gokhale in 1905 and Dadabhai Naoroji in 1906.

3. *Contribution of the Moderates to Administrative Reforms* **:** The Moderates criticised the administrative set-up on various accounts. It was very costly. It was full of red tapism. Indians were excluded from higher posts. I.C.S. examination was held outside India. The demand or Indianisation of the higher grades of administrative services was put forward on economic, moral and political grounds. Economically, there were two factors (i) Higher salaries paid to the Europeans (ii) Payment of pension to Europeans, retired and returned to Britain, at a very high rate causing economic drain. Morally, it developed inferiority complex even among the most talented Indians that they were unifit to carry on the work of administration involving responsible duties. Politically, the European Civil Servants ignored the needs of the Indians.

In 1897, Gopal Krishna Gokhale gave a very convincing evidence before the Royal Commission, which proved that there was need for the Indianisation of administrative services. In the Civil Department, there were only 55 Indians out of 1276 officers; only one military officer out of 856 and in military only 25 officers out of 1303 in the same income bracket. In the police, there were just 3 Indians as District Superintendents out of 230.

4. *Contribution of Moderates in Economic Reforms :* The most notable part of the Moderates' political work was their systematic and factual criticism of the economic policy of the British rules through press and publications. They highlighted the evil consequences of the exploitative economic policies of the British rulers pursued in all the three important areas of economy–trade, industry and finance. They vehemently opposed British economic imperialism which led to the subordination of the Indian economy to the British economy. Naoroji's book *Un-British Rule in India,* R.C. Dutt's book *The Economic History of India in the Victorian Age,* Digby's work *Prosperous India* and Lajpat Rai's *Unhappy India* provided a graphic picture of heavy taxation, costly wars, discriminatory tariff policy, neglect of industries, enormous export of India's raw materials, recurring famines, growing national debt, occurrence of epidemics, rising death rate, heavy foreign capital investment and the unending huge drain of India's wealth to England. About the drain of wealth, Dadabhai caustically remarked, "The English stand sentinel at the front door of India.... and carry away by the backdoor, the very treasure they stand sentinel to protect".

The Moderates organised a powerful agitation against almost all important official economic policies. They popularised the idea of *Swadeshi* or the use of Indian goods and launched a movement for the boycott of British goods. In 1896, students in various parts of Maharashta publicly burnt foreign clothes. They launched an agitation for the reduction of heavy land revenue payments. They demanded that the government should provide cheap credit facilities to the peasants through agricultural banks. They urged upon the government to make available irrigation facilities on a large scale. They pleaded for improving the conditions of work of the plantation labourers. They asked for a radical change in the existing pattern of taxation and expenditure which put a huge burden on the poor. They made representations against the abolition of salt tax which hit hard the poor and the lower middle classes.

5. *Contribution of Moderates to the Defence of the Civil Rights :* From the very beginning, the Moderates put up a strong defence for the civil rights i.e. freedom of speech, the press and association. In 1897, the arrest of B.G. Tilak and several other leaders and editors evoked a country-wide protest. About the arrest of Tilak it was said, "There is scarcely a home in this vast country where Tilak is not now the subject of melancholy talk and where his imprisonment is not considered as a domestic calamity".

6. *Moderates' Contribution to diverse issues of National Interest :* The Moderates demanded separation of the judicial powers from executive powers so that people may get protection from the arbitrary actions of the bureau-

cracy and the police. They criticized the high cost of the judicial process as well as delays involved in it. They strongly criticized the oppressive and tyrannical behaviour of the police and other government officials towards the common people. They laid a good deal of stress to undertake welfare activities for the people. They urged the government to take speedy action for the promotion of primary education. They pleaded for greater facilities for technical education. They demanded extension of health and medical facilities. They protested against the aggressive policy of waging wars against India's neighbours. They spoke up in defence of Indian workers, who, on account of poverty, had been compelled to migrate to foreign countries such as Malaya, Mauritius, the West Indies, British Guiana and South Africa.

The achievements of the Moderates included the following :

1. They founded the Indian National Congress.
2. They evolved a common economic and political programme.
3. The programme and activities of the Moderates were based on the hard realities of the country and not on any kind of sectarian or religious sentiments.
4. They did pioneering work in exposing the exploitative nature of British Imperialism in India.
5. The Moderates made the people of India conscious of their right to freedom.
6. The Moderates paved the way for close interaction in national matters.
7. The Moderates helped in popularising the basic concepts of democracy, civil liberties and freedom of the press etc.
8. The moderates initiated the process of imparting political training to the educated Indians.
9. The Moderates built up a strong public opinion on economic and social issues.
10. They worked for promoting national unity irrespective of caste, religion or region.

Limitations/Weaknesses of the Nationalist Movement Under Moderate Leadership.

The nationalist movement under the Moderates suffered from arm-chair discussions, resolutions and appeals and ineffective methods.

The movement in the first phase was confined to a limited section of society. Only educated people took part in its activities. It was confined to 'paper work' which consisted of passing prayers and petitions to the government. The programmes were not action–oriented with the result that the masses had no contribution to make.

Summing up. Taking into consideration the pros and cons of the issue, it can be concluded very safely that the movement was successful to a considerable extent to achieve the goals it set forth before it. It worked quite effectively under the parameters of its aims and objectives.

Dr. Pattabhai Sitaramaya, a former Congress president in the book *The History of the Indian National Congress* has summed up the role of the Moderates in these words, "We cannot blame them for the attitude they adopted as pioneers of Indian political reform anymore than we can blame the brick and mortar that is buried six feet deep in the foundation and plinth of modern edifice. They have made possible the superstructure, storey by storey by colonical self-government, Home Rule within the empire, *swaraj* and the top of all complete independence".

25

National Movement and Constitutional Reforms (1905-1918)

Q. 1 Narrate the causes which gave rise to Extremism in the Indian politics. How did the Extemists differ from the Moderates in their aims and methods. (*Rajasthan University 1997*)

Ans: *Meaning of the Terms 'Extremism' and 'Extremists'*

Extremism implied revolutionary aims and methods for their achievement. It meant defiance of authority for the achievement of freedom from the British rule. Extremists believed that freedom had to be fought for and not to be begged. They believed in inciting people against the tyrannies inflicted on them by the British. Lokmanya Bal Gangadhar Tilak (1856-1928), Bipin Chandra Pal (1858-1932) and Lala Lajpat Rai (1865-1928) popularly known as *Bal-Pal-Lal* were the important leaders. Tilak has been called the *'Father of Indian Unrest'* and Lajpat Rai as the *'Lion of Punjab'*. Pal was popularly known as the *'Father of Revolutionary* thought in India'.

The extremists were opposed to 'meekness' in the field of freedom struggle. They believed that force might be resorted to achieve the desired objective if other methods failed. Tilak's assertion, "Swaraj is my birth right and I shall have it" continued to inspire generations.

The revolutionary traditions in France, Ireland, America and Italy were nearer to their hearts.

The period during the years 1905 to 1918 is usually referred to as the period of militant or extremist nationalism.

Causes which gave rise to 'Extremism' in Indian Nationalism

Broadly speaking, the causes can be grouped under the following two heads:

1. Internal causes
2. External causes

The internal causes included (i) Surcharged political environment (ii) Recognition of the true nature of the British rule (iii) Growth of self-respect and confidence among the Indians (iv) Growth of education among the Indians (v) Increasing unemployment in India (vi) Partition of Bengal (vii) Repressive measures of the British rulers.

External causes included (i) publicity of India's condition abroad (ii) Independence movements abroad (iii) Reforms in foreign lands (iv) Victory of Japan over Russia.

1. *Surcharged political Environment* : As the 19th century was about to close, the political environment in India was already charged on account of persecutions of the leaders, famines, plagues and high expectations of the Indians and British indifference, injustice and arrogance. Then, there emerged Lord Curzon, the new Viceroy of India (1899-1905), who had behaved from his early days as the 'most superior person'. The keynote of his administrative approach was, "The British bureaucracy knows what is for the good of the Indian people". The movement of adopting aggressive postures emerged after the Partition of Bengal in 1905.

2. *Recognition of the True Nature of the British Rule* : The true nature of the British rule was exposed by the poverty it spread, the man-made famines it created, the racial arrogance it displayed, the drain of India's wealth it led to, the exports of India's raw materials it encouraged and the policy of employment it followed in respect of the educated Indians. Although these were invisible evidences for a long time but certain circumstances brought to light their evil effects. The India Councils' Act of 1882 was a complete disappointment. In 1896, plague took a very heavy toll of lives. The 1898 law put restrictions on freedom of speech. In 1899, the Calcutta Corporation Act completely officialised the Calcutta Corporation. The disastrous famines which ravaged India from 1896 to 1900 and took over 90 lakhs of lives, symbolized the evil economic consequences of the foreign rule.

The Indian Official Secrets Act of 1904 restricted the freedom of the Press.

The Indian Universities Act 1904 reduced the autonomy of the universities and such changes were made in the Syndicates, Senates and Faculties of the Universities which led to the predominance of the Europeans. The most severe blow came in the Partition of Bengal in 1905.

The speeches of George Hamilton, Secretary of State for India and Lord Curzon, clearly reflected the true nature of the British rule. On August 5, 1897, Hamilton termed the Indians as 'Criminal lunatics'. Lord Curzon called the Indians 'cheats'.

3. *Growth of Self-Respect and Self Confidence:* Leaders of the new movement tried to develop self-respect and self-confidence among the Indians. Sri Aurobindo asserted, "The fate of the country is in ourselves. It is not in any outward force. It is in hearts, in our courage." Lala Lajpat told the masses, "They would have to strike the blow for freedom. The harder the contest, the more glorious is the triumph". B.C. Pal reminded the people, "self-help and self-sacrifice" was the real force in the field of nationalism. Swami Vivekanand, though not a political leader, asked the people to have confidence in them. He declared, "If there is a sin in the world it is weakness; avoid all weakness, weakness is death... And there is the test of truth-anything that makes you weak physically, intellectual and spiritually, reject as poison,

there is no life in it, it cannot be true". It is of interest to note that he felt the need of arousing political consciousness among the masses. "The only hope of India is from the masses", he said.

4. *Growth of Education Among the Indians* : In the 1900s, the University and collegiate education in India presented a motely picture. On the one hand, there had been considerable expansion of higher education, on the other hand, the efficiency of the new colleges was not very high. The Western education had created a solid class of intellectuals who became conscious of the Western ideals of democracy, nationalism and radicalism.

5. *Discriminating Policy of Employment and Increasing Unemployment:* The development of higher education was very lopsided. Professional education in general, and industrial and technical education in particular remained neglected. There were fewer avenues of self employment for the educated and thus they faced unemployment. Added to this was the lack of avenues in services, and when employed, they received very low salaries as compared with their counterpart Europeans. Thus, the economic plight of the educated made them look critically at the British rule. The anti-India policy of Lord Curzon led to all the more bitterness and discontentment. The view of Lord Curzon was, "The highest ranks of all civil employment must, as a general rule, be held by Englishmen".

6. *Partition of Bengal* : The Partition of Bengal by Lord Curzon in 1905 was seen by the people of India as a clever move to divide the people. The Indian National Congress opposed the move. (Discussed in detail in the next question).

7. *Repressive Measures :* During the anti-partition movement, Government resorted to several repressive measures.

8. *Inspiration from International Events* : The nationalist leaders drew great inspiration from the following international events:

(i) A backward Japan, an Asian country, coming up as a first rate industrial power.
(ii) The defeat of Russia-considered to be a giant nation — by a small nation like Japan.
(iii) The victory of the Ethiopians, an African power, over Italy, an European power.
(iv) Revolutionary movements in China, Egypt, Ireland, Russia and Turkey.
(v) Liberal ideas of Gladstone (1809-1898), a British Prime Minister.
(vi) Second Socialist International Meet at Paris, emphasising the building up of a new culture.
(vii) The philosophy of the Fabian Society in England with its stress on liberalism.

All the above factors led to the development of this popular feeling among the people of India, "What one Asiatic nation has done others can do. If Japan can drub Russia, India can drub England with equal ease. Let us drive the

British into the sea and take our place side by side with Japan, among the great powers of the world".

Differences between the Moderates and the Extremists

	Moderates		*Extremists*
1.	The aim of the Moderates was very limited. They wanted some representation in the running of government.	1.	Swaraj was the ultimate goal.
2.	They emphasised the need of reforms in the administrative and economic structure.	2.	They believed in complete overhauling the administrative and economic structure.
3.	They believed that the British rule, with some reforms could be beneficial to India.	3.	The British rule was considered as a curse.
4.	The Moderates believed that the people of India were not yet fit for self government.	4.	The extremists believed that the Indians were fully competent to handle their own affairs.
5.	The Moderates believed in adopting constitutional methods for the fulfillment of their objectives.	5.	The Extremists believed that constitutional methods would lead them nowhere.
6.	They believed in sending petitions, prayers and resolutions to the Government for consideration and implementation.	6.	They believed that national problems could be solved by agitation.
7.	They believed in conciliation.	7.	They believed in confrontation.
8.	They were allergic to Swadeshi and Boycott.	8.	They considered Swadeshi and Boycott as important weapons.
9.	They had faith in the goodwill and sympathy of the English people.	9.	They did not believe in such notions.
10.	The Moderates hoped that they could get their requests acceded to, without any substantial sufferings and sacrifices.	10.	They were convinced that without hardships and sufferings, salvation of India was not possible.
11.	The Moderates wanted to follow the path of least resistance.	11.	The extremists were prepared to follow the path of active resistance.
12.	The Moderates confined their activities to the small section of intelligentia and assigned a passive role to masses.	12.	They had immense faith in the masses and made them active partners in the national struggle.
13.	The Moderates in general, were loyal to the British.	13.	They were anti-British. (see the next answer also).

Q. 2. In what way did the Extremists differ from the Moderates in the Indian National Movement? *(Delhi University 1998)*

or

Bring out the differences between the Moderates and the Extremists and assess the role of the Extremists in the National Movement.

(Rajasthan University 1996)

or

Discuss the ideological differences between the Moderates and the Extremists *(Rajasthan University 1994)*

Ans: *Extremist Leaders and Moderate Leaders in the National Movement*

The first phase of the National Movement (1885-1905) was primarily led by Moderate leaders like Dadabhai Naoroji, Badru-Ud-din Tyabji, W.C. Banerjee, Gopalkrishna Gokhale, Pherozeshah Mehta and Surendranath Banerjee. The second phase (1905-1918) was dominated by extremist leaders like Bal Gangadhar Tilak, Lala Lajpat Rai and Bepin Chandra Pal. Sri Aurobindo Ghose, before settling at Pondicherry in 1910 and thereafter leading the life of a yogi, was an extremist and a great revolutionary.

Differences between Moderates and Extremists : During the period 1905 to 1918, the earlier approach of 'reconciliation' followed by the Moderates was replaced by the new approach of 'confrontation' with the British rulers. The Moderates believed that there was great scope of progress for the Indians under the British rule which they termed as 'benevolvent control'. The leaders of the new movement were firmly convinced that India could not make any progress under the 'exploitative, ruthless and oppressive' regime of the British imperialists. They found that the British Government was not receptive to the appeals, petitions and resolutions sent by the Moderates to it. They thought that the peaceful methods adopted by the Moderates had not worthwhile impact. The Militants, therefore, adopted aggressive methods to achieve their objective of self-rule in India i.e. rule of the Indians in India not that of the British.

Broadly speaking, the Moderates and the Extremists differed on the following points.

1. Objectives of the Moderates and Extremists.
2. Attitude towards the British rulers.
3. Methods to be used for the realisation of objectives

Objectives of the Moderates and Extremists

The objectives of the Moderates were very limited. They wanted some representation in the running of the Government. They also emphasised the need for reforms in the administrative and economic structure.

While delivering the Presidential address, W.C. Banerjee, the President of the first session of the Indian National Congress laid down the following objectives of the Congress:

(i) The promotion of personal intimacy and friendship amongst all the most earnest workers in our country's cause in the various parts of the empire.

(ii) The eradication by direct friendly personal intercourse of all possible races, creeds, or provincial prejudices amongst all the lovers of the country and the fuller development and consolidation of those sentiments of national unity that took their origin in our beloved Ripon's ever memorable reign.

(iii) The authoritative accord of the matured opinions of the educated classes in India on some of the most important and pressing social questions of the day.

(iv) The determination of the methods by which during the next twelve months it is desirable for the native politicians to labour in public interest.

S.N. Banerjee explained that the object of the Congress was "not the suppression of the British rule in India but the broadening and the liberalising of its spirit.

On the other hand, B.G. Tilak gave the people of India the slogan "Swaraj is my birth right and I shall have it".

Attitude of the Moderates and Extremists to the British Rulers

The Moderates in general were loyal to the British. They believed that the British rule, with some reforms, could be beneficial to India. They had faith in the good will and sympathy of the English people.

Dadabhai Naoroji wrote to the Secretary of State for India, "They (the educated people of India) know that a real regeneration, civilisation, and advancement of India materially, morally and politically depends upon a long continuance of the British rule". In his Presidential address to the Indian National Congress held in 1886, he said, "We desire that the British connection should endure for a long time to come for the sake of material and political elevation among the civilized nations of the world".

Pherozeshah Mehta, another leader of the Moderates said, "I have unbounded faith in the living and fertilizing principles of the English culture and English education".

As against these views of the Moderate leaders, B.C. Pal wrote in the 21st December 1904 issue of *'New India'*, "The belief that England of her own free will help Indians out of their long established civil servitude and establish those free institutions of Government which she herself values so much was once cherished, but all hopes has now been abandoned".

Difference in Methods adopted :

The methods used by the Moderates to achieve their objectives may broadly be expressed in terms of 6P's i.e. Pen, Press, Platform, Posters, Playcards and Petitions, to mould public opinion and to get redressed grievances and demands of the Indian people. The Moderates believed in adopting constitutional methods. Surendranath Banerjee was very critical of the non-cooperation movement. He said, "There are occasions where we must not cooperate and follow it up as a protest. But I altogether repudiate persistent policy of non-coperation, especially when the Government is prepared to move along progressive lines".

The founder of the Congress, A.O. Hume published a pamphlet entitled '*An Old Man's Hope*' in which he appealed to the people of England in these words" Ah men ! well fed and happy! Do you at all realise the dull misery of these counless myriads ! Toil, Toil, Hunger, Hunger, Hunger, Sickmen, Suffering, Sorrow, these alas, alas, alas are the key notes of their short and sad existence". In 1888, it is estimated that Hume organised about 1000 public meetings. A paid agency was established in England for giving publicity to India's needs and their redressal. Several papers were founded. Numerous prayers on people's demand were sent to the Government for necessary action. Delegates were sent to England to educate British public opinion.

Quite contrary to the approach of the Moderates, Lala Lajpat Rai called the annual meetings of the Congress as "annual national festivals of the educated Indians". He had no love for what he called "holiday patriots". Again to quote him, "You can at times successfully appeal to the humanity and benevolence of individuals but to hope for just and benevolence from a nation is hoping against hope." He started two nationalist papers '*Bande Matram*' in Urdu and '*People*' in English. Lajpat Rai thundered stressing the methods of Extremists. "We desire to turn our faces away from Government Houses and turn them to the huts of the people. We want to stop our mouths so far as an appeal to the Government is concerned and open mouth with a new appeal to the masses of the people. This is the psychological effect of the boycott movement".

Bal Gangadhar Tilak founded two papers '*Kesari*' and '*Maharata*' for developing patriotic feelings for the motherland. He was imprisoned several times for his stirring speeches and writings. At a public meeting at Calcutta, Tilak declared, "It is impossible to expect that our petitions will be heard unless backed by firm resolution. The three P's - Pray, Please and Protest backed by solid force. Look to the examples of Ireland, Japan and Russia and follow their methods" Tilak was called the 'father of Indian unrest? People looked upon Tilak as "the man who is to expel the British from India"

A scholar turned revolutionary, nationalist turned saint, Sri Aurobindo, in his '*Essays* on *Gita*' defined killing of national enemies as '*Dharmayuddha*. He was very emphatic that, "The work of national emancipating is a great and holy '*Yajna*'of which boycott, Swadeshi, national education and every other activity, great or small are only major or minor parts".

Summing up : The Moderates tried to win over the British and the extremists wanted to turn them out by all means.

The Moderates wanted to improve the existing constitution, the Extremists wanted self-rule and to reconstruct the constitution accordingly.

The Moderates wanted to work with the existing bureaucracy; the extremists were out to obstruct it.

The Moderates were in favour of peaceful methods; the Extremists believed in agitation approach.

Impact of Extremists: With the untiring efforts of the leaders belonging to the Extremist thought, the movement against the Partition of Bengal assumed national dimension. People showed great enthusiasm in the programmes of the Extremists which included boycott of British goods and educational institutions also. National education received encouragement. Home Rule movement was organised. Tilak was tried for sedition and sentenced to 6 years' imprisonment. Several newspapers were censured. Pal voluntarily courted imprisonment for his writings in the *Bande Matram.* Lajpat Rai led several demonstrations.

The Extremists were successful in getting repealed the Order of Partition of Bengal in 1911.

Q. 3. Give an estimate and contribution of Bal Gangadhar Tilak to the Indian National Movement. *(Rajasthan University 1997)*

or

Estimate the role and contribution of Tilak in the freedom struggle. *(Rajasthan University 1992)*

Ans: *Brief Life sketch of Bal Gangadhar Tilak (1856-1920)*

Born in Maharashtra, son of a primary school teacher; college education at Deccan College Poona; took to journalism, founded two weeklies '*Kesari*' and '*Maratha*', joined Indian National Congress in 1907.

An extremist leader; arrested in 1908 and deported to Burma for six years, started Home Rule Movement in 1916; wrote *'Gita Rahasya';* started Ganpati and Shivaji festivals to arouse national pride.

Role of Bal Gangadhar Tilak in National Movement.

Symbol of India's Freedom. In the words of Pt. Jawaharlal Nehru, "We have in Tilak a symbol of India's struggle for freedom and a man who was not only a brave soldier but a great captain, not a captain of an organised government but a captain of unorganised masses of India".

Passion for Swaraj : Gandhiji paid Tilak the following tribute, "His patriotism was a passion with him. He knew no religion but love for his country. No man preached the gospel of *swaraj* with the consistency and insistence of Lokmanya".

Tilak remembered as Lokmanya (Loved and respected by the people), was the first leader to use the slogan "Swaraj (freedom) is my birth right and I shall have it".

Tilak — a mass leader : Tilak has been described as 'India's first mass leader. He succeeded in arousing a sense of self-respect and self-reliance among the middle class Indians and made them fight against the oppressive laws of the British Government.

Tilak as an Extremist leader : Tilak has been designated as the 'Father of the Indian unrest' and the 'Prince among patriots'. He became an Extremist leader on account of the following (i) Tilak's temperament, he was buoyant bubbling with life and imbued with unbounded nationalist spirit (ii) Influence of Marathas. Lives of certain Maratha leaders, particularly Shivaji inspired him (iii) Repression. The coercive and repressive measures of the British rulers caused a good deal of disillusionment, frustration and anger in Tilak (iv) Failure of the Moderates, to achieve satisfactory results.

Tilak's method of work : Tilak's slogan was : 'Educate, agitate and organise'. The force he wanted to use was 'the force of public opinion and pressure'.

Man of action : Tilak stressed the philosophy of Gita. In his own words, "No one can expect the Providence to protect one who sits with folded arms and throws his burden on others. God does not help the indolent. You must be doing all that you can to lift yourself up and then only you may rely on the Almighty to help you." He justified the killing of Afzal Khan by Shivaji and exhorted the masses to follow the great leader for liberating their motherland from the clutches of the foreigners.

A revivalist: Tilak was eager to revive all that was good and glorious in Indian culture and civilization. He was opposed to the idea of blindly tòeing the line of the West. In his '*Kesari*' a Maratha language weekly founded by him, he wrote, "A number of our educated men began to accept uncritically the materialistic doctrines of the Westerners. Thus we have the pathetic situation of the new generation making on their minds a carbon copy of the gross materialism of the West" At the same time, he was opposed to the one-sided and dogmatic approach of Indians. He did not minimise the importance of English education. He asserted, "A proper knowledge of the old traditions and philosophies must be imparted, to the newly educated classes and the *'Pandits'* and *'Shastris'* must be given information about newly changed and changing circumstances".

Methods to develop national awakening and to achieve Swaraj

Tilak placed before the nation a nine-fold programme of effective political action for the attainment of Swaraj (freedom). These steps were: (i) Boycott (ii) Swadeshi (iii) National education and (iv) Passive resistance. (v) Organisation of Ganapati and Shivaji festivals: (vi) Two weeklies (vii) Social Work (viii) Home Rule and (ix) Publication of books.

(i) *Swadeshi:* Swadeshi meant self help and to depend upon Indian made goods rather than rely upon manufactured goods of Birmmingham and Manchester. Swadeshi was a spirit, economic and political weapon in the hands of Tilak to create confidence in the people of their strength and will, to cripple the British economically by depriving them of India's wealth and also to shake them politically. Tilak proclaimed, "If we do not wish to be White man's slave we should vigorously carry on the Swadeshi movement. It is the only effective method for our deliverance. The object of the movement is to do away with the system under which we are treated like slaves by Europeans".

Swadeshi came to be understood more than simple economic self-sufficiency. It was being increasingly realized that if there could be self-help in the economic sphere, there could be self help in other spheres as well.

The Swadeshi Movement soon got converted into a movement of national regeneration. It began to be seen as a practical application of love of the motherland. Swadeshi proved to be '*Bande Matram*' in action.

(ii) *Boycott :* Tilak asserted that Swadeshi Movement would not have any practical utility till boycott of '*Videshi*'(foreign goods) was resorted to. Boycott was a fiery weapon. It was, in a way, substitute for war. Boycott was a measure to bring economic pressure on the business interests of the British both in India and abroad. It meant refusal of the people of India to purchase British manufactured goods.

But soon the movement took a new turn. Tilak and his contemporaries emphasised that the entire super-structure of the British Indian administration and the British system of rule over India was based upon the cooperation of the people of India. Hence boycott came to be used to shake the foundation of the administrative structure of the British masters. Tilak said, "We shall not assist them to collect revenue. We shall not assist them in fighting beyond the frontiers or outside India with Indian blood and money. We shall not assist them in carrying on the administration of justice. We shall have our own courts and when time comes we shall not pay taxes".

The Moderates in the Congress had hither appealed to the educated and middle class people. Tilak and his co-workers brought the masses into political action.

The Swadeshi — Boycott Movement was an organised attempt for the assertion of the democratic principle that the predominant political opinion of the inhabitants of a country must not be transgressed by the rulers.

(iii) *National Education :* National education was the third pillar of political action. Tilak was of the view that Western education was ruinous to the future and well-being of the nation. Therefore, Tilak and other national leaders stressed the need for starting national schools and colleges which could impart inexpensive education and inculcate among the students the spirit of self-help and self-reliance which was deplorably lacking in government sponsored schools and colleges. National education thus became an integral part of the nationalists' programme.

The Partition of Bengal was the signal for an agitation such as India had not hitherto witnessed. The Bengal National College was formally inaugurated in 1906.

The National Council of Education was registered under the Act XXI of 1860. The movement for National Education was not confined to Bengal alone. It spread to other parts of India also.

(iv) *Passive resistance :* According to Tilak, Swadeshi and boycott were the techniques of passive resistance. Passive resistance did not mean resort to violence. It was recommended for the use of strong constitutional means. He said, "If thieves enter our houses and we have not sufficient strength in our wrists to drive them out, we should without hesitation shut them up". By passive resistance, he also meant 'sacrifices' on the part of the people. Passive resistance was means to an end, not an end in itself. He described passive resistance as perfectly constitutional.

(v) *Organisation of Ganapati and Shivaji Festivals :* Tilak adopted novel methods of instiling a national spirit and spirit of unity among the masses. He founded two festivals, the Ganpati and Shivaji to achieve these objectives. Ganpati is the Hindu deity of learning and removal of obstacles. The basic idea behind organising the Shivaji festival was to give the masses a hero to rediscover their self-esteem and self-respect. These festivals were organised every year. Tilak regarded these festivals as powerful instruments for imparting instruction to masses.

(vi) *Two Weeklies :* Tilak started two weeklies, the "*Maratha*' in English (for the educated class) and '*Kesari*' (for the masses) for national awakening.

(vii) *Social Work* : His political career began in right earnest in 1896 when two disasters–a terrible famine and the plague hit the country. Tilak visited all the areas and organised relief measures. He became a champion of the peasantry whose emancipation became of the important purposes of his life.

(viii) *Home Rule Movement :* When the first war was on and the British were proclaiming that they were fighting to make the world safe for democracy, Tilak demanded self-government for India. Hence in collaboration with Annie Besant, he started Home Rule Leagues in India.

(ix) *Publication of Books :* Jail gave Tilak enough time to devote himself to meditation, reading and writing. His two monumental works, '*Arctic Home in the Vedas*' and Srimad '*Bhagavadgita Rahsya*' were a great source of inspiration for the people.

Tilak's imprisonment and his legal fights

Tilak had to spend a lot of time of his life in jail and in fighting legal battles. He was arrested several times on sedition charges for publishing poems and articles.

In 1908, when he was charged for his two articles *'The Country's Misfortune'* and '*These Remedies are not lasting*', Tilak addressed the Jury for 21 hours, exhibiting his legal erudition. The Jury, of course found him guilty and he told the Jury, "I maintain that I am innocent. There are higher powers that rule the destiny of things and it may be the will of providence that the cause which I represent may prosper more by my suffering than by my remaining free".

Q. 4. Make a comparative contribution of Gopal Krishna Gokhale and Bal Gangadhar Tilak to the National Movement.

(Rajasthan University 1996)

Ans: *Gopak Krishna Gokhale (1866-1915) a Modeate and Bal Gangadhar Tilak (1856-1920) an Extremists.*

Both Tilak and Gokhale were contemporaries, both hailed from Maharashtra; both were patriots of the first order; both made heavy sacrifices in life; both were teachers in their early life; both were life long servants of the people and both set a standard of service in public life and labour in the national cause which rarely has been matched but both were poles apart.

In the following pages an attempt is made to study their ideological conflicts and methods of approach to their politico-social thinking.

Political Objective : Gokhale stood for 'self-government' and Tilak for '*Swaraj*'. Tilak asserted "Swaraj is my birth right and I will have it". Gokhale, on the other hand wanted gradual advance towards self-government on the principle 'first deserve and then desire'

Attitude towards the British : Like other Moderate leaders, Gokhale admired British rule and considered it a 'blessing in disguise'. Tilak on the other hand regarded it as the greatest 'curse'. As such he was of the firm conviction that sooner the people got rid of it better it would be. Gokhale had his own conviction. Once in a reply to Lord Harding who asked Gokhale's reaction of the British troops decided to leave India within a month, he said, "I would be very pleased to hear the news but before you had all reached Aden... We would be telegraphing to you to come back". Gokhale, therefore, believed cooperating with the British administration and Tilak aimed at ousting them.

Political Programmes : Tilak advocated a number of programmes like boycott, Swadeshi, National education, Home Rule Leagues and celebration of festivals like Ganesh festival and Shivaji festival etc. Gokhale preached Swadeshi and national education.

Political Methods : Gokhale believed in the British sense of justice, equality and fair play. Therefore, he appealed to their sense of reason, through 4Ps i.e. petition, prayer, protest and please - constitutional methods. Tilak, on the contrary declared that petitions and prayers would not be heard unless backed by firm action. He always quoted the examples of Ireland, Japan and Russia. He was for the philosophy of 'defiance'.

Passive resistance: Gokhale believed in passive resistance only as a measure of defence rather than attack and was keen to convert passive resistance movement into moral and spiritual movement. He categorically stated that circumstances in India did not permit passive resistance. Tilak considered passive resistance as a very potent weapon to shake the alien imperialism. His philosophy of resistance was rather 'active' resistance. He equated resistance with people's sacrifices and sufferings for the cause of national uplift.

Sphere of Work : Gokhale was keen to mobilise the intelligentsia and win concessions and favours for them. Tilak wanted to generate political consciousness among the masses and prepare them for national struggle.

Social reforms vs political reforms : Gokhale advocated social reform right from the beginning of his life. He was of the view that the problem of political reform could not be divorced from social reform. Tilak also stood for social reforms but he stressed that political reforms must precede social reforms. He took the plea that once Swaraj was attained, social and economic reforms would automatically follow suit.

Concept of Boycott : Gokhale felt that the word boycott had a sinister meaning. It implied a vindictive desire to injure others. He also realised that strict boycott of foreign goods was not at all practicable in the prevailing industrial conditions. Tilak was a champion of the boycott movement.

Place of revolt : Gokhale never talked of revolt for attaining Swaraj or self-government. Tilak, once said to Gandhiji, "I consider an armed revolt also constitutional. The only difficulty at present is that it is not possible. If anyone were to assure me that armed revolt would be successful to the extent of even eight annas in the rupee, I would start the revolt trusting God to give success to the extent of remaining eight annas". There is no doubt that he was in touch with some leading revolutionaries of the times like Shyamji Krishna Verma, Damodar Panth Savarkar, father of V.D. Savarkar, and Savarkar himself.

Oratory: Gokhale was a parliamentary type of orator while Tilak was a simple but effective orator.

Temperament : By temperament, Gokhale was gentle, polite and full of human kindness, a politician who probably never ultered a wounding word in his life. By temperament, Tilak was kind but his thoughts often verged on extremisms or revolution and his pen was vitriolic.

Service and action : The motto of Gokhale was love and service and that of Tilak was action and suffering in general.

In his book *'The History of the Congress'*, Dr. Pattabhai Sitarammya has compared Tilak and Gokhale in these words, "Tilak and Gokhale were both patriots of the first order. Both had made heavy sacrifices in life. But their temperaments were widely different from each other. Gokhale was a Moderate and Tilak was Extremist, if we may use the language in vogue at that time, Gokhale's aim was to improve the existing constitution, Tilak's was to reconstruct it. Gokhale had necessarily to work with bureacracy; Tilak had necessarily to fight it. Gokhale stood for cooperation wherever possible and opposition wherever necessary. Tilak was inclined to a policy of obstruction. Gokhale's primary concern was with the administration and its improvement; Tilak's supreme concern was the nation and its upbuilding. Gokhale's ideal was love and service; Tilak's was sacrifice and suffering. Gokhale's method sought to win the foreigner, Tilak's to replace him. Gokhale depended upon others' help, Tilak upon self-help. Gokhale looked to the classes and the intelligentsia; Tilak to the masses and the millions. Gokhale's area was the Council Chamber, Tilak's forum was the village '*mandap*'. Gokhale's object was self-government for which the people had to fit themselves by answering the tests prescribed by the English. Tilak's object was Swaraj which is the birthright of every Indian and which he shall have without let or hindrance from the foreigner. Gokhale was on a level with his age; Tilak was in advance of his times."

Dhananjay Kher in his book '*Lokmanya Tilak*' has made the comparison between Tilak and Gokhale in these words, "He (Gokhale) believed in social equality and social justice but who welcomed British rule as a divine dispensation. Tilak was self luminous and self-made. Gokhale criticised the government in a parliamentary vein, whereas Tilak agitated against it and faced imprisonment. Gokhale sought interviews with the spokesmen of the British Government and its representatives in India and interpreted the aspirations of the people, impressing upon them the necessity of introducing reforms. He cooperated with the Government where desirable and opposed it very necessary. Gokhale said to the British Government, "We can understand your difficulties, but these measures are neither proper, nor justifiable. It is not good for a government to violate its pledges to the people and flout their aspirations. This will anger them. So, Sir, open your eyes to the realities and grant our demands". Tilak fought with Government and said, "These are the rights of the people and they must have them".

Gokhale tried to understand the difficulties of the rulers. Tilak wore the robe of a rebel and always fought for the interest of the people. *Why did Gokhale and Tilak differ?* S.A. Welpert in *Tilak and Gokhale : Resolution and Reform in the making of Modern India'* stated that Tilak and Gokhale differed in their attitude towards British rule in India primarily on account of their own lives and their environment. Tilak had to fight throughout his life against the machinery of British justice in India. He had no faith in the law courts of the country as he was invariably convicted and punished by them. He came to the obvious conclusion that no matter what he said or did, the official opinion would brand him as a sedition - monger once for all and this convinced him that until India won independence, he and his colleague would not hope to get justice. On the other hand, Gokhale had many happy memories of his contact with the British Government and the Englishmen. He had access to the homes of the British society which were for ever closed to Tilak in the same way as the Jail cells in which Tilak spent many years of his life were not included in the experiences of Gokhle. It was on account of their divergent experiences that their attitudes towards the British Government differed.

Q. 5. Write notes on:

1. The Partition of Bengal *(Delhi University 1992)*
2. Swadeshi Movement *(Rajasthan University 1991)*
3. Boycott Movement (1905)
4. Surat split (1907) *(Delhi University 1995)*

Ans: 1. *The Partition of Bengal (1905)*

The Partition of Bengal was conceived by Lord Curzon. On July 20, 1905, Lord Curzon issued an order dividing the province of Bengal into two parts. One of them called 'Bengal' comprised the western districts of Bengal proper, Bihar and Orissa. The other called the 'Eastern Bengal and Assam' comprised the eastern districts of Bengal proper and Assam. The Bengali speaking Hindus became a minority and Muslims a majority in the newly carved Eastern Bengal and Assam Province. The official justification of partition was explained as the unwieldly nature of Bengal from administrative point of view. But Curzon made the partition in such a way as to serve his political purpose which he explained to his superiors in London, "Bengal united is a power", he wrote, "that power was to be broken by partition". Lord Minto, who succeeded Lord Curzon, fully approved of it as he said, "Crippling of Bengali political power is, in my opinion, one of the strongest arguments in favour of partition". There was also the motive of placating the Muhammadans and creating a solid Muhammadan block against the Hindus in respect of political views. It was clear to all that partition was a measure deliberately adopted to kindle rivalry and animosity between the Hindus and Muslims.

The Indian National Congress and the different sections of the population — Zamindars, merchants, lawyers, students and even women - rose up in spontaneous opposition to the partition and appealed for the immediate cancellation of the Order. But Curzon did not care and cynically and arrogantly, disregarded the popular feelings. Lord Curzon had fired a very big gun but the recoil was tremendous. The Anti-partition Movement was initiated on August 7, 1905, when a massive demonstration was organised in the Town Hall of Calcutta. Surendranath Banerjee, a Moderate leader took up the leadership. He wrote in *Bengalee,* a paper edited by him, "We are on the threshold of an agitation, which for its intent and its universality will be unrivalled in the annals of this province". Never was prophesy more literally fulfilled. The streets rang with the cries of *Bande Matram*, the immortal hymn to Motherland, composed by Bankim Chandra. More than two thousand public meetings attended by both Hindus and Muslims were held in different parts. The Indian Press and large sections of Anglo-Indian Press of many provinces joined in the protest. Extremist leaders like Aurobindo Ghosh and Bepin Chandra Pal actively supported and promoted the agitation.

Oct. 16, 1905 - a day of mourning: The Partition of Bengal came into effect on October 16, 1905. It was declared by the people as Anti-partition Day. A day of mourning and fasting was observed in Bengal as under:

(a) It was declared a day of national mourning throughout Bengal.
(b) It was observed as a day of fasting.
(c) There was a hartal in Calcutta.
(d) People went to the Ganges barefooted in the early morning and took their bath.

(e) Rabindranath Tagore composed a national song for this occasion. It was 'Amar Sonar Bangla', my golden Bengal. The song was sung by huge crowds parading the streets. (The Song in 1971 became the National Anthem of Bangladesh).

(f) There were cries of *Bande Matram.*

(g) The ceremony of *Raksha Bandhan* was observed.

Swadeshi and Boycott. Swadeshi and Boycott became the battle-cries of economic and political struggle against the imperialist injustice. Students played an active pat in spreading these movements in every nook and corner of India. Swadeshi and Boycott Movements became the order of the day in towns like Amritsar, Bombay, Coimbatore, Dehradun, Lahore, Madras, Madurai and Nellore etc.

The whole Bengal rose as one to resist the wrong inflicted by partition. But no weapon could match the armed might of the British. So, people adopted the most practical means of throwing a direct challenge to the British authority by boycotting British goods.

Swadeshi meant self-dependence which in its turn engendered self-confidence in one's own self and in one's own country. When all the people set out to fight for a common cause by the Boycott and *Swadeshi* movements, it was bound to develop a national consciousness among the people. The students of Calcutta, who had already taken the vow of Boycott and *Swadeshi,* played a very crucial role. Shops selling foreign cloth were picketed; burning of foreign cloth was organised at many places. The Swadeshi Movement had an immense success. In the economic field it meant fostering of indigenous industries; so it happened. Many textile mills, soap and match factories, national banks, etc. were opened. It also encouraged national education.

Programme of the Movement: Four pillers of the movement : Within a very sort period, the Partition of Bengal attracted the attention of the nationalist leaders of other provinces. The issue was no more of one or two Bengals, but whether the British rule should continue. The following ideals became the four pillars of the nationalist movement:

(i) Attainment of Self-Government.

(ii) Boycott of foreign goods.

(iii) Promotion of Swadeshi (Indian made goods).

(iv) National Education Movement.

Ruthless Repression : Singing of *Bande Matram* was banned, Public meetings were forbidden, Swadeshi workers were prosecuted and imprisoned, students were pulled down. Gurkha outrage was let loose upon the Hindus. Government servants were dismissed. District Barisal suffered the most. British terrorism was at its height.

Four nationalist militant/extremist leaders namely Bal-Pal-Lal (Bal Gangadhar Tilak, Bepin Chandra Pal and Lala Lajpat Rai) and Aurobindo Ghose emerged, who spread the nationalist movement all over India.

Lala Lajpat Rai thundered about the methods of the Extremists, "We desire to turn our faces away from the Government Houses and turn them to the huts of the people. We want to stop our mouths so far as an appeal to the Government is concerned and open mouth with a new appeal to the masses of our people. This is the psychology, this is the ethics, this is the psychological significance of the boycott movement".

In his whirlwind tour of the country, Tilak declared, "Swaraj is my birth right; and I will have it".

In 1907, Lajpat Rai and Sardar Ajit Singh were arrested in the Punjab and deported to Burma.

The same year, Bepin Chandra Pal was arrested and kept in various jails. Sri Aurobindo Ghose was also arrested for having published certain articles in *Bande Matram.* His arrest, trial and acquittal made him one of the foremost leaders of the new movement.

In 1908, Tilak was arrested, imprisoned for six years, and kept in Burma in virtual solitary confinement in a prison cell.

Ultimately in 1911, the Government had to cancel the Order of Partition.

Swadeshi and Boycott Movements

Swadeshi and Boycott movements were like the two sides of the same coin. Swadeshi literally means 'of one's own country'. It had three important objectives. First was to promote the indigenous industries and strengthen Indian economy. Second was to strengthen self-confidence and develop patriotism among the people of India. The third objective was to hit hard the industries of Manchaster and other industrial centres of Britain by depriving them of Indian markets.

It was realised that 6 P's Prayers, Public meetings, Posters, Petitions, Placards and Protests - constitutional methods used by the Moderate leaders had no impact on the British rulers. More positive and vigorous steps were needed to shake the British administration.

The Swadeshi and Boycott Movements were powerful instruments to hurt the British interests.

About Swadeshi, Lajpat Rai said, "I regard it as the salvation of my country. The Swadeshi movement ought to make us self-respecting, self-reliant, self supporting and last, not least, manly. The Swadeshi movement ought to teach us how to organise our capital, our resources, our labour, our energies and our talents, for the greatest good of all Indians, irrespective of creed, colour or caste. It ought to unite us, our religious and denominational differences not withstanding. In my opinion, Swadeshi ought to be the common religion of the United India. "On the Boycott Movement, he said, "The meaning of the boycott is this ..... The primary thing is prestige of the government and the boycott strikes at the root of that prestige. The illusory thing they call prestige is more powerful and potent than authority itself and we propose to do this by boycott - We desire to turn away our faces from the Government Houses to turn them to the huts of the people".

Programme This movement started first of all in Bengal. Mass meetings were held all over Bengal where Swadeshi or use of Indian goods and boycott of British goods was proclaimed and pledged. In many places public burnings of foreign cloth were organised and shops selling foreign cloth were picketed.

The Swadeshi Movement was an immense success. According to Surendranath Banerjee, "Swadeshism during the days of its potency coloured the entire texture of our social and domestic life. Marriage presents that included foreign goods, the like of which could be manufactured at home, were returned. Priests would often decline to officiate at ceremonies where foreign articles were offered as oblations to the gods. Guests would refuse to participate in festivals where foreign salt or foreign sugar was used."

Impact of the Movement

The impact of the movement was felt in different walks of life as under :

1. *Impact on indigenous Industries.* With the promotion of native goods, production of cottage industries increased.

2. *Encouragement to Industries.* Several textile mills, match factories, weaving establishments, banks and insurance companies were opened.

3. *Opening of Swadeshi goods stores.* Acharya P.C. Ray organised the famous Bengal chemical stores. The great poet Rabindra Nath Tagore helped to open a Swadeshi store.

4. *National Education Movement.* One of the most significant developments of this period was the birth of the concept of national education. The movement of national education was born immediately after the Partition of Bengal and was basically the outcome of the Swadeshi and Boycott movements. The Swadeshi movement, although economic in origin and application, its spirit affected every walk of life. A demand for *Swadeshi* education soon began to be put forward and was immediately strengthened by repeated conflicts with the official policies and the utter failure of Indians to make the officials to realise the Indian point of view in education. The National Council of Education was set up in 1906. The Bengal College with Sri Aurobindo Ghosh was formally inaugurated after two months of the founding of the National Council of Education. The movement for the national education spread to various parts of India.

5. *Awakening among the youth.* The movement stirred the conscience of the students and they boycotted government sponsored educational institutions and joined national institutions.

6. *Awakening among Women.* Hither to women had shown very little interest in the national movement. Now they began to participate in all national awakening programmes.

7. *Hindu-Muslim Unity.* Barring a few sections of the Muslims who were happy with the creation of a Muslim majority province, others took an important part in the Swadeshi movement.

8. *All India nature of the Movement.* The movement was wide-spread in different parts of the country. Bal-Pal-Lal i.e., trio. Bal was very active in Maharashtra, Pal in Bengal and Lal in Punjab - likewise movement became popular in other provinces.

9. *Emergence of Militancy.* The suppressive actions of the British rulers gave birth to militancy and growth of revolutionary terrorism in India.

10. *Split in the Congress.* As a result of differences in ideology and methods of national awakening, the Indian National saw a split in the Surat Session in 1907.

11. *Value of passive resistance.* The agitation brought into prominence the great value of passive resistance as a more effective weapon than petition— making, so far the only method of political agitation known to the country and approved by the Congress. But the partition agitation did much more than this. It awakened into action, the dormant political consciousness of the people, and gave a definite shape to the spirit of nationalism which had been gathering for some time. "Bengal left the beaten track followed by the Congress, conceived new ideals, adopted new methods for their achievement, shed all tears, braved all sufferings and fearlessly faced death". Even Moderate leader Gokhale was convinced that Bengal's heroic fight made a deep impress upon Indian politics. "For the first time since British rule all sections of the Indian community began to act together in offering resistance to a common wrong". Lala Lajpat Rai echoed the same sentiment, "If the people of India will just learn that lesson from Bengal, I think that the struggle is not hopeless".

12. *Cancelling the Order of Partition.* In 1910 Lord Harding succeeded Lord Minto. At Calcutta, he realized the political unrest and terrorism that prevailed due to the partition. He became very anxious for a policy of conciliation in view of the impending visit of the King and Queen to India within a year's time. He declared, "We feel bound to admit that the Bengalis are labouring under a sense of real injustice which we believe to remove without further delay". In the Delhi Durbar of 1911 attended by the King and Queen, announcements were made to cancel the Order of Partition of Bengal and also to shift the British capital from Calcutta to Delhi. To Lord Harding goes the chief credit of undoing the great wrong and uniting the Bengali speaking region. Bihar, Orissa and Chhotanagpur were made into one province under Lieutenant Governor, Assam reverted to a Chief Commissionership. The rest constituted the province of Bengal under a Governor.

(For Swadeshi and Boycott, also see answer of question 3 of this chapter).

4. Surat Split (1907)

Meaning. The split in the Indian National Congress at its annual session at Surat in 1907, between the Moderate leaders and the Extremist leader is known as Surat Split.

Background or Causes of Split. There were sharp differences of ideology and methodology relating to national awakening and regeneration India between the Moderate leaders and Extremists leaders of the Congress. These differences may be summed up as under:

First, the Moderates believed in getting concessions gradually from the British rulers. According to the Extremists, Swaraj was the final remedy.

Second, the Moderates believed in their loyalty to the British Throne. The Extremists regarded the British rule in India as curse.

Third, the Moderates believed in adopting strictly constitutional methods for agitation. The Extremists were convinced that constitutional methods would lead them no where.

Fourth, under the Moderates, the national movement was confined to a few educated sections of the society. The Extremists wanted to convert it into a mass movement.

Fifth, the Moderates believed that the Indians were still not fit for self-government. The Extremists had complete faith in the capacity of Indian to govern themselves.

Sixth, the Moderates wanted to get concessions without undergoing sufferings. Extremists were of the view that without sacrifices and sufferings, Indians would not get anything.

Course of events. In the first five years of the 20th century, the Congress sessions had been presided over by the Moderate leaders of the Congress. The Partition of Bengal (1905) and the policies followed by the Moderates were not in tune with their prevailing mood. The four fold programme of Swadeshi, Boycott, Swaraj and National Education chalked out by the Extremists sent alarm bells to the Moderates and they feared that the Session of the Congress in 1906 might be dominated by the Extremists. The Moderates, therefore, requested Dadabhai Naoroji who was in England, to come to India and preside over the session. Naoroji's presence saved the Congress from split and Moderate leaders accepted the four-fold programme under pressure from the Extremists. There were frequent meetings between the Moderate leaders and the Viceroy. The Congress Session at Surat on December, 27, 1907 witnessed an open and ugly confrontation between the Moderates and the Extremists. After this, the Government took repressive measures against the Extremist leaders. In 1907, Lala Lajpat Rai and Ajit Singh were deported from the Punjab to Burma. In 1908, Tilak was arrested and sentenced to six year's imprisonment. Aurobindo Ghose was prosecuted. The Moderates, who now controlled the Congress did not condemn the arrests of the

Extremist leaders. The two groups were again united in 1916 to frustrate the policy of the 'Divide and Rule' of the British.

Impact of the Split

(i) *Set back to the National Movement.* The split proved harmful to the cause of national awakening. The British Government followed the policy of 'Divide and Rule' and tried to win over the Moderates so that Extremists could be isolated and suppressed.

(ii) *Brith of revolutionaries.* The suppression and oppression policy of the British rulers led to the emergence of revolutionary trends for getting rid of the foreign rule.

(iii) *Morley-Minto Reforms.* To plactate the Moderate nationalists, Government announced constitutional concessions through the Indian Councils Act of 1909.

(iv) *Cancellation of Partition of Bengal.* In 1911, the Government announced the cancellation of the Partition of Bengal.

(v) *Change of Capital.* In 1911, the seat of the Central Government was shifted from Calcutta to Delhi.

Q. 6. Discuss the chief features and importance of the Act of 1909.

(Delhi University 1997)

or

Under what circumstances were the Morely-Minute Reforms intro duced? Explain their main features and assess their value.

or

Write an essay on the Indian Act of 1909.

Ans : *Morely - Minto Reforms (1909)*

Why were the reforms introduced? The constitutional and administrative reforms introduced in India under the India Councils Act, 1909 are known as Morely-Minto Reforms after Lord Morley, the Secretary of State for India and Lord Minto, the Viceroy of India.

It is usually said that the Indian Councils Act of 1892 was passed to take the wind out of the sails of the Indian National Congress and the 1909 Act was passed by the Government of India to rally to its side, the Moderates in the Indian National Congress and the Muslims in order to buttress the authority of British bureaucracy. The Indian Councils Act of 1882 failed to meet the legitimate demands of the Congress and Lokmanya Tilak condemned the policy of the Moderate leaders of the Congress in these words, "Political rights will have to be fought for. The Moderates think that these can be won by persuation. We think that these can be won by pressure".

In brief, following were the important causes that led to the introduction of 1909 reforms:

1. Failure of the 1892 reforms to meet the aspirations of the people of India.
2. Growing popularity of the Extremist leaders in the Indian National Congress and alarming bells to the Government.
3. Lord Curzon's despotic attitude towards Indian.
4. Opposition to the Partition of Bengal leading to serious unrest.
5. Swadeshi and Boycott Movements for putting pressure on the Government.
6. Enthusiasm and a new spirit among Indians on the victory of Japan over Russia, interpreting it as the Victory of Asia over Europe and inculcating among them a spirit of self-confidence.
7. Humiliation of Indians abroad. "The cup of humiliation was filled to the brim when in 1907, the Transval Government passed the Asiatic Registration Act requiring Indians to be registered by means of finger prints". Mahatma Gandhi launched Satyagrah against this Act.
8. The growth of terrorism and attacks on Europeans.
9. Formation of the Muslim League in 1906 and the Policy of the Government to win over Muslims to their side.
10. Encouragement from outside experiences. Dadabhai Naoroji in his presidential address at the Congress Session in 1906 pointedly remarked, "Indians cannot continue to remain subject to despotism, when China in the East and Persia in the West of Asia were waking up".
11. Impoverishment of the Indians and general unrest. This was considered as the direct result of policy of the British rulers to keep away the Indians from the various organs of the constitutional and administrative machinery.
12. Lord Minto's belief. Lord Minto had by this time felt that permanence of the British administration in India "depends upon a sound appreciation of the changing conditions which surround it"

Main Provisions of the Act

1. *Increase in the number of Imperial Legislative Council.* As against 22 members provided for in the 1892 Act, the 1909 Act raised the strength to 69. Out of these 37 were to be official and 32 non-official.

2. *Election/nomination of Members to the Imperial Council.* Of the 69 members, 9 ex-officio members were as : Governor General (i) Commander-in-Chief (i) Governor of the province where meeting takes place (i) and members of the Executive Council (6).

Break up of 60 members is shown as under:

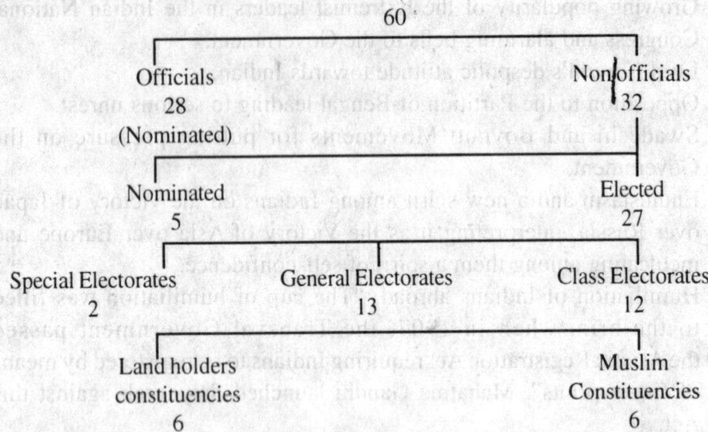

3. *Expansion of Provincial Legislative Councils.* The size of the Legislative Councils of the 7 provinces of Bengal, Madras, Bombay, UP. Easten Bengal and Assam, Punjab and Burma was increased.

There was to be non-official majority in these Councils. However, in several cases, a substantial number of non-official members was nominated by the Government.

4. *Increase in the number of the members of Provincial Executive Councils.* In case of Bombay, Bengal and Madras, the member was raised from 2 to 4. Executive Councils could be constituted for Lt. Governor's provinces.

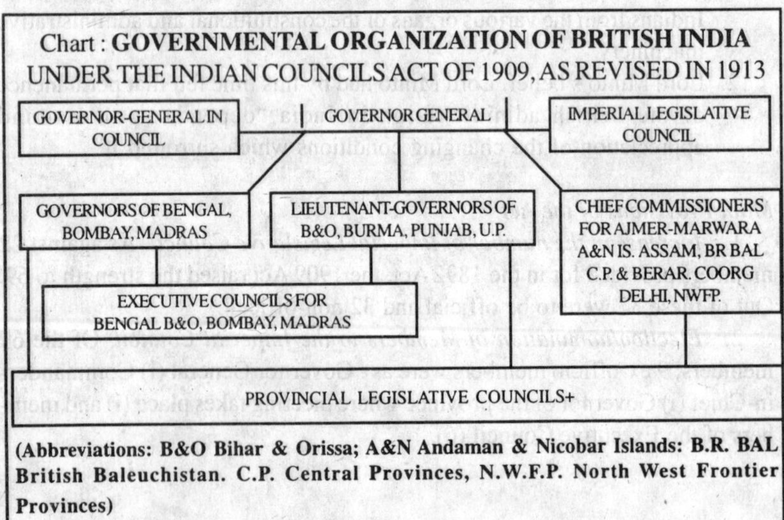

5. *Franchise.* The franchise was discriminatory and restricted.

6. *Enlargement of Functions.* The functions of the Legislative Councils were increased.

7. *Appointment of Indians to Executive Councils.* Provision was made for this.

8. *Separate Electorate.* The Act provided for separate electorate for separate representation to different communities, classes and interests.

9. *Separate representation for Muslims.* Muslims were given separate representation.

10. *Disqualifications for Elections.* Political offenders could not offer themselves for elections.

Observations on the Reforms

1. *No. Introduction of Parliamentary System of Government.* While introducing the Bill, Morley, the Secretary of State for India clearly stated, "If it could be said that this chapter of reforms led directly or necessarily to the establishment of a parliamentary system in India, I for one would have nothing at all to do with it".

2. *Creation of Political barriers.* According to Jawaharlal Nehru, "A political barrier was created round them (Muslims), isolating them from the rest of India and reversing the unifying and amalgamating process which had been going on for centuries".

3. *Excess Representation to Muslims.* For the so-called political importance of the Muslims, they were accorded not only separate communal representation but also representation much in excess to their population on account of their 'services to the empire'.

4. *Communal element - a poisonous element.* The provision for separate eletorates for Muslims was a signal for other communities to agitate.

5. *Stabbing the democracy.* K.M. Munshi pointed out, "They (the British) stabbed the rising democracy".

6. *Shattering of Unity.* The 1909 reforms shattered the National unity forged through centuries. Gandhiji observed, "The Morely-Minto Reforms have been our undoing".

7. *Discriminatory Franchise.* A Muslim graduate of 5 years could vote but not a non-Muslim graduate.

8. *Undue importance to vested interests.* The Act gave undue importance to vested interests like landlords and chambers of commerce by giving them special representation.

9. *Small number of Voters.* In some constitutencies, there were only about a dozen members.

10. *No Voting right to Women.* Women were completely excluded.

11. *Official majority.* Although non-official majority was provided for in the Provincial Councils, the practical result was nothing. The nominated non-official members nullified the impact.

12. *Lack of element of responsibility.* The report on Indian Constitutional Reforms, 1918 observed, "We have at present in India neither the best of the old system, nor the best of the new. Responsibility is the saviour of popular government, and that saviour the present councils wholly lack".

Summing up. The reforms fell short of popular expectations. The Extremists termed the Moderates as 'old fossils' and the reforms as "ingenious fraud". The reforms sowed the seeds of conflict between the Hindus and the Muslims by providing *Separate Electorate*. It is usually held, that the provision of excessive weightage, separate electorate and preferential voting rights for the Muslims, injected a poisonous element in the political life of India which ultimately resulted in the partition of the country. The non-official members were usually 'yes men'. The number of delegates at the Congress sessions began to dwindle. The Congress received a temporary setback. The leaders of the Muslim League felt very happy at the reforms.

Provision of separate electorate for Muslims was an important strategy of the policy of 'Divide and Rule' of the British. Special care was taken to see that "Class was set against class, community against Community".

"The real power remained safely in British hands" as observed by H.C.E. Zacharias.

Q. 7. Write notes on

1. Act of 1909 and Separate Electorate. (*Punjab University 1996*)
2. The Ghadar Movement. (*Delhi University 1993*)
3. Lucknow Pact (1916).
4. Lucknow Session of the Congress (1916).
5. Home Rule League. (*Delhi University 1995 and 1998*)

1. *Act of 1909 and Separate Electorate*

Background. There was a good deal of agitation against the British rulers in India. The agitation against the Partition of Bengal was widespread. The Government resorted to very harsh measures to suppress the movement. However, it thought of winning over the Moderates and the Muslims. It, therefore passed the Indian Councils Acts. The reforms are known as Minto-Morely Reforms after the names of Minto who was the Viceroy of India and Morely, the Secretary of State for India.

Main provisions of the Act

These included the following main provisions:

1. The number of members in the Imperial Council (Central Council) and Provincial Legislative Councils was increased.
2. Official majority was retained in the Centre. Non-official majority was enforced at the Provincial Legislative Councils.
3. The principle of election was introduced for the first time. Very limited number of voters could vote.

4. Separate constituencies for the Hindus and Muslims were constituted.
5. The Councils were given very limited powers.

Meaning of Separate Electorate : Under this system, separate constituencies for the Hindus and the Muslims were created. The Hindus could vote for a Hindu candidate and the Muslims for a Muslim.

Why Separate Electorate Introduced? The chief objective was to divide the Hindus and the Muslims into separate groups so that they would not be united to launch united efforts against the British.

Another objective was to please the Moderates and isolate the Extremists.

Impact of the New System. Separate electorate bred communalism in India. It succeeded to a great extent in keeping Hindus and Muslims at a distance. It was a calculated move to create disunity among Indians.

2. *The Ghadar Party*

The Ghadar Party or the party of Indian revolutionary abroad was founded in 1913, at Stockton in America by Lala Hardayal (1884-1939). It was meant to achieve the goal of freeing India from British rule. The Ghadar Party comprised the Indians who had gone overseas. Most of the members of the party were Punjabi Sikh peasants and ex-soldiers, who had faced the brunt of economic and racial discrimination. They had gone to other countries for livelihood. The leaders of the party were, however, educated Hindus and Muslims. Important leaders of the party were Lala Hardayal, Mohammad Barkatullah, Bhagwan Singh, Jawala Singh, Kartar Singh, Ram Chandra, V.G. Pingle and Sohan Singh Bhakna.

Methods and Techniques. The Ghadar Party was pledged to wage revolutionary war against the British rule in India. The party carried on its propaganda through an Urdu Weekly *Ghadar* which carried the caption *'Angerezi Raj ka Dushman'* (An Enemy of British Rule). It used to make appeals to people for joining its activities. Its advertisement frequented under the caption 'wanted.. heroic soldiers for Ghadar Party' with the following duties and service conditions:

Remuneration - Death
Reward - Martyrdom
Pension - Freedom
Field of Work - Hindustan

In a few months, the party became the supreme organisation of immigrant Indians residing in Canada, Indo-China, Japan, Philippines, Malaya, Singapore, Mexico and the USA. Funds worth millions of dollars were collected to lit the torch of national revolution.

Master Plan of the Party. Rash Behari Bose, Sachindra Sanayal, Ganesh Pingle and Baghi Kartar Singh prepared a master plan for the armed revolt. February 21, 1915 was fixed the date and vigorous preparations were made for that purpose. Messages were sent to leaders in India, especially in the

Punjab. Unfortunately, the British authorities came to know of these plans and took immediate action. The rebellious regiments were disbanded and their leaders were either imprisoned or hanged. Seven hundred men of the 5th Light Infantry at Singapore revolted but the revolt was crushed. Several soldiers were publicly executed and many transported for life.

Almost all leaders of the Ghadar Party in Punjab were arrested. They were tried in the Lahore Conspiracy Case. Out of 291 members, 42 were acquitted and others transported for life/sentenced to death/imprisoned for varying terms. Among the prominent leaders were Baghi Kartar Singh, Bhai Parmanand, and Ganesh Pingle.

3. *The Lucknow Pact (1916)*

The Lucknow Pact marked an important step forward the unity of the Congress and the Muslim League for waging a combined struggle against the British rulers. It is true that it was a temporary truce between the two parties but it had a positive effect on the national movement. Earlier, the Muslim League had supported the Partition of Bengal at its Karachi Session in 1907. The Muslims had been given separate electorates under the Morely-Minto reforms of 1909.

Reasons for the Change in the attitude of the Muslim League. The Muslim League had been a supporter of the British Government but after 1910, certain factors emerged which forced the League to reach an understanding between the Congress and the Leaque. Among the most important factor was the issue of Turkey. Turkey was regarded as the symbol of Islamic greatness. Muslims in general regarded the Sultan of Turkey as the head of Islam. The Turko-Italian War of 1911 annoyed the Indian Muslims. Britain did not help Turkey. The Balkan Wars of 1912-13 in Europe were regarded by the Muslims as a 'crusade' to humiliate Turkey in Europe. The Wars weakened Turkey. In India itself, the Muslim League was not consulted at the time of cancellation of the Partition of Bengal. A militant section of the Muslims was also for national movement. Thus on the one hand, Turkey, which was regarded as the 'Sword of Islam' was fighting for its survival against the onslaught of Britain and its Allied and on the other hand the Muslims felt greatly disturbed inspite of the British assurances. There was thus, a great change in their policy towards the British rulers and the Indian National Congress. Tilak, who had been imprisoned for six years in 1908, was released from jail in 1914. He, along with Mohammad Ali Jinnah played a leading role in bringing the Congress and the League nearer each other. Tilak declared, "When we have to fight against a third party, it is a very important thing that we stand on this platform united-united in race, united in religion - as regards all different shades of political creed". Jinnah, the League president at Lucknow declared, "Hindu-Muslim reapproachment is the first sign of the birth of a United India". This resulted in the Lucknow Pact (1916).

Main provisions of the Lucknow Pact: (i) It specified proportions of Muslim representation in several provinces as well as the Centre. (ii) It included other demands made annually by the Congress, such as shifting imperial or war expenses from the Indian exchequer to the British exchequer, opening of commissioned ranks in the armed forces to Indians and racial equality throughout the empire.

Immediate impact of the Lucknow Pact. The League pledged full support to the Congress aims of self-government and a parliamentary system for India.

In 1916, both the Congress and the Muslim League held their annual sessions at Lucknow. Congress leaders like Mahatma Gandhi and Madam Mohan Malviya attended the sessions of the Muslim League in 1916 and 1917 and spoke from its platform.

The unity between the Congress and the Muslim League had the desired effect on the policy of the British Government. The Secretary of State for India, Montague declared in 1917 that the aim of the British Government was the gradual development of self-governing institutions with a view to the progressive realisation of responsible Government of India, as an integral part of the British empire". It ultimately resulted in the passing of the Act of 1919 and establishment of 'Dyarchy' in the provinces.

4. *Lucknow Session of the Congress (1916)*

The Lucknow Session of the Congress in 1916 bridged the gulf that had been created among the leaders of the Congress at its Surat Session held in 1907. There was a growing feeling among most of the nationalists that disunity in their ranks was harming their cause and that they must put united front against the British Government.

The Moderates, after the death of Gokhale and Pherozshah Mehta in 1915, became leaderless and at the same time there was some change in the attitude of Tilak who was released in 1914 after serving six years imprisonment in Burma. To reconciliate the Moderate nationalists, he declared, "I may state once and for all, that we are trying in India, as the Irish Home Rulers have been all along doing in Ireland, for a reform of the system of administration and not for the overthrow of Government; and I have no hesitation in saying that the acts of violence which have been committed in different parts of India are not only repugnant to me, but have, in my opinion, only unfortunately retarded to a great extent, the pace of our political progress". This cleared the hurdles in the way of unification of the two wings. Thus at the Lucknow Session, both the groups decided to work together.

Announcement of Reforms by the Government. The reapproachment between the Congress and the Muslim League and between the two groups of the Congress, changed the attitude of the British Government. Hitherto, it had relied heavily on repression to subdue the nationalist leaders. Now, in order to appease the nationalist opinion, the British Government announced in August 1917, that its policy in India was "the gradual development of self-governing institutions with a view to the progressive realisation of responsible Government of India, as an integral part of the British Empire".

5. Home Rule Movement or Home Rule Leagues

Background. Home Rule Movement was launched in India by Mrs. Annie Besant and Bal Gangadhar Tilak to put pressure on the British Government to grant self-government to India. There were three important factors which led to this movement. One was that the British Government was preoccupied with its affairs of the First Great War. The second was that with the death of two prominent Moderate leaders namely Gopal Krishna Gokhale and Pherozeshah Mehta in 1915, the leadership of the Indian National Congress had come into the hands of the Extremists led by Tilak and Annie Besant. The Moderates had been great supporters of the British Government. Third reason was that the leaders had before them, the experience of some other countries like Ireland which though under the British empire had devised such a system in which they had an important say in running the affairs of the Government.

Meaning of the Movement. Before the launching of the movement, Mrs. Annie Besant had declared in England in 1914, "India asks only that she shall be recognised as a nation, shall be given self-government and shall form an integral part of the Empire composed of self-governing communities. 'She asks no more than this'.

To build up a vigarous movement for Home Rule, Annie Besant started a daily paper in 1914 called '*New India*'.

Starting of the movement. In 1916, Annie Besant started the Home League from Madras with two of her lieutants namely B.P. Wadia and George Arundale.

Tilak, another protagonist of the Home Rule, considered to be an Extremist, who was released from jail in 1914, appreciated the change in the situation and set out to unify the two streams of Congressmen by modifying his stand. He started the movement from Poona.

In simple words, Home Rule Movement was a movement which was designed to compel the government to provide Indians with sufficient powers to govern themselves. It was far more than merely representation of Indians in the Councils and Provincial Assemblies. It was, however, less than independence for India.

Mrs Annie, while starting the movement said, "I am Indian tom-tom (Indian drum) waking up all the sleepers so that they may wake and work for their motherland".

All India Movement. Soon the movement stirred the country. Besant and Tilak went on a whirlwind tour of the country. In the middle of June the Madras Governor went to persuade Mrs. Annie Besant to give up the Home Rule campaign. The Governor gave this assurance to her side by side, "I will give you a safe conduct to England to take you through". She declined the offer. The Governor made it clear that if she did not give up the Home Rule Campaign, he will have to stop her activities. The reply of Besant was, "You have all the power and I am helpless; and you must do what you like. There is one thing which I should like to say to your Excellency and that is that I believe you are striking the deadly blow against the British empire in India."

Mrs. Besant an English lady but admirer of India's culture and a freedom fighter of India, moved in major cities of India, delivering inspiring speeches and enthusing the people of India for Home Rule. Home Rule branches were established almost in every big city. Public mobilisation took place as never before. The movement soon attracted the anger of the Government. Tilak's entry was banned in Punjab and Mrs. Besant was disallowed to enter Central Province and Bombay. Finally in June 1917, she was arrested. Popular pressure and protest forced the Government to release her in September 1917. Women participated in large numbers. '*New India*' paper was banned. Annie Besant became the most popular figure of Indian politics in the year 1916-17. She presided over the Congress Session in 1917. Students participated enthusiastically in the Home Rule Movement.

Impact of the Home Rule Movement: The voice of the Home Rule Movement became the voice of India. It transformed the national movement into the people's movement. It influenced several British MPs. On 20th August, 1917, Montague declared in the House of Common, that India would be increasingly associated in every branch of administration and there would be a gradual development of self-governing institutions for the progressive realisation of responsible government in India. Accordingly, some steps were taken in this direction after the close of the War.

Q. 8. Discuss the role of the Revolutionaries in the Indian National Movement. *(Delhi University 1996)*

or

Write a note on organisation and methods of revolutionaries. *(Punjab University 1996, 1997 and 1998)*

Ans: *Growth of Revolutionary Movement*

Essence of the revolutionary movement. Revolutionary movement was a movement for the liberation of India led by revolutionary leaders who believed in the use of all types of methods including shedding blood for the achievement of their objectives. They had no faith in the constitutional methods adopted by the Moderates. They also felt that the passive resistance was also not sufficient. They believed in the efficacy of the cult of 'bullets and bombs' etc.

Factors that led to the rise of revolutionary leaders in India. Following were the important factors:

(*i*) Failure of constitutional methods.

(*ii*) Repressive measures adopted by the Government to check national awakening.

(*iii*) Impact of foreign revolutionaries.

(*iv*) Publication of revolutionary literature.

Prominent revolutionary leaders V.D. Savarkar (1883-1966), Madame Bhikaji Cama (1861-1936, Madanlal Dhingra (1887-1909), Rashbehari Bose (1880-1945) and Lala Hardayal (1884-1939) were the most prominent leaders of the revolutionary movement.

Organisation and Methods of revolutionaries: Secret Societies. Gradually it dawned upon a section of the youth that Swadeshi Boycott movement taken up in the wake of the Partition of Bengal was insufficient to achieve the desired end. They were convinced that the British would have to be 'physically expelled' from India. Most violent means were necessary to gain their objective. But it was not possible to organise an open armed revolt against the mighty British power. As such they fell back upon secret societies and action.

Methods and Techniques Employed by the Revolutionaries : The Revolutionaries took recourse to these methods to terrorise the British rulers (i) Organising secret societies (ii) Distribution of revolutionary literature (iii) Organising secret mobs (iv) Taking oaths and pledges for the freedom of the country and to adopt all sorts of techniques for the achievement of their objectives relating to motherland's freedom (v) Gita studies to infuse a spirit of bravery and doing one's duty (vi) Physical training (vii) Weapon training (viii) Making of weapons including bombs (ix) Killing of oppressive British officers (x) Killing of police informers (xi) Looting government treasuries (xii) Looting rich persons for the manufacture and purchase of weapons etc. (xiii) Establishing revolutionary societies abroad (xiv) Creating sedition among the Indian soldiers of the British army stationed outside India.

Revolutionary nationalist were mostly active in Bengal, Maharashtra and the Punjab.

Thoughtful patriots and not terrorists : Since, now they were going to play for high stakes, putting their life on it, their objective was higher, not just to rub out the line of partition from the map, but to wipe out the Britishers from India. The secret societies of this type were the outcome of the new nationalism. It was a further step of the same spirit in an extreme form. Apart from intense patriotism and spirit of sacrifice, they felt the call of a higher life as expounded by Swami Vivekanand. A firm faith in the immortal soul led them to shed the fear of death and bodily pain. Nationalism for them was a religious attitude which made them shed the fear of death and bodily pain. Nationalism for them was a religious attitude which made them realise God in the nation and sacrifice everything at the alter of their Motherland.

These youngmen willingly left their homes, and all that was dear and near to them, to carry on a life-long struggle for freedom, for they could not tolerate the dishonour of their motherland lying trampled under the boots of foreigners. Fear of death and physical torture more terrible than death, did not deter them, obstacles and dangers like Himalayan barriers could not stop or deflect them from their goal. Deserted by friends and relatives, ignored and distanced by their countrymen for fear of police, without food to eat, without means to live, moving fórm shelter to shelter, they carried on the fight from day to day, month to month, year to year, knowing fully well that chances of success were slender but death was sure. They died in order that others may live. One may call them emotional, unrealistic and misguided. But their countrymen, barring a few, never doubted their patriotism which is proved by the homage they paid to them. The country was in tears when Khudiram and others were shot dead or hanged. The news of their death was an event of great mourning in every house, as if someone very near and dear was lost for ever.

Revolutionary Activities in different Parts of India

Bengal. Poems printed on '*Dhotis*' in Bengal, began with the verse, "I shall go to gallows with a smile". It is of interest to note that the Government ordered a wholesale seizure of such '*Dhotis*'. Revolutionary literature in the form of poems, prose writings and press played a leading role in spreading revolutionary ideas.

Papers like *Yougantar, Bande Matram* and *Sandhya* were in the forefront. The *Yugantar* wrote on April 22, 1906, "The thirty crores of people inhabiting India must raise their sixth crores of hands to stop this course of oppression. Force must be stopped with force".

Two famous books *Bhawani Mandir* and *Mukti Kon Pathe* preached the use of force and winning over the soldiers for attaining freedom. The writer of the popular poems titled *Pantha* was sent to jail for 18 months.

Barindra Ghosh, the brother of Aurobindo Ghosh was the main motivating force behind the murders of the British officers. He said, "We are determined and are still so, to take the life of the Lt. Governor of Bengal", for his oppressiveness. In 1908, Khudi Ram, a young boy, was hanged for his murderous attack on a British Officer. Perhaps he was the first martyr in the revolutionary activities. Schools were closed for two to three days as a tribute to his memory. Youngmen began to wear '*Dhotis*' with the name of Khudi Ram woven into their borders.

The revolutionary upsurge in Bengal remained unabated till 1911, when Partition of Bengal was annulled.

Delhi. On December 23, 1912, when Lord Hardinge, the Viceroy of India, was taken in a procession on the back of an elephant in Delhi, a bomb exploded which injured the Viceroy and killed his bodyguard. Rash Behari Bose, who threw the bomb was able to escape. He went to Japan and played an important role in organising the Indian National Army. This incident is also known as Delhi Conspiracy Case. Thirteen persons including master Amir Chand, Bhai Balmukand, Balraj Bhalla, Besant Kumar, Avadh Behari and Dina Nath were arrested and four of them were hanged. Avadh Behari had an interesting inspiring conversation with an Englishman before he was hanged. When the Englishman asked him about his last wish, Avadh Behari's replay was "The end of the British Rule".

Maharashtra. There was a lot of revolutionary political activity at Poona,

Nasik, Kolhapur and Bombay. The statue of Queen Victoria was mutilated at Bombay and similar acts were done at other places. In Maharashtra, several religious festivals, like Shivaji and Ganpati festivals, became the spring-boards of revolutionary activities.

The Marathi press in general, was revolutionary in tone. Papers like *Arunodya, Hind Swarajya, Kal Kesari, Rashtramukh, Vihari* and *Vishvavritta* were very vocal against the policy of oppression and suppression followed by the British. The editors of these papers were arrested and sentenced. Among the revolutionaries, the names of Savarkar brothers come to the forefront. They founded the Abhinav Bharat Society. V.D. Savarkar, who went to England, sent a parcel containing two Browning automatic pistols with ammunition to Bombay, concealed in the fake bottom of a box forming part of the luggage of one Chaturbhuj Amin, who was working as a cook in the India Hose, London. The pistols were to be used by members of the Abhinav Society to murder Jackson District Magistrate of Nasik and other British officers who were very oppressive. This resulted in the Nasik Conspiracy Case in which Jackson was murdered. Three out of 40 youngmen involved, were hanged and the rest were imprisoned.

Punjab. 'Pagri Sambhal O Jatta' (O Peasant ! take care of your turban i.e self respect) was the song of the revolutionaries in Punjab.

The revolutionary group in Punjab, led by Ajit Singh, consisted of Sufi Amba Prasad, Lal Chand Falak, Kishen Singh, Zia-ul-Huq, Ghulam Kadir and others. Ajit Singh used to distribute revolutionary literature through the Bharat Mata Society of Lahore. He was arrested and deported to Burma in 1907. Several Arya Samaj leaders who took part in revolutionary activities were arrested and prosecuted.

Revolutionary Movement Outside India

The revolutionary movement for the freedom of India did not remain confined to India. In England, the prominent leaders were V.D. Savarkar and Shyamji Krishna Verma. It was spread to France by Madame Cama, to America by Hardayal and to Japan by Rash Behari Bose. They helped the movement in a number of ways like, inciting Indian patriots to kill British officers who had committed atrocities on the Indians and had gone back to England, moulding public opinion in foreign lands, organising societies, sending revolutionary literature and weapons to revolutionaries in India.

Berlin, Cairo, Geneva, London, New York, Paris and San Francisco were the important centres of the activities of the revolutionaries.

Achievement and Impact of the Militant/Revolutionary/Extremist Leaders

They helped in developing self-confidence and self-reliance among several sections of the population, especially the educated, the middle class and the youth. They introduced new methods of political struggle. However, in general, the common people, the peasants and workers were still outside the main stream of national struggle.

Q. 9. Discuss the foundation and programme of the Indian National Congress from 1885 to 1919. *(Punjab University 1998)*
(Note: This has already been covered in the previous chapter and in this chapter, however main points are again covered)

Ans: *Founding of the Indian National Congress*

According to Dr. Pattabhai Sitaramayya, a former President of the Indian National Congress and the author of '*History of the Indian National Congress*', the origins of the Congress are "Shrouded in mystery".

Usually two points of view are put forward to explain the foundation of the Indian National Congress.

'Safety Valve' Theory. The foundation of the Congress was laid down by intellectuals who were greatly moved by the impoverishment of the Indian people caused by the economic policies of the British rulers. The Indian National Congress was intended to provide an outlet for the feelings of discontentment and distrust that had been brewing in India against the exploitative and imperialistic nature of the British rule. It is of great interest to know that A.O. Hume (1829-1912), who conceived the idea of founding the Indian National Congress was a foreigner and a retired official of the Indian Civil Service.

According to another version, the Theosophical Society of India was the parent body of the Indian National Congress. But this version is not usually accepted.

There is no doubt that history of the Congress has become almost the history of the struggle of India's independence.

Programme of the Indian National Congress from 1885 to 1919

The programme can be divided into two phases i.e., first phase from 1885 to 1904 and the second phase from 1904 to 1918.

Chief features of the first phase

The first phase was dominated by the leaders who are usually called the Moderates. They included Dadabhai Naoroji, Surendranath Banerjee, Gopal Krishna Gokhale, Pherozeshah Mehta and Badru-ud-din Tyabji.

Main objectives of the leaders of the first phase. The Moderates had three main objectives before them (i) To build up a strong public opinion in India by arousing the consciousness of the people towards administrative, economic and political reforms (ii) To unite the people on one political platform irrespective of caste, religion and region (iii) To persuade the British Government and British public opinion to introduce reforms.

Major demands of the Leaders of the first phase The Moderates worked for the gradual introduction of reforms in the working of administration of India. They asked for more powers for the Indians to the Legislative Councils and election of members. They also demanded major changes in the economic policies of the government for facilitating the growth of industries in India. Other major demands included providing more opportunities for Indians to compete for higher posts in administration, freedom of speech and expression etc.

Methods Used in the First Phase

1. The methods used by the Moderates may broadly be expressed in terms of 6 P's i.e. Pen, Press, Platform, Poster, Placards and Prayers to arouse public opinion for national cause and to get some concessions from the British. In 1888, it is estmated that Hume organised about 1000 public meetings. A paid agency was established in England. Several papers were founded. Numerous prayers on people's demand were sent to the Government for necessary action.
2. The Moderates believed in adopting constitutional agitation within the ambit of law and slow orderly political progress.
3. They framed their resolutions with utmost moderation and clarity.
4. They sent delegations to England to educate British public opinion.

Significance of the Period 1885 to 1905 in the History of Freedom Movement

Taking into considerations the difficulties that the Moderates had to confront with at that time, it goes to their credit that they succeeded in laying a firm foundation of the freedom movement. They created a wide political awakening and made the people of India conscious of the bonds of common economic, cultural and political interest. They popularised among the people ideas of democracy and liberty.

Constitutional Reforms : The passing of the Indian Councils Act of 1892 was regarded as the first fruit of the efforts of the petitions and resolutions passed by the Congress at its sessions. In its sessions the Congress had asked for the expansion of the Councils.

Main programmes in second phase of the work of the Indian National Congress (1905 to 1918)

Usually the second phase is associated with the controversy of the Moderate leaders of the Congress leaders and the Extremist leaders. The programmes of the extremist leaders received great prominence.

Bal Gangadhar Tilak, Lala Lajpat Rai, Bipin Chandra Pal - known as trio of Bal-Pal-Lal, dominated the scene.

The Extremists aimed at Swaraj whereas the Moderates aimed at the betterment of the conditions of the Indians under the British rule.

The Extremists advocated the following methods:

1. Swadeshi i.e. use of Indian made goods.
2. Boycott of foreign goods.
3. Promotion of national education.
4. Passive Resistance.

5. Demonstrations and hartals.
6. Agitation against the Partition of Bengal.

Split and reunion The congress was split into the Moderates and the Extremists at the Surat Session of the Congress in 1907, However both the groups got united in 1916.

Sufferings and Sacrifices The Extremist leaders of the Congress had to undergo extreme hardships under the oppressive methods used by the Government. They were imprisoned for several years, Newspapers were banned. All sorts of harsh measures were adopted by the Government to suppress the freedom movement.

Important events of the period 1905 to 1918 relating to national awakening were as under:

1. Agitation. against the Partition of Bengal (1905) which resulted in Swadeshi, Boycott, National education and passive resistance movements in the country.
2. Split in the Congress (1907); two groups led by Moderates and Extremists were formed.
3. Minto-Morley Reforms (1909) which provided for more reforms and separate electorate for Muslims.
4. Growth of revolutionary movements which believed in the power of force.
5. Home Rule Leagues (1914-16) for putting pressure on the government to grant more power to Indians.
6. Lucknow Pact (1916) leading to unity between Hindus and Muslims for fighting unitedly against the British.
7. Lucknow Congress Session (1916) and reunion of Moderates and Extremists.
8. Announcement of reforms by the Government in 1917-18.

Overall impact of the national struggle. The over all impact of the national struggle was that the Government announced that its policy was "the gradual development of self-governing institutions with a view to the progressive realisation of responsible Government of India, as an integral part of the British Empire".

26

National Movement and Constitutional Reforms (1919 to 1928)

Q.1. Explain the impact of the developments during the First World War and immediate post-war years on the national movement in India.

or

What led to the rapid growth of the National movement after 1919? How would you ascribe it to the advent of Mahatma Gandhi in Indian politics? *(Delhi University 1998).*

Ans: *Impact of the First World War on National Movement*

Backgroun. Two imperialist groups of hostile nations fought the First World War (1914-18). On the one side were Britain, France, Russia and Japan (later on Italy and USA also joined), known as 'Allies' and the other were nations Germany, Austria, Hungary and Turkey, called the 'Axis' powers. The 'Allies' won the war. India, because of being under the domination of Britain had to bear the brunt of the war.

National Movement during the war years. There were four important events during the war that gave impetus to national movement. These were as under:

1. Growth of the revolutionary movements in India and the Ghadar Party outside India for the cause of India's freedom.
2. The Home Rule Leagues started in India by Mrs. Annie Besant and Bal Gangadhar Tilak for self-rule.
3. Temporary reapproachment between the Congress and the Muslim League resulting in the Lucknow Pact and their decision to work together for national cause.
4. Unity between the Moderate leaders and the Extremist leaders of the Indian National Congress, thus strengthening the national movement.

Impact of the immediate post-war years on the National Movement of India

Important factors which led to the resurgence of nationalism in India are described below:

1. *Valuable contribution of India to war efforts and its expectations from the British rulers.* Gandhiji had fully cooperated with the rulers. He said, "it

was our duty to help them (British rulers) win by standing by them in their hour of need".

More than 10 lakh soldiers from India fought at different war fronts outside India. India made an enormous contribution to War Fund and the Red Cross. The British greatly appreciated India's war efforts. But after the War was over, Indian's hope were not fulfilled. The attitude of the British rulers was quite indifferent.

2. *War for freedom slogan belied.* The British Prime Minister regarded Indians as equal custodians of 'Common interests and fortunes'. Montague, the Secretary of State for India referred to the "common loyalty" of Britain and India to the ideal of freedom. President Wilson of America uttered these memorable words that war was meant to make "the world fit for free men to live". Naturally all these sentiments had kindled hopes for India's freedom after war.

3. *War's adverse economic impact on India.* The prices during the war shot up. A large number of industries during war had come up but after the war, no protection to Indian industries was given. Indian industrialists on their part did not share their mounting profits with the labour. This led to labour unrest and trade unionism which affected production. In the villages, the poor people and the peasants were groaning under mounting taxes. With the decline in economic activity after the war, the urban youth were facing acute unemployment. It all resulted in frustration. Thus, people thought national government was the only solution.

4. *Russian revolution - A source of inspiration.* The success of the people of Russia in overthrowing the cruel rule of the Czarists in 1917, influenced greatly the nationalist movement in India. The natural question was, if the Russians could overthrow their own despotic rule, why Indians could not free themselves from the foreign oppressive rule! The Russian Revolution infused courage, confidence and faith in Indians for achieving their objective of self government.

5. *Treatment of the defeated nations.* The imperialist powers did not show any regard to the sentiments of the people of those countries which were defeated in the war. The victorious nations of the Paris Peace Conference, divided among themselves the colonies of Germany and Turkey in Africa. This action on the part of the Allies created suspicion of their motives among the people of countries under foreign domination. India also was affected.

6. *Dissatisfaction and anger of Indian Muslims.* Turkey, a source of inspiration for the Muslims, was dismembered by the Allies after the war. The Sultan of Turkey became a virtual prisoner in the hands of the imperialist powers. The Indian Muslims considered the British Government responsible for the sad plight of Turkey.

7. *Admirable role of Indian soldiers.* Indian soldiers, who had played a significant role in winning victories for the Allies in Asia, Africa and Europe,

on their return to India, imparted some of their confidence to the rural people of India. B.C. Pal wrote in 1919, "Today after the downfall of German militarism, after the destruction of the autocracy of the Czar, there has grown up all over the world a new power, the power of the people determined to rescue their legitimate rights".

8. *Favourable international environment for nationalism.* Disillusionment on the policies followed by the victorious powers in the war led to the resurgence of nationalism all over Asia and Africa. Nationalism also surged forward in Ireland and several Arab countries.

9. *Half hearted Montague - Chelmsford Reforms (1919).* The reforms envisaged in the August (1919) Declaration 'after the end of the War' did not at all inspire the Indians and they began to distrust the British all the more. The prophetic words of Mrs Annie Besant, which she said in 1914, turned out to be true after the end of the war, "India claims the right, as a Nation, to justice among the people of the Empire. India asked for this before the war. India asks for this during the war. India will ask of it after the war, not as a reward but as a right. On that there must be no mistake."

10. *Emergence of charismatic leadership.* Indian nationalism received a great boost under the leadership of Gandhiji who had returned to India, from South Africa after his successful *'Satyagraha'* movements.

Gandhiji and National Movement. After the passing away of the three great leaders namely, Gokhale in 1915, Naoroji in 1917 and Tilak in 1920, a great void was created in the national movement in India. The need for a dynamic leader to guide the masses to participate effectively in the struggle for freedom was greatly felt. This void was filled up by Mohan Das Karamchand Gandhi who had already made his mark in taking up the people's cause in South Africa during his stay there. From 1904 to 1914, he had launched 'Satyagraha' a number of times. On account of his peaceful and untiring efforts, Indians began to be treated as human beings in South Africa.

Gandhiji's country into Indian political scene. In the first phase of his public life, Gandhiji established an Ashram on the banks of Sabarmati in 1915. He joined the Indian National Congress in 1916.

Gandhiji's three successful Satyagrahas at Champaran in Bihar, Ahmedabad and Kheda in Gujarat convinced the people of his qualities of leadership.

Champaran Satyagraha. In 1917, he proceeded to Champaran in Bihar to relieve the cultivators from the oppression of the Indigo plantersie the Britishers. For over 100 years, in Bihar and Bengal where Indigo could be grown, the helpless cultivators were forced to cultivate indigo on their best land, at their own cost, neglecting their own food crops, and to sell them to the European planters for their indigo factories at less than half the market price. They were treated like slaves. If they refused, they were dragged and flogged or locked up in the factory godowns and sometimes killed; their houses were burnt; and all these various acts of oppression occurred before the eyes of the police, judges and magistrates. Gandhiji defied the ban on his entry. When he was tried in the court, he pleaded guilty, but added that he disregarded the order of quitting the place "not for want of respect for lawful authority, but in obedience to the higher law of our being, the voice of conscience". As people all around got ready to join the struggle in response to Gandhiji's courageous act for a noble cause, the Government withdrew the case against Gandhiji and made him a member of a committee to inquire into the grievances of the indigo cultivators. The result was the passing of Champaran Agrarian Bill of 1917, the first triumph in India of *Satyagraha* or Civil Disobedience.

2. *Ahmedabad Satyagraha : Satyagraha* was again used by Gandhiji in an industrial dispute in Ahmedabad in 1918. He led the strike of the labourers for increase of pay. After two weeks, when the strikers were losing the zeal, Gandhiji warned that he would not touch any food till a settlement was reached. So after 21 days' strike, a favourable settlement was reached.

3. *Kheda Satyagraha :* Immediately after the strike was over, Gandhiji plunged into a *Satyagraha* campaign in the Kheda (of Kaira) district of Gujarat, where, under rules, the peasants should have got the exemption from the payment of land revenue as the yield of their corps fell below 25% due to famine and plague. But the Government officials refused to accept the demand of the peasants. Gandhiji advised the cultivators to resort to *Satyagraha.* Gandhiji was joined by Vallabhbhai Patel. The cultivators stood firm. Fear of officials passed away. They faced attachment of property and threat of forfeiture of their land. The Government had to yield. With the triumph of Champaran and Kheda began the third phase of the struggle as the people perceived, that their freedom depended on *Satyagraha* which demanded infinite capacity for suffering and sacrifice.

4. *Roylatt Act Satyagraha.* In 1919, Gandhiji organised an all India Satyagraha for the first time against the enactment of the Royaltt Act (1919) which was intended to impose several restrictions on the civic rights of the people.

Thereafter, the struggle of India's freedom, by and large, began to be associated with Gandhiji.

Q.2 Write a note on the Act of 1919 or Montague Chelmsford Reforms.

Why 1919 Act? During the First World War, the British Government had announced that Indians would be increasingly associated in every branch of administration and there would be a gradual development of self-governing institutions. Accordingly after the war, the British Government introduced these reforms.

The Preamble of the Act declared, "It is the declared policy of the Parliament to provide for the increasing association of Indians in every branch of Indian administration and for gradual development of self-governing institutions.

Main Provisions of the Act of 1919

Central Provisions

1. A bicameral legislature was set up at the Centre i.e, the Council of States and the Legislative Assembly.
2. The Council had 60 members including 33 elected and the rest nominated. The assembly had 140 out of which 103 were elected and the rest nominated-51 General constituencies, 30 Muslims, 2 Sikhs, 7 landlords, 9 Europeans and 4 others.
3. The franchise was extremely narrow. The total number of voters for the Council of States was about 17,350 and for the Central Assembly was about 9,09870 in 1920.
4. The constitutencies were fixed on communal basis.

Provincial Provisions. (1) Each of the nine provinces was to have an enlarged Legislative Council. (2) Each Provincial Council was to have a substantial elected majority.

A system known as 'Dyarchy' was introduced. According to it, the provincial subjects were divided into 'reserved' and 'transferred' subjects.

5. The reserved subjects were to be administered by the Executive Councillors answerable only to the Crown.
6. The Governor could use his veto power to nullify popular decision.

Critical Evaluation of the Reforms. While the King of England termed these reforms as "the beginning of the Swaraj within the Empire", the Congress passed a resolution calling it "inadequate, unsatisfactory and disappointing".

Defects

The reforms suffered from the following defects:

(i) The franchaise was extremely limited. In 1920, out of a total population of about 25 crore in India, there were 9 lakh voters for the Lower House and 17000 for the Upper House (ii) Property qualifications to be eligible to vote were pitched very high (iii) Women could neither vote nor stand for election (iv) The constituencies were grouped on communal basis (v) The Governor could overrule the decision of the Ministers (vi) The Viceroy could overrule his Council. It meant that both the executives — the Governor General and the Governor — were not responsible to the legislatures (vii) Dyarchy or the double executive betrays a lack of confidence in the capacity of Indians and that is why only those subjects were transferred to their care as were politically unimportant. Under Dyarchy a Minister had to serve two masters - the Governor and the legislature (viii) It took away administrative efficiency as Ministers had responsibility without power and legislature had power without responsibility (ix) Subjects vitally related to another were divided into 'reserve' and 'transferred'. Minister of Agriculture did not have 'Irrigation' which was a reserved subject.

Merits:

(1) For the first time Indians were appointed Ministers as the leaders of elected majorities. This was responsible government although to a very limited extent (2) For the first time in the history of British rule, it provided for transfer of power, however was limited it (3) It gave training in the art of government (4) It also gave an opportunity to the people for influencing the action of the Government.

Q.3. Discuss Dyarchy set up under the Government of India Act of 1919. Why did it fail? *(Delhi University 1996).*

or

How was Dyarchy planned under the Act of 1919? What were the major defects of the scheme in Principle, planning and practice?

(Rajasthan University 1997).

or

What do you understand by Dyarchy? Why did it prove unworkable?

(Rajasthan University 1996).

Ans: *Why Reforms under Government of India Act 1919!*

With a view to enlisting the cooperation of the people of India in war efforts, the British Government had declared that they would be given adequate powers after the war. In 1917, Montague, the Secretary of State for India stated in the House of Commons (British Parliament), "The policy of His Majestry's Government, with which the Government of India are in complete accord, is that of the increasing association of Indians in every branch of the administration and the gradual development of self-governing institutions, with a view to the progressive realisation of responsible government in India as an integral part of the British Empire". Accordingly in 1919 reforms at the Central level and Provincial level were introduced in India.

Dyarchy in the Provinces

The most significant changes made by the Act of 1919 were in the field of provincial administration under the system known as Dyarchy.

'Dyarchy' is a derivative of two Greek words '*di*' meaning '*twice*' and '*archie*' meaning 'rule' i.e double government or government by two rulers.

Dyarchy was introduced in 1921 in eight provinces (i) Assam (ii) Bengal (iii) Bihar (iv) Bombay (v) Central Provinces (vi) Orissa (vii) Punjab and (viii) United Provinces. The system continued till April 1937.

Reserved and Transferred subjects. The subjects to be dealt with by the Provincial Governments were divided into parts (i) Reserved subjects (ii) Transferred subjects.

Reserve subjects were administered by the Governor with the help of the Executive Council to be nominated by him and the Transferrcd subjects were looked after by the Ministers who were chosen by the Governor from the elected members of the legislature.

The Reserved subjects were as under:

Administration of Justice, Police, Prisons, Irrigation and Canals, Drainage and Embankments, Water Storage and Water Power, Land Revenue Administration, Land Improvement and Agricultural Loans, Famine Relief, Control of Newspapers etc.

Transferred Subjects included: Agriculture and Fisheries, Cooperative Societies, Education with some exemptions, Excise, Local Self-Government, Hospitals, Public Health, Industries etc.

Powers of the Governors: (i) The Governor was authorised to over-rule his Ministers and the Members of his Council.

(2) Provision was made for the temporary administration of Transferred subjects in case of an emergency.

Responsibility and accountability: A Minister could be dismissed by the Governor at his will. He was responsible to the Legislature also. He had to serve two masters i.e Governor and the Legislative Council.

Working of Dyarchy:

The system of Dyarchy worked in the Provinces for about 16 years i.e. from 1921 to 1937. However, it did not work satisfactorily. The system had several limitations and drawbacks. Following were the major causes for the failure of Dyarchy.

1. *Unscientific division of subjects.* The division of the subjects into Reserved subjects and transferred subject was not done on a rational basis. For instance Irrigation was a Reserved Subject and Agriculture a Transferred subject. There was so much confusion that at occasions it became difficult to pin-point the department to which a particular matter belonged. Shir C.Y. Chintamani, a Minister in U.P. has given an interesting example in which Dyarchy worked. In 1921, an enquiry was conducted in the Department of Agriculture on the question of fragmentation of holdings. When the report was submitted in 1922, it was felt that the question should have been dealt with by the Revenue Department and the case was transferred to that Department. In 1924, it was decided that the case should be dealt with by the Cooperative Department to which it belonged. There were numerous such examples.

2. *Lack of cooperation between Executive Councillors and Ministers.* The Executive Councillors dealing with Reserved subjects were generally members of bureaucracy and the Ministers, the representatives of the people. There was constant friction among these groups.

3. *Weak position of the ministers.* The Ministers had to serve two masters i.e. the Governor and the Legislative Council. Thus a Minister could be turned out by the Governor as well as the Legislative Council. The result was that the Ministers sank to the position of 'glorified secretaries'.

4. *No joint responsibility.* The Governor dealt with each Minister individually. The principle of joint responsibility of the Cabinet did not work.

5. *Department of Finance under the Executive Councillor.* It is accepted that the incharge of finance has always the upper hand. Since the Finance Department was a Reserved subject and with the Executive Councillor, the Ministers had to be at his marcy to get the needed finance for their departments. In other words, representatives of the people were not so much trusted so as to deal with the Finance Department.

6. *Not so cordial relations between the Ministers and the Senior Services.* Several of the key posts in the provinces were held by the Members of All India Services. The Ministers had no control over their appointments and postings. The Ministers had no power to choose their own subordinates when vacancies occurred in their departments. The senior officers did not care for the Ministers.

7. *Governor's support to bureaucracy.* The Governor usually backed the members of all India Services in case of some conflict with the Ministers.

8. *Little freedom of vote in the Legislative Assembely.* The official block, the landlords, the representatives of Commerce and other vested interests always voted for government policies and this weakened the position of Ministers.

9. *Unsuitable political environment.* The system was born under an unlucky star. The political environment in the country was surcharged with distrust and suspicion on account of the Jallianawala Bagh Massaure and the Khilafat Movement. The failure of the monsoons increased the misery of the people who had been feeling the punch of the first World War. Slump had come in the market.

10. *Uncongenial psychological environment.* There was general apathy towards reforms. There was a feeling that more reforms were on the anvail as these reforms were in the nature of a half way house. The people hoped that they were going to get more in the near future.

The term Dyarchy almost became a term of abuse..

Significance of Dyarchy

According to *Professor P. Spear.* "When all this is said, the fact remains that the reforms proved to be solid and substantial achievements. They were an essential milestone on the road to self-government. They gave, by and large, enough inducement to people to work them and enough scope to provide experience. and incentives for the future".

In the words of Coupland, "The most important measure of Indian polity. Limited and checked though it might be, this was a genuine transfer of power".

Punniah has observed, "Dyarchy was a unique experience. Its main object and purpose was to train the people in the art of responsible government".

In the opinion of *Palande,* "Dyarchy was never intended to be an ideal in itself but a stepping stone to a noble consummation, namely, a fully self-governing India".

Dr. Appadorai thinks that it was "a bridge between autocracy and responsibility."

Roberts thinks that "Dyarchy was the best transitional echamism that appeared after a prolonged examination of alternatives".

Summing up A perusal of above would indicate that Dyrarchy did not totally fail. It had its own merits, though to a limited extent.

Q.4. Write notes on :

1. The Rowlatt Act, 1919

2. The Jallianwala Bagh Tragedy. *(Punjab University April 1995,). April 1996, Oct. 1997 and April 1998, Rajasthan Univesity 1995).*

3. The Khilafat Movement. *(Delhi University, 1993).*

4. Non-Cooperation Movement. (1920-22) *(Rajasthan University, 1993)*

1. *The Rowlatt Act, 1919*

Provisions of the Act. The Anarchial and Revolutionary Crimes Act, 1919, usually known as Rowlatt Act was passed by the British Government in India to suppress the revolutionary activities that had been taking place in India since the outbreak of the First World War (1914-1919).

The Rowlatt Act implied (i) Arrest of a person without warrant (ii) Summary trial (iii) No provision of appeal (iv) No open trial (v) Restriction on movement of individuals (vi) Security for good conduct (vii) Any evidence could be accepted even if not according to the Laws of Evidence.

Background of the passing of the Act. Revolutionary activities during the First World War had seriously disturbed the British rulers. So Lord Chelmsford, the Governor General, followed the policy of reform-cum-repression as he was convinced about the effectiveness of the twin policy in India. On December 10, 1917, while he was busy formulating the constitutional reforms, he appointed a committee of five members, including two Indians, to find out the extent of the criminal conspiracies connected with revolutionary activities and to suggest new laws for their suppression. A British judge, Sir Sydney Rowlatt was the President. Two Bills based on the Committee's recommendations were framed without any loss of time and placed before the Governor General's Legislative Council in February 1919. These contained drastic provisions denying protection of law to Indians. All the non-official Indian members of the Council unitedly opposed the measure and four of them resigned by way of protest. Indeed, such a unique opposition of Indians to a Government measure was never witnessed since the Partition of Bengal. The Government just dropped one of the Bills but passed the other as the Anarchial and Revolutionary Crimes Act, 1919, usually known as Rawlatt Act'.

Strong Indian reaction against the Act. The People of India had been promised a democratic set up but the Act came a sudden blow to them. It was a cruel joke to deprive Indians of all liberties and rights and to stop them seeking protection under law. Only suspicion was sufficient to cage them for life or hang them. A widespread public agitation was bound to engulf the country. Gandhiji appealed to the Viceroy to withhold his consent to these obvious measures. When his appeal was ignored. He took the lead and started *Satyagraha,* as a challenge to the Government. A campaign was organised and as a first step, Gandhiji made an all India appeal to observe *hartal* for a day. The date originally fixed as March 30, was changed to April 6. The *hartal* was a unique success. But there were clashes between the police and the people.

Events moved fast in the Punjab where the Lt. Governor, Sir Michael O'dwyer, had already terrorised the whole of the Punjab by his ruthless suppression. He interned hundreds of educated men, gagged the vernacular press and used all sorts of tyrannical methods, as conosiderable part of the Punjab was aflame after the peaceful *hartal* of April 6. In Lahore processions of students and crowds attending meetings were fired upon. In Gujranwala, on April 14, the trouble started over the killing of a calf and hanging it on a railway bridge. Two railway bridges were burnt. In Kasur, the crowd got out of control on April 12, burnt the post office and did such other acts. A train was attacked and two European soldiers were beaten to death.

As there was great popular exitement in both Delhi andAmritsar, Gandhiji was called there. But the police forcibly removed him fromthe train and sent him to Bombay and then set him free. A vast crowd was roused to a pitch of mad frenzy by the news of Gandhiji's arrest and people committed acts of violence in Ahmedabad. Gandhiji did not mince matters. He addressed the people of Ahmedabad, "*Satyagraha*" admits of no violence, no pillage and still in the name of Satyagraha we burn down buildings, loot money, stop trains, cut off telegraph lines, kill people," For such misdeeds, he wished himself to be arrested or hanged.It suddenly dawned upon him that it was a Himalayan miscalculation to call upon people to launch *Satyagraha* without preparing them. He suspended the *Satyagraha.*

2. *The Jallianwala Bagh Tragedy massc are*

A shameless Act. The Jallianwala Massacre of April 13, 1919 on the auspicious day of Baisakhi for the people of Punjab was a calculated act of inhumanity and was unparalled for its ferocity in the history of British rule in India.

Background. Voices of protests swelled from all over the country against the Rowlatt Act which had authorised the government to arrest and imprison any person without trial or conviction in a court of law and which had also denied the right of appeal against it. The whole of India stood as one man against this Act which was called the *'Black Act'* by the people. Gandhiji launched the *'Satyagraha.'* The movement gained momentum in several towns of Punjab, Two *'hartals'* in Amritsar, on March 30 and April 6, passed off peacefully. But on April 9, Sir Michael O'Dwyer deported two prominent local leaders, Dr. Satyapal and Dr. Kitchlew. *Hartal* was immediately declared. A large crowd of demonstrators marched peacefully but indiscriminate firing was opened on them. After that, things seemed settled on the 11th. But things took a bad turn with the arrival of Brigadier General Dyer on the evening of the same day. He immediately declared Martial Law, though it was not officially proclaimed before April 15. He began his regime on 12th by indiscriminate arrests and issue of a proclamation banning all meetings. However, the proclamation of banning meetings and gatherings was not read in many parts of Amritsar. This omission, deliberate or accidential, was very unfortunate, as the people had already announced a public meeting at Jallianwala Bagh on the 13th, the Baisakhi Day, at 4.30 pm.

Brutual Action of Dyer : Dyer took no steps in warn the people not to enter the Bagh or to put troops at the entrance to stop the people from entering. But soon after the meeting had begun, Dyer arrived on the spot with armoured cars and troops with rifles. The Bagh had only one small exist on one side and all the three sides were enclosed by buildings. About 10,000 people had gathered there. Dyer, plugged all possible exists and stationed himself and his troops on a rising ground at the only entrance, and then, without issuing any warning ordered 'Fire' at about 100 yards. 'range'. "The panic-stricken multitude broke at once, but for ten consecutive minutes, he kept up a merciless fusliade-in all 1650 rounds-on that seething mass of humanity, cought like rats in trap, vainly rushing for the few narrow exits or lying flat on the ground to escape the rain of bullets, which he personally directed to the point where the crowd was the thickest."

What happened to the dead and wounded? The wounded lay in their agony and the dead lay putrefying in the heat of Amritsar and the vultures came to tear the flesh of innocent victims of this dreadful holocaust. It was because on the very day (13 April), a curfew order to shoot at sight after 8 pm was issued and, therefore, the anxious and weeping relatives of the wounded and dead remained terrified behind their closed doors and could not come out to take charge of the dead or wounded. Dyer, when questioned by the Hunter Commission frankly said that it was not his job to look after the wounded; it was for them to go to the hospital if they liked. He even admitted that he would not have hesitated from still greater killing if the narrowness of the entry of the Bagh had not compelled him to leave his machine guns behind. He also admitted that he could have dispersed the crowd without firing but that would have lowered his dignity. Such a brute arrogance clearly indicates that some of the rulers of the British colonies and some of their officers considered the coloured Indians worse than slaves, not worthy of being treated as human beings.

Impact of Jallianwala Bagh Tragedy

First, it gave a new turn to the national movement and it became a mass movement.

Secondly, it became a turning point in the history of India. Gandhiji emerged as the most prominent leader and in fact the superme leader of the national movement.

Thirdly, it helped in strengthening Hindu-Muslim Unity, though it was short lived.

Fourthly, several Indians renounced their titles and Rabindranath Tagore was so shocked that in protest, he renounced his knighthood which had been conferred upon him by the Government and he declared, "The time has come when badges of honour make our shame glaring in their incongrous context of humiliation, and, I, for my part, wish to stand shorn of all distinctions, by the side of my countymen, who for their so-called insignificance, are liable to suffer degradation, not fit for human beings".

Fifthly, it gave a fillip to revolutionary tendencies. One of the injured at Jallianwala Bagh was a youngman of 20, named Udham Singh. He was imprisoned for five years after which he went to London for studying engineering. There in 1940, he shot dead Sir Michael O'Dwyer, the notorious ex-Governor of Punjab, responsible for Jallianwala Bagh massacre. He was hanged to death the same year. Udham Singh declared in the court, "I do not mind dying. I am dying for my country. What is the use of waiting until you get old".

Pt. Madan Mohan Malviya, who had earlier been the President of the Indian National Congress in 1909, 1918, became President later on also in 1932 and 1933) collected details of the tragedy which sent such a thrill of horror over the whole country that the Viceroy announced the appointment of a Committee of Enquiry. The British and the Indian members differed in their views on Dyer's conduct.

Sixthly, Gandhiji was so shocked by the grim tragedy that he suspended the 'Satyagraha' campaign on April 8, 1919 and called on the '*Satyagrahis*' to take up constructive programmes, viz, use of Swadeshi goods and unity between Hindus and Muslims.

3 *The Khilafat Movement (1920-22)*

Meaning of the Khilafat Movement. The Khilafat Movement derived its name from the Caliph or Khalifa of Turkey, formally regarded as temporal head of Islam and it arose among Indian Muslims in protest against the treatment given by the Allied and especially Britain to the defeated Turkish empire and Sultan of Turkey (Caliph of Turkey).

Background of the Moement. In the First World War, the Sultan joined Germany and fought against England and her allies. The natural sympathy of the Muslims was with the Sultan and they found it difficult to support the British in the war against the Sultan of Turkey. Suspecting some of the Muslim leaders as disloyal, the British Government put them in internment. Among them were Mohammad Ali and Abul Kalam Azad. The British Government also tried to win the sympathy and support of the Muslims during the war. So the British Prime Minister, in 1918, declared that they were not fighting to deprive Turkey of its territory and gave assurance of sympathetic treatment of Turkey at the end of the war. But all these hopes of the Muslims were doomed after the defeat of Turkey, when portions of Turkish Empire passed under the control of England, France and Greece and the Sultan was deprived of all real authority, even in the remaining dominions. The Muslims regarded this as a great betrayal going against their assurances.

Main demand. The central demand of the movement was that the Khalifa (Sultan of Turkey) retained control of places sacred to Islam and left with sufficient territory to enable him to defend the Islamic faith and its holy places.

Gandhiji's and Congress' role in agitation along with Muslims. In June 1920, the Indian Muslims started a vigorous agitation to bring pressure upon Britain to change her policy towards Turkey. This, known as the Khilafat Movement, received enormous strength and support from Gandhiji as he felt that the Muslim cause was just and he should help them to secure the fulfilment of the assurance given by the British Prime Minister. Gandhiji also looked upon the Khilafat Movement as "an opportunity of uniting Hindus and Mohammedans as would not arise in a hundred years". Gandhiji issued a Manifesto on March 10 embodying the idea of Non-Cooperation, to be pursued in the Khilafat Movement. This Manifesto provides the first definite idea of Gandhiji's Non-violent Non-cooperation: "Non-Cooperation is the most effective when it is free from all violence. It becomes a duty when cooperation means degradation or humiliation." The Khilafat Committee under the guidance of Gandhiji launched the Khilafat Movement in the form of '*Hartal*'. Two issues of the Congress programmes namely agitation against Punjab atrocities, and Swaraj were gradually tagged into the Khilafat Movement.

The boycott of government run educational institutions led to the founding of the Jamia Millia for the higher education of Muslims.

The movement engenered a strong sentiment of Hindu-Muslim unity and the Hindus and Muslims marched together shoulder to shoulder.

The Khilafat Movement collapsed in 1922 and lost its focus for the Muslim world when Kemal Ataurk took power in Turkey and abolished the office of the Khalifa.

4. *Non-Cooperation Movement*

The Non-cooperation Movement (1920-20) is considered the first mass campaign (side by side Khilafat Movement) against the British rule organised by the Indian National Congress under the leadership of Gandhiji. The underlying causes of widespread discontent with British rule were : economic, political and psychological etc. The immediate issues were the repression in the Punjab and Khilafat movement.

Main objectives:

(i) Restoration of the power and prestige of the Khalifa of Turkey.
(ii) Withdrawal of Rowlatt Act.
(iii) Protest against the British over their repressive measures adopted in the Punjab.
(iv) Demand for self-government.

Programmes.

(i) Surrender of honorary titles and posts.
(ii) Boycott of government functions.
(iii) Boycott of government education institutions and establishing national institutions.
(iv) Gradual boycot of Law Courts.
(v) Boycott of all legislatures.
(vi) Boycott of foreign goods.

There was great enthusiasm for the movement. About 30,000 people courted arrest. Several eminent leaders left their practice to join the movement. However, Gandhiji withdrew the movement when violence was committed at the police station of Chauri Chaura in Uttar Pradesh.

(For details see the next question)

Q.5. What were the circumstances that led Gandhiji to start Non-Cooperation Movement, When and why did he suspend it? What were its achievements? *(Rajasthan University 1997).*

Ans: *Non-Cooperation Movement (1920-22)*

Immediate Post-War Period. Immediate post-war years i.e. 1919 to 1922 were marked by several important events which had a remarkable bearing on the history of national movement in India. First, there was the Government of India Act 1919 relating to constitutional and administrative reforms, second, the Rowlatt Act; third, the emergence of Gandhiji, Fourth, the Jallianwala Bagh Tragedy; fifth, the Khilafat Movement and the Non-Cooperation Movement in a way the last phase of the earlier events.

The decision to start the movement was taken at the Calcutta Session of the Congress in September 1920 and endorsed in December at its Nagpur Session in 1920. Gandhiji was the moving figure behind this movement.

Circumstances leading to the Movement : The immediate causes which led to the Non-Cooperation Movement were to protest against the repression in the Punjab by the British rulers, and the Khilafat issue relating to the harsh treatment given to the Khalifa of Turkey by the 'Allies', the victorious nations including Britain after the First World War. The Khalifa (Sultan) of Turkey was regarded as the temporal head of Islam and his humiliation sent a wave of shock among the Muslims.

Essential elements of the Movement. Gandhiji wanted to run the movement on the ideals of *Ahimsa* (non violence) and '*Swadeshi*' (self reliance).

Gandhiji called the movement "a state of peaceful rebellion" and promised that if the people cooperated, he would enable them to get the '*Swaraj* within a year'.

The movement also aimed at making it known to the British rulers that they would not be able to run the administration unless they received the cooperation of the people of India.

The two movements i.e. the Non-Cooperation and the Khilafat based on non-cooperation and non-violence continued side by side but as a single force with united action.

The Hindu-Muslim Unity was spectacular.

Seven point programme of the Movement. The following seven-point programme was approved by the Congress:-

1. Surrendering all honorary posts and titles.
2. Refusal to attend any government function.
3. Boycott of all government and government aided schools and starting National Schools and Colleges
4. Gradual boycott of Law Courts.
5. Refusal of Civilian and Military personnel to serve in Mesopotamia (to protect the oil tanks of Anglo Persian Oil Company).
6. Boycott of all Legislatures.
7. Boycott of all foreign goods.

Non-cooperation Movement at work

A great momentum. The movement picked up fast in the county. There were frequent lathi charges, mass arrests and ban on processions and public meetings.

Student processions and mammoth meetings became the order of the day. The boycotting students adopted a novel method of picketing for preventing others from entering the schools or colleges. A number of them lay flat, side by side, blocking the entrances. Many students resumed their studies in newly started national schools and colleges.

The boycott of foreign cloth was the most sustained part of the movement.

The boycott of legal profession was heralded by the magnificent self-sacrifice of Pandit Motilal Nehru and C.R. Das who earlier enjoyed princely income. Their example was followed by a large number of lawyers including C. Rajagopalachari, Rajendra Prasad and Sardar Patel.

All the Congress candidates withdrew from election contest to the Council. Their seats were filled up by non-Congressmen.

The boycott of titles and honours, as well as government offices was not encouraging. Only a few resigned from their government jobs. Subhash Chandra Bose resigned from the I.C.S.

C.R. Das organised a large number of volunteers to self Khadi.

About 20,000 '*Charkhas*' (Spinning wheels) were distributed for domestic production of cloth.

Imports of cloth were halved.

Though Gandhiji did not subscribe to labour unrest, about 400 strikes took place in industry.

Non-Cooperation Movement among workers on tea gardens and jute plantations in Bengal and Assam added to the pressure on British commercial interest.

The Prohibition Movement in the South cut into state excise revenues.

The most sustantional point of movement was reached with the boycott of the visit of Prince of Wales in November 1921. This further provoked the Government and mass arrests and police brutalities were resorted to against the peaceful demonstrators.

Mass arrests.

Within a few days prisons were filled with political prisoners. Camp prisons were then opened, but they too were filled up in no time. Orders were given to release a large number of old prisoners, but no one would leave prison. The prisoners were thereupon taken forcibly to the prison gate and set free, so that the new flow of prisoners could be accommodated. The British jail had lost its terror and imprisonment became a badge of distinction. Outside prison, arrests were stopped, as there was no place in the prisons and sticks and batons were freely used against the demonstrators. Except Gandhiji, most of the important leaders of the Movement were behind the bars.

Nearly forty thousand Congress workers were in jail in December 1921 when the Annual Congress Session was held in Ahmedabad. The Congress Session decided to organise not only individual civil disobedience but also mass civil disobedience.

Gandhiji's Appeal

Gandhiji then gave an ultimatum to the Viceroy in a letter sent on February 1, 1922: "This lawless repression has made immediate adoption of Mass Civil Disobedience", unless the Viceroy declared a policy of non-interference with all non-violent activities for the redress of the Khilafat or the Punjab wrongs or for Swaraj." Finding no response from the Viceroy, Gandhiji started from Bardoli, his Mass Civil Disobedience Movement including non-payment of taxes. The whole of India watched with suspense.

Suspension of the movement: Chauri Chaura Incident (Feb. 5, 1922): The Congress had asked all satyagrahis to take a pledge to "remain non-violent in word and deed". The movement had spread among the masses. When the movement was at its height, violence occurred at Chauri Chaura, a village in the Gorakhpur District of U.P. when a procession of 3,000 peasants was fired upon by the police and atrocities committed on the processionists. In retaliation, the angry mob took to violence and burnt the police station causing death to 22 policemen.

Gandhiji was so shocked with the violence that he announced the withdrawal of the movement unilaterally when almost all important leaders of the movement were in jail.

Gandhiji was also arrested and sentences to 6 year's imprisonment. During his trial, he told the British judge, that he would "do the samething' again if he was set free. This was regarding launching his Non-Cooperation movement. Gandhiji took upon himself full responsibility for all the events.

Reaction to the Suspension of the Movement. According to Subhash Chandra Bose, "To sound the order of retreat just when public enthusiasm was reaching the boiling point was nothing sort of a national calamity".

According to Jawaharlal Nerhu, "We in prison learnt to our amazement that Gandhiji had stopped the aggressive aspect".

C.R. Das remarked that "Gandhiji 'bungled and mismanaged". He went on to say "The Mahatma opens a campaign in a brilliant fashion, he works it up with skill, he moves from success to success till he reaches the zenith of his campaign but after that he loses his nerve and begins to falter".

Polak states that the withdrawal of the movement created a great gulf in the relations of the Hindus and Muslims. "Muslims wilted under the blow and it was never again possible to restore the confidence and fraternity that he united the two communities during this period of alliance".

Evaluation of the Movement

Failures. The Non-Cooperation Movement failed to achieve the objectives for which it was started. First, it failed to secure the redress and the wrongs done by the rulers in Punjab. Second, the object of saving the office of the Khalifa was not achieved.

After the suspension of the Movement and the imprisonment of Gandhiji, the Khalifat movement lost its momentum. A few months later, in October 1922, Mustafa Kemal Pasha established a Republic in Turkey and after two years abolished the office of Caliph. Thus, the Khilafat Movement also came to an end and its leaders, except one, left the Congress. Abul Kalam Azad of the Khilafat Movement remained a true Congressman. The breach between the two i.e. the League and the Congress was inevitable for the Congress was fighting for India's Independence while the other for a religious cause.

Gains. The Non-Cooperation Movement proved useful in several ways.

Among the several national educational institutions of higher learning established during the period. The Kashi Vidyapeeth, the Gujarat Vidyapeeth and the Jamia Millia of Delhi that still survive have played an important role in national awakening and reconstruction.

The Non-Cooperation Movement converted the Congress from a constitutional body to a revolutionary organisation based on Non-violence and

Satyagraha. In the words of *Coupland,* "He (Gandhi) had done what Tilak had failed to do. He had converted the national movement into a revolutionary movement. He had taught it to pursue the goal of India's freedom, not by constitutional pressure on the Government, still less by discussion and agreement, but by force, none of the less force because it was meant to be non-violent. And he had not only made the national movement revolutionary, he had also made it popular. It had hitherto been confined to the urban intelligentia; made no appeal to the countryfolk. Gandhi's personality had deeply stirred the country side".

Important achievements of the Non-Cooperation Movement may be listed as under:

(1) The general awakening of the masses (2) Loss of faith in the British administration (3) Increased faith in the Congress (4) Strengthening the belief that India can win freedom only by its own efforts and sacrifice (5) Failure of repression to cow down the people (6) Overcoming fear of the British might and readiness to endure hardships and punishments inflicted by the government (7) Congress becoming for the first time, a real mass movement (8) Congress changed from a speech making platform to an organized force with its approach closely resembling non-violent revolutionary nationalism.

Q.6. Write Notes on :

1. The Swaraj Party

2. The Simon Commission (1927-28)

3. The Nehru Report (1928)

4. Revolutionary/Terrorist Movement (1920-1928)

Ans: 1. *The Swaraj Party*

With the withdrawal of the Non-Cooperation Movement, two groups emerged in the Congress. They were the 'Swarajists' led by leaders like C.R. Das and Moti Lal Nehru. The Swarajists were of the view that they should contest elections and fight for their cause from within the Councils and Assemblies. This strategy of Council entry was opposed by the staunch followers of Gandhiji like C. Rajagopalachari (popularly called Rajaji), Sardar Patel, Dr. Rajendra Prasad and Dr. Ansari. They were known as 'no changers' (who did not want any change from the non-cooperation policy of the Congress). However, a special session of the Congress held at Delhi in September 1923, arrived at a compromise by adhering to the principle of Non-cooperation but allowing those Congressmen to contest elections who wanted to enter the legislatures.

Programme of the Swarajists. Their strategy may be described as (i) End the boycott of the Legislative Councils (ii) Contest elections and enter of the Councils (iii) Obstructing the working of the Councils according to official plans (iv) Exposing the plans of he officials (v) Transforming the Councils into arenas of political struggle (vi) Using Councils to arouse public enthusiasm.

The two groups i.e. the Swarajists and 'No Changers' agreed to remain in the Congress but to work in their separate ways. The 'No Changers' engaged themselves in constructive work.

Contesting Elections. Under the Montague-Chelmsford Reforms (1919), elections to the Central Legislative Assembly were held in 1923 and the Swarajists won 42 seats out of 101 elected seats. They agitated in the Assembly through powerful speeches and pleaded for self-government, civil liberaities and industrial development. In due course, they felt that they were not effective in compelling the government to change their authoritative methods. They left the Assembly in 1926. C.R. Das had died in 1925 and a split also occurred among the Swarajists on account of their different views on communalism. Thus, the Swarajists faded away within a short period of four years.

2. *The Simon Commission (1927-28)*

Appointment of the Simon Commission. Elections to the Councils had taken place in 1923 in accordance with the Government of India Act of 1919. The Swarajists led by Motilal Nehru and C.R. Das had joined the Councils and later on walked out of them. On all counts, public opinion was not satisfied with the reforms as envisaged in the 1919 Act. People were getting restive on the apathy of the government. The British Government, therefore, appointed a Commission under the Chairmanship of Sir. J.A. Simon to inquire into the working of the Act of 1919 and to study what changes were needed for the establishment of a responsible government in India.

Faulty Composition of the Commission and Hostility of Indians Towards it. The Commission had all the seven members from the English Community. No Indian was included in it. This sent a wave of anger against the Commission throughout India. The Indian National Congress at its session passed a resolution "to boycott the Commission at every stage". The Commission was boycotted by the Hindu Mahasabha and the Muslim League also. When the Commission landed at Bombay, it had to face a total *hartal* in the city. The cry of "Go back Simon" greeted its members from city to city. The Government resorted to repressive measures and the police lathi-charged the demonstrators. At Lahore, a peaceful demonstration was subjected to repeated baton blows and Lala Lajpat Rai was severely beaten up by the blows and died after 18 days on account of serious injuries. At other places, Jawaharlal Nehru and Govind Ballabh Pant also received lath blows.

Impact of the Commission. The death of Lala Lajpat Rai helped to generate the climate of political revolution aimed at securing freedom for India. The youth was so enraged that on December 17, 1928, three revolutionaries namely, Bhagat Singh, Chandra Shekhar Azad and Rajguru assassinated Saunders, a British Police Officer who had led the '*lathi*' charge at Lala Lajpat Rai.

The report of the Simon Commission was published in 1930. It suggested that the constitutional problems of India should be discussed at Round Table Conferences. This suggestion was accepted by the British Government.

3. *Nehru Report (1928)*

Appointment of the Nehru Committee. The Indian leaders boycotted the Simon Commission because it did not include any Indian as its member. It was decided by the Indian leaders that they would themselves prepare a report on the reforms to be carried out in India for the establishment of a responsible government. An All-Party Conference was held in Delhi under the chairmanship of Dr. M.A. Ansari. The conference constituted a committee with Pandit Motilal Nehru as its chariman. The committee included eminent legal experts like Sir Tej Bahadur Sapru, Sir Ali Imam etc. besides Subhash Chandra Bose and other leaders.

Among the important recommendations of the report were:

Major recommendations:

1. There should be full responsible government in India with Dominion status.
2. There should be two Houses of Parliament i.e. Senate and House of Representatives.
3. The Governor-General should act on the advise of the Executive Council.
4. The statute should embody 19 fundamental rights like freedom of speech, expression and religion etc.

End Result of the Report. The All-Party Convention in 1928, failed to accept the recommendations of the Nehru Report. Jinnah of the Muslim League, did his best to undermine the report. The Congress appreciated the report and insisted that the British Government should accept it before December 21, 1929, otherwise the Congress would declare '*Poorna Swaraj*' as their goal and launch a struggle to achieve it. The Hindu Mahasabha denounced the report as pro-Muslim.

4. *Revolutionary/Terrorist Movement (1920-1930)*

Hindustan Socialist Republican Association (H.S.R.A). The virtual failure of the non-cooperation Movement and the dismay that descended on the nationalist scene created conditions leading to revolutionary, terrorist and militant activities. A meeting held at Kanpur in 1924 which was attended by leading revolutionaries, set up the Hindustan Republican Association. The meeting was attended by old timers like Sachindranath Sanayal, Jogesh Chandra Chatterjee, Surya Sen and Ram Prasad Bismal. The youngsters included Bhagat Singh, Sukhdev, Chandra Shekhar Azad, B.K. Dutt and others. In 1928, the name of the HRA was changed into H.S.R.A.

Objectives of H.S.R.A: Following were its main objectives:

(*i*) To rouse the consciousness of the people of India to the futility of the Gandhian methods of non-violence.

(*ii*) To demonstrate the need and desirability of Direct Action and Revolution in order to achieve complete independence.

(*iii*) To substitute British imperialism in India by a Republic of the United States of India.

Chandra Shekhar Azad became the president of the Association.

Important Activities of the Revolutionaries.

Kakori Conspiracy Case. On August 25, 1925, a few revolutionaries stopped a train near Kakori railway station near Lucknow in Uttar Pradesh and looted the mail van. The revolutionaries were arrested. Four revolutionaries namely Ashfaqulla, Ram Prasad Bismal, Rajendra Lahiri and Thakur Roshan Singh were hanged and many others were given long sentences.

Murder of Saunders (December 1928) A notable activity of H.S.R.A. was the murder of Saunders, the Superintendent of Police at Lahore, who had ordered the brutal lathicharge on the peaceful procession in which, Lala Lajpat Rai had received severe lathi blows that later resulted in his death. The death of Lala Lajpat Rai had greatly enraged the youth of the Punjab.

Bomb in the Central Legislative Assembly (April 8, 1928). The most dramatic act of the revolutionaries was the throwing of a bomb in the Assembly. Bhagat Singh and B.K. Dutt threw two bombs in the Assembly. The aim was not to kill any body. The revolutionaries could have escaped easily but they deliberately chose to be arrested as they wanted to make use of the court as a forum for revolutionary propaganda. They started shouting, "Long Live Revolution", "Down with imperialism" and "Workers of the World, Unite". They also distributed hand bills with the slogan that they have thrown the Bomb"In order that the deaf might listen, the noise must be powerful". After their arrest, the revolutionaries gave historical statement in the court of the Delhi Sessions judge, "The revolutionaries believe that deliverance of their country will come through revolution". Bhagat Singh and B.K. Dutt were sentenced to death.

The Martyrdom of the Revolutionary Jatindranath Das (September 13, 1929). The revolutionaries in jail were treated brutally. They went on a hunger strike for two months. Jatin Das died after 63 days of hunger strike. The unique sacrifice of Jatin Das roused the entire nation as never before.

Bomb at the Viceroy (1929) To protest against the death of Jatin Das, Chandra Shekhar Azad made an attempt on the life of the Viceroy of India. The bomb exploded near the Viceroy's special train near Delhi but the Viceroy remained unhurt.

Martyrdom of Several Revolutionaries. The revolutionaries, including Chandra Shekhar, continued their activities. The government offered a reward of Rs. 10,000 to anyone who could seize him dead or alive. Chandra Shekhar was betrayed and was surrounded by the police as he entered Alfred Park in Allahabad in 1931. He was riddled with bullets and fell dead.

Surya Sen was arrested in February 1933 and soon hanged.

Bhagat Singh, Rajguru and Sukhdev were sentenced to death. Indian leaders pleaded with the Viceroy to condone their death sentences but of no avail. The three revolutionaries were hanged on March 31, 1931. The news of their hanging filled the entire country with great grief. By their heroic sacrifice, and those of several other revolutionaries, they inspired the people of India to work fearlessly and resolutely for the freedom of the country.

27

National Movement and Constitutional Reforms (1929 to 1947)

Q. 1. Write Notes on the following:

1. ***Purna Swaraj* and Lahore Session of the Indian National Congress (1929)**
2. **Dandi March (1930)**
3. **Civil Disobedience Movement (1930-1933)**
4. **Gandhi Irwin Pact (1931)**
5. **Communal Award and Poona Pact (1931)**
6. **Round Table Conference (1930-32)**
7. **Congress Ministries (1937-39)**

1. *Purna Swaraj and the Lahore Session of the Indian National Congress*

Declaration of Purna Swaraj. The midnight of December 31, 1929 is a great memorable day in the history of freedom movement in India as this day was marked by the adoption of *Purna Swaraj* (Complete Independence) as the goal of Indian National Congress.

Background. There was an uneasiness in the mood of people of India in 1929. A change was bound to come. In the first place there was a revival of revolutionary activity as mentioned earlier. There was also a widespread labour unrest. The death of Jatin Das also gave a fillip to the youth movement and student organisations grew up all over India. The Nehru Committee Report (1928) had already been rejected by the Government. There appeared no evidence of the earnest of the Government that it was willing to introduce constitutional reforms in India leading ultimately to India's independence.

Purna Swaraj and Programme Chalked out by the Congress in Pursurance of the Resolution on Purna Swaraj.

A Congress session was held at Lahore on December 29, 1929 in a tense atmosphere. The choice of Jawaharlal Nehru, an embodiment of youthful enthusiasm for independence, as President of the Session, lent a special glamour and courage to the vast assembled Congressmen. The resolution embodied with a spirit of defiance and determination read: "The Congress declares that the word *Swaraj* in Article I of the Congress Constitution shall mean

Complete Independence... and hope that all Congressmen will henceforth devote their exclusive attention to the attainment of Complete Independence for India." The adoption of Independence as the goal of India was hailed with befitting solemnity. As the clock struck midnight between December 31, 1929 and January 1, 1930, Pandit Jawaharlal Nehru came out in a solemn procession to the banks of the Ravi at Lahore and hoisted the tricolour flag of Indian independence.

The Working Committee of the Congress met on January 2, 1930 and decided the following line of action:

1. The members of the legislatures should resign.
2. The 26th of January should be observed all over India as the *Purna Swaraj* Day (Day of Complete Independence).
3. A declaration prepared by Gandhiji should be read out on the occasion.

The declaration contained the following important policy decisions:-

(1) "The British Government has ruined India economically, politically, culturally and spiritually... We hold it to be a crime against man and God to submit any longer to a rule that has caused this fourfold disaster to our country."

(2) We will withdraw, so far as we can, all voluntary association with the British Government.

(3) We will prepare for Civil Disobedience including non-payment of taxes.

(4) Every Indian was to make a declaration of Complete Independence and take a pledge of loyalty to the Indian National Congress and to the sacred fight for India's liberty.

January 26, 1930 was celebrated as the First Independence day all over the country with great enthusiasm. The National Flag was unfurled and every on took the pledge of loyalty to the Congress and to the Freedom Struggle. The Working Committee met again from February 14-16, and authorised Gandhiji to start Civil Disobedience.

2. *Dandi March (1930)*

Dandi March was the beginning of the Disobedience Movement. From 14 to 16 February 1930 the Congress Working Committee met at Sabarmati Ashram and vested Gandhiji with the full powers to launch the Civil Disobedience Movement "at a time and place of his choice." On February 27, the plan of the agitation was declared and Mahatma Gandhi declared that he would first defy the Salt Laws. On March 2, he wrote to the Viceroy. "The British rule in India has brought about moral, material, cultural, and spiritual ruination of this great country. I regard this rule as a curse. I am out to destroy this system of Government...sedition has become my religion. Ours is a non-violent battle. We are not to kill anybody but it is our *dharma* to see that the curse of this Government is blotted out."

On March 12, 1930 Gandhiji left Sabramati Ashram with 78 male inmates of the Ashram on foot to cover the distance of about 350 km to reach Dandi, a village on the sea coast of Gujarat to disobey the Government and break the salt law by obtaining or making salt without paying the salt tax. The villagers flocked from all sides, sprinkled the roads with water, strewed leaves and sunk on their knees, as the peasant like frail figure, with a lathi in hand walking with his followers passed them. Over 300 village headmen gave up their jobs. The slow march on foot, from village to village covering about 350 km, on an average 12 to 14 km a day, was by itself an automatic propaganda rousing the entire countryside and the whole of India to a realistic sense of the coming struggle. On April 5, Gandhiji reached Dandi. On April 6, he picked up a handful of salt from the sea and defied the salt law 'as a symbol of India's refusal to live under British laws'. It was a signal of countrywide repetition of the same. Where natural conditions did not permit for making salt, violation of other laws was resorted to, like openly reading seditious literature and breaking the Law of Sedition (using words to incite people to rebel against authority). Besides these, people began to cut down timber in Central Provinces and Bombay in defiance of forest laws. A campaign for non-payment of taxes and land revenue started in Gujarat, U.P., and in Bengal.

Gandhiji was arrested and his place was taken up by Abbas Tyabji as the leader of the Salt *Satyagraha* but he was also arrested. Then his place was taken up by Sarojini Naidu, who hurried to Dharasana and directed the movement. On May 21, 2500 volunteers from all parts of Gujarat took part in it. Demonstrations continued day after day, but the most demonstrative raid took place on June 7 with 15,000 volunteers. Everywhere, the volunteers were mercilessly beaten. *Mr. Weble Miller,* a foreign correspondent of U.S.A. who was an eye witness wrote: "Suddenly, at a word of command, scores of native police rushed upon the advancing marchers and rained blows on their heads with their steel-shod *lathis.* Not one of the marchers even raised an arm to fend off the blows...From where I stood, I heard the sickening whacks of the clubs on unprotected skulls... In two or three minutes the ground was quilted with bodies. Great patches of blood widened on their white clothes. The survivors, without breaking ranks silently and doggedly marched on until struck down... When everyone of the first column was knocked down... Then another column formed with the leaders with them to retain their selfcontrol."

The newspaper *Bombay Chronicle* wrote about the Dandi March, "In the history of the Indian nation, never before there arouse such a mighty current of patriotism and love for the country as it rose on this occasion. In the history of national movement this even is the most glorious and the most important national event."

3. *Civil Disobedience Movement* (1930-33)

Why Civil Disobedience Movement. There were four important development which led to Disobedience Movement in 1930. The termoil and unrest created by the Simon Commission, the mass participation and the success of the Bardoli Satyagraha under the leadership of Vallabhbhai Patel for the cause of the peasants, the Nehru Report which was rejected by the Government and the 1929 Poorna Swaraj resolution calling upon the people to stop payment of taxes without doing any violence needed some strong steps.

Main Objectives and Features of the Movement

1. To protest against the British rule which had brought about all round ruin of the people of India.
2. To break the salt law as a symbol of Indian people's refusal to obey unjust laws made by the British.
3. To involve the masses on a large scale in the struggle for freedom.
4. To break laws without doing any violence and the movement to remain peaceful.

Movement in action. Gandhiji launched the movement on March 12, 1930. From his Sabramati Ashram to Dandi, a small village on the western sea coast of Gujarat, he covered a distance of 214 miles in 24 days with his 78 followers. He picked up a handful of salt and broke the salt law as a refusal to live under the British rule and British made laws.

The movement evoked countrywide spontaneous response. A wonderful spirit of self-sacrifice and discipline could be seen in the minds of the people. The 'Charismatic' influence exerted by Gandhiji could be witnessed everywhere. On April 10, 1930; he made an appeal to the women of India through his paper *Young India* to take up the work of picketing and spinning. The effect was miraculous. Thousands of women responded, even from orthodox and aristocratic families who had never before come out of their seclusion. They worked and offered themselves for arrests and imprisonment. It was a great accomplishment of the Civil Disobedience Movement towards the emancipation of the women of India. The awakening of women redoubled the activities of the men.

There were several examples of brave deeds. In the North-West Frontier Province, the home of the fierce warlike Pathans, the Red-Shirt volunteers, organised by Abdul Ghaffar Khan (better known as Frontier Gandhi) followed, in a non-violent manner, an intense anti-Government movement including non-payment of taxes. The police fired at them with machine-guns at Peshawar. Many were killed but the brave people refused to budge from their activities or to retaliate with violence. Two Garhwali platoons refused to fire on non-violent demonstrators, taking the risk of long-term imprisonment. Rani Gaidilieu of Nagaland, at the age of 13, raised the banner of revolt and suffered 15 years of imprisonment from 1932 to 1947 when Independent India released her.

Repressive measures of the Government. The Government did not fist take the campaign seriously. Many ridiculed the campaign. The *Statesman* wrote: "The Mahatma could go on boiling sea water till Dominion Status was attained." But before a month passed, the Government realised the gravity and struck hard in a ruthless manner. Repressive laws were made to declare the Congress unlawful and to gag the press. There were wholesale arrests packing the jail with about 75 thousand *Satyagrahis.* Most of the leaders, including Jawaharlal Nehru, were in prison. Finally, Gandhiji was arrested on May 4, 1930. The whole country seemed to be in jail. Laws and arrests were just minor parts of their device to terrorise the people. The brutal assaults made, and atrocities committed on unarmed non-violent men and women, make for horrendous reading. Firing, resulting in maiming and deaths of hundreds of people within minutes, looting of property, burning of houses and torturing people through various devices were the daily normal routine. An English lady, Miss Slades, saw how *Satyagrahis* at Dharasana Salt Depot were being treated by the police. She gave details in *Young India* about the injuries inflicted on the *Satyagrahis:* Lathi blows on stomachs, heads and joints, thrust of lathis on delicate parts, dragging wounded men by legs and arms, throwing the wounded into thorn hedges, riding horses over men as they lie or sit in the ground, thrusting pins into the bodies, using very foul language and 'other vile things, too may to relate'.

Impact of the movement. The movement turned out to be the greatest mass struggle so far. Almost all sections of people of the country—men and women, young and old, the workers and the professionals, the Moderates and the Swarajists, students and teachers—participated in varying degrees. Excepting a few Nationalist Muslim leaders, the Muslims kept themselves aloof from the movement.

The British Government now made attempts to negotiate with the Congress to arrive at some sort of settlement regarded constitutional reforms and this led to Gandhi Irwin Pact (1931).

Revival and suspension of the Civil Disobedience Movement (1932-34). After the failure of the Two Round Table Conferences—first was not attended by the Congress and the second was attended by Gandhiji on behalf of the Congress, the Government again resorted to repressive measures. Gandhiji came back to India on December 28, 1931 and on December 29, he sent a telegram to the Vicerory, expressing his deep concern over the happenings in the country. He specifically referred to the uncalled for shootings in the country. In reply, the Government justified the stand and also refused to grant an interview to Gandhiji. After this Gandhiji announced the revival of the Disobedience Movement. Even before the actual Civil Disobedience Movement was started, Gandhiji was arrested. The Government resorted to repression and issued four ordinances to crush the movement. The Ordianances were (i) The Emergency Power Ordinance (ii) The Unlawful Instigation Ordinance (iii) Unlawful Association Ordinance (iv) Prevention of Molestation and Boycott Ordinance. Within a short time, the number of Ordinances reached 13, covering every activity of national life. The Congress was declared illegal. Swadeshi concerns were also declared illegal. All leading Congress Leaders were put behind bars. 'Lathi' charges on peaceful demonstrators became the order of the day. All various devices to torture and terrorise the Indian masses, as described earlier, were used with all ferocity. Even women were beaten, molested and dishonoured. Punitive and collective fines on villages and seizures of village land and property were to terrify the rural masses.

Two factors namely the Communal Award and the repressive measures adopted by the Government dampened the spirit of the leaders of the Congress and the Civil Disobedience Movement gradually waned. The Congress officially suspended the movement in May 1933 and started Individual Civil Disobedience Movement from August 1, 1933. Gandhiji's prestige suffered to some extent and he temporarily withdrew from active politics. Several important leaders of the Congress felt a sense of despair.

By the beginning of 1934, both the Individual and Mass Civil Disobedience were tailing off. The Individual Civil Disobedience was almost dead. Those who were released from the jail were too tired to face another conviction; so, slowly and silently it faded away, unnoticed, though in some places it dragged on up to May 1934.

4. *Gandhi-Irwin Pact* (1931)

Background. The continuation of the Civil Disobedience Movement had greatly worried the Government. So it called a conference popularly known as the First Round Table conference to discuss the issue of the constitutional reforms in India. It, however, failed to serve any purpose. While winding up the First Round Table Conference, the British Prime Minister declared that "Steps would be taken to enlist the cooperation of those sections of public which had held aloof from the Conference." It was felt that the British Government would have to hold consultations with the Congress. Lord Irwin, the Viceroy of India appealed to the people of India to consider the statement made by the Prime Minister of Britain. He also released the Congress leaders from jail. Discussions between the Viceroy and Gandhiji continued for 15 days and Gandhi-Irwin Pact was signed on March 15, 1931.

Provisions. Following were the provisions of the Pact :

1. The safeguards to be embodied in the new constitutional set-up to be in the interest of India.
2. Civil Disobedience prisoners, not guilty of violence, to be released.
3. Fines, which had not been realised, to be remitted. The fines already realised were not to be refunded.
4. Immovable property confiscated by the Government to be retuned. Where it had been sold, the transaction was to be considered final.
5. Where the posts rendered vacant by resignations had been permanently filled, the Government not bound to reinstate their former employees. Other cases of resignations were to be considered on their merits. The Local Governments were to follow a liberal policy in such cases.

6. Mahatma Gandhi not to press for a public enquiry into the allegations against the conduct of the police in India.
7. The boycott of non-Indian goods to be discontinued if it was exclusively against the British goods with a view to exerting pressure for political ends.
8. The Government of India to withdraw the ordinances promulgated in connection with the Civil Disobedience Movement.
9. The right of manufacturing salt to be conceded to the people living in salt areas.
10. The Congress to withdraw the Civil Disobedience Movement.
11. The Congress to participate in the Second Round Table Congress.

Reactions. Nehruji Commented, "Was it for this that our people had behaved so gallantly for a year? Were all your brave words and deeds to end in this?" Although the Gandhi Irwin Pact was criticised by leading Congress leaders, yet it was endorsed by the Karachi Congress Session in 1931. The Congress leaders were greeted with black flags in Karachi. Gandhiji faced hostile demonstration when he left for London to attend the Second Round Table Conference as the sole representative of the Congress.

5. *Communal Award and Poona Pact* (1932)

While the Civil Disobedience Movement was in full swing in India, British Prime Minister Ramsay MacDonald declared the Communal Award in 1932. This award was meant to create a gulf among different religious groups in India. According to this award, the Muslims, Sikhs, Harijans, Hindus and Anglo-Indians, were given the right to elect their representatives through separate electorates. This award was deemed as an attempt to disrupt national unity and the unity of Hindus. The Muslim League felt satisfied by this award but the Hindus felt a great shock as the Harijans which formed an integral part of Hinduism were given separate electorate.

At that time Gandhiji was in Yervada prison in Poona. He was greatly shocked at this award and he went on a fast. A settlement was arrived at when Dr. B.R. Ambedkar agreed to incorporate certain modifications. This is known as Poona Pact. It had the following points:

(*i*) There would be joint electorates for all the Hindus. This included Harijans also.
(*ii*) The Harijans would remain as the indivisible part of the Hindus.
(*iii*) Seats for the Depressed Classes (Harijans) would be doubled.
(*iv*) Adequate representation to the Depressed Classes would be given in services.
(*v*) The system of reserved seats would be terminated after ten years.

The British Government amended the Communal Award in the light of the Poona Pact.

6. *Round Table Conferences* (1930-32)

Three Round Table Conferences were held in London to discuss issues relating to constitutional reforms to be introduced in India. However, these did not yield any worthwhile result. The first conference was held in 1930-31.

First Round Table Conference. The Report of the Simon Commission was published in June 1930. The continuance of the Civil Disobedience Movement and the British brutal repression made the British Labour Government quite uneasy and worried. The First Round Table Conference presided over by Mr. Ramsay MacDonald, the Labour Prime Minister, and attended by 16 members from the British parties, six from British Indian states and 52 from British India discussed the Report of the Simon Commission and the proposals of constitutional reforms. The prominent leaders of the Muslim League and the Hindu Mahasabha were there but the Congress did not attend as the Civil Disobedience Movement was on. The conference adjourned on January 19, 1931 without any agreement on basic issues. It failed to serve any purpose in the absence of the Congress.

Second Round Table Conference Oct.–Dec. 1931. The Karachi Session of the Congress paved the way for the Second Round Table Conference by ratifying the Gandhi-Irwin Pact. The Congress also decided to discontinue the Civil Disobedience Movement for the time being.

Government released all political prisoners as agreed to in the Gandhi-Irwin Pact.

Gandhiji went to England to attend the Second Round Table Conference (September 7-December-1). The British Government declined to accept the nationalist demand for freedom on the basis of immediate grant of Dominion Status for India. Further, no agreement was reached regarding communal questions.

Third Round Table Conference. (Nov. to Dec. 1932). The British Government called the Third Round Table Conference which lasted from November 17 to December 24, 1934, to review the political situation and to take up constitutional reforms in India. The Congress did not participate in the Conference. There was less enthusiasm among the members as regards a satisfactory settlement better than what was the case a year before.

7. *Congress Ministries* (1937-39)

Under the provisions of the Government of India Act 1935, elections were held to the provincial assemblies. Although the Indian National Congress had severely criticised the 1935 Act, it participated in the elections. It formed its own ministries in seven provinces namely Madras, Bombay, Bihar, Orissa, C.P., U.P. and North West Frontier. It formed coalition ministries in Assam and Sind. In the Punjab, the Unionist Party formed the ministry and in Bengal, the Muslim League and the Krashak Praja Party formed a coalition ministry.

The Congress did extremely well in the elections. The Muslim League failed to make its impact even in the Muslim constituencies.

Functioning of the Congress Ministries:

1. Ministers set their own good examples. Important features of the working of the Congress Ministers were as under: (*i*) They tried to cut all red tapism and bureaucratic delays and attended to people's problems without delay (*ii*) The Ministers worked on nominal salaries (Rs. 500 per month), allowances and perks etc. (*iii*) They tried to set up high standard of honest work and public morality.

2. Work done by Ministers. The Congress Ministries took the following measures for winning the cooperation of the people in the task of national reconstruction in different areas:

(*i*) Political prisoners were released.
(*ii*) Restrictions on the press were removed.
(*iii*) Trade union activities were allowed.
(*iv*) Powers of the police were curbed.
(*v*) Agrarian legislation was passed to provide for tenancy rights to cultivators, security of tenure, rent reduction, and protection to the peasant-debtors.
(*vi*) Prohibition was introduced in selected areas.
(*vii*) Several measures for the uplift of the Harijans were taken.
(*viii*) Greater attention was paid to primary, secondary and higher education.
(*ix*) Basic education was popularised.
(*x*) Technical education was encouraged.
(*xi*) Support was given to Khadi and other village industries.
(*xii*) Modern industries were encouraged.
(*xiii*) Communal riots were firmly handled.

The people regarded the Congress ruled provinces as "islands of self-rule where they could breathe freely and stand upright with dignity."

Jinnah's attack on Congress Ministries

The result of the elections widened the rift between the Congress and the League. At that time Jinnah openly declared, "Muslims can expect neither justice nor fairplay under the Congress Government." The majority of the Muslims accepted this view and began to support the Muslim League. Jinnah suddenly acquired a new personal authority. He now started to complain of the unfair treatment of the Muslims in the Congress ruled provinces and circulated rumours of 'atrocities' which were never proved. When the Congress Ministers resigned in November 1939, Jinnah heaved a sigh of relief and asked the Muslim League to observe a day of deliverance. As the Congress was out of power throughout the war, the British Government had no alternative but to pamper the Muslim League so that the Muslim community might not weaken their war efforts. This also encouraged the Muslims and widened the rift between the League and the Congress.

Second World War and the Resignation of Congress Ministries

The Second World War broke out in 1939 and the British Government declared war against Germany on September 3, 1939. The Viceroy of India proclaimed that India too, was at war with Germany. While announcing this, he did not consult the Central Assembly and the representatives of the people. This was resented by the Congress and it registered a strong protest against the policy of the British rulers. The Congress announced that it would help the war efforts of the Government only if India was declared an independent country after the end of the war, and in this regard it wanted a firm declaration from the British Government. Negotiations between the Congress and the Government failed. Therefore, the Congress Ministries resigned in October-November 1939. The resignation of the Congress Ministries as already stated was hailed by the Muslim League.

Q. 2. Discuss the main features of the Government of India Act, 1935.
(Delhi University 1993)

Or

Comment on the main features of the Government of India Act, 1935. *(Delhi University 1995)*

Or

Why was the Government of India Act, 1935 passed? State its main provisions and comment upon them.

Ans. *Circumstances leading to the 1935 Act*

The Government of India Act, 1919 had failed to come upto the aspirations of the people of India regarding constitutional reforms. The Rowlatt Act had further aggravated the situation by putting severe restrictions on their freedom. The agitation against this Act led to the Jallianwala Tragedy at Amritsar in 1919. The atrocities committed by the rulers along with their humiliating treatment given to Khalifa of Turkey (temporal head of the Muslims) resulted in the Non-Cooperation and Khilafat Movements. Thereupon, the British thought of reviewing constitutional reforms of 1919. The Simon Commission (1928) appointed for this purpose did not include any Indian as its member. This angered the Indians and it was boycotted also and it witnessed black flag demonstrations. The Indian National Congress and others formed the Nehru Committee to suggest suitable constitutional reforms. In the meanwhile the Indian National Congress passed the *'Purna Swaraj'* resolution at its Lahore Session in 1929 and for the attainment of this objective started the Civil Disobedience Movement in 1930. The Government was alarmed at the response of the people to the Civil Disobedience Movement. It held three Round Table Conferences at London to arrive at some decision regarding constitutional reforms. But no unanimous decision could be taken. Nevertheless, Government after taking into consideration the recommendations of the Simon Commission, Nehru Report and the deliberations of the Round

Table Conferences, passed the Government of India Act, 1935. The Act laid down the constitutional and administrative structure of India.

Main Provisions of the Act. Main provisions of the Act may be broadly classified under two heads (*i*) Central Set-up (*ii*) Provisional Set-up.

Central Setup

(1) The Act provided for an All India Federation—Federation of the Provinces, under the direct control of the Government called the British India, and the Princely States, that is, states under the Indian rulers (2) The Federal Legislature was to consist of two Houses i.e. the Upper House and the Federal Assembly (3) The Upper House (Council of States) was to have 156 members from British India and nor more than 104 from the Princely States (4) The Federal Assembly was to have 250 members from British India and 125 from the Princely States (5) The Governor-General was to have a Council of Ministers, not more than ten (6) The Governor-General was to have exclusive power in subjects relating to Defence, External Affairs etc. (7) The Governor-General was given wide discretionary powers.

Provincial Setup

(1) The System of Dyarchy introduced in the provinces under the 1919 Act was abolished (2) The total number of provinces was now to be 11 with the creation of two new provinces of Sind and Orissa (3) Burma was separated from India and was to be no more a part of India (4) Complete provincial autonomy was to be granted (5) The Ministers were to be responsible to the Legislature (6) The Governor was to have several discretionary powers.

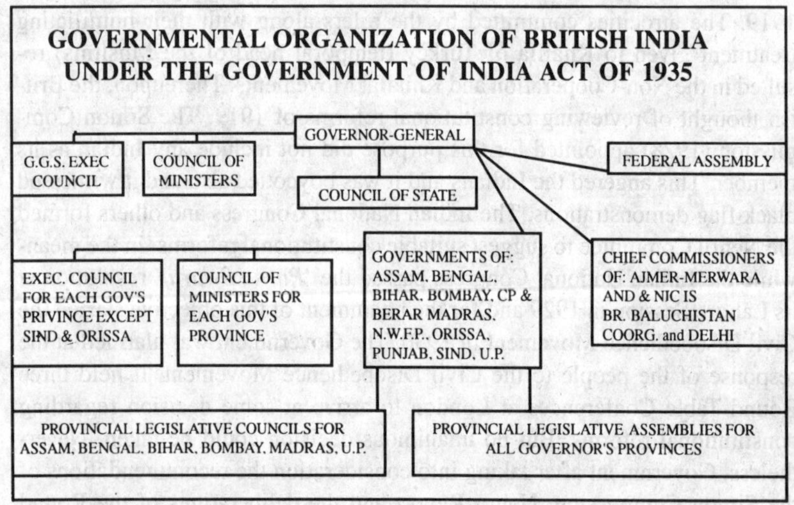

(G.G.'S EXEC. GOVERNOR GENERALS EXECUTIVE COUNCIL)

Critical review of Reforms

Wide powers of the Governor-General. The powers of the Governor-General were so large that even Winston Churchill remarked ,"The Viceroy or Governor-General was armed with all the powers of Hitler and Mussolini. By a stroke of pen, he could scaltter the constitution and decree any law to be passed, or declared Martial Law, which was no law at all. Of all these he was the sole judge. Such a functionary was a dictator and he had a powerful army." His power of patronage was also considerable.

(*i*) *Governor-General's discretionary powers:* These included:

1. Administration of Defence.
2. Administration of Foreign Affairs.
3. Administration of Ecclesiastical Affairs.
4. Administration of Tribal Areas.
5. Appointment and Dismissal of Ministers at the Centre.
6. Presiding at the Meeting of the Council of Ministers.
7. Appointment of Executive Councillors, Financial Adviser, Chief Commissioners, the Governor, and Deputy Governor of Reserve Bank, the Chairman and Members of Federal Public Service Commission.
8. Making rules for the convenient transaction of the work of government and the distribution of work among the ministers.
9. Requiring previous sanction of the Governor-General for the introduction of certain Bills in the Federal Legislature and the Provincial Legislatures.
10. Summoning and proroguing of Federal Legislature, dissolution of Lower House of Federal Legislature.
11. Issuing ordinances.
12. Introducing Budget only on his recommendation. He could restore the items cut or deleted by the legislature. He could certify a bill rejected by the legislature.
13. Having full control over 80 per cent of the budget which consisted of non-votable items.

(*ii*) *Powers exercisable in individual judgement (Special responsibilities).* The Governor-General was required to consult the ministers in case of these matters but was not bound to accept their advice. These included the following:

(*a*) Safeguarding the financial stability and credit for India.
(*b*) Preventing any grave menace to the peace and tranquility of India or any part of it.
(*c*) Safeguarding the legistimate interests of the ministries.
(*d*) Safeguarding the legistimate rights of public services.
(*e*) Preventing commercial discrimination.
(*f*) Preventing discriminatory taxation against the goods of British origin.

(*g*) Safeguarding the interests of Indian princely states and the dignity of their rulers.

Overall criticism of the Act

(1) The Congress felt that the reforms did not go much further as provided in the 1919 Act (2) The Muslim League was not satisfied as it sought more powers for the provinces and fixed number of Ministerships for the Muslims (3) Only 14% of the total population of British India was given the right to vote (4) Defence and Foreign Affairs were outside the control of the Central legislature (5) The Governor-General and the Governors were given special powers to veto the Ministers (6) The Governor-General and the Governors were to be responsible to the British Government only (7) The Governors retained full control over the civil service and the police (8) Foreign rule was to continue as before. Only a few popularly elected ministers were to be added to the British administrative structure in India (9) The Federal part was never introduced (10) The position assigned to the Council of Ministers at the Centre was ornamental.

Criticism and comments against the provisions came from every side. Jawaharlal Nehru described the new set up as a "machine with strong brakes and no engine." Another called it a "grim joke which the joker (The British Government) may enjoy but not those Indians at whose expense the joke is cracked." In the words of M.A. Jinnah, the scheme of 1935 was "thoroughly rotten, fundamentally bad and totally unacceptable."

According to *Prof. K.T. Shah,* "The position assigned under the new constitution to the Council of Federal Ministers is ornamental, responsibility without power, position without authority, name without any real influence."

In the words *of Palande,* "The Council of State was bound to be an assemblage of vested interests, reactionary oligarchs and conservative politicians."

(See also next answer)

Q. 3. Analyse the main features of Provincial Autonomy as introduced by the Government of India Act 1935. *(Delhi University 1998)*

Ans. *Provincial Autonomy under Government of India Act 1935*

Introduction. A new administrative and constitutional structure at the central level and at the provincial level came into being in India under the provisions of the Indian Act of 1935. At the provincial level, the system of Dyarchy introduced under the 1919. Act came to an end.

In August 1935, the long process of administrative and constitutional reforms ended with the passing of the Government of India Act, 1935. It took almost eight long years. The reforms were proposed in 1927, debated in the three Round Table Conferences, drafted and circulated in the form of a "White Paper' (report about the Government's policy) and thoroughly discussed by a Joint Select Committee of the British Parliament. The final Act, 1935, emerged after intense debate in the British Parliament. The Indian National Congress was not consulted regarding the various provisions of the Act.

The Act came into actual operation when elections were held in 1937 for the provincial assemblies.

Meaning of provincial autonomy. Before we discuss whether or not the 1935 Act introduced provincial autonomy, we may briefly go into the meaning and main features of provincial autonomy. Provincial autonomy has the following main characteristics:

(*i*) The provencies *i.e.*, their governments should be free in their internal administration from the control of the Central Government. In other words they should be allowed to carry on administration as independent units of the Central Government.

(*ii*) The provincial legislature must have complete control over the provincial executive.

(*iii*) The provincial legislature represent the largest number of people of the province.

(*iv*) The Ministers should be responsible to the lower house of the legislature.

(*v*) The Governor should only act as the constitutional head of the province.

Main features of the provincial autonomy as introduced under the 1935 Act

1. The Governors of the provinces were given a new legal status and broadly freed from the superintendence, direction and the control of the Government of India and Secretary of State for India except for specific purposes. The Governors derived their authority and power directly from the British Crown.
2. Dyarchy in the provinces was abolished. The distinction between Reserved and Transferred subjects was abolished.
3. The Governor was the head of the provincial executive and was given wide powers.
4. The provincial legislatures *i.e.*, Legislative Assemblies and Legislative Councils were provided in six provinces namely Madras, Bombay, Bengal, U.P., Bihar and Assam. Other five provinces *i.e.*, C.P. and Berar, N.W.F.P., Orissa, Punjab and Sind were to have only Legislative Assemblies.
5. The franchise was lowered but it still remained tied to property qualifications.
6. Communal electorate and weightage were further extended.

Appraisal of the functioning of the Act

In the light of the main features of provincial autonomy as stated above and the provisions contained in the 1935 Act, following observations may be made:

1. *Wide powers of the Government of India.* The scope of 'specified powers' of the Central Government robbed the provinces of their autonomy to a considerable extent.

2. *Enormous powers to the Governors of the provinces.* These powers may be divided under two heads: (*i*) Powers regarding their special responsibilities. (*ii*) Powers in their discretions.

(*i*) *Powers in exercising individual judgement while performing their special responsibilities.* These were as under:

(*a*) Prevention of any grave menace to the peace and tranquility of the province.

(*b*) Safeguarding the rights and legitimate interests of the public servants and their dependents.

(*c*) Safeguarding the interests of the minorities.

(*d*) Prevention of commercial discrimination against Englishmen and their goods.

(*e*) Execution of the orders of the Governor-General issued by him in his discretion.

(*f*) Special powers for specific purposes were given to the Governors of C.P. and Sind.

(*ii*) *Discretionary powers of the Governor.* These included as given below:-

(*a*) A governor could appoint and dismiss ministers.

(*b*) He could issue several ordinances.

(*c*) In certain cases, his sanction was required for the introduction of certain bills in the Provincial Legislature.

(*d*) He appointed members of the Provincial Public Service Commission.

(*e*) He enjoyed large powers regarding the Police Force.

(*f*) He was given large powers to suppress revolutionary/terrorist activities.

(*g*) The non-votable items of expenditure formed about 40 per cent of the budget.

It may be noted that the Governors actually exercised these powers and reduced the autonomy of the legislature.

3. *Very weak position of Provincial Ministers.* There is no doubt that the position of the Minister in the provinces under the Act of 1935 was certainly superior to that of Ministers under the Act of 1919. There were no 'Reserved' subjects and departments. The Governor in theory was expected to carry on the administration of the province according to the advice of the Ministers. However, the powers of the Governors were so vast that the position of the Ministers became very weak. The Governors could dismiss Chief Ministers and Ministers. Fazl-ul Itaq, the Chief Minister of Bengal was dismissed unceremoniously by the Governor. Alla Bux, the Chief Minister of

Sind was dismissed because be gave up the title of *'Khan Bahadur'*. The Governor of Punjab dismissed Shaukat Hayat Khan on flimsy grounds.

4. *Separate representation on communal lines in the Legislative Assemblies.* For instance in Punjab, 175 seats were divided as under:

Bifurcation of Seats in Punjab Legislative Assembly

S. No.	*Category*	*No. of Seats*
1.	Seats for Muslims	84
2.	General Seats	42
3.	Seats for Sikhs	31
4.	Seats for Land holders	05
5.	Seats for Labour	03
6.	Seats for Indian Christians	02
7.	Seats for Muslim Women	02
8.	Seats for Anglo-Indian	01
9.	Seats for Europeans	01
10.	Seats for Punjab University	01
11.	Seats for Hindu Women	01
12.	Seats for Sikh Women	01
13.	Seats for Commerce and Industry	01
	Total	**175**

In Bengal, the Europeans were given the highest representation. Likewise many seats were given to commerce, industry and planting.

The system of giving representation differed from province to province. Thus there was no uniform pattern.

5. *No uniformity in qualifications of voters.* The voting qualifications also varied from province to province. In the case of Punjab, the right of voting was given to those who paid income tax or direct municipal tax amounting to not less than Rs. 50 per year; those who occupied immovable property of rental value of not less than Rs. 60 per year and those who possessed educational qualifications upto the primary standard.

6. *Very limited franchise.* The provincial legislatures did not represent the largest number of people. In practice, a little more than twelve per cent had the right to vote.

The Congress Ministries resigned in 1939 in protest as the British Government declared the Second World War on behalf of the Government of India. There was no issue which involved India into the war. The war was thrust upon India. The Congress leaders demanded that India must be declared free or at least effective power put in Indian hands before it could actively participate in the war. The British Government refused to accept this demand and the Congress Ministries resigned.

From the above details, it becomes quite clear that was a world of difference between the real significance of the word 'autonomy' and the so-called 'autonomy' as given by the British Parliament to India. Provincial autonomy was, by and large, a farce and far from reality.

Some Select opinions on the Act and autonomy

Pt. Jawaharlal Nehru described it a "machine with strong brakes and no engine."

According to *Pt. Madan Mohan Malviya,* "The new act has been thrust upon us. It has a somewhat democratic appearance outwardly, but it is absolutely hollow from within.

In the opinion of *Sir Shanmukham Chetty,* "It is indeed a far cry between the Government of India Act and Dominion Status."

C. Rajagopalachari called the new constitution "worse than dyarchy."

M.A. Jinnah characterised it as, "thoroughly rotten, fundamentally bad, and totally unacceptable.'

Q. 4. What led to the Quite India Movement? Discuss its nature and importance. *(Rajasthan University, 1997)*

Or

In what circumstances was the Quit India Movement launched? How was it different from the other Gandhian movements? *(Rajasthan University 1996)*

Or

Write note on Quit India Movement.

(Rajasthan 1993, Punjab University 1995, 1996, Delhi University 1996)

Ans. *Quit India Movement*

Quit India Resolution. The Quit India Movement was started by the Indian National Congress under the leadership of Gandhiji with the passing of the 'Quit India Resolution' on August 8, 1942.

On July 14, 1942 the Congress Working Committee met at Wardha and passed a resolution renewing the demand that 'British rule in India must end immediately'. After the resolution was passed, Gandhiji said, "There is no room left in the proposal for withdrawl or negotiation. There is no question of one more chance. After all, it is an open rebellion."

The Working Committee referred its resolution to the All-India Congress Committee (A.I.C.C.) which met at Bombay on August 7, 1942. The A.I.C.C., after discussing the resolution on 7th and 8th, passed it with an overwhelming majority. It emphasized the demand for the withdrawl of the British power from India. It sanctioned the non-violent mass struggle under the leadership of Gandhiji. It also instructed, "A time may come when it may not be possible to issue instructions... When this happens, every man or woman who is participating in this movement must function for himself or herself, within the four corners of the general instructions issued." The Resolution declared, "The immediate ending of British rule in India is an urgent necessity, both for the sake of India and for the success of the United Nations... A free India will assure this success by throwing all her great resources in the struggle for freedom and against the aggression of Nazism, Fascism and Imperialism."

Circumstances leading to the Quit India Resolution

Since the outbreak of the Second World War and the failure of the Cripps Mission, there was a feeling of frustration among all sections of the population of India. The Indian National Congress which had done nothing so far to embarrass the Government during the war, apart from demanding a Constituent Assembly for the country and starting for a very brief period limited satyagraha could no longer sit on the fence when events were changing fast not only in India but also in the world.

Now the Congress was looking for positive response from the Government which unfortunately was no where evidence.

Following were the immediate causes that led to the Quit India Movement.

1. *Failure of the Cripps Mission.* The failure of Cripps Mission made a few things very clear to the Congress leaders. The Cripps Mission was not a genuine effort of Britain towards granting even Dominion Status, when India was demanding Complete Independence.

2. *Critical War Stage.* It was perhaps the critical stage of the War and the American pressure that needed some 'show' to assuage the national sentiments.

3. *Pampering the Muslim League.* It was also transparently visible that the Muslim League was being pampered with assurances to foment communal discord and to widen the Hindu-Muslim divide with the aim to weaken the nationalist movement, and if ever India was to be left at its fate, it would be a truncated and chaotic India.

4. *Charchill's negative attitude.* Churchill, Prime Minister of Britain, had bluntly said "No, Sir" to a question asked in the Parliament, whether the famous Atlantic Charter, promising the rights of man—liberty, equality and fraternity to be enforced throughout the world—will be applicable also to India. British mind was very clear: How could they leave India, the largest and wealthiest colony of the empire conquered with so much arduous skill and cleverness and ruled with so much prestige and power and for so long?

5. *Danger of Japanese's invasion.* There was the growing threat of Japanese invasion of India. Gandhiji wanted to save India from that attack and he feared that if the British lost, Japanese might not take their place.

6. *Racial discrimination.* Mahatma Gandhi felt that the Government followed a discriminatory policy in the process of evacuation from Burma. The British provided separate routes for the evacuation of the Europeans and Indians. The result was Indian evacuees had to undergo too many hardships on the road called Black Road for Indians. The White Road was meant for

Europeans.

7. *Nature of the movement and changed attitude of Gandhiji.* There was also a change in the attitude of Ghandhiji. He was hitherto definitely opposed to any mass movement during the World War, but now he again started thinking over it. This was his novel idea of asking the British to quit. At this time the advance of Japan towards India was viewed with great concern. Even then, he wrote in *Harijan,* "Whatever the consequences therefore, to India, her real safety, and Britain's too, lies in orderly and timely British withdrawl from India." (April 26, 1942). Gandhiji once more assumed the leadership of the Congress which he had relinquished during India's negotiations with Cripps.

The circumstances that prevailed then appear to exhaust the patience of Gandhiji and all the people. It will be clear from his ideas expressed in his paper *Harijan:* "The time has come during the war, not after it, for the British and the Indians to be reconciled to complete separation from each other... The presence of the British in India is an invitation to Japan to invade India. This withdrawl removes the bait... free India will be better able to cope with the invasion". (May 10, 1942). "Leave India in God's hands, in modern parlance, to anarchy, and that anarchy may lead to internecine warfare for a time... from these a true India will rise in place of the false one we see." (May 24). Gandhiji's changed attitude to Britain also brought about a change in his method about a mass movement, "I waited and waited until the country should develop the non-violent strength necessary to throw off the foreign yoke. But my attitude has now undergone a change. I feel I cannot afford to wait... That is why I have decided that even at certain risks, which are obviously involved, I must ask the people to resist the slavery." All these go to show how circumstances change men, their ideas, strengthen their invincible determination and transform helplessness into indomitable courage to fight the mightiest without arms, no matter what risks, what fate awaits them."

Do or Die Mantra:

Addressing the Congress delegates on the night of August 8, Gandhiji declared, "I, therefore, want freedom immediately, this very night, before dawn, if it can be had... Fraud and untruth today are stalking the world... You may take it from me that I am not going to be satisfied with anything short of complete freedom... Here is a *mantra,* a short one, that I give you. You may imprint it in your hearts and let every breath of yours give expression to it. The *mantra* is: 'Do or Die". We shall either free India or die in the attempt; we shall not live to see the perpetuation of our slavery."

Quit India Movement in Action and Reaction of the Government

The Government was closely following the activities and the meetings of the Congress. The A.I.C.C. meeting terminated late at night on August 8, 1942. Before the next day dawned, Gandhiji, Azad and all other important leaders of the Congress were arrested. Within a week almost everyone who mattered in the Congress was in jail. All A.I.C.C. and all the Provincial Congress Committees were declared unlawful. The news of the arrest of Gandhiji and other Congress leaders was immediately followed by non-violent popular demonstrations like *hartals* and processions, but when the Government resorted to firing to disperse processions, it led to violence on the part of the people. The official version gives an idea of the nature of the disturbances.

"It was from August 11, 1942 that the situation began to deteriorate rapidly. Apart from the *hartals* and protest meetings, outbreaks of mob violence, arson, murder and sabotage took place, and in almost all cases they were directed either against communications of all kinds (including railways, posts and telegraphs), or against the police. Moreover, these outbreaks started almost simultaneously in widely separated areas, in the provinces of Madras, Bombay, Bihar and also in the Central and United Provinces... The position was at one time extremely serious in the whole in Bihar and in the eastern part of U.P... Assam, Orissa. The Punjab and the N.W.F.P. remained free from serious trouble... and there was comparatively little disorder in Sindh. 104 Railway stations were attacked and damaged, 15 being burnt down... 425 cases of sabotage to telephone and telegraph wires were recorded... 119 post offices were destroyed."

In several parts of Andhra, Bengal, Bihar, Maharashtra, Orissa and Tamil Nadu, the British authorities disappeared for a while. Revolutionaries set up parallel governments in some areas such as Ballia in Uttar Pradesh, Tamluk in Midnapore district of Bengal and Satara district of Bombay. The students, peasants and workers were in the forefront of the struggle. The bureaucracy and the upper class by and large remained loyal to the government.

The repression of the Government knew no bounds. The police and military reigned supreme. The demonstrators were even bombed from the air. Churchill, the then British Prime Minister stated in the House of Commons (September 10, 1942), "The disturbances were crushed with all the weight of the government." K.C. Neogy, a member of the Central Assembly, listed the charges against the administration as "general pillage and arson and wanton damage to property by the police and the military, random shooting on innocent persons when hooligans had already left, assault or shooting of non-violent crowds, whipping and official indignities on all and sundry." The number of the people killed was officially estimated as 1,028, while the popular estimate was about twenty five thousand. Jawaharlal Nehru commented, "Perhaps ten thousand may be nearer the mark."

The movement gained momentum after the escape of Jayaprakash Narayan and his colleagues from Hazaribagh jail in October 1942, when efforts were made to co-ordinate the activities in all the states with the help of Aruna Asaf Ali, Achyut Patwardhan and Dr. Ram Manohar Lohia by remaining underground.

Nature of the Quit India Movement

The violent acts in the 1942 movement were really due to the fact that whatever might have been its original character, the movement merged itself into the revolutionary movement which was always an active political force running on the parallel lines with the non-violent policy of Gandhiji. It is also to be kept in view that Gandhiji had, given the clarion call in his slogan 'Do or Die'. Gandhiji had envisaged that the people of India would spontaneously participate in the movement with courage and face the Government with a determined will. He expected people to undergo supreme sacrifices for their cause of freeing India.

It is pointed out by some thinkers that since the entire strategy of the movement was not properly planned, desirable direction could not be given to the movement when even before the launching of the movement, all the prominent leaders were put behind bars. The movement became directionless and leaderless.

It is rather strange that earlier when Chauri Chaura incident took place, Gandhiji withdrew the Non-Cooperation Movement but this time, this was not done.

The movement was short lived and collapsed shortly.

It is of interest to note the views of the Viceroy of the time, Lord Linlithgow who described it as "the most serious rebellion since 1857, the gravity and extent of which we have so far concealed from the world for reasons of military security."

In the words of Prof. Man Singh, "This was the widest and most bitter mass upsurge against British rule in India." (*Historical Dictionary of India*, 1998).

Assessment and impact of the movement. Opinions do not agree on the issue whether the movement was a failure or success. Mass participation was there, but so did violence.

Q. 5. Discuss the main features of the last phase of freedom struggle of India (1935-47) with special reference to Quit India Movement and I.N.A. *(Punjab University April 1997)*

Ans. *Different approaches to the independence struggle*

During the Second World War (1939-45), the struggle for the freedom of India was waged not only from within India but also from outside. In India, the Indian National Congress was the main party that carried on the struggle under the leadership of Gandhiji and from outside I.N.A. under Subhash Chandra Bose. Both had the same objective in view *i.e.,* attainment of the freedom. Yet both followed different ways. While Gandhiji had full faith in the efficacy of Non-violence and Satyagraha, the other believed in adopting militant and armed techniques. At one time both were in the Indian National

Congress but parted company in 1939.

About this time there was a split in the Congress camp. The Rightists led by Rajaji and Vallabhbhai Patel were not yet prepared to organise the forces of national life for the 'overthrow' of the British Government in India through militancy. The Forwards were led by Subhash Bose, who stood for a bold policy and thought that the time was ripe for an all-out national resistance against the foreign rule. The differences between the Rightists and Leftists came to a head over the election of the President of the next session of the Congress, to be held in Tripuri in the Central Provinces in March 1939. Never since 1920 was there any conflict of views regarding the choice of President, for it depended on the choice of some of the important Congress leaders. Subhash Bose sought for re-elections for Presidentship but the rightists set up Dr. Pattabhai Sitaramaya as a rival candidate. Gandhiji openly supported Pattabhai Sitaramya. Bose won the election but was forced out of office by the right-wingers including Gandhiji who prevented him from securing a favourable Working Committee. Subhash Bose then formed a new group known as the Forward Bloc.

While in 'house arrest' in Calcutta, Subhash Chandra Bose disappeared secretly in 1941 and built an Indian army at Berlin. Thereafter, he became the Supreme Commander of the Indian National Army and waged war against the British rulers.

The 'Quit India Movement' was launched from within the country without any military strength and the other struggle depended upon the army *i.e.*, Indian National Army raised outside India.

Resignation of Congress Ministries (1939). In the Second World War, India was pushed into the flames of war by the British rulers. The war was not fought for the rights of the Indians and was thrust upon them. The Congress Ministries formed in 9 provinces out of 11 in 1937 resigned in 1939 as a protest.

Quit India Movement (1942). The nationalists urged the Government to give them assurance that after the war, they would be given self-government. They were, however, told that they were not yet ripe to manage the administration of their country. On this Gandhiji started the limited Satyagraha. The Government made frantic efforts to win over the cooperation of the people of India. Accordingly Cripps Mission was sent with some proposals which were rejected by the Congress. In the meanwhile Japan with its victories was knocking at the doors of India. Gandhiji thought it to be the proper time to intensity freedom struggle. On August 8, 1942, was passed the Quit India Resolution. The next day (August 9) Gandhiji and all prominent members of the Congress were arrested. Worst kind of repression was let loose on the people.

August 2, 1942 Resolution of the Congress. The Working Committee of the National Congress passed the following resolution at its meeting held on August 2, at Bombay. "The immediate ending of the British rule in India is an urgent necessity, both for the sake of India and for the success of the cause of the United Nations...The ending of British rule in this country is thus a vital and immediate issue on which depends the future of the war and the success of freedom and democracy."

'Do or Die' Mantra. Gandhiji gave the call to the nation in the following stirring words, "I, therefore, want freedom immediately, this very night before dawn, if it can be had. You may take it from me that I am not going to strike a bargain with the Ministries and the like. I am not going to be satisfied with anything short of complete freedom. This is a '*mantra*' a short one that I give you. You may imprint it on your hearts and let every breath of yours gives expression to it. The '*mantra*' is "Do or Die". We shall either free India or die in the attempts; we shall not live to the perpetuation of our slavery."

The government took a serious view and arrested all prominent members of the Indian National Congress. It took stern measures to crush the movement. The Congress was declared illegal.

The movement spread all over India. About one lakh of people courted arrest. Hartals and demonstrations took place everywhere. At some places, people were successful in running 'parallel Governments'. This was the last movement in the freedom struggle. Government started negotiations after sometime. It may be safely concluded that it was the culmination of the struggle. Just after 5 years, its objective was achieved. (For details see the previous answer also).

The Indian National Army (I.N.A.)

Before starting the struggle, on July 6, 1944, Subhash Chandra Bose, popularly known as *'Netaji'*, in a broadcast on *'Azad Hind Radio'* addressed to Gandhiji had said, "India's last war of independence has begun. In this holy war of India's liberation, we ask for your blessings and good wishes."

Subhash Bose is, associated with such slogans as *'Jai Hind'*, *'Dilli Chalo'* (March to Delhi, *'Khoon do, main tumhe Azadi doonga'* (Give me blood and I will give you freedom).

While in India, the Congress carried on the struggle for the freedom of the country, the Indian National Army, under the leadership of Subhash Chandra Bose, was marching from outside towards the eastern frontier of India. Subhash Chandra Bose formed the Azad Hind Fauj or Indian National Army (I.N.A.) in 1943 at Singapore, to conduct a military campaign for the liberation of India. He received valuable help from Rash Behari Bose, an old revolutionary, who was spending his days in exile in foreign lands. Necessary spade work was done by General Mohan Singh who had been a captain in the British Indian Army. A large number of Indian residents in South-East Asia and the Indian soldiers and officers who had been captured by the Japanese forces in Malaya, Singapore and Burma joined the I.N.A. It may be mentioned that out of about 65,000 Indian Prisoners of War, about 20,000 joined I.N.A. Subhash Chandra Bose set up a Provisional Government of free India at Singapore. The soldiers of the I.N.A. fought strenuous battles on several fronts in South East Asia and demonstrated remarkable courage. Intensive military training was given to civilians who had joined the I.N.A. was divided into four Brigades named after Gandhi, Nehru, Azad and Subhash. Captain Lakshmi Sahgal was incharge of the Rani Jhansi Regiment. It was a regiment of Housewives in Singapore.

The Japanese were satisfied of the military skill and efficiency of the I.N.A. Instructions were issued that the main body of the Subhash Brigade would proceed to Kohima. And as soon as Imphal, the capital of Manipur should fall, they should rapidly cross the Brahmaputra and enter Bengal. As such, leaving some men at Haka and Falam, the rest marched towards Kohima, the capital of Naga Hills. Kohima had already been captured by the Japanese forces accompanied by some soldiers of I.N.A. who hoised the tricolour flag on the hill top. A few days later, the Japanese forces and the Subhash Brigade had to withdraw. At a different site, three auxiliary units of the I.N.A. were attached to the Japanese forces attacking Imphal, the capital of Manipur. The Indian soldiers planted the national tricolour flag for the first time on the liberated Indian soil on 19th March 1944. There was tremendous enthusiasm to have set foot on the free Indian soil. But the monsoon started before the fall of Imphal and it became impossible to supply ration and ammunition to the forces besieging Imphal. Thus the Japanese and the INA had to withdraw on account of torrential rains, short supplies, lack of air support and the losses inflicted by American bombers. With the defeat of Japan, I.N.A. also had to surrender. Subhash Bose and his companion. Hbib-ul-Rehman took the plane from Formosa on August 18, 1945 which is said to have caught fire.

Trial for 'treason' of some of the captured officers of INA, such as Shah Nawaz (a Muslim), Prem Sehghal (a Hindu) and G.S. Dhillon (a Sikh) at Delhi evoked patriotic feelings among all sections of the Indian people. Such was the popularity of the I.N.A. that slogans like *'Lal Qie Se Aye Aawaz, Dhillon Sehghal Shah Nawaz'* rent the sky all over the country. Leading lawyers of India appeared for the officers of the I.N.A. and tore the prosecution case into shreds. Several documents presented before the court revealed startling instances of chivalry of the warriors of freedom. Nehruji himself donned the lawyers gown to defend the officers. The British court gave death punishment to the officers, but in people's court they were given the status of 'patriots' and national heroes. So when it caused nationwide protest, the Viceroy thought it proper to use his special powers and the officers were released. Peoples joy knew no bounds on their release.

Q. 6. Describe the main events that took place with the outbreak of the Second World War and led to the independence of India.

or

How did the Indian National Congress react to the Second World War ? Trace the main events leading to the freedom of India.

Ans. *Last Phase of the struggle for Independence (1939 to 1947)*

The years 1939 to 1947 marked the last phase of the struggle of India's independence. This struggle had several facets *i.e.* Non-violent, violent, underground struggle, armed struggle and actual war by the I.N.A. from outside India under the leadership of Subhash Chandra Bose.

Following were the important events around which the national movement revolved and India won freedom. These events may be classified into w/o parts.

I. Events during the War

II. Post-War events.

I. *Events during the War*

There were as under:

1. War thrust upon India and the Indian National Congress's reaction.
2. 1940 August offer of Lord Linlithgow and its rejection.
3. Limited Individual Satyagraha (1940)
4. Pakistan Resolution of Congress (1940)
5. Cripps Mission (1942)
6. Quit India Movement.
7. Wavell Plan (1945)

II. *Post War Events and India's Independence*

1. Changed attitude of the British Government.
2. Change in the equation of balance of power in the world.
3. Shattered military and economic power of Britain.
4. Loss of confidence in Indian forces.
5. I.N.A. trial.
6. Labour unrest all over the country.
7. Freedom struggle in princely states.
8. World opinion in favour of India's freedom.
9. Cabinet Mission.
10. Direct action by the Muslim League.
11. Interim Government.
12. The Constituent Assembly.
13. Prime Minister Atlee's appeal.
14. Mountbatten Plan.
15. Indian Independence Act (1947)

1. War thrust upon India and Indian National Congress's reaction. The Indian National Congress was not consulted when Britain declared war against Germany and involved India also in this war. Since no assurance regarding appropriate constitutional reform was forthcoming from the British rulers, Congress Ministries in the provinces resigned.

2. *1940 August Offer of Linlithgow and its rejection.* On August 8, Lord Linlithgow, Viceroy of India made an offer to expand the Executive Council of Viceroy, with the objective of securing the cooperation of the Indians in the war efforts but the Congress considering the offer inadequate, rejected it.

3. *Limited Individual Satyagraha* (1940). Several efforts were made by the Indian National Congress to cooperate with the Government in their war efforts provided demand for complete freedom to India after the war was accepted. Nevertheless, the Congress did not start any mass movement but only Individual Satyagraha. Vinobha Bhave was the first leader to offer Satyagraha. But it did not create much enthusiam and was suspended after two months in December 1940.

4. *Pakistan Resolution* (1940). On March 23, 1940. the All India Muslim League at its Lahore Session, passed the Pakistan Resolution, which became the Key-stone of the ideological arch of the Muslim League after 1940. The Britishers encouraged M.A. Jinnah in this demand. The idea evoked severe opposition from several quarters including the Indian National Congress.

The ground had already been prepared by the British policy of 'Divide and Rule', Sir Syed Ahmed's role and Aligarh School, Separate electorate, Minto-Morely Reforms and Communal Awards etc. (For details see Communalism).

5. *Cripps Mission (1942).* The nature and dimensions of the Second World War radically had changed. Germany captured Poland, Belgium, Holland, Norway etc. and attacked the Soviet Union on June 22, 1941. In December 1941, Japan also joined war on the side of Germany and Italy and launched a surprise attack on the American fleet at Pearl Harbour. It soon overran the Philippines, Indo-China, Indonesia, Malaya and Burma. It also occupied Rangoon and thus the war was on India's doorstep. England itself was under severe attack. It was subjected to constant bombing by waves and waves of German planes. The I.N.A., under Subhash Chandra Bose, was rising to its full height. The situation was becoming very desparate for the British Government. Now they thought of securing the cooperation of Indians in their war efforts. Sir Stafford Cripps, a Cabinet Minister was sent to India with the following main proposals:

(*i*) India to have Dominion Status after the War.

(*ii*) An elected body to be set up after the war to frame a new constitution of India.

(*iii*) Any province of India to have the right to reject that constitution and to have its own constitution if so desired.

(*iv*) The princely states to be represented in proportion to their population.

The Cripps proposals were rejected by almost all sections of the society. The Congress also rejected these proposals for it was worse than the partition of India and conceding Pakistan by the backdoor. It would mean tearing

India into pieces, each piece representing religion, majority power, vested-interest lobby or autocratic princely rule. Muslims, though happy, rejected it as the proposal of Pakistan was not conceded in that particular form of demand. Other parties like the Sikhs, the Hindu Mahasabha also rejected it.

6. Quit India Movement (1942). Though the 1942 movement was practically crushed in less than a month and finally collapsed within two months, it would be a mistake to consider it a failure. The violent mass upsurge clearly signalled that freedom's battle in India had begun in right earnest. The readiness to suffer and sacrifice everything for the freedom of the motherland displayed by a very large number of people and responded to by the vast country from the Himalayas to Kanyakumari, showed and proved, India's grim determination to free herself from the chains of British slavery. But out of these failures, success came in less than five years.

7. Warell Plan or Shimla Conference (1945). Lord A.P. Wavell, the Viceroy of India from Oct. 1943 to January 1947 proposed a provisional government in the form of Executive Council consisting of the Viceroy, the Commander-in-Chief, an equal member of Hindus and Muslims drawn from the leadership of political parties, one Sikh, and one belonging to Depressed Class, to govern under the Government of India Act of 1935 in the interim, to make proposals for a new constitution and negotiate with the Indian Princes regarding their place in the Dominion of India. This plan was announced in June 1945 on All India Radio.

Simla conference attended by 'eminent persons' could not agree to Jinnah's insistence to nominate all the Muslim members to the proposed Council. There were several other irritants also and the proposals could not be implemented.

II. Post-War Events and India's Independence

Changed attitude of the British Government. There was a radical change in the attitude of Britain towards India immediately after the war came to an end. This attitude, which was the outcome of a large number of factors as given below, went a long way in granting independence to India.

1. Labour Government in Britain. In the general elections which took place in England, Labour Party cameto power. Labour Party was already sympathetic to India's demand for freedom. Lord Attlee, Prime Minister, came to the conclusion that England could not keep India in bondage for a long time.

To begin with, he sent the Cabinet Mission and finally he sent Lord Mountbatten to complete the process of transfer of power in India.

2. *Change in the equation of balance of power in the world.* After the war, the U.S.A. and the USSR emerged as the big powers. Britain's domineering posture was subdued. Both U.S.A. and USSR supported India's demand for freedom.

3. Shattered economic and military power of Britain. The economy of Great Britain was almost exhausted. The Englishmen had too many problems to face at home. The military strength had also been reduced.

4. Loss of confidence in Indian forces. The British Government had so far depended on Indian forces. The I.N.A. factor caused erosion in the loyalty of the Indian army. There were several revolts in the Royal Indian Navy and Air Force at Bombay, Calcutta and Karachi.

5. I.N.A. trial. After the end of the war, the British authorities decided to put on trial in the Red Fort at Delhi, Shah Nawaz Khan, Gurdial Singh Dhillon and Prem Sehgal, officers who had joined the I.N.A. deserting the Indian Army. The people of India, who had welcomed them as national heroes, felt very indignant and angry when they were branded as 'traitors' by the British authorities. After their release, these leaders toured all over India and they were greeted with cries of 'Jai Hind'.

6. Labour unrest all over the country. There was hardly an industry in India in which there was no large scale labour unrest. Peasant movements also acquired a fresh thrust after 1945.

7. Freedom struggle in Princely States: There was popular upsurge in several princely states, such as Hyderabad, Travancore and Kashmir.

8. World opinion in favour of freedom: India's cause of freedom was advocated by a large number of distinguished persons in the world. The Indian point was put forward before the conference at San Francisco which met to finalise the Charter of the United Nations.

9. Cabinet Mission (1946). The British Government led by the Labour Party in England was quite considerate to the demands of India. They sent a Cabinet Mission to India to find ways and means by which Indians could determine their own future set-up. On its recommendations, the work for the formation of an interim began.

10. The Constituent Assembly. Elections to the Constituent Assembly were held in July 1946. The Constituent Assembly met for the first time in New Delhi on December 9, 1946. The Muslim League did not participate in its deliberations. On December 11, the Assembly elected Dr. Rajendra Prasad as its President.

11. Direct action by the Muslim League. Negotiations between the Congress ant the Muslim League began for the formation of the Interim Government. Jinnah of the Muslim League insisted on parity between the Congress and the League. The Muslim League, thereupon called for a Direct Action Day (August, 16, 1946), causing bloodshed in several parts of India.

12. Interim Government. Lord Wavell, the Viceroy of India, invited Pandit Jawaharlal Nehru, the President of the Indian National Congress to form the Interim Government. Jawaharlal Nehru's Government took office on September 2, 1946. After initial hesitation, the Muslim League joined the Interim Government on October 13, 1946. The Interim Government remained in office till the partition of India in August, 1947. The Muslim League created all sorts of trouble in the smooth working of the Interim Government as it had set its eyes on the formation of Pakistan.

13. Prime Minister's Attlee's announcement (Feb. 20, 1947). The next step on the fateful road to India's destiny was the important announcement by the British Prime Minister which fixed June 1948 as the deadline by which the British would quit India and it also envisaged the partition of India.

14. The Mountbatten Plan (June 3, 1947). Lord Wavell was replaced by Lord Mountbatten as the Viceroy of India. Lord Mountbatten's plan of June 3, 1947 became the basis of Indian Independence Act, 1947.

15. Indian Independence Act, (July 18, 1947). The Act partitioned India into two Dominions of India and Pakistan—free countries. Thus India achieved independence on August 15, 1947.

A review of above clearly indicates that apart from the efforts of the Indian National Congress, there were other factors also which played an important role in securing independence to India.

Q. 7. Write Notes on :

1. The Cabinet Mission. *(Punjab University 1994, 1997)*

2. The Mountbatten Plan. *(Rajasthan University 1995)*

3. Indian Independence Act, (1947)

4. All India States People's Conference.

Ans. *The Cabinet Mission (March-June, 1946)*

The Labour Government in England was quite considerate to India's demands. They therefore, sent a Cabinet Mission to India to find out ways and means by which Indians would decide their future. The Mission consisted of Lord Pethic Lawrence, the Secretary of State for India, Sir Stafford Cripps, President of the Board of Trade and A.V. Alexander, First Lord of the Admiralty. Prolonged discussions took place between the members of the Mission, the Muslim League and the leaders of the Congress. The Mission began conducting intensive discussions in India with a wide range of people. It attempted but failed to sort out differences between the Congress and the Muslim League. Finally on May 16, 1946, the Mission announced the following scheme with the approval of the British Government.

1. Formation of Union of India embracing both British India and the Princely States.
2. Immediate arrangements for drafting the future constitution of India.
3. Rejection of Muslim League's demand for Pakistan.
4. The Union of India to deal only with Foreign Affairs, Defence and Communication.
5. The provinces to form regional groups and each group to determine the subjects to be taken in common.

6. Group A to have Hindu majority provinces of Madras, Bombay, United Province (U.P.), Central Province (C.P.) and Orissa. Group B to have Muslim majority provinces of Punjab, North West Frontier Province (N.W.F.P.) and Sind. Group C to have again Muslim majority provinces comprising Bengal and Assam.
   To Group A were added the Chief Commissionerships of Delhi, Ajmer, Marwara and Coorg and to Group B British Baluchistan.
7. Each province left free to come out of the group after elections under the new constitution.
8. The Constituent Assembly to have 398 members, 292 to be elected from Provinces, 4 from Chief Commissioner's Provinces, and others from the Princely states and to be nominated.
9. An Interim Government to be formed at the Centre with 14 members.
10. Communal representation to include Muslims and Sikhs.
11. After the attainment of independence, the Indian Government was free to decide whether to remain in the British Commonwealth or not.

The Cabinet Mission Plan was not implemented as both the parties *i.e.* Congress and the League did not accept the proposals. The Muslim League abandoned constitutional methods and its leader Mahammed Ali Jinnah called the 'Direction Action' by Muslims in favour of Pakistan on August 16, 1946. After the widespread communal violence the road ran downhill to Partition of India.

The Mountbatten Plan (June 3, 1947)

The British Prime Minister, Attlee, declared in February 1947 that the British Government would leave India before June 1948. He observed, "The present state of uncertainly is fraught with danger and cannot be indefinitely prolonged. His Majesty's Government wishes to make it clear that it is their definite intention to effect the transfer of power to responsible Indian hands by June 1948."

In March 1947, Lord Mountbatten replaced Lord Wavell as Viceroy of India. His talks with the Indian leaders convinced him that partition of India was the only viable solution and he therefore put forward his plan on June 3, 1947, in which he suggested the partition of India. The scheme was accepted both by the Congress and the Muslim League.

It may be observed that the Congress leaders in the beginning were averse to the partition of India but gradually they began to reconcile with the situation and ultimately accepted the Mountbatten Plan.

The Plan provided for.

1. Division of India into two Dominions *i.e.*, India and Pakistan.
2. Partition of Punjab and Bengal on the basis of a Boundary Commission headed by Sir Cyrill Radcliff.

3. Referendums in N.W.F.P. and Baluchistan.

Indian Independence Act (July 18, 1947) and Achievement of Independence

On the basis of the Mountbatten Plan, a Bill was introduced in the British Parliament on July 5, 1947 which was passed in both the Houses and it became an Act on July 18 to become operative on August 15, 1947. The Act contained the following main provisions:

1. India to be partitioned and the two Dominions of India and Pakistan to be established.
2. The British Government to have no control over the affairs of the Dominions.
3. The Legislatures of the two Dominions to have full powers to make laws.
4. All treaties and agreements entered upon by the Princely states to lapse.
5. Both the Dominions to have the full powers and rights to leave the British commonwealth of Nations, if they so desired.

Following positions emerged after the implementation of the Independence Act:

A. Territories of India

The following provinces were included (1) East Punjab (2) United Provinces (3) Bihar (4) West Bengal (5) Orissa (6) Bombay (7) Madras (8) Central Provinces (9) Assam exclusive of Distt. Sylhat.

B. Territories of Pakistan:

The following provincess were included (1) West Punjab (2) N.W.F.P. (3) Sind (4) East Bengal (5) Sylhat District of Assam.

Princely States:

A vast majority of Princely states joined India, only a few adjoining states joined Pakistan.

On 15th August, 1947, Lord Mountbatten became the Governor-General of Indian Dominion, and Jinnah became the Governor-General of the Pakistan Dominion. Pt. Nehru was appointed the Prime Minister of India and Liaqat Ali Khan of Pakistan. Neither the British Government nor the British Cabinet were to have any authority over Indian administration. The new system was brought into operation at midnight on August 14.

All India States People's Conference: (Freedom Movement in Princely States)

Two units of India. Under the British Government in India, there were two types of units. One was called British India which consisted of 11 Provinces and a few Chief Commissioner's Territories. The other unit was called Princely States consisting of 562 States. The Provinces were under the direct control of the British Government and the Princely States under the direct charge of the Indian rulers but under the overall charge of the British rulers.

The activities and programmes of the Indian National Congress were confined to British India.

All India States People's conference. The British rulers often used the Princely States to prevent the growth of national unity. Most of the rulers of the Princely states were indifferent and insensitive to the needs of the people. They lived a life of luxury whereas their subjects led a very miserable life. The rulers in general were very autocratic, feudalist and extortionists. There was little freedom of speech.

In 1927, the All India States People's Conference was founded to coordinate political activities in the States. The State Peoples' movement awakened national consciousness among the people of the states.

The Indian National Congress supported the States Peoples' struggle and called upon the rulers of these States to introduce a democratic representative government.

Under the initiative of Jawaharlal Nehru, All India States Peoples' Conferences adopted in October 1937, a resolution supporting the mass movement in the Princely State of Mysore. Within a few months, the movement for an elected government took the shape of a mass movement.

In 1938, the Congress at the Haripura Session declared very unequivocally that the Congress ideal of *Poorna Swaraj* included the independence of Princely States also.

In 1939, Jawaharlal Nehru became the President of the All India States Peoples' conference.

In Orissa, a militant struggle with bows and arrows started in several Princely states namely Dhenkanal, Talcher, Nilgiri and Ranpur. The Congress Socialist leader Nabakrishna Chowdhry (later on Congress Chief Minister of Orissa) and his wife Malati Devi led the Dhenkanal struggle.

The Congress Government was formed in the Princely States of Travancore and Cochin in 1937 and 1938 respectively. Within a short time, the main driving force was in the hands of the socialists and the communists. A.K. Gopalan was the most prominent communist leader who fought against the despotic Dewan, Sir C.P. Ramaswami Aiyar. In Hyderabad, the Arya Samaj launched a powerful movement. Jaipur, Kashmir and Rajkot were the other states where popular struggles were waged.

Zail Singh (1916-1995) who became the President of India (1982-87) was born in the Princely State of Faridkot (Punjab) and he took an active part in the States People's Conference in the 1930s.

28

National Movement: Role of Mahatma Gandhi

Q. 1. Write in brief the role of Mahatma Gandhi before joining the national movement in 1919. Also give in brief his other programmes for freedom.

Ans. *Early Career of Mahatma Gandhi*

Mohandas Karamchand Gandhi (1869-1948) popularly, known as *'Bapuji'*, out of affection, *'Mahatma'*, on account of saintly nature and *'Father of the Nation'* for the regeneration/creation of a nation, free from foreign rule, started his work of public service in South Africa. The year 1893 was a turning point in his career when he was thrown out of a first class train compartment in Durban in South Africa. For about two decades in South Africa (1894-1914), Gandhiji waged his struggle against the discriminatory and humiliating laws through *'Satyagraha'* which meant truth-force or soul-force. Gandhiji remained the most dominating figure in the freedom struggle after his return to India in 1914 from South Africa. He combated with the British with the cooperation of the people of India who very faithfully followed him when he launched several non-violent-Non-cooperation movements against the brutal force of the British rulers.

Gandhiji had implicit faith in the united power of the masses of India. He exhorted to instil in them the spirit of self-sacrifice and discipline to face the mighty power of the British. Satyagraha based on truth and non-violence and fasts were his greatest weapons. Gandhiji had a charismatic appeal which attracted thousands of devoted workers hailing from all sections.

Thousands of people participated in all the movements like Champaran Satyagraha (1917), Ahmedabad Mills Strike (1918), Kheda Struggle (1918), Khilafat and Non-cooperation Movements (1920-22), Civil Disobedience and Dandi March (1930) and Quit India Movement (1942).

Gandhiji made the struggle of freedom a mass movement. He won the cooperation of the peasants and workers. He worked hard to forge Hindu-Muslim unity. He exhorted women and students to rise against the British.

Lawyers, doctors, businessmen, shopkeepers, engineers, teachers etc., participated in the peaceful movements launched by him.

It is an irony of fate that the violence he so detested claimed this man of non-violence as its own victim on January 30, 1948.

Gandhiji's General Ideas and Philosophy Underlying Satyagraha

The word *Satyaraha* is a compound of two words-*satya* (truth) and *agraha* (holding fast). It means 'holding on truth'-no matter what happens. It gives the ideas of 'Truth-force' that is, Truth is force, a power, a weapon. The term was coined in South Africa and Gandhiji himself described it as 'Passive Resistance' but later he made a difference between the two ideas. "*Satyagraha* differs from Passive Resistance as the North Pole from the South. The latter (Passive Resistance) has been conceived as a weapon of the weak, and does not exclude the use of physical force or violence for the purpose of gaining one's end; whereas the former (*Satyagraha)* has been conceived as a weapon of the strongest, and excludes the use of violence in any shape or form."

Non-vilence which forms the very basis of *Satyagraha* is thus explained by Gandhiji—"When a person claims to be non-violent, he is expected not to be angry with one who has injured him. He will not wish him harm; he will wish him well."

About *Satyagraha* Gandhiji says, "*Satyagraha* is the law of love for all. It eshews violence absolutely... The idea behind it is not to destroy or harass the opponent, but to convert him or win him over by sympathy, patience and self-suffering."

Gandhiji referred to non-cooperation and civil resistance (meaning the same thing as Civil Disobedience) as the two offshoots of *Satyagraha.* In addition to these two, the *hartal* (temporary strike), picketing, non-violent raids or marches (as the Dandi March), and fasting are considered by some as different forms of *Satyagraha.*

About *'Swadeshi'* Gandhiji wrote in *'Young India'*, May 13, 1919 as, *"When Hindustan rings with the echoes of* Swadeshi... *When* Swadeshi *pervades the country... And when the* Swadeshi Mantra *resounds in every ear, millions of men will have in their hands the key to the economic salvation of India."*

Q. 3. Describe briefly the main events of the Freedom Movement from 1919 to 1935, with special reference to the contribution of Mahatma Gandhi. *(Punjab University Oct. 1998)*

Or

Critically evaluate the movements begun by Mahatma Gandhi between 1920 and 1934. *(Delhi University 1997)*

Ans. *Gandhiji as Messiah of Indian Nationalist Movement*

Gandhiji emerged as the Messiah of Indian nationalist movement in 1919 and completely dominated Indian politics down to 1947. There was hardly a non-violent movement for the freedom of India in which Gandhiji did not participate. In fact all the movements were inspired, launched and guided by him.

It is generally accepted that as a fighter for India's freedom, Gandhiji had no peer. He was a saint-politician-statesman who always employed moral means for the attainment of political ends. He used 'soul-force' against brute force.

Through his political campaigns of Non-Cooperation and Khilafat Movements of 1920-22, Civil Disobedience Movement of 1930-34, the Individual Civil Disobedience Movement (1940-41) and Quit India Movement (1942) and his numerous fasts, Gandhiji attempted to pressurise and convince the British rulers to appreciate the justness of India's cause.

From a cooperator to a non-cooperator. Gandhiji had supported the British rulers in First World War and had hoped that after the War, the people of India would receive better treatment and their aspirations of self-government would be duly fulfilled. But the events of the year greatly disillusioned him and from a cooperator, he turned a 'non-cooperator'. The passing of the Rowlatt Act, and the Jallianwala Bagh Tragedy, greatly moved him. With a view to enlist the support of the Muslims in the freedom struggle, he launched the Khilafat Non-Cooperation Movement.

Important events and movements with which Gandhiji was associated are as under:

1. Champaran Satyagraha (1917)
2. Ahmedabad Mill Strike (1918)
3. Kheda or Kaira Satyagraha (1918)
4. Non-Cooperation Movement (1920-22)
5. Khilafat Movement (1920-22)
6. President of the Indian National Congress (1924)
7. Purna Swaraj (1929)
8. Civil Disobedience Movement (1930)
9. Dandi March (1930)
10. Gandhi-Irwin Pact (1931)
11. Gandhi-Ambedkar Pact or Poona Pact (1932)
12. Round Table Conferences (1930-32)
13. Gandhi's fasts for purification, (1924, 1932, 1933 and 1934)

Difference in the nature of national movement before and after the entry of Gandhiji in the political field

Gandhiji's entry brought about a revolutionary change in the programmes of the Indian National Congress for the freedom of the country. His entire programme had two basic elements of *Satyagrah* and non-violence. He also believed that political programmes must be accompanied by economic and social uplift of the people.

Gandhiji's active involvement in the political field may be said to have begun with the Non-Cooperation and Khilafat Movements.

The Non-Cooperation and Khilafat Movements differed markedly in objectives and methods as compared with the earlier movements of the moderate phase. The objectives of the earlier movements were limited. They aimed at getting some concessions like government jobs, improving the economic conditions of the people, some participation in running the administrative machinery and involvement in Councils. But the Non-Co-operation and Khilafat Movements had higher aims including self-government.

The Non-Cooperation and Khilafat Movements were very vocal and vehement in their criticism of the British rulers. They believed in boycott of government institutions, legislatures and law courts.

Earlier movements were confined to the few educated intelligentsia. New movements were mas movements. Led by Gandhiji both the movements used peaceful but aggressive methods like picketing, demonstration, Swadeshi and boycott etc. Non-payment of taxes was also resorted to. Laws were disobeyed.

All sections of population including students and women participated in large numbers in the Kihlafat and Non-Cooperation Movements.

Men and women, the rich and the poor saw in the spinning wheel an inspiring message of confidence, dignity and self-reliance.

Before launching these two movements, Gandhiji had written in his letter to the Vicerory in August 1920 as, "Events that have happened during the opinion that the Imperial Government have acted in the Khilafat matter in an unscrupulous, immoral and unjust manner, wrong in order to defend their immorality. I can retain neither respect nor affection for such a government" In the same letter, he wrote, "In European countries condemnation of such grievous wrongs as the Khalifat and the Punjab would have resulted in revolution by the people."

Satyagraha and Non-violence a soverign remedy. Gandhiji had successfully used the weapon of Satyagraha in South Africa and he decided to use the same in India. He said, "I have no doubt that the British Government is a powerful Government, but I have no doubt also that Satyagraha is a soverign remedy."

After the Chauri Chaura incident when Gandhiji withdraw the movement, he told Jawahar Lal Nehru, "If the movement had not been suspended we would have been leading not a non-violent but essentially a violent struggle. The cause will prosper with this retreat. We have come back to our moorings'.

Idealism Combined with : Pragmatism. Gandhiji knew that if the Indians followed a path of violence, the armed forces of the British Government were enough to destroy them. He, therefore, tried to meet their brutal force with the moral force of the people.

Purna Swaraj (1929). Gandhiji played a leading role at the Congress Session held on December 1929 at Lahore in which the resolution of Purana Swaraj (Complete Independence) was passed. A 'Declaration' to be read on January 26, as the Swaraj Day (Day of Independence) was prepared by Gandhiji.

Dandi March (1930). It reflected the resistance of an entire nation to the denial of freedom. The result was the declaration by the British Prime Minister at the end of the First Round Table Conference (1931), that the status of a self-governing Dominion would be conferred to India.

Civil Disobedience Movement (1930-33). Gandhiji was the architect of the Civil Disobedience Movement (Satyagraha Movement) which had the objective of influencing the British Government by demonstrating that the people of India were united in their demand of 'Purna Swaraj'. Following were the main aspects of this movement.

1. To protest against the British rule which had brought about all round ruin of the people of India.
2. To break the salt law as a symbol of Indian people's refusal to obey unjust laws made by the British.
3. To involve the masses on a large scale in the struggle for freedom.
4. To break laws without doing any violence and the movement to remain peaceful.

Launching, Suspending and Resuming the Movement. Gandhiji launched the movement on March 12, 1930. From his Sabramati Ashram to Dandi, a small village on the western sea coast of Gujarat, he covered a distance of 214 miles in 24 days with his 78 followers. He picked up a handful of salt and broke the salt law as a refusal to live under the British rule and British made laws.

Impact of the Movement on National Struggle. There was a mass awakening in the country. Peasants and workers, the young and the old, women and children participated and courted arrest. The movement spread all over the country.

The movement became so strong in certain provinces that it was able to establish a parallal organisation and in certain areas it established an alternative administrative machinery. This spurred Lord Irwin to reach a compromise with Gandhiji in March 1931 and the movement was accordingly suspended.

Gandhiji-Irwin Pact (1931). The Civil Disobedience Movement had rallied massive support for the Congress and virtrally paralyzed the functioning the British Government of India for months. The Government of India was forced to come to terms with Mahatma Gandhi and thus Gandhi-Irwin Pact was signed. Acçording to the Pact, Congress agreed to halt Civil Disobedience Movement and the Government agreed to withdraw the special powers and the punitive police detailed for it. Congress did not agree to modify its demand for responsible government and 'Purna Swaraj' (full independence) but agreed to participate in the ongoing London talks on constitutional reforms.

Poona Pact (1931). Poona Pact was arrived at between Gandhiji and Dr. B.R. Ambedkar on the issue of separate electorate for the Depressed Classes.

Second Round Table Conference (1932). Gandhiji was the sole spokesman of the Congress at the conference that was held in London. The Conference failed as Gandhiji's views on the constitutiónal reforms were not acceptable to British Government.

Gandhiji's fasts. A fast is an other form of *'Satyagraha'*. Gandhiji considered it as the most effective and fiery weapon. Fasting was meant for rare occasions. Gandhiji underfook fast fifteen times. These fasts were dictated by his 'inner light' or the 'candle of his' moral reason'. His fasts undertaken in 1924, 1932, 1933 and 1934 had three-fold objective i.e. moral, political and social.

Q.3. Describe briefly the main events of freedom movement from 1930-47 with special reference to the role of Mahatma Gandhi.

(Punjab University April 1998)

Ans. *Multi-faceted Role of Gandhi in the Freedom Struggle and National Awakening*

Rebindranath Tagore has paid Gandhiji the following tribute.

He is the one luminous, creater of all mahatma.

Always in the hearts of the people enshrined

Revealed through love, intiution and thought, Whoever Knows him, immortal becomes..."

Harbinger of a new civilisation and Messiah of Indian Nationalist Movement. Einstein rightly said, "Generations to come it may be, will scarcely believe that such a one as this ever in flesh and blood walked upon this earth." In the words of Dr. Radhakrishnan, "Gandhiji will ever be remembered as the great prophet of moral and spiritual revolution without which this distracted world will not find peace."

Gandhiji's work of national awakening included the following aspects:

1. National awakening through Non-violence and *satyagraha* techniques.
2. Rural uplift.
3. Prmotion of Swadeshi.
4. Encouragement to Khadi.
5. Uplift of the Harijans.
6. Prohibition.
7. Basic Education.
8. Hindu-Muslim Unity.

Gandhiji awakened the people of India through his numerous journals like *'Indian Opinion'*,*'Young India'*. 'Harijan' and including *'Hind Swaraj'*. *'Elhical Religion'* and a two volume autobiography *"Story of My Experiments with Truth"*

Gandhiji's Personality and work at a Glance

Popularly known as *Bapuji* out of love and respect, Mahatma, on account of saintly virtues of simplicity, truth and non-violence and Father of the Nation for creating the nation, Gandhiji defied the might of the British empire through his weapon of Satyagraha. He started his political life in South Africa through several Satyagrahas.

Important events of his life were as under:

(1) Champaran Satyagraha, (1917) (2) Ahmedabad Mill Strike, (1918) (3), Satyagraha of Peasants in Khaira district (1918); (4) Non-Cooperation Movement (1920); (5) President of the Indian National Congress, (1924); (6) Civil Disobedience Movement (1929); (7) Dandi March (1930); (8) Gandhi Irwin Pact (1931); (9) Second Round Table Conference (1932); (10) Limited Individual Satyagraha (1940); (11) Quit India Movement (1942); (12) Pilgrimage to Noakhali (West Bengal) to check Hindu-Muslim riots (1946); (13) Fasts for purification and polical issues (1924, 1932, 1933, 1934 and 1947).

Gandhiji made the national struggle a mass movement in which all sections of population including children, students and women participated.

Limited Individual Satyagraha (1940). The All India Congress made several offers to cooperate with the British rulers subject to acceptance of their demand of complete freedom to India after the end of the war but the British rulers gave no assurance. On the contrary, they tried to put the Muslims and other minorities and also the Princes against the Congress. The Ramgarh Session of the Congress held in March 1940, presided over by Maulana Abul Kalam Azad reiterated, "Nothing short of complete independence can be accepted by the people of India." It also contemplated the Civil Disobedience Campaign under the leadership of Gandhiji. But Gandhiji was now in favour of Individual *Satyagraha* and not mass *Satyagraha,* because he felt that Mass Civil Disobedience at a time when Britain was engaged in a life and death struggle would not be appropriate, but it was necessary to impress that India was not interested in the war. So, in October 17, 1940 Gandhiji started the individual/limited Satyagraha. Gandhiji, in a letter to the Viceroy of India, explained the aim of this movement in these words, "The Congress is as much opposed to Victory for Nazism as any Britiser can be... And since you and the Secretary of State for India have declared that the whole of India is voluntarily helping the war efforts, it becomes necessary to make clear that the vast majority of the people of India are not interested in it. They make no distriction between Nazism and the double autocracy that rules India".

Vinobha Bhave was the first leader to offer Satyagraha. Thousands were arrested. But it created little enthusiam. Gandhiji suspended it on December 17, 1940.

(for other events, sea the previous chapter)

Limitations of Gandhiji's Movements

Some critics state that by calling off the All India Non-Cooperation Movement and by allowing Quit India to proceed in 1942 without adequate training or preparation, Gandhiji retarded the process of independence and not advanced it. Notwith standing his criticism, Gandhiji's charistmatic personality had the power to move lakhs of people to offer satyagraha and participate in his constructive programme.

Summing up. He took up causes which were not entirely political but touched every one very intimately the life of the large masses of people. Gandhiji's greatest contribution was that he taught us how it was possible for us to successfully fight the mighty British Empire without arms. He has given us and the world a 'moral substitute' for war.

29

Communalism, Partition, Left Movement and Uplift of Depressed Classes

Q.1. Trace the rise and growth of communalism in Indian Politics between 1905 and 1929. *(Delhi University 1995)*

or

Trace the rise and growth of Communalism in India upto 1929. *(Delhi University 1998)*

or

Discuss the causes that led to the growth of separatism in India and evaluate the role of Aligarh Movement. *(Rajasthan University 1996)*

Ans. *Communalism—A Curse*

The term communalism has acquired a special meaning and significance in our country. It is usually treated as synonymous with religious intolerance. It is cancerous and if unchecked initially, will have devastating effects. India has already paid a very heavy price on account of communalism. The unity and integrity of this country which remained, by and large, in tact for thousands of years, was destroyed by communal forces in 1947.

Communalism is a strong force that hinders the process of national integration.

One of the most important causes of communalism is the description and interpretation of the events of the past. Communalist historians attempt to present the past of their religious community in bright colours and exaggerate the weak points of others. As a matter of fact so much such element has been incorporated in history that even a genuine reader of history finds it difficult to sift fact from fiction.

Phases of Communalism. Though it is very difficult to divide scientifically different phases of communalism or to assign any particular year or event when communalist tendencies began or when a particular phase ended and the other started, yet an attempt is made to divide it into four broad phases. While doing so, it has to be remembered, that the movement grow continuously and take clue from the past. These phases are as: (*i*) Upto 1904 (*ii*) Between 1904 to 1929 and after 1929 leading to the partition of the country. (*iv*) 1947 to date present phase.

Beginning of communalism in India. Communialism that grew in 1905 was the result of certain earlier events which had a great bearing on the growth of communalism in 1905. The entire environment had been surcharged so much that it took a serious direction in 1905 when certain events gave all the more strength to communalism.

Sir William Hunter's work. The year 1871 marked the beginning of the rise of Muslim Communalism in India when Sir William Hunter published his book entitled *'The Indian Mussalmans'*. It was contended that the Muslims were too weak for rebellion (1857). "It was expedient now to take them into alliance than continue to antagonise them" Thus the theory of "Divide and Rule' on the basis of religion can said to have taken its birth and the British rulers followed it religiously and vengeancely to strengthen their hold in India by dividing the Hindus and Muslims. Inherent was their patronage to Muslims who became an easy prey to the mischief of the imperialists.

Principal Beck's Contribution to communalism. Theodore Back who had earlier worked at Oxford also, joined Mohammedan Anglo Oriental College, Aligarh and in 1883 became its Principal, played a very important role in winning over the Muslims to the English side. He was essentially a politician and his real mission was to forge an Anglo-Muslim Alliance and he achieved a great success while working at Aligarh. He was able to convince the nationalist Sir Syed Ahmed Khan that "While an Anglo-Muslim Alliance would ameliorate the condition of the Muslim community, the nationalist alignment would lead them once again to sweat, toil and tears." His influence was so great that Syed Ahmed, who had described beautiful bride that was India" became a communalist. Other two Principals of the A.O. College namely Theodore Morrison (1899-1905) and William A.J. Archbold (1905-1908) also encouraged communalism.

Muslim Memorial to British Parliament (1889). Principal Beck organised the Muslim opposition to Bradlaugh's Bill in the British Parliament for giving representative institutions to India. The 'Memorial' sent on behalf of the Muslims claimed that the introduction of democratic institutions was not suited to India because she was not a nation.

Mohammedan Defence Association (1893). Beck was one of its secretaries. The object of this association was to prevent the Muslims from joining the Congress. Beck wrote, "The object of the Congress is to transfer the political control of the country from the British to the Hindus... Muslims can have no sympathy with these demands. We, therefore advocate loyalty to the Government and Anglo-Muslim collaboration."

Partition of Bengal (1905). Although the official reason given by Lord Curzon for the partition of Bengal was to create two viable administrative divisions for the efficient functioning of the government but the real reasons were quite differnt. The British rulers realized that Bengal was the centre of nationalism in the country. It was the birth place of social and religious reforms. It had a composite culture. It had the capacity to lead the nationalists in other states. So with a view to weaken the nationalist movement, the British rulers followed the policy of 'Divide and Rule' in respect of Hindus and Muslims. At that time Bengal included Bengal, Bihar, Orissa and some districts of Assam. In 1905 Bengal was divided into East Bengal and West Bengal-East Bengal with 15 eastern districts of East Bengal and Assam with a population of 31 million-West Bengal with a population of 18 million Bengalis and 36 million Biharis and Oriyas. Thus a new Muslim majority province of Bengal was created. Appropriate course was to separate Bihar and Orissa from Bengal.

Muslim demand for Separate electorate (1906). William A.J. Archbold, Principal of A.O.M. College Aligarh organised a Muslim deputation which waited on the Viceroy Minto at Simla on Oct. 1, 1906. The deputation led by Sir Agha Khan pleaded for separate electroates to the Muslims. Lord Minto's reply was. "... I am entirely in accord with you." In his diary Lord Minto described the day on which the deputation of the Muslims met him as "an epoch in Indian history."

Sir Syed Ahmad–The forerunner of the two-nation theory

Congress not a nationalist party. Sir Syed Ahmad-the nationalist, appeared in the garb of a staunch communalist when he expressed suspicion about the bonafides of the Indian National Congress as a nationalist organisation. In 1887, he openly advised his Muslim brothern to Keep aloof from the Congress. In a letter to Bardruddin Tyabji the then President of the Congress, he wrote, "I do not understand what the words Indian National Congress mean. Is it supposed that the different castes and crceds living in India belong to one nation or can become a nation and their aims and aspirations be one and the same? I think it is quite impossible, and when it is quite impossible, there can be no such thing as a National Congress nor it can be of equal benefit to all people." He further wrote, "I object to every Congress in any shape or form whatsover which regards India as one nation."

Competitive examinations harm Muslim interests

Syed Ahmad opposed tooth and nail the Congress proposal to hold competitive examinations in India as it would be helpful to the Hindus only. He suggested selection by the Government as the Government would prefer Muslims to Hindus.

Representation by election not in the interest of Muslim Community

He opposed the system of representation by election as most unsuited to

India where education in the modern sense had not made an equal or proportionate progress among all sections of population.

Formation of Associations on communal basis. He was instrumental in establishing two associations viz. United Indian Patriotic Association (1888) and Mohammedan Anglo-Oriental Defence Association (1893) as a counter-poise to the Indian National Congress. The latter association consisted of loyalists who were committed to the prevention of political agitation among Muslims.

Safegards of Muslim interests under British rule. He often stated that there was a much better opprtunity for the preservation of Muslim religious rights under the British Raj rather than any revival of so-called Hindu Raj. He remarked, "the large community would totally over-ride the interests of smaller community and the ignorant public would hold government responsible for introducing measures which might make the differences of race more acute and create more violence than ever."

No Bengali domination. In February 1888, he said, "If our Bengali friends want to trample under foot his fallen nation (Muslims), they should not expect that we will submit."

Conferring title of K.C.S.I.-Knight Commander of the Star of India. The British made the most of the opportunity by honouring him with the title of K.C.S.I. in 1889.

Lala Lajpat Rai, once a great admirer of Syed's national outlook and activities expressed utter disgust at such a changed attitude in a letter, "...is it the blindness of old age which has permitted you to remind one of the fall of Adam just as '*Satan*' is said to be the cause of the fall of that progeniture of our race...It is the winter of despair when we see her own sons deserting the cause of awakening India." He further appealed to him, "Sir Syed, for Good sake reconsider your position and do not disappoint us just when the morning of hope has begun to dawn over us and our motherland."

Aligarh School

Syed Ahmad Khan drew around him a band of dedicated followers and it began to be called the 'Aligarh School'. Among the important ones were Chirag Ali, Altaf Hussian Hali (an Urdu poet) Nazir Ahmad, Maulana Shibli Nomani and Khuda Baksh. It is generally believed that most of the leaders of the Aligarh School were guided by the idea of separatism and they helped the British rulers in weakening the national movement.

The All India Muslim League

Introduction. The birth of the Muslim League in 1906, and its subsequent role in the political field, proved very harmful to the unity and integrity of India. It led to the birth of two-nation theory which became responsible for the partition of India; first into two countries i.e. India and Pakistan and then into three, with the division of Pakistan and the creation of Bangladesh.

Objectives of the Muslim League

The Muslim League was founded in 1906 under the leadership of the Agha Khan, the Nawab Salimullah of Dhaka and Nawab Mohsin-ul-Mulik. The birth of the Muslim League may be ascribed to the policy of 'Divide and Rule' followed by the British. It was founded as a loyalist, communal and conservative political organisation. It was dominated by the big Muslim Nawabs and landlords. In the rise of the separate tendencies along communal lines, Sayed Ahmad Khan had played an important role. He had laid the foundations of Muslim communalism in 1880's when he declared that the political interests of the Hindus and the Muslims were not the same but different and even divergent. He also preached obedience to British rule.

The final shape to the programme of the Muslim League was given at its Karachi session in 1907. Its objectives were spelled out as under:

(*i*) Promotion of loyalty towards the British.
(*ii*) Protection of political and other rights of the Muslims.
(*iii*) Generating friendly feelings among the Muslims.

At its session at Amritsar (1908), the Muslim League supported the Partition of Bengal, demanded separate representation and a large share of jobs for Muslims. The same demands were repeated next year.

Separate electorate: Morely-Minto Reform (1909)

The Government accepted the demand of separate electrorate and representation for the Muslims when they declared Morely-Minto Reforms in 1909.

Lucknow Pact

On the persistent demand of the Muslim League of separate representation to the Muslims, the Congress signed an agreement with the League, known as *Lucknow Pact* (1916), accepting separate electorate.

Nehru Committee Report (1928). The Muslim League participated in All Parties Confrence and put forward a 14 point programme of Constitutional reforms, pleading more representation to Muslims. The Committee rejected the demands of the Muslim League.

In 1930, the Muslim League raised the demand for Pakistan and in 1934, at the League session at Lahore, M.A. Jinnah put forward the 'Two Nation Theory' i.e. Hindus and Muslims form two separate nations. As usual, the British rulers followed the policy of 'Divide and Rule' and supported this theory and ultimately despite Gandhiji's opposition, the Congress accepted the proposal of the creation of an independent separate state of Pakistan in 1947.

Hindu Mahasabha and Communalism

The Hindu Mahasabha was formed in 1915 as a political party to counteract the activities of the Muslim League and for the protection of Hindu interests. It resented to the extra weightage given to Muslims in the provinces by the system of separate electorates introduced in 1909. In due course its goal was declared to be "the maintenance, protection and promotion of the Hindu race, Hindu culture and Hindu civilization for the advancement of the Hindu Rashtra". (Hindu nation). However, it failed to make little impact on the political scenario. It was completely overshadowed by the nationalism of the All India Congress and its leaders.

Summing up. Communalism grew in India on account of the following factors:

1. 'Divide and Rule' policy of the British.
2. Role of Principal Beck of A.O.M. College Aligarh.
3. Role of Sir Syed Ahmad Khan.
4. Role of the Aligarh School.
5. Backwardness of the Muslims in education, trade and industry.
6. Getting more opportunities in Government services and employment by Muslims.
7. Bias in the writing and teaching of Indian history.
8. Psychological fears among the Muslims regarding Hindu domination.
9. Economic backwardness of the Muslims.
10. Domination of the landed aristocracy in the Muslim society and their loyalty to the English Raj.
11. Formation of the Muslim League.
12. Religious reform movement and their narrow approach to religious issues.
13. Militant nationalists among Muslim youth.
14. Hindu communal writers and workers.
15. Emergence of Hindu Mahasabha.
16. Personal ambition of Muslim leaders like Jinnah.
17. Rejection of Nehru Report by the Muslim League.
18. Communal Award.
19. Elections and importance to religious issues.

Communalism and Partition of India

Q. 2. Enumerate the factors that led to the partition of India. Could it be avoided? *(Rajasthan University 1993, 1995, 1997)*

or

Delineate the causes for the rise of communalism in Modern India. How for was Muhammad Ali Jinnah responsible for the partition of the country in 1947? *(Rajasthan University 1996)*

or

Discuss the political events during 1937 to 1947 that necessitated India's partition and assess the role of Jinnah in it.

(Rajasthan University 1996, Subsidiary Paper)

or

Trace the growth of the Muslim Separatist Movement from 1919 to 1940. *(Rajasthan University 1993)*

or

Discuss the growth of communalism in India between 1928 and 1947. *(Delhi University 1992)*

Ans. *History of Communalism and Separation of India into Pakistan and India*

Seeds 1871 and fruit 1947. The seeds of communalism and partition of India were sown in 1871 by Sir William Hunter when he published his book, *'The Indian Mussalmans'*. The book's conclusion was, "It was expedient now to take them (the Muslims) into alliance (by the British) rather than continue to antagonise them." This was the beginning of pampering the Muslim community by the British and alienating them from the mainstream of Indian nationalism.

The seeds took about 76 years to bear fruit. The seeds were manured and watered by Sir Syed Ahmad and the Aligarh School. Fence to the seeds was provided by Lord Curzon when he divided Bengal. The seeds grew into a tender plant under the care of Morely-Minto. The plant grew into a tree with the nourishment supplied by the Muslim League. Efforts of the Hindu Mahasabha to remove the fence and uproot the tree helped in strengthening the tree. The tree began to provide shade under the protection of Sir Muhammed Iqbal. M.A. Jinnah provided care, nourishment and protection to the tree and the tree bore two fruits-one sweat for the Muslim League and the sour rather poisonous for India. Tree still exists and in case vigorous efforts are not made to uproot it, it may again bear poisonous fruit.

Theory of 'Divide and Rule'. The most acceptable theory relating to the partition is the theory of 'Divide and Rule' followed by the British, which pitted Muslims against Hindu at each stage of constitutional reform and delaying responsible government. Partition is a permanent blot on the record of British rule in India. It failed to solve communal problems on the Indian Subcontinent and it created new security and psychological burdens for the successor states of India, Pakistan and Bangladesh.

Sir Muhammed Iqbal (1873-1938) as the fore runner of Pakistan

Muhammed Iqbal, a noted poet, a religious philosopher and at one time a nationalist also turne a communalist in the later years of his life after his return from Europe. He was honoured by the Government with Knighthood in 1922. He was elected by the Muslims as a member of the Punjab Legislative Assembly in 1927. In 1930, he was elected as the President of the annual session of the Muslim League at Allahabad. His address as President clearly contained the demand for a separate homeland for Muslims. He said in his address, "I would like to see the Punjab, the North-west Frontier

Province, Sind and Baluchistan amalgamated into a single state, Self-government within the British Empire or without the British Empire. The formation of a consolidated North-west Indian Muslim state appears to mee to be the final destiny of the Muslims." In his speech he further said, "To base a constitution on the conception of a homogenous India or to apply to India the principles dicteded by British democratic sentiments is unwillingly to prepare her for a civil war." In a letter to M.A. Jinnah on May 28, 1937, he again repeated that it would be "necessary to redistribute the country and to provide one or more Muslim States with absolute majorities."

Jinnah as the architect of Pakistan

Muhammad Ali Jinnah (1875-1948), an ardent nationalist and a Congressman in the initial stages who became a staunch communalist at a later stage, became the architect of a new state of Pakistan. It is of interest to note that this Messiah of the Muslims and the creator of Pakistan—a Muslim state could neither speak Urdu—the popular language of the Muslims nor donned a *'sherwani'* and *'pajama'* in the public nor had interest in the religious prayers or rituals of Muslims. He dominated the Muslim League from 1927 onwards to the formation of Pakistan. Jinnah's changed outlook from that of a nationalist to a rank communalist is partially attributed to his domestic circumtances viz. unhappy married life, eventual separation from his second wife and virtual dependence upon his communal minded fanatic sister Fatima Jinnah who looked after her brother.

P.C. Roy Chaudhary's analysis of his dealings with the Congress leaders reveals that Jinnah was essentially an "introvert and narcissist with an insatiable craze for going to the top." Gandhiji seemed to have eclipsed him he was in the Congress. He left Congress in 1921 when Gandhiji emerged as its most prominent leader. Partially, the British were also responsible for giving him undue importance and treating him as the custodian of Muslim interest.

Opposition to Nehru Committee Report (1928). Jinnah's fourteen-point demands on behalf of the Muslim League were rejected by the Nehru Committee and this greatly annoyed him. The League demanded separate communal electorate. Jinnah later described the episode as the parting of ways "between the League and the Congress."

Deliverance Day

The failure of the Muslim League to form its Ministry in any of the eleven provinces after the 1937 elections convinced it to adopt such a strategy which would make them the sole representative of the Muslims. In the elections it could barely get 51 seats out of 482 seats in all provinces. Muslim League was yet a feeble force, Muslims of Punjab voted for the Unionist Party. The Muslims in Bengal followed the Krishak Party of Fazul Huq. The U.P. Muslims preferred the Nationalist Agricultural Party of Nawab of Chhatari. The

Independent Muslim Party of Abdualla Harun won Muslim votes in Sind. The N.W.F.P. was fully swayed by Khan Abdul Ghaffar Khan, whose followers were affiliated to the Congress. In other provinces, the Congress party won handsomely. In these circumstances, M.A. Jinnah raised the cry of 'Islam in Danger'. The League raised a lot of hue and cry that the Congress Ministries were not protecting the Muslim interests.

Jinnah appealed to the Muslims to observe Friday, December 22, 1939 as the 'Day of Deliverance' and 'thanks giving' on account of resignation of Congress Ministries.

Two-nation theory. In a letter to Gandhiji in January 1940, he emphasised, "I have no illusious in the matter and let me say again that India is not a nation, nor a country. It is a sub-continent composed of nationalities, Hindus and Muslims being the two major nations". He explained his two-nation theory as, "The Hindus and Muslims belong to two different civilizations which are based on conflicting ideas and conceptions. To yoke together two such nations under a single unit must lead to growing discontent and final destructon of any fabric that may be so built up for the governance of such a state."

Pakistan Resolution (1940). (Punjab University Oct. 1997, Delhi University 1996).

The Muslim League passed the Pakistan Resolution on March 23, 1940. The first part of the resolution runs thus, "Resolved that it is the considered view of this session of the All India Muslim League that no constitutional plan would be workable in this country or acceptable to Muslims unless it is designed on the following basic principles, namely, that geographically contiguous units are demarcated into regions which should be so constituted, with such territorial readjustments as may be necessary, that the areas in which the Muslims are numerically in a majority as in the North-western and Eastern Zones of India should be grouped to constitute 'Independent States' in which the constituent units shall be autonomous and sovereign."

Thus the Lahore Resolution was the highest culmination of Muslim aspirations roused by leaders from Syed Ahmad's times.

The Pakistan Resolution insisted on the accptance of the principle of division of the country.

Pakistan Day. The Cripps proposals of March 1942, recognised the claim of the Muslim League of Pakistan. The Pakistan Day was celebrated all over India on March 23, 1942. In his message on that day in 1942, Jinnah exhorted the Muslims "to stand solid by our goal of Pakistan...either we achieve Pakistan or Perish."

Condemnation of Gandhiji's movements. Jinnah condemned the famous Civil Disobedience Movement and described the 'Quit India' movement as fraud.

Acceptance of the Demand for Pakistan by the Indian National Congress

Adamant attitude at Simla Conference (1945). Jinnah claimed himself to be the sole representative of the Muslim community and insisted on the right to appoint all Muslim members to the Excutive Council of the Governor-General. This led to the failure of the Conference convened by Lord Wavell~the then Viceroy of India.

Direct Action. To undo the Cabinet Mission Plan, Jinnah sounded a clarion call for the 'Direct Action' on August 16, 1946 to achieve the goal of Pakistan. Jinnah said, "To-day, we bid good by to the constitutional methods." Thus the death-knell to the Cabinet Mission Plan was sounded.

The Muslim League now took a course of action which had no parallel in the recorded history of the British period. It declared 16th August 1946 to be observed as 'Direct Action Day' for holding meetings all over the country to achieve Pakistan by getting rid of British slavery and future Hindu domination. In Calcutta, the orgy of murder and arson continued for four days. It was followed by similar happenings in Noakhali and Tipperah (East Bengal). In Bihar retaliation started.

The 'Direct Action' begun in Lahore followed the pattern of Calcutta and spread to Multan, Rawalpindi, Amritsar and N.W.F.P.

On February 20, 1947 Attlee made the historic announcement of transferring power not later than June 1948. Lord Mountbatten was sent to replace Lord Wavell for transferring the responsibility for the government in a manner best suited for the future happiness of India. Now, rethinking started. The Muslim League also joined the Interim Government. The bitter experience of six months of working in the Interim Government of joint Congress and the Muslim League taught the Congress that the only way of deliverance from anarchy and bloodshed caused by the breakdown of administration, is to create Pakistan.

No Congress leader liked the idea but had to accept it as an evil necessity. Patel's experience of working with the League members in the Executive Council had convinced him of the impossibility of working with the Muslim League. As he said, "Whether we like it or not, there were two nations in India." Dr. Rajendra Prassad felt that by accepting Pakistan, it would be possible to govern the remaining position, in a better way. Pandit Nehru felt, "A large India would have constant troubles, constant disintegrating pulls. And also the fact that we saw no other way of getting our freedom in the near future. And so we accepted it and said, "let us build up a strong India." Gandhiji was fully against partition. When opposition to the acceptance of Partition was running very high in the A.I.C.C. meeting on June 14, 1947, Gandhiji spoke urging the acceptance of the partition. He concluded by saying that he was steadfastly opposed to the idea but sometimes certain decisions, however unpalatable, had to be taken.

Q. 3. Examine the main trends in the development of the Left Movement in India between 1920 and 1947. *(Delhi University 1998)*

Ans. *Present Position.* At present left movement is organised primarily by the following parties in India.

A. National Parties recognised by the Election Commission

(*i*) Communist Party of India (CPI)

(*ii*) Communist Party of India (Marxist) (CPM)

B. State Parties recognised at the state level

(*i*) All India Forward Block (FBL)

(*ii*) Revolutionary Socialist Party (RSP)

C. Registered Unrecognised Parties

(*i*) The Great India's Revolutionaries (TGIR)

(*ii*) All India Kisan Mazdoor Sabha (AIKMS)

(*iii*) Bharat Ka Samaj Wadi Dal (Marxist Lenin Wad) BKSD (ML)

(*iv*) Bolshevik Party of India (BPI)

(*v*) Communist Marxist Party Kerala State Committee (CMPKSC)

(*vi*) Forward (Socialist) FB(S)

(*vii*) Hind Kisan Mazdoor Party (HKHP)

(*viii*) Marxist Coordination (MCO)

(*ix*) Orissa Socialist Party (Kerala) (PSP) (K)

This list is an illustrative one. There are numerous splinter groups in the left movement.

CPM is quite strong in West Bengal and Kerala.

Beginning of Socialist Trend. From the beginning of the national awakening in India, socialist ideas have greatly influenced it. Reference may be made to Dadabhai Naoroji who attended the International Socialist Conference at Amsterdem in 1904. However the 1930s saw the rapid growth of socialist ideas within and outside the Congress which had a great bearing on the national movement.

Factors leading to the emergence of Left Movement in India

Following factors are usually assigned to the emergence of left movement in India :

1. Crippling economic consequences of the First World War and hardships faced by the common man.
2. The success of the Russian Revolution.
3. The romantic appeal of the revolutionary ideas of Marx to the Indian intellectuals.
4. Gandhiji's work for the peasants and the workers and their participation in the national struggle.
5. Congress labelled as a weak force and not very receptive to the interest of the weaker sections—charge of radicals.
6. Stable economy of USSR in the 1930's when almost all industrialised and capitalist countries faced 'Economic Depression'.

Two main streems of the Left Movement. (1) Communist Party as a branch of the International Communist Movement; (2) Congress Socialist Party within the Indian National Congress.

First Phase of the Leftist Movement. M.N. Roy who had earlier attended the Second Congress of the Communist International in 1920, played a leading role in founding the Communist Party of India.

The Communists, individually and collectively, functioning inside and outside the Indian National Congress, worked for the complete independence from British rule. They were also active in the trade union movement and started *'kisan'* or peasants movements in some areas. In the Meerut conspiracy of 1929, thirty one trade union officials who controlled the Communist Movement were arrested and this gave a great set-back to the left movement in India.

In 1928, Chandra Shekhar Azad organised the Hindustan Republican Association. Its main objective was to establish India as a Socialist Republic. The Association believed in the slogan 'Revolution by the masses for the masses'. The Association captured the popular imagination of the masses and helped them to rally around the Civil Disobedience Movement. Bhagat Singh was also a member of this Association.

The Peasants and Workers in the Freedom Movement. Gandhiji was firmly convinced that the prosperity of India was to be determined by the prosperity of the rural masses. He championed the cause of peasants in Champaran in Bihar and organised Satyagraha Movement. Rajendra Prasad, Desai and J.B. Kriplani worked with him in this Satyagraha. A similar opportunity came up in Khaira Distt. in Gujarat. The crops had failed in the years 1918 but the authorities insisted on full land revenue. Gandhiji organised the peasants Satyagraha against collection of land revenue. The peasants refused to pay and the Satyagraha succeeded. This success impressed Sardar Patel who was at that time an important Barrister. He became a follower of Gandhiji. Later he became the incharge of Bardoli Satyagraha Movement in 1928. The success of this movement earned him the title of 'Lion of Bardoli'.

The All India Kisan Sabha also mobilised the peasantry against imperialism.

Second Phase of the Left Movement. The Communist Party of India almost disappeared from the scene when the national movement under the leadership of Gandhiji made giant strides during 1930's. In 1934, the CPI was declared an illegal organisation on account of its indulging in revolutionaries conspiracies.

Socialist trend in Indian National Congress. The 1930s were an era of economic depression for most of the countries of the world. Soviet Russia, however, remained unaffected. It did not suffer unemployment as other countries did. The socialist ideas therefore gained a special appeal. Workers and peasants were attracted to the new ideology that promised them better economic status in the society. Inside the Indian National Congress, the socialist trend resulted in the election of Jawaharlal Nehru as the President in 1936. At the Lucknow session of the Congress in 1936, Nehru pleaded for the acceptance of socialism as the Congress goal. Nehru was followed by Subash Chandra Bose who was well-known for his new ideas.

The socialist trend was equally visible in the leadership outside the Congress. It led to the setting up of the Congress Socialist Party in 1934 by Acharya Narendra Dev, Ram Manohar Lohia and Jaya Prakash Narayan.

In his presidential address to the Lucknow Session of the Indian national Congress in 1936, Jawaharlal Nehru urged the Congress to accept socialism as its goal. He said, "I am convinced that the only key to the solution of the world's problems and of India's problems lies in socialism, and, when I use this word, I do so not in a vague humanitarian way but in scientific, economic sense...That involves vast and revolutionary changes in our political and social structure, the ending of vested interests in land and industry, as well as the feudal and autocratic Indian States system. That means the ending of private property, except in a restricted sense, and the replacement of the present profit system by a higher ideal of co-operative service. It means ultimately a change in our instincts and habits and desires. In short, it means a new civilization, radically different from the present capitalist order".

The CPI of India served as a nursery for the growth of several minor leftist parties in 1939-40.

Third Phase: Second World War. When the Second World War broke out, the Communist Party of India adopted anti-Imperialism policy but in 1941, it reversed its stand. When Hitler of Germany attacked the Soviet Union, the 'Fatherland of Socialism', the Communists in India termed the war as 'people's war'. The Communist Party was rewarded by the Government of India by declaring it as a legal organisation. The Communists vehemently opposed the Indian National Congress and the Quit India Movement. It is stated that the Communists extended all possible support to the British rulers and even acted as the 'spies' for them.

In 1942 itself, the CPI declared that India comprised 16 nations.

In 1946, CPI put forward before the Cabinet Mission a plan for the division of India into 17 separate sovereign states.

By 1947, the CPI was in complete disarray.

Rajini Palm Dutt (1896-1974)

Rajini Palm Dutt, whose father was an Indian and mother a Swedish, played an important role in developing the Communist movement in India. He was one of the founders of the British Communist Party. His book '*Modern India*' written in 1926 served as an important primar of Marxists in India. Dr. Dutt hated western parliamentary democracy. He exhorted the working class to write and gathered round a popular national programme.

In 1946, R.P. Dutt suggested that the Communists should not support the Muslim League's demand of Pakistan.

S.A. Dange (1899-1994)

Dange was one of the earliest members of the Communist Party of India. In his book *'Gandhi Versus Lenin'* (1921), he expressed his dissatisfaction with the Non-Cooperation Movement of Gandhiji. He was always pro-Russia. He took a leading part in the trade union movement. He was imprisoned from 1929-1935 and from 1939-43.

Dr. Ram Manohar Lohia (1910-1968)

Dr. Ram Manohar Lohia expressed his views on socialism in his book *"Marx, Gandhi and Socialism"* He presented a compromise between the two opposing views of Gandhi and Marx.

Q. 4. Write notes on the following:

Contribution of Dr. B.R. Ambedkar in Depressed Class Movement.

(Punjab University Oct. 1998; April 1997; Oct. 1997)

Give an account of the contribution of Jotiba Phule and Dr. B.R. Ambedkar for the uplift of the Depressed Classes.

(Punjab University, April 1998)

Ans. *Jyotiba Phule* (1829-90)

He worked for raising the status and standard of the lower classes.

Jyotiba Phule was born, in a *'Mali* caste (his family supplied *Phool'*—(flowers), garlands, etc., to the family of Peshwa at Poona. Hence he came to be known as Phule.

The outlook of Phule was changed on account of the arrogance of the Brahamans, shown to him on various occasions. On one occasion, he was scolded and insulted by a Brahaman when he joined a marriage procession of the Brahamans. He was also vehemently opposed by the Brahamans when he started a school for the lower castes and women. He was compelled to close the school. He was also compelled to leave his family house.

Jyotiba was very critical of the attitude of the Brahamans who under the pretext of religion tyrannized other castes and wanted to turn them as their slaves.

Jyotiba felt that the Indian National Congress was not doing enough for protecting the interests of the weaker sections.

In 1873, Jyotiba started the Satya Shodhak Samaj (Truth Seeking Society) with the objective of securing social justice for the weaker sections of the society.

Jyotiba opened a number of schools and orphanages for the children and women belonging to all castes.

As a member of the Poona Muncipal Committee, he did a lot of work for the Depressed Classes.

Jyotiba's important publications include *'Dharma Tritiya Ratna' (Expo-*

sure of the Puranas), 'Ishara' (A warning), *'Life of Shivaji'* etc.

B.R. (Bhima Rao) Ambedkar (1891-1956)

Bhima Rao, born in a Mahar (Hindu Untouchable) caste, was a great crusader in the cause of the uplift of the lower classes.

Ambedkar with two Doctorates, one from Columbia University, New York and the other from the London School of Economics began his active public career as an educationist, jurist, politician and a social worker.

The humiliation and indignities that the lower caste people suffered filled his sensitive mind with anguish and bitter resentment against the social system. He remained critical of caste ridden Hindu society as well as of Gandhiji and the Indian National Congress as he was convinced that they were unlikely to grant social equality to the Depressed Classes.

Organisations for the uplift of Depressed Classes. In 1924, Ambedkar founded the *'Bahishkrit Hitkarm Sabha'* (Depressed Classes Organisation) for the moral and material progress of the untouchables.

In 1936, he founded the Independent Labour Party.

In 1942, he established the Scheduled Caste Federation.

Agitations. Ambedkar resorted to several types of agitations including *'Satyagraha'* for the civic rights of the untouchables to enter the Hindu temples and draw water from public wells. His Nasik Satyagraha to enter a Hindu temple attracted All India attention.

Entry into politics. Ambedkar entered national politics and he demanded separate electorates for the untouchables. He was nominated as a delegate of the three Round Table Conferences (1930-32). The British Government announced Communal Award in 1932 which provided for separate electorates for the Depressed Classes. This meant that the Depressed Classes were not Hindus and it hurt Gandhiji very much and he went on fast unto death on this issue. Finally after negotiations a compromise was arrived at between Ambedkar and Gandhi, which is popularly known as Poona Pact (Sept. 24, 1932). It provided reservation of seats for the Depressed Classes in the general constituencies. This provision was incorporated later on in the Indian Constitution in 1949.

Embracing Buddhism. In 1956, Ambedkar announced that the Scheduled Castes would leave Hindu fold and he along with several followers conbraced Buddhism at a mass meeting.

Work in the Constituent Assembly. On the eve of independence, Ambedkar was nominated by the Congress Party as a member of the Constituent Assembly. As Chairman of the Drafting Committee (1946-1949) of the Constitution, he played an important role in framing the Constitution. He was a Law Minister in Nehru's first Cabinet. Ambedkar drafted constitutional provisions and piloted important legislation providing social equality and justice for all. The Untouchability (Offences) Act 1955 spells out the punishments to be awarded for offenders under this Act.

Equality as the foundation stone of a democratic set-up. After the finalisation of the draft of the Constitution, on the the eve of its adoption on November 26, 1949, he addressed the Constituent Assembly on November 25.

During his address, he observed, "We must begin by acknowledging the fact that there is complete absence of two things in Indian Society... equality and fraternity... The down-trodden classes are tired of being governed. (by the monopoly of a few). They are impatient to govern themselves. This urge for self-realization develops into a class struggle or class war. This would indeed be a day of disaster. He further appealed to resolve not to be "tardy in the recognition of the evils that lie across our path and not to be weak in our initiative to remove them. That this is the only way to serve the country. I know of no better."

30

Eminent Leaders of the Indian Nationalist Movement

A. Moderate Leaders

Allan Octavian Hume - A. O. Hume (1929-1912)

A Scottish and a member of Indian Civil Service - ICS. Held high posts. Voluntarily retired from service in 1882 but remained in India.

He became critical of the British indifference to the welfare of their Indian subjects especially during the Viceroyalty of Lord Lytton (1876-1880). Earlier his life had been saved by his Indian friends during the Revolt of 1857.

Hume firmly believed that the British rule must be based on enlightened principles. On March 1, 1883, he exhorted the Calcutta University students, in a letter, to work for the uplift of their motherland: "Even if fifty among you cannot be found with sufficient power and sacrifice and love and pride in your country...there is no hope for India."

He addressed the following lines to the people of India.

"Sons of Ind, Why set you idle?
    Wait Ye for some Deva's aid?
Buckle to, be up and doing!
    Nations by themselves are made!"

In 1883, he tried to form Indian National Union, an orgaination of educated Indian drawn from the cities of Bombay, Calcutta and Madras for encouraging personal acquaintancehip and discussing political issues but he could not create a net work.

However this organisation was renamed as the Indian National Congress at its Bombay meeting of seventy two delegates in 1885. Hume worked as its secretary for a number of years.

At its annual session in 1912, Congress formally recorded its gratitude to Hume, naming him "father and founder" of the organisation.

The early Congress leaders hoped to use Hume as a "Lightening Conductor'. Hume published a pamphlet entitled "*An Old Man's Hope*" in which he appealed to the people of England in these words, "Ah Men! well fed and happy! Do you at all realise the dull misery of these countless myriads? Toil, Toil, Toil, Hunger, Hunger, Hunger, Sickmen, Suffering, Sorrow, these alas, alas, alas are the keynotes of their short and sad existence."

In the words of Surendra Nath Banerjee, "His name will stand forth in the golden records of Indian history as one of the greatest builders of Indian national life." About Hume, Motilal Nehru observed, "He taught us how to fight bloodless battles of constitutional reforms."

Dadabhai Naoroji (1825-1917)

Affectionately called the 'Grand Old Man of India', Dadabhai Naoroji was one of the foremost reformers and leaders of the national movement in India. Even during his professorship at Elphinstone College Bombay, till 1855, he devoted himself whole-heartedly to various kinds of reforms - educational, political religious and social.

He left for England in 1885, to manage a famous Parsi business firm. He launched a paper '*Voice of India* in London to voice the feelings of India regarding reforms. He formed the East Indian Association in London.

During 1892-95, he was the first Indian to be elected to the British Parliament on the Liberal Party ticket. There was hardly any important issue concerning India which he did not bring to the notice of British Parliament.

Dadabhai became the President of the Indian National Congress three times, in 1886, 1894 and 1906. He advocated the concept of moral foundations of political power.

Dadabhai was a pioneer not only in the political awakening of the Indian masses, but also was the first to bring to the notice of the world that India was being made economically destitute on account of constant 'draining' of her revenue to foreign coffers.

In 1901, he published his famous book '*Poverty and Un-British Rule in India*' and explained that India's poverty was on account of continuous exploitation of Indians by the British. He wrote, "Europeans occupy almost all the higher places in every department of government directly or indirectly under its control. While in India they acquire India's money, experience and wisdom, and when they go, they carry both with them."

Naoroji acted as a peace-maker between the 'Moderates' and the 'Extremists.'

Naoroji was also a great social reformer.

Gopal Krishna Gokhale (1866-1915)

At the age of 20, Gokhale became a Professor, at 22, a Member of the Bombay Legislative Council, at 36 a member of the Supreme Council and at 39, the President of the Indian National Congress."

Gokhale was a Moderate. He firmly believed that the situation required "not the policeman's baton or the soldier's bayonet but the statesman's insight;

wisdom and courage." From 1905 to 1915, he virtually dominated the Congress, thwarting the bid of Extremists to control it. He played the role of a 'reconciler':

He criticized the Salt Tax on the ground that the poor were hit by it. He disapproved the policy of the Government of India, of excluding Indians from higher posts. He denounced the Partition of Bengal. He persuaded Gandhiji to come to India from South Africa. He worked for the poor peasants. He was in favour of constitutional methods for the realisation of the goal. He had no faith in revolutionary methods. He made these observations regarding his approach to national issues, "The Englishman who believes that India can be governed much longer on the same lines as in the past, and the Indian who thinks that he must seek a destiny for his country outside his empire ~ of which now, for better or worse we are a part - both sides alike show an inadequate appreciation of the realities of the present situation."

In 1905, Gokhale launched the Servents of Indian society for undertaking public service programme and creating a group of public spirited individuals. He wrote in the Premble to the constitution of the society, "A sufficient number of our, countrymen must now come forward to devote themselves to the cause in the spirit in which religious work is undertaken. Public life must be spiritualised. Love of the country must so fill the heart that all else shall appear as of little movement by its side."

Gandhiji called Gokhale his "Political Guru". Lokmanya Tilak described Gokhale as "the diamond of India, the jewel of Maharashtra and the prince of workers." He has been described by many as a "constructive statesman of the first rank, harbinger together of the East and the West and prophet of the new era of interracial goodwill and cooperation".

B. Extemist Leaders

Bal Gangadhar Tilak (1856-1920)

Remembered as '*Lokmanya*' (Loved and respected by the people), Tilak was the first leader to use the slogan, "Swaraj (freedom) is my birth right and I shall have it." He waged a fierce struggle against the British with his three P's, Pen-Press and Platform as against three P's of "Pray, Please and Protest." He founded two papers *Kasari* and *Maharata* for developing patriotic feelings for the motherland. He is called a militant nationalist. He was one of the most ardent champion of the Swadeshi movement and an outspoken critic of the Partition of Bengal. He was imprisoned several times for his stirring speeches and writings. He was a great terror and nightmare to the British Government. Apart from Indian jails, Tilak was put in Mandalay jail (Burma) from 1908 to 1914. At a public meeting in Calcutta, Tilak declared, "It is impossible to expect that our petitions will be heard unless backed by firm resolution backed by solid force. Look to the examples of Ireland, Japan and Russia and follow their methods." Tilak was often called 'The father of Indian unrest'. He believed that power in India must be with the People of India. Tilak used the following methods to awaken people.

1. He started newspapers for arousing nationalist feeling among the masses.
2. He organised the Ganpati festival with a view to infuse among youngmen, both religious and patriotic fervour.
3. He started the Shivaji festival in 1895 with a view to inspire the youth of India to follow the example of Shivaji.
4. He organised meetings and gave fiery speeches.
5. He started Home Rule League.
6. He kept up nationalist momentum by advocating signing the Lucknow Pact with Mohammad Ali Jinnah to ally the All India Muslim League with Congress goals.
7. He wrote '*Geeta Rahasya*' while in jail and acted upon the philosophy of action.

(Lala) Lajpat Rai (1865-1928) – (Delhi University 1996)

Popularly known as '*Punjab Kesari*' or '*Sher-e-Punjab*' (Lion of Punjab) for his fearlessness and strength, he owed his patriotic feelings for the motherland to the influence of Arya Samaj. He was an eminent journalist, a prolific writer, a fiery speaker, successful lawyer and a staunch fighter against the British rule. He was arrested several times for his anti-British activities. He spent seven years in Japan, U.K. and U.S.A. in lecturing and mobilising public opinion in favour of India. His work for awakening patriotic sentiment among the people may be summarised as:

1. He participated in several movements. He was one of the trio–Lal-Bal-Pal—all associated with Extremists in the Congress.
2. He started two nationalist papers namely *Bande Mataram* in Urdu and *People* in English.
3. He wrote short biographies of Mazzini, Garibaldi, Shivaji, Sri Krishna and Swami Dayanand etc. to develop the sentiments of patriotism, fearlessness and spiritual consciousness.
4. He wrote books on cultural, economic, educational and political issues to awaken the people regarding the wrongs done by the British to the people of India. Among his important publications are—*The Arya Samaj, Young India, The Political Future of India, England's Debt to India, Unhappy India* and *Problems of National Education in India.*
5. While in U.S.A., during the period 1914 to 1919, he did his best to enlighten the people of America about the miserable conditions in India. He wrote several pamphlets and books on different aspects of India's problems. Some of these books are: '*Young India*'; and *Interpretation and History of the Nationalist Movement from Within*; 'England's *Debt to India*'; '*Political Future of India*' and '*Problems of National Education for India.*
6. He along with several other leaders protested against the withdrawal of

the Non-Cooperation Movement in 1922 and formed the Swaraj Party along with C. R. Das and Motilal Nehru. He entered the Central Legislature as a Swarajist in 1925.

7. In 1920, he was elected to preside over the special session of the Indian National Congress. At first, he was not in favour of Non-Cooperation Movement launched by Gandhiji but later on fell in line with him.
8. He proposed the boycott of Simon Commission in 1928, suffered a 'lathi' blow while agitating against it which proved fatal. At a public meeting the same day he said, " I am not going to associate with the Commission in any shape or manner... Every blow that was hurled at us was a nail in the coffin of the British empire."

Bipin Chandra Pal (1852-1932)

Popularly known as 'the father of revolutionary thought in India,' he along with Lala Lajpat Rai and Bal Gangadhar Tilak, became the 'Lal, Bal, Pal' trio usually associated with Extremists. He carried the message of the *Swadeshi*, the *Boycott* and the *Swaraj* to every nook and corner of India. His paper *New India* became the mouthpiece of resurgent Indian nationalism. His eloquence had no parallel in those days. He was considered as the 'arch-seditionist' in India by the British for which he was jailed. He once wrote, "Indian money is taken away by Feringis (the British), while the people starve for want of money. The Indians should not be afraid of jail and must be ready to go to any jail at any moment shouting only *Vande Mataram*." While in London, B.C. Pal lectured widely condemning the policy of violence and terror let loose by the British in India. He also published a fortnightly called *Swaraj* while in England. About the freedom movement he said, "Freedom is man's birth right. It is inherent in the very making of man, Prince or peasant, Brahman or Pariah, man or woman, Hindu or Mohamedan, Buddhist or Christian, rich or poor, ignorant or learned, we are eternally free...Our faith is in God and because we have this faith, we believe in the success of our Movement namely that of Swaraj."

In the second phase of political struggle, he gradually faded out. He died unsung and unheard. His opposition to Gandhiji's Non-Cooperation Movement (1920-22) and his suggestion about India to be a component of Imperial Federation cost him heavily. He retired from active politics and turned to the study of Vedanat.

Revolutionaries

(Lala) Hardayal (1884-1939)

He inspired the revolutionaries from abroad and especially from San Francisco (US A) and this therefore was very ususual.

Born in Delhi, Hardayal went to England in 1905 as a state scholar for studies at Oxford for his Honours Course in Modern History and Ph.D. from the London University. In London, he came into contact with Indian revolutionaries like. V. D. Savarkar and Madame Cama. He threw away his scholarship and devoted himself whole heartedly to the cause of India's freedom. In 1913, he went to America and founded the Ghadar Party. He was arrested for his fiery speeches and revolutionary activities. He jumped bail to reach Switzerland and then Germany and then to Sweden. In 1927, he returned to America and served as a Professor of Sanskrit at various universities. He died under mysterious circumstances.

The latter half of his life was devoted to writing and lecturing. He wrote the famous book '*Hints for Self Culture*' in which he placed high ideals before the people. His last publication was '*Twelve Religions and Modern Life*'

(Shaheed) Bhagat Singh (1907-31)
(Delhi University 1997)

One of the very few young patriots to face gallows at the age of just 24, he is remembered as '*Shaheed-e-Azam* (Martyr of martyrs).

He belonged to the family of freedom fighters of Banga Village in Lyallpur district of Western Punjab. At the time of his birth, his father Kishen singh and uncle Swarn Singh were in jail for their nationalist activities. His another uncle Ajit Singh was in Mandalay jail.

Once his father, who had a farm took him to his friend Mehta Anand Kishore, also a nationalist. Mehta during his conversation asked him:

What are you doing these days?

"I sow guns and rifles, replied Bhagat Singh in a trimphant note.

"Rifles", exclaimed Mehta with surprise

"Yes, rifles."

"What makes you do that?"

"To make my country free."

"What is your religion, my boy?"

"Patriotism (*'dish bhakti'*)" pat came the reply. (as narrated by M.M. Lal in `*Among the great Indians*' (1997)

A product of D.A.V. School and College Lahore, run by the Arya Samaj, from an early age, he participated in agitations against the British rule.

After the Jallianwala Bagh tragedy, Bhagat Singh went to that place to pay his homage to the departed souls.

Bhagat Singh greatly admired Ghadar hero Kartar Singh Sarbhe who was sent to the gallows in the Lahore Conspiracy Case in 1915 when he was just nineteenth years old. He usually carried his photo with him.

Bhagat Singh used to sing patriotic songs and act as hero in the inspiring plays like' Samrat Chandragupta,' arranged by a dramatic club of the college.

When Bhagat Singh was a B. A.- student, he came to know about his proposed marriage. He is believed to have written two letters to his father. "This is not the time for marriage. The country is calling me. I have taken an oath to serve the nation bodily, mentally and monetarily. (*tan*) *man the than nal*'. When his father again proposed, Bhagat Singh declined again, "You are only caring for '*dadi*' (*grand mother* but I think of '*Bharat Mata*' mother of 33 crore." Further he told his friends, "Death shall be my only bride."

In 1926, at Lahore, Bhagat Singh founded an association called '*Naujawan Bharat* Sabha' and became its secretary. Its aims were based on socialism. Later on in 1928, it was renamed Hindustan Socialist Republic Association.

On November 17, when Lala Lajpat Rai succumbed to the injuries as a result of '*lathi*' blows while leading a procession against the Simon Commission, Bhagat Singh vowed to avenge the death by killing J.A. Scott, the Superintendent of Police who had ordered the '*Lathi*' charge.

On December 17, 1928, Chandra Shekhar Azad, Bhagat Singh and others went to the office of Scott. They mistook an English officer Saunders to be Scott and finished him by firing bullets.

Subsequently Bhagat Singh managed to leave Lahore for Calcutta in the disguise of a '*Sahib*' clean shaven and with a hat, although there was a heavy police force at the railway station.

On April 8, 1928, when Viceroy's proclamation enacting the Public Safety Bill and Trade Dispute Bill, despite the opposition of the majority of the Members of the Central Assembly was to be made at Delhi, Bhagat Singh and B. K. Dutt threw a bomb each on the floor of the Assembly from the Visitors' Gallery. Simultaneously they raised the slogans 'Down with British Imperialism' and '*Inqlab Zindabad*' (Long Live Revolution). They also threw leaflets in the Assembly with a view to acquainting the members and the public with the objects of their mission.

Bhagat Singh and B. K. Dutt did not leave their place in the gallery and got themselvers arrested. They were tried and ultimately they were sentenced to transportation for life on June 12, 1929. They were shifted to Lahore Central Jail and tried in the Saunder's Murder Case, which came to be known as Lahore Conspiracy Case 1929.

In Lahore Jail, Bhagat Singh got the following books from his brother Kulbir.

1. *'Militarism'*, 2. *'Why Men Fight'*, 3. *'Soviets at Work'*, 4. *'Left Wing Communism'*, 5. *'Fields, Factories and Workshops'*, 6. *'Civil War in France'*, 7. *'Land Revolution in Russia and Spy'*, 8. *'Theory of Historical Materialism'* and *'Darling's Peasant in Prosperity and Debt'*

Bhagat Singh and his associates were hanged on March 31, 1931 at 7 p.m. Their dead bodies were taken stealthily to Hussainiwala near Ferozepur on the banks of the Sutlej.

His last poetical outburst expressed in his letter from Central Jail Lahore to his brother Kaltar Singh 20 days before his execution read as under.

Khush raho ahle Watan
Hum to safar Karte hain.'

(Be happy, countrymen, we are off on a journey to the other world).

(Veer) Vinayak Damodar Savarkar - V. D. Savarkar (1883-1966)

Savarkar was the first person to term the Events of 1857 as the 'First War of Indian Independence.'

The revolutionary activities of V. D. Savarkar began with the formation of a secret society, 'Mitra Mela', for the freedom of the country, while he was just 16 years of age. The society later on took the shape of Abhinav Bharat Society (New India Society). He drew inspiration from Tilak and Chaphekar brothers who killed the oppressive British officer Rand, of Nasik. In 1909, he published a pamphlet which contained several inflamatory verses. In one of the poems he said, "Take up the sword and destroy the Government because it is foreign and aggressive." The title of another poem was: '*Who obtained independence without a battle*?' Savarkar went to London where he lectured on the events of 1857 which he called "India's First War of Independence." Under his influence, Madan Lal Dhingra shot dead Sir Curzon Willie in 1909. Sir Willie used to watch the activities of the Indian students in England. Savarkar qualified for the Bar but was not allowed to practise as he refused to give an undertaking that he would not participate in the freedom struggle. He was arrested in England and sent to prison. He was to be deported to India. While being sent by ship to India, Savarkar created history by escaping throught the port hole of the ship and swam in the sea to reach Marsellies, on the French soil. But he was captured and brought to India where the court sentenced him for two consecutive life transportations (50 years transportation) on charges of treason. For 10 years (1911-21) he was in Andaman Jail. For 3 years (1921-24). He was in Yervada, Nasik and Ratnagiri jails in Maharashtra. For 13 years (1924-37) he was not allowed to leave Ratnagiri district where he carried out social reforms. After the removal of restrictions, he was elected the President of the Hindu Mahasabha. Among his several books of poems, philosophy and history, two books *Hindutva* and *India's First War of Independence* deserve special mention.

Leaders of the Last Phase of India's Struggle for Freedom

Mahatma Gandhi (See Chapter 28)

Jawaharlal Nehru (1889 to 1964)

First in Various fields of national awakening and movement. It was under his presidentship that the Indian National Congress passed the *'Purna Swaraj'* (Complete Independence), resolution on the banks of the river Ravi at Lahore on December 31, 1929. It was under his leadership that the Independence Oath was taken for the first time on january 26, 1930. It was he who was invited by Lord Wavell to form the Interim Government. It was he who on August 15, 1947, took over as the first Prime Minister of free India and led the nation to the path of reconstruction. He tried to put India on a dynamic, non-communal, progressive, secular and scientific way of life. He established firmly the foundations of Parliamentary democracy in India.

Usually called the architect of modern India, among the freedom fighters, he comes next only to Gandhiji. Born in a very rich family; educated in England; Left practice and richly life for the sake of India's freedom; Started political career by participatiing in the Non-Cooperation Movement in 1920; courted arrested several times in Satyagraha; Imprisoned many times; Became General Secretary of Indian National Congress (1923-25); Presided over the Lahore Session of the Indian National Congress Session; was chosen the second Satyagrahi in 1940; Moved the Quit India Resolution in 1942; Prime Minister in the Interim Government in 1946 and in the Independent India till his death. His memorable words from his historical speech 'Tryst with Destiny' on August 14, 1947, on the eve of India's independence were, "The service of India means the ending of poverty and ignorance and disease and inequality of opportunity." He was author of distinction; his popular books include *Jawaharlal Nehru; An Autobiography; Glimpses of World History; Letters from Father to His Daughter.*

Maulana Abul Kalam Azad (1888-1958) (Delhi University 1997)

One of the greatest scholars of Muslim culture and finest interpreter of the '*Quran*' and ardent nationalist, Maulana Azad was the President of the Indian Nationalist Congress from 1940 to 1946 and also President earlier in 1923. In his '*Al-Hilal*', an Urdu weekly, he challenged the loyalist attitude towards Britain espoused by the Aligarh Movement among Indian Muslims. He disputed the claim of the Muslim League to represent all Muslims.

During the First World War, he took up the cause of the Muslims abroad. He condemned European imperialism in the strongest terms. He took prominent part in the Khilafat Movement.

In 1921, he was prosecuted for his two objectionable speeches in connection with the Non-Cooperation Movement. His statement in Urdu during his trial is generally known by the name of '*Qual-e-Faisal*' or the 'Final Verdict', He said, "I believe that liberty is the birth right of every nation and individual. No man nor any man-made bureaucracy possess the right of enslaving human beings. It is against the will and canons of God. Therefore I refuse to admit the present Government as a valid authority. He further said, "Allow me to occupy this place (in the court) repeatedly and you may also go on writing your judgement with equal agility. There will be the court of the Lord where Time will act as the Judge; it will pass the judgement and that will be the final judgment".

Maulana Azad actively participated in the Non-Cooperation Movement, Boycott of Simon Commission, Civil Disobedience and the Quit India Movement.

Although he opposed the policies of the Muslim League but he never attacked any of its leaders.

Maulana Azad was an outspoken champion of nationalism and 'progressivism' in all spheres of national life.

He conducted negotiations for independence with Sir Stafford Cripps in 1942, and Lord Wavell and the Cabinet Mission in 1946.

He was passionately opposed to Partition and blamed Congress leaders for it as much as Mohammed Ali Jinnah.

His autobiography '*India Wins Freedom*' is a very valuable source of information for the national struggle.

Subhash Chandra Bose (See INA). Chapter 27. (*Rajasthan University 1997*)

Sardar Vallabhbhai Patel (See Chapter 31). Integration of Princely States.

31

Post Independence Era : India

(1947-1950)

Q. 1. Give an account of the making of Indian Constitution.

(Punjab University, April 1998)

Ans : *A Constitution Making a Challenging Task*

The making of a constitution for a country as big as India was a very difficult and challenging task. There are so many diversities by way of religion, language and culture, All these had to be taken care of. The nation had to be bound together. Due care and concern was to be shown to regional aspirations. Constitution is a fundamental legal document according to which the government of a country functions. It is concerned with two aspects–the relation between different organs of government and between the government and the citizens.

On account of these considerations, the main political party i.e. the Indian National Congress whose leaders were in the forefront of the freedom struggle took special care to ensure that eminent jurists and scholars even not belonging to this party are found place in the Constituent Assembly. Dr. B.R. Ambedkar, a great critic of the Congress as well as Gandhiji was sponsored as a Candidate to the Constituent Assembly and he was duly elected.

The framers of the Indian Constitution studied the constitutions of a number of countries so as to incorporate the salient features in our constitution suiting our aspirations and needs.

It took 2 years, 11 months and 18 days to prepare and pass the constitution. As many as 308 learned scholars worked on it. An expenditure of Rs. 6.4. crores was incurred in the process of constitution making.

Elections to the Constitute Making Body. The constitution was formulated by a Constituent Assembly whose members were elected indirectly in 1946 from the provinces of British India and the Princely States. It had members belonging to different communities and regions. The seats for the members of the Constituent Assembly were fixed in each province and were distributed among the three main categories, Muslims, Sikhs and General, on the basis of million. Members of each community in the Provincial Legislative Assembly elected their representatives by the method of proportionate representation with a single transferrable vote. The total number of members elected from the British Provinces was 292 and from the Princely states it was 93. Thus originally the constituent Assembly had 385 members.

Representative Character of the Constituent Assembly. The Constituent Assembly was a representative body of nearly all communities and regions of India. It included some of the foremost men and women of India who distinguished themselves in various walks of life. The best available legal talent in the country was associated with the framing of the constitution. The Assembly had in it several political leaders who had fought for the freedom of the country, Dr. Rajendera Prasad, Jawaharlal Nehru, Sardar Patel and Maulana Azad were the acknowledged leaders of the Indian National Congress. Competent persons like Dr. Shyama Prasad Mookerjee, Sardar Baladev Singh, Frank Anthony and H.P. Modi were associated with the framing of the constitution even though they were not members of the Indian National Congress. Frank Anthony and H.P. Modi represented the Anglo-Indians and Parsees respectively. Constitutional experts like Alladi Krishnaswamy Ayyar, B.R. Ambedkar and K.M. Munshi were also members of the Constituent Assembly, Mrs. Sarojini Naidu and Mr.s Vijaya Laxmi Pandit deserve special mention.

B.N. Rao, an eminent jurists was the constitutional Adviser.

Functioning of the Constituent Assembly. The first meeting of the constituent Assembly was held in the Central Hall of the Parliament on December 9, 1946. The Muslim League decided to withdraw its members from the Constituent Assembly of India. Thus the number of members was reduced to 299. On December 11, the Constituent Assembly elected Dr. Rajendra Prasad as its President. On 15th December, Jawaharlal Nehru moved his famous 'Objectives Resolution' which declared the Assembly's solemn resolve to make India a Sovereign, Independent, Republic wherein the territories which comprised British India or the Indian States should form a Union wherein the said territories shall possess and retain the status of autonomous units together with residuary powers and exercise all powers and functions of govenment save and except such powers and functions as are vested in or assigned to the Union wherein all power and authority of the independent Sovereign India, its constituent parts are derived from the people and wherein shall be guaranteed and secured to all the people of India justice, social, economic and political, equality of status, of opportunity and before the law, freedom of thought, expression, belief, faith, worship, vocation, association and action subject to law and public authority, wherein adequate safeguards shall be provided for minorities, backward and tribal areas and depressed and other backward classes, and the ancient land makes its full and willing contribution to the promotion of world peace and welfare of makind'.

The task of drafting the constitution was assigned to a committee of 8 members. Dr. B.R. Ambedkar was the Chairman of the Drafting Committee. The Constituent Assembly appointed a large number of committees such as the Union Constitution Committee, the Union Powers Committee and the Committee on Fundamental Rights etc and discussed the reports of these committees thoroughly.

The Drafting Committee studied the constitutions of a number of countries such as Canada, France, Switzerland, U.K. and U.S.A. etc and gathered the best features of these constitutions. The cultural, historical and philosophical traditions of India were also kept in view.

The framers of the constitution took into account the programmes of the Indian National Movement with its drive for economic development, social reform and political independence.

Another strong influence on the framing of the constitution was the British legacy of liberal assumptions and procedural conventions of the Westminister model parliamentary democracy.

The third influence on the constitutional markers was their own experience gained from the functioning of provincial governments and Central Government and also the integration of Princely States with the Indian Union.

By February 1948, the Draft Constitution was ready. It was published in the leading newspapers of the country. Suggestions were invited from all sections of population. The Drafting Committee carefully studied the suggestions received and made necessary changes in the original draft.

On November 4, 1948, the Draft Constitution was presented to the Constituent Assembly. The second reading was completed on October 17, 1949 and the third reading in November 1949.

On November 26, 1949, the constitution was finally signed by the members of the Constituent Assembly and it came into effect, three months later.

There is a special reason for this. It was on January 26 in the year 1929 that at its Lahore Session, the Indian National Congress had adopted the attainment of '*Purna Swaraj*' (Complete Independence) as its final goal. To honour this historic day, it was decided to enforce the constitution with effect from January 26, 1950.

Q. 2. Write a note on the main features of Indian Constitution.

Ans: *Indian Constitution*

General. Indian Constitution finalised and signed by all the member of the Constituent Assembly on November 26, 1949, came into effect on January 26, 1950 - the 20th anniversary of the resolution passed by the Indian National Congress demanding *'Purna Swaraj'* or Complete/Full Independence from the British rule. It contains a Preamble, 395 Articles and 12 Schedules.

Articles, 5,6,7,8 and 9 dealing with 'Citizenship, Article 60 'Oath' or 'Affirmation' by the President', Articles 324 'Elections', 366 'Definitions'; 367

'Interpretations, 392 'Powers of President' and 393 'Short Title' came into force with effect from November 26,1949 and the remaining provisions came into force on January 26, 1950.

Main features of the Constitution

1. *Preamble.* Preamble is an introduction of objectives of the constitution and serves as a 'lighthouse' which throws light on the aspirations and urges of the Indian people. It sets out the ideals that the state should follow. It shows the way how the government is to be run.

Preamble is not a part of the Legal section of the constitution. No one can approach a court and say that the contents of the Preamble have not been enforced by the Government.

The Preamble states

"We, the people of India, having solemnly resolved to constitute India into a SOVEREIGN SOCIALIST SECULAR DEMOCRATIC Republic and to secure to all its citizens:

JUSTICE, social, economic and political;

LIBERTY of thought, expression, belief, faith and worship,

EQUALITY of status and opportunity,

and to promote among them all

FRATERNITY assuring the dignity of the individual and the unity and integrity of the Nation.

IN OUR CONSTITUENT ASSEMBLY this twenty sixth day of November, 1949, do HEREBY ADOPT, ENACT AND GIVE TO OURSELVES THIS CONSTITUTION.

(**Note:** Words SOCIALIST SECULAR integrity were added in 1977).

2. It is a very lengthy and detailed constitution.
3. It sets out appropriate goals.
4. It aims at providing equal opportunities to all the citizens irrespective of sex, caste, colour and religion. It contains 90,000 words and perhaps it is the lengthiest written constitution in the world.
5. It provides suitable safeguards for the uplift of the weaker sections of the society.
6. It vests the supreme power in the people of India.
7. It guarantees certain Fundamental Rights.
8. It includes duties of the citizens.
9. It incorporates Directive Principles of State policy which the State should apply in making laws.
10. It provides for the parliamentary form of Government.
11. It divides responsibilities between the Union and States.
12. It establishes the system of impartial and independent judiciary.
13. It prescribes universal adult franchise.
14. It enjoys every person to profess any religion.
15. It makes untouchability an offence.

B. *Integration and Reorganisation of States*

Q. 3. Discuss the process of the integration of the Indian Princely States and evaluate the role of Sardar Patel in it.

(Rajasthan University, 1994, 1996, 1997)

or

Write a note on integration of Princely States

(Punjab University 1996, 1997, 1998)

or

How was the integration of Princely States brought about by the States Ministry under the leadership of Sardar Patel?

(Punjab University, Oct. 1997)

Ans: *A Rare Feat of Unitying 562 Princely States: Sardar Patel's Splendid Role*

The unique feat of merging the 562 mutually exclusive and fiercely self-regarding, small and big princely states into the wider unity of India goes to Sardar Patel, usually known as the 'Iron Man of India', on account of his 'iron will'. There is no doubt that the Princes also made great sacrifices in discarding several of their centuries old privileges and in fact their separate identities. It was a blood-less revolution accomplished with a great vision and sagacity of Sardar Patel at a time when the armed forces of India were extremely inadequate. In fact this task was unification was the best example of the application of Non-violence technique by a strong man.

In takling the problem of the Indian Princely states, Sardar Patel was helped by Lord Mountbatten and V.P. Menon.

The States Ministry was set up under Patel. An appeal was made to the Indian States to join the Union of India. The result was that a large number of states joined India even before August 15, 1947.

Nehru's role in this task was secondary but nontheless important.

Congress policy of Princely states. In 1938, at the Haripur Session of the Congress, the following resolution was passed, "The *'Purna Swaraj'* or Complete Independence, which is the objective of the Congress, is for the whole of India, inclusive of the states, for the integrity and unity of India must be maintained in freedom".

On June 15, 1947, the All India Congress Committee (AICC) laid down its policy towards the Indian States, "The AICC cannot admit the right of any state in India to declare its independence and to live in isolation from the rest of India. That would be a denial of the course of Indian History and the objectives of the Indian people to-day".

Pt. Nehru concluded his address with the following warning, "I should like to say and other countries to know that we shall not recognise the independence of any state in India, further that recognition of any such independence by any foreign power will be considered an unfriendly act".

Constitutional Position of Princely States in Indian Independence Act (1947). The Indian Independence Act passed on July 18, 1947, by the British Parliament included the following provision as regards Princely States, "The British paramountcy on the Indian States would lapse and these states would be able to join India or Pakistan or to remain independent". Thus the task of uniting India by the integration of more than 560 Princely States was a formidable one. They were at liberty to adopt any course they liked.

Under the British Government, there were two types of units or territories. One was called British India which consisted of 11 provinces and a few Chief Commissioner's Territories. The provinces were under the direct charge of the British Government. The other unit comprised Princely States under the direct charge of the Indian rulers but under the overall charge of the British rulers. The rulers of the Princely States enjoyed several powers and privileges and were very loyal to the British rulers.

The Indian National Congress was active in the provinces only. In the states there was some notional activity under the auspicious of the All India States People's Conference.

Incentives to Princely States to Join India. Sardar Patel, while seeking the willing consent of the Princes, provided for the arrangement whereby the Government of India agreed to guarantee the Princes (Maharajas), tax free pensions which sometime ran into lakhs of rupees. They were allowed to retain their ownership of jewellery, properties, land shares and securities. The Nizam of Hyderabad got a tax free pension of Rs. 50 lakhs and also income from his Jagirs. The Nawab of Bhopal was given a tax-free privy purse of Rs. 11 lakhs and his properties. These are some of the examples.

At the time of accession to the Indian Union, 284 of he Princes were qualified to receive privy purses, These were abolished after the Derecognition of Indian Proclamation introduced by Indira Gandhi Government in 1971.

Process of Integration of Princely States. It revolved around three steps:

First, merger of the smallest/Princely States into the neighbouring Princely States or Provinces.

Second, consolidation of Princely States into Centrally Administered areas.

Third, formation of the Princely States' Union.

According to the Merger Instrument/Agreement, the ruling Princely States surrendered to the Indian Dominion Govenment "full and exclusive authority, jurisdiction and power for and in relation to 'governance" of their states and agreed to transfer their administration January 1, 1948.

Junagarh was ruled by a Muslim Nawab but it was predominantly (80 percent) inhabited by the Hindus. His intentions were not clear. A Muslim League politician of Karachi was appointed as the Dewan of the State and the Nawab came under the influence of the Muslim League. The Nawab let loose a reign of terror on the Hindu population which revolted. Law and order situation in the state collapsed. The Congress leaders of the state established a provisional Government. Indian troops were sent to control the situation. Finding no help coming from Pakistan, the Nawab ran away to Pakistan with his family members and the jewellery etc. As soon as normal conditions were restored, the Government of India arranged a referendum of the people of Junagarh with regard to the question of accession. Out of about 2 lakh voters, only 90 voters voted for Pakistan. In this way, Junagarh acceded to India.

The Nawab was reluctant to join the Indian Union. The state had no geographical continuity with Pakistan. Parts of the states which had acceded to India were interspersed with Junagarh territory and access to them was possible only through Junagarh.

Hyderabad occupied a pivotal position. The Hindus formed more than 80 percent of the population. The Nizam of Hyderabad declared that he would be completely independent sovereign ruler. The activities of Razakars - a semi military force organised by Kasim Rizvi posed a great threat to the Hindus as well as on the people of neighbouring states having common border with Junagarh. Kasim Rizvi urged the Muslims of Hyderabad not to sheathe their swords until their objective of Islamic supremacy was achieved. The Hindus were subjected to all kinds of brutalities. Appeals from Indian leaders fell on deaf ears. As there was no alternative, the police action against the state started on Sept, 13, 1948 and within three days, the Nizam surrendered and Hyderabad acceded to India.

Jammu and Kashmir State did not initially join either India or Pakistan but the all out invasion of the Muslim raiders from outside the state, which also inlcuded the soldiers of Pakistan Army on leave, created such a critical situation for the state that the Maharaja of Jammu and Kashmir acceded to India.

Merits of Integration of Princely States

Complete Change in Political Map of India. As a result of the efforts of Sardar Patel, the political map of India was completely changed. Of the 562 states, 216 were merged in the provinces, 312 were consolidated into 6 unions, 5 were put directly under the Centre as Chief Commissioner's provinces, 21 Punjab Hill states formed the Himachal Pradesh and 2 states were made into separate provinces.

Loss of India made up by merger of States.- It is rightly pointed out that as a result of partition in 1947, India had lost 3.6 lakh square miles of territory with a population of 81.5 million. By the integration of states, India acquired 5 lakhs square miles of territory with a population of 81.5 million. By the integration of States, India acquired 5 lakhs square miles of territory with a population of 86.5 millions.

India saved from Balkanisation. Michal Brecher pointed out that integration of the states was 'Patel's master achievement'.

Geoffvery Tyson in his book on Nehru has very aptly described the significance of Patel's work, "If the integration of several hundred princely

states had not been carried out with a skilled and sure hand by the late Sardar Patel, the Sub-continent might easily have suffered divisions into a third major segment in which the smaller princely states would have grouped themselves round the more powerful rulers in independent blocks with resultant 'balkanisation' of a large part of land".

The Indian rulers at that time were capable of doing a lot of mischief. The lead was given by Hyderabad and Bhopal. Indore made no secret of its intentions to follow Bhopal. There were reports of joint action by the two states to create an 'independent pocket' in the heart of the Indian Union and enter into a treaty with Pakistan. The forces at disposal of Indian Union were inadequate. Hence the policy followed by Sardar Patel was the only policy practicable at the moment. As regards Privi Purses, these were abolished by the Government of India after amending the constitution.

Mahatma Gandhi wrote, "The taks of dealing with the princes was truly formidable, but I am convinced that Sardar was the only man who could have coped with it."

Q. 5. Write a note on Reorganisation of States.

(Rajasthan University 1995)

Ans: *Reorganisation of States*

Sriramula Polli's (1901-1952) name will be ever remain associated with the issue of reorganisation of States. His 58 day fast to death undertaken for the cause of separae Telugu speaking state (Andhra) to be separated from the State of Madras was the starting point for the reorganisation of states. After the integration of Princely states, there had emerged a growing demand for the re-demarcation of the boundaries of the states.

In 1953, the Government of India appointed the States Reorganisation Commission to explore the feasibility of giving the linguistic factor an important consideration in demarcating state boundaries. The Commission included 4 members. S. Fazal Ali (Chairman), H.N. Kunjru, K.M. Panikkar and P.C. Chaudhri.

The Commission observed that "It is neither possible nor desirable to recorganise states on the basis of a single test of either language or culture, a balanced approach, which takes all relevant factors into account is necessary.

The report of the S.R.C. was followed by a States Reorganisation Act in 1956.

Following new states were created on November 1, 1956

(1) Andhra Pradesh (2) Haryana (3) Madhya Pradesh (4) Rajasthan (5) Tamil Nadu

The process of reorganisation of states continued and Delhi was the last state in the series. It was declared a state in 1994 (with restricted powers).

32

Indian Society : Immediate Problems Facing Free India, Foreign Policy

Q. 1. Describe the main features of the traditional Indian Society and its impact on Modern Indian Society.

Ans. Traditional Indian Society and Its Impact Upon Modern Indian Society.

Caste system and joint family system were the two characteristics of the traditional Indian society. Caste system became very rigid during the course of time. Our leaders realised the harmful influences of the caste system. Since independence many measures have been taken to do away with caste distinctions. Our Constitution guarantees equality of opportunity. Article 15 provides that the state shall not discriminate against any citizen on grounds of caste or creed. It states that every citizen has right to use public wells, tanks, bathing ghats, hostels, restaurants, cinema houses etc. Articles 16 provides that no citizen should be prohibited to have access to places of worship on grounds of caste and creed. Article 17 abolishes the practice of untouchability.

A number of social reformers have worked against this social evil during the last two centuries. Raja Rammohan Roy (1772-1833) who founded the 'Brahmo Samaj' was the first to have raised his voice against caste system. Later Swami Dayanand (1824-1883), the founder of the Arya Samaj preached against social distinctions based on caste. Gandhiji (1869-1948) launched a mass campaign against untouchability. To him the so-called untouchables were '*Harijans*' (sons of God). '*Bhangi Colony*' (the colony where mostly sweepers resided) was his favourite place for stay in New Delhi.

In order to bring at par with the other sections of the Indian society, the Scheduled Castes and Scheduled Tribes are granted various concessions.

In spite of all these measures the economic and social status of the lower castes, in general, still remains far from satisfactory. Old customs die hard. Vigorous efforts are needed in this direction to mould public opinion. In this context we may remember that social evils cannot be abolished by legislation alone.

Joint Family System. Joint Family system is another characteristic of the traditional Indian society. It was a necessity when the wants of the people were very few as compared with the modern society. Agriculture was the main occupation. Besides it was done with traditional simple implements. It was not mechanised. With the introduction of modern techniques of farming and other occupations, there has come about a great change in the concept of joint family system. Many new occupations have emerged. The processes of industrialisation and urbanisation have affected the traditional joint family system. Joint family system has both merits as well as demerits.

Social Stratification and Mobility

Indian society may be broadly divided into three social classes. These are upper class, middle class and lower class. The middle class may be further divided into three sub-classes—upper middle class, middle class and lower middle class. The lower class people constitute about 70 per cent of the total population. They are mostly agricultural and industrial labourers, low paid employees and daily wage earners.

Class stratification and casteism are still observed in the rural areas to a considerable extent.

Mobility from one occupation to another has been gradually becoming common.

Main Features of the Indian Society as Envisaged in the Constitution.

1. Indian society to be based on democratic values.
2. Indian society to be based on socialist values.
3. Indian society to be based on equality of status and opportunity.
4. Indian society to be based on egalitarianism.
5. Indian society to be based on justice.
6. Indian society to be based on liberty of thought, expression, belief, faith and worship.
7. Indian society to be based on fraternity assuring the dignity of the individual and unity and integrity of the Nation.

Q. 2. What is the meaning of social goals? Give in brief the provisions in the constitution for achieving these goals.

Ans. MEANING OF SOCIAL GOALS

Social goals imply that Indian state should work for a society which is based on social equality and social justice. There should be no discrimination on the basis of caste, colour, creed and sex. Worth and birth should determine the merits. The deprived classes which have suffered for centuries should be provided all possible opportunities for their upliftment. The social status of the women should be raised. Without the achievement of social goals, Indian state cannot become a Socialist Secular Democratic State.

CONSTITUTIONAL PROVISIONS FOR THE ACHIEVEMENT OF SOCIAL GOALS

There are several provisions in the Constitution of India for the realisation of the social goals mentioned above. A brief account of these provisions is given here.

The Preamble of the Constitution

It '*interalia*' mentions Social Justice and Equality of Status and Opportunity. It also refers to secularism, socialism and democracy which have several social implications.

Fundamental Rights

Article 14, 15 and 16 guarantee equality before law, prohibition of discrimination and equality of opportunity in matters of public employment.

Abolition of Untouchability

Article 17 abolishes untouchability in any form. It is declared an offence punishable under law.

Right to Education

Article 21 A. It provides right to free and compulsory education to all children of the age of six to twelve years.

Directive Principles of State Policy

Article 38. State to secure a social order for the promotion of welfare of the people.

The State to strive to minimise the inequalities in income and endeavour to eliminate inequalities in status.

Article 39. (a) Citizen's right to adequate means of livelihood.

(b) Equal pay for equal work.

Article 39 A. Equal justice and free legal aid.

Article 41. Provision for just and humane conditions of work and maternity relief.

Article 43. Living wage etc. for workers.

Article 45. Provision of early childhood care and education.

Article 46. Promotion of educational and economic interests of Scheduled Castes, Scheduled Tribes and other weaker sections.

Q. 3. Explain the problems faced by India in the wake of India's independence.

Ans. Immediate problems Faced by India in the wake of its Independence

Immediate problems facing India on its becoming Independent were as under :

1. Rehabilitation of the displaced persons.
2. Integration of Princely States. (Already explained).
3. Framing the constitution of India. (Already explained).
4. Liberation of Indian Territories Under France and Portugal.
5. Planning for the reconstruction of the economy of the country. (see next chapter).
6. Formulation of the Foreign Policy.

Rehabilitation of Displaced Persons

With the partition of the provinces of Punjab and Bengal at the time of independence of India in 1947, India was faced with the unprecedented influx of displaced persons particularly from Punjab. Large scale killing had taken place. By November 1947, about 8 million displaced persons had come to India.

The rehabilitation of the displaced Hindus and Sikhs posed a serious challenge to the government as vast majority of them had come to India almost penniless. They had left behind their life-long earnings and belongings.

The Central Government of India, the Punjab Government and the people of India showed great concern and made strenuous efforts to heal their wounds.

Following were the important measures that proved very helpful in the speedy rehabilitation of the displaced persons who were initially termed as **'refugees'.**

1. Relief camps were set up at different places.
2. Food and lodging were provided free of cost.
3. Rehabilitation Ministry was set up at the Centre to look after the problems of the displaced persons including exchange of properties with those who migrated from India.
4. Several new cities were set up for rehabilitating the displaced persons.
5. Special colonies in big cities were built for the displaced persons.
6. Houses/lands were provided at cheap rates to the displaced persons.
7. Reservations in services were made for them.
8. Educational facilities like fee concessions were provided to their children.
9. Double shift system of schooling was introduced in some big cities like Delhi.
10. Loans were provided to them.
11. Compensation in the form of land, houses and cash were given in lieu of their assets left behind in case exchanges did not materialise.

Fortunately, the problem was solved in a comparatively short period and in a very satisfactory manner.

Above all, it may be emphasised that the displaced persons themselves showed courage, enterprise and patience of a very high order.

Merger of Areas Under the Domination of France and Portugal

Apart from Princely States, there were small territories owned by the French and Portuguese imperialists. The French had five territories—Chandernagar, Pondicherry, Karaikal, Yanam and Mahe. By 1954, all these colonies became an integral part of India. Portugal had five colonies namely Goa, Daman, Diu, Dadra and Nagar Haveli. Dadra and Nagar Haveli were liberated on August 2, 1954. Goa was liberated on December 19, 1961 when an armed expedition defeated the Portuguese army in Goa. Daman and Diu were simultaneously liberated.

The struggle for independence of Goa goes back to the year 1928 when Triston Braganza Kunha, the 'Father of the Independence of Goa' established the Goa Congress Committee with the specific aim of liberating Goa and integrating it with India. Meetings and demonstrations were banned in Goa in 1943. Braganza Kunha and several other leaders were arrested and some sent to Portugal and some to Portugal's African colonies. Duttatrey Deshpande was released only after India became free. Braganza Kunha was released from jail but not allowed to enter Goa. In 1953, he escaped from Portugal, returned to Goa and built up the Goa Action Committee. A section of the Goa Congress took to arms for the freedom struggle and came to be known as Azad Gomantak Party. In 1954, Dadra and Nagar-Haveli were liberated. The Portuguese resorted to terrible repression. Several people were killed during the armed struggle. Hundreds were arrested. In 1955, a non-violent Satyagraha movement was launched. Satyagrahis went to Goa from different parts of India. The Portuguese ruthlessly killed many of them with bullets. On December 19, 1961, an Indian army operation known as '*Operation Vijay*', under the command of Lt. General Jayanta Chowdhury began and within 26 hours, the Portuguese army surrendered unconditionally and the Indian National Flag flew all-over Goa, Daman and Diu.

Q. 4. Explain the meaning and importance of foreign policy. State the determinants of India's foreign policy after it became independent.

Ans. Meaning and Significance of Foreign Policy.

MEANING OF FOREIGN POLICY

The way we think about and act in our relations with foreign countries represent our foreign policy. It implies the principles, interests and objectives which a country formulates and conducts its relations with other countries for the maintenance of proper relations and participation in international cultural, economic and political relations.

Following are the important definitions of the foreign policy.

According to Padelford and Lincoln, "Foreign policy is the key element in the process by which a state translates its broadly conceived goals and interests into concrete courses of action to attain these objectives and preserve its interests."

In the words of Ruthaswany, "The foreign policy now is the bundle of principles and practices that regulate the intercourse of a State with other States."

George Modelski defines foreign policy as, "The system of activities evolved by communities for changing the behaviour of other States and for adjusting their own activities to the international environment."

According to A.H. Doctor, "Managing one's relations with other States is a necessary activity of every State. This activity may generally be called the framing of foreign policy."

Significance of Foreign Policy

Prof. Rajni Kothari, a great thinker and scholar has described the importance of the foreign policy of a country in these words, "Any discussion of the performance of a political system must sooner or later come to grips with the fact that it forms part of a large world setting with which it interacts almost continuously."

Foreign policy of a country is largely concerned with the promotion of its own interests while conducting relationships with other countries.

Determinants of India's Foreign Policy

Internal/Domestic Factors	External Factors
1. Self Defence.	1. International Peace and Understanding.
2. Age old Ideological Roots.	2. India's Role in International Affairs.
3. Geographical Factors.	3. Rise of Third World Countries.
4. Economic Development Factors.	4. India's Attitude to Freedom Movements.
5. Exchange of Cultural Elements.	5. Power Politics of Super Powers.
6. Interests of Indians Abroad.	6. Race for Armaments or Disarmaments.
7. Constitutional Obligations.	7. International Organisations.
8. Personal factors/Charismatic Leadership.	8. International Economic Order.
	9. Globalisation
	(Last two elements did not figure in 1950's).

Basic Parameters of India's Foreign Policy

Jawaharlal Nehru, the undisputed maker of India's foreign policy enunciated the basic parameters of India's foreign policy in September 1946 : "We propose, as far as possible, to keep away from the power politics of groups aligned against one another, which have led in the past two World Wars and which may even lead to distress on an even vaster scale. We believe that peace and freedom are indivisible and the denial of freedom anywhere must endanger freedom elsewhere and lead to conflict and war. We are particularly interested in the emancipation of colonial and dependent countries and peoples are in the recognition in theory and practice of equal opportunities for all races. We seek no domination over others and we claim no privileged position over other peoples."

Principle of Freedom and Sovereignty.

India believes that every country has the right to safeguard its sovereignty and has the freedom to pursue its own path which should not be interfered with by any country or any international organisation.

PANCHSHEEL

Meaning : Panchsheel or the Five Principles which were enunciated by Pt. Jawaharlal Nehru, the first Prime Minister of India, were incorporated in the Preamble to an agreement arrived at between India and China on June 28, 1954 at New Delhi. The agreement was signed by Nehru, the Prime Minister of India and Chau-En-Lai (1898-1976), the Prime Minister of China.

The Five Principles are :

1. Mutual respect for territorial integrity and sovereignty.
2. Non-aggression.
3. Non-interference in each other's internal affairs.
4. Equality and mutual benefit.
5. Peaceful co-existence.

Why Panchsheel : After the Second World War, there developed an environment of Cold War among big powers of the world. It was feared that mutual conflicts among the nations of the world and especially among the two powers blocs, might disturb the world peace and that there was an urgent need to take some positive steps to ease the situation.

Secondly, the newly freed countries had embarked upon the process of building up a viable political and socio-economic system on the basis of the ideals and values they had cherished before their independence.

Historical Background of Panchsheel : More that 2500 years ago, Gautam Buddha laid emphasis on five principles. Ashoka the Great got them engraved on the rock edicts, spread over different parts of the world. These were tolerance (*Bahu-Sruta*), harmony (*Samavya*), sharing with all (*Samvibhaga*), purity of relationships (*Dharam Sambandha*), and gentleness (*Mardavam*). The United Nations Charter had also provided for settling mutual disputes through mutual consultation.

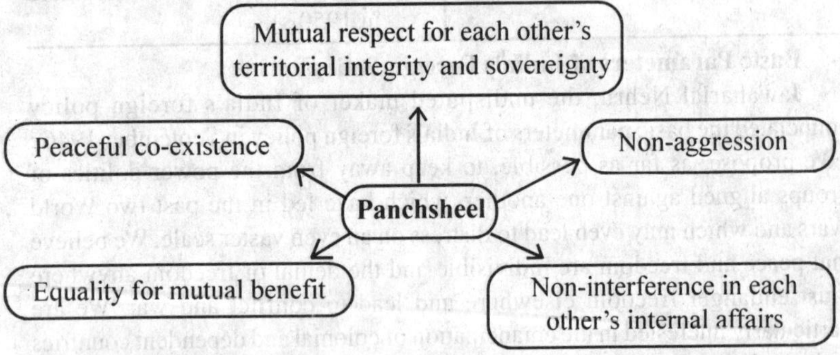

Disregard of Panchsheel by China : It was very unfortunate that China, a signatory to the agreement, violated these principles in 1959 when it attacked Tibet and unleashed a reign of terror. Dalai Lama, the spiritual head of Tibet fled to India and established Government in exile at Dharamshala in Himachal Pradesh. The greatest shock to India came in October 1962 when China carried out an aggression on India in flagrant violation of the Panchsheel. The sweet slogan of '*Hindi Chini Bhai Bhai*' coined by the Indian people at the time of the agreement in 1954 received a great jolt.

Nevertheless, India has always been guided by these Five Principles in matters relating to its foreign policy.

Later on, policy of Non-Alignment also emerged.

33

Empowerment of Women

Q. 1. State the position of women in ancient India and medieval India.

Ans. High Status and Widespread Education of Women in Ancient India.

People in ancient India fully realized that women play a prominent role in the cultural, economic, political life of a country. Accordingly they accorded a reasonably high status to them. More than 400 verses in the Vedas are ascribed to 24 women seers. In the Vedas, women have been called '*Updeshtri*' of 'knowledge. Women worked as teachers during this period.

Here a few quotes from the Vedas and other ancient literature are given which bring out the factual position of the status and education of women in earlier times in our country.

Just as boys acquire sound knowledge and education by the practice of '*Brahmacharya*' and then marry girls of their own, who are young, well educated, loving and of nice temperament, so should a girl practise '*Brahmacharya*', study the Vedas and other sciences and thereby perfect her knowledge, refine her character, give her hand to a man of her own choice, who is young, learned and loving. (*Atharva Veda,* XI.16.3.18).

In the battlefield, in the absence of the king, the queen should take command of forces and should inspire them. (*Rig Veda,* X.159.2).

O Learned Lady ! All life is dependent upon you because you impart education to all. (*Rig Veda*, 2, 49.17).

From the point of view of reverence due, a teacher is ten-fold superior to a mere lecturer, a father a hundred fold to teacher, and a mother a thousand fold to father. *Vashisht Dharmsutra* (13.480).

Where women are respected, there the gods delight, and where they are not, works and efforts come to naught, there is no hope of rise for that family or country where they live in sadness. (*Manusmriti*).

What can the fire not burn!
What cannot merge into the ocean!
What can the weaker section not achieve!

And what can escape death! (*Ramcharitmanas, Ayodhyakand*)

Position of women during the Medieval Period

Society as a whole became somewhat prejudiced against females.The '*purdah*' system prevailed. Infanticide gained recognition. Education of women was neglected.

Q. 2. State the Social evils that have adversely affected the status of women in India. What steps were taken to promote their welfare and states during the British rule?

Ans. Social Evils Affecting the States of Women

A very paradoxical situation regarding the states of women has existed in India. Traditionally she was been hailed as **'Lakshmi'** (Gooddess of Wealth) **'Saraswati'** (Goddess of Knowledge) and **'Shakti'** (Gooddess of Power). On the other hand, she has suffered from several social ills. Here we refer to the following :

1. **'Sati Pratha'** (Practice of **'Sati'**).
2. Infanticide.
3. Widowhood and Denial of Marriage.
4. Child Marriage.
5. Lack of Education.
6. Denial of Property Rights.

Ban on Sati

'Sati' is the traditional Hindu practice of a widow on immolating herself on her husband's funeral. **'Sati'** thus implied a virtuous woman. A woman who died burning herself on her husband's funeral fire was believed to directly go to heaven. Such a woman was worshipped as a goddess and temples were built in her memory. The opponents of **'Sati'** termed it as suicide. The enlightened opinion considered it as a barbarian and inhuman practice. Governor General Warren Hastings (1772-85) and Cornwallis (1786-93) took some steps to restrict the practice of 'Sati'. However these steps proved ineffective. Indian social reformers led by Raja Rammohan Roy launched frontal attack on this evil. William Bentinck (1828-35) took several steps in social reforms. In December 1829, the practice of **'Sati'** was banned by him.

Infanticide Declared Illegal

Infanticide means killing the infant daughter at birth. It is said that it was particularly common among the Bengalis and the Rajputs. Females were considered as an economic burden. Moreover it was considered a social disgrace in case the parents could not arrange for their daughters. Dowry put a heavy burden on them. Enlightened Indian as well as British opinion condemned this price. In 1795, infanticide was declared to be a murder by Bengal Regulation Act XXI.

Widow Remarriage Legalised

The widows in the society led a very miserable life. Several social reformers started the movement for the remarriage of Hindu widows. Pandit Ishwar Chandra Vidyasagar (1820-91), Principal Sanskrit College, Calcutta spearheaded the movement. He quoted Sanskrit references to prove that Vedic texts sanctioned widow remarriage. In 1856, the Hindu Widow's Remarriage Act was passed which legalised marriage of widows.

Native Marriage Act (1872)

In 1872, the Native Marriage Act popularly known as Civil Marriage Act was passed. The marriage of girls below the age of 14 and boys below 18 years was prohibited. However this Act was not applicable to the Hindus, Muslims and other recognised faiths. The Sharda Act (1930) further raised the marriage age of boys to 18 and girls to 14. This removed the earlier anomaly.

An improvement was made by the Child Marriage Restraints Amendment Act, 1978 which raised the marriage age of girls from 15 to 18 and of boys from 18 to 21.

WOMEN EDUCATION

Touched by the work of missionaries in the field of education, several great Indians lent their support to the cause of female education. Among them, Raja Rammohan Roy, Pandit Ishwarchandra Vidyasagar and Swami Dayananda played a prominent role.

Swami Vivekananda has emphasised, "If you do not raise the women, who are living embodiment of the divine mother, don't think that you have any other way to rise."

Gandhiji stated the importance of women education in these words, "I am strongly of the opinion that women should have the same facilities as men and even special facilities where necessary."

Jawaharlal Nehru very rightly observed, "Education of a boy is the education of one person, but education of a girl is the education of entire family."

In view of the importance of women education in national development, the University Education Commission 1948-49 remarked, "There can't be any educated people without education of women. If general education had to be limited to men or to women, then opportunity should be given to women, from them it would more surely be passed to the next generation."

Similarly, the Kothari Commission 1964-66, stated, "For full development of human resources, the improvement of human beings and for moulding the character of children during the most impressionable years of infancy, the education of women is of great importance than that of men."

WOMEN'S WELFARE : SOME MILESTONES DURING BRITISH RULE

S.No.	*Year*	*Act/Effort*	*Details*
1.	1815	Women's Education	The Amitya Sabha, founded by Raja Rammohun Roy, emphasised the importance of education of women.
2.	1815	Attack on 'Sati System'	The noted social reformer Raja Rammohun Roy (1774-1833) wrote the first book in Bengali in which he attacked Sati – the practice of burning widows on the funeral pyres of their husbands.
3.	1829	Sati Abolition Act	William Bentinck, the Governor-General of India passed the Sati Abolition Act.
4.	1956	Widow Remarriage Act	Widows were allowed to remarry.
5.	1872	Civil Marriage Act	Some changes were introduced in marriage rules.
6.	1917	Franchise for women	A delegation of women met the Secretary of state for India and pleaded for franchise for women.
7.	1927	Women's Conference	All India Women's Conference was set up.
8.	1928	Sharda Act	It raised the marriage age of boys and girls.

Q. 3. State the provisions of the Constitution of India relating to equal status and empowerment of women.

Ans. Constitutional Provisions Relating to Equal Status and Empowerment of Women.

Apart from the Preamble of the Constitution, there are several provisions in PART III Fundamental Rights, PART IV Directive Principles of State Policy and PART X Elections which enjoin upon the State to provide equality to women.

Part III - Fundamental Rights

Article 15 : Prohibition of discrimination on grounds of religion, race, caste, sex or place of birth.

1. The State shall not discriminate against any citizen on grounds only of religion, race, caste, sex, place of birth or any of them.
2. No citizen shall, on grounds only of religion, race, caste, sex, place of birth or any of them, be subject to any disability, liability, restriction or condition with regard to –

(*a*) Access to shops, public restaurants, hotels and places of public entertainment; or

(*b*) The use of wells, tanks, bathing ghats, roads and places of public resort maintained wholly or partly out of state funds or dedicated to the use of the general public.

3. Nothing in this article shall prevent the state from making any special provision for women and children.

Article 16 : Equality of opportunity in matters of public employment.

(2) No citizen shall, on grounds only of religion, race, caste, sex, descent, place of birth, residence or any of them, be ineligible for, or discriminated against in respect of, any employment or office under the State.

Right against Exploitation

Article 23 : Prohibition of traffic in human beings and forced labour.

(1) Traffic in human beings and begar and other similar forms of forced labour are prohibited and any contravention of this provision shall be an offence punishable in accordance with law.

Part IV - Directive Principles of State Policy

Article 39 : Certain principles of policy to be followed by the State.

The State shall, in particular, direct its policy towards securing :

(*a*) That the citizens, men and women equally, have the right to an adequate means of livelihood;

(*b*) That there is equal pay for equal work for both men and women;

(*c*) That health and strength of workers, men and women, and the tender age children are not abused and that citizens are not forced by economic necessity to enter avocations unsuited to their age or strength.

Article 42 : Provision for just and humane conditions of work and maternity relief.

The state shall make provision for securing just and humane conditions for work and maternity relief.

Article 44 : Union civil code for citizens.

The State shall endeavour to secure for all citizens a uniform civil code throughout the territory of India.

Part XV - Elections

Article 325 : No person to be ineligible for inclusion in, or to claim to be included in a special, electoral roll on grounds of religion, race, caste or sex.

There shall be one general electoral roll for every territorial constituency for election to either House of Parliament or to the either House of the Legislature of State and no person shall be ineligible for inclusion in any such roll or claim to be included in any special electoral roll for any such constituency on grounds only of religion, race, caste, sex or any of them.

34
Reconstruction of Indian Economy
(Harmful Impact of de-industrialisation and Commercialisation of agriculture Under British Rule)

Q. 1. What were the causes of decline of cottage industries in India during the British rule? State its impact.

Ans. The British policy of Discrimination.

It led to the near destruction of Indian handicrafts. Prior to the coming of the British, India exported large quantities of cotton textiles, silks and muslins, metalwares, ivory, glass, jewellery, sandalwood, etc. Large quantities of the goods were also used by wealthy Nawabs, Rajas, Nobles, etc. But the British Government, with a view to discouraging the use of Indian goods by the British people, banned the import of Dacca muslin in 1720. Indian handicrafts were starved as there were not enough of Indian buyers, since the place of nobles, who loved to patronize industries, was taken over by the British civil servants who were indifferent to Indian interests. With the Industrial Revolution in England, large quantities of British machine-made goods flooded the Indian markets and the local manufacturers could not complete with them either in price or in the durability of goods.

Important Causes of the Decline of Cottage Industries.

Among the important causes, following may be mentioned:

(1) *High handedness of the British Rulers :* After the battles of Plassey and Buxar, the English turned trade into plunder. They committed all sorts of atrocities on the craftsmen. They even went to the extent of cutting off their thumbs if they refused to work for the Company.

(2) *Lack of Patronage of Indian Rulers :* As state after state fell into the British hands, the rulers were no longer in a position to extend patronage to the artistic and rare products of the Indian handicrafts industry.

(3) *Policy of Free Trade in India and its Reverse in England :* With a view to encourage the sale of British made goods in India, all restrictions on their

import to India were revoked. On the contrary, Indian goods were subjected to various duties when exported to England.

(4) *Cheaper Goods :* Cost of production of goods with the help of new machines was considerably low in England, with the result that handmade goods of Indian craftsmen could no longer compete with them.

(5) *Speedy Means of Transport :* The railways enabled British manufactures to reach the remotest villages of the country and uproot Indian products.

(6) *Neglect of Industrial Development in India :* The tragedy of the artisans and craftsmen in India was heightened by the neglect of modern industries in India. Thus, the ruined artisans and craftsmen had little opportunities to find alternative employment.

(7) *Loss of Raw Materials :* As the Industrial Revolution in England progressed, there was scramble for India's materials. Thus the artisans not only lost patronage but also raw materials.

On the one hand, the Indian artisans were deprived of the home as well as European markets, on the other the English manufacturers, industrialists and traders enjoyed the monopoly of supplying civil and military requirements to the Government of India. The Indian articles languished in comparison.

Impact of the Decline of Cottage Industries

1. Craftsmen became unemployed.
2. Craftsmen faced financial hardships.
3. Agricultural sector became overburdened.
4. Indian industries remained backward.
5. People became poor.
6. The drain of wealth from India occurred.
7. Famines became widespread.

Q. 2. Explain the meaning of de-industrialisation of India. What were its causes?

Ans. **See chapter 21.**

Q. 3. Explain the meaning of commercialization of Indian agriculture. What factors were responsible for it? State its compact on Indian economy.

Ans. Meaning of commercialization of Indian Agriculture.

Commercialization of Indian agriculture implies production of agricultural commodities for business purposes. The process of commercialization of agriculture in India emerged in the latter half of the 19th century. Hitherto agriculture in India had been a way of life rather than a business enterprise. Certain special crops began to be grown for sale in the internal and external markets of India. The consumption element receded to the background. Commercial crops like cotton, groundnut, jute, oilseeds, sugarcane and tobacco, etc. became more remunerative than foodgrains.

Likewise the cultivation of crops of condiments, and spices became popular. Fruit and vegetables also began to be grown on a large scale. The highest level of commercialisation process was visible in the development of plantations, *i.e.*, coffee, rubber and tea, etc.

Factors which Encouraged Commercialization.

Among the important factors of commercialization, the following factors deserve special mention :

1. Spread of money economy.
2. The emergence of wide market on account of expansion of rail and road transport.
3. Entry of the British capital in India.
4. Growth of internal and external trade.

Impact of Commercialization of Indian Agriculture.

1. It was alien to Indian tradition of farming.
2. Less quantity of foodgrains became available and it led to scarcities resulting in famines and malnutrition.
3. Profit motive became more predominant.
4. The Indian peasant became more dependent on the money-lender.
5. Commercialization of agriculture became a forced process.
6. For meeting the high revenue demand of the government and high rates of interest charged by the money-lenders, the cultivators were forced to divert a part of the harvest into the market and sell it at whatever price it could fetch. A large number of poor cultivators had to buy back after a few months, part of the crop they had sold away at lower prices at the time of harvest.
7. Agriculture began to be influenced by widely fluctuating prices in the world.
8. The slump prices in the 1870's hit the cultivators very hard. Agrarian riots and famines took place in the Deccan.

The situation created by the phenomena of commercialization of agriculture led to a agricultural stagnation during the period 1890-1947.

Q. 3. What was the need for the reconstruction of Indian economy in independent India?

Ans. Indian Economy in 1997 and The Need for Its Reconstruction.

The economic policy of the British rule in India was subservient to their larger interest. Jawaharlal Nehru in this regard observed. "British and Indian economic interests conflicted all along the line."

He had further observed in 1946, "Nearly all over problems today have grown up during British rule and as a direct result of British policy the prices, the minority problem, various vested interests, foreign and Indian, the lack of industry and the neglect of agriculture, the extreme backwardness in the social services and above all, the tragic poverty of the people."

Now when India was free it got the opportunity to change the trend.

The partition of the country had all the more adverse effect on Indian economy as is evident from the following.

1. India received 77 per cent of geographical area but 82 percent of the population.
2. Partition created a serious problem of shortage of raw material for jute mills of Calcutta and textile mills of Bombay and Ahmedabad. As a result of partition all the 112 jute mills remained with India while 75 percent jute growing area went to Pakistan. This created the problem of raw material for Indian mills.
3. The problem of raw material was also faced by paper mills, leather industry and some chemical industries.
4. The provinces of West Punjab and Sind were known as foodgranaries of India. As a result of partition, these areas went to Pakistan. India was faced with the problem of food shortage.
5. 68% of irrigated land of undivided India went to Pakistan.
6. The communial disturbances, riots and mass migration of people caused severe loss of property worth crores. Large number of people became homeless and unemployed. This had an adverse impact on country's economy.

With a view to reconstruct its economy, India adopted the process of planning.

Q. 4. What is the meaning of economic planning? State its significance. Give the objectives of planning in India.

Ans. Meaning of Economic Planning in Operational Terms.

In operational terms, planning includes determination of 'what', 'where', 'who', 'why' and 'when' to develop direct and implement programmes for the socio-economic development of a country. It implies the optimum use of country's 3 Ms, *i.e.,* Men, Money and Material. It involves the assessment of economic as well as social needs of the country, available resources, determination of priorities, target fixing, periodical review or evaluation and then making necessary changes in the light of the experience gained.

According to the World Development Report 1992, "Development is about improving the well-being of people. Raising living standards and improving education, health, and equality of opportunity are all essential components of economic development. Ensuring political and civil rights is a broader development goal. Economic growth is an essential means for enabling development, but in itself it is a highly imperfect proxy of progress".

Significance of Each Letter of the Concept Planning.

The concept of planning in its various functional dimensions may be illustrated by pinpointing the significance of each letter forming the word 'planning'.

P stands for (i) Purposes (objectives), (ii) Policies, (iii) Priorities, (iv) Public participation, (v) Public and private sectors—their roles, (vi) Perspective plan.

L stands for (i) Long-term and short-term planning, (ii) Legislation needed to implement decisions where legislation is needed, (iii) Liaison among different authorities engaged in the formulation and implementation of the plan.

A stands for (i) Attitude formation, (ii) Administrative structure, (iii) Advisory bodies, (iv) Appraisal of the plan from time to time.

N stands for (i) National development, (ii) Numbers (Data or statistics needed for the plan).

N stands for (i) National income, (ii) New needs and objectives.

I stands for (i) Investment to be made, (ii) Inputs — Indigenous resources, (iii) International assistance needed, if any

N stands for (i) New priorities in the light of appraisal, (ii) Nomenclature of the administrative structure, (iii) National needs.

G stands for (i) Gross Domestic Product (GDP), (ii) Gross National Product (GNP), (iii) GNP per capita income.

SOCIO-ECONOMIC PROFILE OF INDIA ON THE EVE OF INDEPENDENCE. HARMFUL CONSEQUENCES OF THE BRITISH RULE NEED FOR PLANNING

Planning is needed in all areas of national development of all levels. It assumes all the more importance in a country which had been subjected to foreign domination of the British for about two hundred years. India's economy was in a very bad shape. Agriculture was very backward. There was little industrialisation. Social services facilities were very negligible. There was great shortage of foodgrains. India had to make heavy imports to feed its teeming millions.

MAIN OBJECTIVES OF PLANNING IN INDIA

1. To increase national wealth.
2. To remove poverty.
3. To lay down the foundations of a self-generating and self-reliant economy.
4. To distribute national wealth in such a way that economic inequalities are minimised.
5. To remove unemployment.
6. To promote social justice.
7. To expand and improve agricultural production.
8. To build industrial infrastructure.
9. To remove illiteracy.
10. To eliminate diseases.
11. To give incentives to entrepreneurs for export-oriented and import-substituting production.
12. To make the Indian economy modern, competitive, efficient and self-reliant.

13. To provide basic minimum needs for a dignified living.
14. To conserve ecology and protect environment.
15. To free the economy from foreign control.
16. To remove the traditional constraints on various oppressed sections of society like the Scheduled Castes, Scheduled Tribes, Backward Classes, women, etc.

Q. 5. State the Constitutional provisions regarding planning in India. Explain the functioning of the Planning Commission.

Ans. Planning in India : Constitutional Provisions

Article 38 and Article 39(a), (b) and (c) relate to economic development and social justice.

Article 38 states, "The State shall strive to promote the welfare of the people by securing and protecting as effectively as it may, a social order in which justice, economic and political shall form all the institutions of the national life".

Article 39. "The State shall, in particular, direct its policy towards securing

(a) that the citizens, men and women, equally, have the right to an adequate means of livelihood.

(b) that the ownership and control of the material resources of the community are so distributed as best to subserve the common good;

(c) that the operation of the economic system does not result in the concentration of wealth and means of production to the common detriment".

Article 43 and 43A relate to the participation of workers in the management of industries and living wages.

Article 46 relates to educational and economic interests of Scheduled Castes, Scheduled Tribes and other weaker sections.

PLANNING MACHINERY : PLANNING COMMISSION

The Planning Commission was set up in India in 1950. The Resolution on Industrial Policy (April 6, 1948) envisaged the role of the Planning Commission as, "The nation has now set itself to establish a social order where justice and equality of opportunity shall be secured to all people ... For this purpose, careful planning and integrated effort over the whole field of national activity are necessary, and the Government of India proposes to establish a National Planning Commission to formulate programmes of development and to secure their execution".

The terms of references of the Planning Commission are to :-

1. Make an assessment of the material, capital and human resources of the country, including technical personnel, and investigate the possibilities of augmenting such resources as are found to be deficient in relation to the nation's requirements ;
2. Formulate a Plan for the most effective and balanced utilisation of the country's resources ;

3. On a determination of priorities, define the stage in which the Plan should be carried out and propose the allocation of resources for the due completion of each stage ;
4. Indicate the factors which are tending to retard economic development, and determine the conditions which, in view of the current social and political situation, should be established for the successful execution of the Plan ;
5. Determine the nature of the machinery which will be necessary for securing the successful implementation of each stage of the plan in all aspects ;
6. Appraise from time to time the progress achieved in the execution of each stage of the Plan and recommend the adjustments of policy and measures that such appraisal may show to be necessary and
7. Make such interim or ancillary recommendations as appear to it to be appropriate either for facilitating the discharge of the duties assigned to it ; or on a consideration of the prevailing economic conditions, current policies, measures and development programmes; or on an examination of such specific problems as may be referred to it for advice by Central or State Government".

Composition of the Planning Commission and the Process of Planning in India.

The Planning Commission is a high powered Central Agency constituted to prepare a blue-print for development of the country. It has been entrusted with the task of assessing the resources of the country, drawing up plans for the development and utilisation of resources within the framework of specified national priorities and determining conditions, modalities and adjustments, needed for the success of the planning process. The Commission also appraises the progress of the Plans from time to time.

The Prime Minister is the Chairman of the Commission. In order to achieve coordination among the States in implementing the Plans and to achieve targets set in the Plans, an advisory body called National Development Council (NDC) was set-up in 1952, with the Prime Minister as Chairman and Chief Ministers of all the States and Administrators of the Union Territories as members.

Central Objective of Development in India

The central objective of development in India has been to achieve "growth with social justice". This has been clearly spelt out in the Preamble of the Indian Constitution and Part IV entitled 'Directive Principles of State Policy'. This is embodied in terms like the 'socialist pattern of society'.

The Lok Sabha in 1954, affirmed that "the objective of our economic policy should be a socialist pattern of society. In January 1955, Jawaharlal Nehru, the first Prime Minister of India and the architect of planning concept

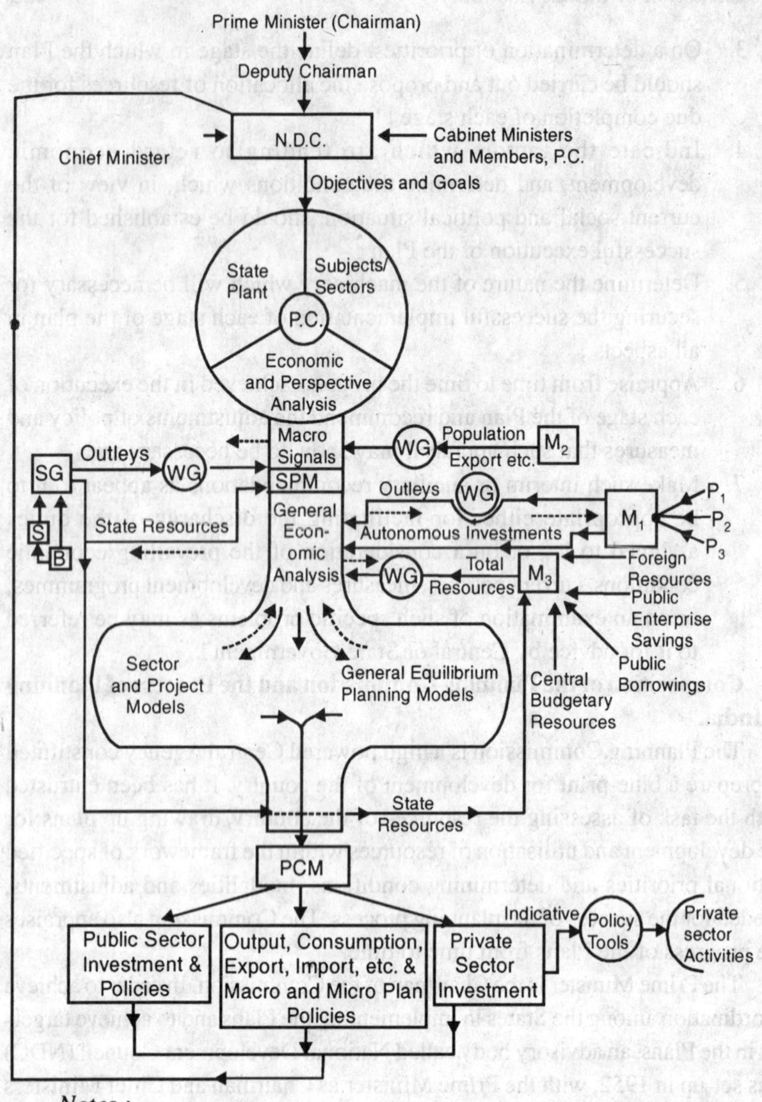

Notes :

P	=	Project
B	=	Block
M	=	Ministries
PC	=	Planning Commission
PCM	=	Planning Commission Meeting
S	=	Sector
ST	=	Stage Government
SPM	=	State Planning Meeting
WG	=	Working Group

Fig . Plan Formulation Process in India.

moved a resolution at the Avadi Session of the Indian National Congress which reaffirmed the principle of establishing a socialist society in India.

In 1976, with a Constitutional Amendment, the word 'Socialism' was inserted in the Constitution of India.

Broadly speaking the national plans are formulated and finalised in three stages. In the *first stage,* the rough projections and estimates, prepared by the Planning Commission in consultation with the Central Ministries and State Governments against the background of the long-term perspective, are approved and modified, if necessary, by the NDC in the form of preliminary instructions.

In the *second stage*, state governments/union territories prepare their own plans and send them to the Planning Commission, which dovetails these schemes, programmes and projects into an integrated plan called the "Draft Plan". The Draft Plan is then released for public discussion.

The *third stage* consists of prolonged discussion between the members of the Planning Commission and the representatives of different Central Ministries, State Governments and the Union Territories, for arriving at an agreement on the nature and the size of the plans.

These tentative agreements are sent to the National Development Council (NDC) after examination by the Union Cabinet. In the light of the recommendations of the NDC, the Planning Commission gives the final shape to the Plan, which is placed before the Parliament for approval and subsequently becomes the official national plan.

Till date, the Planning Commission has drawn up Ten Five Year Plans in addition to Annual Plans and Perspective Plans. Each Plan covers a period of five years, beginning from 1st April of the concerned year and ending on 31st March of the fifth year.

Q. 6. Give a brief review of Five Year Plans in India.

Table : Five Year Plans at a Glance.

Plan and Period	*Focus of the Plan : Main Objectives*
First Plan : April 1951-March 31, 1956	(*i*) *Increase in agricultural production.* (*ii*) *Equitable distribution of production, income and wealth.*
Second Plan : April 1, 1956-March 31, 1961	(*i*) *Increase in industrial production* (*ii*) *Development of heavy industries.*
Third Plan: April, 1, 1961-March 31, 1966	(*i*) *Self-sufficiency in foodgrain production* (*ii*) *Generation of more*

		employment opportunities.
		(*iii*) *Reduction is inequality.*

Three Annual Plans/April 1, 1966 - March 31, 1969

Fourth Plan :	*April 1, 1969-March 31, 1974*	(*i*) *Accelerating the process of growth and development.* (*ii*) *Stability in prices.*
Fifth Plan :	*April, 1, 1974-March 31, 1979*	*Raising the living standards of the people with a focus on weaker sections of the society.*

Annual Plans/April 1, 1979 - March 31, 1980

Sixth Plan :	*April 1, 1980-March 31, 1985*	(*i*) *Removal of poverty.* (*ii*) *Reduction in inequality.* (*iii*) *Development of infrastructure.*
Seventh Plan :	*April, 1, 1985-March 31, 1990*	(*i*) *Generation of more employment opportunities, and* (*ii*) *Increase in agricultural productivity.*

Two Annual Plans/April 1, 1990 - March 31, 1992

Eighth Plan :	*April, 1, 1992-March 31,1997*	(*i*) *Fuller utilisation of manpower by the turn of the century.* (*ii*) *Universalisation of elementary education.* (*iii*) *Strengthening of infrastructure.*
Ninth Plan:	*April 1, 1997-March 31 2002*	(*i*) *Agricultural and rural development.* (*ii*) *Growth of the economy with price stability.* (*iii*) *Checking the growth of population.*
Tenth Plan :	*April, 1, 2002 - March 31, 2007*	(*i*) *Improving the quality of life through better health and educational facilities and improved levels of consumption.* (*ii*) *Reduction in inequality.*

Monitorable Targets for the Tenth Plan and Beyond

- Reduction of poverty ratio by 5 percentage points by 2007 and by 15 percentage points by 2012. This implies that after 2007, the people below the poverty line will constitute 21 per cent and after 2012, the percentage would be 11 per cent.
- Providing gainful and high-equality employment in addition to the labour force over the Tenth Plan period. In other words, every year 10 lakh jobs would be created.
- All children in school by 2003 ; all children to complete 5 years of schooling by 2007;
- Reduction in gender gaps in literacy by at least 50 per cent by 2007;
- Reduction in the decadal rate of population growth between 2001 and 2011 to 16.2 per cent;
- Increase in literacy rate to 75 per cent within the Plan period ;
- Reduction of infant mortality rate (IMR) to 45 per 1000 live births by 2007 and 28 by 2012 ;
- Reduction of maternal mortality ratio (MMR) to 2 per 1000 live births by 2007 and to 1 by 2012;
- Increase in forest and tree cover to 25 per cent by 2007 and 33 per cent by 2012 ;
- All villages to have sustained access to portable drinking water within the Plan period ;
- Cleaning of all major polluted rivers by 2007 and other notified stretches by 2012.

Table : Selected Indicators of Development (1950-51 — 2004-2005)

	1950-51	1960-61	1970-71	1980-81	1990-91	2000-01	2004-05
Economic Indicators							
1. GDP at factor cost							
(i) At current prices (Rs. crore)	9547	16220	42222	130178	510954	1917724P	2843867
(ii) At constant prices (Rs. crore)	140466	206103	296278	401128	692871	1198685P	23936716
2. Per capita net national product at 1993-94 prices (Rupees)	386	4429	5002	5352	7321	16223	19649
3. Index of industrial production (Base : 1993-94 = 100)	7.2	15.6	28.1	43.1	91.6	162.6	204.8
4. Index of agricultural production (Base: triennium ending 1981-82)	46.2	68.8	85.9	102.1	148.4	167.3	179.2
5. Gross domestic capital formation (as per cent of GDP)	8.7	14.4	14.4	20.3	26.3	24.0P	30.1
6. Gross domestic savings (as per cent of GDP)	8.9	11.6	14.6	18.9	23.1	23.4P	29.10

7. Output							
(a) Foodgrains (million tonnes)	50.0	82.0	108.4	129.6	176.4	199.5	204.6
(b) Finished steel (million tonnes)	1.0	2.4	4.6	6.8	13.5	29.3	39.3
(c) Cement (million tonnes)	2.7	8.0	14.3	18.7	48.8	97.6	39.3
(d) Coal (including lignite) (million tonnes)	32.3	55.2	76.3	119.0	225.5	309.6	412.9
(e) Crude oil (million tonnes)	0.3	0.5	6.8	10.5	33.0	32.4	412.9
(f) Electriclty generated (utilities only) (Billion KWH)	5.1	16.9	55.8	120.8	264.3	499.5	34.0
8. Wholesale price index* (Base: 1993-94 = 100)	6.8	7.9	14.3	36.8	73.7	155.7	608.6
9. Consumer Price index (Base: 1982 = 100) @ @	17	21	38	81	193	444	187.2 520
10. Plan outlay (Rs. crore)	260##	1117	2524	15023	58369	185737	2692.67
11. Foreign Trade							
(i) Exports							
Rs. crore	606	642	1535	6711	32553	203571	361879
US $ million	1269	1346	2031	8486	18143	44560	8.540
12. Impoerts							
(i) Rs. crore	608	1122	1634	12549	43198	23387	490532
(ii) US $ mill.	1273	2363	2162	15869	24075	50538	109173

(source : *Economic Survey 2005-2006*)

35

Overview of Significant Events (1858-1947)

(Viceroys of India)

An attepmt is made here to present the chief events in a nutshell during the period of the rule of the Crown in India (1858-1947). Details of these events are given separately while discussing policy matters.

Following were the Viceroys during the period under reference.

Lord Canning	1858-62
Lord Elgin I	1862-63
Sr. Robert Napier (officiating)	1863
Sr. William T. Denison (officiating)	1863
Sir John Lawrence	1864-68
Earl of Mayo	1869-72
Sir John Strachey (officiating)	1872
Lord Napier of Merchistoun (officiating)	1872
Earl of Northbrook	1872-76
Baron (Earl of) Lytton I	1876-80
Marquess of Ripon	1880-84
Earl of Dufferin	1884-88
Marquess of Lansdowne	1888-93
Earl of Elgin II	1894-98
Lord Curzon	1899-1904
Lord Ampthill (officiating)	1904
Lord Curzon	1904-05
Earl of Minto-II	1905-10
Baron Hastings of Pensnurst	1910-16
Baron Chelmsford	1916-21
Earl of Reading	1921-25
Lord Lytton II (Officiating)	1925
Lord Irwin	1926-31
Earl of Willington	1931-34
Sir George Stanley (officiating)	1934
Marquess of Linlithgow	1934-36

Following were the Governors - General and Crown Representatives under Act of 1935.

Marquess of Linlithgow	1936-37
Baron Brabourne (officiating)	1938
Marquess of Linlithgow	1938-43
Lord Wavell	1943-47
Lord Mountbatten	1947

Main Events (1858-1947)

Lord Canning: (1856-58 Governor - General of India, 1858-62 Governor General and Viceroy)

(i) Revolt of 1857 (ii) Government of India Act, 1857 (iii) Queen Victoria's Proclamation, 1858 (v) Act of 1861 regarding constitutional reforms (v) penal Code of 1858 (iii) Setting of Universities at Calcutta, Bombay and Madras (1857).

Lord Elgin I (1862-63)

Revlot of Wahabis (Religious -political creed among Muslims) living on the North-West Frontiers of India.

Lord Lawrence (1864-68)

1. War with Bhutan and peace treaty.
2. Policy of 'masterly inactivity' relating to Afghanistan.
3. Famines in Orissa and other places.
4. Tenancy Acts in Punjab and Oudh.

Lord Mayo (1869-72)

(i) Founding of the Mayo College Ajmer for the education of the Princes of the Indina Rulers.

(ii) Introduction of the electric telegraph.

Lord Northbrook, (1872-76)

1. Kuka movement in Punjab - Ram Singh was the leader.

The movement was against idol worship and caste distinctions etc. The followers of this movement raided butcher shops and liquor shops. The British authorities suspected them and took stern action against them.

2. Famines in Bengal and Bihar.

Lord Lytton (1876-80)

1. Terrible famines in Madras and other places.
2. Establishment of a Muhammadan Anglo-Oriental College at Aligarh which later on developed into Aligrh Muslim University.
3. 'Forward Policy' towards Afghanistan and Second Afghan War.
4. Passing of the Vernacular Press Act which was discriminatory against the Indian Press.

Lord Ripon (1880-1884)

1. Reforms of Lord Rippon.
2. Repeal of Vernacular Press Act (1881).
3. Liberal Policy towards Indian States.
4. End of Second Afghan War.
5. Age limit of entrance to the Indian Civil Services raised from 18 to 21.
6. Introduction of Local self-government.

7. First Factory Act passed (1881)
8. Appointment of Hunter Commission on Education (1882)
9. Decision to make census every 10 year - First census in 1881.

Lord Dufferin (1884-88)

1. Founding of the Indian National Congress (1885).
2. Third Burmese War (1885).
3. Annexation of Burma (1886).

Lord Lansdowne (1888-93)

1. Revolts in Manipur and Kalat.
2 Misgovernment in Jammu and Kashmir and appointment of Council of Regency.
3 Second Census (1891).
4 Durand Agreement with Afghanistan - fixng of boundary between India and Afghanistan.
5 Indian Councils Act (1892).

Lord Elgin I (1893-99)

1 Trouble in Chitral and restoring order
2 Suppression of revolt of Frontier Tribe.
3 Plague and famine
4 Opium Commission and reduction in the quantity of opium export to China.

Lord Curzon (1899-1905)

1 Reforms of Lord Curzon
2 Creation of a new province of North Western Frontier Province
3 Partition of Bengal
4 Famine and Plague; death of about 10 lakh people

Lord Minto (1905-1910)

1 Political unrest and National Movement
2 Minto-Morley Reforms

Lord Hardinge (1910-16)

1 Delhi Durbar and presence of King Georg V (1911)
2 Capital changed from Calcutta to Delhi (1911)
3 Cancellation of Partition of Bengal (1911)
4 Attempt on the life of Lord Hardinge (1912)
5 Outbreak of First World War (1914)

Lord Chelmsford (1916-21)

1 Rowlatt Act (1919)
2 Jallianwala Bagh Tragedy at Amritsar
3 Government of India Act (1919)
4 Non-Cooperation Movement (1919-21)
5 Khilafat Movement (1919-21)
6 Third Afghan War

Lord Reading (1921-26)

1 Boycott of the visit of Prince of Wales
2 Khilafat and Non-Cooperation Movement.
3 Chauri Chaura Incident (1922)

Lord Irwin (1926-31)

1 Boycott of Simon Commission (1927)
2 Lathi blows on Lala Lajpat Rai and his death (1928)
3 Independence Declaration by the Congress at Lahore (1929)
4 Civil Disobedience Movement and Dandi March (1930)
5 First Round Table Conference (1930)
6 Gandhi Irwin Pact (1931)
7 Second Round Table Conference (1931).

Lord Willingdon (1931-36)

1 Communal Award and Poona Pact (1932)
2 Third Round Table Conference (1932)
3 Earthquakes in Bihar and Quetta
4 Government of India Act (1935)

Lord Linlithgow (1936-44)

1 Implementation of the Government of India Act, (1935)
2 Elections in 1937
3 Congress Ministries in nine out of eleven Provinces (1937)
4 Split in the Congress (1938-39)
5 Beginning of First World War (1939)
6 Cripps Mission (1942)
7 Quit India Movement (1992)

Lord Wavell (1944-47)

1 End of Second World War (1945)
2 Simla Conference (1945)
3 Trial of INA Officers (1945)
4 Cabinet Mission Plan (1946)
5 Direct Action by Muslim League (1946)
6 Elections for the Constituent Assembly (1946)
7 Interim Government headed by Jawaharlal Nehru.

Lord Mountbatten (March 1947 to June 1948)

1 Plan for the Partition of India (June 3, 1947)
2 Independence Act passed by British Parliament (July 8, 1947).
3 Division of India into two independent countries *i.e.*, India and Pakistan.
4 India becoming independent (August 15, 1947).

36
Important Questions

A. Essay Type Questions: Quick Revision With Hints

1. Discuss the economic and social life in India in the first half of the 18th century. To what extent were they related to contemporary political development? (Ans. 1, Chapter 1).
2. Discuss the main causes for the decline and fall of the Mughal empire (Ans. 3, Chapter 2).
3. Discuss the role of Peshwa Baji Rao I and Balaji Baji Rao in the Maratha empire. Why did the Marathas fail to establish political system (Ans. 3 and 4, Chapter 3).
4. Discuss the causes and effects of the Third Battle of Panipat. Why did the Marathas fail? (Ans. 4, Chapter 3)
5. Discuss the comparative importance of the Battles of Plasey and Buxar (Ans. 3, Chapter 4).
6. Why did India fail to provide a political power capable of providing a substitute to the Mughal Empire in India in the 18th century? (Ans 5, Chapter 4).
7. Discuss the merits and demerits of the Dual system of Government set up by Lord Clive in Bengal (Ans. 3, Chapter 5).
8. Discuss the relations of the British with Hyder Ali and Tipu Sultan (Ans. 1, Chapter 6).
9. Discuss the Anglo-French struggle in India (Ans. 1, Chapter 5).
10. Write an essay on Anglo-Sikh relations and the circumstances leading to the annexation of Punjab by the British. (Ans. 2, Chapter 8).
11. Discuss the causes of the dawnfall of the Maratha power (Ans. 4, Chapter 7).
12. Write a critical note on the changes brought about by Warren Hastings and Lord Cornwallis in the administrative system. (Ans. 5, Chapter 11).
13. Do you think that Lord William Bentinck was a Liberal? Explain (Ans. 1, Chapter 12).

14. Explain 'economic drain' in the context of economic policies of the British and the impact on India. (Ans. 2, Chapter 13).
15. Discuss the statement, "Raja Rammohan Roy was the father of Modern India". (Ans.1, Chapter 14)
16. Explain Doctrine of Lapse and its emplications. (Ans. 2, Chapter 15).
17. Explain the causes, nature and consequences of the Revolt of 1857. Give some opinions of scholars. (Ans. 4, Chapter 17).
18. Explain the reforms of Lord Ripon. Was he a different person (liberal) in the imperialist era? (Ans. 1, Chapter 19).
19. Give a critical view of Lord Curzon's reforms. In what respects was he different from Lord Ripon. (Ans. 2, Chapter 19).
20. Discuss the main trends in the policy of East India Company with regard to Princely States before and after 1857. (Ans. 1 and 2, Chapter 20).
21. Explain the development of the system of education in India in the light of Macaulay's Minute (Ans. 1, Chapter 21).
22. Explain Auckland's Afghan Policy. What were the causes of its failure? (Ans. 3, Chapter 22).
23. Explain how Brahmo Samaj and Arya Samaj represented the streams of Renaissance Movement in India. (Ans. 6, Chapter 23).
24. Examine the factors that led to the growth of national consciousness in India. (Ans. 1, Chapter 24).
25. What did the natinoal movement in its early phase (1885-1905) try to achieve? How far did it succeed? (Ans. 2, Chapter 24)
26. Explain the causes which gave rise to Extremism in Indian Politics. In what respects did the Extremists differ from the Moderates in their aims and methods? Assess their achievements. (Ans. 2, Chapter 25).
27. Make a comparative contribution of Gopal Krishna Gokhale and Bal Gangadhar Tilak to the National Movement. (Ans. 4, Chapter 25).
28. Discuss the chief features and importance of Morley Minto Reforms of 1909. (Ans. 6, Chapter 25).
29. Discuss Dyarchy set-up under the Government of India Act of 1919. Why did it fail. (Ans. 3, Chapter 26).
30. Comment on the main features of Government of India Act, 1935 with special reference to pronvincial Autonomy. (Ans. 3, Chapter 27).
31. What led to the Quit India Movement? Discuss its nature and importance. (Ans. 4, Chapter 27).
32. Explain the role of Mahatma Gandhi in the freedom struggle covering the events and the methodology adopted by him. (Ans. 2 and 3, Chapter 28).
33. Trace the rise of communalism in India. Explain how it became responsible for the partition of India? How far Muslim League and Jinnah were responsible for it? (Ans. 2, Chapter 29).

34. Trace the circumstances leading to the Partition of India. Was it avoidable? (Ans. 6, Chapter 27)
35. Examine the main trends in the Left Movement in India. (Ans 3, Chapter 29).
36. Give an account of the contribution of Jotiba Phule and Dr. B.R. Ambedkar for the uplift of the Depresed Classes (Ans. 4, Chapter 29).
37. Write Notes on:
    (i) Lajpat Rai (Ans. Chapter 30)
    (ii) Shaheed Bhagat Singh (Ans. Chapter 30)
    (iii) Maulana Abul Kalam Azad (Ans. Chapter 30)
    (iv) Subhash Chandra Bose (Ans. Chapter 30).
38. Give an account of the making of Indian Constitution (Ans. 1, Chapter 31).
39. Discuss the process for the Integration of the Indian Princely States and the role of Sardar Patel in it. (Ans. 2, Chapter 31).
40. Expalin the achievements made in industrial and agricultural development in India since independence. (Ans. 3, Chapter 31).
41. State the contribution of anyone Moderate, one Extremist, one revolutionary and one leader of the last phase of freedom struggle. (Chapter 30).

B. Short Answer Questions: Quick Revision With Hints

Q. Answer the following in about 100 words each.

Significance of the Battle of Buxar. (Ans. 2, Chapter 4)
Khilafat and Non-Cooperation Movement. (Ans. 4 Chapter 26)
Rowlatt Act, 1919. (Ans. 4, Chapter 26)
Jallianwala Tragedy. (Ans. 4, Chapter 26)
Quit India Movement. (Ans. 4, Chapter 27)
Consequences of Third Battle of Panipat. (Ans. 4, Chapter 3)
Reorganisation of States. (Ans. 5, Chapter 31)
Organisation and Methods of Revolutionaries. (Ans. 8, Chapter 25)
Pakistan Resolution of Muslim League. (Ans. 6, Chpater 27).
Simon Commission. (Ans. 6, Chapter 26)
Swaraj Party. (Ans. 6, Chapter 26)
Development of Transport and Means of Communications. (Ans. 6, Chapter 21).
Signficance of the Battle of Plassey. (Ans. 1, Chapter 4)
Ramakrishna Mission (Ans. 4, Chapter 23).
Home Rule League (Ans. 7, Chapter 25).
Indian National Army. (Ans. 6, Chapter 27)
Partition of Bengal (Ans. 5, Chapter 25)
Cabinet Mission (Ans. 6, Chapter 27)

Cripps Mission (Ans. 6, Chapter 27)
Indian Independence Act 1947. (Ans. 6, Chapter 27)
Education Policy of the British. (Ans. 1, Chapter 21).
Nadir Shah. (Ans. 2, Chapter 1)
Nana Phadnavis. (Ans. 1, Chapter 7)
Brahmo Samaj. (Ans. 2, Chapter 14)
Subsidiary Alliance. (Ans. 1, Chapter 15)
Queen's Proclamation, 1858. (Ans. 1, Chapter 18)
Aligarh Movement. (Ans. 5, Chapter 23)
Surat Split. (Ans. 5, Chapter 25)
Separate Electorate. (Ans. 7, Chapter 25)
Lucknow Pact. (Ans. 7, Chapter 25)
Ghadar Movement. (Ans. 7, Chapter 25)
Purna Swaraj. (Ans. 1, Chapter 27)
Communal Award and Poona Pact. (Ans. 1, Chapter 27)
Round Table Conferences. (Ans. 1, Chapter 27)
Aligarh School. (Ans. 1, Chapter 29)

C. Very Short Answer and Objective Type Questions with Answers

Q. 1. Answer the following questions:

1. Give the names of any two Peshwas of the 18th century.
2. When and between whom was the battle of Buxar fought?
3. Give any two reforms of William Bentinck.
4. Write the names of the any four states annexed by the 'Doctrine of Lapse'.
5. What were the two main causes of the uprising of 1857?
6. What was Mahalwari System?
7. Who was the Prime Minister of England when India achieved independence ?
8. When was the first telegraph laid in India? Which were the two cities linked by it?
9. Who was the most important leader of the Aligarh Movement?
10. What is the name of the best known novel of Bankim Chandra Chatterjee.
11. When was Bhima Rao Ambedkar born? State caste also.
12. Who laid the foundation of the Indian National Congress and when?
13. Give the name of home town of Lala Lajpat Rai.
14. Who was the Viceroy of India when Bengal was partitioned?
15. Who said, "If thieves enter our home and we have not sufficient strength to drive them out we should shut them up and burn them alives?
16. General Shah Nawaz, Colonel Gurdial Singh Dhillon and Major Prem Sehgal were associated with which organization ?

17. In which year was the Third Battle of Panipat fought? Who won the victory?
18. Who established dual system in Bengal? Who was responsible for abolishing it?
19. Give two reasons for the destruction of indigenous industry at the hands of the British Government.
20. Who was the founder of the Aligarh Movement? Name any two more leaders of the movement.
21. Who laid the foundation of the Brahmo Samaj and at which place?
22. What were the two aims of the Muslim League? (1906)
23. Name the two leaders of the Home Rule Movement in India.
24. What was the name given to the Indian Council's Act 1909 and why?
25. Why was Bhagat Singh hanged. Name any two person who were hanged with them.
26. Name the first Governor General of India after independence?
27. When was the Constituent Assembly established? Who was elected President of this Constituent Assembly.
28. When was the constitution of India passed and from which date it came into force?
29. Write two causes responsible for the decline of Mughal power in India.
30. In which year was the third Battle of panipat fought? Who lost this battle?
31. Between whom and in which year was the Battle of Plassey fought?
32. Name any two aspects of Dual Government of Clive.
33. Name any two provinces where Permanent Setlement was established?
34. In which year and at which place was the Indina Association formed?
35. Write any two causes of the failure of mutiny.
36. What was Khilafat Movement? Name two of its leaders.
37. How and in which year Gandhiji started his Civil Disobediance Movement?
38. In which year and at which place did the Jallianwala Bagh Incident take place?
39. In which year and by which Viceroy was the declaration of Indian Independence made in India?
40. Who was defeated by whom in the Third Battle of Panipat?
41. Write two results of the Battle of Plassey.
42. Write two results of the Battle of Buxar.
43. Write two causes of rural indebtedness.
44. When was the first railway line established in India and during whose administration?
45. Write the immediate cause of the uprising of 1857 AD.
46. Write any two activities undertaken by the Rama Krishna Mission for the welfare of society.
47. Between whom and when was the Lucknow Pact signed?

48. What was the main result of the Third Battle of Panipat?
49. Who were the Peshwas?
50. What was the important resolution passed in the historic session of the Indian National Congress in 1929? Who was the President of that session?
51. When did the Muslim League pass the resolution of Pakistan and at what session?
52. Who established dual system in Bengal?
53. Who is the author of Anand Math? Mention its famous song.
54. Write the names of two leaders of the Swaraj Party.
55. Who was the main person who worked for the integration of Princely States?
56. When was the first Interim-Government formed in India and who was appointed as its first Prime Minister?
57. Name any two papers started by Bal Gangadhar Tilak
58. Name any two Moderate leaders of the Indian National Congress.
59. Name any two Extremist leaders of the Indian National Congress.
60. Name two Sultans associated with Mysore.
61. Name any two observatories built by Jai Singh.
62. Why is Maharaja Suraj Mal famous?
63. Name the two fort cities built in India by the English.
64. How many Carnatic wars were fought?
65. Who was Duplix? Why did he fail?
66. Name the parties in the Treaty of Amritsar. (1809)
67. Who is said to be the originator of the English System of Education in India ? In whose period was it introduced?
68. Who introduced the Permanent Settlement in Bengal? When was it introduced?
69. Name any two social reforms advocated by Arya Samaj.
70. Name any two leaders of the 19th century who worked for the uplift of the Depressed Classes.
71. Name the most important work of Swami Dayanand. What was the essence of his teaching?
72. What was the messge given by Swami Vivekanand at the Parliament of Religious held at Chicago?
73. Why was Bengal partitioned?
74. Name any two revolutionaries who worked in foreign countries for the freedom of India?
75. What does Lal-Bal-Pal signify?
76. Name any four prominent who leaders played a bading role in the freedom struggle.
77. Mention any two events which made Subhash Chandra one of the greatest leaders of the national movement.

78. With what objectives did Gandhiji start the Sabarmati Ashram?
79. When was the Quit India Movement started? What was Gandhijis' Mantra?
80. Who was the originator of the Basic System of Education? What was its chief feature?

Answers

1. (i) Balaji Vishwanath (ii) Baji Rao-I
2. 1764. Between the English and the Confederacy of Mir Kasim, Nawab of Bengal, Shuja-ud-daula, the Nawab of Oudh and Shah Alam, Mughal Emperor.
3. (i) Abolition of '*Sati*' (ii) Checking infanticide.
4. (i) Satara (ii) Jaitpur (iii) Sambhalpur (iv) Jhansi
5. (i) Use of cartridges greased with fat of pig and cow.
   (ii) Annexation of states by Lord Dalhousi.
6. A system of land revenue in which '*Mahal*' meaning a village or an estate was the unit.
7. Lord Attlee
8. (i) 1853 (ii) Calcutta and Agra
9. Sir Syed Ahmad Khan
10. (i) 'Anand Math'
11. (i) 1891 (ii) Mahar
12. (i) A.O. Hume (ii) 1885
13. Village Dhudika in Ferozepur District (Punjab)
14. Lord Curzon
15. Bal Gangadhar Tilak
16. INA Indian National Army
17. (i) 1761 (ii) Ahmad Shah Abdali
18. (i) Lord Clive (ii) Warren Hastings
19. (i) Commercial and industrial policy of the East India Company.
    (ii) Lack of patronage from Indian rulers.
20. (i) Sir Syed Ahmad Khan (ii) (a) Chirag Ali (b) Nazir Ahmad
21. (i) Rammohan Roy (ii) Calcutta
22. (i) Promotion of political and other rights of Muslims.
    (ii) Promotion of loyalty to the British Government.
23. (i) Mrs. Annie Besant (ii) Bal Gangadhar Tilak.
24. (i) Morley, Minto Reforms (ii) (a) Morley, Secretary of States for India (b) Minto, Viceroy and Governor General of India.
25. (i) For the murder of Saunders, an Assistant Superintendent of Police (2) Rajguru (3) Sukhdev
26. Lord Mountbatten
27. (i) 1946 (ii) Dr. Rajendra Prasad.
28. (i) November 26, 1949 (ii) January 26, 1950

29. (i) Policies of Aurangzeb (ii) Weak successors of Aurangzeb.
30. (i) 1761 (ii) The Marathas
31. (i) English East India Company and the battle led by Lord Clive (ii) Nawab of Bengal, Siraj-ud-daula
32. (i) Internal administration of Bengal under the Nawab
(ii) Collection of revenue under the East India Company
33. (i) Bengal (ii) Bihar
34. (i) 1876 (ii) Calcutta
35. (i) A large number of Indian rulers did not join
(ii) Very week organisation of the rebels.
36. (i) The movement launched to give proper treatment to the Khalifa of Turkey.
(ii) (a) Mohmmed Ali (b) Shaukat Ali
37. (i) 1930 (ii) Salt Satyagraha: Dandi March
38. (i) 1919 (ii) Amritsar
39. (i) 1947 (ii) Lord Mountbetten
40. (i) The Marathas (ii) Ahmad Shah Abdali
41. (i) It paved the way for Britihs supermacy in Bengal
(ii) It marked the beginning of the British policy of 'Divide and Rule'.
42. (i) Laid the solid foundation of British supermacy in Bengal.
(ii) The Mughal Emperor was reduced to the position of a 'servant' of the Company.
43. (i) Poverty of the peasants. (ii) Unproductive expenditure.
44. (i) 1853 (ii) Lord Dalhousi
45. Use of greased cartridges composed of fat derived from beef and pork.
46. (i) Opening of educational institutions
(ii) Opening of dispensaries.
47. (i) Congress and the Muslim League (ii) Lucknow
48. Political and military prestige of the Marathas suffered enormously.
49. The Peshwas held the post of Prime Ministers but usurped all powers of the king.
50. (i) *'Purna Swaraj'* (ii) Jawaharlal Nehru
51. (i) 1940 (ii) Lahore Session.
52. Lord Clive
53. (i) Bankim Chandra Chattopadhyay
(ii) 'Bande Matram'
54. (i) Motilal Nehru (ii) C.R. Das
55. Sardar Vallabhbhai Patel
56. (i) 1946 (ii) Pt. Jawaharlal Nehru
57. (i) '*Kesari*' (ii) '*Mahratta*'
58. (i) Gopal Krishna Gokhale (ii) Surendra Nath Banerjee.
59. (i) Bal Gangadhar Tilak (ii) Lala Lajpat Rai
60. (i) Hyder Ali (ii) Tipu Sultan

61. (i) Jaipur (ii) New Delhi
62. He established Jat Kingdom at Bharatpur
63. (i) Madras: Fort Saint George
    (ii) Calcutta: Fort William
64. Three
65. (i) French Governor in India (ii) Lack of support from French Government.
66. (i) Maharaja Ranjit Singh (ii) The English East India Company
67. (i) Lord Macaulay (ii) Lord William Bentinck
68. (i) Lord Cornwallis (ii) 1793
69. (i) No caste system (ii) uplift of women
70. (i) Jyotiba Phule in Maharashtra
    (ii) Narayana Guru in Kerala
71. (i) Satyarath Prakash (ii) Back to the Vedas
72. (i) Help not fight (ii) Assimilation and not destruction.
73. (i) Bengal was partitioned by Lord Curzon to create a Muslim Majority province and weaken the nationalist movement.
74. (i) Shyamji Krishan Verma (ii) Madam Cama
75. (i) Lala Lajpat Rai (ii) Bal Gangadhar Tilak
    (iii) Bipin Chandra Pal
76. (i) Mrs. Aruna Asaf Ali (ii) Sarojini Naidu
    (iii) Raj Kumari Amrit Kaur (iv) Madam Bhikaji Rustam Cama.
77. (i) Escape from house arrest in 1941
    (ii) Organisation of the Indian National Army for fighting with the British.
78. (i) To carry out experiments in truth and non-violence.
    (ii) To take up constructive work.
79. (i) 1942 (ii) Do or Die.
80. (i) Gandhiji (ii) Craft centred Education

D. Question Bank on National Movement (1885 to 1904)

1. When and where was the Indian National Congress founded ?
2. What was the most prominent organisation prior to the founding of the Indian National Congress ?
3. Who is called the founder of the Indian National Congress ?
4. By what name are those leaders called who had their hold over the Congress or national movement from 1885 to 1905 ?
5. Name any two national writers on Indian languages of the last phase of the 19th century.
6. Who wrote the book Poverty and Un-British Rule in India ? In which year was it written ?
7. Name the leader who celebrated the Ganpati festival. When was it celebrated ?

8. Who organised the Shivaji festival ? When was it organised ?
9. Name any two moderate leaders of the Indian National Congress.
10. What was the name of the weekly journal published from London for presenting India's case before the British public ?
11. When did Gopal Krishan Gokhale join the Congress ?

Ans. **1.** 1885, Bombay **2.** Indian Association of Calcutta. **3.** A.O. Hume **4.** Moderate Leaders **5.** (i) Bhartendu Horish Chandra (Hindi), (ii) Subrahmanya Bharati (Tamil) **6.** Dadabhai Naoroji, 1904. **7.** Balgangadhar Tilak, 1893, **8.** B.G. Tilak, 1895 **9.** Dadabhai Naoroji, W.C. Bonnerjee **10.** India **11.** 1889.

1905 to 1918

12. Who were Bal-Pal-Lal ? To which Congress group are they associated ?
13. Who partitioned Bengal and when ?
14. Who was the President of the Indian National Congress in 1905 ?
15. Which two papers were published by B.G. Tilak ?
16. Mention the names of any two founders of the Muslim League. When was it founded ?
17. When and where was the Congress split ?
18. When were Lajpat Rai and Ajit Singh departed to Mandelay ?
19. When was Khudiram Bose, the freedom fighter, executed ?
20. When did Madan Lal Dingra shoot dead Carzan Wyllic in London ?
21. When did Delhi become the capital of India ?
22. When was a bomb thrown at Lord Hardinge on his state entry into Delhi ?
23. Name any three nationalists who threw the bomb at Lord Hardinge in 1912.
24. Name the revolutionary party formed outside India for the freedom of the country. When was it founded ?
25. When was Tilak released from jail ?
26. Who started the Home Rule Leagues ?
27. When did Gandhiji launch the Champaran Satyagraha ?

Ans. **12.** Balgangadhar Tilak, Bipin Chandra Pal, Lala Lajpat Rai. Militant/ Extremist group **13.** Lord Curzon, 1905. **14.** Gopal Krishna Gokhale **15.** 'Maratha' and 'Kesari' **16.** Sir Agha Khan and Salimullah Khan, Nawab of Oacca. Oct. 1906 **17.** 1907, Surat **18.** 1907 **19.** 1908 **20.** 1909 **21.** 1912. **22.** 1912 **23.** Amir Chand, Bhai Balmukand. Avadh Behari **24.** Ghaddar Party 1913 **25.** 1914. **26.** Mrs. Annie Besant, B.G. Tilak **27.** 1917.

1918 to 1947

28. When did Jallianwala Bagh (Amritsar) massacre take place ? Who was responsible for it ?
29. When did Gandhiji start the Non-Cooporation Movement ?
30. Name the year of the Khilafat Movement.
31. Which incident did compel Gandhiji to suspend the Non-Cooperation Movement ?

32. Give the names of any two prominent leaders of the Swarajist Party.
32a. When was the Simon Commission appointed ?
33. When did Bhagat Singh and his comrades throw a bomb in the Imperial Legislative Assembly ?
34. When and under whose presidentship was declared 'Purna Swaraj' (Complete Independence) as the goal of the Congress ?
35. When did the Congress pass the Civil Disobedience Resolution ?
36. When did Gandhi begin the Dandi March ?
37. When was Gandhi-Irwin pact signed ?
38. When was the Communal Award announced ? Name the pact by which it was modified.
39. When was the government of India Act passed ?
40. When were the Congress Ministries formed ? When did they resign ?
41. When did Muslim League adopt 'Pakistan Resolution' ? At which session was it adopted ?
42. When did the Congress start the Individual Civil Disobedience Movement ? When was it suspended ?
43. When did the Congress Working Committee adopt the Quit India Resolution ?
44. When did Subhash Chandra Bose announce the formation of the provisional government of Free India ?
45. When was the Simla Conference called by Lord Wavell ?
46. When did the Cabinet Mission visit India ?
47. When were elections to the Constituent Assembly held ?
48. Who headed the Interim Government in 1946 ?
49. When did Lord Mountbatten announce transfer of power to India ?
50. When was Indian Independence Act passed by the British Parliament ?

Ans. **28.** April 13, 1919. General Dayer. **29.** 1920. **30.** 1920-22. **31.** Chauri-Chaura **32.** Chitranjan Das, Motilal Nehru. **33.** 1927. **33a.** 1929. **34.** 1929. at the Lahore Session of the Congress. Jawaharlal Nehru. **35.** 1930. **36.** 1930. **37.** 1931. **38.** 1932. Poona Pact. **39.** 1935. **40.** 1937, 1939. **41.** 1940 Lahore Session of the Muslim League. **42.** Oct. 1940, December 1941. **43.** July 1942 **44.** Oct. 21, 1943. **45.** June 1945. **46.** March-June 1946. **47.** July 1946. **48.** Jawaharlal Nehru. **49.** Feb. 20, 1947. **50.** July 1947.

Selected Passages from the Speeches of Prominent Freedom Fighters

Introduction

The following passages are included for two-fold purpose. First, it is to enable the students to make their answers to questions more effective by quoting the relevant passage or lines from the passages. Second to prepare them for making their communication more impressive and inspirational.

PASSAGES

1. "The loyal heart is a stronger weapon than any, that the hand of the tyrant will ever forge. It is therefore necessary that some reasonable scope should be now given to their just and legitimate aspirations. Such timely concessions given with grace and without asking, will carry with them a force of gratitude, which cannot be attained by yielding to pressure and with a bad grace. All unnecessary obstacles should be removed. Something needs be done, by which those natives who have talents and attainments, may be able to enter the various services, with only as much trouble as Englishmen are put to. The problem is clear, and there is no use shirking it".

—*Dadabhai Naoroji* (1825-1929). Speech on May 2, 1867 at the East India Association

2. "The impoverishment of an Indian people under British administration is a more serious calamity than any defeat or disaster which had been known in the history of British Rule in India".

—*R.C. Dutt* (1849-1909) Letter to Lord Curzon in 1900.

3. "I hold strongly British rule has produced disastrous results. On this point, I claim some right to speak, for I have been studying this phase of the question for nearly twenty years now.... The only solution that is possible—a solution demanded alike by our interests and by your interests, as also by your national honour—is the steady introduction of self-government in India".

—*Gopal Krishna Gokhale* (1866-1915). Speech in England on 'Indian Affairs' under the auspicies of the New Reforms Club.

4. "It is difficult to realize unless one goes thoroughly into it. It has been my belief for the past twenty-five years, that every little product of the Indian handloom purchased by us, puts a little money into the hands of some poor countrymen of ours. I therefore look upon it as a religious duty to purchase an article of indigenous make whenever we can get it, and even at a sacrifice if we can afford to make it, in preference to an article of foreign make.

—*Madan Mohan Malaviya* (1861-1946). Presidential address at the Second United Provinces Conference at Lucknow in December 1908.

5. "I want to say from this platform that every blow that was hurled at us this afternoon was a nail in the coffin of the British Empire. We have to avenge ourselves of this cowardly attack, not by violently attacking them but by gaining our freedom. I wish to warn the Government that if a violent revolution takes place in this country, the responsibility for bringing it about will fall on such officers as misbehaved themselves this afternoon. Our creed still stands and we are pledged to a struggle of peaceful non-violence. But if the Government officers continue to behave like this, I would not wonder if the young men were to go out of our

hands and do whatever they choose with the object of gaining the freedom of their country. I do not know whether I shall be alive to see that day. But whether alive or dead, if that day is forced on them by the Government, my spirit from behind will bless them for their struggle."

—*Lala Lajpat Rai* (1865-1928) speech on October 1928 at a public meeting held to condemn the brutality of the British on peaceful demonstrations.

6. "I again say that the demand for Swaraj involves no sedition. It has nothing to do with the invisible sovereign government. The essence of Swaraj is that we should manage our domestic affairs according to our wishes... and it is with this purpose in view that I have chosen this subject for today's discourse."

   "We want our rights. We want a particular kind of rule that will secure our happiness. I believe that we shall get it. We have to exert ourselves in the right direction and set ourselves to the task in the full faith that the work is our own. I am perfectly sure that by the grace of God, even if you do not get the fruit of your labour in your lifetime, the next generation will not fail to reap the benefits."

   —*Lokmanya Bal Gangadhar Tilak* (1856-1920) Speech at Belgaum on May 1, 1916.

7. "India demands Home Rule for two reasons : One essential and vital, the other less important but weighty. First, because Freedom is the birthright of every Nation, secondly, because her most important interests are now made subservient to the interests of the British Empire without her consent, and her resources are not utilised for her greatest needs. It is enough only to mention the money spent on her Army, not for local defence but for Imperial purposes as compared with that spent on primary eduction."

   —*Annie Besant* (1847-1933) Presidential address at the annual session of the Indian National Congress in 1917.

8. "Here is a *mantra,* as short one, that I give you. You may imprint it on your hearts and let every breath of yours give expression to it. The *mantra* is : 'Do or Die.' We shall either free India or die in the attempt : we shall not live to see the perpetuation of our slavery.... and will die, if need be, to attain that goal. Take a pledge with God and your own conscience as witness, that you will no longer rest till freedom is achieved and will be prepared to lay down your lives in the attempt to achieve it. He who loses his life will gain it, he who will seek to save it shall lose it. Freedom is not for the coward or the faint-hearted."

   —*Mahatma Gandhi (Mohandas Karam Chand Gandhi (1869-1948).* Speech on August 8, 1942 at Bombay at the All India Congress Committee meeting.

9. "Soldiers of India's Army of Liberation ! Today is the proudest day of my life. Today it has pleased Providence to give me the unique privilege

and honour of announcing to the whole world that India's Army of Liberation has come into being. This army has now been drawn up in military formation on the battlefield of Singapore-which was once the bulwark of the British Empire."

"Comrades ! Soldiers ! Let your battle-cry be—"To Delhi, To Delhi !" How many of us will individually survive this war of freedom, I do not know. But I do know this, that we shall ultimately win and our task will not end until our surviving heroes hold the victory parade on another graveyard of the British empire-the Lal Kila or Real Fortress of ancient Delhi."

—*Netaji Subhas Chandra Bose (1897-1945)*
Speech at Singapore on July 5, 1943.

10. "Long years ago we made a tryst with destiny, and now the time comes when we shall redeem our pledge, not wholly or in full measure, but very substantially. At the stroke of the midnight hour, when the world sleeps, India will awake to life and freedom. A moment comes, which comes but rarely in history, when we step out from the old to the new, when an age ends, and when the soul of a nation, long suppressed, finds utterance. It is fitting that it this solemn moment we take the pledge of dedication to the service of India and her people and to the still larger cause of humanity."

—*(Pandit) Jawaharlal Nehru.* (1889-1964).
Speech at Midnight 14-15 August 1947.

37

University Question Papers

DEVI AHILYA VISHWVIDYALAYA, INDORE
PAPER–I, 2000

Q. 1. How was the British rule established in Bengal ? What were its consequences ?

Ans. Pages 37 to 39.

Or

Evaluate the deeds and character of Tipu Sultan.

Ans. Pages 60 to 62.

Q. 2. What were the causes of the great outbreak of 1857 ? Do you regard it as a National War of Independence ?

Ans. Pages 152, 162, 163, 171 and 172.

Or

Write short notes on any two of the following :

(i) Regulating Act

(ii) Permanent Settlement of Bengal

(iii) Liberal Policy of Lord Rippon

Ans. (i) 95 and 96

(ii) 111 to 114

(iii) 186 to 187

Q. 3. Write notes on any two of the following :

(i) Indian National Congress

(ii) Act of 1909 A.D.

(iii) Raja Ram Mohan Roy

(iv) B.G. Tilak and Home Rule Movement

Ans. (i) Pages 263 to 265

(ii) Pages 294-295

(iii) Pages 130 to 132

(iv) Pages 302-303

Or

Throw light on the causes of the First Afghan War.

Ans. Pages 214 to 215.

Q. 4. Assess the contribution of Mahatma Gandhi to the political and cultural advancement of India.

Ans. Pages 364 to 367

Or

Write notes on any two of the following :

(i) Subhas Chandra Bose (ii) Bhagat Singh

(iii) Poona Pact (iv) Nehru Report

Ans. (i) Pages 354-355

(ii) Pages 393-394 (iii) Pages 338

(iv) Pages 329

Q. 5. Explain the 1942 Movement.

Ans. Pages 348 to 352.

DELHI UNIVERSITY
2000

Time : 3 Hrs *M.M. : 100*

Note : Attempt any five questions :

Q. 1. "From the point of view of the British supremacy, Buxar is more important than the Battle of Plassey". Discuss.

Ans. Page 35, Q. 3.

Q. 2. Discuss the main features of the Permanent Settlement of Lord Cornwallis with special reference to the government, zamindars and peasants.

Ans. Page 111, Q. 3.

Q. 3. How did Wellesley make British the paramount power in India ?

Ans. Page 139, Q. 1.

Q. 4. Critically examine Lord Auckland's Afghan policy.

Ans. Page 218, Q. 3.

Q. 5. Was Dalhousi responsible for the Revolt of 1857 ? Discuss.

Ans. Page 146, Q. 4.

Q. 6. Describe the various socio-religious reforms movements in the 19th country.

Ans. Page 224, Q. 1.

Q. 7. Give a brief description of the Indian National Movement from 1885-1905.

Ans. Page 266, Q. 1.

Q. 8. Discuss the main features of the Government of India Act, 1919.

Ans. Page 313, Q. 2, Page 315, Q. 3.

Q. 9. What were the causes of the Partition of India in 1947 ?

Ans. Page 377, Q. 2.

Q. 10. Write short notes on any three of the following :

(a) Baji Rao

(b) Treaty of Amritsar, 1809

(c) Regulating Act 1773

(d) Non-Cooperation Movement

(e) Simon Commission

Ans. (a) Page 22. (b) Page 79, Q. 2 (c) Page 94, Q. 1 (d) Page 322, Q. 4 (e) Page 327, Q. 6.

DELHI UNIVERSITY

B.A. (Pass) IInd Year 2001 (Regular)

History of Modern India (1707-1950)

Time : 3 Hrs *M.M. : 100*

Note : Attempt any five questions :

Q. 1. Which factors would you like to assign primary while examining the downfall of the Mughal Empire ?

Ans. Page 13, Q. 3.

Q. 2. Discuss the relationship between the East India Company and Nawab Siraj-ud-Daula of Bengal. What was the political significance of the Battle of Plassey ?

Ans. Page 30, Q. 1.

Q. 3. Write a critical note on the Subsidiary Alliance System of Lord Wellesley.

Ans. Page 138, Q. 1, See also Delhi University B.A. Pass (2001), Q. 3.

Q. 4. What was the economic impact of British rule in India ?

Ans. Page 123, Q. 1.

Q. 5. What were the undergoing causes of the Revolt of 1857 ? Write a note on the nature of the movement.

Ans. Page 162, Q. 3, Page 165, Q. 4.

Q. 6. Discuss the role played by the Moderates in the Indian National Movement.

Ans. Page 269, Q. 4.

Q. 7. Describe the main features of the Government of India Act of 1909.

Ans. Page 294, Q. 6.

Q. 8. Examine the factors responsible for the growth of communalism in India. How far was the partition of India inevitable ?

Ans. Page 377, Q. 2.

Q. 9. Write a note on the Peasant Movement in India under the British rule.

Ans. Page 382, Q. 1.

Q. 10. What was Gandhiji's unique contribution to the National Movement ?

Ans. Page 365, Q. 2. Page 369, Q. 3.

DELHI UNIVERSITY

B.A. (Pass) IInd Year 2001 (External)
History of Modern India (1707-1951)

Time : 3 Hrs *M.M. : 100*

Note : Attempt any five questions :

Q. 1. Analyse the causes of the downfall of the Mughal Empire.

Ans. Page 13, Q. 3.

Q. 2. Discuss the main features of the Permanent Settlement of Bengal. What were its effects on the Zamindars, peasants, state and society ?

Ans. Page 111, Q. 3.

Q. 3. How did the Subsidiary Alliance System help expansion of British Empire in India ?

Ans. Important Contribution of Subsidiary Alliance System to the Expansion of British Empire in India.

In the words of Spears, "In the words of Clive and Warren Hastings, the Subsidiary System was a defensive instrument to safeguard the company's possessions; in the hands of Wellesley it was an offensive device with which to subject independent states to British Control."

The system served the double purpose of asserting British supremacy in India and at the same time of saving India from the menance of invasion of Napolean of France. It played a very significant role in the expansion of the dominions of the East India Company.

Origin of the System. Ever since the governorship of Lord Clive, the system had been applied by almost Governor and Governor-General of India, in varying degrees. Wellesely greatly developed and elaborated the system and applied it in the case of Indian States.

Terms and conditions on which Sabsidiary Treaty was negotiated with the Indian Ruler by Lord Wellesely.

1. The Indian state to surrender the external relations to the care of the company and to make no wars.

2. The Indian state to conduct negotiations with other states through the company.

3. The bigger state to maintain an army within its territories, commanded by British officers for the 'preservation of public peace'. In case of inability of a bigger state to keep such an army, the state to cede some territory in full sovereignty for the manitenance of this army. A smaller state to pay some tribute in cash to the company.

4. The state to accept a British Resident at its headquarters.

5. The state not to employ any European in its service without consulting the company.

6. The company not to interfere in the internal affairs of the state.

7. The company to protect the Indian state against foreign enemies of "every sort or kind."

States Accepting the Subsidiary System Treaty

1. The Nizam of Hyderabad
2. The Ruler of Mysore
3. The Raja of Tanjore
4. The Nawab of Oudh
5. The Peshwa
6. The Bonsle
7. The Raja of Berar
8. The Sindhia
9. Jodhpur
10. Jaipur
11. Macheri
12. Bundi
13. Bharatpur

Advantages of the Subsidiary System to the Company

1. The Subsidiary System disarmed the Indian states and they came under the British protictorate.

2. The company was present by proxy in every Indian state that accepted the Treaty.

3. The Treaty prevented the Indian states from forming any confederacy against the British.

4. The treaty enabled the company to maintain a huge standing army at the expense of Indian Princes.

5. The stationing of the troops of the company in the capitals of the Indian states gave the company the control of strategic and key positions in India without giving any cause of jealousy to other European nations.

6. The treaty enabled the company to counteract effectively any possible French moves in India. The subsidiary ally was under obligation to dismiss all French from its services.

7. The treaty allowed the company to become the arbiter in inter-state disputes.

8. The treaty closed all avenues of direct contact between Indian states and foreign powers.

9. The officers of the company commanding the subsidiary forces were well paid. This put a considerable strain on the financial position of the states.

10. The company acquired territories in full sovereignty' from the Indian states and expanded its dominations in India.

Disadvantages of the Subsidiary Alliance to Indian States

1. In the words of Sir Thomas Munro;" A state purchased security by the sacrifice of independence, of rational character and of whatever renders a people respectable."

2. The state accepting the subsidiary alliance faced financial bankruptcy.

The subsidy demanded by the company was very heavy—usually one third of the annual revenue of the state. The rulers of the Indian states, therefore, taxed the people heavily.

3. The subsidiary system supported even the oppressive and the weak ruler. The people were deprived of any chance of protest as the ruler enjoyed the patronage of the company.

4. On several important matters, the British Resident stationed at the capital of the state interfered in the day-to-day affairs of the state.

Summing Up

Karl Marx very aptly observed that the native states virtually ceased to exist from the moment they became subsidiary to the company or protected by it.

Q. 4. Discuss the relations of Maharaja Ranjit Singh with the British.

Ans. Page 78, Q. 2.

Q. 5. Evaluate the main causes of the revolt of 1857. **Why did** to fail ?

Ans. Page 155, Q. 2.

Q. 6. Estimate the contribution of Brahma Samaj and the Arya Samaj in the social and cultural awakening of India during the 19th century.

Ans. Page 232, Q. 3. Page 245-246.

Q. 7. Discuss the causes for the growth of extremism in Indian National Movement. Why were the extremists more popular than Moderates ?

Ans. Page 277, Q. 2.

Q. 8. Analyse the main features of the Government of India Act, 1919.

Ans. Page 313, Q. 2. Page 315, Q. 3.

Q. 9. What led to the Partition of India in 1947 ?

Ans. Page 377, Q. 2.

Q. 10. Write short notes on any three of the following :

(a) Battle of Plassey

(b) Baji Rao

(c) William Bentinck

(d) Quit India Movement

(e) Indian National Army

Ans. (a) Page 30, Q. 1.

(b) Page 22,

(c) Page 122.

(d) Page 348, Q. 9.

LUCKNOW UNIVERSITY
B.A. Part-II Examination 2001
First Paper
(History of Modern India 1740-1947)

Time : 3 Hrs *M.M. : 50*

Note : Answer Question No. 1 and any four of the remaining questions. All questions carry equal marks.

Q. 1. Write brief notes of 100 words each on any four of the following :

(i) Mir Kasim

(ii) Treaty of Allahabad, 1765

(iii) Anglo-Nepal War, 1814-16

(iv) Wood's Depatch

(v) Ideology of Moderates

(vi) Indian Independence Act, 1947.

Ans. (i) Page 38.

(ii) Page 34 and 35.

(iii) **The Anglo-Nepal War 1814-16**

Both the Gorkhas of Nepal and the East India Company wanted to expand their territories. In May 1818, the Gorkhas attacked the three police stations of Butwal which belonged to the East India Company. According to the Gorkhas, the police stations did not belong to the East India Company. Lord Hastings the Governor General sent a large army of 34,000 soldiers against the Gorkhas army of 12,000. The campaign of the East India Company failed miserably. The English prestige suffered a great setback.

Undaunted, the English renewed their efforts and captured Almora in the Kumaon Hills in 1815. The fort of Malan was also wrested from the Gorkhas.

Treaty of Sagauli

The Gorkhas opened negotiations for peace and entered into the Treaty of Sagauli in March 18.

According to the treaty, the Gorkhas surrendered to the company the districts of Garhwal and Kumaon, including a great portion of Tarai. The Gorkhas accepted a British Resident at Kathmandu and permanently withdrew from Sikkim.

Impact of the Treaty

The English obtained the sites of the hill stations of Simla, Mussorie, Ranikhet, Landour and Nainital.

The friendship between Nepal and the English subsisted till the British rule tasted in India, the Gorkhas, known for their fighting qualities and spirit, joined the army of the company and helped in the expansion of their dominion in India. Nepal remained as an independent country.

(iv) Wood's Despatch, Pages 203 and 204.

(v) Pages 266 to 268.

(vi) Pages 362 and 363.

Q. 2. Trace the circumstances leading to the Battle of Plassey.

Ans. Pages 30 to 34.

Q. 3. Discuss the provisions of the Pitts India Act and point out its significance.

Ans. Pages 96 and 97.

Q. 4. Show light on the causes and consequences of the First Anglo-Maratha War.

Ans. Pages 63-64.

Q. 5. Evaluate the character and achievements of Haider Ali.

Ans. Pages 58 and 59.

Q. 6. Write a note on the Permanent Settlement of Bengal. What were its acts ?

Ans. Pages 111 to 114.

Q. 7. Examine the reforms introduced by William Bentinck.

Ans. Pages 118 to 122.

Q. 8. Discuss the causes of the Revolt of 1857.

Ans. Pages 153 to 158.

Q. 9. Discuss the circumstance leading to the establishment of Indian National Congress.

Ans. Pages 257 to 262.

Q. 10. Estimate Curzon as an administrator.

Ans. Pages 187 to 190.

Q. 11. Bring out the salient features of the Government of India Act, 1919.

Ans. Pages 313 to 318.

NAGPUR UNIVERSITY

B.A. (Final) Examination 2002

Time : 3 Hrs *M.M. : 100*

Note :

(i) All questions are compulsory.

(ii) All questions carry equal marks.

Q. 1. Examine the internal policy of Lord Curzon.

Ans. Chapter 19. Pages 186 to 190, Q. 2.

Or

Describe the contribution of Lokmanya Tilak in Indian National Movement.

Ans. Chapter 25, Pages 281 to 284, Q. 3.

Q. 2. Write the answers of the following in 10 or 15 lines only.

(a) Why did Gandhiji stop Non-Cooperation Movement ?

(b) Write a short note on 'Quit India Movement'.

(c) What were the main provisions of Cabinet Mission ?

Ans. (a) Pages 323 to 327, Q. 5.

(b) Pages 348 to 352, Q. 4.

(c) Pages 360 to 361, Q. 7.

Or

(a) Point out the importance of Lahore Congress (1929).

(b) Write a note on Sardar Bhagat Singh.

(c) What do you know about Indian National Army ?

(d) What were the main provisions of the Mountbatten Plan.

Ans. (a) Pages 332-333

(b) Pages 393-394

(c) Pages 354-355

(d) Pages 361-362

Q. 3. Write the answer of the following in 10 to 95 lines.

(a) Role of Sardar Vallabhabhai Patel in Integration of Indian States.

(b) British policy towards Indian Agriculture.

(c) Ramakrishan Mission.

Ans. (a) Pages 402 to 404.

(b) Chapter 13.

(c) Pages 249-250.

Or

Write notes on.

(a) Dalit Movement under the leadership of Dr. Ambedkar.

(b) British policy towards industries in India.

Ans. (a) Chapter 29

(b) Chapter 13

(**Note :** Questions relating to modern Indian History only)

DELHI UNIVERSITY

B.A. (Pass) IInd Year 2002

(Modern India 1707-1950)

Time : 3 Hrs *M.M. : 75*

Note : (i) Attempt any five questions.

Q. 1. Briefly describe the political, social and economic conditions of India during the 18th century.

Ans. Page 1, Q. 1, Page 17, Q. 1.

Q. 2. Discuss the causes of the conflict between the Nawabs of Bengal and the East India Company between 1757 and 1765. Examine the results of the wars.

Ans. Page 30, Q. 1, Page 37, Q. 4.

Q. 3. Give an account of the administrative, judicial and revenue reforms introduced by Lord Cornwallis.

Ans. Page 106, Q. 2.

Q. 4. Discuss the causes and results of the First Afghan War.

Ans. Page 215, Q. 2.

Q. 5. Examine the causes and nature of the uprising of 1857.

Ans. Page 162, Q. 3, Page 165, Q. 4, Page 165.

Q. 6. Evaluate the contribution of the Brahmo Samaj and the Ramakrishna Movement to the social and cultural transformation of India.

Ans. Page 239 and Page 243.

Q. 7. What did the national movement in the early phase (1885-1905) try to achieve ? How far did it succeed ?

Ans. Page 269, Q. 4.

Q. 8. Bring out the salient features of the Act of 1919.

Q. 9. Was the Partition of India inevitable ? Discuss.

Q. 10. Write notes on any three of the following :

(i) Baji Rao I.

(ii) Subsidiary Alliance.

(iii) The Ghadder Movement.

(iv) Quit India Movement.

(v) Charks Woods Despatch.

(vi) Cabinet Mission Plan.

Ans. (i) Page 22 (ii) Page 138 (iii) Page 306. (iv) Pages 348. (v) Page 203. (vi) Page 360.

BANGALORE UNIVERSITY

B.A. Final Examination, 2002

(History, Paper III, Modern Indian Education)

Time : 3 Hrs *M.M. : 100*

Instructions : Answer all questions as directed.

SECTION-A

Q. 1. Mark on the outline map provided, the expansion of the Mughal Empire under the Peshwas. Write a note on Baji Rao I. 10 + 10

Ans. Pages 22 to 24.

SECTION-B

Answer any two :

Q. 1. Give an account of the establishment of the British Empire in India.

Ans. Page 150 to 152.

Q. 2. Maratha Imperialism reached its climax under the first three Peshwas". Discuss.

Ans. (i) Balaji Vishwanath (Page 22)

(ii) Balaji Rao (Pages 22 to 24)

(iii) Balaji Baji Rao (1740-61)

Extension of Empire

Balaji set in right earnest to expand the power of the Marathas both in the north and south. On account of his efforts, the Maratha power reached the territorial zenith, extending from 'Kaltack to Attock'. Gujarat, Malwa and Bundelkand came under direct Maratha administration. Maratha arms penetrated eastward into Bengal. The Marathas ravaged the Carnatic, humbled the Nizam of Hyderabad and wrested several important territories from the ruler of Mysore. The whole of the Punjab passed under Maratha rule. The Marathas exercised tremendous influence at Delhi.

However, the Maratha lost to Ahmad Shah Abdali in 1761 in the Third Battle of Panipat.

Administrative Reforms

Balaji Baji Rao established a strong system of administration. He took several measures to improve justice. Working of the civil and criminal courts was improved. He reformed the Panchayat System. He paid due attention to the development of trade. He built and improved the roads.

The Peshwa gave liberal donations for religious purposes. He built a number of temples. For carrying out such measures, Balaji Rao earned the goodwill of the people of Maharashtra.

Q. 3. Critically examine the causes of the revolts of 1857. Account for its failure.

Ans. Pages 162 and 163. Pages 177 to 189.

Q. 4. Describe the causes for the growth of Nationalism in the 19th century.

Ans. Pages 257 to 264.

SECTION–C

Answer any four :

(i) First Carnatic war
(ii) Regulating Act of 1773
(iii) Raja Ram Mohan Roy
(iv) Local self government
(v) Jhansi Rani Lakshmi Bai
(vi) Dayanand Saraswati
(vii) Aligarh Movement
(viii) Gopal Krishna Gokhale
(ix) Act of 1909

Ans. (i) Page 44
(ii) Pages 96 and 97
(iii) Pages 130 to 134
(iv) Pages 183-184
(v) Pages 373
(vi) Pages 228 to 232
(vii) Pages 373
(viii) Pages 389-390
(ix) Pages 294 to 298

NAGPUR UNIVERSITY 2005
B.A. (Part - II) Examination
HISTORY
(History of India from AD 1760 - 1950)

Time : *Three Hours*] [*Max. Marks* : 100

N. B. : (1) All questions are compulsory.
(2) All questions carry equal marks.

1. Describe the social and religious movements in the 19th century. 20

OR

Write about the causes of the Revolt of 1857.

2. Write the causes of the rise of Indian Nationalism. 20

OR

Describe the circumstances responsible for the rise of extremist movement and throw light on its working. 20

3. Answer the following questions in 10 to 15 lines each :

(*a*) How did British establish their power in Bengal? 5
(*b*) Write a note on 'Haidar Ali'. 5
(*c*) Write in short about the Treaty of Surat (1775). 5
(*d*) Write a note on Maharaja Ranjit Singh. 5

OR

(*i*) Write a note on battle of Buxar. (1764 A.D.). 5
(*ii*) Give the importance of Treaty of Salbai (1782). 5
(*iii*) Write the significant features of Subsidiary Alliance. 5
(*iv*) Why did Lord Dalhousie abolish the principle of adoption? 5

4. Answer the following question in 10 to 15 lines each :

(*a*) Write about Non-Cooperation Movement. 5
(*b*) Write a note on Dandi March (1930 A. D.). 5
(*c*) Write a note on 'Netaji Subhas Chandra Bose'. 5
(*d*) Write about 'Mountbatten plan'. 5

OR

(*i*) Write a note on 'Lala Lajpat Rai'. 5
(*ii*) Write a note on "Puna Pact 1932". 5
(*iii*) Write two significant features of Act of 1935 A.D. 5
(*iv*) Write a note on 'Cripps Mission Plan'. 5

5. Answer the following questions in 10 to 15 lines each :

(*a*) Write a note on Chamber of Princes. 5
(*b*) Write a note on Sardar Vallabhbhai Patel. 5
(*c*) Give two significant features of Indian Constitution. 5
(*d*) Give information about the social problems that arose in partition of India. 5

OR

(1) Discuss : The Indian Constitution is partially flexible. 5
(2) "India adopted Parliamentary System." Explain it. 5
(3) Give information about the Economical Problems that arose in partition of India. 5
(4) Write a note on Planning Commission. 5

KUVEMPU UNIVERSITY
THIRD YEAR B.A. DEGREE EXAMINATION
APRIL - MAY 2005
HISTORY - PAPER III
HISTORY OF INDIA FROM 1857 - 1964

Time : 3 Hours *Max. Marks* : 80

SECTION–A

1. Answer the following question in 3-4 pages. 12

What were the causes for the genesis of Indian nationalism?

OR

Critically examine the administrative policies of Lytton.

2. Answer any **TWO** of the following in 15-20 lines each. 2×4 = 8

(a) How did the greased cartridges affair lead to the Mutiny of 1857?

(b) State the significance of the 'Queen's Proclamation of 1858'.

(c) What is the importance of the Illert Bill controversy?

SECTION–B

3. Answer the following questions in 3-4 pages. 12

Describe the role played by Gopal Krishna Gokhale and Balgangadhar Tilak in the Indian National Movement.

OR

4. Answer any **TWO** of the following questions in 15-20 lines each. 2×4=8

(a) What is Drain Theory? What were the economic effects of the drain?

(b) Mention the significance of the 'Khilaft' Movement in the Indian freedom struggle.

(c) Write a note on Bhagat Singh.

OR

Describe the administrative reforms of Lord Curzon.

SECTION-C

Answer the following question in 3-4 pages.

5. Describe the 'Quit India Movement' and its importance. How did the British Government react to it? 12

OR

Describe the economic progress of India during the Nehru era.

6. Answer any **TWO** of the following questions in 15-20 lines each. 2×4=8

(a) What is the role played Chandrashekar Azad in the Freedom movement of India?

(b) Describe the Indo-Pak relations from 1947 to 1964.

(c) Write a note on Dr. B. R. Ambedkar.

SECTION-D

7. On the out line map provided :
Mark the areas affected by the Revolt of 1857. 5

(*i*) Barrackpoore
(*ii*) Meerut
(*iii*) Jhansi
(*iv*) Delhi
(*v*) Lucknow

SECTION-E

8. Answer the following questions in 3-4 sentences each 5+2=10

(a) Why did Rani Lakshmi Bai of Jhansi fight against the British?
(b) What is the significance of the World Parliament of Religions held at Chicago in 1893?
(c) What is Surat Split?
(d) What is Ghaddar Movement?
(e) Where was the Azad Hind Fauz organised?

Nagpur University 2005
Second B.P.E. Examination
HISTORY
PAPER–V

Time : Three Hours] [*Maximum Marks* : 80

N.B. : (1) Solve any **FIVE** questions.

(2) All questions carry equal marks.

1. Write in detail the results of Third Battle of Panipat. 16

2. Write in detail the causes of downfall of Marathas. 16

3. Critically examine the value of Clive's works in Bengal as an administrator. 16

4. Describe the reforms done by Lord William Bentinck. 16

5. Why is Lord Dalhousie considered to be the creator of Modern India? 16

6. Throw light on the nature of the movement of 1857. 16

7. Write an essay on Raja Ram Mohan Roy. 16

8. Trace the development of National Movement from 1919 to 1947. 16

9. Write the main features of federal system under the Act of 1935. 16

10. Write short notes on any FOUR : 4×4

(*a*) Nana Fadnavis

(*b*) Mahadaji Shinde

(*c*) Lokmanya Tilak

(*d*) Ranjeet Singh

(*e*) English-Maratha Relationship

(*f*) Warren Hasting.

Gulbarga University 2005

B.A. Third Year Degree Examination 2005

History (N/S) (Comp.)

Paper-III Modern India (1707-1964)

[*Time* : 3 *hours*] [*Max. Marks* : 100]

Note :

(1) Answer all questions from Section 'A'.

(2) And any four from Section "B".

(3) And any two from Section 'C'.

SECTION-A

1. Answer the following questions in not more than three or four sentences. 10×2=20

(1) Where Balaji Vishwanath was born? When did he become the Peshwa?

(2) When and between whom the Battle of Third Panipat took place?

(3) What is 'Dual Government System'?

(4) When and between whom the treaty of Bassein was concluded?

(5) Where and when Ranjit Singh was born?

(6) What is 'Doctrine of Lapse'?

(7) Who wrote the book entitled. 'The First Indian was of Independence' & where it was published?

(8) In which year Indian National Congress was established and who was its first President?

(9) Who was responsible for the partition of Bengal? In which year Bengal was divided?

(10) What is the original name of Swamy Dayananda Saraswati and when he was born?

SECTION-B

Medium Size answers 4×10=40

(11) Sketch the life and achievements of Robert Clive.

(12) Examine the Subsidiary alliance system of Lord Wellesly?

(13) Analyse the Doctrine of Lapse of Lord Dalhousie.

(14) Give a brief account of the life and achievements of Ranjit Singh.

(15) Examine the internal policy of Lord Lytton?

(16) Narrate the Non-Co-operation Movement of 1920?

SECTION-C

2×20=40

(17) Describe the life and achievement of Baji Rao I?

(18) Analyse the causes and Results of the Revolt of 1857?

(19) Explain the reforms of Lord Curzon?

(20) Give an account of Socio-religious Movement of the 19th Century?

38

Self Evaluation Model Test Papers

Guidelines for Scoring High Grades/Marks

Self evaluation : It is generally acknowledged that the habit of writing down answers by students must be cultivated to score good grades and marks. Keeping in view this fundamental principle, students are advised to write out in full the answers of all questions given in the following test papers.

In this regard, following guidelines may be followed :

1. Place yourself in the position of an examinee in the examination room. Here you yourself are the supervisor/invigilator.
2. Note down the time when you start the paper.
3. Stop writing after three hours.
4. Do plan your time and set your own pace. On an average you have twentyeight minutes per question, allowing time for reading the question paper and revision.
5. After finishing the test, evaluate your answers by comparing them with the answers given in this book.
6. Thereafter find out your shortcomings and remove them.

In the Examination Hall

1. Read the instructions very carefully.
2. Keep in view as to the number of questions to be done and also if there is any compulsory question.
3. Go through all the questions, before attempting any question.
4. Organise your time limit for each question.
5. Well begun is half done. So begin with those questions which you can answer confidently and readily.
6. Avoid getting bogged down on any one question.
7. Remember quality is more important than quantity. You may find some students rushing for additional answer sheets when you yourself are only halfway through first sheet and with no likelihood of needing anymore sheet. Do not feel disturbed. Probably others have large and sprawling handwriting.
8. The language you use must be as simple and direct as the subject allows.

9. Long answer may be divided into several paragraphs.
10. If inspite of your best efforts you find very little time for the last one or two questions, give main points and do not use complete sentences.
11. Do not forget to write down your roll number on the answer sheet.

TEST PAPER – I

Time : 3 Hours M.M. 100

Instructions

1. All questions of Section I and II carry equal marks i.e., 14 marks each.
2. Attempt any three Questions from each Section I and II.
3. Section III is compulsory.

SECTION – I

1. Discuss the comparative significance of the Battle of Plassey and Buxar.

OR

Who is usually regarded the founder of the British empire in India? Support your answer with logic.

2. Critically examine the Doctrine of Lapse.

OR

State the merits and demerits of the Subsidiary System.

3. Explain how Brahmu Samaj and the Arya Samaj represented the stream of 'Renaissance Movement in India'.

OR

State the agricultural and industrial policy of the British rulers in India. Examine its impact.

4. What were the causes of the Revolt of 1857?
Why was it not successful?

OR

Review the administration of Lord Curzon.

SECTION – II

5. In what respects did the Moderates in the congress differ from the extremists?

OR

State the contribution of the Revolutionaries to the freedom movement of India.

6. Examine the chief features of the Act of 1909.

OR

Critically examine the Non-Cooperation Movement of 1920-22.

7. What led to the Quit India Movement? Discuss its nature and importance.

OR

Trace the rise and growth of communalism in Indian politics during the period from 1919 to 1947.

8. Explain the role of Mahatma Gandhi in the freedom struggle of India.

OR

State the chief features of the Indian Constitution.

SECTION–III

Marks 16

Write notes on any eight of the following. Each question carries 2 marks.

(i) Jallianwala Bagh Tragedy.
(ii) Reorganisation of States.
(iii) Azad Hind Fauj.
(iv) Indian Independence Act 1947.
(v) Partition of Bengal.
(vi) Sati.
(vii) Purna Swaraj.
(viii) Lucknow Pact.
(ix) Nadir Shah.
(x) Nana Phadnavis.

TEST PAPER–2

Time : 3 *Hours* M.M. 100

Instructions:

1. All Questions of SECTION I and II carry equal works i.e., 14 marks each.
2. Attempt any three sections from each of the sections I and II.
3. Section III is compulsory.

SECTION–I

1. Explain the measures taken during the British rule to improve the conditions of Women.

OR

"The Maratha empire reached its climax under the first three Peshwas." Discuss.

2. Discuss the economic and social conditions in India during the first half of the 18th century.

OR

What were the circumstances leading to the Third Battle of Panipat? Examine its impact.

3. Give an assessment of the achievements of Maharaja Ranjit Singh.

OR

Explain the various Charters issued by the British Government to extend their control over the East India Company during 1800 and 1857.

4. Discuss the development of education in India between 1835 and 1928.

OR

Explain the Anglo-Sind and Anglo-Oudh relations.

SECTION–II

5. Explain the causes of growth of nationalism in India.

OR

Explain the causes which gave rise to extremists in the Indian politics. In what respects did they differ from the Moderates?

6. Explain the meaning of Dyarchy with reference to the Government of India Act of 1919. Why did it fail?

OR

Write notes on Simon Commission (1927-28) and the Nehru Report (1928).

7. Why was the Dandi March organised? What was the reaction of the British Government to it? State the impact of Dandi March.

OR

Analyse the main features of the Provincial Autonomy as introduced by the Government of India Act 1935.

8. Give in brief the political developments in India after the Quit India Movement.

OR

State the factors that led to the Partition of India. Could it be avoided?

SECTION–III

9. Answer any four questions. All questions carry equal marks. 8

(*i*) When was the Lucknow Pact signed? Between whom was it signed?

(*ii*) What does Lal-Bal-Pal denote?

(*iii*) Name the two fort cities built in India by the British?

(*iv*) Name any two observatories built by Jai Singh.

(*v*) Who is the author of Anand Math. Mention its famous song.

(*vi*) Name two Sultans associated with Mysore who fought with the British.

(*vii*) Why was Bhagat Singh hanged?

10. Multichoice Questions. Answer any eight. Each carries one mark. 8

1. The first Indian ruler who joined the Subsidiary Alliance.
   (*a*) The Nawab of Oudh (*b*) The Nizam of Hyderabad
   (*c*) Peshwa Baji Rao II (*d*) The King of Travancore.
2. Arrange the following in the sequence order :
   (i) Dandi March (ii) Simon Commission
   (iii) Purna Swaraj Resolution (iv) Partition of Bengal.
3. The Indian Association that played an important role in arousing national consciousness through the formation of
   (i) Indian National Congress (ii) Bengal British Indian Society
   (iii) Indian National Conference (iv) British India Association.

4. The Chairman of the Constituent Assembly was
   (i) Dr. B. R. Ambedkar (ii) Sardar Patel
   (iii) Dr. Rajendra Prasad (iv) Dr. Radhakrishnan
5. The Chairman of the Drafting Committee of the Constituent Assembly was :
   (i) Pt. Moti Lal Nehru (ii) Mahatma Gandhi
   (iii) Dr. B. R. Ambedkar (iv) Dr. Zakir Hussain.
6. Mahatma Gandhi called him his political 'guru'.
   (i) Lala Lajpat Rai (ii) S. N. Bannerjee
   (iii) Dadabhai Naoroji (iv) Gopal Krishna Gokhale.
7. Minto-Morley Reforms were announced in the year
   (i) 1905 (ii) 1909
   (iii) 1919 (iv) 1929.
8. Purna Swaraj Resolution was passed at the Congress Session of
   (i) Lahore (ii) Lucknow
   (iii) Delhi (iv) Ahmedabad.
9. Mountbatten Plan was announced in
   (i) 1935 (ii) 1942
   (iii) 1947 (iv) 1950
10. Gandhi-Irwin Pact was signed in
    (i) 1931 (ii) 1921
    (iii) 1941 (iv) 1925
11. The Ramakrishna Mission was founded by
    (i) Swami Vivekananda (ii) Swami Dayananda
    (iii) Rabindranath Tagore (iv) Dr. Radhakrishnan.
12. The book Indian's First War of Independence was written :
    (i) V. D. Savarkar (ii) Bhagat Singh
    (iii) Lala Lajpat Rai (iv) Subhash Chandra Bose.

ANSWER

1. b

2. Partition of Bengal, Simon Commission, Purna Swaraj, Dandi March.

3. (iv) **4.** (iv) 5. (iv) **6.** (iv) **7.** (ii)

8. (i) 9. (iii) 10. (i) **11.** (i) **12.** (i).

Appendix : Expansion of British Empire

(Ideologies of Expansion : Mercantism, Orientalism, Utilitarianism and Evangelicalism)

Origin and Meaning of Mercantalism

The doctrine of 'Mercantalism' which became popular from the fifteenth to the eighteenth centuries put emphasis on the importance of maintaining an excess of exports of goods and services over imports as the sole means whereby a country without gold or silver mines could obtain a continuous inflow of the precious metals regarded as essential to national wealth and strength.

Five Essential Elements of Mercantalism

Jacob Viner in an article published in ***'International Encyclopedia of the Social Sciences'*** has stated the following essential elements of mercantalism.

(1) Policy should be framed and executed in strictly nationalistic terms, that is, national advantage alone is to be given weight; (2) In appraising any relevant element of national policy or of foreign trade, great weight is always to be put on its effect, direct or indirect, on the national stock of the precious metals; (3) In the absence of domestic gold or silver mines, a primary national goal should be the attainment of as large an excess of exports over imports as is practicable, as the sole means whereby the national stock of the precious metals can be augmented; (4) a balance of trade in favour of one's country is to be sought through direct promotion by the authorities of exports and restriction of imports or by other measures which will operate indirectly in these directions; (5) economic foreign policy and political foreign policy are to be pursued with constant attention to both plenty and "power" (including security under this latter term) as coordinate and generally mutually supporting national objectives, each capable of being used as a means to the attainment of the other.

Export of manufactures was favoured over exports of agricultural products ready for consumption. Several European countries set up trading companies. The British Government gave all encouragement to the East India Company which established political power in India.

The Company initially had two aims :

(1) To have a favourable balance of trade i.e., (to export more and import less).

(2) To promote flow of bullion to home. In due course, the East India Company was able to eliminate all rival European Companies in India.

Utilitarianism

Utilitarianism is a term that has no precise meaning. It has political as well as philosophical connotation. In the context of British imperialism, it implied utility – to conquer more lands and to impose their own legal sanctions and institutions.

Orientalism

The term 'orientalism' is derived from a Latin word 'Oriens' referring simply to the rising of the sun, to imply "The East" in a relative sense. This is the opposite of **'occident'** meaning the West. In due course orientalism became associated with the culture of India. The British wanted to spread their own culture in India. They dubbed orientalism as inferiorism.

Evangelicalism

The term 'Evangelicalism' refers to anything implied in the belief that Jesus is the saviour. The missionaries wanted to spread Christainity in India. Thus this was one of the factors which prompted the British to expand power. To conclude, Gold, Glory and God (spread of Christainity) motivated the European countries to conquer other lands.